Child and Adolescent Development

To our mentors:

Donald M. Baer
Sidney W. Bijou
Jacob L. Gewirtz

Whose teachings and
guidance have shaped our views of
the science of behavioral development.

To our parents:

Alex Novak and Sophia Novak
Roberto Peláez and Carmen K. Peláez

Whose unconditional love and support
in all our endeavors have shaped our lives.

Child and Adolescent Development

A Behavioral Systems Approach

GARY NOVAK • MARTHA PELÁEZ

California State University, Stanislaus   Florida International University

SAGE Publications
International Educational and Professional Publisher
Thousand Oaks ▪ London ▪ New Delhi

For information:

Sage Publications, Inc.
2455 Teller Road
Thousand Oaks, California 91320
E-mail: order@sagepub.com

Sage Publications Ltd.
6 Bonhill Street
London EC2A 4PU
United Kingdom

Sage Publications India Pvt. Ltd.
B-42, Panchsheel Enclave
Post Box 4109
New Delhi 110 017 India

Printed in the United States of America

Library of Congress Cataloging-in-Publication Data

Novak, Gary.
Child and adolescent development: A behavioral systems approach /
Gary Novak, Martha Peláez.
        p. cm.
Includes bibliographical references and index.
ISBN 978-0-7619-2698-6 (pbk.)
    1. Child development. 2. Adolescence. 3. Developmental psychology.
I. Peláez, Martha B. II. Title.
HQ767.9.N68 2004
305.231—dc21

                                        2003013999

14   15   16   17   10   9   8   7

Acquisitions Editor:	Jim Brace-Thompson
Editorial Assistant:	Karen Ehrmann
Production Editor:	Melanie Birdsall
Copy Editor:	Linda Gray
Typesetter:	C&M Digitals (P) Ltd.
Proofreader:	Mary Meagher
Indexer:	Sylvia Coates
Cover Designer:	Michelle Lee Kenny

CONTENTS

PREFACE

Another developmental psychology textbook? In recent years there has been an explosion of texts in this area, reflecting the enormous popularity of the field. So why another one?

We think this one is unique. Here is why:

A Coherent Approach. Both of us have been college professors for some time. Our experiences tell us that many students come away from a course in developmental psychology with their heads filled with the facts of development but without an overall picture of the process of development. Students may know Freud's theory for identification, Piaget's for cognition, and Skinner's for behavior problems. Yet they have no consistent approach to all human development.

Likewise, students may have studied the latest research findings in these areas (many of which appear to contradict each other) but are left without a consistent overview of how the theories and data fit together. In this book, we try to provide a framework, in the form of a coherent approach to development, on which students can understand the facts of development.

In the field of assessment of student learning, the problem would be characterized as the students receiving a lot of "surface learning" that they will quickly forget once a test is over because the information is so unconnected. We would like to avoid the loss and have students develop some "deep learning". We try to do this here by taking a perspective on developmental psychology called a *behavioral systems approach.*

Behavioral Systems Approach. This approach combines the views of dynamical systems concepts with a behavioral/learning view of development. The behavioral dynamic systems view reflects an emerging consensus in modern developmental theory. It is an approach that incorporates both person and environment influences. It views developmental outcome as a constant learning process resulting from reciprocal interactions (or transactions) between nature and nurture. The result of these ever-changing transactions signifies a continual reorganization of the person–environment systems.

The behavioral approach has long been underrepresented in developmental psychology. Its emphasis on process, interaction, environmental influences, and the individual makes it a good fit with a dynamical systems approach. We think the synthesis of these views—the behavioral systems approach—provides a powerful and coherent view of the process of human development.

Emphasis on Process. The two fundamental questions in developmental psychology are these: (a) What develops? (b) How does it develop? The "what?" is largely a question of developmental *structures*. The "how?" is primarily a question of function or *process*. We take the latter approach. Developmental psychology has become increasingly concerned with questions of process, but most texts do not give a clear view of how development actually occurs. We think this one does.

Developmental Psychology as a Natural Science. Our approach views child development as a natural process, one that can be understood from a scientific perspective. Early on, we attempt to place developmental psychology in its relationship to other sciences. We try to analyze the process of development in a way that is consistent with analysis in other sciences. In doing so, we hope to reach our goal of providing a coherent approach to the field.

Development as a Parallel Process to Evolution. One way in which we provide a natural science approach is to present the process of child development as paralleling the process of *evolution*. Developmental psychology focuses on changes in individuals, whereas evolution focuses on changes in species. We try to show how both the person's evolutionary and learning histories interact, but the focus is on natural selection of individual behavior as the process of individual development. This "selectionist" approach carries into the next point.

Emphasis on Learning as a Natural Process. For many years, developmental texts have ignored or de-emphasized the role of learning in human development. It has often been relegated to the status of a special process reserved for use by parents and teachers to deal with behavior problems. We choose to emphasize the role of learning as the key process that, in interaction with genes and other person variables, determines developmental outcome. We think learning is a key thread that unifies this approach to understanding child development. Moreover, because many of our students are interested in the teaching profession, it is important to know how to use learning principles to foster development of their students.

A Nonlinear Approach. We view human development as an open system simultaneously involving multiple influences. Furthermore, the product of the interaction of these influences changes the process in complex ways. We believe approaches that view development as a set of simple interactions factors are doomed to failure. Development must be viewed as involving ever-changing dynamic systems whose effects result in a reorganization of the systems involved. For this reason, we are interested in some of the developments in a new field called chaos science.

A Contextual Approach. In a behavioral systems approach, when systems are reorganized, the context of development is constantly changing. Development is affected by the current context as well as by past learning histories.

Development Should Be Analyzed at Different Levels of Systems. We have found that students have difficulty grasping how the different content areas covered in developmental textbooks relate to each other. For example, how does learning relate to cognition? How do both relate to schools? We think the key to understanding these relationships is understanding that we are analyzing interlocking systems at different levels. Thus, we have organized this book on the basis of four system levels, from basic processes to society and culture. We use the metaphor of a painting by Seurat to illustrate how our perspective determines on which of the simultaneously present systems we choose to focus.

Systematic, Not Encyclopedic. If you look at the majority of other developmental textbooks, you are impressed by their sheer size. Each appears to try to outdo the other in the number and currency of the studies they cite. Even in their enormous girth, they can't contain all the possible studies relevant to development. We all have to make decisions about what research or theories to include. Our goal is more modest. We would like students to come away with a good understanding of how children develop. Our experiences are that only a limited number of concepts may be reasonably mastered by students studying each chapter. Much of the rest gets lost in the enormous task of trying to retain it all for a test. Often, students do not see the forest because of the huge growth of underbrush. Our goal is to provide a framework for understanding the process of development. We think such a framework will be more useful to students in the long term. As research discovers new facts and revises others, we think this approach will continue to provide a structure for understanding the process of human development.

Finally, we think this book offers teachers and students an alternative approach to the study of development. By focusing on issues rather than details, we provide flexibility in how child development is taught. We find encyclopedic texts constraining. The sheer amount they cover (as well as their cost) makes assigning readings or other material nearly impossible. We think these more limited goals open up exciting (and more flexible) possibilities for the study of child and adolescent development at *both* the undergraduate and graduate level.

ACKNOWLEDGMENTS

The writing of a textbook involves the input and assistance of many colleagues and students.

Students contributed to this endeavor in many ways. Many provided feedback on earlier versions of this book, and we give our continued thanks to them. Among the individuals helping us on this book, several deserve special thanks:

- Anna Perez for contributing the summaries at the end of each chapter
- Marylou Vallina-Raymat for assistance with Chapter 4 on prenatal development and most specially for her contributions with information on maternal diseases
- Felicia Barrera and Sabrina Bica for their assistance with revisions on Chapter 10 on socioemotional development
- Luzmary Amesty, Alberto Arca, and Jenny Rodriguez for their contributions to Chapter 14 on adolescence
- Bethany Duart and Annie Ervesun for their assistance with Chapter 15 on behavior disorders
- Tahir Chaudhary for assistance with locating graphs and figures and for help with the glossary
- Martha, Carla, and Tanya Nogueras for their assistance with photographic material
- Pedro Nogueras for his assistance with some graphs
- F. Phil Hardy for his feedback on education and school issues
- Karen Robinson and Melissa Frieder for their help with new terms for the glossary

We would also like to thank our colleagues who helped us, especially Emily Branscum, who assisted with an earlier version of this book and made some contributions to Chapter 11 in this one. We would also like to express our appreciation to Jack L. Gewirtz, Edward K. Morris, Hayne Reese, and Phil Hineline for their verbal feedback and nagging us about what was wrong and what needed to be changed. Yvonne Barnes-Holmes, Gina Green, Hayne Reese, and Julie Skinner-Vargas were very kind in contributing material that we incorporated.

We would also like to thank our reviewers, Jacob L. Gewirtz, Philip Hineline, Pete Peterson, Jesus Rosales-Ruiz, Michael W. Vasey, and Anne C. Watson, who made excellent comments and provided valuable criticism and support. Phil Hineline was especially generous with his assistance and important suggestions. Pete Peterson also should be singled out for his careful review and support.

Dr. Steven Hayes of Context Press was instrumental in the publication of an earlier version of this book by Gary Novak.

We would also like to thank James Brace-Thompson, Karen Ehrmann, Melanie Birdsall, Linda Gray, and others at Sage Publications for their support and help in bringing this project to fruition. We worked especially close with Linda, who greatly improved the clarity of our writing and helped tie up loose ends.

Finally, we would like to thank our families for their love and support and for putting up with us for all the time we took away from them so that we could write this book.

Our heartfelt thanks goes out to all the above and to many others who helped in many ways.

ABOUT THE AUTHORS

Gary Novak is Professor of Psychology and Child Development at California State University, Stanislaus. He has taught at CSU, Stanislaus for more than 30 years. He was twice Psychology Department Chairperson, founded the campus Child Development Center, and received the university's Outstanding Professor Award. He has many publications and professional presentations on children's language, cognitive and behavioral development, and behavioral systems approaches to development. His current research focuses on the role that early parental interactions play in the development of children's cognitive, language, literacy, and social behaviors. He is a board-certified behavior analyst and has a B.A. in psychology from Rutgers University and an M.A. in psychology from Temple University. He earned his Ph.D. in developmental psychology from the State University of New York at Stony Brook.

Martha Peláez is Associate Professor of Psychology at the Department of Educational and Psychological Studies, Florida International University. She has conducted numerous investigations on infant learning phenomena, including attachment, social referencing, fear of strangers, fear of the dark, maternal depression, moral development, rule-governed behavior, and stimulus equivalence. Dr. Peláez has continued to expand her research program in mother–infant interactions and has applied interventions with infants at-risk, and, more recently, she has studied the relation between language, intelligence, and derived relational responding with adult subjects. She is a Fellow of the American Psychological Association and past Program Chair of APA Division 25; she was also Program Co-Chair for the Association for Behavior Analysis (ABA). Currently, she is a member of various editorial boards for scientific journals and serves as a member of the Articulation Coordinating Committee (ACC) of the Florida Department of Education. She received her Ph.D. in developmental psychology in 1992 from FIU, winning the International Dissertation Award from the International Society for Infant Studies (ISIS) for her research on infant social referencing. In 1994, she completed a postdoctoral fellowship at the University of Miami Medical School, studying the behavior of depressed mothers and the effects on their infants' social and cognitive development.

INTRODUCTION

You are about to embark on one of the greatest scientific expeditions of all time—the exploration of how human beings develop. Humans are just like any other living creatures, yet in so many more ways they are remarkably different. Within a few years, a human goes from a simple single cell to a person capable of building craft that will take its species to the stars, teaching its children to read and write, and curing diseases. Unlike many scientific journeys, this one need take us no farther than our families or ourselves. We are intimately familiar with the subjects we will study, yet, paradoxically, this intimacy makes it difficult for us to be objective: We have many biases that have been difficult to set aside.

In this book, you will learn about many of the important factors that can help determine a child's outcome. Among the myriad issues we will investigate are the important role of parents in children's language development, how children develop prosocial and antisocial skills, what is effective in schools, and what is the most effective treatment of various behavior disorders, including autism. We will present the basic processes of **development** and what influences their outcomes. We will focus on the science of human development and the applications of this science.

As you will soon discover, development occurs at many levels. The organization of the book follows this scheme. We begin with the basics of development, such as genetics, physical development, and learning, and proceed to increasingly broader perspectives of individual, social, and cultural complexities.

The book examines the processes that underlie the complex developmental changes individuals undergo during their lifetimes. It tells the story of the amazing transformation of each individual from a simple single-celled organism to a mature adult composed of billions of cells. But this book is about much more than physical development. It is primarily about the development of increasingly complex and diverse relationships between what a person does and the environment in which he or she does it. As a single-celled organism, the individual's interactions with the world are limited to primitive, life-maintaining activities, but as physical complexity increases, so do our psychological complexities. As infants, our possible behavioral interactions are largely restricted to the reflexes we arrive with at birth. This quickly begins to change. As an adult, a person possesses a rich repertoire of actions. For example, we can watch the TV news, read a book, go for a jog, or think about what we will do this weekend. Which action is performed at any given time depends, in large measure, on the person's past history of interactions with the environment and present conditions in effect. The acts of reading and understanding the words in this book are the result of such a process. Your complex repertoire of behaviors requires much more than a certain level of physical development. These acts also require a certain level of psychological development determined by the history of your interactions with your world.

A BEHAVIORAL SYSTEMS APPROACH ●

This book merges two previously separate approaches to understanding development. It combines dynamical systems principles with those of **behavior analysis**. By focusing on behavior-environment relations as the main phenomena of psychology, behavior analysis has discovered many powerful principles relevant to human development (e.g., Gewirtz & Peláez-Nogueras, 1992a). In recent years, behavior analysis has expanded its province to include the analysis of larger units of behavior and, in doing so, has recognized the importance of dynamical systems principles (e.g., Galbicka, 1992; Marr, 1992, 1996). This book seeks to address some principles of dynamical systems and behavioral perspectives relevant to human development. The result is a natural science approach to development that emphasizes constant, reciprocal interactions between behavior and environment called **behavioral systems theory** (Novak, 1996, 1998).

A DYNAMICAL SYSTEMS APPROACH ●

In our view, development involves constantly changing dynamical systems. The ever-changing person is in constant and reciprocal interaction with a continually changing environment. This environment both is affected by and effects changes in the person. In turn, the person both is affected by and effects changes in the environment. In **dynamical systems**, the person and the environment are in continuous, reciprocal interaction. This book will treat psychological development as the outcome of progressive interactions between the person and the environment. Neither nature nor nurture alone is responsible for development; both are. The structures of biology interact with the effects of the environment over the life span of the individual. From the moment of conception, who you are is determined by these ever-changing, ongoing interactions. A dynamical systems approach attempts to view development from this perspective.

Dynamical systems approaches have only recently had an impact on mainstream developmental psychology. For example, Esther Thelen (Thelen & Smith, 1994; Thelen & Ulrich, 1991) and Richard Lerner (Ford & Lerner, 1992; Lerner, 1991) have championed systems approaches to the study of development that have aspects in common with the dynamical systems approach proposed in this book.

● WHAT IS DEVELOPMENT?

Development means change over time. In this book, we are not studying physical development alone. Nor are we studying motor, emotional, perceptual, moral, intellectual, or social development alone. Instead, we are viewing development from a more holistic perspective. Bijou and Baer (1961, 1978) viewed psychological development as progressive changes in the interactions between the behaviors of a person and the events in his or her environment. This definition identifies three important aspects of psychological development: First, the focus is on changes in interactions; second, these changes are progressive; third, these changes occur over time and, ultimately, over the lifetime of the individual.

Changes in Interactions

Psychologists study behavior. A **behavior** is an action of a living thing in relation to events in the environment. In studying psychological development, we are concerned not only with changes in behavior but with changes in the person-environment relationships. Not only does behavior change, but behavior in relationship to environmental events changes; we learn under what conditions to emit behaviors. We learn what to do and when to do it. What develops are new relationships between behavior and environment, not merely the behaviors themselves. As we develop, the events and objects in our environment take on new functions.

For example, if you give a set of keys to a 1-year-old child, she is likely to place them in her mouth to explore them. Although you could put the keys in your mouth too, it is unlikely that you would behave the same way in relation to the keys. For you, the functions of the keys would be tied to the doors they open, the cars they start, or, in some contexts, their usefulness in prying open the lid of the jar. Not only is your behavior more complex, but it is more complex in relationship to the things and events in your environment.

Progressive Changes

Development is progressive in the sense that it is cumulative. That is, development is built on what has come before. At conception, specialized cells from the child's mother and father combine to produce a new single-celled organism with a unique genetic makeup. For the rest of his or her existence, changes will occur based on what already exists as well as what is occurring now. For example, the elderly person with failing vision and hearing due to deterioration of his or her physical structures adapts to the environment in increasingly complex ways to compensate for the physical deterioration. Because that person can no longer see or hear as well, he or she may learn new behaviors, such as squinting or asking questions, behaviors that were previously unnecessary. In short, later changes are built on what has already occurred.

Note that *progressive* does not necessarily imply a higher level of functioning. With deterioration of biological capabilities, changes may result in diminished behavioral abilities. Nevertheless, such changes are "progressive" in the sense that new skills are built on earlier ones. Note too that progressive does not require unidirectional change toward an ultimate, idealized goal or form. Rather, progressive implies that behavior change has occurred on the basis of the environment-behavior interactions that precede the change (Rosales & Baer, 1994).

Behavior-environment changes can often be accounted for by the progressive complexity (or simplicity) of the current stimulus patterns that control behavior too (Peláez-Nogueras & Gewirtz, 1997). For example, we may start by first learning to read letters (simple stimuli) but later learn to read letter patterns as words (complex stimuli), words as sentences (more complex stimuli), sentences as paragraphs, and, ultimately, paragraphs as books. The stimulus patterns we learn in order to read have become increasingly complex.

Changes Occur Across the Life Span

Developmental psychologists are interested in progressive changes over time. Child psychologists are interested in a relatively short span of time. Some study only infants, others study larger spans of childhood. A relatively recent trend among developmental psychologists is a life span approach. This "womb to tomb" approach enables us to get a broader overview of the entirety of human development.

● A NATURAL SCIENCE APPROACH TO DEVELOPMENT

We can use many methods to obtain knowledge of the phenomena that interest us. Artists and musicians can stir our emotions. Novelists can reveal truths about the human condition. Philosophers can apply introspection and logic to provide accounts of human behavior. All these perspectives have their own validity in helping us understand human nature and its relationships to the world around us. Since the emergence of the scientific method during the Renaissance, science has been one of the most efficient ways of enabling us to understand our world. A natural science approach applies the principles used by all sciences to study phenomena that occur in the real world.

The Scientific Method

All sciences share a common set of methods that define them as sciences and distinguishes them from the other methods of understanding nature. The primary characteristics of the **scientific method** are (a) reliance on systematic observations made under well-specified conditions and (b) using special techniques (including quantitative ones such as statistics) for organizing and summarizing the descriptions of those observations. Science is said to be "objective" and "empirical" because the validity of a scientific statement does not depend on who said it. To be sure, some scientists, such as Einstein, become well-known or even famous for their ability to discern orderly relationships between complex sets of observations, but the "hypotheses" in which these relationships are summarized are open to evaluation by anyone who is able to undertake the relevant observations.

Frequently, the process of conducting science include formulating a **hypothesis**; conducting direct observations on the phenomenon to test the hypothesis; accepting, rejecting, or modifying the hypothesis; and positing new questions from the data obtained. This emphasis on direct observation and manipulation of hypothesized variables is what sets sciences apart from the other ways of drawing inferences about natural phenomena.

To free the observations from the personal biases of the investigator, a scientist attempts to make the observations as objective as possible. Other important aspects of the scientific method include validity of the observation (the scientist is actually measuring what is supposed to be measured), replication of the observation, and control of extraneous variables. Many of these and other concerns of scientists, such as internal consistency, predictability, and **parsimony,** are considered in judging the adequacy of development theories discussed in Chapter 2.

THE CONTINUUM ●
OF SCIENTIFIC DISCIPLINES

In this book, we approach the study of **child development** from the perspective of the natural sciences. Just as physics, chemistry, and biology have been able to reveal basic laws and principles about the dynamical systems that concern them, we feel that a natural science approach is the best approach to understanding development.

To understand the unique position of developmental psychology, it is helpful to place it in the context of other sciences. In fact, it is possible to place various sciences along a continuum based on the complexity of the dynamical systems that are their focus. At one end of the continuum, we examine dynamical systems involving interactions of subatomic particles (**molecular**). At the other end, we view dynamical systems at the aggregate level of culture and society (**molar**). We start at the most molecular level, with physics, and proceed along a continuum, finishing with anthropology, the most molar level.

Physics

Physicists study the physical building blocks of the universe. At its most basic level, physics is the study of electrons, protons, neutrinos, quarks, and other basic building blocks of atoms and subatomic particles, which are themselves the basic building blocks of all things, living and inert, in our universe.

Chemistry

Unique combinations of protons and electrons yield unique elements. The periodic chart of elements depicts the particular combinations that result in each of the 115 known elements. Each has properties that are quantitatively as well as qualitatively unique. For example, hydrogen can be distinguished quantitatively from iron based on the quantity of electrons each possess. The physical characteristics of the subatomic atoms (these include protons, neutrons, and electrons) that make up all the pieces of the universe are identical. The number and arrangements of these subatomic particles make hydrogen different from iron, that make actinium unique from zinc. Chemists study these unique properties. Furthermore, they are also interested in how chemical elements combine to produce substances with properties that emerge that are qualitatively different from their individual elements. Hydrogen and iron can also be easily distinguished based on their unique emergent qualities—one is a gas and the other a solid—but, at the subatomic level, they are made of the same particles that could be switched from one atom to the other.

Neale and Liebert (1980) suggest an example of how the properties of chemical compounds are lost when they are reduced to their components. Chlorine (Cl) is a gaseous element that, if inhaled, will produce severe burns, even death. Sodium (Na) is a very unstable metal which, when immersed in water, will burn vigorously. You would not make contact with either of these elements without taking precautionary measures. Yet when sodium and chlorine are combined, the resulting compound, table salt (NaCl), is something we ingest practically everyday. The resulting compound is not only essential to our health (in small amounts) but also makes life a little more palatable. The compound that emerges from the two elements has properties that cannot be understood by reducing it to the smallest basic elements studied by physics. The phenomena studied by chemistry are at a higher level and, if reduced to a more basic level of analysis, lose their unique (or emergent) properties.

Biology

Biology differs from chemistry in that it focuses on the unique combination of organic molecules that when combined produce whole living organisms and their component systems. Notice that on this continuum there are transitions between the scientific disciplines where those working at the lower-level science are interested in phenomena of the next higher one. Organic chemistry is such a discipline. Notice, too, that some people working in this area are primarily chemists interested in the chemical compounds of living creatures, and some are principally biologists whose first interest is in the study of living organisms and only secondarily in their chemical makeup.

What is next on our continuum?

Psychology

Many textbooks define **psychology** as the science of behavior. However, as noted earlier, this definition is incomplete. Psychologists are not simply interested in an individual's behavior—that is, what he or she does—but in the relationship of that behavior to the environment in which it occurs. For example, if a parent complains to a psychologist that her daughter is noncompliant, the psychologist needs information about the child's social environment before deciding what treatment (if any) is needed. In one environment (e.g., a physically abusive home) noncompliance may be a sign of psychological health, whereas in another environment it could be a sign of a clinical disorder. This suggests a more complete definition. **Behavior-analytic psychology** is the scientific study of the interactions between the behavior of individuals and the events in their environment.

In the molecular-molar continuum, our behavioral systems approach falls midway, given that it is interested in analyzing interacting variables ranging from physical-biological conditions of the organism to sociocultural systems. We analyze both individual as well as group variables.

Sociology

Sociology is concerned with the unique characteristics of groups, not the individuals that make them up. Consequently, sociologists study the causes and effects of variables such as membership in ethnic or racial groups, socioeconomic class, and gangs. These are analyzed as group variables, not individual ones.

Anthropology

As the last science on our continuum, the phenomena studied by anthropology are the most complex. Anthropology is interested in the unique phenomena emerging at the level of cultures. Although cultures are composed of individuals, the effects brought about by the culture transcend the analysis of the individual. Thus, whereas individuals may be best understood by using psychological principles, such as reinforcement and socialization, cultural differences may need a unique set of anthropological principles to be understood. For example, cultures vary greatly in terms of the sexual stereotypes they promote, and it may be necessary to understand the values of a culture to understand the gender-related behaviors that emerge in it.

● METAPHORS FOR UNDERSTANDING DEVELOPMENTAL LEVELS

The universe consists of many systems. As our look at the continuum of scientific disciplines illustrates, these systems may be analyzed at different levels of complexity. For example, human behavior may be analyzed at the level of the person in the environment or, at a lower level, the action of the person's biological systems. We may even analyze behavior at yet lower (i.e., more molecular) levels, such as the action of chemical neurotransmitters or even the person's electrons or neutrons. At all these levels, we are analyzing systems—the interactions between parts. It is important to keep in mind that all levels of these systems are present simultaneously. That is, while we are looking at a person interacting with the environment, there are also biological, chemical, physical (lower-level systems), social, and cultural events (higher-level systems) taking place. We normally choose to view or analyze one level of a system at a time. Psychologists choose to look at the behavior-environment systems; biologists look at biological systems, and so on.

While all levels exist simultaneously, which level you choose for your analysis depends on your question for analysis and perspective. Let us illustrate this point with a metaphor. A famous painting by the 19th-century French painter, George Seurat, called *A Sunday on La Grande Jatte* hangs in the Art Institute of Chicago. It is a huge canvas, filling nearly an entire wall. If you were to analyze it for an art appreciation class, what would you say about it? Where would you start? Your analysis would depend on your perspective. If you stood very close to the painting you could see the thousands of individual colored dots on the white canvas (see Figure 1.1). At this level, the dots are just arrays of colors, not making any sense, but you would be able to talk about the artist's technique. You could talk about the basic processes that made up the school of painting founded by Seurat, pointillism.

Now, as you step back from the painting, the dots begin to merge into organized shapes and forms (see Figure 1.2). You see people, a dog, a tree emerge from the individual dots. You could analyze how the bold use of colors makes up the forms, and you could talk about how the forms look or how they are different from real people. Maybe you could compare the forms with those painted by Manet, Monet, or Van Gogh.

Stepping back further, you begin to see how the forms relate to each other. You could comment on how the little girl and the woman are holding hands and what that says about this presumed mother-daughter relationship. They relate as aesthetic objects and as human beings. Their placement was carefully planned by Seurat, and, at this level, you could write about what is called "composition."

Figure 1.1   Seurat's *A Sunday on La Grande Jatte,* Close-Up

SOURCE: Courtesy of the Art Institute of Chicago. Georges Seurat, French, 1859-1891, *A Sunday on La Grande Jatte–1884*, 1884-1886, oil on canvas, 207.6 × 308 cm, Helen Birch Bartlett Memorial Collection, 1926.224.

Finally, you may be interested in analyzing the painting as social commentary—an afternoon at a working-class leisure spot. You could analyze what the subjects are wearing and what they are doing and perhaps compare

Figure 1.2   Seurat's *A Sunday on La Grande Jatte*

SOURCE: Courtesy of the Art Institute of Chicago. Georges Seurat, French, 1859-1891, *A Sunday on La Grande Jatte–1884*, 1884-1886, oil on canvas, 207.6 × 308 cm, Helen Birch Bartlett Memorial Collection, 1926.224.

the scene with other contemporary paintings of middle-class life. You could point out what the painting tells us about late 19th-century culture.

Which level is most important? That depends on the question of your analysis and your perspective. Are you taking a course in "Techniques of Painting" or "Capitalist Influences in Art"? Are you interested in paint or people? Depending on your perspective, one level of analysis may be more appropriate than another. Also, certain paintings may be more appropriately analyzed at some levels and not others.

Note that all levels exist simultaneously. You could step back and do your social commentary or step forward and describe the processes of pointillism. Note also that one level cannot exist without the other. The characters are created by the technique, but the technique would not exist without the figures that emerge. When you look at the big picture, you do not notice the pointillistic dots, but the forms and the culture they produce would not exist without the basic points of paint. Likewise, what point gets painted and where is determined by the artist's cultural and societal values in his view of "the big picture." Yet sometimes we may be concerned with one level of analysis and with a different level at another time. It is easy to miss the relationships among these four levels of painting. However, analyzing people's behavior is more difficult than analyzing the complexities in a painting. In real life, levels interact in a dynamic manner, and changes are ongoing and constantly evolving.

Looking at a painting, we may analyze it in many ways. At its most basic level, we may look at the canvas and the brushstrokes. At a much higher level, we may look at the social and cultural messages it conveys. The same principle of micro- through macro-analysis may be applied to the sciences we have looked at on our continuum. If we look at a person, we may analyze him or her as atomic, chemical, behavioral, societal, or cultural processes. We can do the same when we look at human development. For example, if we look at language development, we can look at the biology, the words that emerge, the social use of **language,** or the differences in languages across cultures. All are present simultaneously. Often, we tend to focus our analysis on one level because of the perspective we have taken from our formal training and informal experiences. When we focus our analysis at a lower level, we are engaging in what scientists call **reductionism**.

REDUCTIONISM AND ANTIREDUCTIONISM ●

Reductionism is the reducing of a phenomenon to a lower level of analysis. For example, reducing table salt to its individual elements, sodium and chlorine, is reductionism. The unique properties that result when table salt is formed is lost. In psychology, reductionism occurs when one attempts to explain behavior in terms of physiological (i.e., biological) mechanisms rather than in terms of the behavior of the whole organism interacting with its environment (i.e., psychological). Reductionism may be worthwhile when it is effective in producing an **explanation**. However, it is important to point out that it may be more useful to explain a particular phenomenon at the higher level of analysis. For instance, although NaCl may be reduced to its atomic components, you lose the essential nature of the unique chemical compound that we know as table salt. In a similar fashion, when behavior is reduced to the physiological processes that accompany the behavior (e.g., the firing of neurons), you may lose the essential psychological aspects of behavior. Just as sodium and chlorine ingested separately do not taste like salt, neuron firings do not capture the essence of person–environment interactions.

Let us provide you with an example of how different disciplines might approach a common problem of human behavior: stress-induced hypertension or high blood pressure. Physicians and psychologists might both treat this disorder. How would their approaches differ? Physicians (who are actually applied biologists) would likely take a particularly biological approach to treatment, perhaps stressing medication to reduce blood pressure, reduce cholesterol, and control heart rate. Medication might be prescribed to reduce tension as well (e.g., "Take two Prozacs and see me in the morning"). Thus, the focus of intervention would be on the biological organs and processes. Clinical psychologists, on the other hand, are more apt to reduce the number of stressors or try to change the person's reactions to the stressors in the environment rather than directly reduce the physiological reaction to stress. Thus, psychologists would be more likely to teach coping skills and stress reduction techniques, such as progressive relaxation training and systematic desensitization, so as to change the way the person interacts with his or her environment. The focus would not be on changing the body's reaction to stress but, rather, to change the person's reaction to the stress-inducing situations in the environment. Choosing between the two would require a cost–benefit analysis of both treatment approaches.

In recent years, there has been a blurring of these disciplinary borders. The fields of holistic health alternative approaches and behavioral medicine incorporate many psychological principles into the treatment of human disorders. Likewise, advances in biologically based treatments have influenced the practice of psychology. Yet it is important to understand that there are phenomena that may be best understood at a particular level of analysis and that reductionism is not always productive. The study of psychological phenomena is most appropriately studied at the level of the whole organism's interactions with its environment rather than attempting to reduce it to the actions of biological, chemical, or atomic systems.

● BEHAVIORAL SYSTEMS AND DEVELOPMENTAL PSYCHOLOGY

What is developmental psychology? **Developmental psychology** is the study of the progressive changes in the relationships between an organism and its environment over the life span of the organism. Psychologists are concerned with two parallel processes: **developmental phylogenesis** and **developmental ontogenesis** (Sheppard & Willoughby, 1975).[1]

The Evolution of Species and Behavior

Skinner (1981) made a case for the parallelism between the processes in the evolution of species and the development of behavior. He identified the unifying process as selection. Recently Hull, Langman, and Glenn (2001) argued that selection is a process that is generally applicable to the study of changes in many sciences, including biology, immunology, and, of interest here, behavioral change or learning. The selection process does seem to provide a way for mechanisms occurring in nature to bring about changes in species or individuals. We look at these changes called phylogenesis and ontogenesis.

Developmental Phylogenesis

Phylogenesis is the study of behavioral changes within a species over phylogenic (or evolutionary) time. Psychologists who study the evolution of behavior across species are called comparative psychologists, and their field of study is called **comparative psychology**. Comparative psychologists study, for example, the similarities and differences in perceptual, motor, and social behaviors of organisms across the range of complexity from, say, mitochondria to man. Today, a new term, **evolutionary psychology,** has become popular for a field that makes inferences about how human behavior evolved as a result of inferred conditions of natural selection. As Catania (1998) has noted, behavior leaves very little direct evidence in the fossil record. Mostly, behavioral changes across species must be inferred and not directly observed.

Box 1.1   Of Dishes and Organisms: A Metaphor

Let us provide you with a metaphor about **phylogenic** and **ontogenic contingencies.** Recently, many problems one of us (GN) had with the local cable TV provider, prompted a switch to satellite TV. I did not really notice what kinds of dishes were available and how they worked. I remembered the early days of satellite and the enormous dishes they needed, but now that I needed one myself, I started doing some consumer research on what was best, and I also began to notice the differences and similarities of dishes wherever I went. I began to think of why these differences and similarities existed and that led me to this metaphor:

Imagine that you are a visitor from space and you arrived in the ol' US of A on Super Bowl Sunday. You go in search of the inhabitants. There are no people in sight (they are all inside watching their super heroes on the tube), so you might mistake some inanimate object as one of the inhabitants. You might mistake all the satellite dishes as living creatures (after all, you come from the very far out planet, *Anorexia*), all oriented toward some unseen power source, like flowers oriented toward the sun.

As you travel the countryside you make two observations in your flight log. First you notice that the physical makeup of the creatures changes as you travel from area to area. In the congestion of the city, all the creatures look virtually the same. They are the same size and shape. They all seem to inhabit high places like the eaves of roofs. About the only physical difference is in the markings on their dishlike heads. As you travel into the rural countryside, the creatures begin to change. There is more variation. As a whole, they are much larger than the city species, with wiry frames and mounted on substantial feet. They seem to be ground dwellers. On the other hand, it looks as if the smaller city species is beginning to intrude.

Your second observation is with respect to the roosting behavior of the dishes. Individuals living nearby seem to face in the same direction. Local populations roost like an enormous flock of metallic birds perched with their body parts permanently oriented toward some great invisible sun.

How do these observations relate to our discussion of phylogenic and ontogenic contingencies? First, let us look at the physical makeup of the "creatures." In the early days of satellite TV, signals were very weak, so large antennas were necessary to pick up the faint signals. Such large dishes were very unsightly and neighbors complained about them. Because their size was a problem in high winds, they had to be constructed from wire so that the wind could pass through them. Dishes were expensive. They required a lot of space. Because they were so heavy, they needed a firm foundation, and, once installed, they could not easily be moved. Thus, the only viewers who selected these large beasts were those whose location away from the city made reception via antenna or cable impossible. As technology improved and satellite signals became stronger, consumers selected smaller dishes that were not an eyesore. Because they were smaller, they could be mounted high on the house so that line-of-sight to the satellite could be improved. Thus, various species occupy various environmental niches. In the development of organisms, those that are optimally adapted to their environments are selected by these environments and survive to reproduce. In the satellite TV world, dishes selected by consumers are reproduced by their manufacturers. They successfully compete with other organisms in that environment. These are Sheppard and Willoughby's (1975) phylogenic contingencies for selecting the characteristics of the species over evolutionary time. We call these phylogenic contingencies **natural selection**.

One important feature in the evolution of the satellite dish was an adjustable mount. Once the dish was small enough to be mounted on the building, a dish that could adjust its orientation to the satellites in the sky was better than one that only could be mounted with a single orientation. At installation, the technician is able to move the dish until the feedback on the signal strength meter shows that the signal is locked in. This ability to adapt to the specific environment the individual finds itself in is an example of adapting to ontogenic contingencies. These are Sheppard and Willoughby's (1975) ontogenic contingencies for selecting behaviors within the lifetime of the individual. We call the effects of these ontogenic contingencies **learning.**

Notice that in this metaphor, the effects of the phylogenic and ontogenic contingencies interact so that responding to ontogenic contingencies (i.e., in our metaphor, movement of the antenna) is facilitated by those produced by the phylogenic contingencies (i.e., the ability to move is determined by whether a rotor has been selected). In the development of living organisms, the influence of phylogenic and ontogenic contingencies are inseparable. The manner of interaction is the topic of the next chapter.

Developmental Ontogenesis

Ontogenesis is the study of changes in individuals over their lifetimes. Most developmental psychologists study developmental ontogenesis. Developmental psychologists may differ with respect to the part of the life span they study or with respect to the approaches they take to the study of ontogenesis.

Phylogenic Contingencies and Ontogenic Contingencies

Renewed interest in the genetic determination of behavior has led developmental psychologists to examine the relationship between biological and environmental determinants of behavior. One way to view this issue is in terms of the ways in which genetic and environmental factors affect the development of individuals.

Sheppard and Willoughby (1975) contrasted phylogenic and ontogenic contingencies. A **contingency** is an if–then relationship. In behavior analysis, a contingency is any event or force that depends on behavior. Phylogenic contingencies are the forces that shape the development of species over evolutionary time. For example, in the Arctic, if a bear is born with white fur, then it is more likely to escape detection by predators, find food, and, most important, have offspring, than a bear with brown fur. For brown bears in the Arctic, the reverse is the case. Thus, over time, genes responsible for white, furry bears will predominate in the gene pool. The environmental forces that determine the physical and behavioral characteristics of species operate through the process of natural selection. In natural selection, physical and behavioral characteristics that better fit the demands of the environment are possessed by an organism better adapted to survive and produce offspring. Over time, the effect of phylogenic contingencies is that those characteristics that result in better adaptation are the ones that will be present in the genes of the organisms.

Ontogenic contingencies are the forces that shape the behavioral development of the individuals over their life spans (Skinner, 1981). These if–then contingencies work through the processes of development that we will study in this book, primarily the processes of learning. For example, if a baby finds a rattle and discovers how to shake it and produce a sound, then it is more likely to repeat the same action again. Notice that the change occurred within the lifetime of the individual. In short, the baby has learned because of the ontogenic contingencies. Generally, changes in an individual's behavior resulting from the consequences provided by the environment characterize ontogenic contingencies.

Although a behavioral systems approach acknowledges the importance of both nature and nurture, it regards much human behavior as learned. Behavioral systems theory rejects explanations of behavior in terms of instincts and innate habits. Instead, it proposes that behavior is a function of selection of behavior by consequences involving both phylogenic (nature) and ontogenic contingencies. Thus, phylogenic contingencies correspond to the *evolutionary history of the species* and work through survival and reproductive mechanisms. In contrast, ontogenic contingencies correspond to the *developmental history of an individual* and work through reinforcement of behavior (Midgley & Morris, 1998). In short, phylogenetic contingencies are "nature" and ontogenic contingencies are "nurture," and both are essential.

Learning may be viewed as a parallel process to natural selection. Whereas the latter applies to the adaptation of species, characteristics over evolutionary time, learning applies to the adaptation of behaviors of a single individual to the environment over a life span. In both cases the relevant contingencies produce characteristics that allow the organism to function more successfully in its environment.

Developmental Ontogenesis and Dynamical Systems

Developmental ontogenesis (or simply, development) is the topic of this book. The view taken here is that development can be best understood as a process involving behavioral systems. The characteristics that human development shares with other dynamical systems include the following:

1. Development involves the *relationship* between elements, specifically the person's behavior and the environmental contingencies.

2. In development, the relationship between these elements is constantly *changing*.

3. The effects of the elements on each other are *reciprocal*. That is, not only does the environment affect the person, but the person affects the environment.

4. Development is characterized by a large number of factors acting simultaneously. That is, there are *multiple influences* or determinants operating at the same time (e.g., biological, genetic, environmental, social).

5. In development, there are multiple ongoing interactions (e.g., bidirectional and even multidirectional sources, such as mother, father, and siblings) influencing one another.

6. Development is *nonlinear*. The trajectory of development is not a smooth, straight-line progression. Although we assume continuity in development, there may be sudden changes in the rate or form of development (called **phase shifts**). These phase shifts are not the same as what developmental psychologists call "stages of development." Development is *emergent*. The result of person–environment interactions is not simply changes in the number of cells or behaviors. Instead, new patterns of behavior emerge. The organized patterns, called **strange attractors** by dynamical systems theorists, are not just simple additions of elements but newly organized patterns. Qualitative changes may appear as a result of organized quantitative changes in behavior.

7. Development involves multiple directions of outcomes. Changes in behavior may occasion new pathways of development.

Levels of Analysis of Developmental Behavioral Systems

Just as it is appropriate to view science as existing simultaneously at different levels of systems (e.g., physics, chemistry, biology), so too, it is appropriate to view human development at different levels of systems. Modern developmental theory (e.g., Bronfenbrenner & Crouter, 1983) views the child as part of many systems. For example, the child may be viewed as a contributor to the dynamics of the family in which she lives or the school she attends. This systems approach is very compatible with our definition of development that emphasizes the progressive changes in interactions (i.e., transactions) between the person and the environment.

Two questions remain: At what level of systems shall we focus when we look at development? How can stimuli and responses relate to the important context of culture and society? Horowitz (1987) suggests that the answer lies in viewing the process of development as occurring simultaneously at four different levels of systems. We may choose to look at one level of systems for our analysis or move among them for a more comprehensive understanding of the phenomena. Horowitz uses the metaphor of a series of nested boxes to depict the relationship between four levels of systems. We have chosen the levels of Seurat's painting to represent the different levels of systems.

Level 1: Basic Processes

The most fundamental level of analysis of human development is System Level 1. At this level, we see development as a set of basic processes and components. We will be working at Level 1 when we look at the principles of genetics and learning. For example, meiosis in genetics and reinforcement in learning are processes viewed at Level 1. In the painting metaphor, this is at the level of the dots of paint on the canvas.

Level 2: Patterns of Behavior

As we move up to System Level 2, we look at larger chunks of development. At this level of analysis, there emerge from the Level 1 processes new units to be analyzed. The basic units are organized and reorganized. These higher-order units include characteristic behaviors such as intelligence, personality, creativity, or their facets. We can still analyze them using the Level 1 processes, particularly learning, but now we look at larger units. In the painting, the emergence of figures from the dots would be a Level 2 analysis.

Level 3: Social Interactions

At System Level 3 we view processes as bidirectional interactions. "Motherese," the simplified talk used by mothers to their infants, is a Level 3 phenomenon. It develops because the mother's talk is shaped by the slowly changing nature of the child's behavior toward the mother. Analyzing the relationship of the figures to each other in the painting is equivalent to viewing the painting at a Level 3 analysis.

Level 4: Society and Culture

Finally, analyzing at the system's System Level 4 involves looking at the effects of society and culture on the child. These involve higher-order transactions, not merely transactions between the child and another, but with culture and society, which are pervasive and form the largest context for development. In the painting metaphor, Level 4 would include the societal and cultural implications of the art.

To recap, it is crucial to keep in mind that development is occurring at all levels simultaneously. It is our human limitations that make us analyze at one level of system at a time. These levels involve a system within a system within a system within a system. The power of this metaphor is in understanding that development can be analyzed at all or any of these different levels. All levels contribute to an understanding of development. As you move to the higher levels, you increase the breadth of your understanding of development. As you move to the lower levels, you become more precise.

As an example, let us look at sex role development. What causes it? We can explain it at Level 4 by looking at the sex role stereotypes in our culture and society. We can add more to our understanding by moving to a Level 3 analysis involving the transactions between parents and the child. At this level, we may use concepts such as "modeling" and "direct tuition" to explain how sex roles develop. (But note that we move back to Level 4 to describe what the culturally based stereotypes are that parents model and train and to Level 1 for the basic processes to explain how modeling and direct tuition work.)

At Level 2, we explain the differences by saying that girls have an expressive sex role and boys have an instrumental one. These are labels for the organized classes of behaviors that emerge out of, and are different from, the environment–behavior processes we talk about at Level 1.

Yet all these levels of talking about development are occurring simultaneously. We telescope back and forth along these levels of systems to understand development more fully. In this book, we will begin our analysis at Level 1, viewing our painting from up close, looking at basic principles of the organism and environment interactions. We end at Level 4, seeing the "big picture," viewing the unique contributions of society and culture as they are mediated by families and the schools.

THE CENTRAL ROLE OF ● LEARNING FOR DEVELOPMENT

Learning is a basic process in human development. It is a crucial process in ontogenic development. It is responsible for change brought about by an individual's experiences. Learning is defined as a relatively permanent change in behavior in relation to the environment that is due to experience. Unfortunately, the study of the role of learning in children's development virtually disappeared as a central topic in developmental psychology in the mid-1970s (Stevenson, 1983). What was lost was an understanding of the primary process that produces developmental change. Fortunately, there is now a rebirth of learning in the developmental literature (Siegler, 2000).

There are three parts to the definition of learning:

1. Learning is a change in the behavior–environment relationship. Behaviors may change, but they do so in relationship to events in the environment. For example, as toddlers, we learn to say "cat" when we see a cat. Later, when we learn to read the word cat aloud, the behavior that produces the sound "cat" does not change compared with just saying the word; what changes here is not the form of the mouth movements saying "cat" but the behavior's (i.e., the mouth's movement) relationship to the environment (the written word cat versus a cat itself).

2. This change is relatively permanent. Thus, changes are not merely momentary, such as when we sneeze, or drive a car, or complain about a pain, but they are lasting. When we learn to walk, that change remains just as it does if we reliably read cat. If the behavior is not relatively permanent (i.e., we say cat one time but do not respond another), we have not yet learned the behavior. Why do we need the qualifier "relatively"? Sometimes behaviors disappear after we have learned them, as when we forget what a word means or forget how to play a passage on the piano. The exact length of time required to demonstrate learning is vague, but researchers often explicitly define learning as a number or percentage of correct responses in a row.

3. The final part of the definition is that learning is due to experience with the environment. What else could produce relatively permanent changes? Physical growth or physiological changes (e.g., sickness) can change behavior. **Maturation** is a term to describe physical and behavioral changes due to biological growth. Yet one must keep in mind that the effects of biological growth may also be influenced by the environmental experiences occurring, so that maturation may also involve learning as well as physical growth.

● THE EVOLUTIONARY SIGNIFICANCE OF LEARNING

What separates humans from other species is the human species' remarkable ability to adapt to the environment. What would be the evolutionary importance of inheriting increased ability to learn? Unlearned behaviors are fine as long as the environment remains undemanding, nonthreatening, and stable. Animals that have brief lifetimes do not need or, indeed, have the time to learn. Animals may have elaborate patterns of unlearned, instinctual behavior elicited by particular environmental stimuli. Ethologists call these patterns **fixed action patterns** and the stimuli that elicit them **innate releasing mechanisms**. Indeed the stimuli are fixed and cannot vary once the automatic response is released by the species-specific stimulus.

The evolutionary significance of such innate patterns is that they provide behaviors that enable members to survive in environments typical for that species. Equipped with these innate releasing mechanisms, bees will signal the location and distance of honey, a wolf will fight another wolf but not slash its throat because a white patch of fur on the exposed throat of the subdued wolf serves as an innate releasing mechanism, and the lowly freshwater stickleback fish will engage in an elaborate mating dance. But using an unlucky stickleback, we may illustrate the adaptive limits of such innate inflexibility.

An innate releasing mechanism for the courting dance of the male stickleback is the red belly of the female in spring when she is ripe with eggs. The males, in whom the dance is released, build a nest and lure the female into the nest where the eggs are fertilized. This ensures the survival of the species, and presumably the best dancers are the fittest.

But woe the poor male stickleback living in a stream that falls victim to a stream filled with red Christmas tree balls (the result of a train derailment accident). The red spot is a brighter and larger stimulus, which ethologists refer to as a **supernormal stimulus**, and is a more effective releaser of the male dancing behavior than the gravid females' spots. The poor males in this stream dance and dance into the night and to exhaustion. Alas, no little sticklebacks are born in that stream that spring and the population is threatened.

Learning is much more adaptive for humans and, in the long run, for all the species. Species that can learn can adapt to short-run changes in their environment. They may even change the environment based on what they have learned. Individual humans are extremely adaptable to the environments. Over evolutionary time, they have been selected on the basis of their ability to learn. As a consequence, humans exist in a wide range of environments . . . we have even walked on the moon. We do this through our ability to change with respect to the environment as no other species can.

A PARALLELISM BETWEEN EVOLUTION AND LEARNING ●

Recall Sheppard and Willoughby's (1975) concepts of phylogenic and ontogenic contingencies. Recall that natural selection is the process in evolution, and learning is the process in individual development. We may take this parallelism further and point out that both are forms of adaptation to the environment (Baum, 1994; Hull et al., 2001) For natural selection, the adaptation to the ecological niche works over phylogenic time. Learning is adaptation to the ecosystem of the individual over his or her lifetime.

How Does Learning Relate to Development?

What is the difference between learning and development? Development is the overall process—the progressive changes in the interactions between behavior and environment. Learning is a process (or the process) that determines development. The question is, Does learning play only a minor role along with many other process (Is it *a* process?), or is it the main process (Is it *the* process?)?

Is Learning *a* Process or *the* Process in Development?

The question is significant, and the answer is not simple. The answer depends on what behaviors you are asking about. Some behaviors are present at birth, such as basic perceptual behaviors, production of early language sounds (e.g., cooing or babbling), or reflexes. For these behaviors, learning is only one of the processes in their development, meaning that behaviors are essentially hardwired in the child's physiology due to his or her genetic inheritance. Yet even with these simple behaviors, exposure to a **species-typical environment** is necessary for the behaviors to develop (Gottlieb, 1991b, 1997). Thus, development of even these reflexive behaviors requires environmental experience. Learning is therefore a process in development of these types of behaviors.

Why is a species-typical environment necessary for the development of these behaviors? The selection of genes that hard wire these species-characteristic behaviors would have happened in the environment that the species normally found itself. In this way, the selected behaviors would have been the product of genotype–environment interactions. Natural selection did not occur in an environmental void. Stimuli in species-typical environments may be necessary to bring them out.

As they become more individual and unique, they show more influence of ontogenic contingencies. These basic behaviors show greater influence by the environment contingencies, and therefore learning plays the major role in their development (also see Horowitz, 1987). So for the great majority of human behaviors, learning plays *the* role in development.

Where Does Learning Fit in Human Development?

Learning is the major process in development, but where does it fit with respect to other developmental topics, such as language, cognitive, and social development? To help understand this relationship, we turn again to our painting metaphor. In our metaphor, learning is the dots of paint that make up the picture. We might extend the metaphor to suggest that biology is the canvas. These are basic processes of development that occur at Level 1 of analyzing the systems of development. The basic processes of genetics, biological growth, and learning underlay all development. To understand development at three other levels, we necessarily need to know how learning works.

Behavior Analysis, Dynamical Systems, and Development

Behavior analysis is a field in psychology. It is concerned with the environmental influences and contingencies that determine behavior change. It has identified powerful laws of behavioral change that have been viewed mostly from Level 1 as basic processes. Behavior analysts (e.g., Hoyert, 1992; Marr, 1992, 1996; Nevin, 1992) have incorporated dynamical systems principles into their theory and principles. In this book, we attempt to integrate the basic principles of behavior analysis with these basic processes of development and principles of a dynamical systems approach to better explain the developmental process. This synthesis is the essence of behavioral systems theory (Novak, 1998).

WHAT DO DEVELOPMENTAL ● PSYCHOLOGISTS DO?

Developmental psychologists may focus on a specific part of the life span. Some specialize in child psychology. Others may limit their interests to an even smaller segment, such as infancy. A relatively recent trend is the study of the full life span. Those interested in this "womb-to-tomb" approach are called life span developmental psychologists and may refer to their field as human development. Those with more limited interests may call their field child development and refer to themselves as child psychologists. Others focusing on the opposite end of the human life span are called gerontologists.

Developmental Psychologists as Researchers

Most developmental psychologists serve as researchers and teachers at colleges and universities. They received their Ph.D.s at research-oriented universities and continue studying the processes of development. Some researchers are interested in basic issues about how behavioral development occurs. They may study perception or cognition with little regard to the immediate impact of their findings for practical problems of development. Others focus their research on applied problems related to development, such as parent training or learning disabilities. Increasingly, however, this distinction between basic and **applied research** is fading (Whitehurst, 1989).

The traditional perspective on development taken by most researchers is characterized by a **naturalistic approach**. This approach has focused on the observation and description of development in its natural surroundings. For example, the researcher may describe the sequence of language development or the development of reaching in infants. The naturalistic approach has some distinct advantages. Foremost is that this approach is very likely to describe how development occurs in real life rather than in the laboratory. To the extent the researcher describes rather than interprets, the approach yields good descriptions of what actually occurs. The primary weakness of the naturalistic approach is that its lack of control over variables makes the determination of causal variables impossible. For example, because so many things (e.g., objects to describe, parents' words, the child's increasing linguistic ability, etc.) are occurring simultaneously in language development, it may be impossible to "tease out" which variables are responsible for change. Sometimes we want to know why things happen, not just what happens.

Beginning in the early 1960s, there was an increasing emphasis on determining cause–effect relationships in developmental research through the use of the **experimental method.** By bringing children into the highly controlled environment of a laboratory room or by creating special laboratory schools, researchers could control extraneous variables and determine the variables at work in the process of development. The strength of this approach was the discovery of causal variables in development, but there was a price to pay in the possible loss of accuracy in describing what happens in the real world. For example, if it is determined under controlled conditions that reinforcement of infant vocalizations by social stimuli increases the vocalizations (see, e.g., Rheingold, Gewirtz, & Ross, 1959), one may legitimately ask, Is this how it happens in the natural environment?

Research in **basic** and **applied behavior analysis** has emphasized **single-subject designs.** This method has several advantages from a dynamical systems viewpoint. Chief among these advantages is that the multiple developmental variables unique to the individual are controlled by the use of the individual as its own control. A second advantage of a single-subject design is that individual patterns of change are not masked by averaging the changes out as group methods do. The main disadvantage is that generalizability may be reduced by this focus on the individual. This can be overcome by systematic replication with multiple individuals (see Hayes, Barlow, & Nelson-Gray, 1998).

In recent years, the trend in developmental research has been away from overreliance on any single research approach (Reese, 1998). Criticisms of each approach have led to greater awareness of the limitations and benefits of each. New advances in statistical analysis, particularly multivariate analysis; structural modeling procedures; and single-subject designs have enhanced the ability of naturalistic researchers to ask cause-and-effect questions. Likewise, sensitivity to issues of artificiality has improved the quality of experimental research.

Today, developmental psychologists are more likely to advance their science through the use of a strategy involving a **confluence of research methodologies** (Wicks-Nelson & Israel, 2003). Such a strategy may follow a logical progression (although each research question may have its own requirements). A logical sequence of steps in answering a research question might involve (a) naturalistic observation to identify the existence of the problem and potential causal variables in the real world, (b) bringing the phenomena under control in a laboratory environment to identify the processes involved, and (c) returning to the real world to verify that the processes found in the laboratory function in the outside world.

In behavioral systems theory, changes in dependent variables are difficult to understand outside the network of the multiple variables determining behavior. Although some behavioral theorists have recognized the importance of context in development (e.g., Bijou & Baer, 1961, 1978; Gewirtz, 1972; Kantor, 1959; Michael, 1982; Morris, 1988; Skinner, 1938), it was not until recently that researchers began to explicitly develop programs of research to demonstrate the **contextualistic approach to development** (Morris & Midgley, 1990). Today, researchers are developing methods to investigate the dynamical and interactive nature of the relationship between the individual and the multiple determinants of behavior.

At the beginning of the 21st century, the promise of developmental research is more exciting than ever before.

Applied Developmental Psychologists

One reason for the excitement in developmental psychology is that **basic research** is producing more and more direct applications. Developmental psychologists may be involved in the prevention of developmentally based problems as well as the treatment of problems once they become clinically significant. Examples of this preventive approach spawned from basic developmental research abound, and in each chapter we will examine examples ranging from the prevention of mental retardation to the prevention of child abuse in families. Applied developmental psychologists may pursue their interests as members of university faculties or in hospitals and other agencies in the community. **Behavioral pediatrics** is a recent field in which specially trained psychologists in medical settings may work on preventing developmental problems. The burgeoning field of **behavioral gerontology** includes researchers and applied psychologists interested in issues involving the aging process and the elderly. With the increasing number of people living to advanced age, new problems face developmental psychologists. Coupled with new interest in basic research on aging, this is an exciting new field.

Child Clinical Psychologists

These psychologists are engaged in treating existing problems of the child. Traditionally, they may be trained as clinical psychologists with additional training in developmental psychology and child treatment rather than in developmental psychology programs with an emphasis on research. They may receive their training in a clinical program approved by the American Psychological Association, including an internship in treating child cases. They may differ from other applied developmental psychologists in that their training may emphasize treating problems that already exist at levels that are significantly severe enough to result in the child's referral for treatment. Although child clinical psychologists may address relatively common problems of normal development, such as discipline problems or bed-wetting, they are also likely to target problems considered abnormal, such as autism, hyperactivity, or phobias.

● SUMMARY

The *behavioral systems* approach to the study of development is a synthesis of *dynamical systems* principles and *behavior analysis. Development* means change over time. *Psychological development* is thought to involve progressive (cumulative) changes in the relationship between behavior and environment.

The behavioral systems approach to studying development constitutes a natural science approach to studying development through application of the principles of the *scientific method* to studying phenomena. Integral aspects of the scientific method include (a) formulation of a *hypothesis*; (b) direct observation; (c) acceptance, rejection, or modification of hypotheses; and (d) the generating of new research questions based on results. The scientific method lends a relatively objective means of studying development when validity, replicability, and control of extraneous variables can be demonstrated.

Various sciences can be thought of as lying along a continuum in terms of the degree of complexity of the dynamical systems with which they concern themselves. A unit of analysis can be *molecular* (as in the study of subatomic particles) or *molar* (as in the study of culture). In the science of psychology, the behavioral systems approach falls somewhere in the middle, with interest ranging from basic physiological mechanisms to entire sociocultural systems. Although for some questions a reductionist approach will suffice, for others a higher level of analysis may be more useful in explaining a particular phenomenon. The appropriate level of analysis one chooses depends on one's research question and worldview. In psychology, it may be considered more productive to study at the level of the whole organism's interaction with its environment. In the study of development, it is important to keep in mind that regardless of what level of analysis we choose to study, we are analyzing systems that function and interact with other systems simultaneously.

It has been posited that the development of behavior in species and individuals can be likened to the process of evolution. In this sense, behaviors are thought to be selected through *phylogenic* and *ontogenic contingencies,* respectively. Phylogenic contingencies shape the development of species over evolutionary time, whereas ontogenic contingencies shape the development of individuals across the life span. Behavioral systems theory posits that behavior is a function of selection of behavior by consequences of both types of contingencies over time. Phylogenic contingencies might be considered the "nature" influence and ontogenic contingencies the "nurture" influence.

The process of human development seems to share characteristics with other dynamical systems in that (a) it involves the relationship between behavior and environmental contingencies, (b) relationships are constantly changing, (c) the effects of each element on one another are reciprocal, (d) it is the result of multiple influences, (e) there are multiple ongoing interactions, (f) development is nonlinear, and (g) it involves multiple directions of outcomes.

Learning is thought to play a central role in human development. It is defined as a relatively permanent change in behavior in relation to the environment due to experience. Learning is thought to have evolutionary significance in terms of providing means of developing behaviors that enable members of a species to survive in environments typical of that species. Learning can be thought of as a form of adaptation to the environment.

Developmental psychologists may choose to focus on a specific part of the life span and may concern themselves with *basic research* or *applied research*. Research can be carried out in either a naturalistic or laboratory setting and may involve single or multiple participants. Each of these approaches has its strengths and weaknesses. As such, there is a trend toward a research strategy involving a convergence of methodologies.

● NOTE

1. Sheppard and Willoughby (1975) use the terms *phylogenetic* and *ontogenetic*. We choose *phylogenic* and *ontogenic* so as not to suggest genetic inheritance with both terms. Either usage is technically correct.

CHAPTER 2

MODERN DEVELOPMENTAL THEORY

● THE IMPORTANCE OF THEORY

A **theory** is a broad set of statements describing the relation between an observed set of phenomena and the factors assumed to affect those phenomena. We use theory to organize our thinking. It helps to bring some coherence to the many individual observations we make about our world. A theory does not stop at organizing observations; it also attempts to explain the observations by portraying the special kinds of relationships we call cause and effect. A theory often provides avenues for new knowledge by suggesting further research questions.

Clashing Theories

Theories may derive from a more general overarching theory, but they may also clash and come into conflict and opposition. As an illustration, let us consider two theories about language acquisition. Children enter the world unable to speak or understand a language. However, by the age of 5, most of them can understand and generate an unlimited number of grammatical utterances. Most of what they say is grammatical. Furthermore, much of what they say and understand is novel. These are the observations. Now let us look at how two theories help organize and explain these observations.

The first theory has been called "the miracle theory." It states that the human brain contains an innate device that enables this transition from no language to fluency in a few years. The role of the environment is minimized. The second theory has been dubbed "the impossible theory." It states that language is learned as a result of millions of parent–child interactions. By this view, language develops in the same manner as other behaviors—through imitation and reinforcement. Here, the role of genetic inheritance is minimized.

How would we go about choosing between these two theories? If we can teach language to an animal with a brain much less sophisticated than humans—a parrot, for example—this would lead us to reject the miracle theory. Similarly, if the evidence showed that imitation could produce only mimicry and not novel grammatical utterances, this would lead us to reject the impossible theory.[1]

The pragmatic criterion of "successful working"—that is, of assessing which theory is more efficiently working on the goals to be accomplished by the researcher—is more consistent with a guiding rationale of behavior analysis.

As the two proposed theories just discussed suggest, theories in developmental psychology are frequently examples of overarching general theories or **worldviews**. Worldviews dominate the questions that psychologists ask and the answers they propose about their subject matter. One example of a worldview might be that nearly everything is caused by heredity and that children are already preprogrammed for development at birth. Another worldview might be that nothing is inherited and that children are born as blank slates (or Locke's *tabula rasa*). These dominating worldviews bias our interpretation of data. In other words, scientists, including psychologists, tend to interpret data in ways consistent with their worldviews. Thus, many scientists conclude that we determine the very nature of what we study not by some absolute standard of truth but by the general views of the world that we hold. This **relativistic view of science** suggests that our conclusions, and even the basic observations we make, are colored by the scientist's own views. Thus, science is not perfect but is influenced by the imperfect human beings who conduct it.

Box 2.1   Developmental Theories and Worldviews

Traditionally in mainstream developmental psychology, each theory has been grounded in a broader set of philosophical assumptions or worldviews. Based on the original worldviews proposed by Pepper (1942/1960), behavioral, humanistic, cognitive, and other developmental theories have been classified as following one of three main philosophical assumptions: the mechanistic, the organismic, and the contextualistic.

The **mechanistic** model conceives human beings as operating like machines, as a collection of parts (responses) that can be separated or taken apart. The mechanistic model assumes that behavior is passive and changes as a result of outside external influences. The assumed change under the mechanistic model is continuous, gradual, and cumulative.

The **organismic** model, in contrast, views the individual as a whole being who cannot be studied by taking apart its responses. Under this model, organisms are seen as active in their development and progressing by following a series of discontinuous stages (e.g., Piaget, Erikson, and Kohlberg's theories). Maturation is the main process that triggers the developmental change under these approaches.

The **contextualistic** model is the approach that the present textbook favors. The contextualistic worldview treats behavioral development as the product of dynamic interplay between an individual and the environment. Under this model, both the individual and the environment actively participate in development. The behavioral changes are the result of learning, and they are both qualitative and quantitative in nature. Development does not follow a series of predetermined stages but can proceed along many different paths depending on the history of dynamic interactions and the contextual determinants operating at a given moment.

The philosophical position in our textbook is that the mechanistic and organismic accounts may be insufficient for explaining behavior development (Morris, 1998). The growth changes that have taken place in behavior analysis within the last decade suggest that behavior-analytic theory, although not exactly undergoing a paradigm shift, may be evolving, constructively influenced by contextualism and its overarching framework (Hayes, Hayes, & Reese, 1988; Morris, 1988; Sarbin, 1977). There have been differences among behavior theorists about the ideal higher-level metamodel for the behavior-analytic theory of development. This is evidenced by the variety of "mechanistic" and "contextualistic" theoretical approaches that exist today (see Marr, 1993a, 1993b; Morris, 1993a, 1993b) and that appear to overlap in some underlying assumptions. Baer (1993) has observed that, in use, mechanism and contextualism have so many meanings that in effect they no longer have dependable differentiated meanings.

● FOUR DIMENSIONS ON WHICH THEORIES DIFFER

Theories of human development are abundant. If development was easy to understand, there would be only one theory. However, due to the complexity of human development, we have many theories from which to choose and learn. Some theories take a very broad view of development but may be very scanty in details. In turn, other theories may be very limited in scope, focusing on a narrow part of development, such as language comprehension or short-term memory, but give much detail on this narrow topic. Developmental theories differ on many dimensions. We will describe four of these: *structure* versus *function, description* versus *explanation*, *nature* versus *nurture*, and *continuity* versus *discontinuity*.

Structure Versus Function

A theory may concentrate on explaining the **structure** of behavior and knowledge, whereas another theory may focus on its **function.** Let us say that your nontechnologically oriented friend just bought a personal computer and comes to you for help. He asks you an apparently simple question: "Do you *know* about computers?" The answer is not that simple because "knowing about computers" has at least two distinct meanings. The first sense of knowing about computers is knowledge about what computer scientists call their "architecture" (i.e., its structure). This involves knowing about the parts of the computer and how they work in relationship to each other. Thus, you may know about the differences between Celerons and Pentiums, between Pentium 3s and Pentium 4s, and even between Intels and Athelons. You may "know" their central-processing differences and the various advantages they may have in speed and multimedia capabilities. You may know the differences between PCI and AGP slots, between EDO and PCI memory, and endless lists of other possibilities. You may be able to predict that certain components will function well together and give you distinct advantages over other arrangements. You know about the structure of computers. You know of what computers are made. Your knowledge is a **structural knowledge.**

On the other hand, you may know a great deal about computers without knowing anything about what is inside them. For you, comparing hardware is like comparing, well, Apples to PCs. Instead, you may be able to sit at the machine and get it to perform an endless number of tasks, from balancing the budget to writing a term paper with it. You may be able to make great graphs, surf the Internet, and download the best music. You know computers, but what you know is "how to make them work." That is, you know how they function. You don't need to know if they have a Pentium or Athelon. You know the right sequence of clicks to perform a task. You may know the computer's language and be able to write programs to do whatever task you require. And although certain components may speed up operations, you do not need to know which CPU is inside in order to make it perform. You know *how* a computer and its programs function. Your knowledge is a **functional knowledge**.

In both cases the answer to the question is "Yes, I know about computers." Yet the sense in which you know about them is quite different. In the first sense you have a structural knowledge, and in the second, a functional knowledge. Similarly, our knowledge of human development can be either structural or functional. For example, by studying language acquisition in a child, we may know about the changes in grammatical structure from single words through complex sentences. Or we may know how child–parent activities function to produce the changes. Both approaches are valid, although they represent different ways to understand human development.

Theories in developmental psychology that have a structural focus often emphasize the neurophysiological structures believed to underlie behavior. Some structural theories may also emphasize inferred structures called **hypothetical** constructs, such as intelligence or memory storage (Zimmerman & Whitehurst, 1979). From this viewpoint, input to the organism and the organism's responses are of interest because they provide a basis for inferring the structures that underlie them. Returning to the computer analogy, you could systematically enter certain sequences of keystrokes and see what consistently appears on the video display of the computer and from this infer that the computer has a certain CPU or is running a particular structured language.

In human behavior, functional explanations focus on the relationships between what happens to the organism (i.e., the history of behavior-environment interaction) and the behavior of the organism (i.e., response). We are generally not concerned with known or hypothesized internal structures, such as short-term memory or cognitive schemata. Instead, the emphasis is on identifying what events lead to what outcomes and how. From this view, it is not useful to infer hypothetical cognitive "schemata" if one is interested in determining that certain specific experiences lead to certain specific intelligent behaviors.

Both structural and functional approaches can provide complete and adequate explanations. They focus on different aspects of development. A psychologist may dislike a particular theory because he or she favors structural explanations, but the theory is providing a functional one (or vice versa). For example, to someone who wants to know what cognitive structures have changed during development, a theory that emphasizes environmental reinforcement of behavior will be rejected as inadequate.[2]

Finally, some researchers have illustrated how, at times, function and structure are intrinsically confounded. For instance, in the study of language, the analysis of language structure is important in determining its function (Peláez & Moreno, 1998). By virtue of cultural transmission and transfer of learning from one context to another, many rules acquire functional control over behavior without requiring direct learning on every occasion. Thus, the study of the contingencies specified in the rule (i.e., the form) becomes relevant to its potential function.

Description Versus Explanation

Description and explanation are two goals of science and developmental psychology. Unfortunately, they, too, are often confused because virtually all explanations are descriptions, but we in behavior analysis do not accept all descriptions as explanations. The issue, then, is knowing which descriptions we accept as explanatory. Description means to "delineate" or "give an account of." It is one of the earliest goals of any science. In the early days of a scientific approach to human development, it was important to describe adequately the characteristics and nature of the phenomena studied. This was also true in the early days of developmental psychology. The first scientific studies of children were baby biographies. In these journals, scientists and educators described the changes in their own children as they grew. Some early biographers of the 19th century, such as the German educator, Tiedeman (1748–1803), and the Swiss, Pestalozzi (1746–1827), made significant contributions to the early description of child development by chronicling the development of their own children. One such biographer, Charles Darwin (1809–1882), provided the field with scientific credibility by lending his scientific stature to the study of his own child.

In developmental psychology, it is important to give an accurate account of the characteristics of children and adults at various stages, especially the behaviors they perform and the sequences (often arranged hierarchically) in which they appear. Those who focus on the development of hypothetical structures miss some of the observable behavioral phenomena that are of importance in development. Therefore, careful description is a necessary activity of developmental psychology, as it is of any science. As a science matures and we become aware of what it is that we are studying, the goal often switches to an attempt to explain the phenomena.

Explanation is one of the main basic goals of science. But what constitutes an explanation? To *explain,* in this context, means "to make clear a cause or reason." For most scientists, explanation is important because it allows prediction and control. One form of explanation is to identify a particular behavioral occurrence as an exemplar of a general class of occurrences. Another form of explanation is to describe a relation between independent and dependent variables that has greater reliability and generality.

Prediction

When there is a consistent relationship between two factors across changes in the individual factors, we say these two factors are correlated. For example, there is a positive correlation between the amount of storybook reading done by parents and their children's later reading performance; that is, the more time parents devote to reading storybooks to their children, the higher their child's reading scores are later. Therefore, given the amount of time a parent reads to the child, we can predict, with some accuracy, how well or how poorly the child will perform on reading tests in school.

Even when two factors are correlated, this does not imply that one factor caused the other. We cannot conclude that storybook reading by parents causes the level of reading achievement in their children. It may be that children who have good reading (or prereading) skills encourage their parents to read to them. In short, **correlation** does not imply causation.

We should remember that a theory must predict when something will *not* happen, as well as when it will. Many famous prognosticators (e.g., Jean Dixon) claim to have predicted many significant life events (such as wars and tragedies), but the problem is that they keep silent about the many other events they pre-dicted that did not come to pass.

Often, we think we can explain the cause of behavior by using the word *because* as in "He won't sit still *because* he's hyperactive." "Because" is usually the answer to the question, "Why?" as in "Why isn't he able to sit still?" Ross (1980) suggests that the real question to be answered in an explanation is not, Why did the behavior occur? but, rather, Under what conditions does the behav-ior occur? What events control the behavior?

Think about prediction and control together. If you have a true explanation of behavior, then you should be able to both predict and control the behavior. That is, when we are able to control the events that affect (i.e., that are func-tionally related to) the behavior, we should be able to predict when the behav-ior will occur, and if we can control the occurrence of the functionally related events, we can control whether or not the behavior will occur. That is a "true" explanation of the behavior.

Control

Control is necessary to determine if there is a cause–effect relationship. Researchers conduct experiments in which they investigate whether changes in one variable control[3] changes in another variable while controlling for all possi-ble confounding extraneous variables. For example, to exercise control, we could take a sample of 100 children and randomly assign 50 to the experimen-tal group and 50 to the control group. Both groups will be matched on their pre-experiment reading test scores so that there is no initial difference between the groups on reading ability. Both groups should be matched for gender and age and be treated exactly alike by the researchers, except that the parents of the experimental group will be trained and encouraged to read storybooks to their children and the control group's parents will not. The children will be tested on standardized tests of reading achievement (before and after training of parents in the experimental group), and differences will be analyzed statistically between groups and within each group.

Assume that the researchers obtain the following results: The experimental group did much better, on average, than the control group. From these results, we can tentatively conclude that providing increased storybook reading to children causes improved reading scores. We now conclude a tentative cause–effect relationship because by manipulating the variable of parental reading in the two groups, we controlled for the level of reading in the children. We now may be more confident that parental reading causes increased reading skills in their children rather than reading skills being increased by some other causal relationship. In practice, prediction and control of a phenomenon constitutes an adequate explanation in science.

Developmental psychologists try to establish how hereditary and environmental conditions cause the development of progressive changes in behavior. It is not enough to merely describe the ongoing changes in an individual's behavior; as scientists, we also want to identify what produced the observed changes. A description merely depicts the status of things, whereas an explanation establishes cause-and-effect relationships (functional relations) between the behavioral phenomena and the hereditary and environmental events that cause the phenomena. In a behavioral systems approach, we speak of control as inherently **reciprocal**; that is, the behavior has control on the environment (it operates on the environment) and the environment reciprocally controls and maintains such behavior.

Circular Versus True Explanations

Unfortunately, as mentioned above, descriptions sometimes masquerade as explanations. Indeed, there are many cases in psychology where descriptions pose as explanations. Some descriptions count as explanatory, others do not. We often find educational psychologists telling their students that preschoolers "Can't keep still and listen to long stories because they have short attention spans." On the surface, it seems that the concept of "short attention span" explains why children fuss and look away if you fail to present new things every few seconds. But think about that sentence—it seems to be an explanation due to the word *because*. However, "short attention span" is not an acceptable explanation. Rather, it is a **circular explanation**.

Let us look at this alleged weak circular explanation. Why do preschoolers look away after a brief period? They do so because they have a short attention span. How do you know they have a short attention span? Because they look away after a brief period! This argument takes us in circles. A short attention span is merely a summary description of the behavior of children who do not keep still and look away after a brief period. Thus, what the psychologist was really saying was that preschoolers "can't keep still and listen to long stories because they can't keep still and listen."

Descriptions often parade as explanations in the area of learning disabilities. One of the most common specific learning disabilities is dyslexia. We use the label **dyslexia** for children who, for no apparent reason (e.g., mental retardation, blindness), are significantly behind grade level in reading. Many psychologists and educators explain that the child can't read because he or she has dyslexia. However, you probably see that they should say dyslexia is a summary description, not an explanation. It describes children who, for no conspicuous reason, cannot read at grade level. As Ross has said: "Dyslexia is an attempt to say in Greek that the child can't read" (p. 168). Thus, a word of caution: If someone uses the word *because,* he or she is not necessarily providing a true explanation—it may be a circular one, and a weak one.

The Problem With Reification

Often in developmental psychology, a term may serve the purpose of **reification**, in that it becomes the explanation of a phenomenon while at the same time it is also the object of study. Schlinger (1992) has asserted:

> The problem of reification leads to another troublesome verbal practice in developmental psychology. Locating the causes of behavior inside the child makes it easier to describe the child as the originator of his or her actions. Thus, after contact with environmental stimulation the child is said to "sense," "perceive," "remember," "think," "judge," and "decide," and so on as if these verbs referred to real [observed] actions. (p. 1398)

Most typically, reification occurs when a verb is replaced with a corresponding noun. For example, "thinking" gets reified as "thought," "remembering" gets reified as "memories" which in turn become "representations" that are said to be stored and retrieved. The problem is that, once described in this way, behavior can be more easily attributed to mental activities. That is, behaviors are not attributed to the real external contingencies and conditions responsible for the actions. These are words of common usage that divert attention away from the controlling variables of the behavior in question; thus, reification occurs. These activities clearly illustrate reification; they become both the presumed explanation and the object of study. Thus, in the above illustration, when reading problems become reified as "dyslexia," dyslexia becomes a thing that the child has, and this thing explains why the child is having reading problems.

Nature Versus Nurture

Another basic issue pertaining to theories of development is the nature–nurture controversy. This issue addresses the question of which is more important, one's nature (i.e., heredity) or one's nurture (i.e., environment). This debate has probably raged from when humans first questioned their origins; it involves political and ethical as well as scientific questions.

Modern-day developmental psychologists have renounced this question for its presupposing that heredity and environment can function separately. Sheppard and Willoughby (1975) have called the nature–nurture issue "a false dichotomy," meaning that it is wrong to divide the process of development into two separate parts. In a classic paper, Anastasi (1958) observed that the real question is not "how much" is heredity and "how much" is environment but, rather, "How do heredity and environment work to produce development?" Reflecting this view, it is common for present-day developmentalists to respond to the question of "how much" with the answer, "It's 100 percent heredity . . . and 100 percent environment." Still, despite the widely acknowledged problems with separating nature and nurture, the approach is still very much alive, as recent books such as *The Nurture Assumption* (Harris, 1998) demonstrate.

Behavioral Approaches and the Nature–Nurture Dichotomy

Behavioral approaches to development have been mischaracterized as falling exclusively on the nurture side of the nature–nurture dichotomy. However, an examination of B. F. Skinner's behaviorism, by Midgley and Morris (1992; 1998) reveals that Skinner acknowledged both nature and nurture as determinants of behavior. In behavior analysis, we do reject explanations of innate and acquired behavior in terms of instincts and habits, arguing instead that innate and acquired behavior are a function of selection by consequences—selection at both phylogenic and ontogenic levels (Skinner, 1966).

These contingencies of selection can be distinguished themselves in three ways: according to (a) their temporal relation to behavior, (b) their consequences, and (c) what they select. Phylogenic contingencies correspond to the evolutionary history of the species; they work their effects through the differential survival and procreation of members of the species with particular characteristics, and they bridge past and present via genes. Ontogenic contingencies, in contrast, contribute to the behavioral history of an individual, they work their effects through the reinforcement of behavior, and they bridge past and present via nongenetic biological factors. The variables of which innate and acquired behavior are a function—phylogenic and ontogenic contingencies—represent the behavior-analytic version of the nature–nurture dichotomy.

The reason nature–nurture is a false dichotomy is that, from the moment of conception, both genetic inheritance and interactions with the environment are both important causal factors in the individual's development. Biological influences (e.g., heredity and maturational forces) and environmental influences (e.g., culture, child-rearing practices, schooling) both contribute to development and interact. No genetic material can become an organism without interacting with its particular environment and vice versa. To analyze the contribution of one without the other is meaningless. However, in behavior analysis, we concentrate on manipulating variables found in the external environment of individuals, and we prefer to leave the study and engineering of genes and DNA to the field of biogenetics.

Midgley and Morris (1998) concluded that if behavior analysis reconsiders the nature–nurture dichotomy, it may turn to alternative conceptualizations such as "developmental dynamic perspective," which conceptualizes inheritance as reaching beyond genes, studies the role of development in both acquired and innate characteristics, and takes a contextualistic and selectionistic perspective of causality. A developmental systems perspective of nature–nurture would argue that nature and nurture are not causes but products and processes (Oyama, 1985). As we have indicated, selection is the operative process in development.

Continuity Versus Discontinuity

Is development a continuous process, or are there many dead-ends and new starts in development? Do new characteristics evolve from old ones, or do they just appear or unfold when it is time for them in the course of development? For example, in language development, does adult grammar emerge from child grammar or is adult language completely different? Does adult grammar develop for its own reasons (de Villiers & de Villiers, 1999)?

Although there are many meanings of continuity in development, we shall focus on what Rutter (1987) calls continuity in "structure, process or mechanism" (p. 1260). Theories that see development as a continuous process see new behaviors developing from the old ones. For example, some theories see that the child's first words are the result of experiences that the child has prior to the words. In this view, words develop from babbles, and babbles from coos. Furthermore, the progression from one-word utterances to whole sentences is a continuous process. Continuity theorists view human development as an accumulative process that occurs gradually, quantitatively, and sequentially without sudden stagelike changes. Behavioral theories tend to emphasize continuity in development as long as there is continuity in the environment that sustains such individual's development.

By contrast, discontinuity theorists describe development in terms of stages and as a series of abrupt changes in behavior. For instance, they see the structure of words as very different from the sounds that preceded them. Discontinuity theorists view the processes and the mechanisms that cause words as being different from the processes and mechanisms that cause babbles. Thus, although babbling may be a necessary stage in development, words do not directly evolve from babbles. They are separate structures involving separate processes and mechanisms.

Continuous does not mean constant. Development often occurs by fits and starts. Sometimes development is slow, and at other times it is rapid. Sometimes entirely new behaviors will emerge. But the inconsistencies in development do not mean that development is discontinuous.

How Versus What and When

For some developmental theories, the primary question to be answered in studying human behavior is "how" does development occurs. How do individuals do what they do and how do they progress through time? For other theories, the primary questions are "what?" and "when?" That is, what does an individual do and when does it happen? As each kind of theory gets elaborated, it begins to address the alternative kind of question, but given different standing points, theories often are in disagreement regarding the kinds of questions or results that are important.

JUDGING DEVELOPMENTAL • THEORIES: SEVEN CRITERIA

There are many theories in developmental psychology. Each developmental theory has its followers, and some have stood the test of time. How shall we judge them? What makes one theory better than another? Thomas (1985) presented nine criteria to use in evaluating developmental theories. However, before presenting these criteria, we must issue one warning: Although most developmental psychologists would likely agree on these criteria, the simple act of selecting the criteria biases our evaluation of theories in a particular direction. These criteria emphasize an academic–scientific view, whereas some other criteria might emphasize aesthetic or emotive ones. With this caveat, let us look at the criteria.

1. *Accuracy.* A theory of the childhood development is better if it accurately reflects the facts of the real world of children. Theories based on observation of real children are better than those based purely on theorists' hypotheses of how children behave.

2. *Clarity.* A theory is better if it is stated in a way that is clearly understandable to anyone who is reasonably competent. "Reasonably competent" means that any intelligent person with some knowledge of development should be able to understand the theory. Confusing, needlessly difficult theories are less desirable.

3. *Predictability.* A theory is better if it not only explains why past events occur but also accurately predicts future events. The more specific the predictions, the better. It is easy to offer an explanation of events after they happen. We do this all the time with the stock market or after an upset in football. It is also easy to make generalizations. For example, it is safe to predict that children will get larger as they get older. It is much more difficult to make specific predictions about individuals, but theories are better if they can.

4. *Practicality.* A theory is better if it offers practical guidance in solving daily problems of child rearing. Some theories are interesting abstractions but are not very applicable to education, child care, or child welfare. Impractical theories are of limited interest to the real world of children. Good theories are practical ones.

5. *Internal Consistency.* A theory is better if it is internally consistent. It is easy to create a theory by changing the meaning of its parts to make it fit new situations. It is much harder, but the theory is better, if terms and concepts are powerful enough that they can be used consistently throughout. Let us look at a simple example of a theory that is not internally consistent. A physiologically based theory might explain reading reversals (e.g., reading b as d, "was" as "saw") as the result of neurological "mis-wiring," which is said to cause the child to see some letters as mirror images of themselves. However, the explanation offered for the b-d reversal is inconsistent with any that could be offered to explain a large number of other perceptual-motor behaviors. For example, the child who reverses b-d can easily reach for a doorknob in the correct place in order to leave the classroom. If he or she is truly seeing the world as a mirror image of itself, the child should reach for doorknobs in the wrong place. A theory that is internally consistent provides the same explanation for letter reversals and grasping doorknobs. The theory just discussed cannot; the explanation offered for reversals must be changed to fit the observations.

6. *Parsimony.* Whereas it is easier to construct a theory that has a new principle to explain each phenomenon, a theory is better if it is founded on as few unproven assumptions as possible and if it requires simple mechanisms to

explain all the phenomena it encompasses. Good theories are "elegant." A few powerful concepts explain much. Behavioral theory is considered parsimonious because a few simple principles, such as reinforcement, punishment, extinction, and shaping are used to explain a great deal. The laws of nature seem to be parsimonious, in that there are a small number of powerful laws that explain many things. Developmental theories should be parsimonious too.

7. *Testability.* A theory is better if it is falsifiable or disprovable. Theories that invoke global terms borrowed from everyday language tend to invoke hypothetical, reified entities that are largely untestable. For example, mentalistic or spiritualistic assumptions are unobservable and thus are untestable. Like the existence of ghosts, the existence of hypothetical mechanisms cannot be directly tested. Few scientists believe in ghosts because assertions about their existence are untestable and so cannot be disconfirmed or confirmed. Likewise, a theory of development that is untestable is a poor one. Theories that invoke global terms as explanations borrowed from the vernacular are not good theories. All concepts and terms that support the theory should be testable.

8. *Productivity.* A theory is better if it stimulates the creation of new research techniques and the discovery of new knowledge. By stimulating new research, good theories provide the database for their revision and improvement.

9. *Self-satisfaction.* A good theory is self-satisfying to us in that it explains development in a way that we feel makes good sense. We already have basic beliefs about children and development before we study any theory. We find theories more satisfying if they are consistent with such preexisting beliefs.

RESEARCH DESIGNS ● IN BEHAVIORAL DEVELOPMENT

In our first chapter, we discussed the scientific method, which dictates that scientists must be objective in their observations and allow their recorded data to confirm their theories. The research method selected by the investigator guides his or her attempts at understanding the dynamic nature of human behavioral development.

Developmental psychologists are interested in examining not only behavior at one particular phase of life but across different segments or periods of our development. Behavior analysts in particular are interested in studying learning and behavioral change over time. In mainstream developmental psychology, traditional methodologies have included three main designs: the *cross-sectional design*, the *longitudinal design*, and the *sequential design*.

In the **cross-sectional design** individuals who differ in age are studied at the same point in time. This design allows experimenters to compare the behavior of individuals in different age groups and to look for age-related differences. But as we will discuss later, in behavior analysis of development, "age" is a hollow variable and we cannot give it causal explanatory value. Participants usually come from different backgrounds and belong to different **cohorts** (or groups who have been exposed to similar cultural environment). So the main problem with the cross-sectional designs is that they confound age and cohort effects. In addition, the cross-sectional (between age-group comparisons) designs tell us nothing about *individual* performance and learning over time.

In the **longitudinal design** the same group of people are followed and studied repeatedly over time. For example, every 3 or 6 months observations and assessments are conducted on the same group of subjects and changes noted. The advantage of this design is that the experimenters can assess the continuity or stability of the behavior and the trend of the behavior changes as well. This longitudinal tracking helps the investigator determine *individual differences* in behavior development. The main problems are that (a) **practice effects** may result from repeated testing and the use of similar assessment tools and (b) **selective attrition** can also occur, which is the nonrandom loss of participants during the study. The loss of subjects results in a nonrepresentative sample. There is also the problem of cohort or cross-generational effects that may limit the conclusions of the study.

Sequential designs are a combination of cross-sectional and longitudinal designs. In this design, individuals of different age groups are followed over time. In this way, various cohorts or generations can be observed repeatedly across time. This research design is often less costly and time-consuming than longitudinal designs but more costly and time-consuming than the cross-sectional research.

Problems With Group Designs

Two fundamental concerns with the between-group data alone that bear heavily on experimental reasoning are now addressed. First, by definition, a **behavioral analysis** is concerned with implementing changes in the behavior of a subject (as in a repeated-measures, within-subjects analysis). Knowing that the average group performance changes in a given direction will tell little about the performance of each individual subject. Hence, faulty interpretations may be drawn if only a group's mean performance is considered. Only by repeatedly measuring the behavior of individual subjects in the presence and absence of the independent variable can the search for the variables responsible for observed intersubject variability begin.

A second problem associated with the mean group performance is that important sources of variability might be lost. "Statistical control is never a substitute for experimental control. . . . The only way to determine whether or not uncontrolled variables are influencing the data is to inspect the data at the finest available level of decomposition, usually point-by-point for each individual subject" (Johnston & Pennypacker, 1980, p. 371).

Because many studies have shown that learning procedures could produce rapid behavior changes, they have become—for behavioral and nonbehavioral researchers alike—the preferred methods for studying processes that otherwise have been inaccessible by the traditional methodologies of nonbehavioral psychology. In this manner, the use of learning procedures and derivative methodologies has progressed enormously in the last four decades, leading to an impressive advance in our knowledge of the child behavior. Experimental advances have been made under basic psychological rubrics such as discrimination, perception, memory, language, information processing, and basic emotional and social themes such as parent–infant reciprocal conditioning effects, attachment, imitation, and social referencing.

Problems With "Age" in Traditional Developmental Methodologies

In behavior analysis of development, we have problems with using the age of an individual as the main independent variable. In a behavioral systems approach, we have had *no* place for age as a causal variable. The paucity of process-theory usage of age may index that principles based on the passage of time alone are inefficient in accounting for development (Gewirtz & Peláez-Nogueras, 1992a). In this context, *age* is seen as an *empty* variable insofar as it constitutes merely the "space" in which the individual's behavior and environment interact dynamically and process variables operate to produce their effects in behavior. Therefore, age as such has very limited explanatory value for the behavior of an individual (Baer, 1970; Gewirtz, 1969). Even so, age norms are available in the developmental literature.

Preferred Methodologies in Behavior Analysis

In behavior analysis of human development, we prefer **experimental methodologies** that permit us to control our variables under investigation. Experimental designs allow us to conduct a more precise assessment of the functional relationship between environmental stimuli and the individual's responses. As we mentioned in Chapter 1, humans learn as a result of multiple dynamic interactions. **Multiple determination** forces the researchers to focus on measuring and evaluating the method to answer the following questions: Does the target behavior (dependent variable) change reliably as a result of the treatment procedures (our independent variable)? Are those behavioral changes observed between baseline and treatment phases of the experiment the result of the researcher manipulations? Has the researcher controlled for potentially confounding variables that may be producing the observed changes in the behavior across time?

In behavior analysis, the methods for demonstrating cause–effect relationships have used single-subject designs for the most part (e.g., Hersen & Barlow, 1976; Kazdin, 1982). Single-subject designs permit us to conduct **functional analysis.** These single-subject designs have made it possible to move beyond the level of simple description of behavior to the level of identifying key processes that account for much of behavioral development and dynamic interactions. Functional analysis allows us to determine which behaviors denoting development could, and which behaviors could not, be susceptible to learning operations. A corollary is that the phenomena that have been identified in descriptive accounts of human development have benefited, or could benefit, from systematic learning analyses.

As we implied in Chapter 1, in behavior analysis, the term *development* is an abstraction for progressive, orderly changes in the organization of dynamic environment-behavior relations. In this way, a functional analysis of infant behavior, for example, must focus on the many variables likely to be directly responsible for behavior change patterns denoting development. To understand behavioral development, experimental analyses are required for (a) changes in the complexity of the controlling environment (including changes in reinforcing stimuli for behavior), (b) early experiences as potential determinants or establishing operations (EO) of later behavior systems, and (c) all the other contextual variables or EOs (including setting factors) participating. The dynamic interplay in human interactions between stimulus and response functions has been the main interest of behavior development researchers.

Behavior-Analytic Designs

Five general experimental designs have been employed in behavior analysis of child development: ABAB reversal design, multiple-treatment design, multiple-baseline design, changing-criterion design, and within–between group designs.

ABAB reversal design is the most commonly used repeated-measures subject design in behavior analysis of development. This design has been widely used to demonstrate functional relations and the learning of infant attachment behaviors such as those denoted in their protest on separation from their mothers. The ABAB design also has been used extensively by behavioral researchers to demonstrate the learning of diverse types of infant fears as a result of maternal attention and to show the reinforcing effects of various social stimuli such as maternal attention and touch on infant learning. In this design (ABAB), the researcher collects baseline data on the target behavior under investigation (A), then systematically introduces the independent variable or treatment (B), then removes it (A) and then reintroduces it again (B). This systematic manipulation is the most crucial and common characteristic of the ABAB designs.

The basic advantage of an ABAB design, then, is that it ensures that changes in the child's behavior are the result of our treatment manipulation rather than some other confounding variable. The design begins with a **baseline** phase, which serves to describe current performance and compare such performance against subsequent treatment effects. However, among the most important limitations of this design are that in many cases the behavior is difficult to reverse, and in most applied interventions its reversibility is also undesired. For instance, a clinical researcher may have trouble reversing self-injurious behavior once this maladaptive behavior has been reduced or extinguished.

Multiple-treatments design allows us to compare the effects of two or more treatments or interventions implemented within an experimental phase, also known as **alternating treatments designs** (ABCBCB). Differences in rate between the two treatments allow the experimenter to determine which of the two is a more effective intervention. A great advantage of this type of design is that it does not require a reversal phase or a return to baseline level. This way, the researcher avoids the ethical issue of reducing or losing the gains already obtained during treatment. One strong limitation is the carryover effects. To prevent these, some researchers have used a second group of subjects receiving the treatments in a counterbalanced order. Some of the studies described later in this textbook illustrate this type of experimental control.

Multiple-baseline designs involve collecting data on two or more behaviors simultaneously. For example, the effectiveness of the same type of instruction could be evaluated using three academic behaviors: reading, writing, and doing arithmetic. These behaviors are then modified sequentially using the same treatment procedure. In the initial phase, baselines need to be obtained on all of the behaviors. Then, in the next step, only one behavior is manipulated (receives intervention) while observations continue on the other untreated behaviors. After a stable rate has been obtained on the first treated behavior, the researcher then intervenes with the second targeted behavior while continuing to collect data on the other behaviors (responses), and the same procedure is later applied with the third behavior, once the data reaches stability. Two versions of this design are multiple-baseline across settings designs (two or more situations) and multiple-baseline across participants designs (two or more people).

The main advantage of the multiple-baseline design is that it avoids the problem of reversing or reinstating (going back to baseline) some problematic undesirable behaviors in order to demonstrate experimental control and to show the effectiveness of the treatment (as in the ABAB). It is convenient and safer to employ multiple-baseline designs when it becomes difficult to recapture the baseline level or reverse learned behaviors. However, long periods of baselines may be problematic because they can produce fatigue, boredom, and frustration. Also, at times, it is difficult to find behaviors that are independent from each other. For example, once you effectively increase the child's reading, his or her writing and arithmetic skills may also increase, making it impossible to show that the change in instruction method was the controlling variable.

Changing-criterion design begins with a true baseline, but then each subsequent treatment phase provides a baseline against which to assess change when the criterion of the previous behavior has been reached. That is, the target behavior is gradually modified in increments in a series of treatments across phases that required different criteria. For instance, the number of correct math responses is increased gradually across the experimental phases. Thus, with the introduction of each new phase, the requirements for criteria are increased (in some cases decreased if reduction of behavior is desired, as in the case of smoking). The main advantage is that it requires incremental changes in the desired performance. However, one serious limitation is that when the criteria are set too high, the participant shows difficulty in achieving them, and adjustments need to be made consistently.

In our experiments we have used **within-subjects designs** combined with **between-subjects designs** to control for carryover effect, counterbalance for order of treatment presentation, and examine different developmental levels. The within- and between-subjects research design involve the following features: (a) two levels of treatment (e.g., contingent maternal stimulation for infant protests vs. noncontingent maternal stimulation for infant protests), followed by a reversal condition (within subjects) and (b) two treatment order patterns (contingent stimulation in departures and noncontingent stimulation in separations [Group 1] vs. noncontingent stimulation in departures and contingent stimulation in separations [Group 2]. We have found the combined design very useful in addressing and controlling for the potentially confounding effects of order, and we have been forced to use larger samples, which increases the external validity of the research.

The five designs just discussed use **control procedures** that are employed routinely in the laboratory. These procedures provide the experimental basis for concluding that certain stimuli, when contingent, can function as reinforcers for particular infant response classes. Such experimental situations also depend on the fact that total removal (via extinction) of that stimulus and the contingency it provides, or its functional removal by stimulus presentations independent of response occurrence, is correlated with a systematic decrease in the same response attribute. Many studies with infants and children discussed in later chapters have been conducted under this paradigm in which there has been experimental manipulation of the relation between a response, its antecedents, and its consequences, and, in this way, the principles of learning have become established empirically. A good deal of the research involved has focused on processes, on delineating *how* behaviors are shaped and maintained by the delivery of patterns of *particular* contingent stimuli in *differing* contexts.

A BEHAVIORAL SYSTEMS APPROACH ●

When we looked at the nature–nurture controversy, we saw the importance of viewing development as the inseparable interaction of the child and its environment. Interactions involving both phylogenic and ontogenic factors determine development. The products of these interactions themselves also interact. For example, a mother responds to her baby's babbling—the latter being the result of mainly phylogenic interactions—by using "baby talk." Because of the mother's baby talk, the babbling changes to real words—the result of ontogenic interactions. Furthermore, the words the child uses changes the mother's baby talk to more advanced language. This constant, two-way change in interactions is what characterizes **transactions**.

A transaction has occurred when the result of previous reciprocal interactions determines current interactions. The analysis of development into ever-changing, inseparable, and interlocking systems is called the behavioral systems approach. Notice that the product of the initial interactions has been reorganized and the existing person and environment conditions are different from the original ones. When mothers interact with their children, the behavior of the mother changes the child's behavior. In turn, the child's behavior changes what the mother does.

Reciprocal Dynamic Interactions and Methodological Problems

One feature of the dyadic interaction is the potential bidirectionality of reinforcement effects—each member of a dyad is influenced by the behavior of the other. However, a problem in the study of spontaneous dyadic interactions, for instance in the parent–infant case, is that the identity and topography of response elements of the set of turn-taking responses (e.g., smiles, touches, vocalizations, turning away) of each member of the dyad can change very rapidly at every turn in the series. For this reason, until recently, behavior analytic researchers studying the effects of reinforcement contingencies on behavior preferred to study the flow of influence in such interaction sequences in experimentally contrived settings. In mother–infant dyadic interactions, the turn-taking response of one dyad member (typically, the mother) is controlled or manipulated, whereas the infant's response that provides the dependent variable is left free to vary (e.g., Gewirtz & Peláez-Nogueras, 1991a, 1992b; Peláez-Nogueras, 1992; Peláez-Nogueras, Field, Hossain, & Pickens, 1996; Peláez-Nogueras, Gewirtz et al., 1996; Poulson, 1983). At the same time, infant–mother interactions can be analyzed in natural interaction settings without contriving to use a limiting experimental procedure as above. For example, the behavior analyst may record the behavior unit elements of each of the two interactors in sequence and then search for conditional relations between adult behavior elements at different turn positions (sequential lags) for each infant behavior of interest (e.g., Haupt & Gewirtz, 1968). By observing the conditional probabilities in sequential-lag analysis, the researcher can examine the impact of presumptive reinforcement contingencies for each infant target response under ecologically valid circumstances while taking contextual variables into consideration (e.g., stratifying for contextual functions).

Models for Studying Reciprocal Interactions

There are several models for studying multiple and reciprocal interactions. For instance, contingency frequency analysis is a data-analytic model that attempts to analyze patterns of multiple interactions in causal fields (von Eye, 1990). The lag-sequential model analyzes the contingency and cyclicity in behavioral interaction (Sackett, 1987). Even so, these tools for identifying functional relations among large numbers of responses in interaction still pose difficult problems. The method of sequential analysis of dyadic responses is not optimally conducive to translating the contingencies implied into reinforcement effects because, at every turn in the interaction sequence, different behavior combinations could be emitted by a dyad member, different numbers of responses can occur concurrently, or a particular dyad member's behavior might occur intermittently or infrequently. Thus, the behavior-analytic researcher may have difficulty isolating the functional relations involved.

In the past, these complications led many behavior researchers to study the flow of influence in two-way parent–infant interaction in experimentally contrived settings in which the responses of one member of the dyad are controlled. It is important to remember that the mother–child system is reorganized as a function of the earlier reciprocal and dynamical interactions.

Five Factors in Reciprocal Interaction

The outcome of development at any point in time is the result of complex interactions and resultant reorganization of dynamical systems. Alan Ross (1980) suggests that behavior is a function of the reciprocal interaction of four factors:

1. Genetic-constitutional makeup

2. History of interactions

3. Current physiological conditions

4. Current environmental conditions

One's genetic-constitutional makeup is inherited at conception. It is not just the genetic inheritance but, rather, the physical and physiological composition of the individual that results from the interaction of genetics and environment that we are concerned with here. This includes gross physiological characteristics such as gender, physique, and race, as well as all the subtle physiological characteristics we inherit. Right from conception, these inherited characteristics interact with the environment, including the intrauterine environment of the fetus; for example, as when the mother intakes drugs while pregnant, causing detrimental developmental damage to the fetus. Another a common experience is that females and males are raised differently by their parents. How they react to the differential treatment is partly due to biological sex differences. As a result of their different social environments, girls and boys assume different sex roles.

The innumerable interactions one has had with the environment composes one's history of interactions. This history determines, in part, how one is likely to behave at any given moment. Kantor (1959) called this history of interactions the reactional biography. It may also be called one's learning history. These past interactions affect the interactions taking place now. For example, a child who has been punished in the past for saying a "dirty word" in his or her parents' presence is now unlikely to repeat that word in their presence. Note that a history of interaction is dynamic, not static, and it has a history. Behavior analysts study sequences or episodes like this that are brief in relation to the person's lifetime, but they are still temporally extended. The third source of influence is the organism's current physiological condition. This is the physiological environment inside the skin. Whether you are sick or well, tired or rested, hungry or fed, contributes to determining how you behave in interaction with the other determinants. Thus, the child in our example with the newly emerging verbal skills is more likely to say, "I'm hungry," if he or she hasn't eaten breakfast than the child with the same genetic and interactional history but who has eaten breakfast.

Current environmental conditions affect our behavior. These include all the sights, sounds, smells, and other properties of events around us. They also include events inside our skin that affect our behavior. Because of all the environmental cues present, the hungry child is more likely to ask for something to eat in the kitchen than in the garage.

This analysis of the factors necessary to understand development is, however, incomplete. We must add a fifth—behavioral dynamics—to Ross's (1980) four factors:

5. Behavior dynamics

By definition, development is the study of behavior change over time. A behavioral approach is inherently dynamic because our primary task is to explain how and why behavioral phenomena transform or change from one time to another. Behavior-environment relationships are in a constant state of flux, influenced by changes in the relationships as they occur. Although progressive, the effects of conditions are not simply additive. That is, developmental outcomes are not just the sums of genetics, history, and current conditions. The ways in which factors interact are complex. They follow principles characteristic of entities in change, called behavior dynamics (Galbicka, 1992; Marr, 1992). The complexity of these interactions means that simple changes can produce complex results. Small changes in the initial boundary conditions may produce dramatic developmental outcomes; qualitatively new behavioral developments may emerge. The dynamical principles that must be considered are outlined next.

Notice the complexities of the interactions that develop. We are not simply the result of our biological destiny, nor are we machines without a biological and psychological history. We are the result of progressive changes in the interactions between our behavior and the events in our environments.

PRINCIPLES OF DYNAMICAL SYSTEMS ●

The dynamical principles of development are the functions that produce the structures of development. Chief among these dynamical principles are multiple determination, equifinality, nonlinearity, emergent properties, phase shifts, coalescent organization, **selectionism** (organization by contingencies, **behavioral attractors**, and **developmental trajectories**).

Multiple Determination

Behaviors result from multiple determinants. That is, even the simplest behavior is the function of the combination of many factors. Likewise, complex human behavior may emerge from the flowing together of simple, but multiple, conditions. The main assumption underlying the present textbook is that behavior change does not always depend solely or straightforwardly on standard behavioral concepts and learning principles (e.g., reinforcement, extinction stimulus control) and environmental operations (e.g., eliciting, evoking, reinforcing). Both contingencies and contextual determinants (historical and present) play primary roles in the prediction, control, and understanding of behavior change. Determination or causation of behavior is multiple. Consequently, the probability of a child learning at a given developmental point will vary as a function of multiple determinants (Peláez-Nougeras, 1996).

Equifinality

It is easy to see that a combination of different factors can produce different developmental outcomes given unique genetic, historical, or environmental conditions. This is the reason "there is no one exactly like you." Yet it is interesting that we can reach similar developmental outcomes by different combinations of interactions. Thus, two individuals who score 70 on an IQ test may have arrived there as the result of different transactions between genetics, histories, physiological, and psychological conditions. One may have had a potentially devastating genetic problem, such as Down syndrome, but through a history of supportive conditions he or she functions near a normal IQ range. Another may have inherited a "normal" set of genes, but through a less facilitative environment he or she reached the same score. This concept is called **equifinality** and refers to situations in which similar outcomes are the result of different interactions.

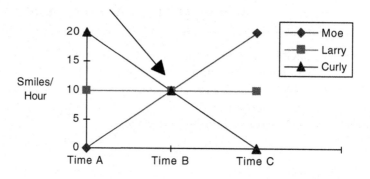

Figure 2.1　　An Example of Equifinality

The term *equifinality* is misleading. It connotes that we have reached an equal and "final" endpoint in development. Yet development is a continual process, and it is only the observer who makes it into a "still photograph," freezing it in time. So these are not true endpoints but merely points along developmental paths. Although different interactions may produce similar characteristics at these points, continuation along the different trajectories of development may mean different rather than "equal" outcomes later.

The graph in Figure 2.1 illustrates this point. It shows hypothetical data on changes in rates of smiling for three children. They start out very differently, at Time A. However, when they are measured later, at Time B, their rates are exactly the same. If we viewed development at this point, we could say this illustrates equifinality. The individuals reached the same endpoint following different paths of distinct combinations of phylogenic and ontogenic factors. Yet development is not arrested by our measurement. It continues, and we may find at Time C that the rates of smiling of the three are no longer equal. Therefore, equifinality is a useful concept but one whose "finality" should not be taken literally.

Nonlinearity and Models of Development

As in our illustration of the smiles per hour (sph) of Moe, Larry, and Curly, one common way to look at development is that it occurs on a unidirectional, straight path. That is, if something happens at point A (for example, you inherit the genetic predisposition to smile), there will be a particular outcome at point B (e.g., happy, grumpy). This is called a **linear model** because it assumes that development proceeds in a straight line. An additional meaning of linear is that the output is proportional to the input. For example, if you are carrying a

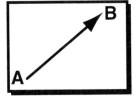

Figure 2.2   A Simple Linear Model

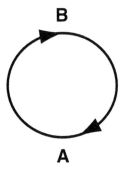

Figure 2.3   A Transactional Model

number of bricks in the back of a pickup truck, with each additional brick the back gets proportionately lower. Doubling the number of bricks doubles the amount of sag. This kind of incremental change in result was the common model for human development. For years, developmental psychologists used this linear model. Most statistical procedures, such as linear regression, still follow it. Figure 2.2 provides a graphical representation of a linear model. Linearity also implies **additivity**, as in analysis of variance in which interaction terms are deliberately minimized or ignored.

As developmental psychology became more sophisticated, psychologists saw the limitations of the linear model and turned to a **transactional model** (see Figure 2.3). This model is transactional in the sense that the causal relationships are bidirectional. This suggests that Event A modifies Event B and that, in turn, B modifies A. The interaction is reciprocal, involving mutual action (Baltes & Reese, 1977). Consider a transactional approach to our example involving smiling. A smiling baby increases smiling in the mother. Considered separately, a smiling mother increases smiling in her baby.

When an image loads from a Web site, the results are seldom linear. Instead, while the meter showing your progress may increase incrementally

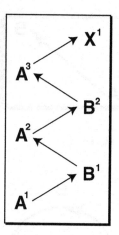

Figure 2.4   A Nonlinear Model

(e.g. 10–15–20%), you may have a completely blank screen. Then suddenly, at some seemingly arbitrary level of input (say 88%), the image pops up all at once and appears in its entirety with the last few percentages of input. Changes like these, which emerge suddenly and nonincrementally, are called nonlinear changes. Human development is filled with such nonlinear changes.

A **nonlinear model** goes beyond the reorganizing effects of bidirectional interactions of transactional modes (e.g., Minuchin, 1999). In a nonlinear model (Figure 2.4), not only does A affect B and B affect A, but the change A produces in B modifies the affect that B has on A, which in turn changes the effect A has on B. At first, this produces a quantitative change, as shown in Figure 2.4, by changes in the superscripts assigned to A and B. A smiling baby (A^1) increases smiling in her mother (B^1). This increased maternal smiling (B^1) may in turn still further increase the baby's smiling (A^2). At this point, the increased smiling of the baby (A^2) has further effects on mother's behavior (B^2). However, now, the high rate of baby smiling may cause mom's smiling to be replaced by an emergent behavior, laughing. As indicated by the notation, (X^1), laughing is qualitatively, not just quantitatively, different from the behavior which came before.

Some work with at-risk children and their parents by Tiffany Field (1986, 1987) and her associates illustrates the **nonlinearity** of mother–child transactions. Field and her colleagues found that mothers who had children who were at-risk for normal development faced special problems in trying to develop positive social interactions through playful exchanges. The problems these mothers faced is that their children provided unusually narrow windows of opportunity for play interactions with favorable outcomes. Most children need some stimulation from parents to play. Parents use special language called "motherese" to get attention; they also tickle and otherwise physically engage the children. Field found that at-risk children required more stimulation than typical children to begin to play back. That is, typical children are more linear in their reactions. Thus, mothers of these children became more stimulated and more active with the children. When infants get overstimulated, they indicate this to their mothers by, at first, looking away. If this "gaze aversion" is not effective in signaling to the mother to back off the stimulation and give the baby a break, the child's gaze aversion shifts to fussing and sometimes crying. Most caregivers quickly (and intuitively) learn to moderate their stimulatory behavior based on the child's behavior, thus keeping the child in playful stimulation and avoiding crying and negative outcomes. Unfortunately, mothers of at-risk children face a "double whammy." Not only does it take more stimulation to arouse them sufficiently for play, but they also get overstimulated more quickly. The shifts from playing to gaze aversion to crying comes much too quickly for most mothers who, it was found, are more likely to miss the child's signals because they are providing more and more stimulation. Field and Peláez's (e.g., Malphurs et al., 1996; Peláez-Nogueras et al., 1996) solution was to conduct several experimental interventions to coach the caregivers in how to become more sensitive and responsive to the child's cues.

A dynamical change may occur during these types of mother–infant interactions. Clearly, the history of child–parent interactions (i.e., the preceding experiences) affects current interactions between them, so they are kind of "transactions." In a nonlinear model, the "transactions" have been reorganized in that the earlier system of smiling/smiling has become a system of smiling/laughing. This is the essence of the dynamical systems approach.

Remember that beyond the bidirectionality of the transactional model, a nonlinear model connotes disproportionality. Consider again the example of the smiling baby and her mother. Initially, small increases in the baby's smiling may cause rather large, disproportional increases in the mother's smiling. However, additional increases in the baby's smiling may lead to no changes in the mother's level of smiling. Still further increases in the baby's smiling may lead to a drastic, disproportional decrease in the mother's smiling—when her smiles are replaced by laughter.

Emergent Properties

Development is a continuous process. From conception to death, the changes in person-environment relationships are based on what has come before. Yet as the nonlinear model suggests, not all changes are simple incremental additions to the person's repertoire. Instead, there may be sudden, abrupt change, as when a baby progresses from crawling to walking. Walking is based on what has come before, the crawling, but it is not just a faster or stronger form of crawling. Walking is qualitatively different. Although based on earlier forms, walking has emergent properties that are not just linear extensions of crawling.

An **emergent property** is a characteristic that suddenly appears, and, although specific precursors can be identified as necessary if it is to occur, the characteristic does not resemble the origins from which it arose. For example, running emerges from walking, but it differs from it in form. This is because it has unique properties, including a unique form or function; while small, incremental changes may occur, at times, change is often more dramatic and irregular. We describe these sudden changes in dynamical terms as **phase shifts.** More traditional developmentalists call them stages, and behaviorists call them cusps.

Behavioral researchers try to avoid the term *emergent* as an explanation and instead prefer to treat emergence as a description. They prefer to trace the origins of the so-called emergent responding to *processes* such as stimulus generalization and transfer of learning. An area of theory and research where the term emergence has frequently been used as an outcome is known as "stimulus equivalence" (Sidman, 1971). A child forms an "equivalence" class when he or she learns two stimulus relations (e.g., A = B therefore B = A *and* B = C therefore C = B), and then he or she concludes a third relation (C = A), which is said to emerge or be derived.

From a behavioral systems perspective, qualitatively new behaviors are said to emerge when many factors, such as increased motor skills, physiological changes, and, most important, environmental conditions all exist, resulting in the new behavior coalescing out of previously hidden skills. Thus, the child may suddenly walk when various factors, including hidden walking skills, come together. Likewise, a child may suddenly form an equivalence relation based on previous experiences and current environmental conditions.

Phase Shifts and Developmental Stages

The continuous nature of development does not mean that it proceeds at the same pace at all times. Rather than just changes in the number of behaviors, or in the strength of them, development may also involve changes in the form of behaviors. Thus, development involves not only quantitative changes in behavior-environment relationships but qualitative changes as well.

In the development of language, for example, we initially see some quantitative changes in babbling. At first, the child's babbling includes all the sounds that appear in all human languages. Then, at around 6 months of age, the number of sounds unique to the child's parents' language increases while the sounds not present in the parents' language decrease and disappear. This is a quantitative change.

However, other aspects of language show changes in the quality of the behavior-environment relationships. At around 9 months of age, the child begins to use his or her own babbling sounds to stand for things, just as we use words to stand for things. Developmental psychologists have used the term *vocables* for the sounds that that child has coined. Developmental psychologists characterize the shift from babbling to vocables as a change from one stage to the next stage. In the same sense, the emergence of true words constitutes a new stage in the development of communication.

Many prominent developmental theories are essentially "stage theories." Developmentalists have used the concept of stage to describe such qualitative changes in behavior or behavior-environment relationships. That is, they suggest that the milestones of development can be understood best by viewing them as qualitatively different states of behavior. Among the most influential of these stage theories are Freud's theory detailing psychosexual stages of personality development and Piaget's theory identifying stages of cognitive development.

Although stages have been widely used in developmental psychology, other sciences have also had to contend with the sudden emergence of qualitatively different states. Physical objects frequently make sudden changes from one qualitative state to another. For example, as water reaches a temperature of 0 degrees Celsius (32° Fahrenheit), there is a qualitative shift to the crystalline structure we know as ice. Gleick (1988) uses the example of applying increasing force to a metal bar. At some point, the bar just crumples, shifting from one state (i.e., straight) to another (bent). This sudden qualitative change in properties is called a phase shift.

Thelen and Ulrich (1991) illustrate the nonlinearity of phase shifts. They point to the sudden shift in the gait of horses from walking to trotting. With just a small increase in speed, the pattern of the horse's hoofs shifts suddenly. Trotting is not just more rapid walking; it is qualitatively different. A completely different pattern emerges from the increase in speed. The switch from walking to trotting is a phase shift.

Phase shifts share four characteristics with what traditional developmental theorists describe as stages. One characteristic of phase shifts is that they are sudden. A child cannot walk at all, and then suddenly takes his or her first steps. A second characteristic of phase shifts is that their order is predictable. That is, we can predict that children will crawl before they walk. A third characteristic is that the new behavior is different in form from the behaviors that preceded it. The walking that emerges is quite different in appearance from crawling. A fourth characteristic is that the form and often the timing of the phase shift is predictable within a species. Thus, Piaget was able to predict a shift at about 2 years of age from the **sensorimotor stage** to the preoperational stage of cognitive development. In addition, he could predict what the differences in behavior would be in a child. However, phase shifts or stages don't explain the shifts in behavior; they are descriptions of it. How, then, do we explain such sudden phase shifts or stages? To do that, we must look at the basic processes that produce phase shifts. One of the most important of these is the dynamical principle of coalescent organization.

Coalescent Organization

Imagine that you can't sleep one night before a big test in your class, Developmental Psychology. As you lie awake in your bed, thinking about child development, your attempts to try to get some sleep are thwarted by the drip . . . drip . . . drip of water from a faucet. Unable to sleep and unable to cram any more facts into your head, you get up, walk over to the faucet and are intrigued by the behavior of the water drops. You notice how the trickle of water gradually builds into a drop and how the drop produces a characteristic shape before dropping into the sink. You also notice the cadence that the sound and the pattern the drops make as they splash. You open the faucet slightly and you find that you can perturb, or upset, the system and produce a completely new pattern and sound of drops. At some point, the flow of water is great enough so that the faucet changes phases from dripping to running. Pleased at finding evidence of dynamical systems even in inanimate substances, you open the faucet, fall off to sleep, and visions of waterfalls flow in your head.

Thelen and Ulrich (1991)[4] have pointed out that just as physical objects and biological systems develop consistent patterns of organization, so, too, do psychological systems. **Coalescent organization** is a term for the dynamical process by which factors come together to produce coherent patterns of behavior. Patterns of behavior emerge because many factors (including genetics, physical structure, previous experiences, environmental conditions, and the task at hand) constrain all possible forms of behavior into the pattern that emerges. For example, the physical structure of most human infants limits the possible forms of locomotion. That is, given our phylogenically selected physique, with a large, heavy body, relatively weak arms, but long and strong legs, we are unlikely to fly. Instead, given a species-typical environment shaped by and including gravity, we are most likely to develop bipedal walking.

Bipedal walking emerges from the coming together of conditions.[5] Given these conditions, behavior is organized into a particular pattern. Because all humans share common species-typical genetic, historical, and environmental conditions, many **universal behaviors** emerge. On the other hand, because of variability between individuals in the same genetic, historical, and environmental conditions, the behavior of individuals differs. In the first 10 to 11 months, the human child's physical structure and learning history make normal bipedal walking universally impossible. Thelen and Ulrich (1991) have shown that because of a large, heavy head, weak muscles, and limited experiences, walking cannot occur without assistance. Given appropriate assistance, such as a parent holding the child up as Thelen & Ulrich (1991) showed, supporting them on a treadmill, the child can demonstrate hidden skills for walking.

An important property of coalescent organization is that the form of the response is assembled by the particular task at hand (Thelen, Kelso, & Fogel, 1987). That is, the form of the response is organized by its function or consequences. In behavioral terms, a group of behaviors controlled by the same consequence is called a functional response class. A segment on the TV show *60 Minutes* several years ago illustrates this point. This segment featured a woman, Bonnie Consuelo, who was born without hands and arms. What made this segment newsworthy and fascinating was, despite the challenges that this severe birth defect presented, this woman was able to perform the functions of everyday life, including selecting fruits and vegetables at the supermarket, cleaning house, and driving a car . . . all with her feet! You can imagine the shock on Mike Wallace's face as he was driven around town by someone using only her feet. Although the forms or topographies of the responses may have been unique and unusual, they came together as functionally producing the effective results.

A second characteristic of coalescent organization is that, although the unique form of the behavior is the result of the coming together of its organismic and environmental elements, the form cannot be predicted from any of its single elements. Again, consider that walking depends on earlier behaviors and changes in neurological, muscular, and skeletal systems. Furthermore, the pattern of walking that emerges cannot be predicted from any of these elements. That is, walking is not just faster crawling or use of bigger muscles. The coming together, or coalescence, of all elements produces the emergent behavior we call walking.

Remembering the principle of multiple determinants, some factors disproportionately affect outcome. Horowitz (1987) calls these elements that have the power to disproportionately affect the system **leading parts.** A mother in a nuclear family is a leading part for much of what develops in that family. For example, a small increase in praise from the mother may disproportionately increase room cleaning by the child. Another example of a leading part in development is the disproportionate effect the emergence of walking has on social behavior. Likewise, the attainment of muscle and bone maturation is a leading part in the development of walking (Thelen & Ulrich, 1991). These conditions that play a disproportional determining role in development have also been called **control parameters** (Thelen & Ulrich, 1991). That is, they are the conditions that control the development of emergent behaviors.

Rosales and Baer (Baer & Rosales-Ruiz 1998; Rosales & Baer, 1994) introduced the concept of behavioral cusps to describe changes in **person-environment interactions** that enable multiple new interactions. That is, a behavioral cusp is a change, such as walking, that, because it has occurred, enables the explosive development of many new interactions, such as social behaviors, exploratory behaviors, and a host of others. Baer and Rosales-Ruiz (1998) liken a behavioral cusp to a node of a tree branch. As with the tree, a behavioral cusp develops from earlier branches, and, like a node, it leads to many later branches, none of which are predetermined or precisely predictable. The explosion of multiple branches of development made more probable by a cusp is consistent with the dynamical principle of nonlinearity.

Selectionism: Organization by Contingencies

As we noted earlier, the two types of behavioral selection are phylogenic and ontogenic selection. *Phylogenic* selection refers to populations of organisms over time, and it results from phylogenic contingencies—those that operated in ancestral environments during the evolution of a species. Phylogenic contingencies involve both gradual and continuous changes taking place over long periods of evolutionary time and others selected following punctuated events that produced massive environmental changes. Selection creates the features of organisms and is also necessary to maintain them. Catania (1998) illustrates this by explaining how the ancestors of whales were once land mammals:

> After they moved back to the sea, the environmental contingencies that made legs advantageous no longer maintained the selection of well-formed legs. Instead selection favored limbs that were effective for movement through water. The legs of the ancestors of whales gradually disappeared. (p. 34)

Ontogenic selection is the kind of selection that produces learning, and that will be emphasized in this textbook. Ontogenic development is one in which the responses of organisms are affected by their consequences; for example, those responses reinforced by food when an organism has been deprived. Thus, ontogenic contingencies are those that operate during interactions between an organism and its environment within its own lifetime rather than over successive generations (Skinner, 1966).

Cultural selection refers to the survival of behavior patterns as they are transmitted from some individuals to others (within the culture or across cultures). These types of patterns of behavior depend on behavior that changes during ontogeny as well as on phylogeny. The transmission of religion and ethnic traditions are good examples in this category.

Bonny Consuelo's behaviors may be unique, but such adaptations to the task are hardly unusual. You are probably aware of how persons who cannot see with their eyes develop other sensory abilities, such as hearing or touching, to a much higher level than most. Such overcompensation is not rare.

This example of overcompensation illustrates the importance of the task for organizing behavior. Behavior is functional. That is, it produces an outcome. Surely, most of us would be unable to pick up a cherry or grapefruit with our feet and bring it to our nose to smell the fruit. However, we perform the same function with our arms and hands—behavior that has the same function, but a different form. Given the phylogenically selected characteristics of these limbs, it is much more probable that reaching and fetching will be done by human hands, not feet. But what if your hands are full and you drop a ball that is rolling into the street, or you are held captive with your hands tied behind your back, but a sharp object is on the floor in front of you? In both cases, you could use your toes as fingers, your feet as hands.

The coalescence of the behavior depends on the results obtained—that is, on the contingencies. Just as the contingencies of natural selection determine the form of the species that emerges, so, too, do the contingencies in the environment organize the form of the behavior that emerges. As an example of contingency, let us return to the Bonnie Consuelo's case; the complex grasping movement of the feet was assembled by the need to pick up a piece of fruit so that it could be placed in a bag. Any behavior that gets the fruit into the bag undamaged will be selected through reinforcement. For most of us, the hand, which evolved with an opposing thumb, is more likely to produce the same outcome, and we develop grasping with our hands that is shaped by the contingencies. The results of these functions are the dynamic structures of development—namely, behavioral attractor states, discussed below.

Thelen (1994) demonstrated how contingencies underlie the development of behavior. She focused on the spontaneous kicking of 3-month-olds, which, under normal environmental contingencies, is random and uncoordinated. Thus, uncoordinated, spontaneous kicking is the norm for 3-month-olds. However, by attaching a string to a soft elastic cuff around the infants' ankles, and attaching this string to a mobile, a new contingency was put into effect: Kick and the mobile moves. Furthermore, Thelen investigated the effects of connecting both ankles together with the cuff versus only one.

What she found was that all infants increased their kicking when the consequence was that kicking moved the mobile. Thus, kicking was no longer random when the contingency was in effect. Moreover, when the legs were cuffed together, coordinated movements of both legs occurred at an age where such movements are not normally observed. That is, the environmental consequences provided in this study assemble coordinated leg movements. However, the coordinated behavior was not strong enough to maintain under normal conditions, and when the cuffs were removed, the coordinated movements disappeared.

Variability in Behavior

As we shall see in detail in Chapter 5, selection of behavior depends on **variability** of behavior. That is, just as in natural selection, where mutation-produced variability in structures is necessary for selection to occur, so, too, is variability necessary for learning. In learning, variability (in this case, behavioral) must occur for contingencies to select new behaviors. Alan Neuringer (1993) has emphasized the importance of variation in behavior for basic learning processes. Recently, Robert Siegler (1994) has recognized the importance of variability in cognitive behaviors for cognitive development to occur. He points out that a common view of cognitive development is that it develops in stages. Most people view the behavior within stages as constant. That is, when a child is at a stage of development, all their behavior is consistent with this stage. Siegler's point is that variability is "pervasive." Variability, rather than consistency, is the norm.

Variability occurs not only across different but related tasks, but it may be seen within an individual solving the same problem twice or even within a single trial. Let us say that the child has to decide which glass (e.g., a tall, thin one versus a short, broad one) has more juice in it. One time the child may pick up each glass and look at it on all sides. Another time, the child may pick up both glasses to see which weighs more. One of these strategies may be better at getting the child more juice to drink and will become the more likely strategy due to the different consequences of the two strategies. Even in cognitive development, variability in behavior is necessary for selection by consequences.

Behavioral Attractors

Behaviors that emerge may have consistent forms or topographies. Thelen and Ulrich (1991) have used the terms "dynamic attractor," "attractor state," or simply, "attractor," for the consistent pattern that emerges as the result of coalescent organization. Thus, crawling, walking, babbling, and other functional response classes having a specific form and assembled by the task at hand (i.e., having a specific function), are attractors.

The term **attractor** may suggest that it is the behavior itself that attracts. In other words, the attractor assembles the components into the emergent behavior. However, the term attractor is a description of the emergent behavior. The attractor is the pattern that is assembled by the coalescence of conditions brought together by the task at hand. For example, the whirlpool pattern that emerges when water goes down a drain is an attractor. It is assembled by the coalescence of conditions, such as the amount of water, shape of the sink, size of the drain, gravity, and the location of the sink (e.g., the whirlpool rotates in a clockwise direction in the northern hemisphere, but it spins counterclockwise in the southern hemisphere). The whirlpool emerges from the coalescence of factors; the whirlpool does not organize the factors into itself.

Thelen and Ulrich (1991) characterize attractors as "soft assemblies." This means that the patterns of behavior that emerge are rather fragile and easily disrupted by changes in the conditions that assembled them. Thus, attractors are dynamic. For example, consider your own experience in learning a skill that has a particular form to it, such as a tennis swing. Given certain conditions that exist while you are taking a lesson (such as balls being propelled from a machine at you at a particular speed, height, and position and a teacher who is telling you to "keep your wrist flat"), your swing "really comes together." A nice pattern has emerged in your swing. The swing has become an attractor; it functions very well at returning the ball.

However, what if the conditions change? What if the speed increases or the teacher now says, "Keep your elbow in"? It is likely that your nice, effective pattern will be disrupted or perturbed. Even a slight change in conditions may throw off the swing considerably. Sometimes such perturbations in attractors provide the basis for variability that will be selected by the environment, and a new attractor, better suited to the current conditions, will emerge. Thus, after a short period during which your swing has "gone to pot," a new, better swing will emerge.

Developmental Trajectories

Thelen and Ulrich (1991) characterize development as a "dynamic, multi-level, non-stationary process" (p. 27). Many levels of systems are involved. Because of the transactions between the person and environment, the influences of each on the other are dynamic and constantly changing. As a dynamic process, development is often viewed as a pathway or **trajectory**. From a dynamical systems view, this means that transacting behavior-environment systems can be seen as tracing a path through time and space.

In simplest terms, the path, or trajectory of behavior, can follow one of three patterns: Behavior can remain stable, it can continue on the same linear or curvilinear trajectory, or it can exhibit sudden phase shifts.

Given consistency in the conditions determining behavior, behavior is likely to remain stable. That is, with no changes in organismic or environmental conditions, there should be no changes in person-environment interactions. However, even in the absence of changes in conditions, behavior may continue on its dynamic trajectory. That is, behavior-environment relations that are moving in a particular direction, at a particular rate, may continue on that trajectory. This is the principle of **developmental momentum** (Nevin, 1992). Unless conditions change to disturb the person from this path of development, the tendency of the organism is to continue to develop on this path. Conditions that can perturb this developmental trajectory can include genetic-constitutional ones (such as changes in neurological, skeletal, and muscular structure), history of interactions, and environmental conditions, especially control parameters. Some of these changes will be a function of the changes in the organism-environment relations that result from previous transactions.

Finally, as conditions change, behavior-environment relations change. Thus, when transactions produce changes in conditions, trajectories of development change, too. Behavior developing along a particular path may be perturbed and a new trajectory may emerge. Thus, discontinuities or nonlinearities of development (i.e., phase shifts) may result from the ongoing processes of dynamic transactions (Thelen & Ulrich, 1991). In summary, development is dynamical in two ways. First, developmental outcome, although cumulative and progressive, is essentially nonlinear. Second, the factors determining development are multiple and nonadditive.

Behavioral Cusps Instead of "Stages"

As we mentioned earlier, Rosales and Baer (Baer & Rosales-Ruiz, 1998; Rosales & Baer, 1994; Rosales-Ruiz & Baer, 1997) introduced the concept of **behavioral cusps** to describe changes in person-environment interactions that enable multiple new interactions. Cusps are behaviors that have significant and far-reaching implications for further developmental changes. That is, a behavioral cusp is a new behavior, such as walking, that, because it has occurred, enables the explosive development of many new interactions, such as social behaviors, exploratory behaviors, and a host of others. Another behavioral cusp is fluency in reading because it opens pathways to an enormous number of other developments. So the fluent reader can follow directions to use a computer program; in turn, this computer program allows that person to get on the

Internet; in turn, this allows him or her to buy a ticket to Tahiti; which in turn, allows the discovery of a new culture, and so forth. This is just one branch of behaviors that are enabled by the development of a behavioral cusp. Cusps also enable many other "branches" as well. This is why they are important. The notion of **cusp** is consistent with the dynamical principle of nonlinearity.

ORGANISM–ENVIRONMENT MODEL ●

In this chapter, we have emphasized that developmental outcomes are products of the dynamic interactions between the organism and the environment. The organism provides the structures of development, and the environment provides the functions. The result is a constant interaction between the structures of the organism, such as arms, limbs, and brain, and the functions of the environment—the contingencies that shape development. Therefore, not only is the organism changed by the environment, but the changed organism affects what the environmental influences will be.[6]

Horowitz (1987) presents an organism-environment model that further analyzes these dimensions. In her model, the organisimic dimension is composed of two continua. The first ranges from impaired to unimpaired and represents the amount of physiological damage the organism brings to the interactions. The second organisimic dimension ranges from vulnerable to invulnerable and represents the sensitivity of the organism to environmental harm (the result of the interaction between **genetic–constitutional make-up** and the individual's history of environmental interactions). Developmental outcomes, which run from nonfacilitative to facilitative, are the result of the interaction between this organisimic dimension and the environmental dimension. Thus, in this model, development outcome depends on the interaction between organism and environment.

What Behavior Developmentalists Study

Organisms are living beings. What is important from a psychological perspective is that they do things—that is, they behave. At any given time the organism has certain characteristics consisting of a genetic makeup, physiological structure, and a repertoire of behaviors.

Psychologists study behavioral development. Behavior is what an organism does, and behavior change includes events both outside and inside the skin. Examples of external behaviors include running and talking out loud. Examples of private behaviors include thinking, feeling, and physiological events. Although nonobservable behavior may lead to problems for the scientist (e.g., they cannot be objectively observed by two people), internal behaviors such as thinking or physiological arousal play important roles in development.

Horowitz (1987) makes a distinction between the development of universal and nonuniversal behaviors. Some of the universal behaviors, such as reflexes and basic perceptual abilities (e.g., detecting light from dark, hearing certain sounds) are highly (but not exclusively) determined by the child's genetic. Other universal behaviors that appear in virtually all children, such as crawling, walking, and talking, take much longer to develop and are much more highly influenced by environmental effects. Nonuniversal behaviors, on the other hand, are unique to individuals, and, while they have a genetic–consistitutional component, are largely the result of environmental processes.

Horowitz (1987) explains that nonuniversal behaviors are those "that are the result of learning opportunities determined by cultural values and variations in functional environments" (p. 149). Thus, what makes each of us so different from others is the role of cultural and socially determined environments trans-acting with our genetic makeup and interactional histories. Note that interac-tions are crucial here. Unlike universal behaviors in which the environment constrains the influence of the genes, with nonuniversals the genetic makeup constrains the role of the environment. Thus, no matter how facilitative the environment, our genetically based body structure will not allow us to flap our arms and fly. We must develop very different behaviors to accomplish that task.

Facilitative Functions of the Environment

Facilitative means that with respect to the behaviors involved, the charac-teristics of the environment are optimal. Thus, given a particular set of organis-mic characteristics, a facilitative environment will maximize outcomes, and a nonfacilitative environment will minimize outcomes. For example, "crack babies" are often exposed to nonfacilitative environments in which nutritional, social, and educational deficits work to minimize developmental outcomes. Such babies may have parents who provide inadequate nutrition and poor socializa-tion experiences, and fail to provide an adequate language environment (e.g., are less likely to read to their children).

Thus, the developmental outcome of a particular characteristic, such as intelligence, language, or social skills, depends on the transactions between organismic and environmental factors. We see how the dynamic interactions of factors fit here. Genetic-constitutional makeup and the history of interactions are organismic factors. Current physiological conditions and current environmental conditions are environmental factors. Their dynamical interactions produce different developmental outcomes.

A given organismic characteristic (e.g., Down syndrome) could have different developmental outcomes (e.g., IQ) depending on the facilitative attributes of the environment. We also can see how equifinality can occur, where two different sets of organismic and environmental characteristics could produce the same developmental outcome.

DEVELOPMENTAL ● QUESTIONS FOR RESEARCH

As we saw in our look at the controversies in developmental psychology, developmental psychologists have a diverse set of views and theories. What unites them and distinguishes them from others who study or work with children is their interest in developmental questions. Developmental questions ask about the causal and functional processes involved in the progressive changes we see in the individual over time. This means that the developmental psychologist is not interested in merely describing phenomena existing in children or in the aged but, rather, in explaining how these phenomena came about.

Earlier, we introduced the notion of behavioral cusps to illustrate how learning to crawl suddenly and dramatically increases the child's development. A crawling child now is able to get to things previously unobtainable and can come into contact with aspects of the environment not previously available. The crawling child can play with toys, chase a cat, explore pots and pans, and contact an unlimited number of things not previously possible. Walking, talking, and reading are just some examples of behavioral cusps. One task of developmental psychologists in asking **strong developmental questions** is really discovering and identifying the behavioral cusps for the developing child.

Thus, development is not a constant, even process. Instead, it is marked by sudden fits and starts, with the development of some behaviors disproportionately influencing the development of subsequent ones. However, development is a continuous process in which current development is a result of the earlier experiences and changes in the individual. Simply identifying stages of development does not lead us to an understanding of individuals. Nor does describing cusps alone allow us to understand the process of how development occurs. To do so, we need a theory of development that acknowledges the ever-changing, dynamic, and nonlinear processes in development.

Box 2.2   Chaos, Contingencies, and Kids

The problems facing the scientist in predicting human development are not that different from those facing the scientist attempting to predict the weather. Both involve large, ever-changing dynamical systems. Both involve a seemingly infinite number of initial conditions from which we must select those on which to base our predictions. Both seem to involve rapid, random, and apparently unpredictable changes. It was from the science of weather prediction, meteorology, that arose a new science, **chaos** science (Gleick, 1988). Some of these new ideas may be relevant to the science of developmental psychology as well (Barton, 1994). Let us look at some of the principles of chaos science and their relevance to development.

Chaotic Systems. In predicting the path of a hurricane, or even the flow of a molecule of water down a stream, simple linear models are of limited use. Up to a point, our predictions are reasonably accurate, but, once past this point, a predictable event tumbles into seeming randomness—chaos. In nature, it seems that chaotic behavior is inherent in large systems; we can predict that systems will reach a point in which they are unpredictable. The laws of Newtonian physics are powerful and useful—they have produced a technology that has sent man to the moon and discovered cures to diseases—yet there are points at which predictions based on linear models fail. These failures to predict do not invalidate the Newtonian principles, but they do call for elaboration of them. The same may be seen as true for current developmental predictions. We may make some predictions about children in general with a fairly high probability of accuracy. Yet our linear models may be insufficient to predict individual development in detail. Chaos may be inherent in the system of human development too.

Nonlinearity. This may be demonstrated by your opening of a bag of potato chips. You start to tear the top, but nothing happens. You apply more force. Still nothing happens. Finally, you reach a point where the bag suddenly ruptures, dumping chips all over you and on the floor. This is a case of nonlinearity. Rather than tearing gradually and tearing faster as you increase the force, the bag does not tear at all and then suffers complete failure. A phase shift has occurred in which the bag went from one state (closed) to a qualitatively different one (empty). Development may be like this. Experiences may have no observable effect, and then suddenly a new behavior may appear as if out of nowhere. The child suddenly gets up and walks and never again needs to crawl. The effect of past experiences is crucial, but the importance of each experience is not simply additive. Traditional developmental theory based on linear models would fail to see the major role played by discrete, minor events in the development of behavior during childhood.

Horowitz's (1987) leading parts may be an example of the nonlinearity of development. Remember, leading parts are experiences or influences in development that seem to have a disproportionately large effect compared with other conditions. For example, early mother language interaction with the infant may influence later language development more than would be predicted from a simple count of interactions. Or having one good friend might insulate the child from the effects on divorce more than would be predicted from the child's overall popularity. Linear regression models might miss the unusual significance of these influences. Chaos science suggests that such leading parts may be more characteristic of development than originally thought.

Horowitz's leading parts concept may also reflect the chaos science principle of sensitivity to initial conditions. If you start two identical balls rolling down a plane, where they stop will be influenced to a significant extent by where they started. That is, by the initial conditions. Development clearly is influenced by initial conditions, including genetic makeup and early interactional history. These may function as leading parts.

Another issue raised by chaos science is how we measure things. The yards, feet, meters, or miles we use to measure the coastline of California are arbitrary. The length of the coastline will be different if we use a tape measure that is accurate to one foot or one-one thousandth of an inch. Likewise our measures of intelligence and social development are arbitrary and affect our findings. Within behavior analysis, there is a debate between those pursuing a microanalysis of behavior and those taking a more molar approach. Chaos science may help lead us to better understanding of the relationship between various measures of development and behavior.

In sum, Chaos science is new and has created an impact among scientists. It may serve to improve rather than replace current scientific principles. It is too soon to tell whether it will yield principles that lead to better prediction and control than current theories. Still, it has led scientists in all fields to question their current theories and find ways to improve on them. Behavior analysts have incorporated its principles into their science (see Galbicka, 1992; Hoyert, 1992; Marr, 1992; Nevin, 1992). It may be useful to the science of developmental psychology, too (Barton, 1994).

● SUMMARY

A *theory* is a set of statements that attempts to describe the relationship between observed phenomena and the factors thought to affect it. Theory provides a coherent framework for conceptualizing this subject matter. A good theory should help us organize and explain observations, as well as generate new research questions. Theories tend to reflect general theories or worldviews of theorists that color how we observe and explain outcomes. Theories differ in the extent to which they emphasize *structure* versus *function*, description versus explanation, nature versus nurture, and *continuity* versus *discontinuity*.

Although theory with a structural focus may concentrate on elucidating the structure of behavior and knowledge, a functional focus is concerned primarily with the relationship between behavior and the environment. Although each focus on different aspects of development, both structural and functional accounts prove to be useful in understanding the process. Although description is necessary in the study of development, the ability of a theory to explain is essential because it allows for prediction and control of the process. It is important to be able to differentiate description from explanation to avoid circular reasoning. Similarly, *reification* can be problematic because of its tendency to divert attention away from variables controlling behavior. Emphasis on the degree of influence of nature and nurture in theory detracts from the more important question of how heredity and environment interact to produce development. Although behavioral approaches tend to have the reputation of being squarely in the nurture camp, in reality, many behavioral theorists acknowledge that innate and acquired behavior are a function of selection by *phylogenic* (concerning the evolutionary history of species) and *ontogenic* (concerning the behavioral history of an individual) *contingencies*. Finally, theories differ in that some conceive of development as a continuous process, whereas others perceive the process in terms of discrete stages.

It is suggested that nine criteria be taken into consideration in the judging of developmental theories: accuracy, clarity, predictability, practicality, internal consistency, *parsimony*, the degree to which it is testable, its usefulness in generating new knowledge and research, and the degree to which it makes sense.

The *behavioral systems* approach is concerned with the analysis of development in terms of inseparable and interlocking systems that are constantly in flux. Although analyzing development at this level is essential to a coherent understanding of it, the sheer scale and complexity of the process creates methodological problems. Alan Ross (1980) suggests that behavior is a function of the reciprocal interaction of four factors: (a) genetic-constitutional makeup, (b) history of interactions, (c) current physiological conditions, and (d) current environmental conditions. We also suggest that to understand development, researchers must also understand behavior dynamics. Important principles of *dynamical systems* include *multiple determination, equifinality, nonlinearity, emergent properties, phase shifts, coalescent organization, selectionism, behavioral attractors,* and *developmental trajectories.*

Multiple determination refers to the idea that even the simplest behavior is a function of the combination of many factors. *Equifinality* refers to the concept that similar developmental outcomes can be achieved through different combinations of interactions. A *nonlinear* conceptualization of development allows for the possibility that interacting factors may have more than simple, consistent, incremental relationships with each other that produce quantitative as well as qualitative changes. *Emergent* properties are qualities of a product not discernable by the examination of the elements that comprise it. The surfacing of emergent properties is sometimes referred to as phase shifts. *Phase shifts* are sudden and differ from preceding behavior. Their order, forming, and timing are predictable within a species. *Coalescent organization* is a dynamical process by which factors come together to produce coherent patterns of behavior. It is one of the basic processes that produce phase shifts. Important properties of coalescent organization are that the form of a response is dependent on its function or consequences, and that form cannot be predicted from any of its single elements. *Leading parts* are elements that disproportionately affect outcomes and have also been termed *control parameters. Behavioral cusps* broaden the spectrum of possible interactions, and, ultimately, outcomes. Selectionism can operate on both phylogenic and ontogenic levels and depends on variability of behavior. *Behavioral attractors* are emergent behaviors having a specific form and function. They are easily disrupted by changes in the conditions that assembled them. Finally, developmental *trajectories* refer to the various pathways development can take. They can remain stable, continue in a linear or curvilinear fashion, or exhibit sudden phase shifts.

It is clear that development is a complex, dynamic process and that the scope of its study can be daunting. However, a behavioral systems approach offers a coherent framework for understanding it to the best of our ability.

NOTES

---

1. The terms "miracle theory" and "impossible theory" have been applied frequently in the past to describe the psycholinguistic and behavioral theories of language acquisition, respectively. The theories will be considered in some detail in Chapter 8.

2. Phil Hineline (Hineline & Wanchisen, 1989) has distinguished also between mediational versus nonmediational theories, which is a distinction that is similar, but not identical, to the "structural/functional distinction."

3. Notice that the word *"control"* in this context does not mean the same thing as in the expression "control group." The former refers to causing changes in a variable to occur. The latter refers to a group that provides the comparison for the experimental group.

4. The term "coalescent organization" is used in this text because it more clearly connotes that it is a coming together of factors. "Self-organization" carries the connotation of the organism (the self) doing something to bring the factors together. Thelen and Ulrich (1991) noted this concern.

5. Paul Andronis and his colleagues (Andronis, 1983; Andronis, Goldiamond, & Layng, 1997) have used the term *contingency adduction* for a complex skill that is assembled from component parts by reinforcement contingencies.

6. For an earlier treatment of this model see Bijou and Baer (1961, 1978).

CHAPTER 3

BEHAVIOR GENETICS

● THE HUMAN GENOME

One of the greatest scientific adventures of all time is the unraveling of the **human genome.** This is the unraveling of the entire human genetic code. A complete first draft of the genome was announced on June 26, 2000, and, for the first time in history, scientists identified all the locations of all the human genes. A **genome** is the entire genetic code of a species. This "genetic roadmap" provides us with great potential for identifying genes responsible for many physical human traits, including many diseases.

In this chapter we will look at **genes** and how they work with the environment to produce human traits or characteristics.

● CONTROVERSY: THE ROLE OF GENETICS IN DEVELOPMENT

In Chapter 2, we saw that the nature–nurture controversy was one of the most basic and oldest in developmental psychology. The predominant worldview has swung back and forth over the years between the relative importance of nature and nurture. In recent years, the pendulum may have swung too far in the favor of genetics (Plomin, 1999). Developments, such as the cracking of the human genome, may tend to overemphasize the role of genes in behavioral development.

As we have seen, we cannot separate the influence of heredity and environment in development. Genes do not directly cause behavior. Genes must interact with the environment to produce the physical structures of the person. These physical structures (e.g., the brain and other organs) must then interact with the physical and social environment to produce behavior. Rather than asking if development is due to heredity or environment, we need to ask how do heredity and environment work together, over time, to produce developmental outcomes (Plomin, 1999; Plomin & Daniels, 1987). This chapter attempts to explain the ways in which genes and environment interact dynamically over the course of the life span. We will first look at behavior genetics, and then we will examine how genes and the environment fit into the overall scheme of development.

BEHAVIOR GENETICS: THE STRUCTURES ●

Behavioral genetics is a field that studies both *behavioral* and *genetic* aspects of development. Genetic analysis describes the genetic structure of each species and is used to study the individual differences in the expression of a trait, the behavior. Behavior-genetic analysis is a method to examine how much a particular behavior is genetically influenced. The nature–nurture controversy discussed in the previous chapter emerged as a result of researchers' attempts to determine how much a behavior pattern is influenced by heredity and how much by environment. The behavior-genetic analysis approach, which asks the question "How much is heredity and how much is environment?" perpetuates the rationale that spawned the nature–nurture controversy.

Why Study Genetics?

The topic of genetics sometimes seems too technical or too biological for the average student of human development. It is technical, but we think there are two good reasons to understand genetic processes. First, genetics is a good example of how parsimonious causes can produce highly complex results. As we shall see below, enormous complexity comes from relatively simple genetic mechanisms. We think this provides a good physical example of the same situation that exists in psychological development, where relatively simple causes can produce enormously complex behavioral outcomes.

The second reason for studying genetics is to understand "how" they contribute to development. Most of society agrees that genes are important in development, but few have taken the time to understand how genetic codes actually affect behavioral development. That is the topic of the second part of this chapter. First, we start with the mechanisms of genetics themselves.

The genetic process produces unique individuals. It ensures variability among individuals of a species. This variability enables natural selection to occur and means that all of us will be unique individuals. Even before conception, processes are underway that virtually guarantee hereditary uniqueness. To understand how we start our existence unlike anyone else who ever lived requires some basic knowledge of the genetic code.

DNA: Secrets of the Genetic Code

An absolute wonder of nature is the genetic code. A simple but enormously powerful set of universal mechanisms is responsible, in large measure, for producing all living things in their infinite variety. Although humans have only existed for perhaps 3 to 4 million years, it is estimated that **DNA**, the basic building block of the genetic code, has been around for billions of years. DNA is the universal basis of life. You share the same genetic building blocks with all living things that have ever lived, including your distant relatives, the trees (Sagan, 1980)!

A molecule of DNA is configured as a double helix, a coiled structure of double-stranded DNA. Each strand of DNA is like a spiral staircase consisting of sequences of chemical "building blocks" or bases. Remarkably, there are only four distinct chemical bases in all DNA molecules that have ever been. These four, and only these four, determine the genetic makeup of all living things. How can this be? How can only four simple bases be responsible for all our inherited attributes and the genetic uniqueness of living things? The answer is that although the elements of the genetic code are extremely simple, the sequences of these elements can be extremely long and complex. The genetic code has a small "alphabet" but an enormous vocabulary!

The alphabet consists only of the letters A, C, G, and T. These stand for adenine, cytosine, guanine, and thiamine. These are the only four chemical bases in DNA. These base letters produce syllables (called codons) that are three letters long. Thus, a codon could be AAA, ACA, TTT, or any base combinations. The syllables produce meaningful units, the genes, just as syllables produce meaningful units called words. The sentences made up of these words can be thousands of letters long. Each unique word, or sequence of bases, may produce a unique characteristic. Thus, AACAGAT could mean blue eyes while CACCAGT could mean brown. Furthermore, not only is the sequence of the letters significant, but the position of the words in the sentences is crucial as well. Just as the positioning of the words in "The dog bit the man" and "The man bit the dog" is crucial, the positioning of the sequences of bases at different locations is decisive. These locations of base-pair sequences that determine physical or behavioral characteristics are called *genes,* and the sequences of bases determining the form of the gene are called *alleles.* Figure 3.1 illustrates the relationships between the various genetic structures. It shows how DNA is comprised of bases, how the DNA comprises a chromosome, and how all the chromosomes in a cell comprise the genome.

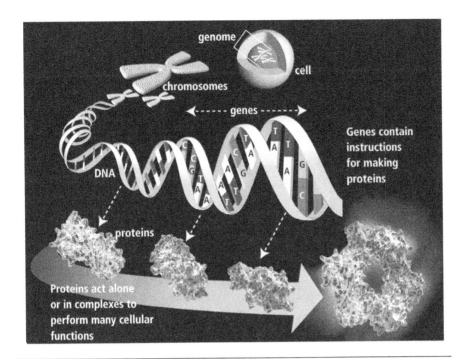

Figure 3.1 From Genes to Proteins

SOURCE: Human Genome Program, US Department of Energy, 2001.

Chromosomes

Each species has a unique number of **chromosomes**. A chromosome is a threadlike strand of DNA that contains the genes. Humans have 23 pairs of chromosomes or a total of 46 chromosomes in the nucleus of each cell. The number of functional locations (or genes) varies from chromosome to chromosome. The number of genes on a chromosome ranges from as few as 295 on the tiny Y chromosome to as many as 3,951 on Chromosome Number[1]. It is estimated that the X chromosome has 1,850 genes or more than 6 times the number that are on the Y. Until very recently, it was estimated that the number of genes in the human genome was as high as 80,000 to 120,000 (Human Genome Program, 2001). One of the astonishing findings of the human genome project was that the number of genes in the human genome was much less than this earlier estimate. Only approximately 30,000 to 40,000 genes compose the genetic code that makes each individual unique and, at the same time, provides them with the common genetic code that helps make them a member of the human species. Moreover, all humans share 99.9% of their genes, so only an extremely

Homo sapiens genome view

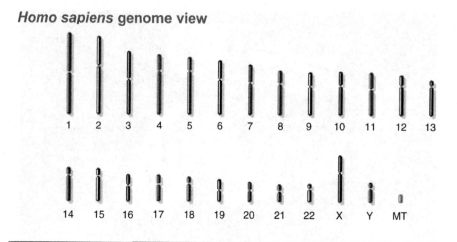

Figure 3.2   Relative Size of the Human Chromosomes

SOURCE: National Center for Biotechnology Information
(http://www.ncbi.nlm.nih.gov/mapview/map_search.cgi?chr=hum_chr.inf&query)

small number of genes are responsible for the differences among individuals. Figure 3.2 shows the relative size of the chromosomes that make up the human genome.

What Are Genes?

Genes are therefore locations on strands of DNA that are called chromosomes. To continue our metaphor, genes are the words made up of letters that stand for the bases. Chromosomes are the sentences, and these make up the book of life that is your genome.[1] The same "book" resides in the nucleus of every cell in your body. Unlike most books, in this one, the sentences that are the chromosomes, the meaningful words, are relatively few and buried among large sequences of nonsense words. These nonsense words are sequences of bases on the chromosomes that provide no genetic information. Each human chromosome has from 50 million to 250 million pairs of the bases A, C, G, and T.

Figure 3.3 shows that a segment of a chromosome representing a gene is made up of chemical bases. Each cell in your body contains your entire genetic code.

The number of possible sequences of bases making up a gene is enormous and varied. There are 3,164.7 million bases making up the human genome. The average gene is made up of about 3,000 base pairs, but the largest known gene

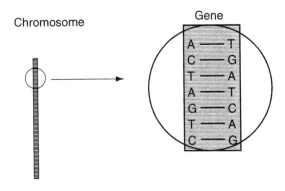

Figure 3.3   Locations on a Chromosome = A Gene

is composed of a sequence of 2.4 million bases (Human Genome Program, 2001). Therefore the variability of characteristics among organisms, even within the human species, is virtually infinite. Sagan (1980) pointed out that there are combinations for putting together humans that have not yet evolved.

GENETIC FUNCTIONS ●

Your unique genetic makeup is established at conception in the single cell, the zygote, which is the fertilized ovum. Therefore, the zygote contains half of the pairs of chromosomes from the father's sperm and half from the mother's ovum. At that point, cellular development proceeds by the process called mitosis. In **mitosis,** a cell divides into two new cells (ironically, multiplication by division!), and the chromosomes are duplicated so that each new cell has exactly the same genetic code as the original cell and all others.

Mitosis

How does every body cell of an individual come to contain exactly the same genetic code? Figure 3.4 shows two identical chromosomes, shown at the gene level. Because of the enormous complexity underlying your genetic code, how can the critical sequence of bases in all the hundreds of thousands of genes be duplicated exactly? The answer to this lies in the double helix of the DNA's

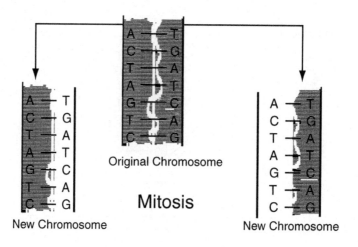

Original Chromosome

Mitosis

New Chromosome

New Chromosome

Figure 3.4   Replicating Chromosomes Through Mitosis

structure. In the early stage of cell synthesis, the DNA double helix unzips. This leaves two half-strands of DNA, each with one of the bases in its exact position in the sequence. Thus, we now have two half-complete DNA replicas of the original molecule. Now remember, each base can be paired only with another single base, its complement (i.e., adenine can pair only with thiamine and cytosine only with guanine.) In the latter part of constructing new molecules, an enzyme binds the complementary base onto its existing partner up and down the molecule. The result is that the original double helix yields two new double helixes that are the mirror image of each other. For every new cell that your body produces, the enormous complexity of the genetic code is duplicated exactly.

Biparental Reproduction

Where do the particular combinations that make up our genes come from? They come from our parents, of course. One of the great evolutionary breakthroughs was the natural selection of biparental reproduction. With two parents, an organism receives half its genetic makeup from its mother and half from its father. Thus, the offspring is genetically different from either parent, ensuring variability within the species.

If each cell contained all 46 chromosomes from each parent, the resulting zygote of the offspring would contain 92, and the next generation 184 and so on. Much too many to fit into our tiny cell nuclei. Fortunately, specialized sex cells or **gametes** are involved in biparental reproduction. Gametes, the female's ovum (or egg) and male's sperm, are produced by the process called **meiosis**.

Meiosis

Meiosis involves several stages, but the essential part of the process is an alignment of the individual chromosomes into pairs. The individual chromosomes touch, and then separate again. Next, one from each chromosome pair moves into one of two resulting daughter cells. Consequently, meiosis produces two "daughter cells," each of which has 23 single chromosomes, or one-half the parent's genetic makeup. Therefore, at conception, the union of the 23 single chromosomes in the ovum and 23 single chromosomes in the sperm yield the full complement of 46 (23 pairs) chromosomes of the new zygote. These 46 will be the basis for all the individual's genetic code as development now proceeds to duplicate these through mitosis.

GENETIC VARIABILITY ●

Mendelian genetics had the problem that by itself it provided no mechanism for variation. Dominant and recessive genes in one generation determined their manifestation in the next. But without variation, natural selection has nothing to work on.

Biparental variability, mediated by meiosis, ensures that each offspring will be different from either parent. Although some similar characteristics will be inherited, the result is variability in the species. Why is variability important?

It is important for the survival of the species. Natural selection dictates the survival of the fittest. Those who are better adapted to the environmental conditions will survive and carry on reproduction. Because environments are continually changing (e.g., global warming/global cooling), species that are unable to adapt may become extinct. The dinosaur extinction is a case where extreme environmental changes outpaced the species' ability to adapt.

Three main factors ensure genetic variability in species. The first two, **random assortment** and **crossing over**, occur during meiosis in the production of the gametes. The third, **mutations** are random (i.e., erroneous) changes in the DNA sequence that occur during mitosis or meiosis.

Random Assortment

Recall that during meiosis the chromosomes sort themselves into 23 pairs. When the two daughter cells are formed, one of each pair is "shuffled" into one or the other cells. However, which one of the pairs winds up in which daughter cells is entirely by chance. This "random assortment" (also called independent assortment) occurs for each of the 23 pairs. Hence the probability of a particular combination (such as 1a, 2b, 3a, . . . 23b) is 2^{23}. This calculates as $2 \times 2 \times 2 \times . . . 2$ (a total of 23 times). When combined with the same random assortment from the other parent, this equals 64,000,000,000, or 64 trillion possible combinations from the same mother and father. Thus, the likelihood of your receiving a particular genetic combination from one parent is one in 64 trillion! That is more than all the people who have ever lived!! So it is highly probable that you will inherit a unique genetic mixture from each parent. Furthermore, one cannot calculate which of the two combinations will ultimately be the one that contributes to the zygote. Every time a sperm is produced, a new assortment of chromosomes occurs.

Crossing Over

If the odds for genetic variability were not already enormous, then crossing over makes them even more astronomical. Crossing over involves the actual exchange of parts of genetic material, as segments of one chromosome in a pair changes places with segments of its complement. The chromosomes pair up and touch along their lengths during meiosis. At this point, parts of the chromosomes (containing many genes) may trade places. When they unzip, we have two chromosomes that are unlike the originals, being composed of parts from both complements. Thus, new combinations of genes appear on these chromosomes produced by crossing over. This process is random and unpredictable. When it occurs, it increases the variability in offspring because it produces chromosomes that have different values of genes. The locations on the chromosomes are the same as the originals, but the sequences are different. Figure 3.5 illustrates the process of crossing over.

What Can Go Wrong? Mutations

Does the process ever result in a mistake? Occasionally, the wrong base is attached and the enzyme that "proofreads" the combinations does not correct this. The resulting proofreading error produces what is called a mutation.

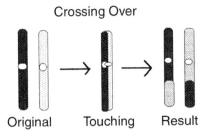

Figure 3.5   Crossing Over: Chromosome Segments Switch

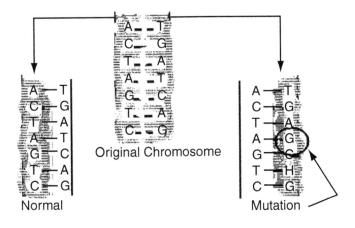

Figure 3.6   A Mutation Produces a Different Sequence on the Right

Mutations, which are proofreading errors that result in a new sequence of DNA bases, are the third process producing variability. If an error is made during chromosome replication, a new sequence of bases is the result. Figure 3.6 shows a mutation. Normally adenine (A) only combines with thiamine (T). Through a proofreading error, guanine (G) has been inserted instead. When this is duplicated, the new chromosome has a segment that reads TGAGCAG instead of the original TGATCAG. If duplicates of this mutated chromosome become a zygote, this new genetic code is transmitted.

Many mutations are genetically "nonsensical" and cause significant imperfections or malfunctions in development. Most are lethal. A few of these new combinations produce characteristics that enable the organism to better adapt to its environment. These are "naturally selected" and are passed on to offspring. This is how new genes evolve.

Genotype

Genotype is the genetic endowment that an organism inherits. One's genotype is expressed as a **phenotype** (the observable and measurable characteristics). The actual genetic makeup contributes to many phenotypic characteristics, at least indirectly. Previously, genotyping was performed by a chemical staining method called **karyotyping**. This method produces the banding shown in photographic enlargements of chromosomes. Of course, **monozygotic twins** share 100% of their genetic code (not withstanding any mutations) because they separated after the zygote was formed by fertilization of an ovum by a sperm. On the other hand, **dizygotic twins** are the same as any other sibling pair from the same parents in that they each receive half of their genetic makeup from the mother and half from the father. Of course, the half from each is extremely variable due to the effects of crossing over and random assortment in forming the gametes that we studied earlier.

Alleles: Dominant and Recessive

Biparental inheritance would be irrelevant if the values of each gene at equivalent locations on each pair had the same strength. That is not so, and these differences are the real power behind biparental inheritance. Each alternative form or value (that is the sequence of DNA bases) of a gene is called an **allele**. (Actually, an allele can mean either the different forms of genes or merely refer to the gene on one chromosome, even if the other is the same form). In a simple example, the alleles for eye color include blue and brown. Because we inherit 23 chromosomes from each parent and because each gene is a location on these chromosomes, at each pair's location there are two alleles, one from either parent. Both the alleles for each gene can be the same value (homozygous) or they can be different (heterozygous). The terms **homozygous** and **heterozygous** refer to the values (or sequences) of alleles at the level of actual genetic makeup, or genotype. An individual with two alleles for blue eyes would have a genotype that is "homozygous, blbl." A person with one allele for blue and one for brown would by "heterozygous, blbr." These genotypes represent their actual genetic makeup. But what of their actual eye color? Before we get to that, however, we need to understand the way genes and environment interact. When we deal with the actual expression of a genetic trait we mean the phenotype. The **genotype-environment interaction** determines the phenotype. Some phenotypes, such as eye color, are so strongly influenced by the genotype that environment has little influence.

Phenotypes that are deeply entrenched along a path of development from which it is difficult to deviate are said to be **canalized**. Other phenotypes, especially many psychological characteristics such as intelligence, are more obviously the result of the genotype interacting with a far more influential environment.

Major Recessive Hereditary Diseases

Most genetic problems are recessive traits that a close relative (grandparent, uncle) may have had. These hereditary diseases will not appear unless both parents carry the troublesome allele and the child inherits this particular gene from both parents. Among some examples of *recessive* hereditary diseases are *cystic fibrosis* (when a child lacks enzyme that prevents mucus from obstructing the lungs and digestive track), *diabetes* (lack of the insulin hormone to metabolize sugar properly), and *hemophilia* (the child lacks a substance that causes the blood to clot).

Is Development Canalized Only by Genes?

Until recently, developmental psychologists defined canalization as the restriction of development to a single pathway by the action of genes. This genotype-only view of canalization was the result of the influence of Waddington (1957), a geneticist. Thus, the view common among developmentalists was that if a developed characteristic was difficult to influence by changing the environment, the canalization meant that the characteristic was genetically determined.

Recently, Gottlieb (1991b) has suggested that the environment can also cause development to be restricted. That is, canalization can also be due to the long-term effects of the environment. This **experiential canalization** suggests that behavior can be organized by the action of environment-gene transaction, not just genes. For example, an individual's scores on an intelligence test may be difficult to change much. One may assume that this is because IQ is strongly determined by genes. That is, that it is genetically canalized. However, an IQ score is a sample of complex human behavior. Many of these behaviors may be difficult to influence because of the long-term person-environment interactions that have occurred over a lifetime. Gottlieb's point is that behaviors do become canalized, but canalization may be the result of environmental as well as genetic factors. This latter view is consistent with a behavioral systems approach.

Let us return to eye color to see how the genotype determines the phenotype. With homozygous genotypes (e.g., blbl or BRBR) the relationship is simple. With a normal species-typical environment, the homozygous genotype will be expressed in the phenotype (blue eyes or brown eyes, respectively). Yet in heterozygous genotypes, the relationship between genotype and phenotype is a bit more complex. Some alleles are relatively stronger than others and are more likely to be expressed if present in the genotype. These alleles are called **dominant**. Those masked by the presence of a dominant allele are called **recessive**. The rule is that dominant alleles (represented by capital letters) are expressed in the phenotype whether they are homozygous (e.g., BRBR) or heterozygous (e.g., BRbl). Recessive alleles are expressed in the phenotype only when they are homozygous (e.g., blbl). Because you receive one eye color allele from each parent, it is possible for a blue-eyed child to have two brown-eyed parents (each heterozygous BRbl). This is how a characteristic can "skip a generation." Figure 3.7 shows the possible outcomes associated with the matings of various genotypes producing offspring with particular phenotypes. Note, however, that in cases where both parents are homozygous for a characteristic, as is necessarily the case with blue-eyed parents (each homozygous blbl), the only possible phenotype their children can have is blue eyes (blbl). Of course, parents who are both homozygous for brown eyes (BRBR) can produce only homozygous brown-eyed offspring (BRBR).

Sex-Linked Characteristics

Certain characteristics, including red/green color blindness, hemophilia, and the dreaded MPB (male pattern baldness) occur more frequently in males than in females. We call these **sex-linked characteristics**. They occur because of the unique characteristics of the **sex chromosomes**, the X and Y chromosomes. In the other 22 pair of chromosomes, both chromosomes are identical in length, so they carry the same gene locations on each strand. On these **autosomes**, only the value (i.e., dominant or recessive) of the genes (or alleles) differs. For a person to express a recessive characteristic in the phenotype, two recessive alleles must be present. The sex chromosomes present a different case. The X chromosome is longer and carries more genes than the Y chromosome. (The reason it is called the X chromosome is that with two of these long strands joined at the center, they look like the letter X. The short Y joined with the longer X strand makes it look like the letter Y.)

Gender is determined by which of the sex chromosomes the child has. A zygote with two Xs (XX) will be genetically female, whereas one with an X and a Y (XY) will be male. Because the ovum develops from the mother, who is XX, it always contributes an X to the child. It is the sperm from the XY father that determines the gender of the child. If it is the result of a sperm that contains the Y chromosome, the zygote will be a male. With an X, the zygote will be a female.

	Mother (Brown Eyes)	
	BR	bl
Father (Brown Eyes) BR	BRBR (Brown)	BRbl (Brown)
bl	blBR (Brown)	blbl (Blue)

Figure 3.7 How a Trait Skips a Generation: Both Mother and Father Have Brown Eyes, Baby Has Blue!

Because the Y chromosome of the male is lacking the sites for some genes, it means that males are more vulnerable to the influence of recessive genes. Instead of needing two recessive genes for the characteristic to appear in the phenotype, a single recessive gene on the extra arm of the X chromosome will manifest itself. This is because there will be no dominant gene to mask its effects. Because there is no gene on the Y chromosome, a male must inherit the recessive gene from his mother, a carrier who may not show the characteristic herself. Besides the simple dominant–recessive relationship, there are other possibilities in single gene inheritance patterns.

Codominance

Codominance occurs when two heterozygous but equally powerful alleles produce a phenotype in which both genes are fully and equally expressed. A gene does not always follow the simple dominant–recessive pattern. Instead the phenotype produced is a compromise between two genes, and codominance takes place. Here characteristics of both are expressed in the phenotype. Blood type is an example of codominance (Shaffer, 1989). The alleles for Type A and Type B blood each act as dominant if heterozygous with Type O. In that case, the person will have either Type A or Type B blood, respectively. Yet a child who inherits Type A from one parent and Type B from the other (AB phenotype) will have type AB blood. So codominance means that both characteristics appear in the phenotype.

Incomplete Dominance

Another interesting characteristic is **incomplete dominance** (Shaffer, 1989). If a person has one allele that shows incomplete dominance, only some of its characteristics will be evident. This occurs in sickle cell disease where if the person is heterozygous for sickle cell, mild symptoms appear. If the person has two sickle cell alleles, the disorder is much more severe.

Single-Gene and Polygenic Inheritance

We have been looking at simple **single-gene inheritance** patterns of the kind that Mendel used to derive his very basic laws of genetic inheritance in the 1860s. Yet it is likely that many characteristics, particularly behavioral ones, involve the influence of many genes. Such **polygenic inheritance patterns** are apparently very common. Yet one must be cautious not to invoke the idea of polygenic inheritance only because a single gene cannot explain the development of a complex characteristic. It may be that the genotype-environment interaction is a better explanation for such complexity of development.

● SOURCES OF DEVELOPMENT: THE COMBINED ROLES OF HEREDITY AND ENVIRONMENT

We have already looked at the mechanisms in biparental inheritance that virtually guarantee that each individual will be genetically unique (save for the case of identical twins who start as a single zygote that splits after fertilization and who therefore share the same genotype). Crossing over, random assortment, and chance fertilization of a single ovum from millions of potential sperm are responsible for this uniqueness. The zygote contains all the person's genetic potential, but how is that potential realized over a life span?

Genes signal the production of cells at particular times and sites. Thus, they produce the physical being. Their effects on behavior may be significant but indirect (Liebert & Wicks-Nelson, 1981). Plomin (1989) suggests that the effect of genes on behavior is **multifactorial**—that is, not fitting the single-gene model. Among the factors are the influence of many genes and the environment. He concludes that genetic influence on a specific behavior involves many genes, each of which has a small effect by itself. Thus, human behavior is polygenic. These genes may contribute to behavior by determining the physical structures (e.g., the central nervous system, muscles, etc.) that interact with the environment to produce behavior.

Heritability

Heritability is a statistical concept. It is the amount of the variability, across individuals, of a characteristic—for example, IQ or temperament (Thomas, Chess, & Birch)—that can be attributed to genes. Generally, heritability statistics are computed from twin studies. In these studies, **concordance rates** are calculated to establish the correlation between two persons on a measure such as IQ or personality. If two people score similarly on a measurement, such as IQ, their concordance rate is high. If their scores are dissimilar, then the concordance rate is low. Generally, comparisons are made in the concordance rate differences among groups based on the strength of their genetic similarity. This ranges from the same genetic makeup of identical twins through the random makeup of unrelated individuals.

According to Plomin (1986), individual differences in IQ are estimated to be 50% heritable (i.e., 50% of the variance in scores is due to genetic makeup). Yet if a characteristic is heritable, that does not mean genes alone are responsible. Instead, behavior geneticists have identified several important sources of influence.

Sources of Influence: Twin Studies

Formerly, twin studies were viewed as comparing the effects of the same genes (identical twins) with different genes (fraternal twins, siblings, unrelated persons). They also viewed the environment as the same (reared in the same home) or different (twins separated shortly after birth and reared in separate homes). Thus, they were seen as a clear test of heredity versus environment in that they were comparing the effects of same or different genes with rearing in the same or different environment.

We now see this as conceptually naive. Whereas the genetic differences were valid, the environmental ones were not as simple as first thought. Identical twins have the same genotype, but people living in the same house do not have the same environment. Correlations for siblings (not just twins) living in the same home for characteristics such as cognitive abilities ($r = .40$), personality $(r = .20)$, and psychopathology $(r = .10)$ are low (Plomin, 1988). This means that the home environment does not function to make siblings very much alike.

What then are the sources of influence on development of the phenotype in estimating heritability? Plomin (1989) has identified the following three: genotype, shared environmental influences, and nonshared environmental influences. In addition, because our estimates of human characteristics such as intelligence and personality are not perfect, we need to add another influence to our estimates—measurement error. Thus, behavior genetic estimates of what determines human development is composed of (a) estimates of genotype, (b) shared environmental factors, (c) nonshared environmental factors, and (d) measurement errors.

Shared Environmental Factors

It is argued that all individuals living in the same household partly share the same environmental influences. This is the basic assumption behind adoption studies that attempt to estimate the amount of genetic influence on a characteristic. For example, if identical twins are raised together, it is assumed that, in addition to having the same genotype, they share the same environment. By comparing their scores on a characteristic (such as IQ) with scores from identical twins reared apart, in two separate households, it is believed that the amount of **shared environmental influence** can be separated from the amount of genetic influence.

Nonshared Environmental Factors

Even if two people live in the same household they have different environments. Because no two things can occupy the same space, no two organisms can have the same environment. Although their physical environments may appear similar, their functional environments may be very different. The unique effects the environment has on the individual are called **nonshared environmental effects**. Dunn and Plomin (1990) have argued that nonshared environmental factors appear to have the major influence on an individual's behavioral development.

Rowe and Plomin (1981) provide a way to calculate the approximate strength of nonshared environmental effects. They argue that by taking the correlation for identical twins living together (i.e., same genetics and shared environmental influences) and subtracting it from 1.00 (the correlation if all effects were included), the result is what is due to nonshared environmental influences. A hypothetical illustration follows: Suppose the correlation for the IQ scores of identical twins is .70. The nonshared environmental influence would be .30 (1.00–.70).

To recap, we have three identified sources of influence: genotype, shared environmental factors, and nonshared environmental factors. There is a fourth factor that influences our estimates of heritability—measurement error.

Measurement Error

We measure human characteristics in calculating concordance rates and correlations. To measure intelligence, we use IQ tests. To measure personality, we use various personality tests. Sometimes we measure behavior directly (e.g., the mean length of utterance is a common direct measure of language development). Many of our measures are standardized samples of behavior called tests. In every case, we make a certain amount of error in our measurements, just as there is often error in measuring the dimensions of a window or the amount of flour that goes into a recipe. The more reliable our measurement, the less error it contains.

We also commit errors in our measurement of human characteristics. Although tests are constructed to be reliable and limit the measurement error, no test is close to achieving 100% reliability or validity. In addition, reliability on many tests may be acceptable for the overall measurement of groups of individuals but may be quite poor in measuring single individuals. Even our ability to measure genotype in identical twins may contain some error. Although improved measurement techniques such as karyotyping has reduced much of this type of error, which happened in earlier studies, researchers still make mistakes. In the early days of twin studies, the techniques were so poor that twins thought to be identical turned out to be fraternal (see, e.g., McGraw, 1935).

In sum, four factors determine the correlations between nature and nurture: genotype, shared environmental factors, nonshared environmental factors, and measurement error. These are factors relating to the "how much?" question. Let us turn to the question of "how?"

DOES BEHAVIORAL DEVELOPMENT ● RESULT FROM INTERACTIONS?

Both heredity and environment affect behavioral development. This influence of one factor on another is called the **interactional view.** Furthermore, the role of heredity and environment appears to be more complex than a simple interaction. Not only does the environment affect development, but the changes in development then affect the environment. The mutual or reciprocal modification of effects of one on the other that result from simple interactions is *also* called a transaction. Transactions are characteristic of dynamical systems, including developmental systems.

WHAT FACTORS TRANSACT ● IN HUMAN DEVELOPMENT?

To recap from Chapter 2, Ross (1980) identified four sources of influence that transact to produce development: (a) genetics-constitutional makeup,

(b) previous interactional history, (c) current physiological conditions, and (d) current environmental conditions. We also add (e) behavioral dynamics.

Genetic–Constitutional Makeup

Genetic makeup is your genetic inheritance and the resulting physical characteristics of the individual. As we discussed earlier, for practical purposes, genetic makeup is fixed at the moment of conception when you receive half your genetic code from your mother and half from your father. At conception, this single cell (called the zygote) begins to multiply. As each new cell emerges, it contains the same genetic code as the original. That same exact genetic makeup is duplicated in the nucleus of every cell in your body. This source of influence is the subject of this chapter.

Box 3.1   Behavior Genetics: Much Ado About (Almost) Nothing

The field of behavior genetics has received a great deal of coverage in the media because it has reported finding apparent genetic causes of many human characteristics, such as personality, language usage, and intelligence. Unlike most developmental psychologists, behavior geneticists embrace the nature–nurture dichotomy and attempt to determine the relative importance of each. The behavior genetics approach is in strong contrast with the behavioral systems one, taken in this textbook, which is interested in the process by which nature and nurture interact. A reasoned critique of the behavior genetics position was recently provided by the eminent developmental psychologist Hayne W. Reese (2002).

Reese points out some common misconceptions about behavior genetics. Behavior genetics is not at all related to behaviorism. In fact, it is not interested in directly observed behavior but, rather, in individual differences on IQ tests, personality tests, or other indirect measures of behavior. Finally, behavior genetics is concerned with whether nature or nurture is responsible for individual differences in traits, not in how traits or behavior develop.

Reese outlines many of the problems with behavior genetics research. Most of these shortcomings can be seen in the numerous questionable assumptions behavior genetics makes about genotypes and environments. He begins by presenting the basic equation that underlies the goals of behavior genetics research: $P = G + E$, where P stands for the phenotype, G for the genotype, and E for the environment. So far, so

---

good. But behavior genetics assumes that both the genotype and environment are quantifiable; both very questionable assumptions. For example, genotypes are usually quantified by making (faulty) assumptions about the genetic similarities of monozygotic twins, dizygotic twins, other siblings, and unrelated people. Similar faulty assumptions are made in estimating the functional shared and nonshared environments.

All told, Reese finds that 23 assumptions are used in behavior genetics research. He points out that each of the assumptions on which the findings of behavior genetics research are based, like the assumption that the home environment has exactly the same effect for everyone living there, are of dubious merit. These assumptions apply to the research designs they use (i.e., family research, twin research, and adoption research) and to the measurements they take, both of genotypes and phenotypes. For example, regarding family research done to determine if a trait runs in certain families, Reese points out that when such a pattern is found, behavior genetics assumes that it is due to genetics. It is also true that environments run in families, but behavior genetics ignores this. Thus, it is impossible to separate the effects of each unless the traits are single-gene ones—a situation that does not apply to the multifactorial nature of human nature.

In sum, Reese concludes that despite an enormous amount of research and wide public appeal, behavior genetics research is of very little merit and has had minimal influence on mainstream behavioral science. In short, there is much ado about (almost) nothing.

Previous Interactional History[2]

Development is a continuous process of *change*. Once a change has occurred (due to learning or maturation), the organism is different. The individual is the product of his or her previous transactions. Horowitz (1987) points out that once learning occurs, its influence shifts from the environmental to the **organismic** dimension. That is, when learning is occurring, it is determined by the environment. Once learning has occurred, the history of interactions are part of the organism's history and will render the person more or less vulnerable to ongoing environmental influences.

Who we are now is determined by what is happening now and what happened before. The longer we are on a particular path of development, the more difficult it is to divert us from that path. This is due to the cumulative effects of our interactional histories.

Current Physiological Conditions

We are also affected by the current physiological conditions. So lack of key elements (e.g., nutrients, stimulation), diseases, and other conditions will prevent growth of the developing organism. On the other hand, good nutrition and freedom from disease or injury will promote desirable development.

Current Environmental Conditions

Current environmental conditions affect development. For instance, right from the moment of conception, interaction is present. The plight of the zygote is dependent on what Horowitz (1987) calls the **functional environmental surround**. This is the part of the environment that comes into contact and actually affects the child. There will be many things present in the environment, but, because they do not have an affect on development, they are not considered part of the functional environmental surround. The functional environmental surround for the zygote is initially one of the fallopian tubes where fertilization occurs. From the start, the quality of the environment interacts with the genetic makeup of the child. For example, a blocked fallopian tube would stop development entirely, whereas a healthy prenatal environment contributes positively to development.

In addition, many similar functional aspects of the current environment affect our behavior outside the womb. They are the changes in light, sound, touch, and social conditions influencing behavior. Most important, they are the events inside and outside the skin that produce learning. Inside the skin, thoughts are stimuli for other thoughts or external actions. Outside the skin, events signal and strengthen our actions.

Behavior Dynamics

Ongoing changes in behavior produce ongoing changes in the environment and the organism. Consequently, these constant dynamical interactions affect ensuing behavioral outcomes. Often, these dynamics keep development progressing along consistent, gradual paths, producing what we call developmental trajectories, discussed in Chapter 2. These trajectories are characterized by small, regular changes along consistent pathways of development, as in the slow, regular increase in vocabulary development when a child first learns to speak. Sometimes these dynamics produce the conditions for many factors to come together under current environmental conditions; coalsecent organization occurs, and the trajectory shows a sudden phase shift, as in the case of a vocabulary growth spurt, or a new behavior emerges (e.g., reading), as in a shift from listening to words to speaking them to reading them.

HOW DO GENES AND ● ENVIRONMENT INTERACT?

Because genotype is fixed at conception, it makes sense to view the genotype as setting the limits on development. That is, the development cannot exceed the range (up or down) set by the genotype. Within this range of potential or range of reaction (Gottesman, 1963) shared, and especially nonshared, environmental influences determine the ultimate influence of the genotype on the phenotype.

However, this restricted range of reaction view has been challenged. Gottlieb (1991a) has pointed out that there are no preexisting, fixed limits within which the environment reacts. He suggests instead that we view the role of genotype as establishing a norm of reaction as suggested by Platt and Sanislow (1988). That is, certain genotypes make potential limits more probable than others but do not determine limits of development by themselves. Rather, because of the constant dynamical interaction of multiple factors, including genetic, neurological, and environmental ones, prediction of a specific developmental outcome is unlikely to be very accurate.

Different genotypes have different ranges of reaction. Some characteristics, particularly physical ones such as eye color, have small ranges of reaction, so the environment has little influence. These characteristics with strong genetic limits and small ranges are said to be highly canalized. Some universal behaviors show strong genetic canalization and small ranges of reaction. Given a normal species-typical environment, little variability in universal behaviors will be due to environmental effects.

Other behaviors have hypothetically much broader ranges of reaction and are less canalized. The environment has more effect on their ultimate expression in the phenotype. Universal behaviors, such as walking and talking, and especially **nonuniversal behaviors,** such as reading, writing, or playing sports, have increasingly wider ranges of reaction. Shared and nonshared environmental effects are potent.

Note that these concepts apply not only across different characteristics of a given individual but also across individuals for a specific characteristic. For example, two individuals may have different ranges of reaction for their IQ. It is estimated that the average range of reaction for IQ under current environmental conditions is 20 to 25 points (Zigler & Seitz, 1982). Yet this may vary from genotype to genotype—that is, from person to person. The range of reaction for an individual with a genotype for Down syndrome may be more restricted than one without the condition.

The **rubber band hypothesis** is a metaphor to help understand the role of the environment with various genotypes. Genotypes are depicted as different types of rubber bands, some short and thick, some long and thin. Some may be stretched more (have wider ranges of reaction) than others. In this metaphor, it is the environment that stretches the range of rubber band. The ultimate expansion of the rubber band is the interaction between the genotype and the environment. Horowitz's (1987) environmental dimension reveals another facet of this metaphor. The environment may run from nonfacilitative to facilitative. In the metaphor, a facilitative environment would exert more stretch on the rubber band.

Genotype–Environment Interactions

Earlier, we suggested that genes do their work indirectly. How might a genotype indirectly produce behavior in the child? One place to look is at geno-type-environment effects (Scarr & McCartney, 1983). In these effects, genotypes interact with the environment, producing behavior in one of three ways: passively, evocatively, or actively.

Passive Genotype-Environment Effects

Parents may provide an environment that is compatible with the child's genotype. These environmental events facilitate the development of the phenotype. For example, parents may enjoy reading to a child. A child with a genotype for hearing will benefit from this. In other words, in an environment containing parents who read to them, children's genotypes cause them to read, whereas children with a genotype for hearing impairment will not so benefit.

Evocative Genotype-Environment Effects

Some genetically determined characteristics of the child (e.g., small size) may evoke different responses (e.g., protectiveness, gentleness) from the parents or others in the social environment. A large baby might evoke independence or roughhouse play from the parent. In turn, this child will develop more independence, vigorous activity, and exploration due to the parenting styles his or her genotype evoked.

Active Genotype-Environment Effects

People with certain genotypes may actively select certain environments. Scarr and McCartney (1983) call this seeking out of compatible or stimulating environments "niche picking" or "niche building." A person with a high IQ may pick a very different environment than one with a low IQ.

Scarr and McCartney (1983) suggest a developmental sequence for these effects. They suggest that passive genotype-environment effects are most frequent in the early years as the parents provide much of the child's functional environment. These become less important, and the active genotype-environment effects dominate as older children and adults select their own environments. The dramatic changes brought about with the appearance of crawling and walking illustrate a change to active effects. Evocative effects occurring over the life span as the environment reacts with the person's characteristics.

A BEHAVIORAL VIEW: ●
PERSON–ENVIRONMENT INTERACTIONS

Genotypes can influence the course of environmental transactions. Transactions, particularly of the evocative and active type, could explain the correlations for identical twins even when they are reared apart. It suggests that they have genetically based characteristics that evoke or select certain interactions from the environment. Over time, these interactions serve to maintain similarities in environments rather than leading to vastly changing environments over developmental time. But are genes the only basis for producing consistency in behavior over time? Are our personalities caused by genes?

Because environment-behavior interactions cause consistency in behavior over time. In his view, not only are characteristic behaviors reinforced by our environments, but we also emit behaviors that select a consistent environment (Baer, 1976). That is, people are likely to choose environments that are typical for themselves and evoke and maintain behaviors that are typical for them. Reinforcement of characteristic behavior is more likely in these "person-typical" environments.

We emit behaviors that keep the environment consistent and more reinforcing. We have the same friends, go to the same places, and do the same things because these are likely to be reinforced. If we wind up in a drastically different environment, our repertoire of behaviors does not work. We act like "a fish out of water." We may find that we are a "different person" at home and at school.

As we have emphasized, although emphasizing the learning rather than the genetic aspect, Baer's (1976) view shares many parallels to genotype-environment effects. We may instead view these as person-environment dynamic interactions or transactions that involve passive, evocative, and active person–environment effects.

Passive Person–Environment Effects

The person has acquired characteristics that enable him or her to respond to events in the environment. The role of the environment is to evoke and reinforce certain behaviors that the person has acquired. Behaviors that are not functional will not be reinforced and will disappear (extinguish). Other behaviors will strengthened or "shaped" (see Chapter 6) into new ones. Passive genotype-environment effects occur when the rearing environments that biological parents provide are influenced by the parents' own genes and hence are correlated with the child's own genotype (Shaffer, 2002).

Evocative Person–Environment Effects

The behavioral repertoire evokes certain events in the environment. These events bring consistency to the environment based on the characteristics of organism. The way you dress affects what your environment is like. A soldier's uniform affects how others respond to him or her. Likewise a person may speak a different way "on the street" or in a college class because the different speaking styles evoke different reactions from different environments. Evocative genotype-environment correlations occur when our heritable characteristics affect others' behavior toward us and thus influence the social environment in which our behavior develops.

Active Person–Environment Effects

This is the notion that we seek to relate to that which is most compatible with our perceived genetic predispositions. For instance, we call friends, go to familiar places, select certain things to read or watch. In each case, we select a certain environment. These environments strengthen behaviors already in our repertoires. However, in Baer's (1976) view, the consistency in our behavior patterns is due to the consistency in the contingencies in our environments.

How Does the Influence of Genetics Change Over Time?

The heritability of many human traits increases consistently from infancy through childhood, adolescence, and adulthood (McGue, Bouchard, Iacono, & Lykken, 1993). At first blush, this may suggest that genes themselves may continue to canalize behavior. However, the genotype-environment and person-environment effects discussed produce these changes. Although many may attribute these changes to genes, it is the environmental interactions that produce the changes.

A BEHAVIORAL SYSTEMS APPROACH ●

Dynamical Interactions

The interplay between the factors discussed in this chapter is significant in a behavioral systems approach. Each individual will be unique due to the unique ways in which genetic, historical, and environmental factors act on each other. Two children could be raised in apparently similar, depressed environments. A parent may be absent, nutrition may be substandard, social and educational opportunities may be lacking. One child may become a high school dropout, get arrested for a violent crime, and die before the age of 21. The other may become good at sports, go to college, and become a lawyer. One becomes a casualty because of the environment, the other a success, seemingly in spite of the environment. How can the environment produce such opposite effects?

The answer is that the effects of any of these factors are not simple. Development is a continuing series of complex transactions between all five factors (i.e., genetic-constitutional makeup, history of interactions, current physiological conditions, current environmental conditions, behavior dynamics), producing unique coalescent reorganization of behaviors. Prediction may not be made from only one factor. Prediction of developmental outcomes is difficult because of the ever-changing, dynamic transactions between all factors.

Predictions made on the basis of group generalizations are not likely to predict individual development. Because each individual has a unique set of initial organismic and environmental conditions that are critical, group generalizations are likely to yield only crude probabilities about individual development.

Returning to our interactional view, both heredity and environment produce changes. Our behaviors react to, evoke, and actively select our environments. These behaviors are the result of our genes, our history, and our current environment. The coalescence of these factors means that highly consistent physical and behavioral characteristics emerge, in what we view as canalization. Plomin and his associates (Plomin, Reiss, Hetherington, & Howe, 1994) have found that environmental factors, such as the mother's positive and negative behavior directed at the child, are, in part, a result of the child's genetic characteristics. Their findings suggest that characteristics of the child determine to some extent the reactions of the environment toward him or her. So even nonshared environmental effects may be the result of a long interactional history involving organismic and environmental characteristics in a complex, nonlinear fashion.

In recent years, the pendulum that is our dominant worldview has swung toward the nature side of the controversy (Plomin, 1999). We expect to find—and as a result, therefore do find—increased evidence for genetic determinants of behavior. Like the pessimist who finds the glass half empty, we now find development to be half genetic where formerly it was half environmental. We have begun to take an increasingly simple genetic view of development.

Robert Plomin (1989), one of our most respected behavior geneticists, has offered some wise words of caution:

> Genetic effects on behavior are polygenic and probabilistic, not single gene and deterministic. The characteristics in the pea plant that Mendel studied and a few diseases such as Huntington's disease and sickle-cell anemia are due to single genes that have their effects regardless of the environment or the genetic background of the individual. The complexity of behaviors studied by psychologists makes it unlikely that such a deterministic model and the reductionistic approach that it suggests will pay off. There is no firm evidence for a single-gene effect that accounts for a detectable amount of variation for any complex behavior. . . . Behavioral genetic research clearly demonstrates that nature and nurture are important in human development. (p 110)

Ten years later, Plomin (1999) reconfirmed this view and suggested that scientists search to "find not the gene for a trait, but the multiple genes that affect the trait as a probabilistic propensity, not as predetermined programming" (p. 250). Thus, multiple genes affect behavior indirectly, by enabling physical characteristics that interact with the environment to determine behavioral outcomes (McGuffin, Riley, & Plomin, 2001).

SUMMARY ●

The mapping of the *human genome* has provided us with the opportunity to identify genes responsible for many human traits. It also provides us with a unique opportunity to expand our understanding of how genes work in concert with the environment to affect development. *Behavioral genetics* is a field that studies both behavioral and genetic aspects of development. Behavior genetic analysis is a method used to examine to what extent behavior is genetically influenced. Although this course of study has contributed to our understanding of the role of genetics in development, it has become increasingly clear that pursuing the question of "how much" of development is attributable to genetics will ultimately be nonproductive. Instead, a more productive question would concern determining "how" heredity and environment work together to produce developmental outcomes.

The genetic process ensures the variability in characteristics of organisms that is necessary for natural selection to occur. A molecule of *deoxyribonucleic acid* (*DNA*) takes the form of a double helix containing sequences of chemical bases (adenine, cytosine, guanine, and thiamine). Metaphorically, combinations of these bases in groups of three can be thought of as of syllables (codons) that constitute *genes,* which may be thought of as words. Furthermore, *chromosomes* can be thought of as sentences that make up the book that is the genome. The process of *mitosis* ensures that identical genetic information is present in every cell of the body. The processes involved in *biparental reproduction* ensure genetic variability. *Meiosis* is an aspect of this phenomena that involves the processes of *random assortment, crossing over,* and, sometimes, *mutation.*

One's genetic endowment constitutes a *genotype* that is expressed in a *phenotype* (set of observable characteristics). The genotype-environment interaction determines phenotype. Some phenotypes, however, are influenced differentially by genotype. *Canalization* is the restriction of development to a single pathway and has been thought to work by means of both genetic and environmental influences. *Heritability* is the amount of variability across individuals of a characteristic that can be attributed to genes. Heritability has commonly been determined by twin studies. It is important to note that *shared environmental factors, nonshared environmental factors,* genotype, and measurement error influence our estimates of heritability.

The emerging paradigm in the study of development is an interactional view. Transactions (the reciprocal modification of genetics and environment on one another) are characteristic of dynamical systems, including development. The factors of (a) genetic constitutional makeup, (b) previous interactional history, (c) current physiological conditions, (d) current environmental conditions, and (e) behavioral dynamics are thought to transact to produce development. From this viewpoint, a process of development has been posited in which specific genotypes make potential developmental limits more probable than others and have different ranges of reaction to the environment. Also, genotypes may interact with the environment passively, evocatively, or actively to produce behavior.

Development is a continuing series of complex transactions between factors producing a unique coalescent reorganization of behaviors. Accurate predictions about development are unlikely because of constant flux in the dynamic process.

● NOTES

1. Ridley (1999) also uses the book metaphor to describe the human genome. His more detailed account is as follows:

There are twenty-three chapters, called *chromosomes*. Each chapter contains several thousand stories, called *genes*. Each story is made up of paragraphs, called *exons*, which are interrupted by advertisements called *introns*. Each paragraph is made up of words, called *codons*. Each word is written in letters, called *bases*. (p. 6)

2. At this point, we prefer to use the term "transactional history" because we are talking about reciprocal interaction.

CHAPTER 4

PRENATAL, BIRTH, AND POSTNATAL PERIODS

The moment of conception fixes your genetic makeup and sets into motion the complex interactions between the person and environment that typically will continue for approximately 80 years. From that moment, it will take about 260 days for the one-celled zygote to become a 200-billion-cell fetus about to be born. It will have increased in size 200 billion times. It will emerge from its highly specialized environment capable of surviving in the world of human beings. Let us look at this process.

The menstrual cycle lasts an average of 28 days. Approximately halfway through the cycle, an ovum, one of many eggs, is released by one of two ovaries. If the ovum is not fertilized, it will eventually break down and be sloughed off along with other mucus membrane material and blood.

However, if a sperm penetrates the cell wall of an ovum moving in the fallopian tube, fertilization takes place. Which ovum will be fertilized by one of the hundreds of thousands of sperm is determined at random. Once one sperm fertilizes the ovum, the cell's membrane protects it from any further penetration. With 23 chromosomes from the mother and 23 from the father, the child's genotype is now fixed and completed. Only mutations can now change this code.

PERIODS OF PRENATAL DEVELOPMENT ●

Prenatal development encompasses the time from conception until the beginning of the birth process. Indeed, it is a developmental period with its own set of unique milestones and wondrous processes. Psychologists divide the **prenatal period** (conception to birth) into three periods based on the structures and functions developing in each.[1] These are the periods of the **ovum**, **embryo**, and **fetus**. Each period has its own length that depends on the distinct structures and functions occurring during each. Unique features mark the end of one period and serve as the beginning of the next.

The Ovum-Germinal Period

The establishment of the fertilized ovum, now called the **zygote,** marks the beginning of the period of the ovum or **germinal period**. It lasts approximately from Day 2 to Day 14. The name "germinal" period comes from the word *germ,* meaning "the rudiment of a living organism" (Stein, 1973).

Indeed, the rudiments of what is to become the child begin here. As the zygote moves through the fallopian tube, it begins the process of mitosis. The first cell divides, producing 2 identical cells. These 2 divide to yield a total of 4. The 4 divide into 8 and so forth until, gradually, a mass of cells begins to develop. When it reaches 32 cells in size, it is called a **morula**.

At this early stage, the cells are undifferentiated. That is, there are no differences among the cells. Not only do they have the same genetic makeup, but they also look alike and function alike. At this point, a cell could be moved from any one spot to any other without affecting development. This will not be so later when cells are earmarked for certain parts of the body.

A malfunction during mitosis at this early stage of development may cause a parting of the cells into two separate spheres. If these two spheres continue to multiply on their own, twins will occur. Twins of this nature originate from the same zygote and therefore have the same genetic makeup and are called identical, monozygotic, or **paternal twins**. In contrast, dizygotic twins are formed when at conception two unique ova are fertilized by two separate sperm. Therefore, these twins are no more similar in genetic makeup than any two siblings from the same parents.

As the number of cells continues to increase, it becomes a hollow ball of cells called the **blastula** or **blastocyst**. The journey through the fallopian tubes takes about 3 to 4 days. Near the end of this time, cell **differentiation** begins to occurs. Within the blastula, a group of cells develops at one end into a grouping, called the inner cell mass, or **embryoblast**. The embryoblast will develop into

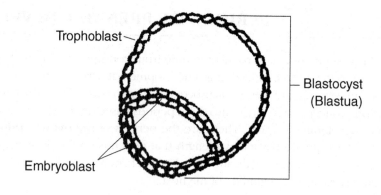

Trophoblast

Embryoblast

Blastocyst
(Blastua)

Figure 4.1   The Blastula

the organism proper. This growing inner mass of cells will develop into all of the
body parts such as the heart, skin, bones, and muscles. Another group of cells
forms a distinct layer making up the exterior of the blastocyst. This outer, protective layer of the blastula, called the outer cell mass or **trophoblast**, ultimately will develop into the membranes surrounding the developing child. The
amnion, chorion, placenta, umbilical cord, and allantois all will develop from the
trophoblast. Figure 4.1 shows the components of the blastocyst or blastula.

At around 7 days, the blastocyst consists of 100 to 150 cells. It floats free
inside the uterus for a few days before making contact with the uterine wall. The
lining of the uterus is, as part of the menstrual cycle, engorged with blood.
Normally, this lining sloughs off, carrying an unfertilized ovum with it during
menses. But if the blastocyst begins to send tendrils into the lining of the sensi-
tized uterus, hormones inhibit the menstrual flow. This embedding of the blastocyst (more specifically, the trophoblast) is called **implantation**. This event,
around the 14th day after conception, marks the end of the germinal period and
the beginning of the embryonic period.

The Embryonic Period

Once implantation occurs, more dramatic changes take place. This formerly
free-floating blastula is now connected to the mother's body. At first, hairlike
blood vessels from the trophoblast burrow their way into the mother's uterus,
establishing a connection with the mother's blood system. During the **embryonic period** these will become the **placental barrier**, a semipermeable membrane. The placental barrier functions as the interface between the blood supply
of the mother and that of the child. The barrier allows the child to receive

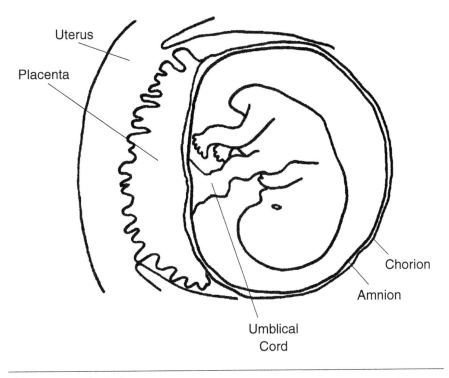

Figure 4.2   An Embryo

nutrients and discard waste products. Figure 4.2 shows the developing embryo.

Other organs that develop out of the trophoblast include the following: The **allantois** becomes the **umbilical cord,** the conduit for substances between the child and the placenta. The **chorion** is the protective membrane that surrounds the child and amnion. The **yolk sac** is the initial source of embryonic blood cells. The **amnion** is an inner membrane surrounding the embryo and containing amniotic fluid.

The Three Layers of the Embryo

What was once the embryoblast is now the embryo. The next major change after implantation is the differentiation of the embryo into three distinct layers: the **endoderm, mesoderm,** and **ectoderm.** The individual's organs will emerge from those layers. The innermost layer is called the endoderm. During the next few weeks, the inner organs will develop into the digestive tract, respiratory system, pancreas, and the circulatory system. The middle layer is called the mesoderm and will yield the muscles, bones, circulatory and excretory systems, and the inner layer of skin. The outer layer, or ectoderm, will turn into the skin, hair, and nails. Curiously, this outer layer is also the origin of the central nervous system. The location of the spinal cord along the back and the brain at the very top reflects the legacy of their origins in the ectoderm.

The embryonic period lasts from approximately the second through the eighth week. During this brief span, all the organs of the body arise. Once all the basic structures are formed, we cease to call the organism an embryo. We now leave the embryonic period for the last prenatal stage, the period of the fetus.

The Fetal Period

The **fetal period** is by far the longest period of prenatal development. It lasts from approximately the 9th week until birth at about the 38th week. It is a period marked by fetal growth and further differentiation and refinement of the organ systems. At the beginning of the fetal period, the fetus is about 1.5 inches long. At birth, the average male baby is about 20 inches, about a 14-fold increase in length.

Much more than an increase in size or weight occurs during this period. Notably, all basic structures of organs that emerged during the embryonic period are refined during the fetal period. At the beginning of the period, the fetus has only the most elemental forms of its organs. During the fetal period, the organs are increasingly refined to the point that, at birth, the organ structures can support life outside the mother's body. The turning point, called the age of viability, occurs around the 26th week. At this time, the child's structure is sufficiently developed to sustain life outside the womb.

● PRINCIPLES OF PRENATAL DEVELOPMENT

The prenatal period initiates the beginning of the lifelong interactions between the person and the environment. Already processes of development are occurring that follow basic principles. Among these principles are some general laws regarding the order in which developments occur.

The Laws of Developmental Direction

The **laws of developmental direction** are generalizations that state the order in which characteristics emerge. The laws are not restricted to physical development or to prenatal development. They are general guidelines that seem relevant also to motor development and to early postnatal development. The three specific laws and their combined effects are as follows.

The Cephalo-Caudal Law

The **cephalo-caudal** law of development means literally that development proceeds from head (cephalo) to tail (caudal). In other words, characteristics closer to the head (eyes, nose, arms) will develop before things closer to the lower parts of the body (legs, toes).

The Proximo-Distal Law

The **proximo-distal** law of development implies that things nearer to the center of the body will develop before those that are more extreme. It suggests that the heart will develop before the hands, that the elbows will develop before the fingers (this makes intuitive sense: if you were going to make a sculpture, would you ever start with the fingers and work to the middle?).

The Gross-Fine Law

The **gross-fine** law of development states that general, unrefined characteristics develop into specific, refined ones. For example, the basic unrefined characteristics of the embryo turn more specifically into the finely honed features of the newborn. At the beginning of the embryonic period, hands are just nubs. At birth, they are elongated, composed of many bones, covered with skin, and the fingers have fingernails.

The General Law of Developmental Direction

Although these guidelines are stated as if they are three separate laws, it is essential to be aware that they are interrelated. Considered in combination, they help us predict which characteristics will emerge relative to others and when internal general features located near the head will emerge before refined parts of the lower extremities. For instance, the laws suggest that toenails be among the last parts to emerge.

The Role of Timing in Development

The laws of developmental direction reflect the importance of timing in development. The timing of an event often determines its impact. Growth is more rapid during the prenatal period than any other stage of development. If the 200 billion-fold increase in size continued, we would be around 476 billion feet tall when we reached our first birthday. Imagine the bottles of formula this would require or the diaper disposal problem it would create! Fortunately, growth is not always so rapid.

The velocity of growth in length during prenatal development and the first 2 postnatal years is the most rapid of the life span. Note that after a slow start, growth of length accelerates rapidly and is fastest around the 4th prenatal month. The velocity for weight follows the same pattern, except that the peak velocity is reached later, at the 34th prenatal week.

Timing and Teratogens

This rapid growth has important implications for development, particularly when things go awry. **Teratogens** are agents such as diseases, chemicals, or radiation that cause physical or psychological abnormalities frequently referred to as birth defects. The term *teratogen* comes from the Greek word for "monster." Birth defects are not usually so dramatic as this word suggests, but they do have the potential for affecting developmental outcomes.

When growth is rapid, events that halt it will have much greater effects than when growth is slower. Many more cells will be affected in the same short time. Thus, the presence of teratogens during the germinal period may be catastrophic; the result at this period is to prevent the blastocyst from even implanting. The mother will not even know conception had occurred. Teratogens present during the embryonic period may cripple entire organs or systems. Because basic organs are present, albeit not fully refined, the effects of teratogens during the last months of pregnancy are frequently less severe than if teratogens are present during the embryonic period.

Different organs will be affected by teratogens present at various times. Some teratogens, such as rubella, have their most damaging effects only during the first trimester. This is during the embryonic period when the central nervous system and related organs are developing. Rubella is a mild disease for an adult, and also for a fetus. Yet its effects on the embryo can be devestating because this virus may produce blindness, hearing problems, and mental retardation. A teratogen such as this is dangerous because the mother is often unaware of its presence. By vaccinating all women of childbearing age prior to conceiving, the devastating effects of this disease could be prevented.

Box 4.1   Benefogens?

Scientists use the term teratogen for environmental agents that have harmful effects on the prenatally exposed child. In contrast, recent research has shown that prenatal exposure to other environmental agents may have beneficial effects. Two that are discussed below are folic acid and AZT.

Folic acid is a B vitamin that is naturally present in foods, especially dried beans, green leafy vegetables, and members of the broccoli family. Folic acid is necessary for the proper formation of the neural tube through which the spinal cord runs. The absence of folic acid has been linked to spina bifida, a common birth defect. Spina bifida occurs in nearly 1 of every 1,000 live births and is characterized by small or large openings in the spine so that parts of the spinal cord protrude. Because the nerves have very little protection, the spinal cord is likely to be injured or infected. This usually results in paralysis, mental retardation, other major disability, or even infant deaths from infection.

Some of the effects of spina bifida can be prevented through surgically enclosing the spinal cord. It may be possible, however, to prevent spina bifida itself. It has been reported that women who take folic acid vitamin supplements in the earliest stages of pregnancy may reduce the likelihood of having a child with spina bifida ("Use of Folic Acid," 1991). It is believed that American women follow diets that are too low in folic acid (Willett, 1992). Even taking a multivitamin may not provide enough folic acid to prevent many defects.

Because the defects are likely to occur in the embryonic period, even before women are aware that they are pregnant, the Federal Drug Administration has proposed fortifying flour and other grain products with folic acid (Williams, 1994). The *New York Times* (Kolata, 1995) has reported that although the importance of folic acid in preventing this common birth defect is well established, the importance of supplementing the diets of females of childbearing age is still not widely understood, and attempts to alter dietary habits have been unsuccessful. To that end, the American Academy of Pediatrics (AAP) endorses the U.S. Public Health Service (USPHS) recommendation that all women capable of becoming pregnant consume 400 µg of folic acid daily to prevent neural tube defects (AAP, 1999). Studies have demonstrated that periconceptional folic acid supplementation can prevent 50% or more of neural tube defects such as spina bifida and anencephaly (AAP, 1999).

The drug AZT (or Zidovudine; also called ZDV) may be considered a **benefogen** for children of mothers infected with the AIDS virus, HIV. Originally found to slow down the development of AIDS-related symptoms in adults with the virus, AZT has been found to offer protection to the prenatal child. In a study by Boyer et al. (1994) only 1 of 26 (4%) mothers treated with AZT transmitted HIV to their children. This is in contrast to the nontreated group in which 12 of 42 (29%) of the mothers transmitted HIV to their children prenatally. Similarly, another study involving 477 HIV-infected pregnant women found only 8% HIV infection among the children of the AZT group versus 15% of those receiving a placebo (Cowley, 1994). This discovery caused the researchers to abandon the placebo and administered the AZT to all participants.

Unlike the use of folic acid to prevent spinal tube defects, the use of AZT is not without controversy. In many views, it is quite different to add an inexpensive, natural substance (Vitamin B) to food (although this, too, is not without its critics), and yet another to administer AZT. AZT is expensive, has potential side effects (U.S. Department of Health and Human Services, 1998), and therefore requires that mothers be tested to determine if they are HIV positive. Ethical concerns revolving around a person's right to privacy versus the benefits of AZT therapy for the child have been raised (Bayer, 1994). In 1995, however, the U.S. Public Health Service developed guidelines that strongly urged that all pregnant women voluntarily obtain an AIDS test as early in the pregnancy as possible. The Centers for Disease Control and Prevention (CDC) estimated that with testing and administration of AZT before, during, and after birth, the number of babies who could be saved from HIV infection through the voluntary guidelines would be significant. Indeed, the CDC has reported remarkable success with the use of AZT and other therapies during the past decade. "During the early 1990s, an estimated 1,000 to 2,000 infants were born with HIV infection each year. In 2001, an estimated 100 cases of perinatally acquired AIDS cases were diagnosed in the U.S." (CDC, 2003, p. 1). Of course, prevention of HIV infection in all individuals, including pregnant women, would be even more desirable, but, short of that, the benefogenic effects of AZT have been enormously valuable.

● THE EARLIEST ENVIRONMENT

Thus far, we have focused mainly on the developing child. Now we must turn our attention to the highly specialized context in which the prenatal organism develops—its mother's body. The progressive interactions between the person and environment that characterize behavior start immediately at conception. The amniotic sac is the entire functional environmental surround for the child's first 9 months. Over our species phylogenic history, the mother's body has evolved special characteristics that truly place it in the category of a species-typical environment. All members of the species develop in the specialized structures of the child's protective membranes and its mother's body.

The *ovaries, oviduct,* and *uterus* are structures that serve very specialized functions. They transact with the characteristic of the developing organism. The structures of the mother's body change as the developing child changes. Each affects the other. These structures play very specific roles. For example, the oviduct has evolved to function as a conduit to transport the blastula into the uterus. Its tiny, hair-sized tubing is unsuitable to nourish the body to full term.

Unfortunately, things can go terribly wrong even in the earliest stages of the mother–child interaction, and a blastula can implant in the oviduct rather than in the uterus. This ectopic pregnancy is lethal to the developing embryo and a serious medical emergency for the mother, requiring surgical treatment. The much more spacious chamber of the uterus evolved as the appropriate species-typical environment for the growth and development of the embryo and fetus. In addition, maternal diseases may have adverse and permanent effects on the fetus. The mother's body may determine the potency of potential teratogens. Because of the difference in maternal reactions to various teratogenic agents, such as diseases, maternal systems may increase or decrease the embryo's exposure to the teratogens. Likewise, some embryos and fetuses may be more susceptible than others to particular teratogens because of genetic factors. In sum, exposure alone to teratogens does not doom the prenatal child to specific developmental outcomes. Instead, we may look at exposure as providing a possibly nonfacilitative environment, with the outcome dependent on the transactions between this environment and the vulnerability of the prenatal child.

A CLOSER LOOK AT TERATOGENS ●

Unfortunately, the placental barrier does not only bring nutrition in and wastes out. The mother's body is also the environmental source for many teratogens. If the substances are small enough to pass through the semipermeable membrane, the placenta transmits these as well. Researchers (Vorhees & Mollnow, 1987; Wilson, 1973) have looked at many suspected environmental teratogens. Following is a list of environmental agents concerning their detrimental effects.

Maternal Diseases

Toxoplasmosis

Toxoplasmosis is a disease caused by a microscopic parasite called Toxoplasma gondii and is a potentially serious health risk to humans. The mother usually acquires the infection by eating undercooked meat containing tissue cysts or by exposure to occysts in soil contaminated with cat feces. Transmission to the fetus occurs when the virus passes through the placenta, transplacentally, and into the fetus's environment. Symptoms include loss of vision, mental retardation, loss of hearing, and even death in severe cases.

Cytomegalovirus

Cytomegalovirus (CMV) is a member of the herpes virus family and is found all over the world. Newborns can be infected with CMV before birth or during the birth process, almost always because the child's mother developed CMV infection during pregnancy. Usually the infected infant shows no symptoms at birth, but, in some cases, symptoms appear over the next few years. These symptoms may include neurological, growth, and developmental problems; sight or hearing problems; and dental abnormalities. In rare cases, a newborn may have a life-threatening infection. Infants can be infected with CMV during or soon after delivery as they pass through the birth canal of an infected mother, consume breast milk from a mother who has the virus, or receive a blood transfusion contaminated with CMV.

Rubella

Rubella is a viral infection caused by a togavirus of the genus Rubivirus. The effects of rubella infection in adults are minor, with fever and flu-like discomfort. The embryo or fetus may get infected through the mother if she contracts it. If the fetus contracts rubella beyond 16 weeks after conception, there is generally no known effect, although some growth retardation may occur in third-trimester fetuses. If infection of the embryo or fetus occurs prior to 16 weeks after conception, however, significant hearing, vision, cardiovascular, and neurological damage can occur (Webster, 1998). Because the early infection is so damaging and because it can occur even before a woman knows she is pregnant, universal immunization for rubella is an important preventive measure.

Genital Herpes

Genital herpes is a contagious viral infection caused by the herpes simplex virus (HSV). The virus remains in certain nerve cells of the body for life, causing

Table 4.1   Maternal Infections and Prevention Strategies

Maternal Infection	Potential Fetal Complication	Maternal Prevention Strategies
Toxoplasmosis	Visual defects, blindness, cerebral defects, seizures, mental retardation, hearing loss, hepatomegaly, intrauterine growth retardation, low birth weight	Avoid consumption of undercooked meats Avoid handling soiled cat litter prior to conception or during pregnancy
Cytomegalovirus	Chorioretinitis, mental retardation, microcephaly, neurological dysfunction and hearing loss	Wash hands frequently and practice good hygiene Avoid exposure to CMV + toddlers
Rubella	Visual defects, blindness, deafness, cerebral defects, seizures, lethargy/irritability, large anterior fontanel, hepatomegaly, splenomegaly, jaundice, cardiovascular and cutaneous defects	Rubella immunity at least three months before conception
Genital herpes	Herpes exposure: Visual defects, blindness, cerebral defects, cutaneous lesions	Safe sexual practices to avoid exposure to syphilis

periodic recurrences in some people. Newborns can become infected with herpes virus in the following ways: through the uterus, passing through the birth canal (the most common method of infection), or in the time immediately after birth. If the mother has an active genital herpes infection at the time of delivery, the infant is most likely to become infected during the birthing process. A pregnant woman who develops a first episode of genital herpes can pass the virus to her fetus and may be at higher risk for premature delivery.

With early detection and therapy, many serious complications can be lessened. Because of the danger of infection to the baby, however, the physician will perform a cesarean section if herpes lesions are detected in or near the birth canal during labor. A baby born with herpes can develop encephalitis (inflammation of the brain), severe rashes, and eye problems. Acyclovir, a drug used to treat genital herpes, can greatly improve the outcome for babies with neonatal herpes, especially if they receive immediate treatment.

Table 4.1 outlines some maternal diseases, fetal complications, and maternal prevention strategies.

Drugs

There are many substances categorized as drugs that when taken by the mother during pregnancy have the potential to act as teratogens. Nevertheless, the link between many substances and prenatal risks is not clearly established. Among the most widely studied drug sources are two of the most common, alcohol consumption and cigarette smoke.

Alcohol Intake

Women who drink moderate amounts of alcohol may place their children at risk for developing detrimental effects such as a lower IQ, attention deficits, learning deficits, and reduced social competence. In addition, women who drink heavily during pregnancy place their children at risk of developing fetal alcohol syndrome (FAS), characterized by growth retardation, craniofacial anomalies, and mental retardation. "The deficits associated with this disorder are long lasting and pervasive" (Jacobson, 1997, p. 199). Evidence shows that many fetal alcohol syndrome deficits can be detected at infancy and remain through adolescence into adulthood. In particular, an abnormally small head circumference, and behavioral, emotional, and social problems can become more pronounced (Jacobson, 1998).

Deficits and problems are relevant not only to the quantity of the alcohol consumed but also to the timing of the consumption. First-trimester exposure is related to skull and facial abnormalities, whereas the effects on growth, especially postnatal growth, are related to alcohol exposure later in pregnancy (Jacobson, 1998). Early detection of alcohol-affected infants, both those with FAS and those less obviously affected, could provide the opportunity for significantly improved services for both mothers and infants.

Cigarette Smoking

Maternal smoking during pregnancy has long been recognized as having permanent and damaging effects on the unborn fetus. Women who smoke early in pregnancy increase their chances of having an ectopic pregnancy, when the embryo implants in a fallopian tube or other abnormal site instead of the uterus. As we have noted, ectopic pregnancies must be removed surgically or with drug treatment to protect a woman's life. Smokers are more likely to suffer a miscarriage than nonsmoking women.

Smoking significantly increases a woman's risk of having a low birth weight baby. Low birth weight babies, who weigh less than 5.5 pounds at birth, are at an increased risk of serious health problems that include chronic disabilities (such as cerebral palsy, mental retardation, and learning problems), and even death. Low birth weight can result from poor intrauterine growth, preterm delivery, or a combination of both. Smoking has also been known to slow fetal growth.

Pregnant women who do not smoke should avoid exposure to other people's smoke. Studies suggest that regular exposure to secondhand smoke also may reduce fetal growth and contribute to learning and behavioral problems.

Environmental Hazards

Radiation

The developing fetal brain is quite vulnerable to abnormalities caused by exposure to radiation. The most vulnerable period seems to be the time from approximately the 8th through the 15th week of pregnancy. Effects include decrease in intelligence test scores, changes in the occurrence of major features of physical development, impaired school performance, susceptibility to seizures, and, possibly, other effects.

Maternal Characteristics

Maternal Age

The mother's age is an influential factor in assessing the likely well-being of her fetus. In particular, some adolescent mothers are especially likely to expose the developing embryo or fetus to negative consequences. Some of the long-term consequences of teenage mother births are increased high school dropout rate, increased unemployment, and increased welfare dependence. In addition to the socioeconomic consequences for adolescent mothers and infants, a number of negative medical consequences may occur, including increased risk of severe birth-related complications (Pan, Gross, & Gross, 1996). Repeated pregnancies during adolescence can also increase the risk of perinatal death. Lack of prenatal care, a typical characteristic of adolescent pregnancies, can result in a disproportionate number of low birth weight babies and increased risk of birth defects and developmental delays. Some of these effects can be moderated if the teenage father continues to be involved with the mother and child.

Figure 4.3   An Adolescent Mom

Nutrition and Development

Another important factor in growth and development is the availability of nutrients. Initial growth during the prenatal period is slow. An important limitation of the free-floating blastula is the lack of available nutrition. It can ingest available nutrients only by absorption through the cell membranes, a process called **phagocytosis**, which is a very inefficient way to take in food. This lack of nutritional supply is part of what makes implantation in the uterus lining such a phase shift and cusp Now, with the availability of substances in the maternal blood supply, growth can accelerate. Let us look at this mother-embryo connection.

Initially, the trophoblast sends its hairlike tendrils burrowing into the lining of the uterus. Eventually, some cells of the trophoblast form the placenta. The placenta is the interface the allows nutrients from the mother to move to the child and waste products from the child to travel to the mother's body where they can be eliminated. These exchanges occur because the placenta is a semi-permeable membrane that functions through **osmosis**. Substances flow from a location of high concentration to one where there is a low concentration. As a semipermeable membrane, this placental barrier allows small molecules through, but it keeps large particles, especially blood cells, from crossing between the two blood systems. Thus, the two blood systems are separate. This is why the mother can carry a child with different rh antigens without her immune system producing antibodies against this foreign substance. Because the blood cells and their antigens are kept separate, they do not trigger an immune response.

The ability of the placenta to exchange nutrients and wastes between the two blood systems is striking. The placenta is very convoluted and filled with tiny hairlike capillaries. This gives it an immense surface area, facilitating the exchange of substances. To fully appreciate the enormity of the placenta's surface area, consider one estimate of the size of its surface area relative to the size of the child it nourishes. Although the weight of the placenta is only 14% of the weight of the child at birth, Eichorn (1970) estimated the surface area of a newborn is about .22 square meters or about two square feet, while the surface area of the placenta is about 11 square meters or about 99 square feet. This increased ability to obtain nutrients enables the prenatal child to grow at a prodigious rate.

REPRODUCTIVE RISK •
VERSUS CARETAKING CASUALTY

Reproductive risks are those that occur prior to birth, such as genetic disorders or teratogens, or at birth, such as anoxia (lack of oxygen). For years, the linear model that dominated developmental theory had us focus on reproductive risk. In this view, exposure to a teratogen or other nonfacilitative condition, such as anoxia, produced a poor developmental outcome. This idea was based on assumptions and backed by faulty research findings supporting the view that some of the above teratogens and birth complications such as anoxia carried a near 100% probability of later developmental problems. To recap the linear model, if something happened at A, it caused a difficulty at B.

Sameroff and Chandler (1975) took issue with the linear approach inherent in the term "reproductive risk." They cited improved research that showed that mild anoxia usually did not lead to long-term problems for the children. They argued that long-term parental caretaking over a period of years was more influential than a single early event in affecting developmental outcomes. Thus, they argued for replacing the term reproductive risk with the **continuum of caretaking casualty**. A continuum emphasizes the long-term and continuous nature of the caretaker's role. The idea of caretaker casualty implies the importance of the environmental dimension mediated by the caretaker. Thus, the expression "continuum of caretaker casualty" suggests that interactions between genetic, historical, and current environments are crucial. Although the term *continuum* sounds linear, their thinking was transactional. Thus, they found that the effects of mild anoxia gradually disappeared over a period of years if caretakers provided a facilitative environment.

The transactional model seems particularly useful when viewing prenatal development. It will be helpful to refer again to Horowitz's (1987) model. Genetic makeup falls on the organismic continuum, contributing to where the child falls on the impaired–unimpaired and vulnerable–invulnerable continuum. For example, a child with Down syndrome has certain impairments that will influence physical, intellectual, and social development. Likewise, inherited characteristics, such as ear canals that retain fluid, make the child vulnerable to developing language problems because the child's hearing is affected. The prenatal environment the mother provides falls on the environmental dimension. Conditions in the environment, such as appropriate nutrition or diseases, determine the child's placement on the nonfacilitative–facilitative dimension.

The effects of the environment on the child become part of the organismic dimension. For example, if a mother's exposure to high concentrations of alcohol (nonfacilitative environment) produces detrimental effects, the child will be more impaired on the organismic dimension. The long-run effects also fall on the environmental side, with sensitive child rearing, remedial education, and other facilitative events eradicating the early nonfacilitative ones.

● GETTING READY FOR THE WORLD

The intrauterine environment provides a mostly facilitative environment for the fetus. During the last months of development, the fetus is acquiring the physical structures that will ensure survival in the outside world. At the same time, basic behavioral adaptations are taking place that will enable it to adapt to its environment. As a result, it enters the outside world ready to profit from the full range of potential learning experiences in this new functional environmental surround.

POSTNATAL DEVELOPMENT: ● THE REMARKABLE NEWBORN

After some 266 days, the newborn emerges from the highly protective environment of its mother's body. It has spent the time not only developing physically but behaviorally as well. Not only has it acquired the biological structures necessary for survival but also the ability to interact with the outside world.

Birth is an event that changes the child's environmental surround. Auditory stimuli were muffled, visual stimuli were dim or nonexistent, but birth has changed that. The newborn enters an environment filled with multiple stimuli. Is the newborn capable of sensing these? Do newborns react to the stimuli immediately, or do they first need to experience the world for a while before they can react to it? William James, the preeminent American psychologist of his day, described the newborn's world as "one great blooming, buzzing confusion" (James, 1890, p. 462). Today, a century later, we know that the newborn enters this new world already capable of responding to it in systematic ways. Such response capabilities set the stage for rapid learning. What are these capabilities? When do they begin? How do we assess them? These are questions to be answered about the remarkable newborn.

The newborn is also known by the technical term "neonate." **Neonate** literally means newborn, and we use those terms for the child for the first two weeks of life. The full-term neonate averages 20 inches (51 cm) and weighs between 6 and 9 pounds (2.7–4.1 kg) at birth. Hormonal changes signal the mother's body to produce changes that induce labor. On average, labor for first-borns lasts sixteen to seventeen hours (Lamb & Bornstein, 1987).

Assessing Baby's Condition: Apgar Test

The Apgar test, is named for its developer, Dr. Virginia Apgar. Created in 1953, Apgar also stands for the five areas it measures: appearance (color), pulse (heartbeat), grimace (reflex), activity (muscle tone), and respiration (breathing). Each of these measures is rated from 0 to 2 by the observer. A total of 10 points is perfect, and a 7 is considered good. The test is usually given at

Table 4.2   Using the Apgar Test to Assess Newborns

Apgar Test Characteristic	Score		
	0	*1*	*2*
Heart rate	Absent heartbeat	Slow (fewer than 100 beats per minute)	Adequate heartbeat (over 100 beats per minute)
Respiratory effect	Not breathing	Weak cry, irregular breathing	Strong cry
Muscle tone	Flaccid, limp	Some flexing or bending	Strong, active motion
Color	Pale or blue	Body pink, extremities blue	Completely pink
Reflex irritability	No response	Frown, grimace, or weak cry	Vigorous cries or withdrawal

1 minute after birth and again at 5 minutes after birth. Subsequent testings may be given if the score is low. The Apgar gives a quick indication of the newborn's vital functions and alerts the medical staff to any immediate life-threatening problems. The scoring for the Apgar is shown in Table 4.2.

Brazelton's Neonatal Behavioral Assessment Scale

The Apgar is a very general measure of the child's vital life signs. Brazelton's Neonatal Behavioral Assessment Scale (NBAS), developed by Dr. Berry Brazelton (1984), takes a more detailed look at the child's physical and behavioral functioning shortly after birth. The NBAS was developed in 1973 and, despite having never been standardized, is used to assess behavioral capabilities of newborns up to 20 days of age. A new, briefer scale, the NBAS–R (Neonatal Behavioral Assessment Scale–Revised) (Brazelton Institute, 2000) has just been developed to be more objective and standardized. The NBAS–R looks at 28 behavioral and 18 reflex items to give a profile of the newborn's functioning in seven areas: habituation, social interaction, motor, state organization, state regulation, autonomic system, and reflexes.

After 9 months of development in the specialized and largely protective environment that the mother's body provides, the human neonate arrives in the outside world with the capabilities to survive, learn, and develop. The rest of this book is about those processes. Our adventure begins in the next chapter as we look at the newborn's sensory, perceptual, and motor capabilities.

Already the neonate is brimming with the capacity to respond to the external environment. These capacities have been detected even prior to birth. Sakabe, Arayama, and Suzuki (1969) measured changes in the **EEG** (electroencephalograms) of fetuses in the 32nd to 38th week following conception. The study measured changes in brain waves that occurred when changes in sound were presented. These brain wave changes not only indicate that perceptual capabilities may already exist 1 month before birth, they also show that exposure to external stimuli is possible while the fetus is still in utero.

THE NEONATE'S ABILITY TO ● RESPOND TO THE ENVIRONMENT

Sensory Capability

Two capabilities are necessary to respond to the environment. The first is the ability to detect changes in the environment. This is the sensory capability of the child. The second is the ability to behave or respond. We start by looking at the first of these, the sensory capability of the neonate.

There is a sudden bright flash of light. What is it? What color is it? Is it a photo flash, an explosion, or what? What did you see? We can look at this event (the flash of light) in many ways.

Sensation

First thing we need to know is whether it had an effect on the person. If a tree falls in the woods . . . is there a sound? This philosophical question deals with the act of sensation. **Sensation** is the actual stimulation of sensory receptors and their connection to neurons traveling to the sensory center in the central nervous system. Sensation is the detection of the presence of stimuli.

Humans have five basic senses: seeing (visual), hearing (auditory), smelling (olfactory), tasting (gustatory), and feeling (touch, pain, proprioceptive). Each of these senses involves a relationship between an event in the environment (i.e., stimulus) and a specific sensory receptor. Receptors are stimulus specific; only certain stimuli will fire them. Visual receptors detect changes in light; sound receptors detect changes in sound waves. Likewise, receptors tend to be located at specific sites, such as the retina of the eye or the outer, middle, and inner ear.

The stimuli that fire the visual receptors are changes in light. Light is physical energy occurring in waves of a distinctive length. Specifically, the visual spectrum for visual receptors is energy in wavelengths from 380 to 700 nanometers. Other organisms have receptors that can sense light in the ultraviolet or infrared parts of the spectrum, but we cannot.

Several specific types of cells are receptors for vision. All are located in the eye. The retina, the lining of the back of the eyeball, contains these cells. Two specific visual receptors are the rods and cones. Each of these is sensitive to a particular aspect of the visual stimulus—light. Cones, concentrated in the central portion of the retina called the fovea, come in different varieties. These different cones are sensitive to light of a specific wavelength, corresponding to colors. Because the fovea contains a high density of many cones, vision is most acute in this area.

Rods are cells located in the periphery of the retina and fire in response to small changes in light. Thus, they are light–dark receptors, but they cannot detect color. When a dim object such as a shooting star is detected, it is because of the sensation of these rods.

Sound also takes the form of waves of energy, but sound waves are larger and travel much more slowly. They are detected by receptors in the inner ear after being enhanced by the action of the ear drum and parts of the middle ear. These organs respond to the presence of waves of energy in the auditory range. Note that although sound waves also consist of physical energy, because of the wavelength differences we do not see sounds or hear light. Nevertheless, if sound waves are slow enough (as in the deep bass of a drum) and amplified enough, we may sense them with something other than our ears. With a good stereo (or when someone is riding by with a boom box in his or her car) we not only hear the sound, we feel it with the pressure sensors in our bodies.

In short, because of natural selection, we have evolved certain cells that serve the role of specialized receptors. These receptors are sensitive to particular events in our environment. Thus, for purely physical reasons, some parts of our environmental surround will be sensed and others not. We will now turn to another reason why some stimuli affect our behavior and others do not.

Perception

Perception is the organized response to a stimulus. Perception requires sensation but entails more than that. The firing of a cone by a stimulus is sensation, but an awareness of blue in our "mind's eye" or responding to that sensation with the word *blue* or pushing a key or feeling an emotion is perception. Perception involves an integrated response to a stimulus. It is an integration of a sensation with the activation of appropriate response systems. A question arises: Is our perception of "blue" innate or acquired?

Nativism Versus Empiricism

In the field of perception, the nature–nurture controversy becomes the nativism versus empiricism controversy. **Nativism** proposes that perception is innate, that it is hardwired and present at birth. In contrast, **empiricism** states that we acquire perception through experience. As in the nature–nurture controversy, there is probably no way to make a clear determination of which is true.

Our physiology provides us with some hardwired universal behaviors. Among these are basic sensory responses to stimuli. We detect light versus dark, horizontal versus vertical lines, and other innate perceptual responses. In addition, apparently we have hardwired responses to stimuli called reflexes. Some reflexes may be complex enough that we consider the response of the child as demonstrating that she is perceiving the stimulus, not merely sensing it.

For example, in a series of experiments, Meltzoff and Moore (1977, 1983) have reported that within hours of birth, neonates imitate the gestures of adults. The authors (Meltzoff & Moore, 1985) stated that "our working hypothesis is that human newborns have an innate ability to appreciate equivalencies between their acts and the acts they see" (p. 155). This "appreciation of equivalencies" is perception inferred from the neonate's organized imitative response. Seeing a newborn stick out its tongue after an adult does, or opening its mouth after an adult does, leads us to the conclusion that the child *perceives* the adult behavior as something to be imitated.

How Do We Know the Sensory and Perceptual Capabilities of the Infant?

As James's (1890) famous quotation implies, we underestimated the newborn's sensory and perceptual capabilities. We did this because of the difficulty in assessing these capabilities. To assess the visual acuity of adults, we present them with an eye chart and ask them to tell us what line they can read. We use a similar procedure to assess auditory perception. Yet how do you ask newborns what they can see or hear? The difficulty in posing the question meant we had little data on infant sensory capabilities.

This dilemma was solved by Robert Fantz, a psychologist at Case Western Reserve University in Cleveland. Fantz (1958, 1961) devised a simple procedure to test visual acuity. Like many breakthroughs, his method, called the **visual preference method,** was simple. Yet it was so powerful in its conceptualization that it led to the development of many other methods and revolutionized the field.

Methods Used in Perceptual Research

Let us look again at how adults are tested. You give them a line of letters and ask them to tell you what letters they see. You stop when they can no longer give you a response that correlates with the stimulus. Or you change the pitch of a sound and you ask them to tell you if they hear it. In both cases, you present them with a change in stimulus (e.g., letters, pitch), and then you see if there is a correlated change in behavior (e.g., "f," "e," or "yes, I hear it").

Fantz recognized that this relationship between a change in the stimulus and a change in behavior was common to all measures of perception. His problem was to identify a neonatal response that was reliably related to visual perception. Again the solution was simple—looking, itself, was correlated with perception. If a change in what the child was looking at followed a change in the stimulus, it could be concluded that the child could detect or see the change.

Fantz realized that if the child spent more time looking at one stimulus over another that this *preference* indicated that the child could tell one stimulus from the other. Admittedly, in some cases the child would show no preference, even though he or she could perceive one as different from the other, as, say, a circle from a square or a Coke from a Pepsi. Such a lack of a preference would not allow us to attribute the lack to perception or motivation. If the child does show a reliable preference, looking longer at one stimulus than the other, however, then it means he or she can tell one from the other. That is, the child can perceive a difference.

To use this preference method, Fantz created a visual chamber. The child could be placed on its back inside the chamber. Lying in an infant seat, the infant would be facing the top of the chamber. On this "ceiling" Fantz could place two pictures that were his stimuli. By carefully lighting the chamber, an image of what the child was looking at was reflected on the cornea of the child's eye and could be seen by an observer looking through a peep hole in the top of the chamber. By carefully recording the amount of time each stimulus was reflected in the child's eye, the observer would have the total duration that the child looked at each stimulus.

If the amount of time were equal for both stimuli (after reversing the location of the square and circle to prevent a "side bias"), this could mean one of two things: either (a) the child could not tell one stimulus from the other or (b) that the child could see a difference but did not prefer one over the other. Therefore, finding equal durations would be inconclusive regarding visual capability.

However, an infant who spent more time looking at one stimulus over the other showed not only a preference but the ability to perceive a difference in the stimuli. By varying the stimuli and the amount of detail, researchers could use this preference method to determine visual acuity, color perception, and other characteristics of vision.

To measure visual acuity, Fantz chose a neutral gray square for one stimulus. The other stimulus was a box containing lines of specified thickness. These repetitive black-white patterns are called gratings. Varying the thickness of the lines would be like varying the size of the letters for adults. As long as the infant perceived the lines as lines, their complexity attracted the infant's gaze. But as the lines became thinner, they became fuzzy. A lack of preference for the lined stimulus over the gray one meant the infant could no longer distinguish between the two stimuli and perceived these lines to be the same as the gray stimulus. By measuring the width of the lines at the point at which a preference was no longer shown and comparing that measure with the width at which adults no longer could tell the lines from the solid gray, an estimate of infant acuity could be made.

Fantz's preference method broke the conceptual logjam that had prevented researchers from designing methods to test infant perceptual capabilities. Within a few years, other researchers developed methods that have enabled us to know much more about how the infant perceives its world. Some of these methods are described below.

Visual Cliff

The question of whether depth perception is innate or develops due to experience prompted Walk and Gibson (1961) to develop the **visual cliff** apparatus. The visual cliff is a large glass covered table with a "shallow end" and "deep end." The shallow end has a checkerboard pattern of black and white squares immediately under the glass. The deep end has the same pattern placed on the ground, a few feet below the glass. The infant is placed on a board between the two ends and is enticed by its mother to crawl to her, either over the shallow or the deep end.

Walk and Gibson (1961) showed that children at 7 months avoid crawling on the deep end, indicating they perceive the "depth" of the deep end, despite the feel of the glass sheet. You probably can see, however, why this method cannot answer the nativism–empiricism question. You need a child who can crawl (about 6 months of age) to use the cliff. Later Campos and his colleagues (Campos, Langer, & Krowtiz, 1970) tested noncrawlers using the visual cliff by lowering them onto the deep side and measuring their heart rate. They found children (as young as 2 months of age) showed a change in heart rate (a *decrease).* This meant that children could detect the depth from visual cues, as a decrease in heart rate is taken as a measure of attention. About a month after learning to crawl, the same procedure produces an *increase* in heart rate. This is associated with fear responses and suggests perception of depth is possible prior to crawling but that fear of falling is acquired with the experience that comes with crawling.

Habituation–Dishabituation

In this procedure, the researchers record a consistent, ongoing response such as a newborn's sucking response to a nipple. (This can be done systematically by using a high-tech nipple: one with a microswitch attached to a recording device.) Now the researcher introduces a sound such as the phoneme "ba." The sucking stops as the child orients to the sound. If you continue the "ba" sound, the sucking will resume. This is habituation (see Chapter 5) and involves adaptation to a repeated stimulus (e.g., "ba"). Now change the stimulus slightly, from "ba" to "pa." If the neonate stops sucking again, then it perceives the difference between these two auditory stimuli. This reversal of a habituated response is dishabituation. This is the procedure used by Eimas and his colleagues (1971) at Brown University to show that infants as young as 6 hours could discriminate "ba" from "pa." Among the most frequently used responses in the habituation–dishabituation procedure, besides sucking, is heart rate (Miller, 1987).

Operant Conditioning Procedures to Study Perception, Memory, and Early Socialization

Many procedures used to assess neonatal perceptual capabilities involve operant conditioning (Gewirtz & Peláez-Nogueras, 1992a; see Chapter 6). The basic process involves reinforcing the child for differentially responding to stimuli—that is, the infant is reinforced for making one response (e.g., turning head to the right) for one stimulus and a second response (turning head left) for another stimulus. If she now turns her head in the appropriate direction when presented with a given stimulus, perception of this stimulus is inferred.

Stimuli. Stimuli may be presented one at a time or simultaneously. Among the responses used by researchers include head turning (e.g., Siqueland, 1964; Engen, Lipsitt, & Kaye, 1963; Siqueland & Lipsitt, 1966), sucking a nipple at a high (or low) rate (e.g., DeCasper, & Fifer, 1980), or kicking a mobile (e.g., Rovee-Collier, Griesler, & Earley, 1985).

Reinforcers. Reinforcers for the neonate have included the mother's voice (e.g., DeCasper & Fifer, 1980; Barrett-Goldfarb & Whitehurst, 1972), milk (e.g., Siqueland, 1968), visual stimulation (e.g., Rovee-Collier et al., 1985), and even a recording of the intrauterine heartbeat (DeCasper & Sigafoos, 1983). Thus, in operant conditioning methods, a wide range of **stimuli, responses,** and **reinforcers** may be employed with young infants (Gewirtz & Peláez-Nogueras, 1992a). Taken together, the use of various operant conditioning procedures has been very effective for studying a wide range of infant perceptual capabilities.

Operant Learning Studies on Cognition and Memory

In the cognitive studies, the work of Rovee-Collier and associates (Boller, Rovee-Collier, Borovsky, O'Connor, & Shyi, 1990; Greco, Hayne, & Rovee-Collier, 1990; Rovee-Collier & Fagen, 1981) illustrates the impact of operant methodology in the study of infant memory. Infants placed faceup in a crib, viewing an overhead mobile, kicked their legs to produce, as a consequence, a proportional movement of the mobile. That is, the more they kicked, the more the mobile twirled. This correlation of the magnitude of the reinforcer to the magnitude of the response is called **conjugate reinforcement**. During the conjugate reinforcement phase, the mobile's movement was activated by a ribbon connected from the infant's ankle to the mobile. A stimulus cue, such as an X, was used to signal that the conjugate reinforcement contingency was in effect. Remembering was tested by returning the child to the testing condition after different time periods. Infants immediately responded to the cued stimulus by kicking, indicating that they had remembered the stimulus. This conditioning procedure facilitated the delineation of short- and long-term memory processes, indexed by retention of cued responding, after delays of hours, days, and weeks. Variations of this mobile conjugate reinforcement paradigm have also been employed to assess the contextual determinants of retrieval in early infancy (e.g., Rovee Collier et al., 1985). In sum, much of what is known about infant memory derives from use of the operant conditioning paradigm.

Operant Learning Studies on Early Perception

How operant learning has been used to study infant perception and learning can be illustrated by the work of DeCasper and associates, who demonstrated the impact of systematic prenatal auditory exposure on postnatal learning (DeCasper & Prescott, 1984; DeCasper & Sigafoos, 1983; DeCasper & Spence, 1986). After instructing mothers to repeatedly read aloud specific stories during the last 3 months of pregnancy, their newborns exhibited increased nonnutritive sucking to produce the acoustic properties of a speech passage their mothers had recited repeatedly compared with a passage their mothers had not recited. That is, the newborns preferred the passages their mothers had read, indicating that the maternal passages were reinforcers (DeCasper & Spence, 1986). In another study, the maternal voice, to which the fetus was exposed during gestation, was found to function as a more effective reinforcer for the newborn (as evidenced by high sucking response rates) than did a stranger's voice to which the infant was never exposed (Spence & DeCasper, 1987). These studies suggest that in utero auditory experience can affect postnatal behavior and learning in human infants (Gewirtz & Peláez-Nogueras, 1992a).

Operant Learning Studies on Early Socialization

Operant conditioning studies on infant social and emotional phenomena has been grouped in the literature under headings such as attachment and separation distress discussed in Chapter 10 (e.g., Gewirtz & Peláez-Nogueras, 1991a, 1991b; Wahler, 1969), crying (e.g., Etzel & Gewirtz, 1967), imitation (e.g., Baer & Sherman, 1964; Kymissis & Poulson, 1990), fear, jealousy, depression, and social referencing (Gewirtz & Peláez-Nogueras, 1992b, 1997; Peláez-Nogueras, 1992).

For example, in this area of infant social and emotional development, the work of Gewirtz and Peláez-Nogueras (1992d) demonstrated that infant social referencing (i.e., being cued by the mother's facial expressions) and subsequent behavior can result from operant learning generated by positive and aversive contingencies for differentially cued infant behavior in ambiguous contexts. They showed that, in uncertain contexts, maternal facial response cues need not be limited to those providing affective or emotional information to their infants, such as those of joy and fear, as proposed by Campos (1983). Their research suggests that the extent to which an infant turns to search its mother's face for discriminative expressive cues in contexts of uncertainty depends on success in obtaining such information, its validity, and its utility. That is, for the referencing response to be maintained in the infant's repertoire, maternal facial expressive cues must be consistently contingent on infant referencing behavior and must predict reliably the environmental consequences of the infant's ensuing action in ambiguous contexts.

In sum, the operant-learning paradigm has been remarkably fruitful in generating diverse research questions and answers concerning cognitive and social phenomena. Behavior analysis has shown itself to be an effective and powerful approach for adding to our knowledge of infant behavior capacities, learning, and development. As demonstrated in the work listed in this chapter, behavior-analytic research has progressed beyond mere demonstrations of the acquisition of simple human behavior and has attained a level of conceptualization adequate to organize diverse complex processes during infancy.

In the above section we presented various methods and variations used by developmental psychologists to determine the perceptual, cognitive, and social capabilities of very young infants. Now we turn to a more detailed overview of what these capabilities are.

SENSORY ABILITIES ●

Visual Abilities

Acuity. The acuity of the newborn is not as good as that of the normal adult, but during the first 6 months acuity improves by three- to fourfold (Dobson & Teller, 1978). It is possible that the poorer vision occurs because the neonate does not use the fovea, which contains the largest concentration of cones, for focusing.

Color Perception. Regarding sensitivity to different stimuli on the visual spectrum, 1- and 3-month-old infants have about the same range of sensitivity to colors as adults (Powers, Schneck, & Teller, 1981). Furthermore, based on habituation data produced by Bornstein (1981), Anslin (1987) concluded that by 4 months, infants group wavelengths into the same categories that adults do.

Auditory Capabilities

Studies by Sakabe et al. (1969) using **EEG** and Grimwade, Walker, Bartlett, Gordon, and Wood (1971) using heartbeat indicate that the auditory system is already functioning prior to birth. In addition to detecting sounds within the normal adult range, auditory discrimination may develop surprisingly early.

Box 4.2 Sound Localization: A Developmental Problem

It is pitch dark. You hear a ticking sound. Tick . . . tick . . . tick. Where is that watch? You listen and turn your head a bit and then you quickly walk over and pick up the watch you never saw. We have found a solution to a very common problem. The problem is called **sound localization**.

Bower (1977) presents an interesting illustration of the interaction of biological maturational structures and learning in the problem of sound localization. Biology is important. Our biological makeup includes a biaural hearing system. That is, we have two ears; one on either side of the head. In the case of sound localization, it is true that two ears are better than one. Since the sound has to travel through your head to get to the opposite ear, when a sound emanates from your left, the sound wave hits your left ear microseconds before it reaches your right one. The difference is called the **interaural time difference.** The differences are maximal when the sound is 90 degrees to the side. As the sound travels directly in front or to the rear of you, the delay differences disappear. In fact, we have difficulty knowing if something is directly in front or directly to the rear of us because there is no time discrepancy to use as a cue. Although a matter of microseconds, this difference is sufficient enough for adults to readily identify the source of the sound.

Is such localization ability hard-wired? Ashmead, DeFord, Whalen, and Odom (1991) presented some data relevant to this issue. They found that the precision of the infant's sound localization abilities does increase dramatically during the first year. The increase, however, is not as great as the increase in our ability to detect interaural time differences. At 10 weeks, there must be a difference of at least 170 microseconds for the neonate to detect the difference. By 80 weeks, a much smaller difference (63 microsec) is detectable (adults can detect differences as small as 20 microsec). So our abilities to detect differences improve significantly during a few short months.

Why should our localization ability lag behind our sensitivity to sound differences? Bower suggested that it is because of physical changes occurring over the first year. During the first year, head size increases from 60% of adult size to nearly 85%. To make his point, consider the illustration of changes in head size shown in Figure 4.4. Notice that as the head size increases, the distance, and, therefore, the time it takes for the sound to reach the right ear increases too. The interaural time difference is greater. This means we have to constantly recalibrate these interaural timed differences to the position of a sound to accommodate changes in head size if we are to successfully localize a sound. Are we able to do this? Such recalibrations require transactions between the child and her experiences. It requires learning the relationship between a sound and its visual location. This is a skill made more difficult by the constant change of head size that changes the interaural time difference for something in the same place.

Because nearly all humans learn to localize sounds, it is a universal behavior. But it is a universal behavior that requires constant adjustment between physiological changes and environmental events.

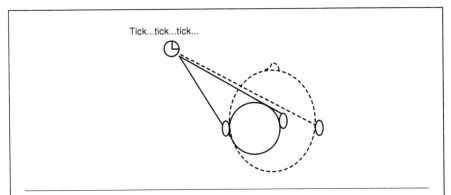

Tick...tick...tick...

Figure 4.4   Recalibration in Sound Localization

NOTE: To identify the location of a sound, such as a ticking clock, as the distance
between the ears increases (as head sizes increases in development), small increases in
the time the sound reaches the left ear versus the right must continually be recalibrated.

Sensory Integration

Sensory integration consists of the infant detection of shared absolute features
of stimuli. These **amodal** features are not unique to a given sense modality
(Bahrick, 1988, 1992, 1994, 2000, 2001; Lewkowicz, 1996; Lickliter & Bahrick, 2000,
2001; Slater, 1999). For example, tempo, or rhythm, is one such amodal feature that
can be common to most stimuli, regardless of whether the stimuli are visual, auditory, or tactile. Thus, at a dance, the music, strobe light, and body movement can all
pulsate to the same beat! Watson and Chase (2002) discuss sensory integration studies and interpret them within the framework of a behavior-analytic approach. In
their description, they explain that research suggests that a large portion of the
human cortex is devoted to integration of information between sensory modalities,
particularly sound and vision, but also tactile information. Sensory integration can
be studied in infants using the habituation paradigm we explained earlier in this
chapter. In these sensory integration studies, 1-month-old human infants show differential responding in the presence of synchrony or asynchrony between seeing
and hearing the impact of an object on a hard surface (Bahrick, 1988, 2000).

PERCEPTUAL ABILITIES ●
AS UNIVERSAL BEHAVIORS

Basic perceptual abilities fit Horowitz's (1987) definition of universal behaviors.
They are hardwired responses to stimuli that all normal human infants

possess at birth. They are the result of the interaction of genetic and prenatal environmental variables. Most important, they enable us to learn from our environment even before the moment of birth.

● REFLEXES AS UNIVERSAL BEHAVIORS

We also enter this world with certain behaviors (or responses) that are made to certain events (or stimuli). We call these behaviors **reflexes.** They too are universal behaviors. All normal newborns possess these reflexes. These relationships between certain stimuli and certain responses are part of our genetic makeup. Table 4.3 lists the reflexes of the neonate.

Psychologists believe that natural selection has produced these reflexes that are common to our species. They reason that it is adaptive for the infant to possess these from birth. The alternative would be that we would have to learn these behaviors. This is a sobering thought . . . imagine a mother needing to teach her newborn to suck or to swallow to keep it alive. Fortunately, our inborn nature provides these functions for us.

Note that a reflex is not just the behavior. It is a relationship between an environmental event (the stimulus) and a behavior (the response). Because this behavior is unlearned (or unconditioned), we may look at it as an unconditioned response. Because the stimulus that causes it is also an unlearned relationship, we may call it an unconditioned stimulus. To recap, a reflex is a relationship between an unconditioned stimulus and an unconditioned response. Because the stimulus draws out or brings forth the **reflexive** response, we say the stimulus "elicits" the response. You can see the enormous number of environment-behavior relationships, called reflexes, with which the child enters the world. They form the initial repertoire of human behavior.

● HOW DO REFLEXES CHANGE?

The universal behaviors we call reflexes comprise most of the initial behaviors in the newborn's repertoire. At birth nearly all person-environment interactions are reflexive ones. Although they start us on the path of developmental change, reflexes themselves are very inflexible. Humans are characterized by their ability to change in relation to their environment, but reflexes are hardwired. They change very little over time. Reflexive behaviors may take four developmental paths.

Table 4.3 Neonatal Reflexes

Eyelid Responses		
Other activity (i.e., body movement)	Opening	
Touching the eye, lid, lashes, forehead, nose, etc	Closing	
Pupillary Responses		
Weak light	Pupil dilation	
Strong light	Constriction	
Strong stimulation of the skin	Pupils widen	
Ocular Responses		
Moving stimulus	Ryes follow	Pursuit
Approaching stimulus	Rotation of eyes	Saccadic
Cold (20 degrees C.), rotation of body	Rapid eye movement	Nystagmus
Face and Mouth Responses		
Touch stimuli around mouth	Opening	
Touch stimuli around mouth	Closing	
Tongue and jaw motions—tactile and taste stimuli; hunger	Sucking	
Bitter, salt, sour tastes, pricking of nose	Grimacing, twisting of face and mouth Yawning	
Bitter, salt, sour tastes rejected	Tongue pushing Licking	
Touch about mouth	Lip pursing	
Smells of ammonia	Sneezing Coughing	
Tongue stimulation, bitter tastes	Gagging Swallowing Hiccoughing Vomiting	
Head Responses		
Tactile stimulation of the side of the mouth	Turn in that direction	Rooting (or search)
Tactile stimuli to face or nose, touch on cheek, bright light away		Head turning
Bitter tastes	Head shudder Head balancing	
Hand and Arm Responses		
Tapping on shoulder blade		Radius reflex Scapulohumeral
	Contraction of arm and shoulder	

(Continued)

Table 4.3 Continued

Tactile stimulation to fingers or palm	Hand closes	Grasping
Sharp tap or pinprick to hand	Withdrawal	Flexion
Tickling stimuli to face, irritation of mucous membrane of nose, strong odors	Face rubbing Random movements	
Sudden strong stimulation	Outward flinging of hands and arms	Startle
Trunk Responses		
Nose pinching, being held upside down, crying, and stimulus producing dorsal head response	Back arching	
If chest held, pelvis twists in opposite direction of head	Trunk twists in same direction as head is rotated	Twisting
		Abdominal reflex
Sexual Responses		
Tactile stimulation of inner thigh	Raising of testes	
Foot and Leg Responses		
Pressing on the sole of the foot	Curling in of the toes	Plantar
Gently stroking the sole of the foot	Fanning back of the toes	Babinski
Tapping patellar tendon		Knee-jerk reflex Achilles tendon
Needle prick to foot or leg, pushing head down towards chest	Flexion of leg	
Gentle push sometimes strong enough to support baby's weight	Extension of leg	
Free foot kicks at other when other is restrained, leg is pinched	Kicking	
When held upright, feet touching surface	Stepping	
Coordinated Responses		
Body tickled stroked	Concave bending of side of body; leg on stroke side extends, contralateral leg flexes	Back bone reflex
If held horizontally in the air, when head is raised, rump rises too	Lifting head and rump	
When head is turned	Faced arm extends, other flexes faced leg extends other flexes	Fencing
If held upright	Inclined slightly forward, arms extend and legs are flexed	Springing
	Back arches, head arches back, leg extend, arms extend over head	Stretching

(Continued)

Table 4.3 Continued

Sudden loud noises, falling, sudden touches, sudden widespread change in temperature over surfaces of body, sudden blow to chest or abdomen, and also at random moments in absence of any obvious stimulus	Head thrown back, arms thrown apart from body, fingers extend and fan out, legs extend, crying inextreme cases	Startle response
In prone position	Arms and legs drawn in under body, head lifted; feet may push against traction, and arms will move too	Creeping
Urination	Shivering, trembling	
Pressing on palm when arms are raised	Mouth opens	Babkin

Reflexes May Stay the Same

Many reflexes remain virtually unchanged from birth. A puff of air still elicits an eye blink reflex, and a bright light elicits pupillary dilation across the life span.

Reflexes May Disappear

Many reflexes disappear over the first year of life. These include the moro, swimming, and Babinski reflexes. Let us look at these three. The moro reflex is elicited by stimulation of the balance organs in the middle ear, as occurs during a fall. The child first arches his back, next opens his arms, and then closes the arms in a grasping motion. The swimming reflex is elicited by cold water. The child holds his or her breath and makes basic swimming movements. The Babinski reflex is the fanning of the toes when the sole of the foot is lightly touched.

As other behaviors develop and physiological development of the brain proceeds, the cortex suppresses these subcortical responses, and they disappear during the first year. Therefore, when you fall (e.g., in an elevator) you do not respond with a moro reflex. In fact, the reappearance of these responses is used as clinical evidence of cortical damage.

Reflexes May Be Elicited by New Stimuli: Respondent Conditioning

As we interact with our environment, stimuli become associated with the stimuli that elicit reflexes. As this association continues, a new stimulus comes to elicit the response. For example, mom regularly talks to baby as she feeds him. The nipple elicits the sucking reflex, but soon baby is sucking to mom's voice, even before she gives him the nipple. This is a form of learning known as respondent conditioning. It is the topic of the next chapter.

Reflexes May be Elaborated Into New Behaviors: Operant Conditioning

Finally, behaviors elicited in the newborn may develop into behaviors that are sensitive to the changes they produce in their environment. For example, some crying may start as a reflex to pain, but it becomes crying that gets mother to pick up the child. This is what is called operant conditioning and is the topic of Chapter 6.

However, not all behavior develops from reflexes. Indeed, only a small percentage of human behavior originates in this way. Most behavior appears to develop through other principles of operant conditioning.

So at birth, a neonate senses its environment and responds to it in ways that will help it survive. From this excellent start, the child embarks on a journey involving an infinitely large number of reciprocal interactions with its environment. To understand the basic principles of this process, we must understand how learning occurs and how it relates to development.

● SUMMARY

The moment of conception crystallizes *genotype* and marks the advent of the interplay between the person and environment that characterizes the course of human development. Prenatal development is composed of the time between conception and the beginning of the process of birth.

The *prenatal period* consists of the *ovum, embryo,* and *fetal* periods. The period of the ovum is characterized by the differentiation of cells and implantation of the *blastocyst* into the lining of the uterus. This marks the end of the ovum period and beginning of the *embryonic period*. During the embryonic period, what was previously known as the blastocyst becomes the *trophoblast* and establishes the *placental barrier*. During the course of this period, other important organs develop out of the trophoblast. Also, the organism develops into the embryo and differentiates into three distinct layers: the *endoderm, mesoderm,* and *ectoderm,* from which the individual's organs will emerge. Once the basic structures are formed, the organism enters the period of the fetus, the longest period of prenatal development, marked by fetal growth and refinement of the organ systems.

Basic developmental principles are already at work during the prenatal period, including the *laws of developmental direction.* These are generalizations delineating the order in which characteristics will emerge. Taken together, the *cephalo-caudal, proximo-distal,* and *gross-fine laws* indicate that internal general features located near the head will emerge before refined parts of the lower extremities. These laws have important implications for the timing of events during development. For instance, *teratogens* (contaminants producing abnormalities commonly known as birth defects) present during the earliest prenatal stages, characterized by rapid growth and the advent of development of vital organs, are likely to have a much more devastating effect on the organism than if they are present during the latter part of the prenatal period, characterized by slower growth and refinement of preexisting organs. Exposure to teratogens in and of itself, however, does not determine outcomes. Instead, exposure holds the potential to provide a nonfacilitative environment where outcomes depend on the transactions between the organism and its environment. Some common factors that constitute teratogens include toxoplasmosis, cytomegalovirus, rubella, genital herpes, alcohol intake, cigarette smoking, and radiation. Other factors, such as maternal age and nutrition, also bear on developmental outcomes.

In assessing the effects of teratogens and nonfacilitative conditions on development, a dynamic transactional model seems better suited to account for development than a linear model. Such a model conceptualizes development in terms of probabilities based on the transactions between the environment and the organism.

The neonate emerges with the biological structures necessary to survive as well as the ability to interact with its new environment. Tests such as the Apgar and Brazelton Neonatal Behavioral Assessment Scale assess the newborn's adaptation and behavioral repertoire and neurological well-being, respectively. The ability the detect changes in the environment and the ability to behave or respond are necessary for adaptation. *Sensation* is the detection of the presence of stimuli. By virtue of our physical makeup alone, some aspects of the environment are sensed, whereas others are not. *Perception* is the integration of sensation and organized response.

The nature–nurture controversy is paralleled by the *nativism–empiricism* controversy in the field of perception. As in the nature–nurture controversy, it is impossible to make a determination as to whether perception is innate or the product of experience. Basic perceptual abilities are the result of the interaction between genetic and prenatal environmental factors that enable learning to occur. Methods of perceptual research and operant conditioning procedures have lent much to our understanding of infant perceptual and behavioral capacities, learning, and development.

The presence of *reflexes* substantiate that at least some of our behaviors are hardwired. They constitute the primary catalog of human behavior, characterizing nearly all person-environment transactions at birth. Over time, they may remain the same, disappear, come to be elicited by new stimuli (respondent conditioning), or become elaborated into new behaviors (operant conditioning). It is important to note, however, that the majority of behavior seems to be the result of other principles of operant conditioning.

● NOTE

1. A different way of dividing up the prenatal period is to use trimesters. The segments are based not on the functional or structural differences but by simply dividing the 9-month prenatal period into three equal segments. Thus, the first trimester is from 0 to 3 months, the second trimester is from 3 to 6 months, and the third trimester is from 6 months until birth. Although the trimester system is in common use, it does not at all correspond to the same as the germinal, embryonic, and fetal period. Indeed, the germinal and embryonic periods are completed and the fetal period begins all during the first trimester.

CHAPTER 5

LEARNING 1

Habituation and Respondent Learning

I n Chapter 1, we described how, for most behaviors, **learning** is the single most significant process in producing the changes we call **development**. Learning involves relatively permanent changes in behavior-environment relations due to experience. In this chapter, we look at three types of learning: habituation, respondent, and operant. The first two will be described in some detail in this chapter, but we devote all of Chapter 6 to operant learning because of its importance and its complexity. First, we start with some comments about the learning processes in general.

● LEARNING AS A NATURAL SELECTION PROCESS

Learning and natural selection are parallel processes, as noted earlier. In fact Hull, Langman, and Glenn (2001) offered selection as a general process that can be applied to biology, immunology, and learning, as well as to most other aspects of nature. Learning involves the contingencies in ontogenic development, whereas natural selection involves the contingencies in phylogenic development. Recently, it has been argued that selectionism is the basic process in ontogenic as well as phylogenic development (Donahoe, Burgos, & Palmer, 1993; Donahoe & Palmer, 1994). That is, learning functions as a type of natural selection too. The difference is that selection of an individual's behavior is made by contingencies that work directly on the individual during his or her lifetime.

Selectionism implies that there is no set complex plan but that processes occurring in nature can yield complexity in creatures and their behavior. Three processes that occur in nature are required for selectionism to function (Donahoe & Palmer, 1994): variation, selection, and retention.

Variation in Learned Behavior

Selection means choosing from among what already exists. If all items were exactly identical, only duplication would occur. For example, when you buy a car, you do not start with an unpainted one, mix the colors, and paint your own. Rather, you select from a range of colors that the manufacturer provides. Some manufacturers offer many possibilities; others offer few. There was a famous saying about the Model T Ford that "you can have any color you want . . . as long as it's black."

Variation is the rule in nature. In Chapter 3, we saw how enormous variation in genotype occurred. Thus, the process of natural selection has many possible genotypes from which to select those that produce phenotypes that best fit the demands of the environment. Variation is also the rule in behavior. Some behaviors are more variable than others. One reason we practice a skill such as a golf swing, a phrase in a foreign language, or a speech to be given in front of a class is to reduce variability in the forms of the behavior. We want the same behavior to occur with no variation. Even seemingly simple behaviors, such as walking and talking, have some variations. They do not occur precisely the same way each time. When behaviors first occur, they are likely to be the most variable.[1] Because this variation happens, it provides for the natural selection of behaviors that best fit the contingencies in the environment.

Selection in Learned Behavior

Once various options are available, there needs to be a process that results in a particular one being kept. In buying a car, you can call your sales adviser, fill out a form, or make a click online. In each case, one car of a particular color is selected, and the others are eliminated. In phylogenic selection, particular individuals survive because they have phenotypic characteristics that make them more capable in some ways; hence, those are the ones whose genes are available to produce offspring. They survive because they can better adapt to their environments than can others with other phenotypes. Because they can better compete for food, avoid physical destruction by predators or disease, and compete with others for mates, they survive. The environment "selects" those that best fit.

So, too, does the environment select behaviors that fit best. Some of these behaviors will be selected by the same contingencies that affect phylogenic development. The results are the universal perceptual and reflexive behaviors that have important adaptive significance for the species. Most human behavior patterns, however, are selected by the environment during ontogenic development, thus enabling the *individual* to adjust to varied and quickly changing environments in ways that the species as a whole cannot.

In the case of phylogenic development, selection occurs specieswide. Selection occurs within the individual in the case of ontogenic development. When structures or behaviors are selected by the environment, the variations that then arise range around the one newly selected.

Retention of Learned Behavior

There must be a way to keep the changes that have been selected by the environment so that changes are not lost. In phylogenic development, changes are retained in the genes. There is still much debate over the retention mechanisms for ontogenic development and learning. Although it is generally assumed that the brain is the major organ responsible for retention in learning, so far, it is unclear exactly how specific brain structures and functions are involved. The identification of the retention mechanisms for learning will be the result of future research.

Still, this does not mean that the functional characteristics of learning and its retention cannot be studied without identifying the underlying physical structures. Clear functional relations can be established between environmental events and long-term changes in behavior. Learning will best be facilitated through environmental adjustments rather than through measures that focus directly on the underlying physiology, even if or when the latter is well understood. Consider the futility of trying to specify, in physiological terms, a day care arrangement that would nurture children's cooperative behavior. The environmental elements to accomplish that would be much easier to identify.

Learning as Relations Between Behavior Patterns and Environmental Events

Remember our definition of *development:* Progressive changes in the interactions between a person and his or her environment. This definition is consistent with the role of learning in development. We should use new terms, however—technical terms—to describe what changes in learning. To analyze at the level of basic processes, we need to be more precise about the person and the environment. Specifically, we will focus on what the person does and how that relates to the environmental events that precede or follow. Behavior includes all the actions or changes that individuals do. Snapping your fingers, walking, talking, whispering, and writing a letter are all behaviors Although they are covert and thus difficult to study, imagining a sunset and thinking about what you will do tomorrow are also activities and thus constitute behavior patterns. In contrast, actions, by their nature, are overt. The overt–covert distinction does not prevent both from being instances of behavior, for the feature of privacy is a relation between the behavior and the observer and does not imply a difference-in-kind, such as mental versus physical.

Are thoughts appropriate phenomena for those studying behavior? In a word, yes. As early as 1953, Skinner (1953) wrote about the role of thoughts in natural science. He referred to thoughts as private events. That is, they are like other behaviors of an individual, such as walking or talking, but unlike these public events, thoughts are observable only to the individual producing them. They are internal responses. This may make them difficult to objectify, but they are behaviors and, as such, are governed by the same basic principles that affect all behaviors. The main difference is that they occur inside the skin and are therefore private, not public.

In analyzing the environment, we talk in terms of stimuli. A **stimulus** is an environmental change or event. A flash of light, a ringing bell, the letter A: These are all environmental events or stimuli. In looking at the environment, we can identify countless stimuli. Normally, however, we are interested only in those aspects of the environment that have a **functional relationship** to behavior. That is, we are most interested in stimuli that actually have an effect on the context of behavior. (Peláez-Nogueras & Gewirtz, 1997).

CLASSIFYING STIMULI ●

We can categorize stimuli in a number of ways. A common way is to classify stimuli based on their physical characteristics; this is a structural approach. The classes are based on what the stimuli look like, not what they do. Bijou and Baer (1978) identified four physical stimulus classes:

1. *Physical:* Objects and natural phenomena (e.g., tools, furniture, plants, trees)

2. *Chemical:* Gases that have an effect at a distance (e.g., the aroma of roast turkey, perfume, smoke); liquid solutions in contact with the skin (e.g., water, soap)

3. *Organismic:* The organism's own biological structure (e.g., stimulation from breathing and digestive processes, kinesthetic and proprioceptive stimulation)

4. *Social:* The appearance, action, and interaction of people and animals

● FUNCTIONAL STIMULUS CLASSES

Although physical classifications are a common way to look at stimuli, in psychology, it is more important to identify the **functional stimulus classes.** The function of a stimulus is the effect it has on behavior. We exist in a sea of stimuli. Not all stimuli have an effect on (or a function for) our behaviors. Many stimuli in the environment are outside the limits of our abilities to sense them. A dog whistle may have a function for Fido, but its pitch is too high for most people to be affected by it. A nearsighted person may not respond to a stimulus that a person with 20/20 vision would. Other functions are the result of our developmental history. If you grow up in the United States, the French word *sortie* (the word for "exit") may not have an effect on your behavior. So although we may analyze the environment as composed of an infinite number of stimuli, in behavioral psychology we are concerned only with the functional environment affecting the behavior and development of individuals. That is, we are concerned with those events in the environment that actually have a function for our behavior. Although still large, the number of possible functional events is limited and consists of stimuli that function universally (i.e., for all humans) and those that are unique to each individual.

● TYPES OF LEARNING

In this chapter, we look at three types of learning. The first two, *habituation* and *respondent learning,* are specific to behaviors called reflexes. The third is called *operant* learning and is the primary process in producing **instrumental behaviors,** which make up the largest class of human behaviors. We start with the simplest learning process—habituation.

● HABITUATION

Consider the following story: In an attempt to discourage a pesky crow from eating her crop, Farmer Joan decided to install a loudspeaker system in her fields and broadcast the sound of a shotgun blast at regular intervals. At first, this tactic successfully scared the bird and it flew off, only to return much later. After repeated shots, however, the bird failed to respond at all. Expressed in the technical language of the behavioral sciences, the bird's flight response habituated to the auditory stimulus produced by the speaker system. As generally defined (e.g., Fantino & Logan, 1979; Jeffrey & Cohen, 1971), **habituation** is a decrease or elimination of response to a particular stimulus as a result of repetitive presentations of that stimulus. So when the sound of the shotgun blast was repeated several times, the bird stopped responding.

Nonhuman Studies

There is an extensive history of research reporting habituation in nonhumans, including spiders (e.g., Peckham & Peckham, 1887), rats (e.g., Prosser & Hunter, 1936), and cats (e.g., Sharpless & Jasper, 1956). For example, Crampton and Lucot (1991) exposed cats to a "motion sickness" stimulus, which initially **elicited** a retching response. With repeated exposure to the stimulus, there was a pronounced decrease in the incidence of retching, which suggested habituation. Habituation has also been demonstrated in a large variety of other species, including frogs, birds, earthworms, and squirrel monkeys (Catania, 1984).

Infant Studies

In a study conducted around 1950 in the Soviet Union, Bronshtein and Petrova (1967) found that nonnutritive sucking habituated to the repeated presentations of each of a variety of auditory stimuli (e.g., a whistle, a harmonica) in neonates as well as in older infants. In a classic U.S. study, Bridger (1961) reported the habituation of both accelerated heart rate and startle response to auditory stimulation in neonates. Subsequent research demonstrated habituation in infants not only to auditory stimuli but to visual and olfactory stimuli as well (see Jeffrey & Cohen, 1971). Furthermore, habituation has been demonstrated with fetuses as well. For example, Madison, Madison, and Adubato (1986) applied vibrating stimuli to the abdomens of women between 28 and 37 weeks pregnant. After repeated presentations, fetal movements habituated.

Defining Characteristics of Habituation

The previously cited definition of habituation identified two necessary conditions: (a) There must be a decrement in responding; (b) this decrement must follow the repeated presentations of a particular stimulus. To distinguish habituation from related behavioral phenomena, however, additional conditions must be met. A third necessary condition is that it applies only to those stimulus-response relations commonly called *reflexes* (Catania, 1998). As we saw earlier, a reflex is an automatic and unlearned relation between narrowly defined stimulus and response (S–R) classes. However, whereas reflexive S–R relations do not require any prior experience with the stimulus, the waning of reflexive responding characteristic of habituation does require that the organism experience repeated presentations of the stimulus. In short, although reflexes are unlearned, the habituation of reflexive responding is a type of learning.

A fourth necessary condition for habituation is that the decrement in responding must not be the product of other processes such as satiation or fatigue. For example, an infant's rate of drinking decreases as the baby becomes satiated. This is not a result of habituation, however, but a result of physiological processes accompanying ingestion of water. Unlike the infant exhibiting habituated responding, the satiated infant is unresponsive not to a particular food-related stimulus but to food-related stimuli in general. Similarly, a response decrement that is the result of muscle fatigue is not an example of habituation. The fatigued muscle is unresponsive to all stimuli that normally elicit its contraction, not just to a particular stimulus (Fantino & Logan, 1979).

How then do you distinguish habituation from these other types of decreased responding? Jeffrey and Cohen (1971) suggested a procedure that has come to be widely used: Present an infant with a novel stimulus from the same sensory modality as the habituated stimulus. If the infant's response returns to its earlier level, the response decrement was probably habituation; if it does not, the response decrement was probably the product of another process. For example, if you repeatedly clap your hands in the presence of an infant, his or her orienting response to that auditory stimulus will decrease. If you then ring a bell in the infant's presence and he or she orients to the sound, the response decrement following repeated hand clapping was probably habituation.

In summary, there are four necessary conditions for habituation:

1. There must be a decrement in responding.

2. This decrement must follow the repeated presentations of a particular stimulus.

3. The initial S–R relation must be a reflex.

4. The decrement in responding must not be the product of other processes, such as satiation or muscle fatigue.

These four necessary conditions, taken together, constitute a sufficient condition for habituation.

Why Study Habituation?

There are two principle reasons why those interested in child development should study habituation. First, habituation is a form of learning that plays a critical role during a child's life. As William James (1890) put it, the child is exposed daily to a "buzzing, blooming confusion" of stimuli. The ability to stop responding to some stimuli while continuing to respond to others has implications for long-term survival. For example, a nursing infant is likely to stop feeding when exposed to a loud auditory stimulus. After repeated presentations of this stimulus, however, the infant's orienting response habituates; the baby no longer stops feeding when it hears the sound. As Fantino and Logan (1979) expressed it, "The organism that continues to respond to an innocuous stimulus is wasting valuable time and energy engaging in uneconomical behavior" (p. 41).

Second, habituation needs to be understood by students of child development because of the role it frequently plays in infant studies, as we discussed in Chapter 4. For example, the fact that an infant has habituated to a particular stimulus is useful as a way of determining whether the infant recognizes or remembers a stimulus. Researchers have indeed used habituation to determine whether infants recognize or remember particular faces. Similarly, if an infant has habituated to a stimulus and then is presented with both it and a novel stimulus, the fact that it responds only to the novel stimulus is taken as evidence that it can discriminate between the two stimuli.

CONTIGUITY AND LEARNING ●

Contiguity is a very important process for learning because it strongly affects learning by association (Baum, 1973). The principle of contiguity states that whenever two or more events that produce sensations occur together often enough (either in time or space), they will become associated by the observer. After several occasions of being contiguous, whenever only one of these events (a stimulus) occurs, the other will be experienced (or remembered), too (by the observer responding to it) (Gallistel, 1980). Have you noticed that after a young child has learned to sing the alphabet letters, if one sings "a, b, c," the next sound that automatically comes to the child is "d"? They have heard those letters together many times. Contiguity plays a major role in the associative learning processes of respondent (classical) and **operant conditioning**.

● RESPONDENT LEARNING

Respondent learning is also called **classical conditioning** or **Pavlovian conditioning**. This type of learning focuses on the learning of reflexes or so-called involuntary physiological responses, such as those involved in fear: faster heartbeat, pupillary constriction, and galvanic skin response (sweating of the palms), which are often called **respondents.** They are automatically triggered by stimuli in the environment. Through this process of classical conditioning, humans and animals can learn to respond or react to a stimulus that was originally neutral and had no effect.

Consider again the story of Farmer Joan. While she was busy trying to keep the crow from feeding in her fields, her 2-year-old daughter, Jenny, conducted her own training program with a bird of another feather. On a number of occasions when her mother was outside, Jenny used a large spoon to strike the cage of the family's pet parakeet, Frankie. Frankie responded to these disturbances by excitedly flapping her wings in an attempt to escape. As a consequence, whenever anyone with a spoon in hand now comes within close proximity of the cage, Frankie flaps her wings in a similar fashion. Frankie has been conditioned to fear spoons.

In the earlier discussion of habituation, unlearned S–R relations, such as a bird's fear response to auditory stimulation, were identified as reflexes. However, because this term has a number of popular meanings, it lacks the precision necessary for scientific discourse. Therefore, *reflex* will now be replaced with the more precise term: *respondent.* Respondent S–R relations in humans include increased illumination eliciting pupillary constriction, a loud sound eliciting the eye blink, and a frightening stimulus eliciting an increase in heart rate. What then is respondent learning?

In a respondent S–R relation, the stimulus is termed the **unconditioned stimulus** (UCS) and the response, the **unconditioned response** (UCR). Note that conditioning is a synonym for learning. Therefore, unconditioned means unlearned. In our example involving Frankie, the UCS is the loud noise and vibration produced by the spoon, and the UCR is the flapping of wings and other related behaviors. Prior to Jenny banging the cage numerous times with the spoon, the presence of a spoon was a **neutral stimulus** (NS). It did not elicit the flapping of wings. As a result of Jenny pairing presentations of the UCS (the noise and vibrations produced by the spoon) with presentations of the NS (the spoon), however, the spoon is no longer a neutral stimulus. It is now a **conditioned stimulus** (CS), and the response it elicits (the flapping of wings, etc.) a **conditioned response** (CR). Frankie has learned to respond in a new way to the presence of spoons. The relation between the presentation of a spoon and the behavior of wing flapping is a conditioned respondent relation.

Discovery of Respondent Conditioning Through Animal Studies

Does the name Pavlov ring a bell? Ivan Pavlov was a Russian physiologist at the turn of the 20th century who received the Nobel Prize for his study of the physiology of digestion. As notable as that achievement was, however, Pavlov is best remembered for his discovery of the importance of respondent learning, also known as classical or Pavlovian conditioning, as has been mentioned.[2] During his research, trying to determine how long it took a dog to secrete digestive juices after it had been fed, Pavlov noted that the dogs would begin to salivate when they saw the person who normally brought them their food. He hypothesized that the dogs had somehow associated the sight of the attendant with the presence of food in their mouths. Pavlov tested this hypothesis by ringing a bell immediately before feeding the dogs. Following several bell–food pairings, Pavlov presented the sound of the bell alone. The dogs salivated. In technical terms, the presence of food in the mouth was the UCS, and salivation was the UCR. Before conducting the experiment, the bell was an NS. However, after pairings of the food presentation with the bell, the previously neutral sound of the bell became a CS eliciting the CR (salivation).

Since Pavlov's time, there have been many studies investigating respondent learning with nonhumans. For example, Harlow (1959) trained infant rhesus monkeys by pairing presentation of a tone (the NS) with an electric shock (the UCS). After completion of training, the presentation of the tone alone elicited movement. In an experiment with newborn albino rats, Caldwell and Werboff (1962) paired the presentation of a vibrotactile stimulus (the NS) with an electric shock (the UCS) to the forelimb. After a number of such pairings, the vibrotactile stimulus alone (now the CS) elicited movement (the CR).

Infant Studies on Respondent Learning

The case of Little Albert is the most famous respondent learning experiment involving an infant. During the initial stage of their classic experiment, Watson and Rayner (1920) presented a friendly white rat to their subject, 11-month-old Albert (see Figure 5.1). Albert approached the rat and played with it. During the next stage of the experiment, a loud noise (produced by striking a

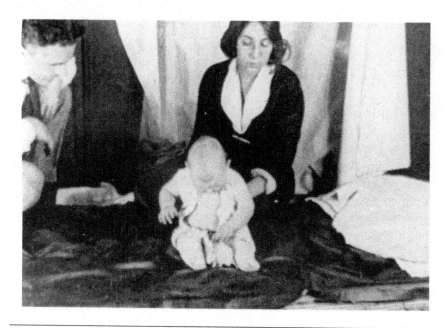

Figure 5.1   Little Albert With J. B. Watson and R. Rayner

metal rod with a hammer) was paired with presentation of the rat. The loud noise elicited crying.

Eventually, the presence of the rat alone elicited crying. Furthermore, other similar objects (e.g., cat, fur coat, Santa Claus mask) reportedly also elicited crying (see Novak, 1990).

Additional respondent learning experiments have been conducted with fetuses (e.g., Ray, 1932; Spelt, 1948) and infants (e.g., Kolata, 1987; Levin & Kaye, 1964). For example, Spelt (1948) paired a loud clapper (UCS) with vibrotactile stimulation (the NS) in an experiment with fetuses between 7 and 9 months of gestation. Eventually, the vibrotactile stimulus became a CS, eliciting fetal movements. Lipsitt and Kaye (1964) paired presentation of a tone with the insertion of a nipple in the mouths of newborns 3 or 4 days old. Eventually, the presentation of the tone alone elicited a sucking response.

Defining Characteristics of Respondent Learning

Three necessary conditions for **respondent conditioning** have been identified: First, the initial S–R relation must be an unlearned, automatic, respondent relation—a UCS–UCR reflex. Second, the UCS must be paired with an NS. Third, presentations of the CS alone must elicit the response. A fourth necessary condition is that the response must not be the product of other processes, such as sensitization. In sensitization, presentation of the UCS alone might stimulate the infant to respond to the previously neutral stimulus. In this case, the capacity of the previously neutral stimulus to elicit the response is not the product of pairing the UCS with the NS; rather, it is the result of simply presenting the UCS, thereby sensitizing the infant to many other previously neutral stimuli. One way to distinguish respondent learning from sensitization is to use a control group that is presented with the UCS alone and not paired with the NS. If the previously neutral stimulus fails to elicit the CR in the control group but does elicit the CR in the experimental group (i.e., the group trained with UCS–NS pairings), it is likely that the experimental group exhibits respondent learning and not sensitization.

Generalization

When a conditioned response is established, the CR is elicited not only by the CS but by other stimuli that are similar to the CS. For example, in the Little Albert study, Albert showed fear not only in response to the rat but also to a rabbit, cotton wool, and even Watson's hair. **Generalization** explains how new stimuli not directly present can come to elicit conditioned responses. Our fears are often the result of generalization after respondent conditioning to a stimulus. For example, a child may fear a teacher because she yells at him or her. The teacher has become a CS that elicits fear. Because other teachers resemble the first, they, too, come to elicit the same fear response.

Discrimination

Discrimination is demonstrated by the *lack* of a response to other stimuli similar to that involved in the original conditioning. At some point in his research, Pavlov was also able to teach dogs discrimination—to salivate to one tone but not to others that were similar. In his experimental preparations, he and his students ensured that the food always followed one tone and not any other. In the Watson and Rayner (1920) study of Little Albert, wooden blocks did not elicit a CR, only a metal rod did. Albert showed respondent discrimination to the blocks.

Respondent Extinction

The defining characteristic of **respondent extinction** is that the CS no longer elicits a CR. The CS has returned to serving as an NS. If a CS is created by the pairing of an NS with a UCS, extinction is brought about by presenting the CS without the UCS. Many CS-alone presentations may be necessary to produce **extinction**. When a particular tone is presented repeatedly, but it is not followed by the unconditioned stimulus (e.g., food), extinction occurs.

At first blush, respondent extinction may appear to be the same as habituation because, in both cases, the response to the stimulus decreases. Note, however, that the stimulus that loses its power to elicit the response is different in habituation and respondent extinction. In habituation, we stop responding to the UCS. In respondent extinction, we stop responding to the CS. In extinction, the stimulus ceases to function as a CS and functions as an NS again.

Why Study Respondent Learning?

Students of child development should study respondent learning for a number of reasons. First, like habituation, respondent learning plays a critical role in helping the child successfully adapt to the environment. Some common examples may be a child who fearfully avoids a dog that has bitten it or a child opening its mouth in the presence of food. Both examples show the child behaving in ways that enhance its chances of surviving. We can help individuals to risk anxiety-producing situations voluntarily and successfully by respondent training. For example, we can use desensitization with a student who is afraid and anxious of speaking in front of the class, starting with a very small audience and using some notes and then gradually increasing the class size and ultimately eliminating the notes. These and many other adaptive responses are products of respondent learning.

Second, the process of respondent learning helps explain the wide variety of emotional responses a child makes to the world. Consider a young boy who has been strongly admonished by his father for going outside without his pants. Months or years later, that same boy may blush (an emotional reflex) when he discovers that his pants are unzipped (Bijou & Baer, 1978). Many instances in which we cry, become fearful, anxious, hungry, or become sexually aroused can be trained and reversed in terms of respondent conditioning.

Box 5.1 Can Respondent Conditioning Help Infants Develop New Food Preferences?

Research has demonstrated that newborns are capable of showing preferential responding to distinct tastes and food-related odors. It is not clear, however, whether infants are also capable of responding to distinct food textures. It has been suggested that a history of respondent conditioning may affect these infant preferences.

A study was done to determine if food texture preferences differ during two developmental periods—infancy and toddlerhood—and whether experience with textures influenced infants' food preferences (Lundy et al., 1999). In the research, infants displayed more negative expressions, negative head movements, and negative body movements when presented with more complex textures of food. In contrast, toddlers showed more positive head and body movements and more eagerness for complex textures. The data also suggested that pairing difficult-to-chew textures with more preferred ones can facilitate a preference in infants for the complex textures.

In addition, infants with medical disorders are sometimes placed on special diets that taste pretty terrible. The result is that they refuse to eat the food that has the needed medication added. Although it is usually possible to get older children to eat these diets by convincing them that it is good for them, this option is not available with infants.

Coyle, Arnold, Goldberg-Arnold, Rubin, and Hall (2000) tried to see if they could use infants' responsiveness to smells to respondently condition a smell associated with a preferred food (formula) to a nonpreferred food (water). After measuring baseline rates of sucking the formula and water to establish the preferred and nonpreferred stimuli, the researchers paired the formula bottle with a smell by soaking a small ring in one of two distinctive odors, vanilla or strawberry. In the conditioning phase, one of the rings was placed around the base of the nipple on a bottle containing the preferred formula and the child was allowed to establish the smell (NS)–food (UCS) relationship. That is, every time the child sucked, the smell on the ring was paired with the taste of the preferred food. For half of the infants, vanilla was the olfactory stimulus paired with formula and for the other half, strawberry fragrance was paired with food.

To test that these odors were neutral stimuli, the nonpaired odor was then placed over the nipple on a bottle filled with water. Consumption of water actually dropped by about one-third with this novel olfactory stimulus. When the odor associated with the formula was placed on the bottle filled with water, however, sucking and water consumption increased dramatically. Thus, the research suggests that a previously neutral stimulus, an odor, became a conditioned stimulus for these infants.

This pairing of smells with taste is a frequently occurring natural relationship in the lives of all humans. It is responsible for the elicitation of pleasant feelings (and some saliva) when the smell of warm chocolate chip cookies comes wafting from the oven. It is also the basis of the not-so-pleasant feelings of nausea if a particular food smell has become paired with a food that has made us ill to our stomachs. Such respondent pairing has been implicated in the aversion reactions that some patients experience, elicited by the stimuli associated with chemotherapy.

Advertisers and political handlers have long known that they can influence the ability of products or politicians to elicit pleasant responses by pairing them with stimuli eliciting pleasant responses. Sometimes, even mildly unlikable things become palatable through conditioning procedures. Coyle et al. (2000) suggest that by pairing odors with good-tasting, preferred diets, the odors can become conditioned stimuli that can be used to make unpleasant substances become more pleasant, and infants who need unpleasant medication can take it more easily.

At this point, let us examine more closely some important aspects of respondent conditioning.

Types of Behaviors

As we have noted, a defining characteristic of respondent behavior is that it involves reflexive behaviors.[3] However, are the UCR and the CR the same response, differing only in terms of the stimuli that elicit them? The answer is no. In most cases, the CR will be at least slightly different from the UCR. For example, the arousal produced by a conditioned stimulus (e.g., a white rat) may be lower than that produced by an unconditioned stimulus (e.g., a loud noise). Unless we are careful in our observations, however, the behaviors may appear topographically identical.

What Factors Influence Respondent Learning?

Are We Biologically Prepared to Learn?

Organisms may be prepared by phylogeny to behave in the same way as their ancestors, but they are also prepared to start learning right away, even pre-natally (DeCasper & Spence, 1986; Johanson & Hall, 1979). A variety of behavior is available before learning occurs, and it comes in many forms (Gallistel, 1980): for example, the beating of the heart, the kinesthetic responses and maintenance of balance, and the innate reflexes discussed in Chapter 4. We are born prepared to like or dislike certain stimuli or foods, and thus some stimulus–response relations are easier to establish than others are. Many of us have had the experience of eating something like a hot dog or baloney sandwich and then getting sick to our stomachs. Although the food may have nothing to do with the illness, it is likely that we will make this association. As Catania (1998) suggests, this propensity for associating taste NS with illness UCS may be one reason why cancer patients receiving radiation therapy lose much of their appetites. So although the radiation is the actual cause of the illness, we are much more prepared to attribute the illness to the food we eat. Revusky and Garcia (1970), in conducting experiments on taste aversion, found that a rat stops eating a particular food if it later became sick. Nausea and illness may be associated with the taste of certain foods.

Forward, Trace, and Backward Conditioning

Must the neutral stimulus precede the UCS, or can the UCS come first for respondent conditioning to be successful? Is it more effective for the NS to remain with the UCS present, or is it better that the NS end before onset of the UCS? These are some questions regarding the order of presentation of the stimuli.

First, the order of stimulus presentations seems important. The most effective conditioning occurs when onset of the NS precedes the UCS and terminates either with onset of the UCS or remains present for a time, along with the UCS. This procedure is called **delayed conditioning** (Klein, 1987) or forward conditioning. Delayed conditioning is used in the following example: A nipple on a bottle is a UCS, which elicits sucking (the UCR) in an infant. This is the sucking reflex. Engen, Lipsitt, and Kaye (1963) preceded the onset of the UCS with the onset of a tone (NS). With repeated presentations, the tone alone elicited sucking, demonstrating that the tone had become a CS because it elicited a CR, the sucking to the tone.

Such anticipatory sucking can frequently be observed outside the laboratory. Because mothers often talk to their infants prior to feeding them, a mother's voice often becomes a CS, eliciting sucking even before the nipple is placed in the child's mouth.

A second type of sequence is called **trace conditioning** (Klein, 1987). In this procedure, the NS also precedes the UCS, but the NS is terminated before the onset of the UCS. For example, the mother would stop talking before placing the nipple in the baby's mouth. This procedure produces weaker conditioning than delayed conditioning, particularly if the gap between the end of the NS and onset of the UCS is long.

A third sequence is called **backward conditioning** (Klein, 1987). In this procedure, the UCS precedes the NS. In our example, this would mean that the mother would place the nipple in the infant's mouth and then begin to speak. This is the least effective of the three procedures. The implication is that respondent conditioning is more likely to occur when a neutral stimulus precedes and remains present with the onset of an unconditioned stimulus.

NS–UCS Interval

Is there an *optimal interval* of time that the NS should precede the UCS? We noted that in trace conditioning, a long delay between the NS and UCS will be less effective. Indeed, it is unlikely that an association will be made between a threat (NS) and a spanking (UCS) if the spanking occurs the following day. Too long or too short a latency between NS onset and UCS onset will also inhibit the formation of a CR (Smith & Moore, 1966). One-half second seems to be optimal in adults (Kimble, 1961).

Intensity of the UCS

The *intensity* or magnitude of the unconditioned stimulus affects the development of a conditioned stimulus. Generally speaking, an intense UCS (e.g., loud sound, bright light) will lead to easier conditioning within fewer trials. Highly intense stimuli may produce **one-trial conditioning,** as when fear of an object may be produced by a stimulus that elicits an intense emotional response. Many phobias are the result of such brief, intense exposures.

Respondent conditioning is limited to the class of behaviors that originate as reflexes. As such, they are limited to responses that have a strong phylogenic basis. However, the simple learning that occurs in respondent conditioning extends the functioning of these responses to a wider range of ontogenic stimuli. Of special interest is the development of some of our emotional reactions to the world around us. However, most human behavior is not limited to respondents; new behaviors are acquired in a different manner. We shall examine this important developmental process later in this chapter and the next, when we look at operant learning.

● THE TREATMENT OF FEARS AND PHOBIAS: AN APPLICATION OF RESPONDENT LEARNING

Children's Fears

Children learn to fear animals, doctors, darkness, strangers, heights, and the like because they associate these objects or events with aversive

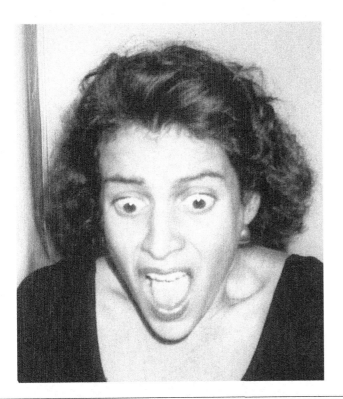

Figure 5.2   A Mother's "Fearful" Face

unconditioned stimuli, such as pain or a sudden loud sound (e.g., thunder). *Fears* can be acquired via both respondent and operant conditioning (Peláez–Nogueros & Gewirtz, 1997). In this section, we will concentrate only on the respondent type of fears. In the next chapter, we will discuss how fears can result from operant learning, where infants learn the meaning of a facial expression of emotions like a "fearful"or "joyful" face (see Figures 5.2 and 5.3).

As we discussed earlier, Watson and Rayner's (1920) classic study with Little Albert is the most famous illustration of the conditioning of fearful responses in infants. A few years later, Watson and another associate, Mary Cover Jones (1924), conducted a study with a 3-year-old, Peter, to countercondition fear.

Counterconditioning

In **counterconditioning,** the conditioned stimulus is paired with an unconditioned stimulus that elicits a response opposite (or counter) to the

Figure 5.3   A Mother's "Joyful" Face

conditioned response. Thus, a new conditioned response is established to counter the original. Mary Cover Jones, a student of Watson's, first reported this procedure in 1924. Jones reported the case of Peter, who exhibited a fear of rabbits (that should be easy to remember). In her study, Jones gave Peter candy to eat and then introduced a rabbit while Peter was eating the candy. This pairing of candy and rabbit led to the rapid elimination of Peter's fear of rabbits.

Her procedure also involved presenting the CS (the rabbit) gradually and repetitively, in a careful way that would not elicit the fear response but would instead elicit a competing (replacement) emotional response (eating). At each session, the stimulus was moved closer and closer while Peter was eating his lunch, until the rabbit no longer triggered a negative emotional reaction.

Many studies followed this classic intervention, and clinical psychologists use a very similar type of fear reduction counterconditioning today. This is considered a form of behavior modification and cognitive behavior therapy to treat school and animal phobias. In the next chapter, we will explain how operant conditioning combined with replacement techniques can explain and reduce infant fear of darkness and strangers.

Extinction

Counterconditioning involves a new conditioning procedure, in which the CS that was paired with the feared stimulus is now intentionally paired with stimuli associated with stimuli evoking pleasant responses. A different method relies on the extinction procedure described above, where the CS is presented repeatedly by itself. This method is called systematic desensitization and is the most frequently used method for the treatment of fears and phobias.

Systematic Desensitization

One impediment to the extinction of some conditioned responses, particularly emotional ones, is that the conditioned emotional response is also accompanied by escape behavior, such as running away or closing the eyes. When this behavior occurs, the child does not experience the CS without the UCS, and extinction will not occur. Psychologists treating the intense fears known as phobias have developed some specialized procedures to reduce the intensity of the conditioned emotional response and to reduce escape behaviors. Counterconditioning addresses this problem by the active pairing of the CS with stimuli such as candy that elicit pleasant, not fearful, responses.

In **systematic desensitization**, avoidance is addressed by creating a hierarchy of stimuli, ranking the intensity of the fear produced by each stimulus from most to least. That is, a child with a fear of dogs may be terrified of petting a snarling pit bull and only a bit uneasy watching Disney's animated film *Lady and the Tramp* (although *101 Dalmatians* may be a bit too intense). The child would be allowed to watch the film without escaping until the film elicited no emotional response at all. Extinction of this first stimulus would make successful desensitization (another term for extinction) to the next stimulus possible. Thus, the child would be presented the second stimulus on his or her hierarchy until it could be presented without eliciting an emotional response. Successive stimuli on the hierarchy would be presented until the child's response to the last stimulus (the snarling pit bull) is also desensitized (i.e., extinguished).

● OPERANT LEARNING

We have seen how environment-behavior relationships change in two ways. First, repeated presentation of a stimulus leading to cessation of a response is known as habituation. In the second type of change, the response came to be elicited by a new stimulus; this is respondent learning. Both relationships were concerned with a small class of behaviors called reflexes that are elicited by a preceding stimulus. No new responses developed, only changes in the relationship of existing reflexes to stimuli. Although these are significant adaptations, they do not begin to account for the major changes in development brought about by the environment. To understand how most voluntary behaviors are learned we must understand the principles of operant learning.

What Is Operant Behavior?

Operant learning involves changes in **operant behaviors,** or simply "operants." Skinner (1938) chose the term **operant** because it connotes a key feature of this type of behavior: It is behavior that operates on the environment and thereby affects it. These effects on the environment determine the operant's frequency and define it. On the other hand, it is the preceding stimuli that determine the frequency of respondent behavior and, coupled with the relatively fixed form of the response, define it. For example, the operant *cleaning* is defined in terms of its effects on the environment. If you are cleaning your eyeglasses, the behavior has the effect of making the world clearer. Furthermore, if the cleaning removes smudges from the lenses, you are more likely to engage in cleaning behavior in the future. However, if the cleaning has the effect of scratching the lenses, you are less likely to engage in that behavior in the future.

Consider now the respondent behavior of pupillary constriction. The number of times your pupil constricts is determined by the number of times a preceding light stimulus (e.g., a flashlight) stimulates your pupil; its frequency is not determined by any effects on the environment the response may have. That is, your pupil will constrict regardless of the **consequences** of the behavior. Furthermore, we define the respondent, the pupillary constriction, in terms of the eliciting stimulus (i.e., the light) and the relatively fixed form of the response, not in terms of the constriction.

Although the occurrence of operant behavior can be affected by antecedent stimuli, it is not elicited in the manner of a reflex. Unlike respondent behavior, operant behavior is **emitted** in an environment but not elicited by any stimulus in that environment. For example, a newborn stretches out its arms, touching objects, some of which make a noise when touched. This behavior is not elicited by any specific stimulus; it just occurs (or is emitted) and is strengthened by the sounds the behavior produces. As we shall see later, however, operant behavior comes to be **evoked** by a preceding stimulus, as when the child learns to reach for specific objects, such as rattles, because of the sounds they produce.

Although we have been considering operants and respondents as independent, there are many operant–respondent relationships. In some cases, operants may originate as reflexes. For example, crying may begin as one of three types of reflexive cries elicited by hunger, anger, or pain stimuli (Wolff, 1966). Respondent crying may become operant crying, however. For example, a child initially cries in response to pain or hunger; when she cries and receives attention or when she cries and gets to stay up late, however, she is engaging in operant crying. What follows crying (i.e., attention or staying up) is what determines the crying in these cases, not some unconditioned or conditioned stimulus.

Although some operant behaviors are elaborations of respondents, most are not. Instead, most operant behaviors originate as emitted responses. They are strengthened or weakened by environmental consequences. In some cases, the consequences may function universally to strengthen the behaviors they follow. For example, in newborns the presentation of milk or skin contact with the mother strengthens the behaviors they follow. Other consequences are unique to individuals in terms of the strengthening or weakening effects they have on the behaviors they follow. As we develop, some consequences strengthen behaviors for some of us, whereas, for others, those same consequences may have neutral or even weakening effects. For example, a health-conscious athlete may find the consumption of brewer's yeast following exercise increases the likelihood that he or she will exercise in the future, whereas the couch potato may find that its consumption weakens any behavior it follows (e.g., opening up the jar!). For still others, it has no effect on the behaviors it follows. Consequences determine the occurrence of operant behavior. We adapt to our environments as we learn behaviors that produce strengthening consequences.

RESPONSE CLASSES AND OPERANTS ●

In behavior analysis, it is not useful to treat every individual occurrence or instance of a response as a different response (Skinner, 1935). For example, every unit of crying behavior should not be treated as a different response. Skinner defined **response classes** instead, where each instance or unit would be considered a member of that class if it is maintained by or holds a functional relation with the same class of consequent stimuli. Skinner defined the response classes as functional units, to avoid finding or looking for topographical or structural features to define each response class. Notice that when individual component responses are controlled by the same type of consequences and context, they form part of the same response class. So if crying occurs in the same context with the same controlling consequences, then that crying should be considered instances of the same response class. In the next chapter, we will come back to this topic.

● HOW DO OPERANTS AND RESPONDENTS DIFFER?

The distinction between operant and respondent behaviors is based on four characteristics:

1. Operants are emitted; respondents are elicited.

2. Operants, once emitted, continue to occur or not occur because of their consequences; respondents occur because of their antecedent stimuli, irrespective of consequences.

3. Operants include a wider range of behaviors; respondents are limited to behaviors that originated as reflexes.

4. Over time, operant learning involves the development *and* shaping of new behaviors: Respondent learning involves an existing behavior (UCR) being elicited by a new stimulus.

Let us examine these differences.

Operants Are Emitted

Operant behavior initially occurs without being predictably preceded by any antecedent stimulus. It is in this sense that living organisms emit operant behaviors. "When a baby puts his hand to his mouth, the movement may be reinforced by the contact of hand and mouth, but we cannot find any stimulus which elicits the movement and which is present every time it occurs" (Skinner, 1953, p. 107). On the other hand, respondent behavior is elicited by a conditioned or unconditioned stimulus. It is a direct response to a stimulus. The eliciting stimulus is present every time the respondent behavior occurs. In general, most operant responses can be seen as voluntary responses instead of reflexive or involuntary.

Operants Occur Because of Their Consequences

You are at the edge of a high cliff enjoying the seascape below. A friend sneaks up behind you and yells boo! The startle reflex elicited by the sudden noise causes you to jump . . . in spite of the rather severe consequences. This is respondent behavior. It occurred because a CS or UCS preceded it. It did not occur because jumping off cliffs in the past produced strengthening conse-quences. In this case, it is the UCS (shouting boo!) that causes the behavior.

Consequences are crucial to operant behavior. We perform responses because they are followed by certain consequences (called **reinforcers**) and do not perform other responses that have no consequences or else aversive ones (called **punishers**). Reflect again on jumping off the cliff. If you managed to sur-vive the plunge by clinging to a bush to the applause and cheering of your friends, you are likely to jump off a cliff in their presence again, sans the boo. Such cliff jumping would be an operant, influenced by its consequences. (Is this how bungee cord jumping got started?)

Consider another example of operant behavior. In the dark, we press a but-ton, and the consequence of the light going on determines the occurrence of the response in the future. If the switch is broken and no light goes on, we soon stop pressing that switch because our behavior has no consequence. If we press a switch and get a shock rather than light, we quickly stop—again, because of the consequence our behavior produced.

As previously noted, operants occur because of their consequences. However, this seems to be contradicted by the example of flipping on a light switch. Doesn't the presence of the light switch in the dark (an antecedent event) cause us to reach out and flip the switch in the same way the "boo!" caused the jumper to jump? No, because the presence of a light switch causes us to turn it on only because of the reinforcing consequence that follows. We flip the switch and the light comes on. Without that reinforcing consequence, the switch would not cause this behavior. This is not the case with our jumper. He or she will jump when startled by a loud sound despite the unfortunate con-sequences. Most operant behavior is signaled or guided by antecedent stimuli. With operant behavior, we say that the **antecedent stimulus** "evokes" the response. The presence of an on-off switch means that pressing responses will occur more frequently than if there were only a blank wall. Yet the function of the antecedent in operant behavior is different from a CS or UCS in respondent behavior. In operant behavior, the antecedent only cues behavior and only does so because the behavior it cues has a certain consequence. Therefore, if a switch is installed backward, we can easily learn to press the "off" side to produce light, because it is that response in the presence of the cue that has the reinforcing consequence of producing light. In short, the switch does not elicit a pressing reflex: There is no such thing. Instead, the switch evokes a pressing response that is reinforced by the consequence of producing light.

Operants Include a Wider Range of Behaviors

Respondent behaviors originate as reflexes—that is, as unconditioned responses to unconditioned stimuli. They are of the universal innate type of behaviors (see Chapter 2). As a class, respondents are restricted to innate reflexes that are part of the organism's phylogenic history. Startle reflexes, orientation reflexes, and physiological fear responses are the respondents that are of the most practical significance in human development.

As previously noted, operants can originate as reflexes, too, as with crying or smiling. Even changes in physiological responses, such as heart rate and brain waves, can come under the control of consequences and be classified as operants. However, operants involve much more behavior than just these former reflexes. Most of what we see emitted by children are operants, determined by the consequences the behaviors have in the environment. This is because most human development—cognitive, language, and motor responses—are operants and follow the principles of operant learning. We will define and discuss carefully *all* types of consequences for operant behavior in our next chapter.

Operant Learning Produces New Behavior

Recall that development involves progressive changes in person-environment interactions. In respondent learning, the response remains the same regardless of whether it is elicited by the unconditioned or the conditioned stimulus. The eye blink reflex or activation syndrome remains the same, and what is learned is that a new stimulus, the conditioned stimulus, elicits that reflexive response, now as a conditioned response.

Operant learning, over time, produces a new response because the effect of consequences is to strengthen some behaviors and weaken others. *Shaping* of behaviors and producing complex *chains* of behaviors are ways that operant learning produces new behaviors. Both processes will be discussed in detail later. Also, in our next chapter, we will discuss in detail the four different principles of operant learning that involve either presentation or removal of positive or aversive consequences for behavior.

SUMMARY ●

Learning can be defined as a relatively permanent change in the behavior-environment relation that is the result of experience. It is a process paralleling natural selection, in that behaviors are selected by the environment through ontogenic contingencies. The selection of behaviors is based on their adaptive value. Variation, selection, and retention of behavior are necessary for selection to occur.

The terms *behavior* and *response* are synonymous. They describe the actions or changes that individuals perform. Behavior can be either covert (private) or overt (publicly observable). Both covert (e.g., thoughts) and overt behaviors are subject to the same basic principles that govern all behaviors.

A *stimulus* is an environmental change or event. Stimuli can be classified on the basis of their topography (physical characteristics) or function (the effects on behavior). The function of a stimulus is of greater importance in the study of development.

Habituation, respondent conditioning, and operant conditioning are three types of learning. Habituation is the decrease or cessation of reflexive responding (an automatic, unlearned response to a stimulus) to a specific stimulus due to repeated presentation of that stimulus, wherein the decrease in responding is not the result of other factors, such as satiation or fatigue. The study of habituation is important not only because of its prevalent role in infant studies but because the phenomena has implications for the long-term survival of an organism.

Respondent learning (also termed classical conditioning or Pavlovian conditioning) involves reflexive behaviors that are automatically triggered by stimuli in the environment. In a respondent stimulus–response (S–R) relation, the stimulus is termed the *unconditioned stimulus* (UCS) and the response, the *unconditioned response* (UCR). Repeated paired presentations of a previously *neutral stimulus* (NS) with the UCS results in the previously NS becoming a *conditioned stimulus* (CS), and the response it elicits, a *conditioned response* (CR). Four necessary and sufficient conditions demonstrate respondent learning: (a) The initial S–R relation is an unlearned, automatic respondent relation; (b) the UCS must be paired with an NS; (c) presentation of the CS alone must elicit the response; and (d) the response elicited by the previously neutral stimulus must not be the product of other processes, such as sensitization. *Generalization* refers to the phenomena wherein once a conditioned response is established, the CR is elicited not only by the CS but by stimuli similar to the CS as well. *Discrimination* is evidenced by a lack of response to stimuli similar to the CS. *Extinction* is the cessation of responding to the CR and is brought about by repeated presentation of the CS without the UCS. Conditioning is most effective when the NS precedes the UCS and terminates with the onset of the UCS or persists for a time with the UCS. Also, in establishing an S–R relation, latency of one-half second between presentation of the NS and UCS has been found to be optimal in adults, with longer delays inhibiting the formation of a CR. The intensity of the UCS also affects the formation of an S–R relation, with a more intense UCS generally leading to easier conditioning with fewer trials— in some cases, one-trial learning. It is important to note that although they may appear topographically identical, the CR and UCR will typically differ at least slightly from each other. Some S–R relations are easier to establish than others due to certain predispositions that we are born with.

The study of respondent learning is important because of its adaptive value for organisms, and it helps explain a wide range of emotional responses to the environment. Also, the principles of respondent learning can be applied to the treatment of fears and phobias through *counterconditioning* and *systematic desensitization.*

Operant behavior is that which operates on the environment, producing *consequences* that determine the operant's frequency and define it. Operants are behaviors that are *emitted* or *evoked* by stimuli in the environment. Although some may originate as reflexes, most begin as emitted responses that are strengthened or weakened by environmental consequences. Although some consequences strengthen or weaken behavior universally, others vary in their ability to do so idiosyncratically. A behavior is considered to be part of a *response class* if it is maintained by or has a *functional relationship* with the same class of consequent stimuli. Respondents and operants differ in four important ways: (a) Operants are emitted, whereas respondents are elicited; (b) the performance of operants is dependent on their consequences, whereas respondents occur because of their antecedents; (c) operants include a wide range of behaviors, whereas respondents are limited to behavior that originated as reflexes; and (d) operant learning involves the development and shaping of new behaviors, whereas respondent learning involves an existing behavior being elicited by a new stimulus. The study of operant learning is important to understanding development because it is the process by which new behavior appear in a person's repertoire.

● NOTES

---

1. Variation itself may be selected. Neuringer and his associates (Denney & Neuringer, 1998; Neuringer, 1993; Neuringer, Deiss, & Olson, 2000) have shown that variability, even near randomness, can be increased through reinforcement. Much earlier, Pryor (Pryor, Haag, & O'Reilly, 1969) showed it was possible to produce novel responding in dolphins by reinforcing a diversity of behavior patterns.

2. Although the discovery of respondent type learning is generally attributed to Pavlov, some have considered an American, E. B. Twitmyer (1905), who completed his doctoral dissertation on the knee-jerk reflex, to be the discoverer of the phenomenon.

3. Turkkan (1989) has argued that Pavlovian conditioning principles can be applied to a more extensive range of behaviors, including physiological responses, such as endocrine secretions and changes at the level of the individual neuron synapse. Although the issues in this area are hotly debated, renewed interest in classical conditioning processes may lead to revisions in how we view this form of learning.

CHAPTER 6

OPERANT LEARNING

We ended our last chapter by comparing respondent learning to operant learning. We noted that operant learning is much more important to understanding development because it is the way that new behaviors appear in the person's repertoire. E. L. Thorndike (1911) was the first investigator to study, in controlled experiments, how animals' nonreflexive, instrumental behavior patterns can be learned as a result of the consequences experienced. He placed cats in puzzle boxes from which they could learn to escape by pulling a string, stepping on the platform, and turning one of two latches on the front of the gate door. On opening the door, the cats could exit and immediately eat some food placed outside. Thorndike's measure of problem solving was escape latency—the amount of time it took the animals to escape the box. In this way, Thorndike formulated the learning principle that he called the **law of effect** (which was later reformulated as **reinforcement** by Skinner). This principle remains as one of the most important processes in the psychology of learning.

It is true that Thorndike's law of effect and Skinner's principle of reinforcement are defined on the basis of the same kinds of phenomena; however, the two conceptions are quite different. Thorndike portrayed the process as the forming of connections. His approach is fundamentally that respondent-like associations are formed, whereas Skinner portrays the process as the selection of response classes. The latter is the conception that has already been developed in the earlier chapters of the present textbook.

● THE CONTRIBUTIONS OF B. F. SKINNER (1904–1990)

Burrhus Frederic Skinner was born in 1904 in Susquehanna, Pennsylvania. He studied English literature at Hamilton College in Clinton, New York, and was fantastic at mechanical inventions. He went to Harvard in 1928, earned his Ph.D. in 1931, and taught there until 1974. Skinner continued writing and conducting research experiments until his death. Eight days before he passed away, on August 18, 1990, Skinner received the first and, to this day, the only citation for outstanding lifetime contribution to the field of psychology from the American Psychological Association. He was always a controversial figure and distinguished himself for his significant contributions to a natural science approach to human behavior. He maintained that private events, such as feelings and thoughts, were not the causes of, or explanations for, behavior but rather were under-the-skin (private or inside the organism) activities and behavior that also could be studied and explained.

Skinner's most important legacies to us were his theory of **operant behavior** and principles of learning. He advocated the principle of positive reinforcement over the use of aversive controls. Unfortunately, many of his contributions have been misunderstood and misinterpreted, mostly by uninformed psychologists and in biased introductory textbooks in psychology. One example is the popular belief that he raised his daughter in an experimental chamber and that she later committed suicide. In fact, his daughter, Deborah, who was raised in a special crib designed to reduce aversive stimuli, is currently an artist living in London.

Box 6.1 The Baby Tender

Many controversies have swirled around B. F. Skinner because many people, holding different worldviews from his, have misunderstood his work. One of the most persistent myths has been over what has been called the *air crib*. To set the record straight, the following is excerpted from the B. F. Skinner Foundation's Web site (www.bfskinner.org):

In 1943, towards the end of the Minnesota years, Yvonne (Skinner) was pregnant again. Knowing of her husband's talent at solving problems with gadgets, she wondered whether he might design a crib that would be safer than the typical crib with its bars that could trap a leg

Figure 6.1

SOURCE: Reprinted with permission of the B. F. Skinner Foundation.

and blankets that could suffocate a baby. He could, and did. Proud of his new invention, an enclosed and heated crib with a plexiglass window, he sent an article to the popular magazine, the *Lady's Home Journal*. Changing Skinner's title to grab attention, the article came out as "Baby in a Box." The *"baby tender,"* as Skinner called his crib, was used only as a bed for the new baby. Deborah had a playpen and spent as much time out of her bed as do other infants. But inevitably confusion occurred between the baby tender and the "Skinner Box." To the end of his life Skinner was plagued by rumors about his second daughter, hearing even that she had committed suicide. In fact, Skinner was an affectionate father and never experimented on either of his children. Deborah is a successful artist and lives in London with her husband. (Vargas, 2002)

That Deborah turned out to be a creative, well-adjusted, free-spirited, motorcycle-riding adult is likely to disappoint some of Skinner's critics, who often like to paint his theories as cold and mechanistic. Their disappointment would be even greater were they to learn that the foregoing passage was written by Skinner's other daughter, Julie Skinner Vargas. Dr. Vargas is a highly respected behavioral psychologist who has written extensively on the application of behavioral principles to education. A former president of the Association for Behavior Analysis, Julie Vargas and her husband Ernie Vargas (also a prominent behaviorist) are retiring after long careers at West Virginia University and moving back to the family home near Harvard where she grew up. The house, which still has Skinner's workshop in the basement, is intended to become the headquarters for the B. F. Skinner Foundation.

Whereas Thorndike (1911) produced the first experiments dealing with consequences that strengthen behavior, Skinner was primarily responsible for the most systematic and comprehensive investigations on the basic properties of reinforcement. One of Skinner's major contributions was to take the study of behavior beyond the disconnected or discrete trials of animals running a maze by instead studying the strengthening and weakening of behavior in the highly controlled, yet less constricted, environment of an operant chamber or "Skinner Box." In this setting, animals were free to make an unlimited number of responses, to be determined only by the environmental conditions.

Free Operant Procedures

Unlike discrete-trial procedures in which a rat is placed in a running maze and each run through the maze constitutes a discrete trial controlled by the experimenter, in the free operant procedure, the organism is placed in an environment and is allowed to behave freely. The frequency or strength of some operant behavior is measured, such as lever pressing by rats, key pecks by pigeons in an operant chamber, words spoken, or the amount of fussing by a child in the home. The concept of the free operant means that the organism's response can occur at any time and can be repeated as long as the animal remains in the experimental space. Instead of using latency as a measure of the response, Skinner used response rate. Critics of behaviorism have claimed that these experimental chambers are artificial environments. However, the reason for studying animals in these boxes is to obtain as much experimental control as possible over the independent variable and to minimize confounding variables. Furthermore, applied behavior analysis frequently studies behavior in real-life environments, such as homes or schools or even supermarkets. The principles of operant conditioning are based on contingencies and were discovered in the laboratory. Today, the principles and their derivative techniques are being used effectively to modify behavior in therapy and to produce new learning, as we will see in future chapters.

WHAT IS A CONTINGENCY? ●

A **contingency** is a dependent relationship, expressible as an if–then statement. The movie *Field of Dreams* had a ghostly voice whisper in the wind, "If you build it, he will come." This mystical theme meant that if the main character built a baseball field in the middle of a cornfield in Iowa, then the character's deceased father would come back to play in the field and resolve a tangled family relationship. This is a simple contingency: The first term, "*If* you build it," specifies the *then* term: "He will come." This type of contingency is the basis for operant behavior: If this response occurs, then this consequence happens. If you press the switch, then the light goes off. If you press it again, then the light goes on. Note that the consequence (light off or on) is **contingent** on the response; the consequence depends on the behavior.

THE THREE-TERM CONTINGENCY ●

In its simplest form, in studying operant behavior, a contingency involves the relationship between three aspects, or terms, of the contingency: (a) the context in which the behavior is emitted (the **antecedent** stimuli, called discriminative stimuli); (b) the response itself (called the *operant*); and (c) the consequent stimuli that follow the response (called the *reinforcer* or *punisher*). In this chapter, we will focus, for the most part, on the four-term contingency.

● THE FOUR-TERM CONTINGENCY

Although the three-term contingency has been the dominant paradigm in behavior analysis, it may be insufficient to account for changes in behavior in development. For that, we need a contextualistic account—one that takes into account the context of development. To accomplish that, we can break down the contingency between environmental events (stimuli) and behavior (responses) into four terms (Bijou & Baer, 1978). This is called the **four-term contingency,** and we will now look at these four terms. Taken in order of occurrence, the four terms are (a) a setting event or establishing operation, (b) a cue or discriminative stimulus, (c) a behavior pattern or response, and (d) a consequence or reinforcing stimulus. This is noted in the following sequence:

Setting Events or Establishing Operation

$$S^d \rightarrow R \rightarrow S^r$$

Discriminative Stimulus → Response → Reinforcing Stimulus

However, what we have depicted here is a static interaction—a still picture. Human interactions are like moving pictures. Although the four-term contingency is the critical unit of operant interaction, it is important to keep in mind that dynamic interactions are continuing streams of ever-changing four-term contingencies. Morris (1992) has attempted to capture the complexity of reciprocal interactions between organism and environment over time by unpacking the four-term contingency. We have adapted this model in Figure 6.2.

Notice that Morris's (1992) analysis firmly embeds the four-term contingency in a historical context that suggests how prior interactions influence the one under current analysis and how the current contingency affects future interaction. Normally, to understand this contingency, we stop the stream of development at one instant in time. This is like taking a still picture—we freeze the interaction at one instant in time. Behavioral change would be better captured as a video, but, for practical purposes, we need to pause it to analyze it. A better representation of the continuity of change is depicted in Figure 6.3.

We will examine in detail one four-term contingency out of the continuous stream of them. With this one contingency, we build our analysis around the most critical term, the response or behavior pattern, rather than discussing them in the order in which they occur in time.

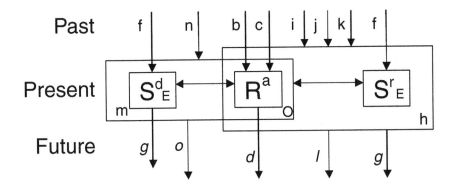

Figure 6.2   The Complexity of the Four-Term Contingency

SOURCE: Adapted from Morris (1992). Used with permission.

NOTES: Letters at the bottom of the figure (*d, g, l* and *o*) are italicized to indicate that these are future effects.

O = the organism

a = current physiological makeup

b = genetic-constitutional makeup

c = biological ontogenic history (e.g., teratogens, reproductive risks, injury, illness)

d = effect on future physiological conditions because of this contingency

E = the environment

f = current physical environmental conditions

g = effect on future environmental conditions because of this contingency

Organism-Environment Interactions' Effects on Reinforcement or Punishment

i = genetic influence on reinforcement/punishment

j = current physiological influence on reinforcement/punishment

k = learning history effects determining acquired reinforcement/punishment

l = effect on future reinforcement or punishment because of this contingency

Effects on Discriminative Stimulus

n = learning history effects on determining S^d

o = effect on future S^d because of this contingency

Contextual Setting Events

h = setting events or establishing operations affecting reinforcement

m = setting events affecting discriminative stimulus

THE FIRST TERM: THE RESPONSE[1]   ●

R

We start with the behavior of interest, the operant response. It is the central segment of our unit of analysis, the four-term contingency. As noted previously,

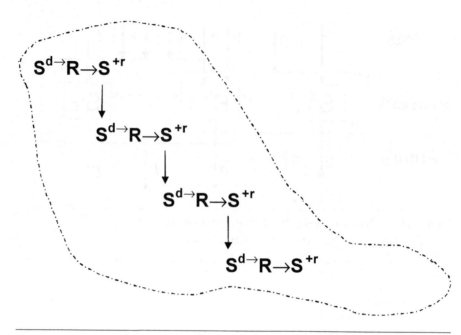

Figure 6.3   Contingency Over Time

a response is any action of a living thing. Operant responses can be classified in three ways: by their topography, their function, and their physical location.

Topographic Response Classes

Responses are often classified by their form or, more technically, their **topography**. That is, we talk about running, button pushing, snoring, and any number of other categories or classes in terms of the form of the behavior patterns. Take jumping, for an example. Members of a **topographic response class** may include jumping over a puddle, jumping up to touch a basketball rim, or jumping rope. What do all of these responses have in common that makes them members of the same class? These responses are placed in a common category by their "look" or form. All running responses are similar in form, as are button pushes and snores. However, it is important to note that there is some variability within these classes. Each stride is not exactly alike, neither is each button push. Nor is each snore. They are similar but vary slightly from each other. Yet it is convenient to talk about running as the behavior pattern, even though we are actually dealing with a rather large number of individual responses, each of which is at least slightly different in form from any other. The observer conveniently lumps them together as a response class defined by topography. However, from our viewpoint, responses are more usefully classified on the basis of their function.

Functional Response Classes

A **functional response class** is composed of operant behaviors that produce the same consequence, regardless of their form. That is, they have the same function. Most functional response classes include many behavior patterns that vary in their topography. For example, because of their effects in producing light, striking a match, flipping a light switch, and opening drapes are all members of the same functional class. Furthermore, each of these response topographies is also a member of another functional response class. For example, the response of striking a match also belongs to the class of responses concerned with smoking, because it produces heat to light a cigarette. Other topographies belonging to this class include operating a cigarette lighter and asking another smoker for a light. In short, topographically different responses can have the same meaning or function. If they have the same function, regardless of their topography, they are members of the same functional response class.

Response Classes Based on Physical Location

Last, operant responses may also be placed into classes based on geography or **physical location**. Thus, we may divide them into classes of behaviors that occur outside the skin, called **public events** (Skinner, 1953), or inside the skin, termed **private events** (Skinner, 1953). (The latter are not to be confused with birthday parties or bar mitzvahs.) Motor activities, such as walking or talking, are part of the class of public events. Internal operant responses, such as talking to oneself, imaging, or hallucinating, are members of the class of private events.

Response Variability and Selectionism

Recall the earlier discussion of learning as a process of selection. Recall also that the first requirement for selection is that there be variability in the response in order that a variety of responses are available to be selected by consequences (Donahoe & Palmer, 1994). Operant behavior is certainly characterized by variability. Even simple motor responses, such as jumping or reaching for a glass, are characterized by variability. That is, even these simple motor responses are never exactly the same each time they occur. Some jumps are higher, or faster, or more tilted than others. This characteristic variability of responses allows selection by consequences (Neuringer, 1991). Variability in behavior also makes it possible that a totally novel behavior, never performed by an individual before, can gradually be shaped and developed. One procedure that makes use of behavior variability is known as shaping (Shahan & Chase, 2002), which is a technique consisting of reinforcing successive approximations to the target behavior. We shall consider this technique in detail later.

● THE SECOND TERM: THE CONSEQUENCE

$$R \rightarrow S^{r+} \text{ or } R \rightarrow S^{r-}$$

Operant behaviors produce environmental effects or changes in the environment, which increase or decrease future likelihood of the operant. A response is strengthened in the sense that it is more likely to occur in the future. Similarly, a response is weakened in the sense that it is less likely to occur in the future. There are two types of consequences: (a) one in which a stimulus is added (+) or produced following a behavior and (b) one in which a stimulus that is present is terminated or removed (−) following the response.[2] The effect of these consequences will be to strengthen (reinforce) or weaken (punish) behavior, respectively.

Selection by Consequences

One way to look at the strengthening effect of consequences is that consequences select certain responses from the wide range of behaviors that occur. Recall that there is variability in behavior. Some responses produce more adaptive consequences and others do not. For example, the better jumps of a skater may be selected by the consequences of the jump—landing upright on the ice—whereas poorer jumps will not be selected because the consequences of the behavior are falls. Thus, from a selectionist perspective, variation in behavior leads to differential consequences, some of which strengthen and some of which weaken behavior. We now turn to how consequences strengthen behavior: reinforcement.

Reinforcement: The Strengthening of Behavior

Behavior increases in strength when it becomes more frequent or more likely to occur. **Reinforcement** is any operation[3] that strengthens behavior;

behavior that has been strengthened is said to have been reinforced. Note that the terms *reinforcement* and *reinforced* are used consistently with their everyday meaning, as in reinforcement of a building or reinforcing a regiment of soldiers. Reinforcement should be defined empirically (Gewirtz & Peláez-Nogueras, 1992a). That is, there must be an observable increase in the behavior to conclude that a behavior has actually been reinforced. There are two types of reinforcement: positive and negative. This distinction is based on the consequences that lead to the strengthening (reinforcement) of the response.

Positive Reinforcement ($R \rightarrow S^{r+}$)

Positive reinforcement occurs when a response adds or produces a stimulus event and, as a result, the response increases in strength (i.e., in frequency or probability). We call the stimulus that follows the strengthened response a positive reinforcer or positive reinforcing stimulus (S^{r+}). Some examples of positive reinforcement follow:

- Sidney shakes a rattle and hears a noise. The shaking behavior occurs more frequently as a consequence of the response producing the noise. The shaking behavior has been *positively reinforced*. The noise is a positive reinforcer.
- Sylvia says "thank you," and her mother responds with "you're welcome." "Thank you" is a behavior that becomes more frequent. "Thank you" has been *positively reinforced*. "You're welcome" is a positive reinforcer for Sylvia.
- Tommy hits Jamie, and she cries. Tommy is more likely to hit Jamie in the future because his hitting behavior has been positively reinforced. Jamie's crying is a positive reinforcer for Tommy. Note that siblings, parents, teachers, and society provide lots of *positive reinforcement* for inappropriate behavior, usually inadvertently.

Note that in each case the behavior has been strengthened as a consequence of the behavior's producing a stimulus. Note also that it is the behavior of the child, not the child himself or herself, that is reinforced. We may be tempted to say, "I reinforced Johnny," but it is more accurate to say, "I reinforced Johnny's behavior."

Negative Reinforcement ($R \rightarrow S^{r-}$)

Negative reinforcement occurs when a response removes, terminates, or avoids a stimulus event and the response increases in strength (in frequency or probability). Note that because reinforcement is involved, the behavior is strengthened. This correct technical usage is contrary to the everyday usage of the term *negative reinforcement*. In everyday language, negative reinforcement applies to situations in which the behavior is weakened. This is incorrect. Technically, these situations actually involve punishment and will be examined later. To repeat, negative reinforcement occurs when a response removes, terminates, or avoids a stimulus and the response is therefore strengthened. We shall call the stimulus that is removed or terminated, as a consequence of the response, a *negative reinforcer, negative reinforcing stimulus,* or *aversive stimulus* (S^-). When a loud alarm wakes us up, its termination is preceded by our turning-off response. In this case, we escape from the alarm noise by performing some behavior that has been negatively reinforced if its frequency increases in the future. The term *negative reinforcement* also includes *avoidance,* in which the response prevents an aversive stimulus from occurring in the first place. An example would be to wake up before the alarm sounds and turn it off.

Here are some other examples of negative reinforcement:

- Don holds his hand over his eyes and shades them from the bright sunlight. The eye-shading behavior is strengthened because it terminates the brightness of the sunlight. The eye-shading behavior is negatively reinforced. Bright sunlight is a *negative reinforcer.*
- Elsie unwraps an unmarked foil package from the uncharted depths of her refrigerator. An unidentifiable, overpowering fowl odor (ancient chicken parts?) wafts through the air to her nostrils. She quickly rewraps the package. The wrapping behavior is more likely to occur again under similar circumstances. Thus, the rewrapping behavior has been negatively reinforced because it terminated the *negative reinforcer* (the odor).
- Jack throws a tantrum when his mother asks him to clean his room. The consequence of the tantrum is that his mother drops the demand. The tantrums will most likely be more frequent in the future. These tantrums have been negatively reinforced because they terminated the *negative reinforcer* (his mother's demand).

Punishment

Consequences can also weaken behavior. Behavior is said to be weakened when the frequency, duration, magnitude, or latency of the behavior decreases. This weakening of behavior due to either of the two types of consequences is called **punishment**. We note that punishing consequences need not be painful, and, on the other hand, painful consequences do not necessarily decrease the behavior that produces them. "Those football linebackers take severe painful events when they attempt to blitz the quarterback, but they keep on coming." Let us now examine the two types of punishment.

Positive (Presentation) Punishment

One way behaviors are weakened is that they add or produce aversive stimuli (i.e., stimuli that hurt in some way). Behaviors that are followed by aversive stimuli are less likely to occur again. Some examples of positive punishment follow:

- Melissa grabs a pot on the stove, producing a burning-hot stimulus. She is unlikely to grab the pot again. The behavior was punished; the hot pot was an aversive stimulus.
- Chucky takes a swig of milk from a carton. This puts sour milk in his mouth. Chucky will not drink again from this carton. His behavior has been punished. The sour milk is an aversive stimulus.
- Amanda drives through a red light. She is stopped and given a ticket. She is less likely to drive through a stoplight in the future. Her driving pattern has been punished. The ticket is an aversive stimulus.

Negative (Removal) Punishment

Negative punishment includes contingencies that result in behavior decreased by its consequences, with those consequences being the removal, termination, or loss of something. In other words, the individual's behavior is followed by the termination or loss of a valuable object or activity. This includes commonly applied procedures to reduce child behavior problems: **time-out** and response cost. For example, Johnny teasing his sister at the dinner table results in loss of weekly allowance and further results in Johnny behaving or teasing his sister less frequently when at the table. Another example is that Jerry occasionally took the bus to school, until after the day in which his wallet was stolen at the bus stop. Figures 6.4 and 6.5 are flowcharts showing how to determine the name of the operation or procedure (Figure 6.4) and the name of the stimulus (Figure 6.5). In both figures, you start at the top and follow the steps until you find the right box.

Operant Extinction

What happens if reinforcement for a particular behavior is no longer forthcoming? If reinforcement of a behavior is discontinued, the behavior will

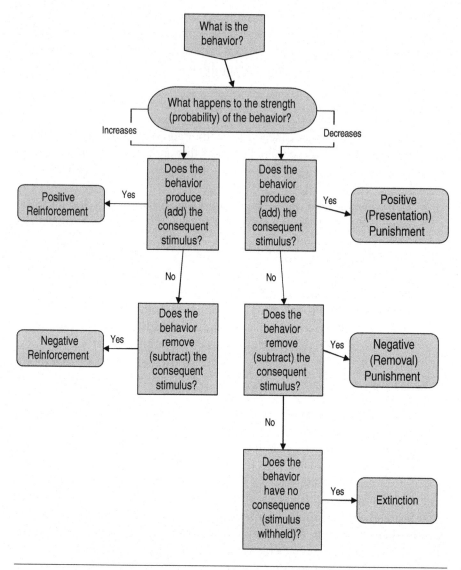

Figure 6.4   Determining the Name of the Operation

eventually stop occurring. If no one answers our telephone calls, we stop calling (Skinner, 1953). Likewise, if we hit a key on our computer keyboard and nothing happens on the screen, we eventually stop hitting the key.

In both examples, the long-term effect of the withholding of reinforcers is the **extinction**[4] of behavior. However, these effects are different from the effects of punishment. With punishment, the weakening of behavior is rapid

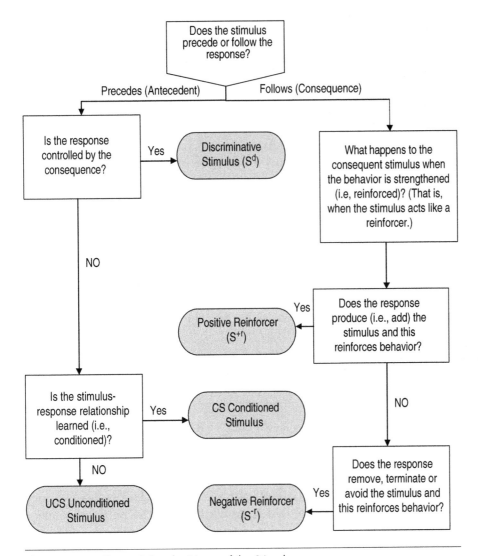

Figure 6.5   Determining the Name of the Stimulus

NOTE: The same stimulus name (positive reinforcer or negative reinforcer) can be retained when applied to punishment contingencies. Thus, **negative punishment** occurs when a response removes, terminates, or avoids a **positive reinforcer**. Likewise, **positive punishment** occurs when a response produces a **negative reinforcer**. Therefore, be certain whether you are naming the operation (reinforcement, punishment, or extinction) or naming the stimulus (positive or negative reinforcer).

(particularly if the consequent stimuli are powerful). The procedure of extinction involves eliminating the contingency between the operant response and its consequence. As a behavioral process, extinction refers to a decline in the frequency of the operant when the extinction procedure is in effect.

In **operant extinction**, the weakening of behavior by withholding reinforcement follows a different pattern. Generally, if reinforcement of a previously **reinforced behavior** is withheld, the initial effect on the behavior is a rapid increase in the frequency, magnitude, and variability of the behavior. Emotional behavior may also be elicited by the withholding of the stimuli. This so-called **extinction burst** may have an evolutionary significance for organisms because the increased responses may cause the reinforcement to occur again. For example, if you press the "f" key on your keyboard and it does not appear on the screen, you do not immediately stop. You press again, a little harder. When this does not produce the reinforcer (screen "f"), you hit the key harder and more rapidly. You may even slam the keyboard. In short, there is initially a burst of activity. However, if none of this produces an "f" on the screen, you stop responding. Your "f"-key-hitting behavior has been extinguished. However, there is an interesting phenomenon called **spontaneous recovery,** which means that after a period of extinction, the rate of the response may increase again to the operant level. If reinforcement continues to be withheld, extinction will occur again followed by another spontaneous recovery, but, over repeated sessions of extinction, the amount of recovery decreases.

● THE THIRD TERM: THE DISCRIMINATIVE STIMULUS (S^d)

$$S^d \to R \to S^{r+} \quad S^d \to R \to S^{r-}$$

We list this element third because the response–consequence contingency is the crucial one for operant behavior. Yet any stimulus that precedes or accompanies the response–consequence contingency may come to evoke the response. Such an antecedent stimulus is called a **discriminative stimulus** or S^d (pronounced "ess-dee"). It signals or cues the response. Look at the shorthand notations at the beginning of this section. The contingency has now become three termed: In the presence of this stimulus (S^d), a particular response (R) will have a particular consequence (S^{r+} or S^{r-}). Consider the example of turning on the light switch. Because flipping the light switch produced the positive reinforcer (light), the switch itself has become a discriminative stimulus for the flipping response. The switch evokes a press that produces light. Similarly, a rattle evokes shaking that produces noise, and a seat belt evokes a buckling-up response that terminates the noise made by the car's auditory reminder. These antecedent stimuli have acquired their discriminative properties because they have been correlated with specific consequences. After time they also acquire reinforcing properties, which will be discussed later.

Note that although there may appear to be a similarity between the operant S^d and the respondent conditioned stimulus (CS) or unconditioned stimulus (UCS), the S^d has acquired its power to "cause" behavior in a very different manner. Let us look at the case of stopping at a red light. As you approach an intersection in your car, you see a red light. You automatically lift your foot from the accelerator and move it to the brake. You come to a gradual stop. Now, if the red light were a CS or UCS, it would have elicited a stopping response regardless of the consequence. The stopping response would have had to originate as a reflex. Maybe in centuries to come, such a reflex will evolve via natural selection. But for now, stopping at a traffic light has been acquired because of the consequences that follow. We stop because of negative reinforcement: Stopping avoids having accidents and getting traffic tickets. If the consequences are changed, we may not stop at red lights. For example, at midnight, in a deserted town, a red light may not always evoke the behavior of stopping.

At this point, we have a three-term contingency; $S^d \to R \to S^{r+}$ (a positively reinforced, discriminated response) or $S^d \to R \to S^{r-}$ (a negatively reinforced, discriminated response). Yet each contingency is affected by the context in which it occurs. Context is a central ingredient in behavior analysis of development because it is what gives behavior meaning (Morris, 1993a).[5] Thus, we come to the last term, the setting event.

THE FOURTH TERM: THE SETTING ● EVENT (SE) OR ESTABLISHING OPERATION (EO)

Dad is smiling. The smile is an S^d that signals the child that approaching his father will be reinforced with a hug. The **setting event** (SE) or **establishing operation** (EO) is the context in which the event may be more or less reinforcing for the child to approach his father. For instance, approaching Dad when not playing with other children (the context) may be more reinforcing by receiving a hug than if Dad is approached when the child's friends are present. Your behavior of going out to buy food is more likely to occur when you are hungry. According to Bijou and Baer (1978), "A SE influences an interactional sequence by altering the strength and characteristic[s] of the particular stimulus–response functions involved in an interaction"(p. 26). Thus, SEs (or EOs) are general conditions that affect the specific stimulus–response relationships.

There appear to be at least two distinct ways in which SEs affect the contingency (Michael, 1993).[6] Some SEs increase the likelihood that the S^d will evoke a particular response by affecting the $S^d \to R$ relationship. For example, in the context of Dad's smiling, his saying "come here" (the S^d) is more likely to evoke the response than if Dad were not smiling.

Some other SEs increase the likelihood that the S^d will occasion a particular response by affecting the R → S^{r+} or R → S^{r-} relationships by determining the degree to which a consequence is reinforcing or punishing. Michael (1982, 1993) preferred to use the term establishing operation (EO) for such a contingency-altering SE. Formally, an EO is defined as any change in the external or internal environment of the organism that momentarily alters the effectiveness of the reinforcing event. It alters the frequency of the behavior that has been followed by that reinforcer.

Thus, a discriminative stimulus (S^d) occasions the behavior that has previously been reinforced in its presence, whereas the EO is a contingency-altering event with an **evocative effect.** The S^d sets the occasion for the behavior to produce the consequence event; in its absence, the consequence event will not occur ("When my Dad is not smiling, he might not hug me"). The SE or EO determines the reinforcing potency of the event ("It does not matter much because I can play with my friends now").

For example, if you have eaten recently, seeing a package of dried prunes will not cause you to pick up the package. If you are food deprived, you are more likely to have the package evoke behaviors that lead to eating the prunes. Being food deprived affects the contingency by making food more reinforcing than it had previously been. **Deprivation,** in this example, is an operation that establishes food as a reinforcer for the response. The more deprived the organism, the more effective the reinforcing stimulus. Thus, EOs such as deprivation and satiation fall into the realm of motivation. They may be viewed as motivational SEs.

To recap, operant behavior can be analyzed as a four-term contingency. Within a particular context (the SE), a particular stimulus (discriminative stimulus) evokes a behavior (response) that affects the environment (produces a consequence), which in turn maintains that response.

● WHAT CHANGES? THE DEVELOPMENT OF ACQUIRED REINFORCING STIMULI

Primary Reinforcers

One of the important developments in the progressive changes between behavior and environment is in what become reinforcing and punishing stimuli. At birth, a number of reinforcers are already functioning. We call this initial class of reinforcers **primary reinforcers**. This connotes that they are the first reinforcers to function; their effectiveness is not dependent on their relationships to other reinforcers. Primary reinforcers are universal, owing their reinforcing function to the genetic inheritance of the child. There are both positive and negative primary reinforcers. Among the primary positive reinforcers are food, water, sucking-produced stimulation, taste stimuli, skin temperature, rest and sleep, and air. Watson (1972) demonstrated that discovery of a contingency between the child's own behavior and its consequence may itself be a primary reinforcer. Thus, noticing that an action (e.g., moving ones head) causes a consequence (e.g., change in visual stimulation) may be what reinforces a repetitive act: A child may do something over and over to determine what the effects (consequences) of the action are.

Primary negative reinforcers may include the escape or avoidance of painful stimuli and a range of physical and chemical stimuli. Bijou and Baer (1965) pointed out that almost any stimulus can be a negative reinforcer if it is sufficiently intense. Loud noises, bright lights, and sudden changes can negatively reinforce behaviors that terminate or avoid these changes.

Primary reinforcers evolved because of their adaptive significance for the newborn child (Gewirtz & Peláez-Nogueras, 1992a). Food, water, visual stimulation, and touch are examples of primary positive reinforcers necessary for survival. Behaviors that produce them are strengthened. Pain, bright lights, and foul odors are examples of primary negative reinforcers. Behaviors that remove, avoid, or terminate them are also strengthened. The adaptive significance of sensitivity to these consequences in terms of the survival of the species should be apparent.

Lipsitt (1979) reported a series of studies on positive and negative reinforcers in newborns. Sucking that produced sucrose was not only stronger than that which produced water, but, if the neonates were first allowed to produce sucrose by sucking, switching them to water reduced their sucking below what it was when water alone had been the reinforcer. This change was affected not only by the withdrawal of sucrose but also by the SE of having the sugar first. This change in behavior, produced not by the reinforcer alone but by the context of the water following the sugar, is referred to as **behavioral contrast** and may be a type of SE.

As part of the biological inheritance of the human species, most primary reinforcers are universal. That is, all children are affected by the same primary positive and negative reinforcers. Because of individual differences in biological makeup, there will be some individual differences in responding to primary reinforcers. For example, a child who is born without sensitivity to light will not respond to visual reinforcers as will the sighted newborn. More subtle differences in sensory capabilities mean that individual children will be more or less affected by specific primary reinforcers. These individual differences become even greater when we consider the effects of secondary or **acquired reinforcers**, also known as **conditioned reinforcers.**

Secondary Reinforcers

Secondary reinforcers are acquired or learned. The distinction between primary and secondary reinforcers is that primary reinforcers strengthen behavior due to the phylogenic history of the organism. They are unlearned. In contrast, secondary reinforcers are acquired, and this is why they are also called **conditioned reinforcers.** They are acquired because they have been paired and are correlated with primary or other secondary reinforcers. That is, they reliably signal that a response will have a certain consequence. (This is the same situation that leads to the development of discriminative stimuli.) Indeed, discriminative stimuli acquire the dual function of secondary reinforcers. Thus, in operant conditioning, when an originally neutral stimulus or event is repeatedly associated with a primary reinforcer, it acquires its reinforcing properties, and it becomes a conditioned reinforcer. Skinner (1938) conducted studies in which rats, after pressing a lever, first received food pellets accompanied by clicking sounds from the pellet dispenser. In the second part of the experiment, the rat's responses (pressing the lever) were no longer followed by food pellets. Instead, lever presses were maintained only by the clicking sound. Of course, the capacity of a stimulus to maintain behavior without often-repeated pairing to the primary reinforcer is very limited. The click eventually loses its effectiveness to function as a reinforcer unless it is again paired with food.

Unlike the essentially universal set of primary reinforcers, each individual develops a unique catalog of acquired reinforcers. The interindividual variability in acquired reinforcers is due to the unique genetic makeup and environmental conditions each child experiences. It is partly the unique set of reinforcers a person acquires that determines that person's special **repertoire of behaviors.**

Note, however, that just as universal genetic similarities produce a common set of primary reinforcers, similar environmental experiences may produce secondary reinforcers shared by most members of a family, society, culture, or even species but different from those who do not share that learning history. In turn, these reinforcers produce similar behaviors in members of the family, society, culture, or species.

What Reinforcers Are Acquired?

We know about what stimuli develop as reinforcers for newborn behavior (Gewirtz & Peláez-Nogueras, 1992a; Rovee-Collier, 1987). An infant's own mother's voice reinforces his or her sucking, whereas a strange female voice or even the voice of the father does not (DeCasper & Sigafoos, 1983). Mother's odor can also be reinforcing (Cernoch & Porter, 1985). Visual stimuli require more time to become discriminated and to acquire reinforcing functions, perhaps because of newborns' relatively poor acuity. The viewing of faces reinforces visual orientation, but Rovee-Collier (1987) concludes that the preponderance of the evidence is that faces play no special function until about 4 months of age (based on Dolgin & Azmitia, 1985).

A Research Illustration of Acquired Reinforcers

Touch provided by a caregiver to an infant can be very reinforcing. Peláez and colleagues (Peláez-Nogueras et al., 1997; Peláez-Nogueras, Gewirtz, et al., 1996) studied the effects of tactile stimulation on the duration of infant eye contact during a face-to-face situation with an adult experimenter. Ten 1.5-month-old to 4-month-old infants participated in a single-subject, repeated-measures design. The researchers compared two conditioning treatments by alternating them.

In the touch treatment, the adult smiled, cooed, and touched the infants' legs and feet when there were infant eye contact responses. In the no-touch condition, adult smiles and coos alone followed infant eye-contact responses, but no touch was given when the infant was not looking at the adult. The findings were that all babies emitted more eye contact, smiles, and vocalizations and spent less time crying and protesting in the touch condition. These results suggest that infants prefer social interactions that include touch. These findings also suggest that touch stimulation can be a primary social reinforcer for infant behavior.

To further validate this assumption, the researchers conducted a second experiment in which the effects of contingent stroking on infant attention and affective responses, such as smiling, were compared with effects of contingent tickling and poking using a synchronized reinforcement procedure. During face-to-face interactions with an adult female, twelve 2-month-old to 4.5-month-old infants participated in a within-subjects, alternating-treatments design. Each subject received the two touch-conditioning treatments in alternation within each of four consecutive sessions. In each session, three 2-minute conditioning periods were implemented. During the stroking treatment, all infants spent a greater proportion of time making eye contact with the experimenter, smiled and vocalized more, and frowned and cried less compared with their responses to the tickling and poking treatment. These results contribute to our knowledge that touch can modulate infant attention and affect in face-to-face interaction with adults, functioning as a very potent *primary social reinforcer* (Peláez-Nogueras et al., 1997).

Classes of Common Acquired Reinforcers

Tangible Reinforcers

Tangible reinforcers are objects that derive their reinforcing effects because they can be touched, viewed, smelled, or manipulated in a variety of ways. This class includes items such as stickers, trinkets, scratch-and-sniff materials, and toys.

Edible Reinforcers

As the name implies, **edible reinforcers** are eaten (Lundy et al., 1999). Most sweets, such as cookies, crackers, and M&Ms, are primary reinforcers. The taste is reinforcing because of the evolutionary history of our species. Others, such as horseradish or liver pate, are often acquired reinforcers, requiring a specialized learning history.

Social Reinforcers

Social reinforcers are acquired reinforcers that develop because they are associated with many primary reinforcers or previously established secondary reinforcers. For example, Mom's smile becomes a reinforcer because it is present when she feeds and fondles her infant. As explained earlier, some social reinforcers appear to be primary. For example, in two of three experiments conducted by Peláez et al. (1997) that examined the effects of providing touch, the infants did not interact with their mothers (their primary caregivers) but instead their responses were reinforced by a female adult who was unfamiliar to the infants.

Cooper, Heron, and Heward (1987) distinguish three types of social reinforcers: (a) physical contact (e.g., pats and hugs), (b) **proximity** (e.g., sitting near someone), and (c) verbal statements (e.g., "good job").

Activity Reinforcers

Activity reinforcers are behaviors that can themselves be reinforcing. The **Premack principle** (Premack, 1959) states that access to high-frequency behavior can reinforce any low-frequency behavior. So if your child often plays with his or her video game (a high-frequency behavior) and rarely does homework (a low-frequency behavior), you may try to use access to the former to increase the latter.

Generalized Reinforcers

Generalized reinforcers are acquired reinforcers that have been associated with many other secondary or primary reinforcers so that they are generally reinforcing. In other words, unlike food, which is reinforcing only when

Figure 6.6   Interacting With Touch

you are hungry, or a coat, which is reinforcing only when you are cold, generalized reinforcers strengthen behavior under many SEs. Examples of generalized reinforcers are money, Mom, attention, and a baby's security blanket. Generalized reinforcers are a special class of conditioned reinforcers associated with a large number of different primary reinforcers. A common example of a generalized reinforcer is money, and it works as such precisely because it can be exchanged for so many different stimuli that are inherently reinforcing or that function as primary reinforcers. Money can be exchanged for food, shelter, and safety. But like all conditioned reinforcers, money depends on its continuous association and repeated pairing (backup) with primary reinforcers. When we travel to certain countries, we may find ourselves unable to use the currency we brought with us; in those instances, money is ineffective as a reinforcer. The mere presence of a mother to her infant can function as a generalized reinforcer, because the moms are the primary providers of all the infants' needs, such as food and water. Another example of a generalized reinforcer is praise, which is used frequently in everyday life. We recommend using descriptive praise in reinforcement interventions with children in schools and home settings whenever possible, but one should avoid being repetitious, to prevent habituation or satiation. When the same nondescriptive praise sentence, such as "very good," is used over and over, it may lose its reinforcing properties.

Token Economies

In a **token economy**, the principle of conditioned reinforcer and generalized reinforcer is evident. The key feature in a token economy is that each individual can earn tokens (e.g., points, poker chips, or gold stars) by performing any of the desired target behaviors. Subsequently, the individual should be able to exchange these earned tokens for a variety of primary reinforcers. The tokens may have different criteria or costs that correspond to the response rate or measure. Money or currency also constitutes a token economy.

Shaping

In working with children, very often our goal is to increase the rate of a particular behavior. For example, a teacher may want to increase the number of cursive writing assignments students complete per week. In such a case, the teacher could use a positive reinforcement procedure and reward each completed assignment with 10 minutes of free time. However, what is a teacher to do when the student has yet to learn cursive writing? How can you reinforce a behavior that a student does not exhibit? Shaping is one answer.

Shaping is a procedure in which one reinforces **successive approximations** of a **terminal behavior.** If, for example, one is trying to teach a child to write, one can first reinforce the child's behavior of simply picking up the pencil. Once this occurs reliably, one can change the criterion for reinforcement. One now reinforces only when the child picks up the pencil so that the lead is pointing downward. In a sense, this places other, regressive, forms of pencil holding, on extinction. Because one has put the old behavior on extinction, the student will display variability in the form of the response. One form of the response is likely to be holding the pencil with the lead pointing downward. When this happens, the teacher can then reinforce the behavior. Once the student is reliably picking up the pencil with the lead pointing downward, one then shifts the criterion of reinforcement to a behavior that is a closer approximation of the terminal behavior—putting the point to the paper. By reinforcing successive approximations of the terminal behavior (shaping), one can use positive reinforcement to teach a new behavior.

Shaping does not always involve the intervention of another person, such as a teacher. Shaping often occurs as a part of normal interaction with the

Figure 6.7   Mom as a Generalized Reinforcer

environment. For example, in learning to pick up a bottle, the child's first responses are likely to involve large muscle movements of both arms and hands. As these behaviors are reinforced, the likelihood of a one-handed grasp occurring and being reinforced is increased. As the single-hand grasp is strengthened, it is more likely that other objects, such as cups, which are smaller in size, will shape finer grasping behaviors. In this way, interaction with the environment shapes new behaviors.

The famous Russian psychologist, Lev Vygotsky (1987), also emphasized the importance of shaping processes that occur during the child's assisted learning in interactions with adults. He defined the zone of proximal development as the range of behavior between what a child can achieve independently and what can be achieved with a more competent member of the culture present, such as an adult or another child. The child's behavior can be enhanced through the use of assisted learning and scaffolding. **Scaffolding** is the support and assistance that the parent (or other competent member, such as a teacher or even a computer) provides for the child's behavior. By successively moving the criteria for reinforcement ahead by small increments, the adult is able to shape new behavior (Burkholder & Peláez, 2000; Novak, 1996). We will discuss Vygotsky's ideas in more detail in the next chapter.

Chaining

Suppose you want your children to make their own sandwiches for lunch. You cannot wait for them to make sandwiches if they do not already know sandwich making. However, if they do know how to perform the individual behaviors that constitute sandwich making, you can assist or teach them to chain those behaviors together. A **behavior chain** is a set of discrete behaviors sequenced in a particular order.

To teach a behavior chain to someone, one must first perform a **task analysis**. In our example, the task of making a sandwich must be analyzed into its component behaviors. In a task analysis, one must identify the discrete behaviors composing the chain and the sequence in which these behaviors occur. Thus, sandwich making might be analyzed as follows: (a) fetch the loaf of bread, mayonnaise, and other ingredients; (b) place them on the table; (c) fetch the knife and so on. After completing the task analysis, one could then teach the students the first behavior and then teach them to perform the first and the second behaviors, and so on, until one finally taught them to perform all the behaviors in the appropriate sequence. This is called **forward chaining**.

In a commonsense method for teaching a behavior chain, one begins by providing an S^d that evokes the first behavior in the chain. In our example, one could say, "Fetch the bread and mayonnaise." Having these items in hand serves as a reinforcer for the fetching behavior. However, the bread and mayonnaise also serve as S^ds for the next behavior: placing them on the table. Similarly, seeing the loaf and mayonnaise on the table is a reinforcer for placing them there, and they are also S^ds for performing the next behavior in the chain. In this way, each response produces a reinforcer and simultaneously an S^d for the next behavior, until all of the behaviors in the chain have been performed.

Chains of behavior also develop without specialized teaching or training. Consider the following example: Kate has learned to push a button to turn on the TV. She has also learned to climb up onto a chair. She has learned to push a chair around. One day, you observe Kate push a chair over to the TV, climb up on it, and turn on the TV. Without being trained to do so, Kate has chained three discrete behaviors together in a sequence. What causes this chain to emerge?

To answer this question, we must first consider another process. In the sandwich-making example, we used forward chaining. We taught our students the first behavior first and then chained it to the performance of the second behavior, until all the behaviors in the chain had been learned in the sequence in which they are to occur. In forward chaining, the reinforcer and S^d for the initial response (getting the bread and mayonnaise) is rather weak. In contrast, the final reinforcer (eating the sandwich) is much stronger. The next procedure, **backward chaining**, takes advantage of this fact.

In backward chaining, the trainer may perform all the behaviors involved in sandwich making except the final behavior in the chain. All that is left for the student to do is the final behavior, which is immediately and powerfully reinforced by the taste of the sandwich. Once the student can reliably perform the final behavior, the trainer would then require the student to perform the last two behaviors in the chain. Then the student performs the last three, in sequence. Eventually, the student learns the first behavior in the chain and can now perform the entire chain. The major advantage of this approach is that during the first lesson, the student immediately contacts the highly reinforcing consequences of eating the sandwich. This does three things: First, the response is quickly strengthened by establishing the relationship between the response and the consequence. Second, the antecedents of the last response quickly become S^ds for its occurrence. Last, because of their role as S^ds, antecedents of the last response become conditioned reinforcers for the next-to-last response.

Let us return to our earlier question about how Kate developed her chain of behaviors. The reinforcer that holds the chain together is seeing a TV show (e.g., *Sesame Street*). Pushing the button is reinforced by this. Touching the button is an S^d for pushing it. It also becomes a reinforcer for a response (climbing on the chair), which is reinforced by touching the button. At this point, you should be able to follow the chain back to its initial S^d. Can you? What would happen to Kate's chain of behavior if the TV broke?

Fading

Fading is a technique that involves transferring stimulus control or cue control from one stimulus to another. We teach our children new responses by using prompts and cues. For example, in the presence of Mary's dad, her mother may ask, "Who is he?" After many of these instances, Mary learns to say "Dad." In the presence of her father, gradually, Mary's mother may only say, "Who . . . ?" and Mary may still emit the same response: "Dad!" Eventually, her mother may completely withdraw the question and her prompts in small steps until just Mary's father's face evokes the correct response. In this example of the fading procedure, gradual transfer of stimulus control from Mary's mother's verbal prompt to her father's facial features occurred.

Schedules of Reinforcement

Some behaviors are always followed by reinforcers. However, this continuous reinforcement schedule is rare. Most often, reinforcement does not follow every behavior but is intermittent. The same is true for punishment, which seldom follows every occurrence of the response. The **schedule of reinforcement** is important because it has an effect on the pattern of responding by the individual. Schedules of reinforcement have been extensively studied in the laboratory (Ferster & Skinner, 1957) and in real life. In our complex lives, the behaviors of people may be under the influence complex schedules of reinforcement. We shall look at some simple schedules and see how they are likely to affect our behaviors.

Continuous-Reinforcement Schedule

Continuous reinforcement (CRF) is the simplest schedule of reinforcement. Every response produces a reinforcer. For example, every time you flip a light switch, the light goes on, or every time a child sucks from a bottle, he or she gets milk. The result is that the response is strengthened most rapidly. Thus, learning is very rapid with CRF because each response gets reinforced. Although CRF occurs naturally, it is also the schedule of choice in teaching someone a response.

Although learning is most rapid under CRF schedules, there are some problems with using it. First, CRF is expensive to employ. Because each response receives a reinforcer, many reinforcers must be delivered. If tangibles are employed, this can literally be expensive. But even with social reinforcers, it can cost the teacher a lot of time and effort. Second, satiation is more likely with CRF. **Satiation** is SE in which the more the person receives the reinforcer, the less reinforcing the reinforcer becomes. For example, the more you eat, the less reinforcing food becomes. Baer and Sherman (1964) showed how children could become satiated to social reinforcers. One way to avoid satiation is to make a wide variety of reinforcers available so that new ones can be substituted for those that are no longer effective. The use of generalized reinforcers, such as praise or tokens (or money), can also be useful because they are not likely to satiate the person.

A third problem with CRF is that it can lead to rapid extinction of the response if reinforcement does not occur. Imagine a child who starts playing a game at a level that is very easy. He has a history of continuous reinforcement, where every move is reinforced by the game's feedback. Now, if the game moves to a more difficult level and several of the child's moves do not produce reinforcement, he is likely to stop playing the game. We then have extinction, which is more likely to occur because the child has had a history of every previous response being reinforced. Thus, although CRF has advantages in producing rapid acquisition, it has some liabilities in practice.

Intermittent-Reinforcement Schedule

The term **intermittent reinforcement** is used for any of the schedules in which only some responses are followed by reinforcers. There are four basic schedules of intermittent reinforcement, based on whether there is a constant (fixed) or varied (variable) basis for reinforcement and whether the reinforcement requires a certain number of responses before reinforcement (a ratio) or a certain passage of time before the response is reinforced (an interval). We shall look at these four simple schedules of intermittent reinforcement next and how they affect behavior.

Fixed-Ratio Schedule

Imagine infant Jill with a jack-in-the-box. Jill turns the crank once and nothing happens. She turns it again; nothing happens. The same for the third time, but on the fourth turn of the crank—boom! The jack pops out with a loud noise. After laughing and enjoying this surprise, Jill pushes the jack back in and cranks again. Again, after four turns, the jack pops out. This pattern continues until Jill is satiated with the toy. Thus, there is a ratio of one pop to four cranks. This is called an FR4 because the four-response requirement is constant or fixed.

What happens to Jill's behavior if 15 cranks are required for the jack to pop out? What if 100 are needed? What happens if the toy breaks, and jack will never pop out?

The effect on behavior of **fixed-ratio** (FR) **schedules** is well documented. The pattern of responding is consistent, with a brief pause after the reinforcer is delivered and then a generally rapid rate of responding that peaks with the response that produces the reinforcer. The greater the number of responses needed to produce reinforcement, the more rapid the responding. So whereas

Jill would turn the crank fairly slowly if the toy popped on a FR4 schedule, her cranking under FR15 would be very fast, and it would occur at a dizzying rate if the jack was made to pop under a FR100 schedule.

What if the toy breaks and jack will no longer pop out? In CRF, extinction would occur rapidly. After a history of every crank turn producing a reinforcer, Jill would quickly learn to stop when no turns produced the effect. Extinction would take only a little more time with a FR4 schedule, but the predictability of the schedule makes the changed contingency easy to detect. Likewise, the additional cranks required for the FR15 and FR100 schedules would mean that extinction would take only a bit longer.

Variable-Ratio Schedules

Mechanical things, such as machines and computers, frequently reinforce on FR schedules. Many times, adults and teachers impose FR requirements for children's behaviors (e.g., "You have to do four laps before you can rest"; "You have to finish 15 problems before you go outside to play"). What they get is the child's behavior matching the reinforcement contingency. There is a high rate of responding until reinforcement is delivered. This is followed by a postreinforcement pause. However, many contingencies in nature do not require a specified number of responses before reinforcement but are more variable. Thus, **variable-ratio** (VR) **schedules**, in which the number of responses before reinforcement vary, are more common. They produce the same rapid responding that FR schedules produce (although they are generally even more rapid), but because it is impossible to predict which response will be reinforced, VR schedules are less likely than FR schedules to produce the pauses when the reinforcer is delivered.

The classic VR schedule is employed with slot machines: Each response has the same probability of reinforcement. The result is that slot machine players show steady and very rapid rates of responding. VR schedules are identified by the average number of responses required between reinforcements, so a VR4 means, on average, every fourth response will be reinforced; but even though there is a 1-in-4 chance that the first response will be reinforced, reinforcement may not occur until the sixth or eighth or even later response. In fact, schedules with higher response requirements generate more rapid responding, as a person works faster to get the reinforcer.

Besides producing high, stable rates of responding, VR schedules are very resistant to extinction. Because the reinforcement is predictable, and each response may be the one that is followed by reinforcement, the person is likely to continue. Because the person has had a history of making many responses without reinforcement only to have the next response reinforced, he or she is likely to continue responding long after the last reinforcer has been given.

Fixed-Interval Schedules

Consider the following: Mac is a sports fan who can't wait to read the latest about his team each morning in the local newspaper. Each morning, he gets in his car and drives to the corner store to buy the paper. The paper is delivered every day at precisely 7 A.M. What pattern does Mac's newspaper-buying (and driving) behavior follow? The pattern is typical of a **fixed-interval** (FI) pattern, in which the first response after the lapse of an interval of time is reinforced. Mac will probably get in his car just before 7:00, drive to the store where he buys his paper (the reinforcer), and then return. He will wait another 24 hours before more paper-purchasing behavior.

Thus, FI schedules produce almost no responding at the beginning of the interval, with a gradual ramp-up of responding just before the interval is due to be up. In Mac's case, he was able to use a clock as a discriminative stimulus, so his responding was at zero until the interval was up and then only one response was emitted. For cases in which the end of the interval is not clearly discernible, several responses may be emitted.

Born and Davis (1974) observed the studying behavior of students enrolled in psychology courses in which tests were scheduled either weekly, monthly, or only at midterm and finals. Thus, reinforcement for studying (the test) was on either a FI 1-week, FI 1-month, or FI 5-week schedule. The study materials were available only in a reserved room, so data could be collected about the amount of studying that was actually done. Students showed the typical FI pattern of behavior in which very little studying was done at the beginning of the interval and a lot occurred just before the test, regardless of whether the test occurred every week, every month, or only twice during the semester.

Although schedules are generally applied to individuals and their behavior, some studies have shown that the same effects can be seen in the behavior of groups. For example, Weisberg and Waldrop (1972) looked at the number of bills passed by the U.S. Congress during each session. Very little bill-passing behavior occurred at the beginning or even during the middle of each congressional session. Instead, a sudden burst of activity occurred just prior to the congressional recess when members of congress returned to their local areas. In a follow-up study, Critchfield, Haley, Meacropolis, Colbert, and Sabo (in press) updated these data by looking at the bill-passing behavior of Congress from 1949 to 2000 and found the same pattern typical of FI schedules as found earlier by Weisberg and Waldrop.

Likewise, Novak (2001) looked at when graduate students posted discussion questions and answers on the class Web site. The initial contingency was that these had to be posted prior to the weekly class meeting. The results showed an almost perfect FI pattern of responding, with nearly no posting early in the interval and the highest rate of responding just before class. Changing the criterion to an earlier time (to give fellow students a chance to reply) changed the day of the week that responding occurred but did not change the FI type pattern.

Variable-Interval Schedules

In **variable-interval** (VI) **schedules**, the first response after the interval has elapsed gets reinforced, but the length of the interval varies around a certain average time. For example, Lisa gets an e-mail from her boyfriend, Josh, once a day, on average. However, 2 or 3 days may pass, and Lisa will receive no mail from Josh. But at other times, she may get more than one e-mail a day from him. The result of this (VI) schedule is that Lisa will continuously check her e-mails at a higher rate compared with when Josh writes once every day.

Other Schedules of Reinforcement

We have been considering schedules based on the number of responses required for reinforcement (ratio) and the passage of time before a response is reinforced (interval). We have also considered the effects of fixed or variable requirements. Other reinforcement schedules exist: **differential reinforcement of high rate of behavior** (DRH) and **differential reinforcement of low rate of behavior** (DRL). In DRH, the person is reinforced for doing the behavior at or above a certain rate. For example, when the child says more than five words a minute, he or she is reinforced. In DRL schedules, the response requirement is the opposite: The child may be reinforced for talking less than one word per minute. What effect do these schedules have? As you might guess, DRH produces high rates of behavior and DRL produces low rates of responding. These schedules can be used to increase behaviors occurring at low rates (DRH) or decrease those occurring at high rates (DRL).

Differential reinforcement of other behavior (DRO), **differential reinforcement of alternative behavior** (DRA), and **differential reinforcement of incompatible behavior** (DRI) are frequently used schedules in the reduction of undesirable behavior. Using the DRA, DRI, and DRO schedules, an alternative behavior is identified, and, when it occurs, it is reinforced instead of the target undesirable behavior. The original behavior is not reinforced and is put on an extinction schedule. DRO is sometimes used as an alternative to punishment to reduce undesirable behavior and to establish constructive replacement behavior.

In addition, we have fixed-time (FT) and variable-time (VT) schedules, where reinforcement occurs once the time interval has elapsed, regardless of whether there is a response or not. For example, the delivery of snail mail in our homes occurs independently of our going to the mailbox or not. Another schedule is called *limited hold* (LH). In LH schedules, the reinforcer is not given and is lost if the person fails to respond within a certain time period. For example, there are many TV game shows in which the participants need to give the correct response within a period of seconds or the opportunity to win a prize or money is lost.

A Research Example Comparing CRF With DRO

In a laboratory experiment, Gewirtz and Peláez-Nogueras (1991a) were able to increase and reduce the crying and protest behavior of twenty-three 6-month old to 11-month-old infants. Their mothers, in successive daily training sessions, were instructed to ignore their infants' protest on separations and to return to their infants only when the babies were playing. Using a single-subject (reversal) design, the infants' separation protests were increased under maternal continuous reinforcement schedule (CRF) and decreased under maternal differential reinforcement schedule (DRO).

Often in behavior analysis, the DRO behaviors are also called **replacement behaviors**. In this study by Gewirtz and Peláez-Nogueras (1991a), play was the replacement behavior under DRO. Play behavior increased, and infant protest behavior decreased. The infant protest rate shifted downward from CRF to DRO treatments and upward from DRO to CRF treatments.

Gewirtz and Peláez-Nogueras (1991a) concluded that infant protests to maternal departures and to brief separations could be conditioned via the operant paradigm. They criticized the mainstream view that infant protests result from an underlying cause, such as "separation anxiety" or "insecurity of attachment". Peláez and Gewirtz's research program has generated useful practical implications from the view of applied behavior analysis regarding advice for parents on how to behave toward their infants during separations to preclude maladaptive behavioral outcomes, how to reverse these behavioral patterns when they have already have been established, and how to establish more constructive developmentally appropriate behavioral patterns in their children.

The researchers carried out a second experiment (Peláez-Nogueras, 1992) with eighteen 6-month-old to 9-month-old infants and their mothers. This within-subjects and between-subjects design replicated the findings with younger infants and demonstrated *conditional discrimination training:* In one condition, babies learned to protest in response to their mothers' departure's cues before separation and not to protest during their absence. A second group was taught the opposite pattern: The babies learned to protest their mothers' absence but not their mothers' departures. This was a demonstration of the role of different contextual cues in controlling behavior of infants.

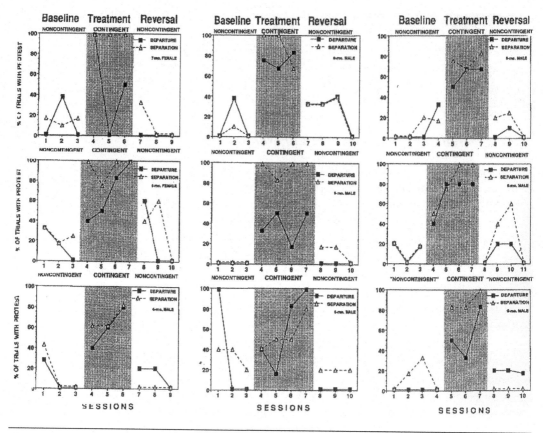

Figure 6.8   Maternal Responses to Infant Protests

Complex Schedules of Reinforcement

So far, we have considered simple schedules of reinforcement. Although pure FR, VR, FI, and VI schedules are often in effect and affect the patterns of behavior, many times complex schedules are in effect. These include multiple and mixed schedules, change and tandem schedules, and concurrent schedules (Catania, 1998). What these complex schedules have in common is that more than one schedule is affecting behavior. When multiple or mixed schedules are in effect, the schedules alternate and are not in effect simultaneously. With tandem and concurrent schedules, when an initial schedule ends, a second begins, such as the individual who must wait till the end of the week to go to a movie (FI) and then goes to several over the next few days (VR). With concurrent schedules, two or more schedules of reinforcement will be in effect at the same time, and we match our behavior to the one that provides the most reinforcement. The intricacies of these schedules and the differences in patterns of behavior produced are well documented under a wide range of situations (e.g., Catania, 1998; Ferster & Skinner, 1957).

A Final Word About Reinforcement Schedules

Schedules of reinforcement can be employed by those wishing to change child and adult behavior. For example, in trying to initially teach a behavior, CRF is the most effective schedule to use because the maximum reinforcement of response produces the fastest acquisition of behavior. With the constant use of reinforcers in CRF, however, satiation is likely to occur so that new reinforcers must be introduced. In addition, CRF is likely to lead to easy extinction when the person with a history of receiving reinforcers for every response now stops getting them. This can be avoided by switching from CRF to an intermittent schedule. This means fewer reinforcers and more **resistance to extinction.** Yet care must be taken to avoid making the schedules too thinly reinforcing too soon, to avoid extinction and loss of behavior. Furthermore, you may find that pattern of responding produced by the schedule in effect is not the most desired.

We have suggested how schedules may be used in contrived reinforcement situations in which you are trying to bring about changes in the behavior of yourself or another. It is important to emphasize that schedules, as with the other aspects of learning we have described here and in the previous chapter, occur naturally, without any intended or contrived intervention. We all respond to the contingencies that occur naturally in our environments, based on our current and previous experiences. Many of these contingencies are scheduled, usually in complex ways, and our behavior is, in part, affected by these naturally occurring schedules of reinforcement, punishment, and extinction.

OPERANT LEARNING AND DYNAMICAL ● PRINCIPLES OF DEVELOPMENT

With this discussion, we conclude our look at the basic processes of development. Recall that learning is a process involved in all development. Even in basic sensory abilities, exposure to a species-typical environment is necessary for change. Recall also that learning plays the central role in the development of the rest of human behavior. But to understand how such seemingly simple processes of learning can produce the complexity of human behavioral development, we must revisit the principles of dynamical systems.

In Chapter 2, we discussed how and why development involves the reciprocal interaction of the organismic and environmental factors. We concluded that the process of development involves the coalescence of genetics, interactional history, current physiological conditions, and current environmental conditions coming together to organize behavior.

Coalescent Organization Revisited

Behavior is assembled by the task and the context (Thelen & Ulrich, 1991). Another way of saying this is that the coalescence of factors occurs through the contingencies of reinforcement in effect for the child. Under certain SEs, a bright, shiny object will evoke reaching. The form of the chain of behaviors of reaching will be determined by the coalescence of many factors, including the genetically influenced shape of the arm and hand, the presence of gravity; the history of reaching for visual stimuli; the consequences of reaching, both past and present; and the existence of hidden skills. All this is assembled by the environmental contingencies presented by the environment. The child goes from one phase of reaching (two-handed) to another (one-handed) as the coalescence of factors enables the child to reach and grasp the object with one hand. Hundreds of tiny influences come together through the contingency of reaching—feeling the object to produce phase shifts in the organized pattern of behavior we call reaching. Shifts happen!

Another Look at the Emergence of Dynamic Attractors

As you remember, the patterns that emerge are called *attractors*. They have a characteristic topography or form based on the limits imposed by the coalescence of factors involved. That is, at a particular time in development, reaching may be limited to picking up objects with two hands by lack of skill and physical strength. The development of increased strength due to physical changes in bones and muscles, coupled with skills learned through environmental contingencies, lead to one-handed reach-grasps. Yet even a basic behavior such as reaching for and picking up an object is organized by the consequences. Think about your own reaching. If the task is to pick up a pin, what will the form of your response be? What if the task is to pick up a 30-pound boulder? What if you need to pick up a 30-pound dumbbell? What determines the form of the response?

The Importance of Leading Parts or Control Parameters

Although many factors coalesce to produce behavioral development, some play larger, more important roles than others. Some factors disproportionately affect development. You have learned the term *leading parts* (Horowitz, 1987) or control parameters for this principle. For example, in the backward chaining procedures discussed earlier, the final reinforcer is a control parameter.

The Issue of Nonlinearity

We often assume that reinforcement has linear effects, that each reinforcer adds the same amount to the strength of a response. You have recognized that this assumption is often not true. Reinforcements and punishments may have little effect on behavior at first, and then a single reinforcement (or punishment) may have a suddenly large effect on the behavior. Thus, the effect of contingencies may be nonlinear.

Nonlinearity also appears in shaping. Very seldom do the successive approximations to the final goal involve evenly spaced steps. More frequently, the approximations are nonlinear. Early steps may be very small, and later steps may be large leaps. Consider children playing a hiding game. One child has to find a hidden toy. Approximations to finding it are reinforced by "You're getting warmer!" and punished by "You're getting colder!" At first, we are likely to see small movements around a local area. Then, the child's searching behavior may involve larger movements, and progress toward the goal may be much faster. At the end of the search, approximations may again involve smaller steps.

SUMMARY ●

Although learning, especially operant learning, is only one of the processes in development, it plays a key role. The contingencies of reinforcement and punishment assemble behavior into loosely organized patterns or attractors. The function of behavior determines its form; form follows function. Forms are continually developing as the effects of biological, historical, and current environmental factors combine to make behavior function more efficiently at producing reinforcement and avoiding, terminating, or escaping punishment. Psychological development is a process of adapting to our environment, and it is learning that provides the flexibility to do so.

B. F. Skinner chose the term *operant* to describe behavior that operates on the environment to produce changes in the environment that, in turn, affect the behavior's frequency and form. An important aspect of *operant behavior* is that it is *emitted* in the environment, not *elicited* by environmental stimuli. However, operant behavior can come to be *evoked* by an *antecedent* stimulus. Some operants have their origins as reflexive behaviors, although most are not. Most develop from emitted responses that are strengthened or weakened by environmental consequences. Some consequences universally strengthen or weaken behavior, whereas others exert an idiosyncratic influence. To understand operant behavior, it is important to understand contingencies. A *contingency* is a relationship between response and stimulus, where the presentation of a stimulus depends on the performance of some type of response. It can be expressed in terms of an if–then relationship.

Operant behavior can be conceptualized in terms of a *four-term contingency.* In such a contingency, within a particular context (*setting event*), a particular stimulus (*discriminative stimulus*) evokes a behavior (response) that produces a change in the environment (consequence). Operant responses can be classified by *topography* (form), *function* (effect on the environment), and physical location (inside or outside of the skin). The variability of operant behavior allows for selection to take place according to consequences. It increases the likelihood that novel behaviors will be developed and shaped.

Operants produce consequences that either increase or decrease the likelihood of such a behavior's occurrence in the future. These consequences consist of presentation or termination of a stimulus. When such operations strengthen behavior, this is known as *reinforcement. Positive reinforcement* involves presentation of a stimulus, whereas *negative reinforcement* involves termination of an aversive stimulus. An operation that weakens behavior is known as *punishment.* Whereas *positive punishment* involves the presentation of an aversive stimulus, *negative punishment* involves removal of a typically desirable stimulus.

Operant behaviors can undergo *extinction* (cease) when reinforcers are withheld or the behavior is punished. An *extinction burst* (rapid increase in responding) often accompanies the withholding of reinforcement. Operant responding is cued by a discriminative stimulus (a stimulus preceding the response–consequence contingency), whereas general conditions affecting the stimulus–response relationship (setting events) determine the likelihood of an S^d's provoking a response or determining the degree to which a consequence is reinforcing or punishing. A variety of reinforcers are already in effect at birth; others are acquired. These are *primary* and *secondary reinforcers,* respectively. Primary reinforcers owe their strengthening effects to the phylogenic history of a species, whereas the effectiveness of secondary reinforcers is the result of their association with primary or other secondary reinforcers. Classes of *acquired reinforcers* include tangible, edible, social, active, and generalized reinforcers (the principles on which *token economies* are based).

The development of a desired operant can be achieved through *shaping*—the process by which the performance of a terminal behavior is achieved through reinforcement of *successive approximations* of that behavior. Shaping can be the result of the intervention of another person or of normal interaction with the environment. Shaping is a central element in Vygostsky's conception of learning. He emphasizes that there is a differential between what a child can achieve on its own and what can be achieved with the assistance of more competent members of society (the zone of proximal development). He used the term *scaffolding* to describe the support provided by such persons to shape new behavior by successive progression of criteria for reinforcement in the process of learning behaviors.

The performance of complex behavioral sequences can be achieved through the process of **chaining.** A *behavior chain* consists of a discrete set of behaviors sequenced in a particular order. A prerequisite to teaching a behavior chain is the performance of a *task analysis,* in which the discrete behaviors composing the chain and the sequence in which they occur are identified. In *forward chaining,* the process begins with presentation of an S^d, evoking the first behavior in the chain. The result is an initial reinforcer that also functions as an S^d for the next response, and so on until the chain is completed, resulting in presentation of the final reinforcer, the effects of which are usually much stronger than the initial reinforcer. A process that capitalizes on this situation is the process of *backward chaining,* where the terminal link is the first behavior performed: the immediate presentation of the final reinforcer. Subsequently, the individual is required to perform an increasing number of links to receive the final reinforcer, regressing back through the chain until it is performed in its entirety.

Schedules of reinforcement are important due to their differential effects on patterns of responding by individuals. Schedules of reinforcement include *continuous reinforcement* (CRF), *fixed ratio* (FR), *variable ratio* (VR), *fixed interval* (FI), *variable interval* (VI), fixed time (FT), limited hold (LH), *differential reinforcement of high rate of behavior* (DRH), *differential reinforcement of low rate of behavior* (DRL), *differential reinforcement of other behavior* (DRO), *differential reinforcement of alternative behavior* (DRA), and *differential reinforcement of incompatible behavior* (DRI). Many times, complex schedules of reinforcement are in effect. These include multiple and mixed schedules, change and tandem schedules, and concurrent schedules. With multiple or mixed schedules, schedules alternate and are not in effect at the same time. With change and tandem schedules, the termination of an initial schedule is accompanied by the onset of a second. With concurrent schedules, two or more schedules of reinforcement are simultaneously in effect. In attempting to modify behavior, consideration must be given to the various ways in which different schedules of reinforcement affect behavior. It is important to choose a schedule of reinforcement that will produce the desired effect most efficiently. It is also important to note that schedules of reinforcement also occur naturally in the environment, affecting the behaviors of all.

Although learning holds a place of importance in the process of development, it cannot account for the whole of human development. It is but one component of a dynamic system. Development is the result of the coalescent organization of genetic factors, interactional history, and current physiological and environmental conditions. The coalescence of factors varies as a function of environmental contingencies. The topographies (forms) of emergent patterns of behavior, called attractors, depend on limits set forth by the coalescence of factors involved. Some factors disproportionately affect development. These are called leading parts or control parameters. The complexity in interaction of the factors involved in development illustrates the fact that the effects of contingencies are nonlinear. Development is best conceived of as a dynamic process of adaptation to the environment in which learning plays an important role by providing us with the flexibility to meet changing demands.

● NOTES

1. We choose to use the term *response* here, which is conventional behavioral terminology. Ferster and Culbertson (1982) caution that using the term for operant behavior may be misleading. Operant behavior is affected by its consequences, not by responding to stimuli, as respondent behavior is. We have considered using B to stand for behavior with C for consequence and A for antecedent. Thus, our contingency would include the ABCs. However, the $S^d \rightarrow R \rightarrow S^r$ notation is more widely used and will be the convention used here.

2. Note that the shorthand notation for the consequent stimulus is either S^{r+} or S^{r-}. These are the technical names for the consequent stimulus. S^{r+} may be read as "positive reinforcing stimulus" or "positive reinforcer." S^{r-} is read as "negative reinforcing stimulus" or "negative reinforcer."

3. Reinforcement is an operation (a specific procedure implemented by the experimenter) involving contingencies that strengthen behavior. A reinforcer is a stimulus that follows the behavior and strengthens it. Depending on whether the consequence of the behavior is to add or remove the stimulus, the stimulus is called a positive or negative reinforcer, respectively.

4. The operation in which reinforcers are withheld is called *operant extinction*. However, behaviors become extinguished, not *extincted*.

5. Morris (1993b) argues that behavior analysts have adopted two types of contexts in their systems. The first type is, as used here, concerned with general setting conditions that alter the other three terms of the contingency. Morris (1993b) believes that this "context-as-place" is what most people mean when they use the word *context*. However, Morris also points out that behavior analysis is also contextualistic because it adopts the

second sense of the word: context as time. This sense of the word places current behavior squarely in the context of a history of interaction, a basic behavioral systems view that is entirely consistent with developmental psychology.

6. Michael (1982, 1993) uses the term *establishing operation* and identifies both the evocative and contingency-altering effects of certain events or operation. The term *setting event* is used here, based on the terminology used by Bijou and Baer (1961). Numerous other researchers have dealt with these contextual variables under different headings: "third variables" (Skinner, 1931), "setting factors" (Kantor, 1946), "setting events" (Bijou & Baer, 1978; Bijou, 1998), "potentiating variables" (Goldiamond & Dyrud, 1967), "contextual determinants" (Gewirtz, 1972b; Morris, 1988) and "contextual interactants" (Peláez-Nogueras, & Gewirtz, 1997).

CHAPTER 7

COGNITIVE DEVELOPMENT

Cogito, ergo sum.

I think, therefore, I am.

This famous quote from the French philosopher René Descartes (1596–1650) underlies the prominence of thinking as the most important human characteristic. What are thinking and thought? How shall we treat them from a natural science viewpoint? How do they develop? How are language and thought related? These are questions undertaken in this chapter.

Cognition means "the act or process of knowing" (Stein, 1973). For most of us, knowing means thinking. For Skinner and other behavior analysts, thinking is an action: It is behavior. In this view, the only difference between some cognitive acts and other operants is their location. Cognitive behavior thoughts are private events occurring inside the skin. But not all **cognitive behaviors** are private events. Cognitive behaviors include many overt behaviors related to the external environment. As Skinner (1989) said, "Cognitive processes are behavioral processes; they are things people do" (p. 17).

Skinner (1953) identified two aspects of cognition: **knowledge** and **ability**. He treated these as operant behaviors. Bijou and Baer (1961) added a third category of cognition, **problem solving**. In addition, we will look at exploratory behavior and creative behavior in this chapter. **Cognitive development** involves the changes in our knowledge and abilities over our life spans. We will examine the development of these behaviors from the viewpoint of behavioral systems theory. However, to put the study of cognitive development into historical perspective, let us look at the first systematic theory of cognitive development—Jean Piaget's.

● PIAGET'S THEORY OF COGNITIVE DEVELOPMENT

Box 7.1 Piaget's Worldview

Piaget transformed developmental theory. It is interesting to see how this theory emerged from Piaget's early training and the existing worldview of his day. Jean Piaget was born in Neuchâtel, Switzerland in 1896. His godfather was a professor of philosophy with a specialty in logic. Although he also studied logic, the young Jean's real interest was biology, and he published his first scientific paper at the age of 10! (It was on his observations of an albino sparrow.) By age 22, he had received a Ph.D. in biology and had published over two dozen papers in his specialization.

The dominant theory in the field of biology during his time was the then still new and controversial theory of Charles Darwin. Darwin's theory of natural selection inspired Piaget's doctoral dissertation on mollusks. Piaget studied the patterns of whorls on shells of different populations of freshwater snails. Using Darwin's theory, he explained how the structure of the snail's shells evolved due to natural selection. Snails in a particular ecosystem had different patterns of shells that allowed for better adaptation to the existing environmental conditions. Thus, some patterns were better fits to their ecological niche.

The basic idea of adaptation marked his viewpoint when he turned his interest to psychology. In Paris from 1919 to 1921, Piaget studied at the Sorbonne and worked on the development of intelligence tests with Theodore Simon. Simon, along with his colleague, Alfred Binet, is credited with developing the first standardized intelligence tests. Piaget began giving individual intelligence tests to children but soon became unhappy following the restricted format of the test. Shortly, he became intrigued by the errors the children made, and instead of just noting the answers as wrong, Piaget began pursuing wrong test answers given by children to try to identify the logic used in producing the errors. His use of this so-called **clinical method,** in which a small number of individuals are examined extensively, led him to a lifelong interest in the intensive questioning of just a few young children. Among the subjects studied were his own children. This method, which is very different from the more widely used method of employing large, randomized pools of subjects, led Piaget to develop a theory of what children know about the world and how they come by this knowledge. After a distinguished career that spanned many decades, Piaget died in 1980 at the age of 84.

What Changes? Structure

In his doctoral dissertation, Piaget was interested in changes in biological structure in phylogenic development. The structures of the snail shells he studied changed in form as they adapted to changes in the ecology. Subsequently, he looked for and found a parallelism in the development of knowledge. He inferred change in the structure of thought. He believed that the structure of knowledge, or mental structures, developed over an individual's life span (note that this is another parallel of natural selection). Piaget called these mental structures schemes.[1]

For Piaget, schemes are mental representations of the world. **Schemes** may be actions, images, or symbols used to interpret interactions with the environment. These organized mental representations are the child's knowledge of the world in the form of miniature models of that world. Changes in these schemes mean changes in the child's knowledge of the world. The schemes that are the representation of the world in infancy are not only fewer than in adulthood, but their type and organization differ as well. For Piaget, development includes qualitative, not just quantitative changes (Phillips, 1975). That is, the types of schemes are different in children and adults. Piaget based his stages of cognitive development on behavior patterns that resulted from the emergence of increasingly more complex and more highly organized schemes.

Schemes

What does the newborn know about the world? What form do its mental structures take? Piaget (1952) believed that the child's first representations of the world were his or her reactions to stimuli in the form of reflexes. Thus, the child's first schemes were behavioral schemes. Remember, a reflex involves the relationship between a stimulus and a response. **Behavioral schemes** are mental representations in the form of actions. So Piaget called his first stage, between birth and about 2 years, the sensorimotor (i.e., stimulus-response) stage.

As development continues, behavioral schemes are expanded to include behaviors other than just reflexes. This process, termed by Piaget (1952) as **circular reactions,** extends other (e.g., operant) stimulus-response relations into more complex and more highly organized behavior schemes. Bruner (1964) called the mental representation of the world by actions **enactive representation**. For an example of a behavioral scheme, think of what you would do if someone asked, "What's a Slinky?" You would probably hold your hands palm up and alternate moving them up and down. That is a behavioral scheme for a Slinky.

During the second year, the child begins to represent the world first with images and then through language. Bruner (1964) called the use of images **iconic representation,** with **language** being labeled **symbolic representation.** Unlike behavioral schemes, images and words do not involve the actual physical activity they represent. Still, an iconic representation (e.g., an image of a sunset) has a physical correspondence to what it is representing (e.g., the actual sunset). **Symbolic schemes** are arbitrary representations of the things they stand for, not the things themselves. The word *sunset* does not look like or feel like an actual sunset. In Piaget's view, symbolic schemes enable increased ability to represent the world, resulting in increased knowledge. Asking you to close your eyes and think of what a Slinky looks like would evoke an iconic representation of it (an image). Asking you what the object is called would evoke a symbolic representation—"Slinky." However, by using words, you could come up with many more ways that a Slinky can be used than you can picture or act out.

Piaget's last category of schemes is the **operational scheme.** In Piaget's view, an operation is a set of mental tasks that follows certain logical rules. Addition, subtraction, and negation are operations. So is reversibility, transforming something into another thing and then changing it back. Being able to perform an operation provides us with greater flexibility and precision in understanding the world.

According to Piaget, what develops is not only the type of schemes (starting with simple behavioral to symbolic and then operational ones) but also the amount and complexity of schemes. The proposed mental representations of the world become not only more numerous but more organized as well. As we develop, our representations increase from "mommy" to "girl" to "woman." Our representation also takes on a hierarchical organization: "mommy" fits under the class "woman." With time, the differentiation of the world produces highly organized structures of schemes. Your knowledge of the world is determined by your schemes. Thus, as your schemes become more organized and differentiated, so does your knowledge of the world. As schemes become more organized and differentiated, they provide a better model for representing the world. Now we turn to the question of "how" development occurs.

How Do the Structures Change? Functions

In the Darwin-driven biology of Piaget's day, **adaptation** was the basic process for change in biological structures. Piaget saw a parallelism to his study of the development of knowledge. For Piaget, mental structures also changed through a process of adaptation. Biologists saw physical structures changing by adapting to the physical environment. Piaget saw mental structures changing through adaptation to the intellectual environment.

Adaptation = Assimilation and Accommodation

Biologists saw adaptation occurring through the action of two reciprocal and complementary processes: **assimilation** and **accommodation**. Both are necessary to produce changes in physical structures. Consider an example:

Imagine that you are really starved after a busy morning at school. You go to the cafeteria, and to your delight you find that there is a special sale on chocolate decadence cake. It seems that the baker thought it said six cases of flour, not six cups, and they have about a dozen cakes too many. In order to sell them, whole cakes are on sale for $1.00 a cake. Not being one who could turn down a bargain (or chocolate decadence, for that matter) you purchase one of the cakes.

Now, what do you do? Not being of reptilian ancestry, unhinging your lower jaw is impossible. You are going to have to do something to be able to take the cake (environmental input) into your existing structures (mouth, esophagus, stomach, intestines). You begin to modify the input to put it into a form that will fit the existing structure: you must assimilate the cake.

What is the consequence of this? (We are all too familiar with this.) Your existing structures assimilate the portion of input that readily fits into current structures. (Biologically, this process would parallel digestion.) Yet often (and unfortunately for those watching their weight) some portion, usually the fat, of the input does not fit into existing structures. So the structures change or accommodate this new input. In the case of the cake, thighs, hips, and stomach are often the accommodating structures. Thus, development is the result of the complementary action of both assimilation and accommodation.

Piaget applied these processes to cognitive development. Both assimilation and accommodation are necessary for changes in schemes to occur. Assimilation involves taking environmental information into existing structures (i.e., schemes). For this to occur, aspects of the information inconsistent with existing schemes are ignored, modified, or changed. For example, a child who already has the symbolic scheme "car," sees a motorcycle go by. She says "car" and sees it as a car. She has assimilated the motorcycle into her existing scheme.

Yet what the child saw was discrepant from the existing scheme—car. This thing had only two wheels, the rider was in the open, and it made a different sound. These discrepancies make the existing schemes change to accommodate the experience. Thus, the scheme for car becomes enlarged or perhaps organized into different but hierarchically organized schemes involving cars, motorcycles, and vehicles.

The result of this reciprocal action of assimilation and accommodation is adaptation. The child's knowledge and ability fits better with his or her environment. Yet the more we know, the more we need to know. The environment of the neonate is a good deal less demanding than that of the adult. A few simple behavioral schemes (the reflexes) are all the newborn knows or needs to know. However, by assimilating new information, the infant allows accommodation to make for increasingly more numerous and complex schemes that better represent the complexity of the real world. Thus, this active interaction between what the child knows and what he or she needs to know produces, in Piaget's view, changes in cognitive development.

Equilibrium–Disequilibrium

What motivates adaptation? Piaget's view is that it is the mismatch between what the child knows and what it needs to know that causes assimilation and accommodation. This mismatch produces a disequilibrium or imbalance in that there is always more to know. **Disequilibrium** is the normal state, whereas **equilibrium** is achieved only temporarily when the cognitive structure matches what there is to know in the environment. If the discrepancy is too large (e.g., teaching an infant about nuclear physics), no assimilation can occur. If there is no discrepancy (e.g., play), everything is assimilated, but accommodation does not occur. Cognitive development occurs when schemes change because there is **optimal discrepancy** between what the child knows and what it needs to know in the environment. This optimal discrepancy occurs naturally as the child actively interacts with its environment. Optimal discrepancy means that there is disequilibrium to produce change, but this disparity cannot be so great that the child cannot assimilate the information. The reciprocal changes in the child's existing knowledge and what it needs to know fit our dynamical model of development. Not only is the child affected by the environment, but the changes in the child now affect the environment as well.

For Piaget, the structures known as schemes are what change to produce development. In contrast, the processes that produce the changes—adaptation through assimilation and accommodation—remain the same over our life spans. They are **invariant.** They work in the same manner across the life span to produce more numerous, complex, and organized schemes. The alteration in the schemes produces the changes in cognitive behavior that Piaget categorized in his stages of cognitive development.

PIAGET'S STAGES ● OF COGNITIVE DEVELOPMENT

Piaget (1952) saw cognitive development occurring in four qualitatively different stages. It is necessary to complete each stage before the child could progress to the next. These stages are determined by the type of schemes that the child possesses. The stages occur in the following order.

Sensorimotor Stage (Birth–24 months)

Behavioral (or sensorimotor) schemes dominate this stage. It has six substages:

1. **Reflexes** (Birth to 1 month): These are the innate reflexes listed in Chapter 4.

2. **Primary circular reactions** (1–4 months): These are reflexes that are repeated over and over because of the bodily sensations they produce. For example, thumb sucking occurs repeatedly because of the pleasure it produces. Behaviorally, we would view these as behaviors that produce **intrinsic** or **automatic reinforcement.**

3. **Secondary circular reactions** (4–7 months): These are repetitive behaviors that produce consequences from the external environment. For example, the child shakes a rattle and hears a noise.

4. **Coordination of secondary schemes** (8–12 months): Consequences of the behavior are more organized. Behavior seems to occur to produce a specific consequence. This is called intentionality. A child may coordinate several behaviors (e.g., grasping, lifting) to move a barrier to get to a toy.

5. **Tertiary circular reactions** (12–18 months): The child accidentally produces a consequence and then varies response to determine what behaviors produce the consequence. Curiosity begins and is influenced by the ability to use symbols.

6. **Symbolic problem solving** (18–24 months): This is the emergence of mental representation. The child can anticipate the whereabouts of objects placed out of his or her hands, and the child may invent new ways to get to the objects by thinking rather than just grabbing for them.

Preoperational Stage (2–7 years)

The child enters this stage poised on the use of symbolic schemes, particularly language. Now with symbolic schemes, the child's representation of the environment becomes more sophisticated and increasingly more flexible. The stage has two substages.

Preconceptual Period (2–4 years)

In this period, the child's thinking is naive and primitive compared with adult thinking. The child thinks by using transductive reasoning, thinking from specific to specific, unable to generalize. With **transductive reasoning** the child does not make cause-and-effect connections. Thus, the sun rises because it is daytime. Other characteristics of **preconceptual** thought are **animism** (giving human characteristics to inanimate objects—as when the child says the wind is blowing because the trees are waving their arms), and **egocentrism** (seeing things from one's own point of view).

Intuitive Period (4–7 years)

The child's thought shows a simple form of reasoning. Still egocentric, the child guesses rather than uses true logical operations to explain events. Without being able to use the operations of **conservation,** the child may not know that the liquid from a tall glass maintains its amount when poured into a flat dish. Instead, the child guesses that the tall glass had more, because the child focused on the height of the glass. Also, without the ability to use operations of addition or subtraction, the child has difficulty with problems involving class inclusion.

For example, when asked if there are more flowers or more roses in a field, the child might guess that there are more roses because he or she fails to see that roses and other flowers are added together to compose the class of "flowers."

Concrete Operations Stage (7–11 years)

As schemes become more numerous and organizationally complex, a new class develops. These classes are called **operational schemes**. These represent the abstract rules that apply to the relationships between objects and events. Schemes for operations such as conservation, class inclusion, and seriation (i.e., putting things in a particular order, such as by height) mean that now the child can use more adultlike logic. Now when presented with the problem of the glass and the dish, the child can apply the operational schemes and conclude that the amount is the same in either. Although the preoperational child's reasoning was from specific to specific, the concrete operational child can use **inductive reasoning** to go from the specific to the general. The child's world is no longer a sequence of still pictures showing the beginning and end states. Operational schemes turn it into a motion picture in which children can view the transformation of the beginning into the end.

Formal Operations Stage (12 years and up)

During this last stage, the schemes are most highly organized and developed. Abstract reasoning characterizes this last stage. The difference between concrete and **formal operations** is that in the earlier stage the child can apply logical operations only to real (i.e., concrete) objects or events. In the latter stage, the child can apply them to abstract or theoretical ideas. Thus, at this stage, thinking is most flexible. The term *formal* refers to the ability to follow the form of the argument without being tied to its content.

Piaget and Function

Schemes have been presented as if they are real things—as if they have a physical existence. They do not. Piaget inferred schemes from the behaviors children gave in responses to their environments. When presented with problems or with questions, children behaved or gave verbal explanations that had an underlying consistency. Piaget attempted to explain this underlying consistency of their behavior (motor or verbal) by attributing the behavior to schemes. Yet no one has ever seen a scheme and, though attempts have been made to find a neurological equivalent in the form of a cell assembly or neurotransmitter, none has yet been found. Thus, Piaget's schemes are really descriptions of behavior and of categories of behavior, not explanations. As we have seen, in behavior analysis we focus on *functional classes* of stimuli (e.g., the function of a car is to transport people).

● VYGOTSKY'S THEORY OF COGNITIVE DEVELOPMENT

Piaget's emphasis on the development and organization of schemes makes it a largely structural theory. Although in his last years Piaget put more emphasis on the processes of development (Belin, 1989), the focus on schemes and stages is a focus on structure. In our brief treatment of Piaget's theory, we have also tried to emphasize the functions involved in cognition so that we understand how change occurs, but Piaget's theory remains very weak on explaining how cognitive development occurs. After Piaget's death in 1980, cognitive psychologists increasingly looked for ways of enhancing his theory. One significant thread was the rediscovery of the work of the Soviet psychologist, Lev Vygotsky (1978, 1987). Although Vygotsky's work was known in the West during the 1930s, it was not until the 1970s, well after his death at age 38 in 1934, that its application to Piaget's constructivism was appreciated. Because Vygotsky put much more emphasis on the role of the social environment in facilitating cognitive development, his theory has been called social constructivism (Nelson, 1999). The interest in Vygotsky's theory has been largely the result of three concepts: the zone of proximal development (ZPD), social scaffolding, and cultural tools (Siegler, 1998). These principles or processes have been interpreted from a behavior–analytic approach (Burkholder & Peláez, 2000).

The Zone of Proximal Development

The **zone of proximal development** (ZPD) is "the distance between the actual developmental level as determined by independent problem solving and the level of potential development as determined through problem solving under adult guidance or in collaboration with more capable peers" (Vygotsky, 1978, p. 86). Thus, the ZPD is the difference between what the child can do alone and what he or she can do with the help of others. Thus, it implicitly recognizes that there are hidden component skills that are more likely to be displayed with the support of others. The ZPD is a descriptive term; it describes the discrepancy between what the child can accomplish on his or her own and with competent social assistance.

Scaffolding

Social **scaffolding** explains, in very general terms, the conditions under which the ZPD exists. Scaffolding is a metaphor grounded in the physical world. Much like ironworkers construct scaffolds as safety nets beneath those working higher up, Vygotsky (1978) suggested that parents and more competent peers provide supports just below where the children are working to construct their knowledge of the world. The supports, in the form of social prompting, are there when the child struggles and assist the child in getting back to the higher levels of cognitive behavior.

Scaffolding is very similar to the behavioral process of shaping. By successively changing the criterion for reinforcement, the behavior being shaped more closely resembles the targeted terminal behavior (Burkholder & Peláez, 2000).

Cultural Tools

Cultural tools are the physical things (such as computers and newspapers) and intellectual tools (such as an alphabet or number system) that are part of the child's cultural experience that help the child develop cognitively (Wertsch, 1999). The most significant of the cultural tools is language. Language is a cultural tool in that it is passed down by the culture of native language speakers and is used in the development of cognition. In contrast with Piaget, who believed that cognitive and language development were independent, Vygotsky (1978) argued that the two interacted in important ways.

In Wertsch's (1999) view, Vygotsky's theory extends the mind "beyond the skin" (p. 316). What this term means is that the development of thinking and cognition is the result of the child's interactions with the external social environment, particularly parents; more advanced peers; and the cognitive tools, such as language and books, that society provides. Thus, in this view, cognitive development is learned through social interaction and not simply through the child's solo actions. One of Vygotsky's important Soviet contemporaries, Alexander Romanovich Luria, summarized this view in the following way:

In order to explain the highly complex forms of human consciousness one must go beyond the human organism. One must seek the origins of conscious activity and categorical behavior not in the recesses of the human brain or in the depths of the spirit, but in the external conditions of life. Above all, this means that one must seek these origins in the external processes of social life, in the social and historical forms of human existence. (Luria, 1981, cited in Wertsch, 1999, p. 315)

Only when cognition is developed "beyond the skin" does it begin to occur "within the skin" as private behavior is reinforced.

● BEHAVIORAL APPROACHES TO COGNITIVE DEVELOPMENT

Behavioral psychologists are often accused of being unable or unwilling or merely uninterested in analyzing **cognition**. Cognition is not a behavior-analytic term, but cognitive behavior is. For years, behavioral psychologists have addressed cognitive behaviors such as knowing and thinking. The behavior-analytic approach is different, focusing on the functions of cognitive behaviors rather than the inferred structures studied by cognitive psychologists. Behavior analysts share the basic view of Vygotsky—that cognitive behaviors develop from interactions with the social environment. Furthermore, as we shall soon see, language is viewed by both Vygotsky and behavioral psychologists as playing an important role in the development of cognitive behavior. But behavior analysts focus on functional behavior.

Behavioral psychologists apply the same principles of learning to cognitive development as they do to other behaviors. They are interested in cognitive behavior, its organization and the processes that maintain it, not in presumed underlying structures such as schemes. What develops is behavior, not hypothetical constructs. Cognitive behaviors may have structures, but these structures are the relationships between behaviors. That is, the way behaviors are organized is the important structure of cognitive behaviors (see, e.g., Commons & Miller, 1998). For behaviorists, cognition is behavior that is related and influenced by the environment, including the social environment. Language and cognition may share many topographies. One of the unique things about cognitive behavior is its location. Cognitive behaviors often occur privately, with only the discriminative stimuli that cue them and the overt responses related to them being public. Even though they may develop with the help of the social environment, cognitive behaviors take place mostly within the skin. They are **private events.**

For Piaget and other cognitive theorists, cognitive structures, such as schemes, are given special explanatory or causal power. Thus, children fail to conserve amounts because they are in the preoperational stage. They are thought to be at the preoperational stage because they have preoperational schemes. For behaviorists such as Skinner (1953), cognition is not due to hypothetical structures such as schemes, but it is behavior in relationship to the environment, just like any other operant behavior. "Thinking," "imagining," and "remembering" are treated like operants and analyzed by using the four-term contingency detailed in Chapter 6.

Knowledge and Ability

Skinner (1968) identified two types of behavior we call cognition. First there is knowing about things. This is what we call knowledge. We "know" how much is 2 + 2. We "know" who the first president was. We "know" what a reinforcer is. The second meaning of knowing is knowing how to do things. This is what we call ability. We are able to add 2 + 2. We are able to find the name of the first president. We are able to change a flat tire.

Bijou (1975) defined knowledge as a class of behavior specified by a particular stimulus. For example, a stimulus ("how much is 2 + 2?") is a cue for the response ("4") that is reinforced. Bijou identified four subcategories of knowledge:

(a) simple discriminative behavior (e.g., taking orange juice when offered a choice between orange juice and tomato juice); (b) conceptual or abstract behavior (e.g., collecting only round stones along the seashore and ignoring their size and color); (c) describing past events (e.g., one's birthday party); and (d) describing how things work (e.g., how to wind up a toy so that it will propel itself). (p. 833)

Bijou (1975) defined ability as two operant classes. The first class is an operant sequence behavior (i.e., a chain) occurring in a certain order, as in solving a problem. An example is knowing how to use an ATM to get cash. Second, Bijou defined an operant with a characteristic response topography (i.e., form), as in riding a tricycle. These abilities are cued by certain classes of discriminative stimuli. Bijou lists three sources of antecedent stimuli for preschool children: (a) the anatomy and physiology of the child's own body (e.g., hopping, skipping, and jumping), (b) physical objects (e.g., scissors to cut with), and (c) people (e.g., participating in a game of tag).

In sum, behavior analysts see cognition as behavior in relation to environmental events. Cognition or thinking is not a thing. It is not a scheme. It is something that a person does in relation to the environment. In knowledge, emitting the right response under specific stimulus conditions is reinforced. Cognition, as all other behavior, is affected by the contingencies in which it occurs. In abilities, certain forms of the response are differentially reinforced. Bijou described some cognitive response classes and their antecedents. But what reinforces cognitive behavior?

Table 7.1   A Three-Term Contingency Analysis of Knowledge Responses

Discriminative Stimulus	Response	Reinforcer
a. Glasses of orange and tomato juice	Drink orange juice	Taste of orange juice
b. Stones varying in size, shape, and color	Pick up round stones	See round ones
c. "How was your party?"	"It was great!"	Friend smiles and nods
d. Girl looks at toy car	"Push the button."	"Car goes like this!"

Natural and Contrived Consequences

Strengthening stimuli that are an inherent consequence of a response are called **natural reinforcers** (Skinner, 1982). The odor that is a consequence of opening a bottle of perfume or the sound made from beating a drum are examples of natural reinforcers. Much cognitive behavior is strengthened by natural reinforcers. Thinking is strengthened by the answers it produces, reading by understanding what is read. Hopping, jumping, and skipping are reinforced by the bodily sensations they produce.

Some cognitive behaviors are strengthened by stimuli that are not naturally occurring consequences but external to the response. These are called contrived reinforcers (Skinner, 1982). We often set up environments to **extrinsically reinforce** cognitive behaviors in others (e.g., when we teach) through the use of praise or feedback. Sometimes we extrinsically reinforce ourselves (i.e., when we employ self-control) by saying to ourselves "good job" or treat ourselves to a cup of coffee for a job well done.

What Reinforces Cognitive Behavior?

There are many reinforcers for the behavior patterns that constitute knowing. Many of these are natural reinforcers, but some are contrived. Below, each of Bijou's (1975) examples of knowledge classes is addressed through an $S^d \rightarrow R \rightarrow S^r$ contingency sequence (where under a certain setting event, a discriminative stimulus evokes a response that produces a reinforcing stimulus). In each case, the child is said to "know" when he or she makes a response that produces reinforcement for each stimulus situation. For example, the child "knows" the difference between orange and tomato juice when he or she reliably chooses one over the other. Table 7.1 provides some examples in these categories.

Table 7.2   A Three-Term Contingency Analysis of Ability Responses

Discriminative Stimulus	Response	Reinforcer
Scissors and paper	Handling scissors and paper	Paper doll
Boys and girls playing game	Spinning the bottle	A kiss
Blank computer screen	Moving mouse	Image returns

Notice that some of these sequences shown in Table 7.1 involve natural reinforcers (a, b, and d) and one (c) involves a contrived reinforcer (although it could be argued that a smile is a natural consequence of such an exclamation). Whenever looking at any contingency, we also must note the importance of the fourth term, the **setting events** that form the context for these knowledge interactions. For example, if it were not morning and the person were not thirsty, the discrimination producing orange juice would not have occurred because the stimulus (taste of the juice) would not reinforce the response (drinking the juice). Table 7.2 provides an analysis of ability responses. Note that in these examples, it is the form of the response that is important.

Abilities involve producing certain sequences or forms of behaviors in relationship to the environment. Again, there may be either natural or contrived reinforcers for these behaviors. For example, what is the reinforcer in being able to hit a baseball (an ability)? Is it a father saying "Good job"? Probably not. The reinforcer is the "crack" of the bat on the ball, the feel of the ball hitting the bat, and the flight of the ball. All these are natural consequences that immediately and automatically reinforce the skill of swinging the bat. But what if the child lacks the skill to make contact? Can we shape the swing with contrived reinforcers? Can we make the natural reinforcers more probable by putting the ball on a tee? Now we have solved a problem.

Problem Solving

In summarizing Skinner's analysis of problem solving, Reese (1994) described a problem as lacking the behavior needed to produce reinforcement. **Problem solving** is defined as emitting behaviors that change the situation in such a way that the behaviors that produce reinforcement will occur. For example, a child cannot open a box because he or she lacks a key. This is a problem because unlocking behavior will not be reinforced. The child may solve the problem by prying the lock open with a nearby screwdriver. Thus, changing the situation so that the screwdriver was not used in the customary way but, rather, in a novel way, led to reinforcement.

To solve a problem, two steps are involved. The first is to change the situation so that a solution is obtained. The second is to emit the problem-solving behavior so that reinforcement of the solving behavior may occur. Behaviors that change the situation are called **precurrent behaviors** (Skinner, 1974). Precurrent behaviors may include simple responses such as feeling, looking at, listening to, smelling, or tasting an object. Precurrent behaviors may also be more complex, such as putting objects (or words) in a group, rearranging the order of things, or using plans or algorithms to serve as discriminative stimuli for behaviors producing the correct solution. The use of algorithms, or sequences of operations, may occur often in mathematics, as when there is an arithmetic problem such as, "How much is 395 divided by 17?" This is a problem because the answer that will produce reinforcement from the teacher is not immediately available. However, by engaging in the precurrent behavior of going through the steps of the long-division algorithm, the correct response can be obtained and reported.

Exploratory Behavior

Bijou and Baer (1965) explained **exploratory behavior** as "a sequence of operant interactions that is strengthened and maintained by contingent ecological stimuli under specifiable setting factors" (p. 5). An **ecological stimulus** is one involving the physical properties of the various objects, social stimuli, or biological stimuli in the child's environment. An environment rich in ecological stimuli has many shapes, textures, colors, smells, sound, and other stimuli. Ecological stimuli are the inherent properties of natural reinforcers. They strengthen behaviors that produce either positive ecological stimuli or the avoidance of aversive ecological stimuli. Turning the handle on a jack-in-the-box produces the jack. Shaking a rattle makes a sound. Ecological stimuli are natural reinforcers for exploratory behaviors (Bijou, 1998).

James Gibson (1979) introduced a concept called **affordance** that is very similar to the ecological reinforcer idea. Affordances are the various properties of objects "at the ecological level that specify how the object relates to the observer and what responses are possible or appropriate" (Schwartz, 1984, p 34). In other words, the various visual, tactile, auditory, and other sensory characteristics of the environment intrinsically and automatically reinforce unique responses to them. Inherent aspects of the environment also serve as discriminative stimuli that prompt responses to them.

The different characteristics of stimuli prompt and reinforce different responses, including different perceptual responses. Consider the following as an interaction between the characteristics of ecological stimuli and the reinforcement of exploratory behaviors they provide:

> When an infant up to 7 or 8 months old detects a potentially graspable object within reach he grasps it, bangs it, shakes it, passes it from hand to hand, and above all, he carries it to his mouth and sucks it. He is only rarely observed to explore it, visually or tactually. It is suggested that the object is perceived as affording grasping, manipulation, noise making, and sucking. Similarly, objects in the intermediate but nonreachable distance afford looking and listening but not reaching and grasping. These appear to be pleasurable activities in themselves. (Schwartz, 1984, p. 51)

If you reread the preceding quotation but this time substitute the word *reinforce* (or *reinforcing*) for the word *afford* (or *affording*), you will see how similar Gibson's affordance concept is to the ecological reinforcer notion of Bijou and Baer. In both cases, inherent variability in characteristics of the environment provide automatic reinforcement for exploratory behavior (Guerin, 1990).

This is not to suggest that exploratory behavior cannot be encouraged by contrived reinforcers and setting events. Besides providing environments rich in a variety of ecological stimuli, adults and peers may prompt and directly reinforce children's explorations. For these children, exploratory behavior may emerge as a functional response class, and the child may be described as "curious about things." Conversely, adults may limit exploratory behavior by prescribing to the child what to do rather than having the child learn about the environment from the natural reinforcers in it.

Exploratory behavior leads to increased contact with the environment. This may lead to the development of knowledge and ability behaviors, including perceptual behaviors. In addition, exploratory behaviors may be the precurrent behavior to problem solving. Behaviors that may originate as exploratory behaviors may become strong knowledge or ability responses through **reinforcement traps**. That is, in the process of emitting an exploratory behavior, the natural reinforcement it produces may increase the likelihood that the same response will occur again. For example, in exploring a rattle, the child may move it and it makes a sound. The child is likely to repeat the movement over and over again.

Creative Behavior

It is difficult to define creative behavior. Definitions have included (a) novelty of the response or (b) novelty of the product, (c) diversity of responses (e.g., "How many ways can you think of to make a house of cards?") or (d) the quality of response or product (e.g., "That was really creative!" vs. "That was really garbage!").

Creativity has been studied as behavior in relation to its environment. Holman, Goetz, and Baer (1977) identified three characteristics of most studies of creativity, novelty, originality, and uniqueness. Taken together they involve "newness." But the phrase "there is nothing new under the sun" applies to creativity. Creative behavior is not entirely new but involves unique combinations of stimulus and response elements.

If creative behavior involves the unique combination of behaviors, under what conditions does creative behavior develop? Two have been identified. First there is the development of a large repertoire of knowledge and ability responses. With many behaviors available, many more combinations can be made. Creative people know about many things and/or can do many things. Still, a large repertoire of knowledge and ability is not sufficient for creative behavior. Many well-read and well-trained people are not very creative. The second condition is necessary as well. This involves a history of reinforcement for making new combinations of knowledge and abilities. Both a history of knowledge and ability, along with a history of being reinforced for unique combinations, leads to creative behavior.

In a series of studies, Goetz and her colleagues were able to increase the diversity of children's block building (Goetz & Baer, 1973), easel painting (Goetz & Salmonson, 1972), felt pen drawing, and Lego building (Holman et al., 1977). The procedures involved selection of a behavior in the children's repertoire (e.g., block building) and then reinforcement of new forms. This produced an increase in new forms that were different from the ones that were previously reinforced. Thus, creativity becomes a generalized class of responses.

● FISCHER'S SKILL LEARNING APPROACH TO COGNITIVE DEVELOPMENT

Theorists have introduced theories of cognitive development that are compatible with a dynamical systems approach (e.g., Commons & Rodriguez, 1993; Fischer, 1980; Fischer & Pipp, 1984). Among the main features of these theories is the view that cognitive development involves a hierarchical system of skills in which later skills emerge from earlier and simpler skills. These theories retain some of the observations of the structure and organization of cognitive development first made by Piaget but are more consistent with behavior analysis and a natural science position. Commons and Rodriguez (1993) call their theory general systems theory. Its 12 stages are logically deduced from analyzing the tasks involved in complex cognitive behavior. A second approach, called skill theory and developed by Fischer in 1980, shall be examined in some detail.

Fischer's Skill Theory: What Develops? Operant Response Classes

Fischer believes that Piaget's concept of schemes is more accurately viewed as operant response classes (or "sets") in relation to the environment. Rather than mental representations of the world, skills are behavior-environment relations. The relation between Piaget's schemes and Fischer's skills may be easy to see at the sensorimotor level, where action in relation to the environment is involved. However, Fischer (1980) points out that thought and language are also behaviors.

If I ask you to imagine a dog riding a bike, this may evoke an image in you. What is this image or iconic scheme? Fischer and behavior analysts share the view that producing an image is an operant just like other behaviors. The image is the product of the response in the same way that when you sit, your lap is the product of that response. Sometimes it is difficult for us to analyze our thinking as behavior. Instead, we accord thinking special status by using words such as *image, consciousness,* or *thought.* Because of our special treatment of private events, it is difficult for us to view private behavior as fitting the four-term contingency. The image seems real to us.

Psychologists have attempted to analyze cognitive behavior through the use of a computer analogy. This approach, known as the information processing approach, is a broad theory that assigns computer metaphors to humans. It is suggested that humans have structures that perform tasks similar to the components of computers, which also process information. Thus, we may have short-term memory storage that is similar to computer RAM, long-term memory similar to a hard disk drive, and a brain that is like the CPU of the computer.

We are often misled into reifying memory storage as a thing, but in humans memory is a function or process: it is remembering. Remembering is something you do. It is responding to a discriminative stimulus that was presented externally some time before. Perhaps a computer analogy can help clarify things here. You can call up to the screen a picture of your dog, Sally, that you have on your hard disk. Thus, we are able to take the image from long-term memory, process it, and view it. How is the image stored in the graphics file on your disk drive? Is it a small image of the dog? Of course not. It is a series of electronic charges at specific locations on the disk. The computer acts on the electronic code to produce a very real image of the dog, but the actual image of the dog is not stored on the disk.

However, we must not lose sight that the computer is only a metaphor for humans, although from the way we talk to (and about) our computers ("It's thinking." "What's it saying?", etc.) one might think that they are living creatures. Humans are living things, and living things behave. Some of this behavior takes place within the skin, and we call it cognitive behavior. Remembering is one type of cognitive behavior in which there is a delay between the presentation of a public stimulus and the response to it. Recall the example of memory research with infants in Chapter 4 (Rovee-Collier, Griesler, & Earley, 1985). As Palmer (1991) has pointed out, the extraordinary feats of remembering listed in the *Guinness Book of World Records* are the result of reinforcement contingencies that shape extraordinary behaviors. Other cognitive behaviors can be directly observed. Those external behaviors often take place publicly. For instance, public verbal behavior is called language.

Cognitive Behavior as Organized Response Classes (Attractors)

Behavior-environment relationships develop into classes of behavior from these internal and external interactions. These classes develop into organized patterns of behavior. At our most fundamental level of analysis (Level 1), contingencies produce individual behavior-environment relationships. At Level 2, contingencies act to organize systems of behavior-environment relationships. Emergent behaviors coalesce into more highly organized systems of behavior. These organized behaviors are called **response classes** or skills and are the structural aspect of skill theory. Skills build on each other, with later structures emerging from earlier ones. Structures change as a result of interaction with the environment. Skills emerge in various ways. Some ways result in linear combinations of skills, as in chaining. Other ways produce nonlinear, qualitative changes that may appear similar to the qualitative changes suggested by Piaget. **Equivalence classes** and relational frames may be examples of such highly organized response classes and will be discussed below.

Knowing and problem solving, not just abilities, are skills. A hierarchical organization of behavior develops into skills in many areas, or domains. Examples of domains are social skills, expressive language skills, and knowledge of mathematics. More advanced skills emerge from the strengthening of more simple behaviors by **environmental contingencies.** As Fischer (1980) summarized, "The child masters specific skills, builds other specific skills upon them, and transfers skills from one domain to another. This mastery process involves qualitative changes in skills, but the specific changes occur gradually, not abruptly" (p. 483).

Levels of Cognitive Skills

Fischer (1980; Fischer & Pipp, 1984) developed a progression in the development of cognitive behavior that shows a great deal of agreement with Piaget's observation of cognitive-developmental stages. However, significant differences between the two approaches are noted below.

At the basic level, the constant interaction of organismic (including learning history) and environmental factors produce continual changes in development. Underlying these changes are the environmental contingencies that bring about changes behavior. Many changes are small additive steps, as when a child reaches farther for an object or grabs a larger peach. Other changes are qualitative and nonlinear. There is a sudden change, or phase shift, in the topography of behaviors, such as when grasping changes from two-handed to one-handed. The dynamical principles of behavior (outlined in Chapter 2) that coalesce bring about the transformations described above and result in the qualitative changes.

Fischer's skill theory specifies four tiers based on the types of behaviors: reflex, sensorimotor, representation, and abstraction. Reflexes are placed at Level 0.[2] The remaining three tiers are each further divided into four levels. These levels overlap specific skills that create the opportunity to begin a new tier. For example, the skill at Level D-Tier 1 is the same as the skill at Level A-Tier 2. This overlapping process produces a total of 10 skill levels within the three tiers. Because each level is built directly on the previous one, there is a hierarchy of cognitive skills, with later skills emerging from earlier ones. Therefore, to reach a higher level of cognitive skill, one must first accomplish the simpler ones. Finally, because these skills are assembled by the events in the environment, there will be independence between the levels of skills for different domains and for different individuals in our behavior-analytic interpretation.

Comparing Fischer's Levels With Piaget's Stages

At first blush, the astute reader will no doubt find some resemblance between Fischer's skill levels and Piaget's cognitive stages. Indeed, there are some similarities, but there are important differences as well. Let us look at the differences.

What Changes? Skills Versus Schemes

In Fischer's theory, skills are operant behavior classes. Changes occur as relationships between response classes become more complex and more organized. The structures are the relationships between response classes. In Piaget's theory, however, schemes are mental structures and networks. They are hypothetical structures; they are mental representations.

How Do Changes Occur? Environment Versus Organism

Both Fischer and Piaget see cognitive development as the result of an environment-organism interaction. Fischer, however, places much more emphasis on the role of environmental contingencies in shaping behavior (Bjorklund, 1989).

Consistency Between Domains of Development: Décalage Versus Synchrony

By emphasizing the role of the environment, Fischer finds that different skills are likely to develop at very different rates. Fischer's theory suggests, for example, that reading skills are likely to develop at a very different rate than mathematics skills or social skills. This lack of consistency across domains was called *décalage* by Piaget and was thought by him to be the exception rather than the norm. Piaget believed, instead, that there was great consistency or synchrony across different cognitive domains such as math, language, and social skills. Thus, in Piaget's view, the child was at a specific level of cognitive development and the schemes at this level brought a consistency to behavior in all domains. This belief is in contrast with Fischer's view that differences among domains are common.

Individual Differences Versus Universal Stages

Based on the unique combination of organismic and environmental factors, Fischer's theory predicts that there will be large individual differences in the development of cognitive skills. In addition, Fischer's theory also supports equifinality, in that different individuals who reach the same cognitive skill level may have reached that level through different combinations of organismic and environmental factors. On the other hand, Piaget's theory emphasizes that all persons pass through the same sequence of stages at about the same time.

Box 7.2 Skill Theory and Behavioral Systems

Although a leading cognitive-developmental psychologist (he is a past president of the Jean Piaget Society), Kurt Fischer was introduced to behavior analysis as a graduate student at Harvard. The skills theory of cognitive development that he proposed shows some of this joint influence (Fischer, 1980). Several points of agreement make skill theories such as Fischer's especially attractive as a model for describing the organization of cognitive behaviors from a behavioral systems view of development. Some of these features are listed below.

Ever-Changing Dynamical Systems

Fischer's view of the dynamic organization and reorganization of skills is based on the development of relationships between response classes or sets. These relationships between response classes constitute systems and even systems of systems at the highest levels within each tier. Thus, Fischer's skill theory is itself a systems theory. What changes are the relationships between the systems?

Nonlinearity

Cognitive skills are built on earlier skills. In many cases, the changes are small and proportionate to the amount of environmental experience. Fischer refers to such changes as microdevelopmental changes. Examples would be the learning of a new name for a dog or adding the "four-times" table to multiplication skills. In a dynamical systems approach, such as a behavioral systems one, small linear changes are expected. Sometimes, however, small changes can produce qualitatively different changes. Often, this is due to the sudden coalescence of "hidden skills" that are present but not obvious by themselves. When these skills come together under certain contingencies, new levels of cognitive skills suddenly emerge. Fischer would call these nonlinear changes macrodevelopmental changes. Changes from one skill tier to another are macrodevelopmental changes. These nonlinear changes in behavior are the phase shifts of a behavioral systems approach.

Skills as Dynamic Attractors

Skills are classes of behaviors that fit our view of dynamical attractors as consistent patterns of behavior organized by the coalescence of organismic and environmental factors. As such, skills should be "loose assemblies," which in their initial formation are easily perturbed. This can be seen in the characteristic of cognitive skills to be easily disrupted by environmental conditions such as stressors or ambiguous stimuli, especially as a child is first acquiring the skill. For example, the child who is just "getting" conservation of amount may be thrown off by the adult asking a leading question such as, "Are you sure there is more in the tall glass?" As skills, including cognitive ones, become more strongly organized, they usually become more difficult, but not impossible to disrupt.

Equifinality

In emphasizing the reciprocal interactions of organismic and environmental factors in producing cognitive development, the skill approach stresses that there may be many paths to development. Thus, children may have different experiences contribute to acquisition of reading or conservation of amount skills. A corollary of this is that there will be individual differences in the levels of cognitive skills obtained.

Décalage

One significant point of disagreement between Piaget and Fischer is over whether the level of cognitive development is consistent across different skill domains, such as mathematics, verbal, or social skills, or whether there is a consistent level of development across all skill levels. Piaget favored the latter view and believed that the general stage of cognitive development determined that all domains would be at the same level. Fischer favored the view that skills develop independently, a view Piaget called decláge. The behavioral systems view agrees with Fischer that individual skills develop largely independently of other skills. Consequently, although the development of some skills may contribute to the development of new ones, there may be wide levels of accomplishment by individuals across skill domains.

Reciprocal Influence

The behavioral systems approach emphasizes the reciprocal interaction of organismic and environmental conditions, including genetic-constitutional makeup, learning history, and current environmental conditions. Change occurs from the coalescence of these factors under an individual's unique developmental history.

Cognitive Skills as Operants

The skills approach is consistent with behavioral principles. Fischer sees cognitive skills as operant response classes. His most basic level skills are simple classes of sensorimotor, representational, and abstract behaviors. As we move up his hierarchy, classes become combined in additive (i.e., linear) and nonadditive (i.e., nonlinear) ways. More highly organized, qualitatively different behaviors may emerge out of many lower-level behavior-environment interactions.

SKILL THEORY AND BEHAVIOR ANALYSIS ●

The Four-Term Contingency

As operant classes, cognitive skills are analyzed by using the four-term contingency detailed in Chapter 6. Skills may be simple classes of individual responses, or they may be organized into compound classes or complex systems of response classes. These response classes are controlled by their consequences. Complex classes and systems emerge because they have more access to reinforcing consequences. Simple response classes have a specified and limited amount of reinforcement. Many cognitive skills produce automatic reinforcement. That is, knowledge or ability responses produce their own natural consequences. Because increased knowledge and ability responses enable better manipulation of the environment, the attainment of these skills allows complex problem-solving responses.

The cognitive operant classes and systems come under the control of discriminative stimuli. Consider the word *stop*. What is the response that it cues? A particular stimulus, such as the word stop, may control whole classes or systems of responses. Stopping is not a simple response with a single form. Stop is a stimulus that specifies a relationship between any number of possible responses and the consequences of stopping. Furthermore, *stop* may mean one thing under one setting event (e.g., "stop that, you're hurting me") and another if the setting event differs (e.g., "stop me if you've heard this one").

● STIMULUS EQUIVALENCE AND COGNITIVE DEVELOPMENT

Recently, much attention has been drawn to the study of stimulus equivalence classes (Fields, 1993; Hayes & Hayes, 1992). A **stimulus equivalence class** (or equivalence class) is a group of stimuli that have the same function as discriminative stimuli. Because each stimulus in the class may be substituted for any other stimulus, they are functionally equivalent. The result is that once they become members of the equivalence class, they can be substituted for other class members and therefore be responded to in ways in which they were not directly trained to be responded to. Thus, we have the emergence of new stimulus–response relationships.

Stimulus Equivalence Classes

An important characteristic of equivalence classes is that **functional equivalence** emerges without direct training. For example, if a child learns that his pet named "Raffles" is a dog, and he learns that *canine* is the same as the word *dog*, he may say that Raffles is a canine without anyone directly teaching him the Raffles-canine relationship. This four-term contingency relationship, called **transitivity**, is the most difficult of the three relationships that must appear in order to say an equivalence class has been formed (Sidman, 1986). The other two relationships are **identity** or **reflexivity** (i.e., Raffles is Raffles, regardless of the context) and **symmetry** (i.e., taught that Raffles is a dog, the child can say that the dog is Raffles). When all three relationships—identity, symmetry, and transitivity—are displayed, an equivalence class can be said to have emerged. Sidman (1986) has used simple formulas from mathematical set theory to describe these relationships:

Identity: $A = A$ (e.g., Raffles is Raffles, is Raffles)

Symmetry: $A = B$ then $B = A$ (e.g., Raffles is this dog; then this dog is Raffles)

Transitivity: $A = B$ & $B = C$ then $A = C$ (e.g., Raffles is a dog; a dog is a canine; then Raffles is a canine)

Relational Frame Theory and Stimulus Equivalence

Steven Hayes (1991, 1994) has proposed a theory to explain the emergence of equivalence classes in human behavior. This theory is called **relational**

frame theory (RFT) because, in Hayes's view, what is learned in equivalence classes are relationships between stimuli, not individual cases. It is as if the rest of the contingency is like a picture frame, and a new, but related, stimulus can be inserted in the place of the original one. For example, once the Raffles–dog and dog–canine relationships have been established, "Raffles" can be put in place of "dog."

According to RFT, the core process underpinning human language and cognition is arbitrarily applicable relational responding (or relational framing). Nonhumans can be trained to respond to the nonarbitrary relations among the physical properties of stimuli (e.g., brighter than and longer than; see Harmon, Strong, & Pasnak, 1982). When this type of relating behavior is itself abstracted and brought under the control of contextual features other than the formal properties of stimuli, the behavior is defined as arbitrarily applicable relational responding. Such responses can be brought to bear on, or applied to, any stimuli encountered in an appropriate relational context. This responding is referred to as arbitrarily applicable because, in some contexts, it is under the control of cues that can be modified entirely on the basis of social whim. Consider, for example, a childhood game in which a child is instructed as follows: "More means less, and less means more." In this example, the functions of "more" are transformed so that they now mean "less," and the functions of "less" are transformed so that they now mean "more" (Barnes-Holmes, 2001).

For a child to be able to respond appropriately to the game in the previous example, he or she must have learned to discriminate between the relevant contextual features of a task (e.g., listening to the instruction) rather than the irrelevant formal features (e.g., observing the physical form of the actual stimuli). From the perspective of RFT, the establishment of symmetrical relations between words and referents in early language development provides a firm basis for this type of discrimination learning. Learning name–object and object–name relations is itself contextually controlled, and a variety of cues indicate the task at hand, including phrases such as, "What's that?" and the juxtaposition of objects and words. According to RFT, training in symmetrical relations across many examples gives rise to generalized symmetrical responding. For instance, when a child is exposed to a novel name–object relation ("This dog is called Raffles"), a derived—that is, untrained or untaught—symmetrical object–name relation may emerge (the child subsequently calls the dog "Raffles").

What differentiates RFT from other behavioral accounts of phenomena such as symmetry and equivalence and naming theory (Horne & Lowe, 1996) is its emphasis on multiple-stimulus relations (i.e., more than, opposite to, part of, etc.) and the transformation of stimulus functions described below. To account for the various patterns of responding to these complex desired relations, RFT employs three key terms as defining features of arbitrarily applicable relational responding. Mutual entailment describes the fundamental bidirectionality of relational responding (if A is related to B, then B is related to A). Although bidirectional relations are mutual, they are not always symmetrical. For example, if A is larger than B, B is smaller than A. Responding on the basis of mutually entailed relations is contextually controlled, such that when, in a given context, A is related in a characteristic way to B, as a result, in that context, B is related in another characteristic way to A. For example, in most normal situations, when given the choice between Coke and Pepsi, you choose Coke because you think it tastes better to you. However, if you are with a new friend who says she hates Coke, you choose Pepsi.

Combinatorial entailment refers to a derived-stimulus relation in which two or more stimulus relations mutually combine. For example, combinatorial entailment applies when, in a given context, if A is related to B and A is related to C, then B and C are combinatorially related in that context. For example, if good is the opposite of bad, and good is the opposite of naughty, then bad and naughty are combinatorially entailed (in this case, bad and naughty are the same, because two opposites make a same relation). The term *transformation of stimulus function* refers to changes that occur to stimulus functions by virtue of their participation in relational frames. Consider the following example. In the verbal community, a child learns that a $10 bill is worth "more than" a $5 bill (even though both bills may be identical in size). As a result, the child is likely to be more excited at the prospect of receiving a $10 bill than receiving a $5 bill, despite having no direct experience of the former. In this case, the increased excitement displayed with the $10 bill is a direct result of its participation in the "more than" relation with the $5 bill.

In the language of RFT, the term **relational frame** specifies a particular kind of arbitrarily applicable relational responding (Hayes & Hayes, 1989). In this way, therefore, a relational frame always refers to an action (i.e., framing events relationally). Families of relational frames specified so far include frames of coordination, opposition, distinction, comparison, and hierarchical and deictic (or perspective taking) relations. According to RFT, any action that involves relationships that participate in relational frames may be defined as verbal behavior.

In its account of language and cognition, RFT attempts to address a range of mainstream phenomena, such as analogy, metaphor, storytelling, humor, perspective taking, understanding false belief, executive function, and so on (O'Hora, Peláez, & Barnes-Holmes, 2003). The complexities of these psychological events are captured by the suggestion that stimulus relationships (trained and derived) can continue to expand virtually to any level of complexity, and concepts such as relational networks and the relating of relational networks to other relational networks are employed for this purpose. Consider, for example, the many relations surrounding the word *teddy*. It is part of many hierarchical classes, such as the classes "noun" and "toy." Other terms are in a hierarchical relationship with it, such as "leg" and "fur." It enters into many comparisons: "It is *smaller than* a house, *bigger than* a snail and *different from* a doll." The participation of the word teddy in these relations is part of the training required for the verbal community to use the stimulus teddy in the way that it does. This complexity is managed by contextual control such that not all derived (unlearned, emergent) relations are psychologically present to the same degree when the word is used.

Many of the key processes stipulated by RFT can be brought together to form a set of theoretical concepts that appear to offer a coherent account of verbal development. Specifically, Hayes, Barnes-Holmes and Roche (2001) stated the following: "RFT stands on three pillars: relational frames, relational networks, and abstraction from and transformation of the **nonarbitrary environment**. Each of these pillars is implicit in the others and all are developing simultaneously, but what is barely seen at one level becomes dominant at another" (p. 153). Barnes-Holmes and Barnes-Holmes (in press) proposed archetypal examples of these three pillars as naming, storytelling, and problem solving, respectively, and argued that the development of these critical repertoires may be essential features of a coherent behavior–analytic account of the development of human language and cognition (O'Hora, Peláez, & Barnes-Holmes, 2003).

In the next chapter, we will look at the development of communication— in particular, the function of language. We will again rely heavily on a skill learning approach in this area.

Do Parents Teach Relational Framing?

It has already been suggested that relational frames are automatically reinforced by naturally occurring consequences in the environment. As part of the child's natural environment, what influence, then, do parents play in the development of derived stimulus relation skills? In the next chapter, data are presented in detail on how parents intuitively teach language skills to their infants and toddlers. Are relational-framing skills taught by parents through the processes of mutual entailment and combinatorial entailment? Does the ability to derive stimulus equivalence relationships, such as reflexivity and transitivity, develop through caretaker–infant interactions?

Fields (personal communication, May 1993) has observed such relational training in the interactions between his sister and her children. Hayes (1991) describes some possible training of reflexivity in how the concept of "Daddy" and other objects is taught. First, the child is taught identity in the following manner:

The child is oriented toward Daddy and has been asked "who's that?" If the child says "Daddy", celebration ensues. If not, the child may again be prompted, "Is that your Daddy?" If the child shows any sign of acknowledgment (e.g., a smile when the name is given), the child is fussed over. Even before the child can speak, parents to some degree assess whether Daddy has control over the word "Daddy." The child may be oriented toward Daddy and asked, "Who is that? Is that your Daddy?" If the child makes a face that indicates agreement, the child may be tickled or playfully shaken and be told, "Yes, that's right, that's your Daddy!" The child in other words is taught to pick the sound "Daddy" (and later to produce it) in the presence of Daddy. (Hayes, 1991, pp. 25–26)

In this case the child is able to pick A (word Daddy) given B (object Daddy).

A similar type of interaction may be responsible for teaching symmetry: The child will be asked "where's Daddy" while Daddy is not immediately in the child's view. Young children will be carried around the room to face various persons and objects. Given the question, signs of recognition when the child is oriented toward Daddy are followed by parental signs of excitement. Signs of recognition elsewhere are followed by retraining: "No, that's not Daddy, that's the doggie!" Later the child will have to search the room visually without assistance or, for a more mobile child, may have to look behind objects to find Daddy given the question "where's Daddy?" (Hayes, 1991, p. 26)

To summarize, Hayes suggests a model for parent–child interactions that should result in the development of equivalence relationships. To put this model to a test, the Hayeses recruited their son, Charlie, to serve as a subject in a series of experiments (Lipkens, Hayes, & Hayes, 1993). Charlie participated in this research for an 11-month period. Training began when Charlie was 16 months old and ended when he was 27 months old. Charlie was shown line drawings of familiar (e.g., baby, ball) and novel stimuli (e.g., strange and prehistoric animals). Familiar (e.g., cat, dog) and novel (e.g., ui, neus) spoken words were also used as stimuli. Charlie's task was to learn relationships between visual stimuli and spoken words. The studies were conducted to see if Charlie would form symmetry and transitivity relationships.

The emergence of symmetry was shown when Charlie, who had been trained on spoken word-pick picture relationships (e.g., "Where is the pig? That's good.") was able to produce the name of the object to a question (i.e., "What is this?"). The symmetrical relationship is said to have emerged because the picture–spoken word relationship for the pictures had not been trained. A similar procedure led to the development of transitivity. In this case, training involved the relationships between a picture and the name of the object (e.g., "This is a dog") and a second relationship between the same picture and the sound the animal makes (e.g., "This animal goes 'woof'"). Charlie demonstrated transitivity when, given the name of the animal, he was able to make its sound (e.g., "What does a dog say?"). Notice again, that the relationship, this time of transitivity, emerged without direct training.

The Charlie studies demonstrate that equivalence may be taught, given appropriate environmental conditions. Further research is necessary to determine, as suggested by Fields (1993), Lipkens et al. (1993), and others, that parents intuitively teach **derived relational responding** to their children. So far, much of the interest in the development of equivalence classes has focused on language or skills at Fischer's (1980) representational skills level. It is likely that the learning of relational responding begins earlier, even at the sensorimotor level. The form of possible sensorimotor relationships is more difficult to conceive than the representational ones that have been so extensively studied. Nevertheless, Commons and Rodriguez (1993) have suggested that there is evidence for equivalence relationships from studies of non-language-using animals (e.g., Zentall, Edwards, & Hogan, 1983; Zentall & Urcuioli, 1993) and human infants (e.g., Watson & Ramey, 1972).

Sidman (1994) has taken the position that equivalence relations are a fundamental part of all natural phenomena. Therefore, when a child learns a concept, identity, symmetry, and transitivity are automatically present. What needs to develop through experience is the discrimination of equivalence into the three distinct relationships. That is, through experience, the child who sees stimuli as equivalent must learn to treat identity, symmetry, and transitivity as special cases. This is in contrast to the view taken by Hayes (1986, 1991), who views responding to stimuli in relational ways as the result of experiences. Thus, *equivalencing* is a term for behavior involving responding to stimuli using identity, symmetry, and transitivity relationships. That is, equivalencing equals relational responding.

Novak (1995) presented some preliminary data that mothers actually do provide conditions for the training of relational framing. They looked at mothers' interactions with their children during toy play when the children were 11, 15, 19, 24, and 30 months of age. Already at 11 months (the earliest age at which they recorded), mothers were providing their children with relational training. For example, mothers would not only label an object, but they would also ask the child "What's that?", requesting the child to label the same object. This "provide a label/request a label" sequence suggests that mothers actually do engage in the same kind of mutual entailment, combinatorial entailment, and demonstration of transfer of stimulus functions that are characteristic of relational training as suggested by Lipkens et al. (1993).

Because child language skills are not well developed at 11 months, these same mothers also provided nonlanguage relational trials too. That is, caregivers constantly pick up toys, manipulate them, and either hand them to the child to manipulate or ask the child to do so. This "manipulation/request for manipulation" sequence provides the same type of identity relational training as described by Lipkens et al. (1993) and Hayes (1991) but at a sensorimotor level. At 11 months, in most mother–child pairs, manipulation relationships are more common than labeling relationship trials. By the time their children are 19 months of age, labeling relations are the most frequent strategy used by all mothers who were observed, but other strategies continue to be employed.

Finally, the data also suggest that symmetry and transitivity relationships may also be taught by mothers who point out, play with, describe, and ask their children to do the same. Thus, the multiple experiences with objects provided by the experimenters to Charlie are observable in mothers actually playing with their infants. There seems to be support, then, for the contention that the ability to develop functional and stimulus equivalence classes in children is a skill that emerges from massive numbers of trials provided by parents with their children.

Why Are Equivalence Relationships Important to the Study of Development?

As emergent phenomena, the development of equivalence classes is consistent with a dynamical systems view. They help us understand that complexly organized, hierarchical behavior-environment relationships can emerge from the basic processes of development, particularly from a history of environmental contingencies. The emergence of relationships that are derived from other exposures and not directly trained produce the nonlinear changes characteristic of cognitive development. Furthermore, the use of relational frames may be seen as a skill that is consistent with the principles underlying the development of all cognitive skills. Finally, researchers and theorists find that relational frames are important to our understanding of language development and communication. After all, language enables us to represent complex relationships between a multitude of environmental features in our environment. Many of these relationships in language emerge rather than resulting from direct training, although, as we have seen, the emergence results from the informal training of relational frames by caregivers.

The next chapter continues to look at the development of skills in the area of communication, including the verbal behavior we call language. Skill theory will be again presented as a way of understanding the development of language as emergent behavior.

Figure 7.1   Face-to-Face Interaction of an Infant and Caregiver During Language Learning

SUMMARY ●

Cognition has been defined as "the act or process of knowing." Cognitive development concerns changes in knowledge and abilities across the life span. *Cognitive behaviors* can be either private or public. Even when private, most behavior analysts consider cognitive behavior to be governed by the same rules that govern public behaviors.

Jean Piaget's approach to cognitive development was shaped by his background in both biology and logic. Influenced by Darwin's theory of natural selection, the concept of adaptation would become a central aspect of his theory. Like the shells of Darwin's mollusks that changed through natural selection, Piaget theorized that the structure of knowledge changed in much the same way. He inferred mental representations of the world called *schemes,* which at birth differ in quantity, type, and organization from those present in adulthood. Although the first schemes are *behavioral schemes* consisting of reflexes, ultimately, *operational schemes* develop, consisting of sets of mental tasks that follow certain logical rules. Piaget considered this type of scheme to provide individuals with the flexibility and precision needed to understand and react to the world in adaptive ways. As development proceeds, behavioral schemes are expanded, becoming more complex, differentiated, and highly organized through the process of adaptation. Adaptation occurs through the reciprocal and complementary processes of *assimilation* and *accommodation*. Assimilation involves modifying input in such a way that it fits existing structures, whereas accommodation involves a change in structure that allows input to be received. The process of adaptation produces a better fit between an individual's knowledge, ability, and environment. *Disequilibrium* (discrepancy between one's knowledge and what one needs to know) causes assimilation and accommodation to occur. If discrepancies are too large, assimilation cannot take place. If there is no discrepancy, accommodation does not occur. Through the processes of assimilation and accommodation, a state of equilibrium may be achieved, but only temporarily. Piaget's conception of development consists of changes in schemes. Piaget's stages of cognitive development consist of the *sensorimotor stage* (birth to 24 moths), the *preoperational stage* (2 to 7 years), the **concrete operations stage** (7 to 11 years), and the *formal operations stage* (12 years and up).

In contrast to Piaget's structural theory, Lev Vygotsky's (1978, 1987) theory of cognitive development focuses on explaining how cognitive development occurs. His theory has been called social constructivism because of its emphasis on the role of the social environment in facilitating development. Development is thought to be the product of social interaction. The *zone of proximal development* (ZPD), *scaffolding,* and *cultural tools* are central concepts. The ZPD is the discrepancy between what a child can achieve independently and what can be achieved with the assistance of others. Scaffolding describes the general conditions under which the ZPD exists (e.g., social supports that facilitate the child achieving higher levels of cognitive behavior). Cultural tools are those physical and intellectual aspects of the child's culture that assist cognitive development (e.g., an alphabet), the most significant of which is language.

Yet another conception of cognitive development has been suggested by Fischer (1980), who asserts that what develops is a conceptualization of behavior-environmental relations. These develop into classes of behavior though internal and external interactions. The classes, in turn, develop into organized patterns of behavior called *response classes* or skills and constitute the structural aspect of skill theory. Structures change in both linear and nonlinear fashions. *Knowledge, problem solving,* and *abilities* are considered skills. Fischer's skill theory delineates four tiers of cognitive skills levels based on the types of behaviors involved (reflex, sensorimotor, representation, and abstraction).

Aspects of Fischer's skill theory that resonate with a behavioral systems approach include (a) a dynamical systems perspective, (b) nonlinearity, (c) similarity of the concept of skills to dynamic attractors, (d) equifinality, (e) reciprocal influence, (f) consideration of cognitive skills as operants, and (g) the ability to analyze skills in terms of the four-term contingency.

Behavioral approaches treat cognition just as any other behavior and apply the same basic principles of learning to cognitive development. Skinner identified two types of cognitive behavior: knowing about things and knowing how to do things. Bijou identified four subcategories of knowledge: (a) simple discriminative behavior, (b) conceptual or abstract behavior, (c) describing past events, and (d) describing how things work. Bijou also identified ability as two operant classes based on (a) sequence and (b) topography that are cued by certain classes of discriminative stimuli.

Problem solving is defined as emitting behaviors that change a situation in such a way that the behaviors that produce reinforcement will occur. Problem solving consists of (a) changing the situation to effect a solution (*precurrent behaviors*) and (b) emitting the problem-solving behavior to produce reinforcement.

Exploratory behavior facilitates the development of knowledge and ability behaviors through increased contact with the environment. Stimuli that are an inherent consequence of a response and serve to strengthen behavior are called *natural reinforcers. Ecological stimuli* are the innate properties of natural reinforcers. Ecological stimuli serve as natural reinforcers of exploratory behavior. Alternately, exploratory behavior can also be influenced by contrived reinforcers and *setting events.* Similarly, *affordances* refer to the sensory characteristics of the environment that intrinsically reinforce specific types of responses. Environmental characteristics may also serve as discriminative stimuli that prompt responses to them. Those stimuli external to a response are called contrived reinforcers.

Creativity is a rather esoteric concept. *Creative behavior* is thought to involve unique combinations of stimulus and response elements. Prerequisites for creative behavior include a large repertoire of knowledge and ability responses as well as a history of reinforcement for making novel combinations of knowledge and abilities.

The development of *equivalence classes* and relational frames is also considered an important part of understanding development. A stimulus equivalence class consists of a group of stimuli having the same function as discriminative stimuli. An important aspect of these classes is that *functional equivalence* emerges without specific training. If *identity, symmetry,* and *transitivity* are all demonstrated, it can be said that an equivalence class has emerged. *Relational* frames involve the development of derived arbitrarily applicable relations among stimuli that are the result of multiple exemplary training *involving mutual entailment, combinatorial entailment,* and *transfer of stimulus function.* Understanding equivalence classes and relational framing is important to the study of development in terms of helping us understand how highly complex, organized, hierarchical behavior-environment relationships arise from the basic processes of development. The concept of equivalence classes and relational frames is particularly relevant when considering development in terms of a history of environmental contingencies.

● NOTES

1. Piaget used the French noun *schéme,* which frequently is translated into the term *schema* (plural is *schemata*). In later years, Piaget (Piaget & Inhelder, 1971) reserved the term *schéma* for mental images. Thus, most psychologists now use the term scheme as the equivalent of Piaget's term for mental representations in general (see Fischer, 1980).

2. Fischer has subdivided his reflex tier into the same four levels as he had done with the other tiers; at this point it is difficult to relate these reflexive levels to the operant levels presented in detail here. This task will be left for some future analysis.

CHAPTER 8

THE DEVELOPMENT OF COMMUNICATION

Most introductory textbooks in developmental psychology devote a chapter to language development. Such chapters often describe the development of verbal behavior in terms of the structure of verbal behavior's products. For example, a child's developing speech may be described as a progression from single-word utterances (i.e., simple structure) to multi-word utterances (complex structure). The ability to speak and understand utterances with varying structure is attributed to mental structures possessed by the language user.

In this chapter, instead of focusing on the structure of linguistic and mental entities, we focus on the function of language (see structural and functional knowledge, Chapter 2): communication. In this context, to communicate means to change via verbal behavior the relationship between a person's behavior and some part of the environment. For example, if we tell you "it's raining," we have temporarily changed your behavioral relationship with umbrellas and raincoats; you are now more likely to reach for them. We first look at two significant theoretical viewpoints that have attempted to explain communication development. Then we look at a transactional view of how communicative behavior develops.

● STRUCTURE VERSUS FUNCTION: CLASHING THEORIES

The traditional debate in this area has focused on language. Throughout the last third of the 20th century, a war (Hebb, Lambert, & Tucker, 1973) raged in the field of language development. On one side were structuralists (cognitive theorists who called themselves psycholinguists). In the other corner were functionalists (behavioral psychologists). The war began when Noam Chomsky, an MIT linguist, wrote a searing review (Chomsky, 1959) of B. F. Skinner's (1957) book, *Verbal Behavior.* In the subsequent counterreviews (e.g., MacCorquodale, 1969, 1970), both sides claimed to have won. Only in recent years does there appear to be some rapprochement, much of it due to the emerging interactional worldview where language is viewed as neither solely nature (i.e., the biological structure) nor solely nurture (i.e., the functional environment). As the battle raged, it was said to have been between the "miracle theory" (i.e., psycholinguistics) and the "impossible theory" (i.e., behavioral theory; see Chapter 2). Psycholinguistics was deemed the miracle theory, in that language just happened in human children without formal training—seemingly, a miracle. The miracle was the human mind that abstracted the rules of language just by being exposed to it. Behavioral theories were deemed impossible because operant principles did not seem adequate to account for language development. Critics argued that it would be impossible to develop language through imitation and reinforcement. Let us turn our attention first to psycholinguistics.

A STRUCTURAL APPROACH: ● PSYCHOLINGUISTICS

A major reason for the gulf dividing these theories was that each was looking at language in a fundamentally different way. **Psycholinguists** emphasized structure. They saw language as an idealized system of symbols. Led first by Chomsky's linguistic theory, they began to focus on word order, or **syntax,** as the basic structure of language. They were much more interested in the structure or form of language than in its actual usage (function). Instead of focusing on what children actually said, psycholinguists focused on determining **linguistic competence.** This was the hypothetical rather than real ability of the child to form language constructions. Linguistic competence is determined by taking a large body of language utterances sampled from a group of people and summarizing the highest level of language used. Thus, psycholinguists try to explain ideal rather than actual language. Mispronunciations, grammatical errors, and dysfluencies that real children made were often seen as errors and were less important than the consistent structure that language had. Structure was what was important, and the structure of the language was thought to reflect the structure of the mind. Competence was what children were capable of doing with language, not what they actually did. Although children often spoke ungrammatically, they were believed to know all there was to know about the structure of language and to develop this competence by the age of 4 or 5. No wonder this is called the "miracle theory."

Nativism

The reason for this emphasis on syntactic structure was Chomsky's argument that language structure was constrained by the structure of the mind. That is, humans have certain **linguistic universals,** or commonalities, in language, whose occurrence arises directly from the structure of thought. Because we are humans we think in a certain way, and that way of thinking determines our language. For example, all languages have subjects and actions (nouns and verbs) because the structure of our thoughts causes our language to include talk about these things. The structure of syntax follows a grammatical set of rules because of the constraints of the human mind to impose a certain order when we speak and to understand a certain order when we hear. Therefore, language is a part of the biological nature of humans. This view is called *nativism* (see Chapter 4).

As nativists, psycholinguists invoke biology as the primary mechanism for language acquisition. They argue that children in all cultures know all the basics there are to know about their language structure by the time they are 4 or 5 years old. To do this with little formal teaching, children must have a type of **language acquisition device** (LAD) in their heads. Some people would like to point to specific parts of the brain that are the physical structures for thought and language, but none have been clearly determined. Instead, the LAD is a hypothetical structure whose existence is inferred from the human ability to learn language. In this view, the human mind has a structure that can deduce the rules of language, despite hearing only a limited number of utterances in early childhood and despite the variability in what is heard. These rules enable the child to generate an unlimited number of novel, yet grammatical utterances, from then on. How can that happen?

The Child as Linguist

Psycholinguists suggest that children learning their native languages are like little linguists discovering a new language. Children are said to follow the same process linguists use. This involves (a) listening to the sounds made and the situations in which they are made, (b) forming a hypothesis about what the sound means, (c) testing this hypothesis by using the sound in a situation, and (d) confirming or discarding the hypothesis. For the child, as for the linguist, language learning involves testing hypotheses about the relationship of sounds to events. For example, the child hears "mama" frequently. Mama is nearly always present when she hears this sound. Thus, the child forms the hypothesis: *mama* is Mama. Now, the child tests the hypothesis by waiting to see that when she hears "mama," her mother will respond. When the test is confirmed, the child has acquired the word.

The Language Acquisition Device (LAD)

Psycholinguists argue that to acquire words with such apparent ease, the child must have a specialized mechanism that takes linguistic input (sounds and sights), processes this information, and produces rules that lead to language. The rules are seen as important because language is viewed as a **generative process.** That is, language is not merely imitative or rote but characterized by an infinite number of grammatical utterances. A finite (i.e., limited) set of rules can produce an infinite number of novel, yet grammatical, utterances. With a LAD, all children in a normal species-typical environment (one with normal linguistic information) can understand an infinite variety of utterances and can also say an infinite number of grammatically correct utterances. Again, we have a miracle.

Changes in Emphasis

The focus of psycholinguistics has shifted over the years. The initial emphasis was on how syntax determined meaning. Grammars were developed that specified the rules generated by children to produce meaningful utterances. Chomsky argued that **surface structure** (the actual ordering of words as spoken) was determined by deep structure (the underlying meaning). He first proposed a phrase structure grammar that parsed language into tree diagrams, revealing the structure of the sentence as consisting of nouns, verbs, and other components hierarchically organized. Later, he proposed a transformational grammar in which specialized rules, called *transformations,* developed. For example, any active sentence, such as "The dog bit John," can be turned into a passive sentence ("John was bitten by the dog") by applying a **transformational rule.** In this case, the rule is to reverse the position of the subject and object and insert an auxiliary verb (was) and "by." Examples of other transformations include negation and questions. Transformational rules expanded the generativity of language by providing simple rules for changing a basic sentence into another form.

Researchers questioned the importance of syntax in determining meaning. Snow (1972) argued that when a child says "mommy sweater," we know the meaning of the utterance not by the deep structure of the utterance but by its context. If the child is cold, we derive one meaning; if the child points to mommy's sweater, we infer another. This study of the relationship of the situation or context to meaning is called **semantics** and has been the focus of cognitive psychologists in recent years.

An even more recent trend is the emphasis on pragmatics. **Pragmatics** deals with the way language is used. Taking turns or using language to ask for things in different ways (e.g., a request with "please" versus a demand) are examples of pragmatics. At this point, the emphasis is no longer on structure but on function. That brings us to look at an approach to language that emphasizes function, **verbal behavior.**

Chomsky's theory itself also changed, with a move away from a central focus on rules and a new emphasis on what he called the principles-and-parameters approach (as cited in Schoneberger, 2000). Still, Chomsky's approach maintains its strong nativist perspective based on primarily logical grounds rather than direct evidence (Palmer, 2000).

Box 8.1 Vygotsky & Behavioral Systems

Since the translation and publication of Vygotsky's work into the English language in 1962, his work has been widely cited and studied by Western European and American developmental psychologists and educators. Although much of the attention has come from traditional cognitive-developmental psychologists in search of a more social-environmental alternative to Piaget's theory, there are important similarities between Vygotsky's theories of language and cognition and modern behavioral theory (see Burkholder & Peláez, 2000; Novak, 1996). Most important, Vygotsky's theory and the behavioral approaches to thought and language are culturally and environmentally based.

As noted in Chapter 7, three of Vygotsky's important concepts—the zone of proximal development, scaffolding, and cultural tools—easily fit the behavioral approach to cognitive and communication development.

Vygotsky's view that the environment influences and changes behavior in different ways, based on the historical and present context, has also been incorporated into behavioral theory by several developmental behavior analysts (Hayes, Hayes, & Reese, 1988; Morris, 1988; Novak, 1998; Peláez-Nogueras & Gewirtz, 1997). That the individual's history with the environment, the current state of the organism, and other environmental influences (along with genetic-constitutional factors) combine to alter the probability, rate, form, and production of behavior is an overriding theme in behavioral systems theory. The idea that a reciprocal interaction occurs between interpersonal and intrapersonal psychology—that is, public and private behavior—has been emphasized by behavior analysis in the study of verbal behavior. The notion that intrapersonal experiences affect interpersonal interactions is embedded in the behavioral notions of rule-governed behavior (see Chapter 10) and relational framing (see Chapter 7).

Similarities also exist between Vygotsky's inner speech and Skinner's private verbal behavior (Burkholder & Peláez, 2000). Both Skinner (1957) and Vygotsky (1987) state that thinking is a process learned from the verbal community, and learning to think is no different from language acquisition or other socially learned behavior. Skinner (1957) goes so far as to say that verbal behavior has no special properties and obeys no special laws when compared with other types of behavior (p. 438). Vygotsky's (1987) "egocentric speech" is considered language (or verbal behavior), but the function of egocentric overt behavior (developing simultaneously with inner speech) is different from the function of vocal verbal behavior (directed speech). The function of egocentric speech is to modify the behavior of the speaker (Vygotsky, 1987). This notion of a changed function, with the internalization of speech, is consistent with Skinner's statements that any speaker can be his or her own listener and that individuals engage in **self-editing**. The similarity of the two positions in the acquisition of language and thought, or public and private verbal behavior, is central to both theories because they philosophically share an externally based causation (i.e., **environmental determinism**).

Both Skinner and Vygotsky omit some mental processes from their interpretations of thinking and inner speech or private verbal behavior (Skinner, 1976; Vygotsky, 1987), such as emotions. Emotions are considered by Skinner to be reactions to environmental stimuli. Skinner (1957) states: "The emotional reaction is usually a by-product of some other verbal function" (p. 155), and Vygotsky (1987, pp. 78, 88) argues that emotions are part of our thinking, which is indirectly influenced by inner speech but is not verbal in nature. Consequently, both Skinner (1957, p. 215) and Vygotsky (1987, p. 88) state that emotions can influence verbal behavior just as they can be influenced by verbal behavior, but they are not themselves verbal in nature.

Although differences between behavioral systems theory and Vygotsky's developmental theory do exist, we have highlighted the similarities. These similarities offer exciting possibilities for collaborative research and expansion of the behavioral methodology and theory in developmental psychology. Vygotsky's emphasis on context and setting and his use of culture make his theoretical approach to child psychology particularly interesting and a good fit within the overall framework of behavioral psychology. Moreover, Vygotsky's focus on the social origins of higher mental functioning seems theoretically consistent with aspects of the behavioral theory of verbal behavior.

A FUNCTIONAL APPROACH: THE ● ANALYSIS OF VERBAL BEHAVIOR

It was Skinner's (1957) book that set off the language "war." In it, he presented verbal behavior as "behavior reinforced through the mediation of other persons" (p. 2). What this means is that verbal behavior is the same as any other operant behavior—it is determined by the four-term contingency. The thing that makes verbal behavior unique is that it must be reinforced by someone whose own verbal repertoires are reciprocally coordinated with it. "Thank you," "gracias," and "merci" are reinforced by speakers and listeners who understand the words and can reinforce their use.

Verbal behavior is not limited to vocal speech in Skinner's (1957) analysis. Sign language, written language, even body language can be verbal behaviors if they are mediated by people who understand their function. Your pet dog or cat may use verbal behavior when it pokes its food dish across the floor, and you reinforce that verbal behavior by filling it with food.

Skinner (1957) listed several categories of verbal behavior based on the functional relationship between the behavior and the environment (not on structural categories), such as nouns and verbs, or even on modalities, such as speech and gestures. The primary verbal behaviors are described as follows:

Mand. The **mand** is operant behavior under the control of a setting event, such as deprivation or aversive stimulation, and reinforced by the stimulus that reduces this deprivation or aversive situation. A person saying "water," "agua," "wawa," "I want water please," writing the word *water,* using gestures or a certain kind of cry or even a puppy pushing its empty water dish with its nose, are all examples of mands: (a) They are controlled by deprivation of water, (b) getting water reinforces each response, and (c) the response will be reinforced only if there is another person in the environment who will mediate reinforcement (give the water). Notice that what is paramount here is not the form the response takes but, rather, its function. A mand is a functional response class. Anything can be a mand if it is reinforced by a particular class of consequences. This is often the thing that it names.

Tact. **Tacts** are classes of verbal operants in which a response of a given form is evoked by a particular object, event, or property of an event (Skinner, 1957). Tacts are specific responses that are controlled by a discriminative stimulus and reinforced by the verbal environment. In a simple sense, tacts are labels, words, or other symbols that stand for something. Thus, "cat," "that's a cat," or "gato" are tacts that the verbal community reinforces (perhaps by saying "yes, that's right") for labeling certain furry little animals. Note that unlike the mand, the object itself is not the reinforcer; the response of a listener who understands and provides a consequence is. The reinforcer for a tact is arbitrary; the reinforcer for a mand is specific.

Echoic. In **echoics** or echoic behavior, the controlling stimulus is verbal (remember, not necessarily vocal), and the response matches the form of this stimulus. Imitation is an echoic if the child's response matches the model's. For example, if a mother says "chair" and her daughter repeats this, the daughter's utterance is an echoic.

Textual. A **textual** is a verbal response whose discriminative stimulus is written or printed. Reading the word *stop* is a textual. So is reading this textbook. What is the reinforcer for that?

Intraverbal. An **intraverbal** is a verbal behavior whose controlling stimulus is the speaker's prior verbal behavior. Chains of verbal behavior (the sentences we speak) require intraverbal behavior because parts of the sentences are controlled by other parts. For example, if I say " Four score and . . .," your response ("seven years ago") is an intraverbal. Likewise, most children learn the English alphabet by singing the song "A-B-C-D-E-F-G." If you stop them, they have to go back to the beginning. Even most adults will have difficulty saying the alphabet in reverse order because of stimulus control by the other letters in their utterance.

Autoclitic. This final category is composed of a heterogeneous class of verbal responses. This is Skinner's most complex category. **Autoclitics** are verbal behaviors that are based on or depend on other verbal behavior (Skinner, 1957). Skinner identified several types of autoclitics. They give language its style and complexity. Syntactical word order, grammatical tagging (e.g., *walks, walked, walking*), assertion ("I'm sure it's going to rain today"), and negation ("He is not stupid") are some of the subcategories of autoclitics (Winokur, 1976). Another subcategory, called *qualifying autoclitics*, is seen in the difference between a speaker saying "It's going to rain today" and "I think it's going to rain today." "Think" is an autoclitic that qualifies the strength of the speaker's conviction that it is going to rain.

This is a necessarily brief overview of Skinner's account of language. It is important to emphasize again the major distinction between verbal behavior and language as characterized by cognitive psycholinguists. For Skinner, verbal behavior is something people do, not a thing that they have. Grammar is a description of behavior, not an explanation. Skinner's theory focused on function; psycholinguists focus on structure. With the change of focus by psycholinguists to more emphasis on syntax and pragmatics has come an interest in function or process. Perhaps it is time to call a truce in this language war. The rest of the chapter looks at a behavioral systems view of communication.

Higher-Order Operants

Is "Naming" the Basic Unit of Verbal Behavior?

Horne and Lowe (1996) used **naming** to link the emergent properties of a stimulus derived though stimulus equivalence training to Skinner's analysis of **verbal behavior.** Horne and Lowe view naming as a higher-order operant behavior. That is, naming subsumes other operants, such as echoics and tacts, and is a generalized behavior. Furthermore, Horne and Lowe view naming as bidirectional, requiring the development of both speaker behavior and listener behavior, two separate aspects of verbal mastery first identified by Skinner (1957). Listener behaviors are responses made by the child to others' speaker behaviors. For example, the mother may say, "That's a shoe, look at the shoe. Can you touch the shoe?" The mother's speech serves as a discriminative stimulus for the child to do some listener behavior, such as look at and touch the object the mother names as a shoe. Mom may use the same word, "shoe," in the presence of other footware. She reinforces the child's behavior that entails listening as well as the child speaking.

According to Horne and Lowe (1996), not only does the child learn the stimulus class of shoe by acquiring listener behaviors, but the child also learns to imitate the mother's vocal behavior (or other speaker behavior, such as a signed symbol) through direct or automatic reinforcement (Palmer, 1996). Once the child has acquired generalized echoic behavior (Poulson, Kymissis, Reeve, Andreatos, & Richards, 1991), the child uses this behavior to learn to speak words that refer to the stimuli that may have been learned through listening. This bidirectional relationship between speaking and listening allows the child to say names for objects that the child was not directly taught to name and to be able to emit behaviors based on listening to stimuli based on a name or the object itself. Thus, naming results in emergent behavior. That is, new relationships between stimulus classes and response classes are derived that are not specifically taught. So children may learn that a lamp, a chair, and a table are all called "furniture." They see that the lamp and chair go into a moving van. From these experiences, they try to move the table into the van. When they see a TV go into the van, they point to it and say "furniture." Thus, new relationships between speaking and stimuli coalesce out of the children's experiences. Horne and Lowe (1996) have suggested that, through this fusion of speaking and listening, naming may be the basis for the development of stimulus equivalence.

Relational Frame Theory and Language

Proponents of **relational frame theory** (RFT) (Barnes, 1996; Hayes, 1996) suggested that use of multiple examples in the development of listener and speaker behaviors are like the conditions used in teaching Charlie (see Chapter 7; Lipkens, Hayes, & Hayes, 1993) relational responding in the laboratory and thus show how caretakers teach relational frames and relational responding in real life. Novak and Scott (1998) have shown that parental play interactions with children as young as 4 months of age are characterized by large numbers of multiple stimulus presentations (visual and vocal) and requests for child behaviors.

These conditions seem to fit well the conditions from the Charlie studies that promoted relational framing. Thus, it appears that most parents provide the kind of intensive trials involving multiple stimuli and response relationships for the development of a generalized behavior of relational responding.

For proponents of RFT (e.g., Barnes-Holmes & Barnes-Holmes, 2002), **relational responding** is a developmental process acquired through social learning. The development of relational frames is just one phase of this development. In their view, naming is one form of relational responding and, although important for language and cognitive development, it is not the only form of relational framing. A second significant cornerstone of relational framing to develop is **relational networks.** These involve relational responding among relational frames. Barnes-Holmes and Barnes-Holmes (2002) suggest that syntactic development and more complex relational behaviors, such as storytelling, are examples of relational networks. The third key component of relational framing is the ability of the child to substitute stimulus properties, depending on the context or setting event. Problem solving, discussed in the previous chapter, is an important example of behavior that relies on this type of generalized relational behavior.

A major source of evidence for stimulus equivalence and derived relational responding as an account of language development is that performance on relational tasks varies with children's language ability. First, young children or children with language-specific deficits fail to demonstrate derived relational responding. For example, Devany, Hayes, and Nelson (1986) and Barnes, McCullagh, and Keenan (1990) found that equivalence responding was absent in language-disabled children. Peláez, Gewirtz, Sanchez, and Mahabir (2000) found similar effects with prelinguistic infants of normal development. Second, in the Charlie studies, Lipkens et al. (1993) tracked the emergence of a simple repertoire of derived relational responding in a single child, and their findings suggested that such responding showed a developmental trend similar to language. Third, in human subjects, equivalence and other complex derived relational performances emerge readily, but nonhuman subjects require extensive training and testing to demonstrate such performances (e.g., Schusterman & Kastak, 1994). Indeed, due to certain characteristics of the training and testing procedures employed in these nonhuman studies, there is some debate as to whether these performances satisfy the necessary requirements for transitivity and derived relational responding.

A Behavioral Systems Perspective

Our behavioral systems viewpoint leads us to look at the ever-changing reciprocal relationships between genetic makeup, history of interactions, and environment to explain communication. Verbal behavior develops as a skill out of the interactions between the individual and the environment (Novak, 1999).

What Is the Role of Genetics?

Although other organisms communicate among themselves and with other species, animal communication is limited compared with human communication. The complex communication behaviors that we call language are unique to humans. It is obvious that we have a common genetic basis for a physiology that enables us to develop such flexible communication skills. The evolution of our vocal apparatus enables us to produce a range of sounds that can be produced with the great precision necessary for vocal language. The localization of certain speech functions in specialized areas of the cortex has been known for centuries. Yet we still know very little about the physiology of language. One may speculate that we may just inherit, to a much higher degree than other organisms, a genetic makeup that enables us to learn the environment-behavior relationships necessary for acquiring and manipulating symbols.

At any rate, we cannot identify at this time the specifics of neurology that lead to language development. We may never be able to. For the purpose of psychological analysis, we do not need to engage in reductionism. Palmer (2000) has suggested that the biologically based differences in behavior that enable humans to be exceptional at developing language may be more quantitative than qualitative. He suggests that the evolved "language faculty" in humans

> may be a heterogeneous assortment of characteristics such as a nimble tongue, control of rapid integrated sequences of motor responses, sensitivity to reinforcement by a wide range of arbitrary stimuli, (and) the ability to adapt a well-practiced motor sequence to the demands of an arbitrary task (as a man juggling oranges is passed a baton and doesn't miss a beat). (p. 52)

Thus, humans may not do anything that some other animals cannot—it may be that they can do the same behaviors much more fluently. Whatever the unique biological capabilities of the human organism, we need look at language in terms of its functional relationships to the environment.

The Functions of Language

The main function of language is communication—that is, the effects that one person's behavior has on the behavior of others. Language develops because of its increasing effectiveness in obtaining reinforcement from the environment. We can adapt better to our environment with language behaviors than we can without them. For example, with language, we can obtain things that are not present and we can talk about things that no longer exist. We can produce positive reinforcers by asking for them, and we can avoid or escape negative reinforcers by asking for someone's help.

EARLY STAGES OF ●
LANGUAGE DEVELOPMENT

The neonate comes into this world with perceptual systems that enable it to interact with a world rich in verbal behavior. Among the universal behaviors the newborn possesses is the perceptual ability to detect human language sounds. This is not such an easy task. Speech is an ephemeral thing. The sounds the child hears quickly change and then are gone. In addition, unlike written language, speech sounds are streams of sound, and these streams are constantly varying. The child must be able to detect the boundaries between one basic unit of sound (a **phoneme**) and the next. It is likely that the ability to chop up the stream of speech into language units is an important universal behavior. The research of Eimas and his colleagues (Eimas, Siqueland, Jusczyk, & Vigorito, 1971) on "pa" and "ba" (described in Chapter 4) suggests that infants can do this during their first month.

Besides the ability to detect differences in speech sounds, children may show differential reactions to speech sounds at very early ages. Watson (1969) found that auditory stimuli were more reinforcing for girls than visual stimuli. For boys, the reverse was true. DeCasper and Fifer (1980) showed that a neonate will suck at a specified rate in order to turn on a recording of the mother's voice. Taken together, the evidence is strong that very young infants perceive variations in human speech and that some speech sounds may be reinforcing.

Neonates also come into the world with a built-in repertoire of communication behaviors. Most notable is the cry. Wolff (1969) identified three types of newborn cries: hunger, pain, and anger. For neonates, these cries are reflexes, each elicited by particular stimulus classes. They also differ in form, with the pain cry being particularly high pitched, loud, and irritating—a sound that no parent could ignore, thus obtaining its evolutionary survival function.

Cries may begin as reflexes, but the functions of crying expand quickly. By the third week of life, infants are developing fake cries. Wolff (1969) described these as having different forms and functions than the reflexive types. Fake cries are combinations of low moans and intermittent cries and do not seem related to the same aversive stimuli that elicit the others. Fake cries are reinforced by attention or, Wolff suggests, the intrinsic reinforcement of the sound of the fake cries themselves.

Of course, operant crying can become the bane of the new parent. An infant may quickly learn how to produce his or her parent's presence—a potent acquired reinforcer—by crying. Do parents who respond to their crying children reinforce such operant crying? As with most dynamical interactions, the answer is not simple.

A correlational study by Ainsworth, Bell, and Stayton (1972) found that mothers who were the quickest to respond to their infants' crying had the children who cried the least at the end of the first year. Why should this be the case? A study by Gewirtz and Boyd (1977) showed that mothers who responded quickly to their infants' cries were also able to respond to other more desirable cues that the infants made. Mothers who delayed responding to their babies' cries inadvertently wound up shaping their children to cry longer and more intensely when the parent was absent. In both cases, the children learned to use vocal behavior to produce changes in their environments. They had learned the function of communication.

At around 3 to 5 weeks of age, infants begin **cooing.** Coos are vowel-like sounds that appear to occur under pleasant setting events. Somewhat later, true babbling occurs (3–4 months). Babbling sounds include most of the basic sounds of language. The same sounds appear in the babbling of all children—those exposed to any language and those, as in deaf children, who are exposed to none. This early babbling appears to be a universal pattern of behavior: The babbling of infants all over the world consists of the same set of sounds. Somewhere around 6 months of age, the babbling of children exposed to different languages and that of deaf children begin to develop on different paths. From a selectionist viewpoint, this universality of babbling sound provides the variability necessary for reinforcement contingencies to select the sounds of the native language. Due to environmental experiences, the sounds that hearing children produce become more and more restricted to the sounds in the language to which the child is exposed. The babbling sounds of nonhearing children begin to disappear. At this point, babbling comes to resemble operant behavior more clearly. It is also at about this point that children begin to gain control over volume, pitch, and phrasing.

Near the end of the babbling period, **echolalic babbling** appears. This is when the baby babbles but has developed the intonation of adult language. The effect is that someone in the next room might think the child is talking, even though the sounds are nonsense syllables. Near the end of this time (10–12 months), infants coin their own words and begin to use their own sounds for certain functions (mands? tacts?). These are called **vocables**. At about this same time (10–12 months), children begin to use gestures to stand for things, such as waving to signify "bye-bye" (Acredolo & Goodwyn, 1985). Finally, around 10 to 12 months, infants begin to use their first true words.

Do Prelanguage Sounds Lead to Language?

Most parents assume that crying, cooing, and babbling are the building blocks of language development. Psycholinguists, taking a discontinuity stance on language development, do not think they necessarily are. Instead, their view is that these **prelinguistic sounds** are necessary for the child to perform, but they do not get shaped into words themselves. Their view is that the prelinguistic stage is a time for effectively exercising the tools for real language. Behavioral psychologists see the prelinguistic sounds as shaped into later language in a continuous manner.

Who Shapes Babbling into Words?

If babbling does become language, who does the shaping? Certainly, the drifting in of babbling across languages and in the hearing impaired suggests an environmental role, but the question remains: "Who dunnit?"

The most obvious agent for shaping babbling is the parent. At first blush, this appears to be the case. Mom and Dad hover over their baby, smiling and laughing and tickling whenever their little one emits a babble. Rheingold, Gewirtz, and Ross (1959) and Weisberg (1963) showed that infant vocalizations could be increased with contingent social reinforcement. The studies involved a researcher who smiles, tickled, and said "tsk, tsk, tsk" whenever the infant vocalized. With this contingent social reinforcement, vocalizations increased.

So there is evidence that adults can reinforce infant vocalizations (for a review, see Poulson, 1984). But how important is their role in real life? Consider the difficulty of trying to shape a babble into a word. It would require much skill and an enormous amount of reinforcement to accurately shape this behavior. Parents do some of this, but they do not do it at the level required to shape all the sounds of the child's language. Parents simply do not stand over their infants, accurately differentially reinforcing every correct sound and ignoring incorrect ones. This is one reason why psycholinguists called the behavioral approach the "impossible theory." There must be another mechanism.

Automatic Reinforcement

Behavioral psychologists have proposed automatic reinforcement as that mechanism (Bijou & Baer, 1965; Vaughn & Michael, 1982). In **automatic reinforcement,** the native speech sounds become acquired reinforcers, and the child, in uttering one of the sounds, hears the sound, and "automatically" the motor behaviors that produced the sound are reinforced. The five-step process is as follows:

1. During parenting, the parents use the sounds of the child's native language.

2. Because of their association with other reinforcers provided by the parents, the sounds of the native language become secondary reinforcers themselves.

3. When the child babbles, by luck, one of these sounds (a response) is emitted.

4. The consequence of the response is hearing the sound (the secondary reinforcer).

5. The response (producing the sound) is automatically reinforced (by hearing the sound produced by the babbling behavior).

In a series of experiments, Sundberg and his associates demonstrated how automatic reinforcement may lead to acquisition of verbal sounds. In the first study, M. Sundberg, Michael, Partington, and C. Sundberg (1996) paired some sounds, but not others, with direct reinforcement, such as tickling. The sounds paired with reinforcement were soon acquired by the children, even though production of the sounds was never directly reinforced. In a second study (Smith, Michael, & Sundberg, 1996), an infant received a positive reinforcer when an experimenter produced a specific sound. This respondent pairing of the sound and the reinforcer produced an increase of the child's production of the sound. Thus, the child was automatically reinforced, as it were, when he produced the sound himself. The behavior was maintained when the adult-produced sound was paired with a neutral stimulus and showed a clear drop when the adult-produced sound was paired with a mild negative reinforcer. Thus, it appears that the pairing of the sound with positive reinforcement made the sound a positive reinforcer so that when the child emitted it, it was automatically reinforced by that sound.

In this view, the child's babbling is shaped into native language sounds through a combination of automatic reinforcement and some parent shaping. The parents provide models of native language utterances that become secondary reinforcers that reinforce the baby's vocalizations that produce the sound.

Symbolic Gesturing

True words are symbols arbitrarily selected by a community to stand for concepts. At about the beginning of the second year, the time that true vocal

Table 8.1   Kate Acredolo's Symbolic Gestures From 12 to14 Months of Age

		Acquired (Months)		
Signs	*Descriptions*	*Age Sign*	*Age Word*	*How Acquired*
Flower	Sniff, sniff	12.50	20.00	Imitation
Big	Arms raised	13.00	17.25	Trained
Elephant	Arm extended from nose	13.50	19.75	Trained
Anteater	Tongue in and out	14.00	24.00	Trained
Bunny	Torso up and down	14.00	19.75	Trained
Cookie Monster	Palm to mouth plus smack	14.00	20.75	Trained
Monkey	Hands in armpits, up-down	14.25	19.75	Trained
Skunk	Wrinkled nose plus sniff	14.50	24.00	Trained
Fish	Blow though the mouth	14.50	17.50	Imitation
Slide	Hand waved downward	14.50	17.50	Spontaneous
Swing	Torso back and forth	14.50	18.25	Spontaneous
Ball	Both hands waved	14.50	15.75	Spontaneous
Alligator	Palms together, open-shut	14.75	24.00	Trained
Bee	Finger plus thumb waved	14.75	20.00	Trained
Butterfly	Hands crossed, fingers waved	14.75	24.00	Trained

SOURCE: Adapted from Acredolo and Goodwyn (1985), "Symbolic gesturing in language development: A case study," in *Human Development, 28,* pp. 40–49. Used with permission from Karger Publishers.

words usually appear, children begin using gestures to represent their environment in the same manner as words. For example, children may flap their arms to represent a bird or blow through their mouths to mean "hot." This has been called **symbolic gesturing** (Acredolo & Goodwyn, 1990). Table 8.1 shows the symbolic gestures used by Kate Acredolo and compares them with the age at first appearance of the gesture and the age at appearance of the equivalent true word. Notice how, in all cases, the use of the symbolic gesture precedes the acquisition of the equivalent word by many months.

The development of both symbolic gesturing and real words seems to coalesce around the functions of communication. Indeed, the first functional class of symbolic gestures to emerge comprises those symbols requesting things, followed by symbols describing attributes of objects, and then by symbols functioning as labels (Acredelo & Goodwyn, 1988). The same order and relative timing for the functions of requests and labeling occurs with vocal words (Griffiths, 1985, cited in Acredelo & Goodwyn, 1990). It is also the same sequence suggested for the acquisition of Skinner's mands (which function as requests) and tacts (which function as descriptions and labels).

Organized by the functions of communication, we see the coalescence of symbolic language usage appear. It requires physiological changes but also a long history of interaction with the environment. Symbolic gestures may coalesce first because of advantages they have in developing (see Acredolo & Goodwyn, 1990; Acredolo, Goodwyn, Horobin, & Emmons, 1999). Some of these advantages may be physiological (dexterity of the arms and hands versus dexterity of the vocal apparatus). For example, Thelen (1991) pointed out that even a one-syllable utterance requires the simultaneous coordination of more that 70 muscles and 8 to 10 body parts. Clearly, making an understandable gesture is easier for the infant, and some advantages are due to the consequences they produce. For example, gestures are present for a longer time than sounds and are present when the reinforcement is applied. Sounds are reinforced after they are no longer present. Furthermore, gestures may look like the things they represent and therefore be directly prompted by the object they specify. Such symbolic gestures may have a higher probability of leading to reinforcement by the environment because their meaning is obvious.

The advantages of symbolic gestures are limited, however, compared with vocal symbols, and true words begin to dominate the communicative repertoire of the child. Vocabulary is not limited to what can be visually represented. True words are arbitrary symbols, so an infinite number of words are possible.

First Words

The child's first true word emerges around the time of the child's first birthday. Nelson (1973) looked at the first 15 words of children. Names for items, including "mommy," "daddy," and pet names, were most common. These, when used as names, would be considered tacts, but if they are demands for "mommy" and "daddy," they may function as mands. What Nelson called "action words," such as *give, bye-bye,* and *up,* were almost as frequent. Many of these action words would fit the category of mands when used to obtain the thing.

The Holophrastic Stage

During the stage of first words, children use single words to stand for entire concepts. This is called a **holophrase.** A child may say "wawa" when it means "I want water," "That's a glass of water," or "There's water on the floor." Snow (1972) suggests that it is the parent who decides what the child means and responds appropriately. Here, the function of language (tact or mand) is ambiguous, with the parent using the context to interpret what the child means and hence reinforcing the verbalization.

The Telegraphic Stage

Between 18 and 24 months, the child begins to put words together to form sentences. At first, these are two-word utterances, such as "Mommy sweater," "Cookie gone," or "More wawa." Because these utterances are missing some unimportant words, they are deemed **telegraphic** speech, in that they resemble the messages sent when people had to pay per word.

Why do children increase the mean length of utterances from one to two and then from two to three words? Why do they leave out words rather than add words in grammatical sequences? The answer is in the communicative function of language. Two-word utterances are more effective in obtaining reinforcers from the social environment than one-word utterances. "More wawa" is more likely to obtain the reinforcer than is "wawa," which an adult may interpret wrong. Then why do we not use fully adult grammatical speech right away?

The answer is that language learning is very difficult. The **law of least effort** suggests that we do the least effortful behavior that is reinforced. In a way, the telegraphic speech child is paying for every word in effort, not in money. Early in development, the child's environment is very supportive of language learning. Patient parents reinforce ambiguous utterances and try to clarify them. Later, when the child's language is stronger, the environment will be less tolerant.

LANGUAGE DEVELOPMENT ● AS SKILL LEARNING

Some researchers (e.g., Brown & Hanlon, 1970) have suggested that parents play little direct role in grammatical development. Others suggest that imitation has no important role either. They argue that imitation can lead only to mimicry and cannot produce the generative quality that distinguishes language. Those who take this position tend to be nativists and look for the innate LAD to explain the miracle of language. Others have looked elsewhere.

Ernst Moerk (1989) has found the LAD—and discovered that it is really a LADY—the child's mother. Moerk's point is that there is ample evidence that the environment, mediated particularly by the mother, shapes language development. Moerk (1986) identifies four behavioral characteristics mothers use in teaching any skill to children. He finds that these same four are used intuitively by mothers to teach language to their children:

1. *High intensity of repetitions of each of the sentence types by the caretaker.* Because very young children usually do not employ rehearsal strategies

themselves, repetition by the mother is very important for learning. The intensity of repetitions has three aspects (Moerk, 1986):

- *Repetitiveness:* Mothers are likely to repeat their modeled utterances over and over again, sometimes with minor variations. For example, mother might say, "That's a car." "See the car." "Look at the people in the car."
- *Priming (or prompting):* Mothers initiate retrieval of utterances in the child by asking the child to name an item or to talk about a subject. For example, mother may ask, "What color is the car?"
- *Combining massed practice with spaced rehearsals:* Mothers enhance language skills by massing three to five repetitions of an utterance closely together. Then, they back off, allowing the child to rest. Moerk (1986) describes this intuitive approach to skill learning by mothers:

The principles guiding maternal techniques seem to be: (1) Initially, the item has to be repeated, densely spaced to be retained in the child's short-term memory long enough in order to be analyzable and transferable to long-term memory. (2) It should not be repeated so often as to lead to fatigue or loss of interest. (3) After several repetitions with short intervals, the speed of forgetting declines and the rehearsals can be reinstated after longer and longer intervals. After a certain degree of learning, testing might replace modeled reinstatements. (p. 210)

2. *The effects of frequency of repetitions by parents on their children.* Findings (e.g., Brown, Cazden, & Bellugi, 1969) show that there is a relationship between the frequency of use of a sentence type by parents and the order of appearance of the sentence type by the child. Although Brown subsequently argued that no such frequency effects exist (Brown, 1973; Cazden & Brown, 1975), Moerk (1986) has reanalyzed the same data and found clear evidence for the effects of parental frequency on the emergence of child language.

The high level of teaching techniques evident in mother–child dyads makes the role of environmental shaping not only seem "possible" but likely. For example, analyzing tapes of one of Brown's mother–child dyads, Moerk (1983) estimated that the child (Eve) would have encountered each major sentence type about 100,000 times per month. The same child responded to all the sentence types between 500,000 and 1 million times per month! In looking at the language of his own children, Bell (1903) found that his two daughters (aged 3 years, 6 months and 4 years, 4 months) spoke 15,230 and 14,996 words per day, respectively. Brandenburg and Brandenburg (1919) counted 14,930 words per day for their 4-year, 4-month-old daughter. Moerk (1986) points out that this is about 1,000 words per working hour and nearly half a million words per month! Given the enormous number of language trials experienced by the child, this theory no longer sounds so impossible.

3. *Knowledge of results (feedback to the child).* According to Moerk (1986), caretakers provide frequent feedback to their children. Both positive feedback (or positive reinforcement) and negative feedback (or punishment) is provided, and the findings are that mothers give either positive or negative feedback on utterances in from 33% (Rogers-Warren & Warren, 1980) to as many as 50% (Rondal, 1979) of their utterances. Positive feedback may take the form of praise, but it need not be limited to this. Indeed, behaviors of the caretaker that demonstrate understanding of the child's utterance (such as giving the child the requested toy or using a more complicated utterance repeating in part what the child said) can serve as positive reinforcement for the child's utterance.

Likewise, negative feedback need not be a verbal rebuff, such as "No!" Instead, parents provide negative feedback to the child in many ways, including corrections and **expansions,** which involve taking a child's partial utterance and making it more complete. Moerk (1983), again analyzing Brown's data, found that mothers may correct their infants' grammar around 50 times per hour or nearly once every minute.

Maternal corrections do not just punish the child's incorrect utterance. This feedback also serves as a prompt (an S^d) to try again, with the mother **modeling** the correct expansion of the child's utterance. In the data, Moerk found that not only do mothers correct their infants' grammatical errors most of the time, but if the mothers correct the children or give them eye contact, the children recommunicate their messages nearly 100% of the time. In contrast, only about 3% of messages accepted by the mother are restated by the child.

4. *Information acquired by the teacher of the learner's failure or success, which allows the mother to modify her talk.* Language learning is a dynamical process involving two-way transactions. In the process of influencing the child's behavior by her own, the changes the mother has produced in the child's behavior affect her behavior as well. Mothers are sensitive to children's level of language skills, as shown in their ability to predict with high precision the level of their children's language abilities (Rondal, 1979).

This maternal sensitivity to the level of their child's language skills allows the mothers to adjust their modeling and feedback to levels that keep them just steps ahead of the child. Early on, this appears in the baby talk or *motherese* used by the mother in interactions with her child. Motherese can be seen as a universal characteristic of mother-to-child interactions that is shaped by the pace of the child's ability to respond to the mother (Peláez-Nogueras, 1997).

Box 8.2 Mother's Vocal Imitation and Motherese Speech as a Reinforcer for Infant Vocalizations

Infant vocalization has been studied as a function of maternal vocal imitation, and motherese speech studied as a reinforcer, in two experiments. In the first experiment, the role of mother's vocal imitation as a reinforcer for infant vocalizations was investigated. Seventeen three- to eight-month-old infants were subjected to a repeated-measures experimental design using two treatments (CRF1–DRO–CRF2). Under continuous-reinforcement conditions (CRF1, CRF2), a mother imitated the topography of her infant's vocal response immediately contingent on its emission. Under the yoked-control DRO condition, a mother responded in a pattern of duration and topography identical to her pattern under CRF1, but never within four seconds of any one of her infant's vocal responses, to preclude reinforcement effects. The results were that fifteen babies did (and two babies did not) show patterns of three-minute vocalization frequencies under both CRF1 and CRF2 that were higher than the three-minute vocalization frequency under DRO densities (frequencies) of maternal vocal stimuli, and were equal or greater under the non-contingent/nonimitative DRO schedule than under each of the two CRF conditions, for every one of the seventeen subjects. Thus, elicitation or stimulation alone could not have accounted for the higher vocalization rate under the CRF conditions. In this frame, the patterns of higher individual infants' vocalization rates under CRF than under DRO treatments indicated that the mothers' contingent imitative vocal responses functioned as reinforcers of infant vocal responses. This first experiment further supported the view of early vocalizations as operants and the assumption that the sound of maternal matching/mimicking infant vocal response (infants "perceiving" similarity) may function effectively as a reinforcer for those infant responses.

In the second experiment by Peláez and associates (Peláez-Nogueras, 1997; Mahabir, et al., 2000), fifty-six three- to five-month month old infants participated in a repeated-measures multiple treatment design $(A_1B_1A_2B_2A_3B_3)$. In the first group, six two minute conditions were implemented sequentially: baseline (A_1), contingent maternal-imitation (B_1), noncontingent-yoked (A_2), contingent maternal-imitation (B_2), noncontingent-yoked (A_3), and contingent maternal-imitation (B_3). In the second group, contingent motherese-speech was used instead of contingent maternal imitation. The results of the first experiment confirmed the hypothesis that maternal imitation effectively reinforces infant vocalizations. The second experiment revealed that maternal-imitation produced the highest rates of infant vocal responses compared to the motherese speech and noncontingent-yoked treatments which produced the lowest rates. Further, motherese was not at all effective as a reinforcer for infant vocal responses. This demonstration of an increase in prelinguistic vocalization rates of three-month-old infants due to contingent maternal-imitation speech lends support to the view of early vocalizations as operant responses that can be shaped and maintained (i.e., conditioned) by imitative maternal vocal responses. Subsequent work will compare the reinforcing power for infant vocalizations and other behaviors of such contingent events as imitative and diverse social and nonsocial stimuli, under similar elicitation–control conditions (Mahabir, N. M., Peláez, M., Cárdenas C., & Calvani T., 2000).

Language Skill Learning in the Home

Hart and Risley (1995) conducted a landmark longitudinal study of the everyday language experiences of children in their homes. Forty-two children and their families were observed and audiotaped for 1 hour once every month for 2.5 years. The study began when the children were, on average, 9 months of age and continued until they were more than 3 years old. The families were divided into three groups based on their income: welfare families (6), working-class families (23), and professional families (13). All told, the researchers coded 1,318 hour-long observations, each of which produced 20 pages of transcripts!

The project was an enormous undertaking, and the analysis of this data took over 3 years. What did Hart and Risley find? Their findings supported at least three of Moerk's claims about the role of the mother in language teaching.

Language Input to the Children

There was an enormous amount of language spoken to children of all three groups during the earlier years. On average, in 1 hour of observation, a family spent 28 minutes verbally interacting with the child, 12 minutes interacting with someone other than the child, and 20 minutes not talking at all. Even though there was a great deal of time when the parents did not engage the child in language interaction, the average for all the parents was 341 utterances per hour to the child.

Hart and Risley (1995) further broke down these utterances, providing estimates of the number of individual words spoken by the parents to the children. Children in the welfare families heard 620 words per hour, those in the working-class families heard 1,250 words per hour, and those in professional families heard 2,150 words per hour. These numbers could be extrapolated to a weekly estimate of number of words heard, by multiplying these hourly rates by the 100 hours per week of family time that the authors estimated. Thus, it is estimated that the average child with welfare parents heard 6,200 words a week, the child with working-class parents heard 12,500 words a week, and the average child with professional parents heard 21,500 words each week. Further expanding this analysis, Hart and Risley (1995) claim that by age 3, the welfare children would have already heard about 10 million words, an enormous number—but not in comparison with the 20 million words that the average working-class child or the 30 million that the child of professional parents would be exposed to. So by the age of 3, children have had an enormously rich linguistic environment directed at them.

Parents do not only provide quantitatively important input; the quality of what they provide is also important. Gelman, Coley, Rosengren, Hartman, and Pappas (1998) looked at how mothers read picture books to their 2- and 3-year-olds. They found that mothers provided a rich range of information beyond mere labels. Using both speech and gestures, mothers typically provided information about the categories that objects, especially animals, fell into. In addition, mothers frequently linked information about two or more pictures.

The Effects of Exposure on the Development of Language

Although the Hart and Risley (1995) data show that children have an enormously large amount of language spoken to them, regardless of social class, the large differences in the number of words spoken by parents in the three samples provide an opportunity to examine the possible effects that amount of exposure has on the children's language development.

One important point is that despite the huge difference in the amount of language the children heard, all of them learned their language. This did not mean that there were not important differences in the resulting level of language development. On the contrary, the data show that large outcome differences were readily apparent.

Figure 8.1 shows the average cumulative vocabulary of the children in each of the observed groups. Notice that by the end of 3 years, the professional parents' children had a vocabulary more than twice as large as the welfare parents' children. Figure 8.2 shows the number of words spoken at home

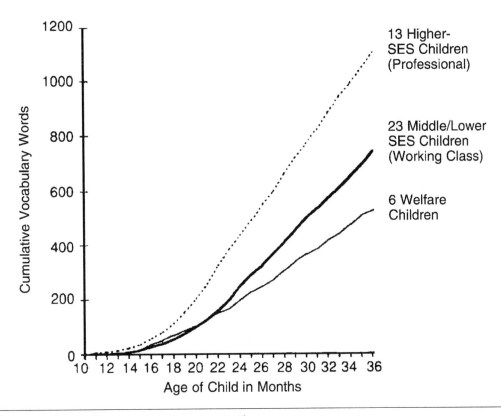

Figure 8.1   Vocabulary and Socioeconomic Class

SOURCE: From Hart & Risley, *Meaningful Differences in the Everyday Experiences of Young American Children.* Copyright 1995. Reprinted with permission of Paul H. Brookes Publishing Co.

NOTE: At each month, the average number of vocabulary words was recorded for that and all prior months for three groups of children from the time the children were 10 months old until they were 36 months old. The children were grouped by the socioeconomic status (SES) index assigned to the occupation of their parents. The 13 higher-SES children (dotted line) were in professional families, the 23 middle- to lower-SES children (heavy solid line) were in working-class families, and the 6 lowest-SES children (light solid line) were in families receiving welfare.

to the children. Again, there is a large difference among the groups, with the children of professional families being exposed to more than 3 times the number of words than the welfare parents' children by 3 years of age. Although the nearly 10 million words the welfare family children hear are enough to teach them language, these children are at a disadvantage when that level of language exposure is compared with the more than 30 million that the professionals' children hear.

There are also differences in the other quality measures given by the parents, to the extent that there is a correlation between an overall measure of

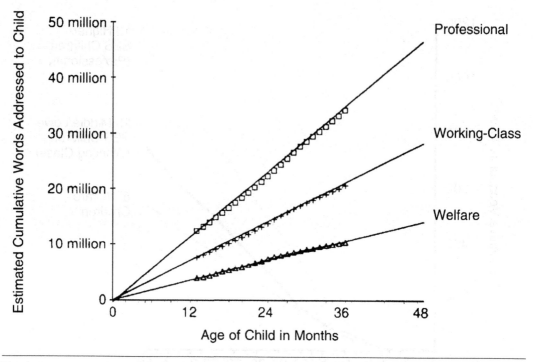

Figure 8.2   Language Experience

SOURCE: From Hart & Risley, *Meaningful Differences in the Everyday Experiences of Young American Children.*
Copyright 1995. Reprinted with permission of Paul H. Brookes Publishing Co.

NOTE: Cumulative number of words addressed to the 13 children in professional families (squares), the 23 working-
class family children (plus signs), and 6 children in welfare families (triangles) extrapolated from birth to 12 months
of age and from 37 to 48 months of child age. The linear regression line was fitted to the actual average cumulative
number of words addressed to the children per hour when they were 12 to 36 months old.

verbal parenting before age 3 and the children's scores on the Stanford-Binet
intelligence test. A clear linear relationship shows that the more parenting, the
higher the child's IQ at 3. Furthermore, although the connection between the
families' socioeconomic (SES) level and the child's academic test performance
in third grade declined, the language exposure the parents gave the children
before 3 years of age was still a very strong predictor of how well the children
would do on academic tests 6 years later. Thus, the density of exposure to language has significant benefits at least several years down the road.

Feedback to the Child

Although Hart and Risley did not tease out the reinforcing and punishing
effects of feedback from the overall events such environments provide, it is

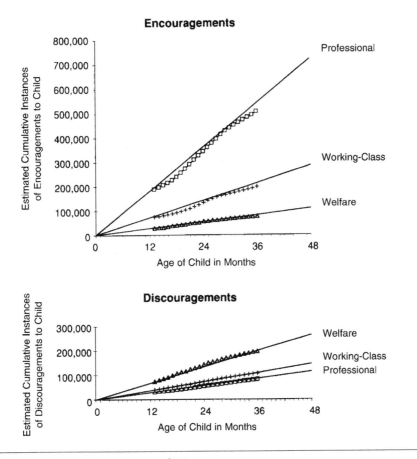

Figure 8.3 Encouragements and Discouragements

SOURCE: From Hart & Risley, *Meaningful Differences in the Everyday Experiences of Young American Children*. Copyright 1995. Reprinted with permission of Paul H. Brookes Publishing Co.

clear that such feedback would differ in these homes and have important effects. Figure 8.3 shows the number of encouragements and discouragements provided by parents in the three SES groups. The welfare parents provided more negative comments and fewer positive comments for talking than did either the working-class or professional parents. The SES groups differed not only in the *number* of encouragements and discouragements of their children's verbalizations but in the *proportion* as well. Although when they were speaking to adults and older children the percentage of encouragements and discouragements used by professional parents was nearly equal, that was not the case when they spoke to their 13- to 18-month-old children: Nearly 80% of their feedback was in the form of positive encouragements (see Figure 8.3). In contrast, when the welfare parents were speaking to their 12- to 18-month-olds,

1.   2.

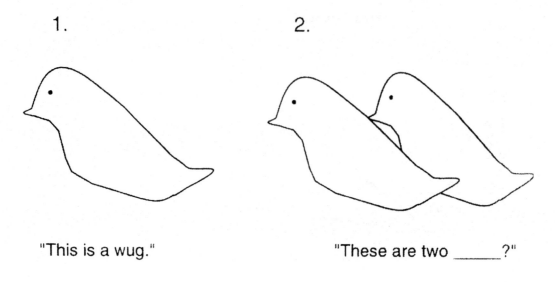

"This is a wug."   "These are two _____?"

Figure 8.4   Wugs

nearly 80% was negative. Hart and Risley (1995) characterize the welfare parents in this study as providing a "consistent and pervasive negative Feedback Tone" (p. 178) as a model to the children of how the family works. Figure 8.3 shows Hart and Risley's (1995) findings that professional parents provide more verbal encouragement and less discouragement of their children's speaking behaviors.

The Role of Imitation

Some have argued that imitation plays a very small role in language development. They base this on logical grounds: If language is generative, characterized by an unlimited number of novel yet mostly grammatical utterances, then mimicry cannot play a role. They argue that if imitation was a process in language development, then children would first have to hear all the utterances they would later produce.

This argument was attacked on logical and empirical grounds. Whitehurst and Novak (1973) conducted a study in which children heard sentence phrases (e.g., prepositional) with a consistent syntax (e.g., "The boy is on the bike," "The squirrel is in the mailbox") to describe a set of pictures. The children were prompted to repeat the modeled sentence and were reinforced when they did. No phrases were provided for a second set. Instead, children gave their own descriptions to this novel set of pictures. The results showed that the children produced their own utterances to the novel pictures. These utterances contained the same type of phrases as learned on the training pictures but were novel in terms of their content. Whitehurst and Novak (1973) called this behavior, which matches some part of the model's utterance (i.e., syntax) but that is novel on another (i.e., what is being talked about), **selective imitation.** Selective imitation may explain the learning of regularities in language that include the use of plurals, tenses, and adjectives as well as sentence structure. For example, look at Figure 8.4. It is a picture of a wug. Now look at the next figure. It shows two . . . You probably said two "wugs." How did you know that? Did anyone ever teach you that two of them are "wugs" and not "wuggen" or "wuggi?" Berko (1958) used this "Wug Test" and showed that children say "wugs," too (or make that, "two wugs.") Caretakers model the "s" sound for nearly all plural nouns and correct for misuse. Children have a history of learning to add "s" for plural.

Selective imitation and not a biological LAD may be responsible for the universal errors that appear in children's misuse of verb tenses and plurals, called **overregularization.** In English, verbs such as walk, touch, and smell are called "regular" verbs because they follow a standard rule: The "ed" sound is added to them. Verbs such as go, run, and see are called "irregular" because the past tenses (i.e., went, ran, saw) do not follow a rule. Some irregular verbs, such as "to be" ("am," "are") and "go," are very frequently modeled by caretakers, and their individual frequencies are high. Thus, children often use the appropriate past tense of frequently used irregular verbs (e.g., "was," "were," "went"). However, increasing vocabulary means that many regular verbs are acquired through the teaching techniques of the caretaker. Thus, children begin to apply the regular past tense form "-ed" more and more. At some point, selective imitation of the regularized form "-ed" is applied to the irregular verbs so that the child now says "goed" instead of "went" and "runned" instead of "ran." This is overregularization. The effects of caretaker teaching, including corrective feedback, results in a mixture of irregular and regular forms, so the child may now say "wented." In time, appropriate use of both irregular and regular verbs appears. Similar sequences occur for plurals and adjectives (Reich, 1986).

The Role of Reinforcement in Imitation and Communication

Several studies have been conducted to show how this expanded view of imitation makes it more likely to view imitation as an important part of language development. Poulson et al. (1991) looked at generalized vocal imitations in infants 9 months to 13 months of age.

Generalized imitation was first studied by Baer and Sherman (1964) and demonstrated that imitative behavior can be a functional response class established by reinforcement of some but not all imitated behaviors. For example, in the Baer and Sherman study, children were reinforced for imitating some of "Jimmy the Puppet's" behaviors, such as head touching and opening their mouths. They were never reinforced for pressing a lever but, when after the other imitative behaviors were reinforced, the children also imitated Jimmy's lever pressing, even though this behavior continued to be unreinforced. Poulson et al. (1991) extended this to language by demonstrating that reproduction of adult verbal sounds (e.g., "EE," "DAH," "EH") that had never been reinforced would occur if imitation of other sounds (e.g., "OO," "MAH") were reinforced. Reinforcement was contingent on descriptive praise (e.g., "Good baby! You said OO.")Thus, the study shows that reinforcement need not be given for every verbal imitation for generalized verbal imitation to play a role in language acquisition.

Poulson's (1991) study suggests that not all imitations must be reinforced but that generalized imitation of language will occur if imitation is intermittently reinforced. Horne and Lowe (1996) include this generalized echoic behavior as a critical component in the development of naming. Still, others have suggested that reinforcement is not important in language development (e.g., Brown & Hanlon, 1970). They argue that parents are more likely to reinforce the truthfulness of children's utterances (e.g., "It rain") than their grammatical correctness (e.g., "It is raining now.").

In contrast, Whitehurst and Valdez-Menchaca (1988) argued that differential reinforcement of language is important and necessary. As evidence, they conducted a study in which 2- and 3-year-olds were exposed to a foreign language (either Spanish or English). If children used the foreign language word to name a toy, their response was reinforced by receiving the toy. One group was differentially reinforced in this manner throughout the study, whereas a second group received reinforcement for naming in both languages and was later switched to differential reinforcement for use of the foreign vocabulary.

The results showed that differential reinforcement with the named toys increased spontaneous use of the foreign words. In addition, formal assessment by tests showed that comprehension and production of language were significantly increased by differential reinforcement. Whitehurst and Valdez-Menchaca (1988) concluded that the role of contingent reinforcement was significant. Virtually no spontaneous use of the new language occurred without differential reinforcement but, with it, a great deal of usage occurred.

Note that the type of reinforcement used was not praise or feedback. Instead, the response was reinforced by delivery of the object requested. This fits Skinner's definition of the "mand" (although it is also a tact because they named an object actually in front of them). Hart and Risley (1968, 1974, 1975) made effective use of this type of contingency in enhancing several categories of language, including descriptive adjectives and compound sentences, with educationally challenged children.

Mand-type contingencies have been shown to be effective forms of reinforcement for verbal behavior, and other parentally mediated reinforcement contingencies may be effective, as well. Petersen and Sherrod (1982) found that mothers frequently provided approval to children's utterances during free play. Moreover, there was a significant correlation between the amount of feedback provided by the mothers and their children's mean length of utterance. Caulfield, Fischel, DeBaryshe, and Whitehurst (1989) found that mothers with children just beginning to learn language were much more likely to provide praise for words and to criticize nonwords. Thus, it can be generalized that in the early stages of language, mothers are most likely to use contingent reinforcement and punishment.

This is apparently the case even in the development of symbolic gesturing. Once Kate Acredolo began to spontaneously use symbolic gestures, her mother, Linda, began a "game" from which 13-month-old Kate learned the gestures of sniffing as a reference for flowers and arms-over-the-head for "big" (Acredolo & Goodwyn, 1990). Soon, other adults joined in modeling gestures, pairing them with objects and providing feedback. By the age of 17.5 months, Kate had acquired 29 signs, more than half of which had been intentionally taught by her parents (see Table 8.1).

Reinforcement for verbal behavior takes many forms, including praise, automatic reinforcement, correction, and obtaining the consequences specified by the verbal behavior itself. When mothers use expansions, they are simultaneously reinforcing what the child has uttered as well as providing a model for a successive approximation to adult speech, a clear form of shaping. Taken together, these types of reinforcers seem to play an important role in the acquisition of language.

Last, Moerk (1990) found strong evidence for the existence of three-term contingency patterns in mother–child language interactions. Early in language development, child behaviors that were followed by maternal agreement were likely to be repeated. Thus, these maternal consequences functioned as reinforcers. The most common three-term contingency, occurring in 30% of the interactions, was a sequence in which the mother used a vocabulary word (S^d) that evoked the use of the word by the child (R), which had the consequences of the mother's agreement (S^{r+}).

Thus, the following contingency is likely in language interactions:

$$S^d \rightarrow R \rightarrow S^{r+}$$

Mother: "Ball" $\rightarrow$ Child: "Ball" $\rightarrow$ Mother: "Yes, that's right."

Later on, expansions by the mother are increasingly likely to follow the child's utterances. Expansions may reinforce the correct part of the child's utterance (as occurs in selective imitation) but also may punish an immediate child repetition. The data show that maternal expansions often terminate an interaction, as in the following sequence (Moerk, 1990):

$$S^d \rightarrow R \rightarrow S^{r+}$$

Mother: "What is the child doing?" $\rightarrow$ **Child: "Running."** $\rightarrow$ **Mother: She is running."**

Thus, maternal expansions that occur frequently in the later stages of language development may serve to strengthen the child's response, but they may punish responses that are too difficult for the child at the time. However, expansions are observed by Moerk (1990) to also function as discriminative stimuli in the form of prompts. Thus, expansions are often followed by child verbal behavior, which is followed by maternal agreement. This is just one set of three-term contingencies (i.e., $S^d \rightarrow R \rightarrow S^{r+}$) observed to occur in mother–child language interactions.

Despite the enormous effects that differences in family language input and consequences had on the language development of children, Hart and Risley (1999) also concluded that all children did learn to talk. Even the most linguistically poor environments are sufficient to teach language, although not to the level that linguistically rich interactions are.

Hart and Risley (1999) described the parent–child language teaching interaction as a type of dance involving three functional phases. They termed the *first phase* "becoming partners." Prior to about 11 months, children only listened, but once they used the first word recognized by the parent, the parent began directing more speech toward the child and encouraging the child to participate, even though the child still had more nonwords than words in his or her utterances.

The *second phase,* "staying and playing," occurred on average at about 19 months. Its beginning was marked by the point at which the child uttered as many words as nonwords. During this phase, the child was increasingly given opportunities to "hold the floor" and extend language skills through conversation.

The *third phase,* "practicing," came at the point where the children's number of utterances exceeded the parents'. In this phase, which typically started at about 28 months, the parents receded into supportive partners, and the children often engaged in soliloquies and private conversations during which they could practice on their own.

Box 8.3   Interactive Storybook Reading and Language

One of the most enjoyable yet most important things parents can do with their children is to read to them. Reading to a child promotes language development and establishes reading as a significant reinforcer for the child. Any type of reading may be beneficial, but storybook reading provides an especially rich opportunity for language learning interactions. Russ Whitehurst and his associates noted this while working with language-delayed children and developed a procedure they called "dialogic reading." The term *dialogic* comes from the word *dialogue* and suggests that reading can involve an interactive dialogue between child and parent rather than just a parental monologue. They reasoned that this "hear-say" method, in which the child first hears some of the story and then is prompted to say part of it, fits the skills notion of learning in which the child learns language by active participation.

Dialogic reading involves seven steps designed to maximize language interaction (Whitehurst et al., 1988):

1. Ask open-ended "What" questions, such as "What's this?" or "What is it doing now?"

2. Follow the child's answers with more questions. This confirms or reinforces the child's utterances and at the same time prompts more language.

3. Repeat what the child says, such as "Yes, that's a turkey." This again confirms and reinforces the child's response.

4. Help the child as needed, such as by providing the answer. This prevents the frustration of extinction and models the correct response.

5. Praise and encourage the child.

6. Shadow the child's interest. For example, if the child seems to really like a particular animal in a story, spend more time on that character.

7. Have fun. This final step reinforces the child's language and participation in the interaction. Furthermore, it helps make reading a reinforcer.

Whitehurst et al. (1988) showed that with two training sessions, mothers using dialogic reading over a 6-week period could significantly increase their 2-year-olds' language skills. In fact, with just 1 month of dialogic reading, children's vocabulary measures increased an equivalent of 6 to 8 months, and the length of the child's utterances also significantly increased. Subsequent studies have shown similar results (e.g., Branscum & Novak, 1995). The method has been adapted to slightly different formats. For example, Valdez-Menchaca and Whitehurst (1992) taught the dialogic reading method to teachers in a Mexican day care center. In turn, the teachers used the method in reading with individual 2-year-olds in their centers for 30 sessions that lasted 10 to 12 minutes each. The results were similar to previous studies: Children participating in the dialogic reading sessions showed significant increases on standardized tests of receptive and expressive vocabulary. In addition, dialogic reading produced significant increases in measures of actual language production skills, such as the mean length and complexity of utterances.

If dialogic reading works in one-on-one situations between parent and child and between teacher and child, would it work in small groups with one teacher working with a few children at a time?

Novak's research group embarked on a series of studies using the "multilogic reading technique" with preschool and school-aged children with English language deficits (Novak, 1993; Novak, Staggs, & Jones, 1993). Two of the studies involved children classified as "limited English proficient" because their parents spoke little or no English and their school language tests identified them as such.

The steps in the dialogic method were maintained, but the procedure was modified to fit the small group setting. This involved arranging the children in a semicircle in front of the teacher (who was an undergraduate or graduate student). The teacher would read a sentence or two while showing the book to the children and then would call on one of the children to answer "what" questions. The teacher followed this with the dialogic steps, randomly calling each child so that all of the children were part of the interaction. The results showed that after 6 weeks of reading, the children's verbal expressions increased in complexity and length. However, receptive vocabulary did not increase. The size of the group did matter, for there was a significant difference in the four-child groups versus groups with eight children. Nevertheless, it seems possible to use interactive storybook reading with small groups of children to increase their language skills. Furthermore, the method was used successfully with school-aged children with language deficits, both in groups or individually.

Lonigan and Whitehurst (1998) compared the effectiveness of parents and preschool teachers using dialogic reading for 6 weeks with 3- to 4-year-old children from low-income families. Although the effects on language skills were significant for the teacher-alone group, the groups with parents alone and parents and teachers combined showed the largest effects. Although the effects of dialogic reading are most clear on expressive language development, Zevenbergen and Whitehurst (2003) concluded that shared reading interventions have positive effects on both literacy and language skills of children.

Parents do not necessarily read books to their young children and, if they do, they do not necessarily adopt a dialogic reading style. Programs have been developed to enhance the language and literacy development of low-income children through home-based storybook reading. One of these programs is the Parent–Child Home Program (PCHP). The PCHP has home visitors bring a book or toy into the homes of 2- and 3-year-olds each week. The home visitor models the use of the item with the child and encourages the parent to adopt an interactive, dialogic style. The books and toys are left with the family to keep and build a collection. A recent study (Levenstein, Levenstein, & Oliver, 2002) showed that the 2 years of PCHP intervention greatly lowered the extra risk of poor school readiness that those not receiving home visits faced.

In sum, interactive storybook reading is a fun and effective way for parents and teachers to promote the development of reading and language learning skills.

Thus, there is ample evidence that the mother-child dyad plays a crucial role in language skill learning (Moerk, 1983, 1992). From a behavioral systems perspective, language development is the result of an interaction between a specialized organism and a specialized environment. The organism has a physiological structure that facilitates linguistic interactions with the environment. The caretaker is a leading part who disproportionately influences the development of communication by providing an enormously high level of environmental contingencies through modeling, prompting verbal interaction, and reinforcement.

● SUMMARY

For the purposes of the present chapter, to *communicate* means to change the behavior-environment relationship through *verbal behavior*. The study of language has been approached via both structuralist and functionalist paradigms. Only in recent years has there been a melding of these views, due, in part, to an expanding view of language development as an interactional process. In the nativist view, the structure of the mind is thought to place constraints on language structure: Language is the product of an individual's biology. From a functionalist view, verbal behavior is subject to the same basic principles of learning as any other operant behavior. However, verbal behavior differs from other operants in that it must be reinforced by someone who understands it.

Verbal behavior can take several forms (sign language, written language, and even body language) so long as it is behavior mediated by people understanding its function. Skinner (1957) identified several categories of behavior: *mands, tacts, echoics, textuals, intraverbals,* and *autoclitics. Naming* is a generalized, higher-order operant behavior that subsumes other operants (e.g., echoics, tacts). It is a bidirectional phenomenon, requiring the development of both speaker and listener behavior, which results in the ability to identify new relationships between stimulus and response classes with no specific training.

From a *relational frame theory* (RFT) perspective, *relational responding, relational networks,* and abstraction and transformation of the *nonarbitrary environment* are processes that underlie language development. From a behavioral systems perspective, verbal behavior is the product of person-environment interactions.

The development of language has adaptive value. Universal behaviors present at birth, such as various perceptual abilities and reflexive abilities (e.g., crying), enable its development. Although the origin of communicative behavior is reflexive, it ultimately develops into operant behavior. From a behavioral perspective, prelinguistic sounds are shaped (through automatic reinforcement and parent shaping) into language in a continuous manner. The first form of language to emerge consists of *symbolic gesturing,* later followed by true words. A child's first true words appear around his or her first birthday. Subsequently, during the **holophrastic stage,** the child uses single words to signify entire concepts. Then, during the *telegraphic stage,* the child begins to combine words to form sentences.

Although some theorists have de-emphasized the role of parents in language development, others emphasize the importance of the mother. Ernst Moerk (1989) described language development in terms of skill learning, with the mother intuitively incorporating four aspects of this process: (a) high intensity of focused repetitions, (b) frequency of verbalizations, (c) feedback, and (d) teacher acquisition of learner's performance, allowing for modification of teacher behavior. Similarly, Hart and Risley (1995) illustrated the importance of amount of exposure and feedback in language development. Imitation and reinforcement have been found to be integral aspects of the process. Last, mother–child interactions can be described in the context of a three-term contingency. Ultimately, it is evident that a behavioral systems approach provides an adequate account of language development and acknowledges the integral role of parent behavior in the process.

CHAPTER 9

PERSONALITY
AND THE SELF

- Who are you?
- What is your best friend like?

Take out a sheet of paper and take a few minutes to answer these questions:

- List all the words you can think of to describe your best friend.
- Now, do the same thing to describe yourself as others see you.
- Finally, list all the words you can think of that describe yourself.

What did you find? What kind of words did you use? How many words did you use? Did the list describing yourself as seen by others differ from the one with which you described yourself? Which of these lists did you find easiest to do? Which was hardest?

These questions deal with personality and the self—the focus of traditional psychology for years. We will look at these and then consider personality and the self from a behavioral systems perspective.

PERSONALITY: BIOLOGICAL THEORIES ●

An Ancient Theory

Personality has been the concern of poets and philosophers for centuries. One of the earliest theories of personality can be traced to the ancient Greek physician Galen. Galen thought that personality was due to biology—specifically, the fluids of the body called "humors." The four humors were thought to be in various proportions in our bodies. If one of these humors—blood, phlegm, yellow bile, or black bile—predominated, the personality would be affected. With blood predominating, the person was sanguine (from the Latin word for blood) or cheerful. If phlegm predominated, the person was slow and lethargic. The word *phlegmatic* (meaning apathetic, sluggish, or cool) comes from this humor. Too much black bile caused melancholia, and too much yellow bile produced choleric behavior (i.e., anger or wrath). Notice that the explanatory role played by the humors in ancient times is similar to the role that is now sometimes assigned to hormones.

Sheldon's Somatotypes

Since Galen's time, theorists have looked to biology as the source of the unique qualities of individuals. Sheldon (1954) developed one of the most important biological theories of the 20th century, asserting that personality was strongly determined by body type. In one of the most ambitious research projects ever done in psychology, Sheldon set out to measure the body types of males. His research was published in the *Atlas of Men* where he reported having measured hundreds of males from photographs. From these measurements, he identified three body types or **somatotypes**. The somatotypes were (a) **ectomorph**, (b) **mesomorph**, and (c) **endomorph**, so named because of the embryological layer from which they presumably originated (see Chapter 4). Sheldon calculated the relationship between somatotype and personality characteristics and found a strong correlation. Ectomorphs were not only thin and frail, but were also introverted, sensitive, and intelligent (remember, the central nervous system originated in the ectoderm). In fact, ectomorphy was correlated with the personality type called *cerebrotonia*. Mesomorphs were not only muscular and strong but also athletic and energetic. This aggressive, risk-taking personality was called *somatotonia*. Finally, endomorphs were round and plump and were likely to have personality traits that included the search for pleasure and social contact, a personality type called *viscerotonia*.

As with many correlational studies, Sheldon was unable to determine what caused this relationship. Did the somatotype cause personality, did personality cause somatotype, or did something else cause both? So although the theory had some intuitive appeal and some empirical data for support, it was too broad and general. It has largely been ignored since the 1960s.

However, in early 1995, Sheldon's name again made headlines. Eighteen years after his death, the press became aware that photographs taken of students attending a few elite colleges in the 1940s through the 1960s still existed. These students were photographed in the nude for Sheldon's study in an attempt to relate somatotype and intelligence. For all these years, photos of thousands of nude undergraduates (among those photographed were former President George Herbert Walker Bush and the wife of President Clinton, Hillary Rodham Clinton) were kept in the archives of Yale University. The public concern (and perhaps fantasies) surrounding the potentially embarrassing photographs led to their destruction (at least we have been told they have been destroyed!). All told, more than 100 pounds of photographs were shredded.

Modern Biological Theories

Although Sheldon's work is no longer deemed scientifically significant enough to pursue, other current personality theories retain a biological orientation. However, the biological mechanism causing personality is very general or unspecified. Instead, today the emphasis is on measuring personality characteristics for the purpose of identifying individual differences. In most cases, the factor analysis method is used. Factor analysis is a multistep statistical process in which: (a) a large number of possible trait descriptions are obtained from a sample of individuals; and (b) statistical analyses are performed on these self-reports to see which of the other trait items they correlate with and which they do not. These correlated items form clusters; and (c) these clusters are examined and an attempt is made to assign a meaningful name to each cluster.

Among the most influential of current theorists is Raymond Cattell (1950, 1965), whose 16 personality factors are thought to have a biological basis in the brain. Another prominent theorist is Hans Eysenck (1964b, 1967), who has identified three personality dimensions: **extraversion–introversion,**[1] neuroticism, and psychoticism. As a way of explaining this approach to personality, consider the first of these three dimensions. Extroversion–introversion is thought to be due to the physiological arousal level of the person. A person with low arousal needs the external stimulation that the extrovert seeks to bring the arousal to a normal level. The introvert is already too aroused and avoids external stimulation.

Biological theories such as these place personality as part of the nature of the organism. Whether the source of individual difference is a trait (Cattell), a type (Eysenck, Sheldon), or even a humor, it is due to a physical entity: the physiological makeup of the individual. Furthermore, behavior genetic research showing that extroversion-introversion and neuroticism are moderately heritable (Henderson, 1982) has encouraged the view that individual differences within the personality dimensions are the product of genetically determined differences in physiological makeup.

Recent factor analyses have suggested that five factors account for all the significant dimensions of personality. Although there is some disagreement about the actual makeup of Factor V (Goldberg, 1993), there is significant consensus on the other four. The so-called Big Five *personality characteristics* are identified as follows:

- *Factor I: surgency or extroversion*—the extent to which a person seeks out others or prefers to be alone
- *Factor II: agreeableness*—the extent to which a person goes along with suggestions or is argumentative
- *Factor III: conscientiousness*—the extent to which a person is reliable, consistent, and able to follow up on commitments
- *Factor IV: emotional stability (versus neuroticism)*—the extent to which a person is emotionally calm or emotionally volatile
- *Factor V: culture, intellect, or openness to experience*—the most controversial of the Big Five factors and thus the disagreement on what to call it

In these theories, personality is a physiological entity; it is something that one has. Measurements, in the form of personality tests, are taken to determine how much of each trait or type a person has. This is the most common and traditional approach to the study of personality. However, because this approach is merely descriptive and does not explain how the progressive changes in individual reactions to the environment occur, it is not a developmental approach.

● PERSONALITY: BEHAVIORAL APPROACHES

Many think behaviorists are, at best, disinterested in, or, at worst, incapable of offering an account of **personality**. If personality is meant only as a thing (something one "has"), then this is undoubtedly so. However, behavioral psychologists are interested in providing an account of personality when it is cast as a summary description of stable patterns of responding across settings. For the behaviorist, attributing a trait or type to someone is based on how that person behaves, not on what physiological structures he or she possesses (see *reification* in the glossary). No one has seen a trait or type; they are only inferred from the behavior of the person. When we asked you to describe your friend at the beginning of this chapter, were the words you wrote down traits? Yes, in the sense that they described the characteristic behaviors of your friend. Words such as *humorous*, *smart*, and *energetic* are descriptions of how a person behaves across many situations, but they do not specify the physiological entities. Some would have you treat these as the causes of your friend's behavior, but they are just descriptions of it.

As we saw earlier, these are really descriptions masquerading as causal explanations. As such, they are circular explanations. We say a person is active, always moving, and vigorous because he or she is energetic. Yet how did we identify the trait as energetic? Because that persons is active, always moving, and vigorous. This is not to say that such explanations are never useful. If someone tells you that John is energetic, you can generally expect that he will work hard at most tasks he is presented. However, in labeling him "energetic," We have not identified the causes of his propensity to work hard. The prediction is based on his previous behavior under various conditions.

Lundin (1961) defined personality as "that organization of unique behavioral equipment an individual has acquired under the special conditions of his [or her] development" (p. 7). Let us look at two of the important features of this definition.

First, personality is not just the sum of the person's behaviors. What leads us to call it personality is that the behaviors are organized. By *organized*, we mean that behaviors have a relationship to one another. This organized nature of behaviors produces the characteristics unique to the individual. Rather than being the sum of individual behaviors, characteristic behaviors emerge that form a pattern organized around particular, and sometimes unique, reinforcement histories. For example, a person may shop for bargains, reuse old items, and cut coupons, all to save money. He may label himself "frugal" (and his spouse may call him "cheap"). Second, personality develops in relation to the individual's unique history of interactions between his or her genetic, historical, and current physiological and environmental conditions. Significantly, these interactions produce a unique set of behaviors and reinforcers based on biological and learning factors. Thus, individuals labeled as introverts have different reinforcers than do extroverts. It is not just that they engage in different behaviors.

Recall also Baer's (1976) suggestion that we behave in ways that maintain consistent environments. We act in ways to maintain familiar cues for our behaviors. For example, we select friends who talk about certain topics or play familiar games. Furthermore, these friends engage in behaviors that produce reinforcing consequences for us. This makes it more likely that we will continue to seek out the same social environment. Friends also provide setting events and discriminative stimuli for the child to behave in characteristic ways. For example, a scout troop dresses in uniforms that make certain behaviors more likely to occur and be reinforced than other behaviors (e.g., helping old people across the street—even against their will).

Is behavior totally characteristic across settings, or is it specific to a situation? That is, is the extrovert always extroverted, or does he or she behave so only under certain conditions? This is one of the great controversies in the field of personality theory. You probably can guess that biological theorists believe that the physiological mechanisms that cause personality produce consistent behavior across situations. They believe that situations play only a minor role. In contrast, behavioral psychologists suggest that the environment plays the major role in our consistent pattern of behavior, but as situations change, so do behaviors. Behavior is specific to the situation.

A BEHAVIORAL SYSTEMS ● APPROACH TO PERSONALITY

A behavioral systems perspective assumes that both physiological and environmental factors play a role in determining consistencies and changes in behavior. More specifically, the theory involves two types of interactions a person has with his or her environment. These are (a) genotype–environment interactions, which emphasize how phylogenic characteristics of the person affect developing transactions, and (b) person–environment interactions, which show how ontogenically developed characteristics influence subsequent transactions. Both were introduced as basic processes in Chapter 3, but here, in the development of personality, their roles come to the fore.

Temperaments

One role for biological factors is the establishment of genotypes involved in the genotype–environment interactions described in Chapter 3. Recall that there are three types of interactions—passive, evocative, and active. Recall also the allusion to a developmental sequence to the appearance of these interactions. One way to look at the contribution of biology is initially through genotypes that react to the environment. These genotypes react first passively, then evocatively, and finally by actively selecting the environment. One area to look at for the beginning of personality may be in the initial behavioral differences called **temperament**. Thompson (1999) defines temperament as the "early-emerging, stable individuality in a person's behavior. More specifically, temperament is defined as constitutionally based individual differences in behavioral characteristics that are relatively constant across situations and over time" (p. 378).

There are many theories of temperament. The first influential theory was proposed by Thomas, Chess, and Birch (1968). Studying 136 children over a 10-year period, they identified the following so-called Big Nine categories of behavioral style that they called temperamental characteristics (Thomas, Chess, Birch, Hertzig, & Korn, 1963):

- *Activity level:* This is whether the child generally is quiet or moving.
- *Rhythmicity:* This is the regularity of biological patterns. It is reflected in the regularity of sleeping, eating, and elimination cycles.
- *Approach or withdrawal:* When touched, does the child respond positively, engaging the caretaker, or does the child withdraw and tense up?
- *Adaptability:* Is the child able to adjust easily to changes in caretaking patterns?
- *Intensity of reaction:* Is the child relatively quiet and passive, or does the child show extremes in crying and fussing?
- *Threshold of responsiveness:* How sensitive is the child to stimuli? Some are unfazed by relatively high levels of noise and light; others are hypersensitive, reacting to the drop of a pin.
- *Quality of mood:* Some children are happy, bubbly infants from the start. Others continually cry and are upset, as in the classic "colicky" baby.
- *Distractibility:* Some infants ignore novel stimuli; others are easily captured by them.
- *Attention span and persistence:* Some infants are able to attend intently for a long time, others flit from interest to interest as new stimuli come along.

Bates (1989) proposed an alternative classification, suggesting agreement among researchers that there are seven major domains of temperament as follows:

- Negative emotionality (e.g., fear, anger)
- Difficultness (e.g., highly intense, easily evoked negative moods)
- Adaptability to new situations or people
- Activity level
- Self-regulation (e.g., soothability)
- Reactivity (e.g., how intense the stimulus must be to evoke a response)
- Sociability-positive emotionality (e.g., pleasure in social interactions)

These two lists include a great deal of overlap in the categories of temperament. Still, Shaffer (1999) points out there this is little consensus among researchers. He suggests that there is better evidence that organized patterns of temperament exist and influence how caretakers respond to the child and vice versa than there is that these characteristics are easily categorized. It is likely that temperaments are uniquely organized behavioral attractors that are the result of the coalescence of biological, historical, and current environmental factors.

How Stable Is Temperament?

Not only are there questions about what and how many categories should be used to describe temperament, but there are questions about the stability of temperaments across situations and over time. Although researchers are convinced that individual children have unique temperaments, this assumption is called into question because a child's parents frequently disagree about their infant's temperament (Wachs, 1999). Studies have shown only moderate interparental agreement, with correlations averaging about 0.41 (Goldsmith, 1996). The modest agreement between the child's mother and father is actually higher than the agreement between the mother and the child's teacher. Thus, there is not high agreement even among various observers who know the child well.

Thompson (1999) provided three conclusions on the issue of stability over time. First, measurements of temperament taken during the first months of the child's life have weak correlations with later measurements of temperament. Second, there is greater short-term stability in temperament measures beginning around the end of the first year. Third, after the second year, there is high longer-term stability in temperament measures. This increased stability supports the view that temperaments are initially highly influenced by biological factors very early in life, but as development continues, the dynamical and reciprocal interactions between the child characteristics and the child's environment work to coalesce individual patterns of behavior into organized "attractors."

Are Organized Patterns of Temperaments Attractors?

On the basis of their original research, Thomas and Chess (1977) found that for more than two-thirds of their subjects the individual characteristics seemed to form an organized pattern in relation to the environment. They identified three such patterns:

1. *The **easy child***: These are children whose characteristics, such as moderate activity level, rhythmicity in biological functions, and positive mood, make care of the child easy. Some of these characteristics passively respond to the environment and others evoke from the environment events that facilitate behavioral development.

2. *The **difficult child***: This child's characteristics include negative mood, short attention span, and nonadaptability. These characteristics react to and evoke environments that are nonfacilitative.

3. *The **slow-to-warm child***: This child's withdrawal and unpredictability in moods and biological patterns mean that the child responds to the environment less strongly and evokes milder reactions from the environment than does the difficult child. Development of a facilitative environment takes longer but probably will occur.

Thomas and Chess found that these characteristics tended to be long lasting. Difficult children are more likely to develop behavioral problems later (Thomas, Chess, & Korn, 1982). Yet there is evidence that parental practices can strongly influence the development of child outcomes (Thomas & Chess, 1977). This illustrates the interaction of possible genetics, early history of interactions, current physiological conditions (e.g., mood, health), and current environmental conditions (i.e., current parental practices). For example, Crockenberg (1986) reported that difficult children receive different treatment from their parents than do other children. They are likely to be given less positive attention and stimulation and more likely to be punished than is an easy child.

As development proceeds, temperamental characteristics become strengthened and organized into what we call personality. Now the child actively seeks environments that cue and reinforce the behaviors in his or her repertoire. Individual personality becomes stronger.

The Role of the Environment in Personality

Individual characteristics may influence how the environment reacts to us. Some of these, such as our physical appearance, may be strongly determined by phylogenic factors. Consider the person with a baby face. Researchers, including Lorenz (1943) and Guthrie (1976), have suggested that people perceive a baby-faced person as childlike. Zebrowitz and Montpare (1992) have shown that not only can people reliably identify individuals with large eyes, a round face, thin lips, and a small nose bridge as baby-faced, but that they perceive baby-faced adults as more childlike. That is, raters found people with baby faces to be more dependent, physically weaker, more naive, more honest, and warmer than mature-faced people.

Thus, a physical characteristic such as a baby face may serve as an S^d that cues responses in other people. Are similar effects possible because of the color of a person's skin, one's gender, or even one's physical size? We may characterize these effects as **genotype–environment** effects. But because physical appearance may often be altered (as in a baby-faced person applying makeup to appear older or a more mature person dying his or her hair), these are actually **person–environment** interactions. These types of interactions (passive, evocative, and/or active) may apply to the clothing we wear, as well as to the things we *say* and *do*.

Indeed, Wachs (1999) emphasizes the important effects that the environment can have on temperament, along with the reciprocal effects that temperament can have on environment. Active children seek more dangerous environments and thus are more likely to be physically injured as showing an active temperament-environment interaction (Matheny, 1991). Several other factors influence the child's temperamental characteristics. These include environmental properties, such as a chaotic physical environment, characteristics of the culture, and parent characteristics, as well as biological characteristics (e.g., genotype, biomedical status) and child characteristics. Wachs's (1999) model is presented in Figure 9.1.

What happens when environments change? Different environments evoke and reinforce different behaviors. Still, we would expect to find many characteristic behaviors because if the environment is not too dissimilar, it will evoke and strengthen the behaviors already strong in the repertoire. As the environment changes, so does behavior. We often hear statements such as, "Johnny's a completely different child at school," or "Mary's a different person at work." Johnny is Johnny and Mary is Mary. It is their characteristic behaviors that are different in the different environments.

These are still person-specific environments for Johnny and Mary. They also influence their environments by the way they behave, even by the clothes they wear. What differences would occur if Johnny wore a school uniform versus

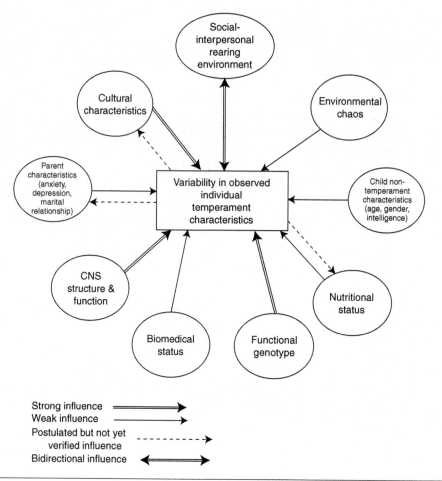

Figure 9.1   Temperaments

SOURCE: Wachs, 1999.

gang colors and an earring to school? But what if the environment is drastically different? On the basis of our history of interactions, we will likely use characteristic behaviors. We may, however, not know the discriminative stimuli, and the rein-forcers may not be present. For example, hostages often undergo dramatic changes in behavior. When Patty Hearst, the heiress to a huge publishing fortune, was kidnapped by the radical Symbionese Liberation Army (SLA), her shy, quiet, conservative, college-student behavior underwent many changes. After months in captivity, she was photographed by a bank camera taking an active part in a violent holdup. She appeared to be "a different person." After the destruction of the SLA and her return to her family, Patty Hearst emerged appearing to be much the same "person" as before. What happened to her personality?

**Box 9.1 How Personality
Changes: The Strange Case of the SLA**

In February 1974, the Symbionese Liberation Army, or SLA, burst onto TV newscasts and the front pages of every newspaper. Earlier, they had claimed responsibility for the assassination, using eight cyanide-tipped bullets, of Oakland, California Superintendent of Schools Marcus Foster. But what grabbed the headlines was their brazen kidnapping of newspaper heiress and UC Berkeley student, Patricia Hearst. The SLA, whose symbol was a seven-headed cobra and whose motto was "Death to the fascist insect that preys on the life of the people," was a small gang of mostly middle-class college students who viewed themselves as radicals intent on liberating "the people" from an oppressive military–government–business society. They appeared at the tail end of the radical antiwar, antigovernment protests of the late 1960s, and their story ended nearly 30 years after it started.

Within weeks of being kidnapped, Patricia Hearst was no more. Instead, she showed up on a bank surveillance camera dressed as a radical guerilla, brandishing a rifle during a holdup. She was heard on audiotape as a newly assumed personality, Tania, rejecting her earlier life and espousing radical rhetoric. In May 1974, "Tania" and two other SLA members were stopped in a store while shoplifting. They escaped when Tania fired a gun. If not for this incident, Tania would have been with six heavily armed members of the SLA who were killed in a shoot-out with police that was televised live on national TV. During the shoot-out, the house they had been hiding in was ignited by police tear gas and burned to the ground with the SLA members inside. Tania was not captured until more than a year later. When police booked her, she gave her occupation as "urban guerrilla."

In March 1976, Patricia Hearst was convicted of bank robbery and sentenced to seven years in prison. President Jimmy Carter commuted her sentence after serving 21 months. Tania disappeared, and Patricia Hearst married her former bodyguard and resumed the life of an heiress. She was recently seen on PBS serving as the hostess of a TV tour of her grandfather's Hearst Castle in California. In 2001, President Clinton pardoned her for her crimes.

Nothing was heard of the SLA for more that 20 years. Then, in 1999, Sara Jane Olson, a middle-class housewife, was arrested in St. Paul, Minnesota. To the shock of her neighbors, who knew her only as a respectable middle-class mother of two children, an actress in the local theater, and a soccer mom, Olson was accused of being Kathleen Soliah, a member of the SLA, and charged with planting two bombs beneath a police car in Los Angeles in 1975.

The following year, three other former SLA members, Emily Montague, who was known as Emily Harris when she served as the triggerwoman in a fatal holdup, her former husband, William Harris, and Michael Bortin were apprehended. Along with Soliah/Olson, all were charged with the murder of a patron in a botched bank robbery in 1975. All four of these SLA members pleaded guilty to the charge of second-degree murder and received prison sentences. A day after their sentencing in November 2002, the last remaining known SLA member, James Kilgore, was arrested in South Africa where he was using an assumed identity and serving as a faculty member at a university. In April 2003, he pleaded guilty to murder charges. This brought to an end the nearly 30-year-long saga of the SLA.

In each case, when these former 1970s radicals were arrested, they were living lives very different from the ones they lived as SLA members. Instead of radical terrorists, each became an exemplary middle-class citizen. Kathleen Soliah was a model mother and amateur actress. In 1978, Emily (Harris) Montague and Bill Harris had been convicted in the same bank robbery as Patricia Harris. After serving 8-year sentences, they divorced, and each fashioned a new career, gave to charity, and had close families. They had become the middle-class individuals against whom they had once rebelled. As one of the law enforcement officials said, "The irony is that the Harrises now have become the people they used to despise." Their personalities as violent 1970s revolutionaries were as different from the contemporary personalities they became as the 1970s Berkeley environment was from the middle-class environments that shaped them into the new persons they became.

When environments are radically different, extinction of existing behaviors occurs. Changes take place in these behaviors through shaping. New behaviors coalesce, come to strength, and are organized into "a new person(ality)."

● GENDER DIFFERENCES

Certain words are associated with one sex or the other. If you hear that someone is "sensitive," "dependent," "pretty," or "indecisive," do you picture a male or a female? Which words come to mind if you are asked to describe the typical male? These are our sex role **stereotypes** and generalizations about each gender. As stereotypes, some may be true about one group or another, but they need not be true for the individual. Some are not even true as generalizations about males or females. Let us look at these stereotypes and then examine how sex differences come about during development.

How Do Gender-Related Behaviors Develop?

The interaction of **organismic** and environmental factors is clear in the area of sex role development. Gender is determined at conception by the presence of other XX or XY chromosomes. Even before birth, the differential treatment of boys or girls is already set in motion though the actions of baby showers, advertising, and other environmental influences. At birth, boys and girls are treated differently by parents, nurses, and others. Not only are all three types of genotype–environment interactions at work producing gender-related behaviors, but societal, cultural, and parental expectations prompt and shape sex role specific behaviors as well.

Sex Role Stereotypes and Societal/Cultural Expectations

Recall Horowitz's (1987) levels of systems. We may analyze the processes that produce gender-related behaviors at any of these four levels. At Level 1, the basic processes, including genotypes and reinforcement contingencies, contribute to the selection of gender-appropriate behaviors. At Level 2, these individual behaviors are organized into gender-appropriate attractors. These Level 2 organized patterns, called gender identity and gender stability, are reached through the action of the basic biological and learning processes of Level 1. At Level 3, social interactions between the child and parents and peers occur, involving existing attractors and basic processes. Finally, at Level 4, the child's society and culture provide gender role stereotypes and determine which behaviors are gender appropriate. All four systems are at work simultaneously to produce the behaviors typical of boys and girls. To understand how the four levels produce these behaviors, we start at the highest level. The society and culture determine which behaviors will be shaped in children.

In most cultures, it is expected that males will develop an instrumental style and females an expressive one. However, this is not universal, and exceptions exist; societies promote their sex roles in many ways. Families, religious and social institutions, and media foster expectations about how boys and girls are supposed to behave consistent with existing sex role stereotypes. These create expectations in parents and others about appropriate gender-related behaviors. How do these expectations translate into the development of gender-related behaviors?

Parental Expectations and Reinforcement

Societal and cultural expectations are transmitted through the transactions between the child and parents. Because of the child's gender, parents have societally based expectations about what behaviors a child should engage in. Rubin, Provenzano, and Luria (1974) conducted a study in a hospital nursery with the parents of newborns. With only brief exposure to their neonates (not enough to detect real differences), both mothers and fathers described their daughters in language that was different from those who had sons. Although independent observers could record no such differences, daughters were described as smaller, weaker, and crying more. Sons, on the other hand, were described as more active and more vocal. Again these were perceived differences or expectations, not observed differences.

The existence of such differences in expectations in the first days of life suggests the importance of societal and cultural expectations (Golombok & Fivush, 1994). These differences are translated into transactional differences suggested in a study by Lyberger-Ficek and Sternglanz (1975). They observed that nurses in an infant nursery interacted differently with girls than with boys. Nurses were more likely to give more attention to boys not only when they were crying but when they were quiet as well.

The power of expectations is also illustrated in a classic study by Rothbart and Maccoby (1966). These authors recorded a child's voice making statements. Parents were asked to write down their reactions to what the child said. Half the parents were told that the voice belonged to a boy; the other half was told it belonged to a girl. Fathers who were told it was a girl were more permissive than those told it was a boy. The reverse was true for mothers. Thus, parents have different expectations for the same behavior in boys than in girls.

Reinforcement of Gender-Appropriate Behaviors

The emergence of gender-appropriate behaviors requires differential reinforcement. Boys' behavior is reinforced when these behaviors are consistent with the expectations of parents, teachers, peers, and others.

Reinforcement is generally not given contingent on behavior that is inconsistent with the sex role stereotype. Further, cross-gender behaviors may be punished by the environment. This may be particularly true with boys when "sissy" behavior is ridiculed or otherwise socially punished. Our society is more tolerant of "tomboy" girls, and such behaviors are less likely to be punished. Yet as the tomboy enters adolescence, her cross-gender behaviors, also may be punished.

The Development of Gender-Specific Reinforcers

Boys and girls may be susceptible to reinforcement based on different stimuli. Watson (1969, 1972) found that there were sex differences in the effectiveness of auditory and visual stimuli in children as young as 14 weeks. Girls learned best with an auditory reinforcer (e.g., a tone) and boys with a visual reinforcer (e.g., a light). As development proceeds, new gender-appropriate stimuli become conditioned reinforcers. For example, in traditional families dolls are likely to be associated with positive reinforcement for girls, and trucks for boys. Beginning in preschool, same-sex peers help establish gender-appropriate reinforcers. Thus, playing with sex role-appropriate toys becomes automatically reinforcing.

Developmental Changes in Gender-Related Behavior

Gender Identity

By the age of 2, most children know their gender (Thompson, 1975) and prefer to play with toys traditionally associated with their particular sex (Weinraub et al., 1984). This knowledge of one's sex is called gender identity. For example, at this age, girls are more likely than boys to play with dolls. By the time they are 3, children act out sex-typed roles (Eisenberg-Berg, Boothby, & Matson, 1979). Thus, at this age, a boy is more likely than a girl to assume the role of a fireman while playing.

Gender Stability

At around the age of 5 or 6, children know that their sex is not going to change. This is called gender stability. Furthermore, at this point, they begin to prefer and imitate those of the same sex (Bryan & Luria, 1978).

Gender Consistency

By the age of 6, most children have developed full-blown gender stereotypes (Huston, 1983). A final characteristic of their stereotypes is gender consistency— the knowledge that sex roles are consistent across settings.

A result of these changes is a solidification of behaviors consistent with their sex role stereotypes. For example, they are likely to maintain that men cannot be nurses and to ridicule any boy who plays with dolls (Marantz & Mansfield, 1977). As children continue to develop, these gender stereotypes broaden and become more divergent. As evidence of this, one study discovered that fourth and fifth graders believe that men and women differ greatly in terms of a number of stable personality traits. For example, these elementary school children viewed women in general as weak and emotional, whereas men were viewed as ambitious and dominating (Best et al., 1977).

Androgyny: Combining Roles

Some have argued that these rigid sex roles are harmful because they limit the behavior of both males and females. Indeed, Sandra Bem (1975, 1978) asserted that individuals who possess both masculine and feminine traits are better able to adapt to different situations because of their sex role flexibility. In short, Bem endorsed **psychological androgyny.** According to Bem, men should respond to some situations by being forceful and to others by being gentle. Similarly, women should be dominant when the situation requires it and defer to others when that is the best strategy.

In an attempt to demonstrate that androgynous individuals are more adaptable than those who are traditionally sex typed, Bem and her colleagues first developed the Bem Sex Role Inventory to allow the differentiation of androgynous people from others. Next, in a series of studies (e.g., Bem, 1974, 1975, 1981), they tested this hypothesis. One study (1975) found that when compared with traditional sex-typed subjects, **androgynous** individuals were more likely to display behavioral flexibility. Specifically, these individuals were more likely to act independently (a "masculine" trait) when the situation required it and to act in a nurturing manner (a "feminine" trait) when that approach was most efficacious. In other studies, androgynous adolescents and college students were compared with those who exhibit traditional sex roles and were found to have higher self-esteem and to be viewed as more likable and well adjusted by their peers (Major, Carnevale, & Deaux, 1981; Massad, 1981; Spence, 1982). Although androgyny has had its harsh critics (e.g., those who charge that it promotes a unisex society), there remains strong evidence that some individuals benefit from having both masculine and feminine characteristics (Spence, 1982).

THE SELF ●

"The self" is one of the oldest and most familiar concepts in psychology, but also one of the most controversial. How shall we look at it from a natural science perspective? What is the self? If the mind is located in the head, where is the self located? What is the relationship between the self and personality?

Skinner (1989) noted that *Webster's Third New International Dictionary* contains about 500 entries that begin with "self." As with personality, many theories look at the self as a thing, as an object. Early on in the study of psychology, William James (1890) drew a distinction between the "self-as-knower" and the "self-as-known." The **self-as-knower** is equivalent to your listing of words to describe yourself. It is the you that you know. The **self-as-known** equates to your listing as others see *you*. It is the public *you*. It is your personality as you think others see you.

From a natural science perspective, personality is the organization of characteristic behaviors under a unique developmental history. The self is verbal behavior describing your own personality (Skinner, 1953). The self is usually private verbal behavior—your thoughts that describe your characteristics—but these self-descriptions may be made public (as when we asked you to describe yourself at the beginning of this chapter). The self-statements may be made with respect to your own evaluation, with respect to how others may see you, or as evaluative statements. Evaluative statements are also taken as indicating self-esteem or lack thereof.

Self-Concept and Self-Recognition

The preverbal child may be said to have a **self-concept**. This self-concept is inferred from the child's behavior with respect to stimuli pertaining to self. Lewis (1987) concluded that there is little evidence for **self-recognition** before 8 months of age. Thus, infants do not differentially respond to photographs of themselves or to their images in a mirror at this age. Not until 12 months of age do children show self-awareness, which Lewis takes as the emotional reaction to seeing themselves in a mirror.

But under what conditions do self-recognition and self-awareness develop? Let us look at a history that will produce self-recognition. First, parents constantly speak the child's name across a wide range of situations. The child also learns *you* and *your*. These verbal stimuli accompany situations involving the child's image in pictures and in the mirror. For example parents ask, "Who's that?" and then say, "That's Mary." The child's image of itself in a mirror or a picture becomes discriminative behaviors with respect to itself. Behaving in front of the mirror produces different consequences than behaving in front of a picture or another person. The movement of a part of the body is accompanied by a change in the stimulus. In the presence of a mirror, the child makes a response that is instantaneously reinforced by a corresponding visual stimulus. With the parents' labeling of the stimulus in the mirror with the infant's name or "you," the self-recognition develops into self-awareness.

Self-Awareness and Perspective Taking

Developmental psychologists have long been concerned with the emergence of self and related phenomena such as perspective taking. Most of the recent research in this area has employed the concepts and techniques of the approach commonly known as theory of mind, or TOM (Baron-Cohen, Tager-Flusberg, & Cohen, 2000; Howlin, Baron-Cohen, & Hadwin, 1999). TOM is the ability of children and adults to behave as if they and others have private thoughts that are distinct from their public behaviors. For example, in one of the measures of TOM, called the false belief task, a child may be shown a crayon box, but the crayons are removed and a coin is placed in the box. The child is asked, "What's in the box?" The answer is "A coin." The key to TOM is shown after another adult, who was not present when the coin was put in the box, enters the room. The child is asked, "What do you think Mr. Smith thinks is in the box?" If the child answers, "Crayons," he or she is said to have a theory of mind.

Behavior analysis has also been concerned with the concept of **self-awareness** and even the "mind." Skinner (1974), for example, emphasized processes such as social contingencies and control by discriminative stimuli in the development of self-awareness in humans and nonhumans alike (Lattal, 1975; Pliskoff & Goldiamond, 1966; Reynolds, 1966; Shimp, 1982). Premack and Woodruff (1978) coined the phrase "theory of mind" in work in which they showed that given her training history, their chimp, Sarah, inferred the "intentions" and "motivations" of a man on a videotape to predict his actions. They believed that Sarah understood the actor's purpose and chose alternative solutions compatible with that purpose. For example, Sarah was shown a man trying to get food that was out of reach or experiencing a machine that would not work. When then given choices between two pictures, one of which was a solution to the problem and the other unconnected, Sarah chose the one that was connected logically. In other words, Sarah acted as if she understood that the man had motives and beliefs.

Other behavioral researchers working under the rubric of **relational frame theory** (RFT), however, have argued that human self-discrimination is functionally distinct from that of nonhumans because the former involves verbal processes, whereas the latter does not (Hayes, Barnes-Holmes, & Roche, 2001). A number of studies demonstrating the derived transfer of self-discrimination response functions via equivalence and other types of relations (Dymond & Barnes, 1994, 1995, 1996) lend support to the view that human self-discrimination is verbal and involves repertoires of relational framing.

RFT argues that an analysis of self-awareness requires an understanding of perspective-taking frames that appear to be essential in the verbal construction of self. Deictic relations, which specify a relation in terms of the perspective of the speaker, are a family of **relational frames** that appear to be critical for the development of perspective taking. The three frames that have been identified as the most important in this regard are the frames of "I and you," "here and there," and "now and then." These frames differ significantly from other relational frames because they do not have formal or nonarbitrary counterparts and cannot be traced to formal dimensions in the environment. The relationship between the individual and other events serves as the constant variable on which these frames are based (and not on nonarbitrary dimensions of stimuli themselves). For example, whereas "bigger" may refer to specific and nonarbitrary aspects of stimuli (e.g., the size of a truck), the perspective of "here" is based only in relation to "there," not on "hereness." From the perspective of RFT, we develop these **relational repertoires** from caretakers who provide many situations and say, for example, "Look who's here" or "What's over there?" and point to the exemplars. Not only do caretakers provide multiple exemplar training of these relational frames, but the child contributes by responding to, and asking, many questions contained within daily verbal interactions with others (e.g., "Mommy, what are you doing there?"). Although the physical environment is different each time an individual engages in questions such as these, the relational properties of I versus You, Here versus There, and Now versus Then remain constant. For example, I is always from this perspective—here—but not from the perspective of another person—there. Abstraction of an individual's perspective on the world, and that of others, requires a combination of a sufficiently well-developed relational repertoire and an extensive history of exemplars that take advantage of that repertoire.

Perspective-taking frames appear to be even more complex because they cannot be defined in terms of particular words (not even *I, you, here, there, now,* and *then*). According to RFT, words used to describe the perspective of the self and others are merely examples of the relational cues that control the perspective-taking frames, and a range of other words and contextual features may serve the same function. Consider, for example, this sentence: "It is after midday and I am at work [here and now], but the children [you] are still at school [there and now]."

Although the RFT approach to perspective taking is relatively new, some authors have highlighted commonalities with the more traditional TOM account. Specifically, Barnes-Holmes, Barnes-Holmes, Roche, and Smeets (2001) suggest that the tasks commonly used to establish TOM indirectly involve training in the three perspective-taking frames. Novak, Long, and White (2000) presented evidence from analyses of early mother–child interactions during the child's first and second years. The results showed that even in these prelanguage children, mothers provide multiple exemplar training with objects, their labels, their properties, and their use. However, in keeping with predictions made by RFT, these researchers (Barnes-Holmes et al., 2001) argue that a more effective means of establishing these repertoires would be to target the relational frames directly, thereby focusing the training on the largely verbal nature of the behavior in question.

In a preliminary RFT study of perspective taking, Barnes-Holmes (2001) developed a protocol for analyzing and training perspective-taking performances as generalized relational activity in young children. The methodology developed in this work consisted of an extensive protocol for targeting each of the three perspective-taking frames directly. The basic format of the protocol distinguished patterns of responding in terms of both relation type (i.e., I–you, here–there, and now–then) and relational complexity (i.e., simple, reversed, and double reversed relations). An example of a simple I–you relational task employed by Barnes-Holmes is as follows. A child and an experimenter are seated adjacent to one another, and before each is placed a differently colored play brick (e.g., the experimenter's brick is green and the child's is red). The child may be instructed as follows: "I (experimenter) have a green brick and you (child) have a red brick. Which brick do I have? Which brick do you have?" This task targets the relational frame of I–you directly and is simple in the sense that the child requires relatively limited perspective-taking abilities to respond correctly. Consider now a more difficult version of the same task in which the relations are reversed and the child is instructed as follows: "If I was you and you were me, which brick would you have? Which brick would I have?" In this task, the I–you relation is explicitly reversed, and the task requires a much more sophisticated repertoire of I–you relational responding. Consider now an even more complex task in which the frames of I–you and here–there are targeted and reversed simultaneously (i.e., a double reversed relation): "If I was you and you were me and if here was there and there was here, which brick would I have? Which brick would you have?" This task requires sophisticated repertoires in terms of both the perspective-taking frames and relational complexity. In the study by Barnes-Holmes (2001), two young children were exposed to testing and training of this kind, and highly sophisticated relational repertoires were established as a result.

In an ongoing program of research extending this early work on relational perspective taking, McHugh and colleagues (McHugh, Barnes-Holmes, O'Hora, & Barnes-Holmes, in press-a) developed a more robust protocol for assessing perspective-taking skills in adults and constructed a developmental profile from the relative performances of five different age groups ranging from early childhood to adulthood (McHugh, Barnes-Holmes, O'Hora, & Barnes-Holmes, in press-b). The findings overall indicated that accuracy on the perspective-taking tasks increased as a function of age. Specifically, the youngest group of participants (aged 3–5 years) produced significantly more errors than all other groups of participants (aged 6–30 years) on all tasks, but few differences were recorded among the other groups.

These findings are interesting for a number of reasons. First, they correlate with findings from the mainstream TOM literature in which it has been demonstrated that children develop perspective-taking abilities around the age of 5. Second, from an RFT perspective, these performances correlate with the level of verbal abilities of individuals of various age groups. In an extension of this research, a number of children are currently being exposed to rigorous training procedures using the relational protocol in an attempt to replicate the earlier findings on the establishment or development of these repertoires of perspective taking. Aside from the practical implications of this work for populations with debilitating deficits in perspective-taking skills (e.g., those with Autistic Spectrum Disorder), that different psychological traditions are drawing similar conclusions seem to suggest that the current approach to perspective taking may well have significant value.

How Do Self-Statements Develop?

Parents encourage their children to provide self-statements. They ask, "How do you feel?" "What do you think?" "Why did you do that?" Hayes (1987) has suggested that this produces **literality**. That is, the parents prompt and then strengthen the equivalence between the child's self-statements, behaviors, and physiological responses. Thus, children behave as if their thoughts were the same thing as their physiological conditions. The words "I am afraid" become attached to the physiological condition of fear.

Parents also encourage the development of reason giving (Hayes, 1987). They ask, "Why did you do that?" and reinforce the child's verbal response, "I did it because . . ." If a child breaks a dish, the parent is likely to ask, "Why did you break that?" and expects the child to state a reason by making an "I-statement." Because parents reinforce the child's providing the I-statements, either by agreeing (i.e., positive reinforcement) or by terminating further demands for an answer (negative reinforcement), reason giving becomes a strong response for the child, and the reasons the child supplies become secondary reinforcers. Thus, the child will engage in reason-giving I-statements even without reinforcement from the parents because these statements are automatically reinforced. It is reinforcing to give reasons. Reason giving continues throughout life. As adults we continue to give reasons for our behavior and treat the reasons as the actual causes of our behaviors. Although the reasons parents teach are often treated as causes, they are usually not. Still, we learn to treat reasons as causes (Dietz, 1986).

The internalization of external behavior that becomes private talk was discussed in the Chapter 7 on cognitive development. Vygotsky (1987) wrote extensively on how the "self-extends beyond the skin." That is, the origins of the self are in the verbal–social interactions the child has with his or her caregivers and others. This source of the self in the public world enables the parents to shape self-verbalizations through prompting and reinforcing the child's public statements. Once these public self-verbalizations are strong, the statements become self-reinforcing through automatic reinforcement. At this point, the process of extinguishing the public self-statements occurs. The result is that children learn to make private self-statements. Dietz (1986) gives this account of his child learning to discriminate between public and private speech:

> I was at the barber shop with my son, Joshua. There were quite a few people ahead of us and we were sitting and waiting patiently. He was being very quiet but soon turned to me and said: "Sometimes you can't hear me talk." "Huh?" I answered. He continued, "Sometimes I talk in my head and no one knows what I'm saying except me." This was an interesting comment on thinking. (pp. 162–163)

Reason-giving I-statements may start out as public verbal behavior that is reinforced by others. However, it becomes private behavior because it is self-reinforcing and because revealing self-talk is often punished as we get older. Some of the reasons given attribute the cause to external events ("It was too heavy." "I didn't see the ball on the stairs." "The other driver cut me off."). Besides being external, these causes are specific to the event. Other causes refer to our own, more permanent, characteristics ("I'm not very strong." "I'm hyperactive." "I'm not a good driver.") Rotter (1966) distinguished between these two stated sources of cause as external or internal locus of control. Furthermore, Rotter (1966) thinks that some children are characteristically "externalizers" and others "internalizers" because they have learned to attribute causes to either an external or internal source.

Stable Versus Unstable Traits

Those viewing the source of control as being an internal condition also view these causes as being stable. That is, a cause due to a trait of the self is rather **stable**. For example, if the child attributes his or her failure to a lack of intelligence, that child is unlikely to behave in a way to change his or her performance. In short, the child is more likely to give up trying. On the other hand, causes that are external are viewed as more likely to change. So if the child attributes his or her failure to bad luck or a hard test or a "stupid teacher," then the child is more likely to try again. These unstable causes are not seen to be part of the characteristics of the self.

Self-Efficacy Beliefs

Bandura (1977a) used the term **self-efficacy beliefs** for self-statements about the ability to succeed in accomplishing specific behaviors. Bandura found self-efficacy verbal statements to be central in coping with stressful situations and to underlie all successful therapeutic interventions. He proposed that the development of self-efficacy beliefs originated from four sources. *First* was the actual successful accomplishment of tasks. A child who is successful has a history of success. *Second*, observing a model who is successful sets the occasion for a child to imitate the behavior and become successful, as in the child who sees an adult fold a paper airplane, and the child follows. *Third*, others can use verbal persuasion, encouraging the child by providing efficacy statements such as, "See, now you can do it too!" *Fourth*, self-efficacy beliefs are enhanced (or weakened) by the emotional arousal of the child. The child who is excited may be more (or if too excited, less) likely to make self-statements about being able to accomplish a task, such as jumping a stream or speaking in front of an audience.

Self-Esteem

Self-esteem includes the evaluative statements about what we can do and how we appear to others. A person with high self-esteem emits self-statements with high positive value: "I'm good at math." "I'm pretty good looking." "People really like me." A child with low self-esteem makes self-statements of high negative value: "I'm dumb at math." "I'm ugly." "People don't like me." Like most self-statements, these are likely to originate from others in the child's social environment: parents, siblings, or teachers. They attribute good or bad outcomes to enduring internal characteristics of the child (e.g., personality, intelligence, aptitude). Positive statements are associated with other positive reinforcers (good math grades, praise), and these type of statements become positive self-reinforcers when the child emits them privately.

The low-self-esteem statements become self-reinforcers as well. Saying the child is dumb "explains" why the child got bad grades and terminates the aversive situation. Likewise, "ugly" explains unpopularity and is negatively reinforcing. Pejorative statements by others become negative self-reinforcers because they terminate aversive events.

Self-Control

A final topic dealing with the self is **self-control.** This area has to do with **resistance to temptation** and delay gratification. In this situation, for example, the child is faced with a choice between obeying a societal rule (e.g., "Don't eat the candy.") and yielding to the sweet siren call of sugarcoated chocolates. Some explanations of children who can resist temptations such as these rely on internalized states or conditions, such as "high ego strength" or a "strong superego." However, from a behavioral systems perspective, we may see the child's dilemma as a choice between behaviors that have different consequences coupled with the history of the child with respect to the differential consequences for these different behaviors.

Walter Mischel studied self-control in preschool children using a series of experiments in which the child had two choices. If the child waited the entire period of time, the child got the more preferred of two reinforcers. However, if the child could not "delay temptation" and rang a bell to signal that he or she could not wait, the child got the less preferred reinforcer. Mischel and his colleagues studied many factors thought to increase the preschooler's resistance to temptation, including attention to the preferred reinforcer (Mischel & Moore, 1973) and distracting the child from attending to the reinforcers (Mischel, Ebbesen, & Raskoff-Zeiss, 1972). In an interesting study, Grosch and Neuringer (1981) developed an analog to the Mischel technique with pigeons as subjects. The researchers studied some of the same variables with pigeons that Mischel and his colleagues had used with preschoolers and found parallel effects in the way they could manipulate environmental conditions to manage the "resistance to temptation" in the birds. Thus, environmental contingencies seem potent in determining whether individuals will yield or resist temptations.

Often, the need for self-control occurs when we have a choice between a behavior that has an immediate but rather small reinforcer (such as the taste of the candy) versus a behavior whose consequence is delayed but with a larger reinforcer (praise from the adult). Much of human development involves choices such as between buying a piece of candy or saving up for a new video game or tasting the smoke of a cigarette versus not smoking and adding years to one's life. Rachlin (1976) presents such dilemmas as choices between behaviors that have small immediate consequences versus those that have large but delayed ones. He concludes that living things follow the **matching law**. This law states that we closely match our behavior to the value of the consequences of each behavior.

Box 9.2   Delay and Choice

Have you ever noticed how all the candy bars are on display right at the checkout stand at the grocery store? Well, the store manager who puts them there understands the classic problem in self-control—that immediate reinforcement nearly always wins out over delay of gratification. One thing that managers and economists also know is that if it takes time to get a reward, the value of the reward becomes less. Kagel, Green, and Caraco (1986) call this change in the value of a reward as a function of increased time delay discounting. For example, you may choose $100 now more than $300 in 5 years. Why do we do this? Kagel et al. (1986) have argued that we have learned that there is risk implicit in waiting and that this delay discounting is an adaptive response to uncertainty in an organism's natural environment.

It turns out that an equation can be constructed that predicts the behavior of various organisms, including pigeons and humans, given various combinations of amounts and time delays. Both pigeon choice of food and human choice of hypothetical amounts of money are discounted in the same way (Rachlin, Raineri, & Cross, 1991). The formula is as follows:

$$V = \frac{A}{(1 + kD)^2} ,$$

where V is the value of a reward; A, the amount of the reward; D the delay of the reward; and k is a constant—the larger the value of k, the greater discounting.

Len Green and his associates (Green, Fry, & Myerson, 1994) wanted to know if this same mathematical function held up in predicting the discounting behavior of young children, young adults, and the elderly. The subjects included groups of 6th graders, college students, and older adults (mean age 67.9 years). Subjects were given binders of file cards with pairs of various monetary amounts and times. One choice was always one fixed large delayed amount (either $100 and $1,000 for the 6th graders, or $1,000 and $10,000 for the adults). There were six different delays for these rewards, ranging from 1 week to 25 years. The immediate rewards ranged from .1% to 100% of the delayed amount with which they were compared. For example, a choice might have been between $1,000 in 10 years or $100 now.

The choices of all subjects in each age group were combined to produce equivalence points. These were the points at each combination of amount and delay in which the immediate reward matched the delayed one. These data were plotted, and mathematically generated curves were fit to the data.

The results showed both similarities and differences in the age groups. All groups showed discounting (reducing the size of the immediate reward they would accept as equal to the delayed one). The same basic mathematical formula given above fit all groups. However, the constants were different. Children discounted much more quickly, suggesting that they did not value the delayed rewards as much. The children were also more sensitive to short delays than adults who were more sensitive to long delays. The result is what we would call *impulsivity*. That is, children will accept a smaller immediate reward in place of a large delayed one, and the delays they will tolerate are very small. The older adults were the most willing to accept large delays for large rewards, and they discounted least.

So the next time you pass the candy display with a child, don't try to suggest that if he waits he can have a better dessert. The child will probably discount what you're saying.

On the basis of the study involving self-control in pigeons (Rachlin & Green, 1972), Rachlin provided a formula that predicts the behavior of a college student faced with a choice between studying versus going to the movies. The formula states that the person will do the behavior for which the consequences have the highest value. The value of the consequences involves both the amount of reinforcement (or punishment) and the time that elapses before the consequence occurs. If both behaviors have consequences that are immediate, such as going to the movie now or taking a final exam now, then the student should study, because passing the exam is a larger reinforcer than watching the movie. Likewise, if both the exam and the movie are the same time in the future, say 1 week away, the student will study. However, if the student can go to the movie now and the exam is a week away, the value of the choice switches, and the student goes to the movie. Green and Synderman

(1980) manipulated amount of reinforcement and delay in matching for pigeons. They concluded that delay is a more powerful determinant of choice than is amount of reinforcement. The matching law explains why it is easier to give in to the temptation of eating a snack versus resisting that temptation and looking slim for swimsuit season.

How do we engage in self-control? We learn to engage in behaviors that change the matching law equation. In other words, we learn to change the value of the consequences. We can do this by increasing the amount of reinforcement. We may do this by adding reinforcers for the desired behavior, such as adding self-praise ("Good, I lost three pounds this week.") or giving oneself a special reward (e.g., buying a new bathing suit). Or we may increase the aversiveness of the undesired behavior (e.g., fining oneself for a transgression or nagging oneself).

Likewise, we can provide small, immediate reinforcers, such as self-praise or a snack, so that they compete with the small, immediate reinforcers for a less desired behavior. Similarly, we can manipulate the value of the less desired behavior. When we use such strategies, we are also making consequences of the delayed behavior more immediate. For example, posting a particularly bad photo of an out-of-shape self on the refrigerator door makes the consequences for eating not only more aversive, but more immediately so.

One way we can control ourselves is to make a **commitment**. For example, we may join a health club and pay yearly dues because we know that this payment is a commitment that will make it more likely we will go to the club and work out. Otherwise, without the commitment, we are likely to find other activities (like lying around watching TV) more reinforcing. Sometimes our commitment is physical restraint, as is increasingly the case with extremely obese individuals who, after trying other "soft" commitments to losing weight through various diets and failing, opt for stomach bypass surgery, in which their stomachs are surgically made into the size of a hen's egg.

Rachlin (1995) has suggested that self-control is indeed based on environmental contingencies, but, rather than focusing on individual consequences, he argues that self-control is determined by overall patterns of contingencies. So when the obese person continually tries to lose weight but instead continually gains, this pattern makes commitment possible.

Commitment is behavior made more likely by our overall responding patterns (although Fantino & Stolarz-Fantino, 2002, view Rachlin's use of "patterns of responding" as contextual variables that function as setting events or establishing operations). For example, he argues that we would not make a commitment to control our own behavior based on the immediate contingencies. Instead, when we continually choose the small, immediate reinforcer (junk TV) over a large, delayed one (a healthy body), we choose to make a commitment (prepay health club dues). Thus, self-control through commitment appears to occur because of the *patterns* of behavior–consequence relationships and not just *individual* behavior–consequence relationships. If only individual contingencies were involved, we would always choose the short-term immediate ones.

Can We Learn Self-Control?

If self-control is affected by learning history and current environmental conditions, can we teach self-control to children? Schweitzer and Sulzer-Azaroff (1988) developed a procedure to increase the selection of larger but more delayed reinforcers over small but more immediate reinforcers in six preschool children. In pretesting, the children demonstrated a preference for smaller, immediate reinforcers over the delayed, larger ones. The method involved a shaping procedure in which the delay to all reinforcers was gradually increased. The results showed that after the teaching, five of the six children showed an increase in preference for the large, delayed reinforcers.

Can such a procedure work with children who are hyperactive? Binder, Dixon, and Ghezzi (2000) used a similar shaping procedure with children identified with attention deficit hyperactivity disorder. Initially the children showed a clear preference for immediate, small reinforcers. By gradually increasing the delays to reinforcement (and adding some verbal instructions), all subjects switched their preference to the larger reinforcer.

The Self Revisited

The term *self* refers to many phenomena and may be used in many contexts. In this chapter, we have looked at several ways in which it has been used, and we have noted that these often include very different aspects of the word. In summary, taken together, the self-statements we make constitute our self-concept. The topics of self-recognition, perspective taking, literality, reason giving, locus of control, and self-efficacy combine to suggest a theoretical approach to self-concept based on the interaction of the person with the environment. The response class of self-statements we make regarding our publicly observable behavior may make up what James called "the self-as-known." This is the self we call "me." The class of self-statements that includes private as well as public behavior about what our behavior constitutes James's "the self-as-knower," or "I."

SUMMARY ●

A behavioral systems approach to *personality* is concerned with providing an account of personality development and acknowledges the role of both physiological and biological factors in contributing to both consistency and changes in behavior.

Personality has been defined as "that organization of unique behavioral equipment an individual has acquired under the special conditions of his [or her] development" (Lundin, 1961, p. 7). Personality is a product of the unique interactional history between genetic, historical, current physiological, and environmental factors that produce a unique set of behaviors and reinforcers. Personality has also been described in terms of the early occurring behavioral patterns called temperaments (Thompson, 1999). As a child grows older, correlations between present and subsequent measures of temperament become stronger. This is in line with observations that, initially, temperament is highly susceptible to biological factors and subsequently comes under greater influence of dynamical interactions between the child's characteristics and the environment; it also reflects the progression of genotype–environment interactions from passive to evocative to active. Ultimately, there is a reciprocal relationship between the environment and temperament.

Societal, cultural, and parental expectations prompt and shape the development of gender-related behaviors through parent–child transactions. The process involves differential reinforcement of gender-appropriate behaviors. Gender-appropriate behavior is strengthened, and gender-appropriate stimuli become conditioned reinforcers. *Gender identity* (awareness of one's sex), gender stability, and gender consistency develop in succession. Rigidity in sex roles has been posited as detrimental. It is asserted that the sex role flexibility evidenced in *androgynous* individuals (those possessing both masculine and feminine traits) affords them greater adaptability.

The existence of a self-concept in the preverbal child is inferred through behavior with regard to stimuli pertaining to self. *Self-recognition* develops into *self-awareness* (the emotional reaction to oneself in a mirror). In terms of *relational frame theory,* the study of self-awareness necessitates a comprehension of perspective-taking frames, thought to be an integral aspect of the verbal construction of the self. Person-environment relationships serve as constant variables on which these *relational frames* are based. Relational repertoires are developed via the interaction of caretaker, who provides multiple exemplar training of relational frames, and child, who provides responses and asks questions. *Perspective taking* requires both a well-developed relational repertoire and a broad history of exemplars that capitalize on that repertoire.

Individuals possessing an **internal locus of control** see causes of outcomes as stable, whereas those possessing an **external locus of control** consider causes more subject to environmental change. *Self-efficacy* refers to one's beliefs regarding the ability to affect the environment. These beliefs are important because of their effects on coping skills as well as their central role in the process of psychotherapy. *Self-esteem* comprises evaluative statements regarding one's abilities and appearance to others and bears heavily on one's sense of self-efficacy. *Self-control* concerns the conflict one experiences in choosing between different behaviors with different consequences. Environmental contingencies weigh heavily on such choices. Engaging in self-control requires that we change the value of consequences. Self-control may be gained through commitments, the effectiveness of which lie in consideration of patterns of behavior–consequence relationships rather than single instances of behavior–consequence. It is somewhat reassuring that it has been demonstrated that people have the ability to learn self-control.

● NOTE

1. In Eysenck's (1970) theory, two of these dimensions are bipolar. That is, they are continual, with opposite endpoints. Extraversion and introversion mark the extremes of the first of these. The second, neuroticism, runs from "stable" to "unstable." The psychoticism factor has no opposite poles but, rather, varies in strength from person to person.

CHAPTER 10

SOCIAL AND EMOTIONAL DEVELOPMENT

● WHY STUDY SOCIAL AND EMOTIONAL DEVELOPMENT?

How critical is a child's early social and emotional development? Children with greater delay of gratification at the preschool age were later found to be adolescents whose parents rated them as more "academically and socially competent, verbally fluent, rational, attentive, playful, and better able to deal well with frustration and stress" (Mischel, Shoda, & Peake, 1988, p. 687). These findings suggest that a child's social and emotional behaviors and his or her interactions with the social environment (parents, peers, teachers) are critical in the child's development. That is, adolescents' self-regulation and restraining behaviors may be related to their early childhood learning experiences. In this chapter, we will discuss different types of socioemotional learning phenomena, explain their functions, and explain how they originate.

● PROCESSES IN SOCIAL BEHAVIOR

In our coverage of operant interactions (Chapter 6), we emphasized the four-term contingency. As you recall, the contingency involved: (a) a discriminative stimulus signaling (b) a response that was followed by (c) a reinforcing stimulus occurring in the context of a general (d) setting event. Recall the schematic below:

$$S^d \rightarrow R \rightarrow S^{r+}$$
(setting event)

In this chapter, we focus on social transactions that also are four-term contingencies. What makes social transactions unique is that one person's behavior functions as discriminative or reinforcing (or both) stimuli for another. Thus, we have reciprocal interactions in which one person's behavior functions as a stimulus for others. These *multiple, dynamic, reciprocal interactions* mutually influence the development of the behaviors of individuals in social transactions (Peláez-Nogueras, 1996).

Consider the following meeting of two individuals, Bert and Ernie:

Bert's contingency:

$$\underset{S^d \rightarrow}{\text{sees Ernie}} \quad \underset{R \rightarrow}{\text{"Hi, Ernie"}} \quad \underset{S^{+r}}{\text{Ernie smiles}}$$
(setting event = walking along)

Ernie's contingency:

$$\underset{S^d \rightarrow}{\text{"Hi, Ernie"}} \quad \underset{R \rightarrow}{\text{Ernie smiles}} \quad \underset{S^{+r}}{\text{Bert smiles}}$$
(setting event = in a good mood)

Notice that the same event ("Hi, Ernie") that functions as a response for Bert functions as a discriminative stimulus for Ernie. Note also that we are analyzing one small segment of a series of interlocking sequences or chains of operant responses (behavior patterns). It is as if we are looking at a still frame of a video. If we were to resume "play" of this transaction, we would note that Ernie's smile serves not only as a reinforcer for Bert's "Hi, Ernie" but that Ernie's smile also serves as an S^d for Bert's next behavior, perhaps evoking a smile from Bert. We could continue analyzing these interlocking chains until the two parted and ceased to function as the stimuli for the other's responses.

Behavior is both an event controlled by social stimuli and as an event that serves as a social stimulus for the behavior of others; this is the essence of social transaction. This is our analysis of social transactions at the level of basic processes (Level 1). This chapter (and the next on antisocial interactions) is about long-term changes in social transactions (Level 3). That is, here we focus on the dynamic outcomes of the basic processes: How reciprocal social inter-actions produce what we call **prosocial transactions** such as those occur-ring in the formation of attachment, the development of separation anxiety, empathy, and **altruism**. Some developmental psychologists have provided behavior analyses of these types of moral behaviors (e.g., see Eisenberg & Mussen, 1989; Gewirtz & Peláez-Nogueras, 1991a, 1991b; Peláez-Nogueras & Gewirtz, 1995).

The Function of Social Behavior

The child enters this world with a set of universal responses and reflexes that enable his or her rudimentary interactions with others. Not only do other people elicit reflexes, but also, the child possesses characteristics (including "cuteness" and "cuddliness") and emits reflexes (such as the smiling reflex) that function to evoke caregiver behavior directed at the child. Ethologists suggest that such universal behaviors evolved because of natural selection. Individuals who evoked caregiving from their parents were more likely to survive the vul-nerable period of infancy to grow to maturity and have offspring of their own who possessed these characteristics as well. Thus, we first examine the phylogenic basis for prosocial behaviors.

Phylogenic Contributions to Social Development

Ethologists have argued that natural selection would have favored the evo-lution of characteristics that promote the development of caregiver behaviors. They argue that vulnerable human newborns would be more likely to survive if they possessed characteristics that elicited or evoked parental caregiving. Among these proposed characteristics of the child are the child's physical appearance and his or her initial reflexive behaviors.

Physical Characteristics

Has there ever been an ugly baby? Certainly not—if you ask parents. Neonates have unique appearances that most of us see as cute. Not only are newborns' heads disproportionately large compared with adult proportions, but their facial characteristics are different too. Lorenz (1943) observed that the large forehead, prominent eyes, flattened nose, and small chin characteristic of newborn humans are also characteristic of other newborn animals. It is suggested that such universal "cute" characteristics evolved through natural selection because they elicit in adult members of the species positive emotions that promote caregiving. However, as we have emphasized in this textbook, a behavior analyst should keep in mind that in the context of organismic/physical and environmental changes, **operant learning** is the one that provides the main basis for human behavioral development (Gewirtz & Peláez-Nogueras, 1996). We will first consider some of the organismic innate characteristics of human beings, such as social reflexes and innate *facial expressions*.

Social Reflexes

Included in the repertoire of reflexes that human newborns are born with are the so-called **social reflexes.** These reflexes, such as smiling, grimacing, and crying, have the function of evoking parental caregiving. Although these behaviors may originate as reflexes, they may soon develop into operant behaviors as well because they produce reinforcing consequences.

Facial Expressions

Izard and Malatesta (1987) have reported ample evidence that most human emotional responses display facial expressions based on specific muscular patterns that are universal. That is, the muscles involved in showing interest, disgust, and smiling are the same for all infants. Following a line of reasoning first suggested by Darwin (1872/1965), Izard and Malatesta conclude that these universal facial expressions are the result of phylogenic contingencies that have selected genotypes for these expressions because they contribute to the survival of the infant by evoking parental caregiving.

Both the expressions of "interest" and "disgust" are present at birth, with the smile appearing 3 to 4 weeks later (Izard & Malatesta, 1987). The novelty of a human face appears to elicit an interest reflex. Painful stimuli can also produce discomfort and elicit the facial expression of disgust. A study by Gewirtz and Peláez-Nogueras (1992c) showed that 9-month-old infants actually learn to *reference* adults' cues or facial expressions signaling "joy" and "fear" when in ambiguous or unknown situations.

Infants in that study were able to learn which maternal cue denoted a positive or negative consequence. Their reaching-for-the-toy response rate increased under the maternal expression that cued positive consequences (a pleasant toy), whereas the reaching-response rate decreased under the maternal expression that cued negative or aversive consequences (i.e., a loud, aversive sound). That is, the infants learned which situations to react in and which to avoid. We will illustrate this phenomenon in detail in a later section titled "Social Referencing."

Similarly, Soken and Pick (1999) found that 7-month-old infants were able to discriminate among videotaped happy or sad expressions. Infants were also found to prefer looking at the happy and interested expressions rather than the sad expressions. From both studies (Gewirtz & Peláez-Nogueras, 1992c; Soken & Pick, 1999), one can infer that children before the age of 1 can learn to avoid negative or aversive situations that may prove to be a danger and actively prefer or seek out situations that are pleasant and less of a threat to their survival or functioning.

Reflexive Crying

Recall (Chapter 8) that at least three distinct cries can be detected in newborns: hunger, anger, and pain. Each is elicited by one of these classes of stimuli (i.e., hunger, anger, and pain) and has the function of causing the caregiver to terminate the aversive stimulus affecting the infant (Novak & Peláez, 2002). The adaptive significance of these behaviors is clear. Of additional significance is that crying can have an influence on parental care even if the parent is at a distance. This is not true of the child's physical characteristics or facial expressions, which require the parent to make visual contact with the child in order to be influenced by them. Crying can evoke parental behavior from the next room (and while the parents sleep!). A study conducted by Miller (2001) found that 2- to 5-month-old infants exhibited discomfort behaviors (e.g., crying, fussiness) significantly more often with strangers than with their mothers. With their mothers, they exhibited more positive vocalizations. Consequently, these infants showed a preference for situations that are known and that have proven to be safe in the past versus the unknown and potentially dangerous. But as we will see in the next section, infants also learn operant-voluntary crying.

Neonatal Imitation

Consider the basic problem in imitating motor behaviors. Let's play the game "Simon Says." One of us is the model. I raise my hand over my head, saying, "Simon says, DO THIS." Go ahead, do it! If I raised my right hand, which one would you raise? How do you know that what you did matches or looks like what I did? Did you look in a mirror to see if your gesture looked like mine? Of course you didn't. Should you have raised your right or left hand? Which is the "correct" imitation? Imitation of gestures seems to require knowledge that the child's own unseen behavior matches that of the observed model. Because he felt such knowledge requires cognitive development, Piaget concluded that true imitation does not emerge until the last quarter of the first year (Anisfeld, 1991).

In the mid 1970s, psychologists (e.g., Meltzoff & Moore, 1977) first reported observations of newborns imitating adult facial and motor gestures. They videotaped the faces of newborns who watched adults model behaviors such as sticking out their tongues (tongue protrusion), smiling, or making exaggerated eye movements. If a child's behavior occurred in the next time interval following a model's behavior and it matched the form of the model's behavior, the child's behavior was considered imitative. Children as young as 2 days old were said to imitate adult facial gestures (Meltzoff & Moore, 1983). Such early appearance strongly suggests that these are universal behaviors that have evolved because of phylogenic contingencies. This raises the question of whether such **neonatal imitation** is the basis for development of later imitation. After carefully reviewing the evidence, it is not clear that neonatal imitation is the same phenomenon as later imitation (Anisfeld, 1991; Poulson, de Paula Nunes, & Warren, 1989).

How Does Neonatal Imitation Differ From Later Imitation? First, it appears that neonatal imitation is more limited and less robust than originally suggested. In his review of 19 well-controlled studies on neonatal imitation, Anisfeld (1991) concluded that the only behavior for which there is strong evidence for imitation is tongue protrusion. Studies attempting to demonstrate the imitation of other behaviors have either failed to be replicated or have strong methodological flaws (Anisfeld, 1991).

Second, even tongue protrusion may be elicited by a stimulus other than the behavior of a model. Jacobson (1979) showed that tongue protrusion in 6-week-olds could be elicited by a ball or pen moving toward the child just as readily as by an adult protruding his or her tongue. She concluded that rather than true imitation, it was behavior released (or elicited) by any stimulus that contained curvature and concentricity.

Third, neonatal imitation seems to disappear around 2 months of age. Imitation of adult behaviors disappears only to develop slowly over the first 9 months (Uzgiris, 1972). Thus, it appears that there is little evidence that neonatal imitation directly leads to generalized imitation (Anisfeld, 1991; Poulson et al., 1989).

However, neonatal imitation may have been selected by phylogenic contingencies because it facilitates the development of social interaction. Bjorklund (1987) felt that one of the functions of early imitation was to focus the infant's attention on the adult's face. In our view, the neonatal behavior may facilitate the development of true imitation by reinforcing the parent's modeling behaviors. Papousêk and Papousêk (1981) have noted that both mothers and fathers model feeding behaviors, such as mouth opening, lip movements, and licking, for their infants. Some of these modeled behaviors may act as stimuli eliciting neonatal imitation. The newborn's matching behaviors may serve as positive reinforcing stimuli strengthening the modeled behaviors of the parent. This makes it more likely that the parent will prompt further imitation. Thus, the neonatal behavior may reinforce the beginnings of the reciprocal interactions between parent and child.

The development of reciprocal interactions may be a hidden skill that leads to the development of true imitation, and generalized imitation might form a basis for later language learning.

Ontogenic Contributions and Operant Learning

Although phylogenetically based universal social reflexes such as tongue protrusion may contribute to the survival of the human species, most social behavior is more varied than this and develops over a long period of time. Thus, we now turn our attention to how social behaviors develop over the life span of the individual. To do this, we must look at the development of social transactions.

● SOCIAL BEHAVIORS AS REINFORCERS

Reinforcer identification is very important, and this is why researchers have explored different methods for assessing reinforcing stimuli with young children (Higbee & Peláez-Nogueras, 1998). **Social behaviors** are strengthened by the actions of others. That is, adult social behaviors can function as **social reinforcers** (see Chapter 6).

Recall that social reinforcers are considered secondary or acquired reinforcers—stimuli that acquire their strengthening characteristics because they are associated with primary and other **secondary reinforcers.** The analysis of a reinforcer is very useful. Unfortunately, critics such as Alfie Kohn (1993) have attacked behavioral practitioners for using "praise" and "tokens" as reinforcers, arguing that these types of "rewards" are counterproductive. His views have created a misunderstanding in the literature about the use and effectiveness of positive reinforcers (Peláez-Nogueras, 1993). Many experiments have documented that stimuli that are reliably present when the child's behavior is reinforced become discriminative for reinforcement and therefore become reinforcing stimuli as well.

For example, Bijou and Baer (1965) describe how mothers (or other caregivers) are likely to emerge early on as social reinforcers. In their analysis, the mother is likely to provide primary positive reinforcers (e.g., food, water, taste stimuli, pleasant temperature, tactile stimulation, visual and auditory stimuli) and to remove negative reinforcers (e.g., roll the child off uncomfortable hard objects, move the child away from harsh light, burp the child to relieve him or her of gas buildup, massage aching gums, drive away pesky older siblings or pets, etc.). Thus, by this combination of providing positive reinforcers and removing, terminating, or avoiding aversive ones, the caregiver may become discriminative for reinforcement. In addition, the caregiver's presence and actions come to strengthen the child's behaviors, which, in turn, produce the provider's presence or actions. Caregivers become acquired positive reinforcers.

Proximity

Bijou and Baer (1965) argued that, at first, the mere proximity or nearness of the mother is reinforcing. That is, the child engages in behaviors that bring the mother near. Some of these proximity-producing behaviors may originate as reflexes, especially the smiling and crying reflexes described previously. In our analysis, these behaviors soon acquire a new function—to bring the mother near.

Attention and Mands

Although the mother's proximity is a reinforcer, Bijou and Baer (1965) suggest that children learn to discriminate that in some situations, just having the mother nearby is less reinforcing than getting her to direct her behavior toward the child. For example, a child cries and her mother picks her up, or a child tugs at his father, who asks, "What's wrong?" Thus, the caregiver's attention, not just proximity, becomes a reinforcer. From then on, behaviors that produce these directed changes in the parent's behavior (i.e., attention) become more frequent.

Children's emotions can come under the positive-reinforcer control of caregiver attention and touch (Gewirtz & Peláez-Nogueras, 2000). Attention-producing behaviors have unique characteristics. Parents may consider verbal behaviors in the form of **mands** (see Chapter 8). Crying "Mommy!", a tug on the mother's arm, or even hitting a younger sibling meet the criteria for a mand in that they are emitted in a state of deprivation of the caregiver's attention and reinforced by the mother's attention (i.e., "What is it dear?", a look down at the child, "Stop that hitting.") As with most mands, attention-seeking behavior is more likely to occur with deprivation of the reinforcer. That is, a child is more likely to emit "Mommy!", tug on an arm, or hit another child when the child is deprived of adult attention.

It is important to remember that children learn socially appropriate or inappropriate behaviors to get their parent's attention. The child's behaviors receive attention, at least intermittently. If appropriate behaviors are not reinforced, the nonreinforced behaviors are likely to escalate into inappropriate ones. Child–parent problems often arise when only the child's high-magnitude behaviors (e.g., cries, biting another child, attempting suicide) trigger the reinforcing attention of others. For instance, parents often fail to see that their reactions to these attention-seeking behaviors, such as yelling at the child to stop, function as reinforcers. However, yelling at the child meets the criteria that define a positive reinforcer if the yelling strengthens the child's behavior that produced the yelling. So parents (and others too) often think they are punishing behavior when in fact they are unwittingly reinforcing it. This principle of human behavior is what underlies the saying, "It's the squeaky wheel that gets oiled."

Ways of Reducing Mands for Attention

Because attention-producing behaviors are often problematic for parents, teachers, and others, finding ways to reduce these behaviors is of interest. There are four primary ways to reduce mands for attention.

Extinction. With extinction, we may try to ignore the behaviors and expect the behavior to slowly decrease. This procedure may eventually work, but it has several problems. First, withholding attention means that the deprivation of adult attention becomes greater and is likely to increase, rather than decrease, demands for attention. Second, ignoring the behavior usually results in an extinction burst (see Chapter 6), so that the behavior in the short run is likely to escalate rather than decrease. That means a mand for attention may turn into a full-blown tantrum. Third, the increased attention-seeking behavior means that it is even more difficult to ignore, thus increasing the likelihood that it will eventually be reinforced. This means that the behavior will be maintained under an intermittent reinforcement schedule (specifically, a variable-ratio schedule). Therefore, the behavior will become increasingly resistant to extinction and continue to occur with intermittent reinforcement. For these reasons, extinction by itself is rarely the answer to reducing attention-seeking behavior.[1]

Differential Reinforcement. A second method called differential reinforcement of other (DRO) behavior combines the extinction of the undesirable attention-seeking behavior with reinforcement of another incompatible behavior. An **incompatible behavior** is one that cannot be done at the same time as the first. For example, sitting quietly with hands folded is incompatible with yelling and flailing the arms to get attention. The advantages of DRO (also called the **incompatible response technique**) are twofold. First, a desired response is strengthened, making the undesired one less likely to occur. Second, attention is provided so that deprivation of the desired reinforcer does not happen. These are the principles behind the advice, "Catch them being good!"

Positive (Presentation) Punishment. A third technique to reduce attention-seeking behavior is **positive punishment** (punishment by hurt; see Chapter 6). Parents may apply some aversive stimulus (e.g., a spanking, a threat) contingent on the attention-seeking behavior in an attempt to reduce the undesired behavior. Unfortunately, as we have seen above, unless the aversive stimuli are strong and consistently applied, the long-term effects may be to reinforce rather than decrease the attention-seeking behavior. The use of these aversive stimuli is likely to be unsuccessful for other reasons. First, adults may be reluctant (for moral or ethical reasons) to administer strong aversives and to do so consistently. Second, aversives may trigger escape behaviors so that the child avoids or escapes from the adult, and his or her behavior is thus negatively reinforced. This escape interferes with the positive role of parenting or teaching.

Negative Punishment (or Punishment by Loss). **Negative punishment** was also discussed on Chapter 6 and is a technique that can be used to reduce undesirable attention seeking. Recall that this involves the contingent loss of positive reinforcers. Taking away privileges, such as TV time or outside play, is sometimes used by adults to reduce undesirable behavior, including attention seeking. Losing tokens is an example of a negative punishment procedure known as *response cost.* These procedures can be effective if the reinforcer that is lost is large enough and if the punishment contingency is immediate. One problem with the procedure is that the loss of reinforcement is often delayed (e.g., "You can't watch TV tonight," "You can't go to the movies on Saturday") or weak (e.g., losing only one or two tokens when the child has 500). It is conceivable that the delays in sending criminals to prison due to complications in legal due process has rendered prison a less effective deterrent to criminal behavior than it otherwise would be.

Another type of negative punishment discussed is called **time-out**. In time-out, an undesirable behavior has immediate consequences—the child is removed from reinforcement. Usually this involves placing the child in a room or corner for a brief period of time. The purpose is to have the undesirable behavior result in the loss of the reinforcers the child was receiving. It is effective if the loss of reinforcers is immediate and brief. Its purpose is to punish the behavior, not to isolate the child. Studies have shown that time-out is effective when a brief time-out from positive reinforcement of 3 to 5 minutes immediately follows as a consequence of undesirable behavior. Again, the purpose of time-out is to punish the behavior by a brief, contingent loss of reinforcement, not to isolate the child from his environment or deprive her from interactions.

Affection

Although attention reinforces behaviors that the provider may find desirable or undesirable, the last of Bijou and Baer's (1965) classes of social reinforcers—affection—is likely to be provided for behaviors that elicit feelings of affection. Usually, affection takes the form of hugs, kisses, smiles, pats, nuzzling, tickling, hair ruffling, special crooning tones of voice, and affectionate words, but the exact form will vary from one parent–child dyad to the next. Bijou and Baer suggest that there is a great deal of variability from dyad to dyad, not only in the form of affection provided, but in the amount. They point out that parents invariably reinforce by being near and providing attention, but they may not give affection. Therefore, there may be some parents who provide little affection as positive reinforcers.

Those who do provide affection often find that because it, unlike proximity and attention, is likely to follow "desirable" behaviors, it strengthens these desirable behaviors. Contingent use of affection is an effective way to shape desired behavior.

> The ease of giving affection for good behavior, and the natural tendency not to present it and to withdraw it when confronted with bad behavior, set up situations which strengthen selectively those behaviors which please the mother, rather than those which displease her. This line of reasoning suggests that children who are maximally responsive to affection as a positive reinforcer are more readily influenced by the mother's goals for them than are children more responsive to her attention than to her affection. (Bijou & Baer, 1965, p. 141)

● OBSERVATIONAL LEARNING

If we were to ask you to say the Polish word for *good,* we could wait for you to pronounce it and then reinforce. Assuming that you do not speak the Polish language, this would take a long, long time, as it is unlikely that you would emit the correct sounds in the course of a normal lifetime! Likewise, we could employ shaping—waiting until you emitted an approximation to the sounds, reinforcing that, and then reinforcing ever-closer approximations to the word itself. Although this would be somewhat faster and more likely to succeed, it would still take a very long time. No, neither of these reinforcement methods would be very effective. Instead, our success would likely be enhanced by modeling the sound "dub-zhe" and prompting you to imitate it. Imitation is the basis for what is called **observational learning**, or changes in behavior brought about by watching the behavior (including the verbal behavior) of others.

How are we to analyze observational learning? Do we need a new set of principles to explain it? Albert Bandura and his colleague, Richard Walters, at Stanford University conducted much of the early work on observational learning. Bandura and Walters published much of their work in an important early text, *Social Learning and Personality Development* (Bandura & Walters, 1963). Bandura followed this description of experimental work with a systematic treatment in his book *Social Learning Theory* (Bandura, 1977b). In his early work, Bandura treated the learning of behavior through the observation of models as following basic learning principles. He believed reinforcement of behavior was important, but he felt that reinforcement affected the performance of the behavior, not the learning of it. This distinction between learning and performance and whether unique processes were involved became key issues in understanding observational learning. These issues with Bandura's approach have been extensively discussed by Gewirtz (1971a, 1971b), who pointed out the importance of overt responding and extrinsic reinforcement for observational learning.

Bandura based the learning–performance distinction on his classic "Bobo" doll studies (Bandura, 1965; Bandura, Ross, & Ross, 1963). In one of these studies (Bandura, 1965), children watched filmed adults (models) emit aggressive behaviors against Bobo dolls. The adults modeled physical (e.g., kicking, hitting with a hammer) and unique verbal (e.g., "Wettosmacko") behaviors. One third of the children saw the model receive severe admonishment. Another third of the children saw the model receive praise and rewards. The remaining third saw a film in which the model received neither reprimands nor praise.

After watching the modeling on film, the children were brought in to an observation room with a Bobo doll and aggressive implements, including a hammer and knife. The children were observed in two postmodeling sessions. In the first, the performance test, children were not given consequences for aggressive behaviors. Under these conditions, the children in both the model-rewarded and model-no-consequences groups performed significantly more aggressive responses than the children in the model-punished group.

In the second session following the film, the learning test, however, all children were told that they would get highly attractive rewards if they could reproduce the model's behaviors. Under these conditions, the differences between the groups vanished. All three groups showed high rates of aggressive responses. Even sex differences disappeared. Girls, who had shown less aggressive behavior than boys in the performance test, emitted nearly as many aggressive behaviors as the boys under the learning test conditions. All children had learned the aggressive behaviors of the model.

Other social learning theorists have used these studies to make two points. First, because all children were able to reproduce the behaviors when offered a reward, they all learned what the model (the authority figure) did, regardless of whether the model was reinforced, punished, or neither. Therefore, Bandura concluded, reinforcement is not necessary for learning behavior but only for the performance of it. Second, Bandura theorized that reinforcement (and punishment) need not be direct but could also be experienced by watching others. Even though **vicarious consequences** (i.e., vicarious reinforcement and vicarious punishment) were thought to be key aspects of observational learning, and which had some effects on performance of behavior, some behavior theorists have raised serious concerns about the need for additional principles other than those offered in the operant conditioning paradigm (e.g., Gewirtz, 1971a, 1971b; Gewirtz & Stingle, 1968), as discussed next.

An Operant Approach to Observational Learning

Although Bandura (1965) felt that new principles, such as vicarious consequences, were needed to explain observational learning, others felt that existing principles of operant learning were sufficient. Gewirtz and Stingle (1968) presented the argument that vicarious reinforcement actually does not function as reinforcement (i.e., to strengthen the behavior of the observer). Instead, they suggested that the behavior of the model is a discriminative stimulus that signals the observer that a behavior that matches the model's behavior will be reinforced. This happens because of a history of interaction in which the observer has developed **generalized imitation** (see Chapter 8). That is, behaviors that match a model's behaviors are frequently reinforced by the consequences they produce. For example, a child watches another child solve a puzzle. When the observer matches the puzzle-solving behavior, his or her behavior, too, is reinforced by the solution to the puzzle. Notice the child's imitative behavior is directly reinforced by the solution. When we view the consequences to the model as discriminative stimuli rather than vicarious reinforcers, we can also understand a phenomenon known as **counterimitation.** In counterimitation, a child observes another child do something that is reinforced, but the observer does not match the model's reinforced behavior. He or she may even do the opposite, or counterimitate. For example, Johnny may watch his older brother get away with cookie-nabbing behavior, but Johnny doesn't try it because he has learned that imitating his brother's behavior is punished, not reinforced. His brother serves as a discriminative stimulus that signals that a matching behavior would likely be punished, not reinforced.

From Gewirtz's perspective (1971a, 1971b), we imitate a model's behaviors when they are discriminative for direct, not vicarious, consequences to the imitator. Thus, if we look at Bandura's (1965) study, we can see that in the absence of offering the child contrived rewards, the child is likely to match the model's behavior if the model receives toys or appears to enjoy hitting the Bobo doll. In the absence of the direct consequences to the contrary, observing a model who is being punished for aggression means that children are not very likely to aggress themselves. Finally, when children are offered extrinsic rewards to imitate the behavior, the verbal cue is a setting event establishing that repeating the model's behavior will be reinforced.

Observational Learning of Respondents: Emotional Behavior

In Chapter 6, we examined how we may acquire fears and other emotional responses by the process of respondent learning. As you recall, a neutral stimulus becomes a conditioned stimulus because of its pairing with an unconditioned stimulus for the emotional response. Thus, we learn emotional responses by observing them in others and then matching the behavior and experiencing the consequences ourselves.

A clever study of college students by Berger (1962) illustrates vicarious respondent conditioning. The students were assigned to one of two groups. In the vicarious-conditioning phase, both groups witnessed the same event: A model was seated at a table; as the light dimmed, a buzzer sounded and the model rapidly jerked his arm off of the table. The control group was told that this was a reaction time study and the model was trying to lift his arm as soon as the buzzer sounded. The vicarious-conditioning group was told that the model was receiving an electric shock when the buzzer sounded and that the jerking of the arm was a response to pain. Thus, this group was led to believe that the model was expressing pain and that the buzzer was associated with electric shock.

Following the observations, the subjects were tested for vicarious conditioning. Individually, in a different room, each student was attached to a machine similar to a polygraph to record his or her galvanic skin response (GSR), a measure of sweating associated with emotional arousal. While they were attached to the equipment, the same buzzer was sounded as when they had seen the model's performance. That is, they were tested to see if the buzzer came to be a conditioned stimulus for the conditioned response of emotional arousal. There were no changes in GSR for the control group. Remember, they were told they were watching a reaction time study. Apparently, the buzzer remained a neutral stimulus for them. However, subjects in the experimental group showed increased GSR activity. The buzzer had vicariously become a conditioned stimulus for those who had thought they had seen the model being shocked. This suggests that we may come to fear (or like) things by merely watching others become conditioned to them, not just by experiencing the conditioning directly ourselves. However, it is conceivable that earlier histories of the subjects (pre-experiment) influenced their responses. Most participants had experienced pain themselves in other situations.

● PROSOCIAL TRANSACTIONS: INTUITIVE PARENTING

How do parents know when and how to interact with their children? Is there a phylogenic basis for social interaction? As noted above, there is some evidence that physical and behavioral characteristics of the infant elicit positive maternal responses. From an ethological viewpoint, it would benefit the species if respondent caregiving responses were hardwired. However, knowing how to interact with a neonate need not require a phylogenic explanation. It is likely that, because of the social experiences parents have had with other adults and children, parents, particularly mothers, may intuitively know how and what to do to take care of and interact with their infants.

Papoušek and Papoušek (1987) have detailed many parental behaviors directed at infants. They have identified the following six ways in which parents intuitively interact with their infants to promote learning:

1. Creating and maintaining an awakened state

2. Presenting a simple structure of stimuli and learning trials

3. Providing a large number of repetitions of trials

4. Gradually ordering tasks so that there is increasing complexity

5. Using adequate reinforcers

6. Being sensitive to feedback signals indicating the child's limits of tolerance

These characteristics that parents use intuitively in early social interactions are conditions that promote the development of learning in their infants. They are remarkably similar to the characteristics described by Moerk (1989) (see Chapter 8) of parent–child interactions in the learning of language. It suggests that early on, parents already know or develop the skills necessary to teach their infants to acquire basic skills and abilities in social, cognitive, and linguistic domains. Parents build on the initial patterns of behavior that may be heavily influenced by the phylogenic characteristics of the child that evoke parenting in the parents. But as parent behaviors produce changes in the child's behavior, these changes in the child's behavior will progressively shape the parents' behavior as well. This parent–child dynamical system continues to evolve.

THE ORIGINS OF SOCIAL PHENOMENA ●

In this section, we examine the origins and learning of diverse social learning phenomena that have been investigated from the behavior–analytic approach. The phenomena discussed include attachment, depression and touch, fear of the dark and fear of strangers, social referencing, and jealousy.

Attachment

Above we described some characteristics of the infant that evoke caregiving behaviors from adults. We also described how these caregiving behaviors are likely to reinforce proximity-, attention-, and affection-producing behaviors in the infant. When the infant's proximity- and security-regulating behaviors become organized around one or more particular caregiver, we say the child is developing an **attachment** (Bretherton, 1987, p. 1063). When we say the behaviors are "organized," we mean that more than just individual behaviors occur. Instead, attachment is characterized by dynamical patterns of behaviors focused on the attachment object (i.e., the caregiver). Bowlby (1969, 1973, 1980) proposed that attachment evolved because of phylogenic contingencies in which behaviors that protected the child from predators were naturally selected. Petrovich and Gewirtz (1985) argued that both phylogenic contingencies and ontogenic contingencies, in which caregivers reinforce proximity, imitation, and identification (Commons, 1991) contribute to attachment. The combination of phylogenic and ontogenic contributions to attachment is consistent with a behavioral systems approach.

Attachment and Separation Protests

Visit nearly any child care center or preschool at the beginning of a new year and you are certain to observe **separation protests,** commonly identified as "security of attachment" (Ainsworth, Blehar, Waters, & Wall, 1978), and "separation anxiety" (Kagan, Kearsley, & Zelazo, 1978). Let us look at the possibility

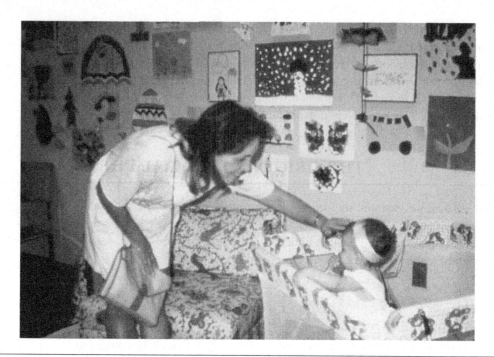

Figure 10.1   A Mother Saying Good-Bye to Her Infant and Holding Her Purse

that separation protest might develop as learned interactions between the child and parent(s) (Gewirtz & Peláez-Nogueras, 1991a).

As we described earlier, the caregiver becomes reinforcing for many infant behaviors. Loss of a reinforcer, as occurs in separation of the parent and child at the start of school, is aversive to the child. The loss elicits some emotional responses as well as evokes behavior that may function to get the mother back, as is the case in extinction bursts. Jack Gewirtz and Martha Peláez have conducted several studies on how the mother–infant interaction influences the development of separation protests and distress. We discuss those studies in the next section.

The Conditioning of Separation Protest. In one of their first studies (Gewirtz & Peláez-Nogueras, 1991b), the researchers hypothesized that contingent maternal responding to the protests shape behaviors such as whining, crying, and throwing tantrums. They further hypothesized that separation protests could be reduced if parents would differentially reinforce behaviors other than protest behaviors, such as playing with toys (see DRO or incompatible response technique, above).

Twenty-three infants, ages 6 to 11 months old, and their mothers were studied in a laboratory setting. Mothers were given cues by a private earphone to signal to the child that she was leaving by standing up, kissing the child, waving, and saying, "Bye-bye, I'll be right back." At this point, the mother left the room for up to 3 minutes, at which point she returned. After a brief reunion, another separation trial was conducted.

The effects of two conditions of reinforcement, continuous reinforcement (CRF) and DRO, were compared. In the CRF condition, every infant protest to the mother's separation cues was reinforced by the mother by stopping, retracing her steps, turning to, speaking to the child, and so on. In the DRO condition, an infant's protests cued by the mother's leaving never received contingent reinforcement from the mother.

The child–mother dyads were given 6 to 8 separation trials daily for 8 to 12 days. An ABA design was used in which successive trials of a noncontingent baseline (DRO) were followed by trials of the contingent responding to protests (CRF), which in turn were followed by a return to the DRO of baseline. As shown in Figure 10.2, the analysis indicates significant increases in protest behaviors during the contingent CRF trials compared with both DRO conditions where play increased drastically.

The authors (Gewirtz & Peláez-Nogueras, 1991b) concluded that separation protests, which have been used by others as a measure of the strength of attachment, could be learned as operants. They go on to suggest that such operant learning is very likely trained inadvertently in the life settings in which it occurs by the maternal reactions that operate under the notion of positive, responsive, "loving" mothering (Gewirtz & Peláez-Nogueras, 1990, 1993b).

In viewing these typical transactions from a dynamical systems viewpoint, we must point out that although the study described above demonstrates how the mother is likely to shape the child's behavior in separation protests, the interactions are reciprocal. It appears that mothers "inadvertently" reinforce protestations because in doing so, the mother is likely to reduce (at least temporarily) the whining and crying. Thus, the mother's behavior is often shaped by the child through negative reinforcement (by avoiding or escaping of the aversiveness of the child's cry) while, simultaneously, the child's protest behavior is shaped by the mother through positive reinforcement (her approach, touch, talking, and smiles).

THE POWER OF TOUCH •

Human touch can be a very powerful reinforcer during interactions (Cigales et al., 1996; Peláez-Nogueras, Field, et al., 1996; Peláez-Nogueras et al., 1997; Peláez-Nogueras, Gewirtz, et al., 1996). Researchers at Florida International University and at the Touch Research Institute at the University of Miami have

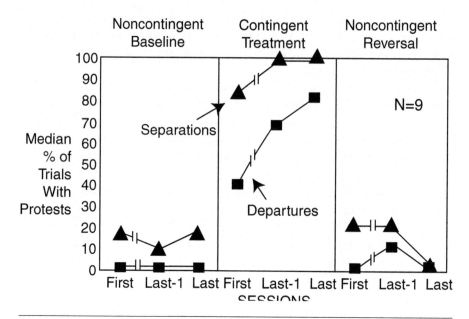

Figure 10.2   Graph on Separation Protest (Median)

conducted a series of studies investigating the usefulness of this variable. Early on in the study of social reinforcers, researchers used touch as part of a package of social reinforcers that also included a smile and vocalization (Rheingold, Gewirtz, & Ross, 1959; Weisberg, 1963). However, without appropriate controls, touch elicits, rather than reinforces, behavior. That is, touching a child might elicit a sound from the child in the same manner that a tickle or pinch would. To verify that touch is reinforcing, it is necessary to keep the number of touches equal but to vary whether the touch is contingent on the behavior of the child or independent (i.e., noncontingent) of the child's behavior (Poulson, 1983). If the number of touches is the same but the child increases behavior only when touch is contingent on the response, then touch functions as a reinforcer, not as an unconditioned (eliciting stimulus).

A study by Peláez-Nogueras, Gewirtz, et al. (1996) showed exactly this. Ten infants from 1 to 3 months old received two types of social reinforcers. In the touch condition, a female adult smiling, cooing, and rubbing the child's legs and feet was provided contingent on the infant making eye contact. The tactile stimulation continued for as long as the child continued eye contact in what they called a **synchronous reinforcement procedure**. In the synchronous reinforcement procedure, the onset of the infant response (eye contact) corresponds to the onset of the consequent stimuli (the touch). As another example, imagine you are driving a car; your car moves only when you press the accelerator, and it stops motion when you release the pedal.

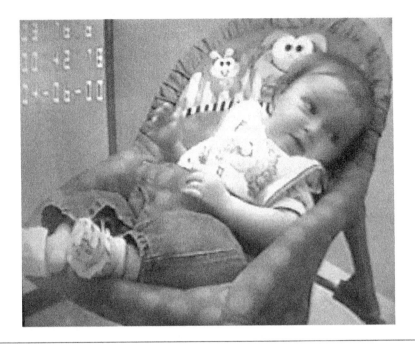

Figure 10.3   Infant Gazing Away From Mother

In the infant experiment, the baby produced as much touch as he or she wanted by making eye contact, and once the infant become disinterested (or aversive), he or she stopped making the eye contact response and gazed away (as in Figure 10.3).

In the no-touch condition, the rubbing was omitted, as shown in Figures 10.4 and 10.5. All infants showed more social behavior (vocalizations and smiles) when their eye contact produced the additional reinforcer that included touch stimulation compared with the condition in which touch was not provided (only smiles and vocal sounds were made contingent on infant eye contact). Moreover, when touch was not included in the reinforcement treatment, infants also spent more time crying, gazing away, and protesting.

In this way, the researchers were able to measure infant preferences for social reinforcers.

Comparing the Effects of Two Types of Touch

To investigate the effects of diverse types of touch and determine which infants prefer the most, Peláez-Nogueras et al. (1997) conducted a study comparing *massage-like touch* with *poking/tickling touch*. The massage-like

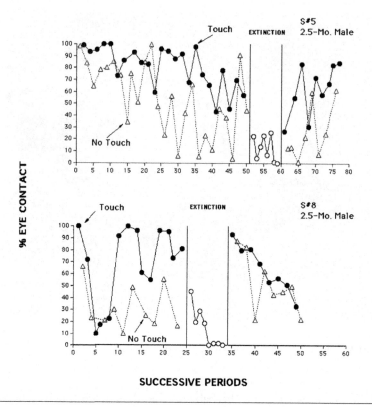

Figure 10.4 Touch as a Reinforcer of Infant Behavior

touch consisted of deep but gentle circular rubs starting at the infant's legs and moving up to the abdomen and forearm. Poking/tickling touch consisted of a pattern of deep but short nudges along the same path on the child's body. Both types of touching were delivered using the synchronous rein-forcement procedure in which stimuli were presented when the child made eye contact and were withdrawn when the child looked away. The results of Peláez–Nogueras et al. (1997) showed that massage-like touch strengthened eye contact more than the poking/tickling touch. In addition, massage-like touch increased smiling and vocalizations more and decreased crying com-pared with poking/tickling. Because the stimulation could be terminated by the infant by looking away, the increases in looking away, crying, and protest-ing suggest that poking/tickling, although gentle, was, nevertheless, a nega-tive reinforcer. These studies demonstrated not only that touch serves as a reinforcer but that it can also evoke and maintain positive affect. Furthermore, the type of touch provided is important. Rhythmical, massage-like touch is more reinforcing than intrusive poking and tickling.

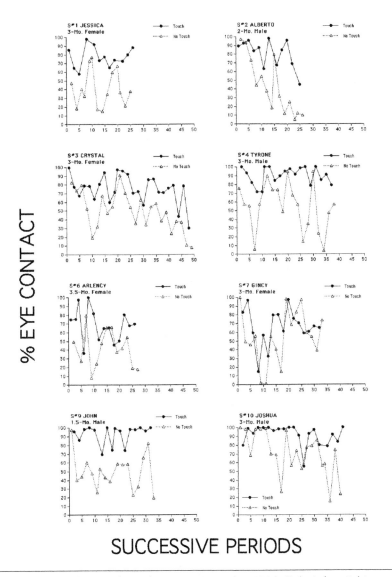

Figure 10.5   Synchronized Reinforcement Procedure With Eight Infant Subjects Under Two Treatments: Touch Versus No Touch

Touch as Therapy for Depressed Mothers and Their Infants

Consequently, the same researchers wondered if they could use touch as therapy for infants of depressed mothers (Peláez–Nogueras et al., 1996). They were interested because depressed mothers frequently have nonfacilitative effects on their infants. In turn, their infants often show less attentiveness, fewer smiles, lower activity levels, and more fussing (Cohn, Campbell, Matias, & Hopkins, 1990; Field, 1984, 1992; Hart, Field, del Valle, & Peláez-Nogueras, 1998). And although Field et al. (1988) found that these infants would continue to act "depressed" with a "nondepressed" adult stranger, that need not be always the case.

In another study, Peláez-Nogueras, Field, Cigales, Gonzalez, and Clasky (1994) showed that children behaved in a less depressed way when interacting with an adult who is familiar with the child (i.e., a nursery school teacher) and who knows how to provide the appropriate contingencies during interactions than when interacting with their depressed mothers. Last, the authors also found in a subsequent study that the interactions the child has with the depressed (i.e., withdrawn) caregiver may elicit protest when their mothers are instructed to pose a flat facial expression or "still face" (Peláez-Nogueras, Field, Hossain, & Pickens, 1996).

In these experiments, the depressed mothers learned to use massage-like touching to produce infant positive affect and attention (Malphurs, Raag, Field, Pickens, & Peláez-Nogueras, 1996; Peláez-Nogueras et al., 1997; Peláez-Nogueras, Gewirtz, et al., 1996). By using massage-like touch, depressed mothers, even in a condition in which they kept a straight, nonexpressive still face, were able to get their infants to smile, vocalize, and make more eye contact. Those studies suggest that depressed mothers can buffer the negative effects of their depressive behavior (e.g., lack of stimulation) and can compensate by touching their infants. Certain kinds of touch can be very effective in overcoming the deleterious affect of depressed mothers.

● FEAR

The crying and screaming of children experiencing stranger anxiety is said to emerge between 6 and 7 months of age and to peak at 8 to 10 months (Sroufe, 1977). Explanations for its development include the development of attachments and the development of a cognitive representation or schema for the mother (Kagan, 1974).

Gewirtz and Petrovich (1982) suggest that an approaching stranger is a discriminative stimulus for the disruption of a child's ongoing, positively reinforced behavior with the mother. They cite a finding by Emde, Gaensbauer, and Harmon (1976) that infants picked up by a stranger in the mother's presence cry more than if the mother is not there. Presumably, crying in the presence of the mother is likely to cause the stranger to put the child down, allowing the previous reinforcing interaction to resume.

With experience, the child learns that other stimuli, such as strangers, may be associated with harm, and these strange stimuli evoke and elicit the crying we call stranger anxiety. This analysis is supported by research that shows that characteristics of the setting (e.g., a strange room) and characteristics of the stranger's behavior (e.g., threatening facial expressions, speed of approach) affect the occurrence of crying.

In the next section, we describe two laboratory studies that have demonstrated the conditioning of fear of the dark and fear of strangers.

The Conditioning of Fear of the Dark and Fear of Strangers

In mainstream developmental literature, infant fear of strangers and fear of the dark have been studied by nonexperimental means. Nonbehavioral researchers have ignored in their entirety the contributions of environmental factors and learning processes to these behavior problems. One of the most important factors contributing to the emergence of fears is the caregiver's behavior contingent on the infant initiations to protest in particular contexts. We refer to this process as "shaping protests." In traditional theories, the fearful protests and avoidance behaviors involved have been conceived to be universal and unlearned (Izard, 1992).

These operant responses, however, may not always be valid indicators of reflexive fear. The protest and approach-and-avoidance responses toward strangers often may result from *operant conditioning*. Also, the fearful response of darkness (as discriminative stimuli) can be conditioned by contingent maternal attention. Attention, as we discussed earlier, can be provided by a well-intentioned and concerned mother functioning as positive reinforcement of inappropriate or undesired behaviors of the child.

Fear of the Dark

Fear of the dark can be conditioned. An experiment on fear of the dark was conducted in our lab by Aida Sanchez, with ten 6 to 8-month-old infants (reported in Gewirtz & Peláez-Nogueras, 2000). The infants sat in a high chair for 25 minutes per day for 10 to 20 weekdays, with their mothers seated immediately behind them where they could receive instructions from an experimenter (see Figure 10.6).

The researchers used a single-subject, alternating-treatments reversal design in the presence and in the absence of light in a room. That is, five infants received either contingent maternal attention as reinforcement when the infants protested (CRF), or maternal reinforcement of other, nonprotest behaviors, such as play (DRO), depending on whether the room was light or dark. These two treatments were compared across four experimental phases:

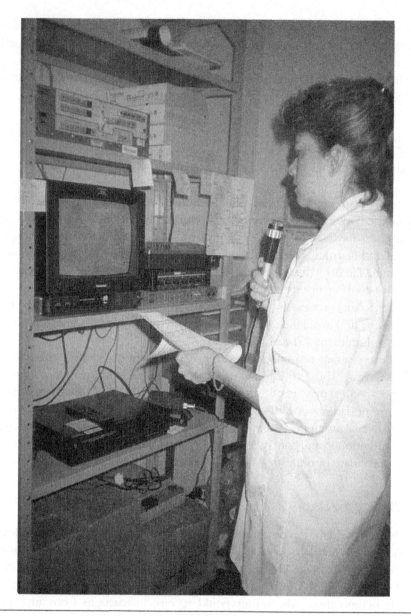

Figure 10.6   An Experimenter Speaking to Mothers

(a) baseline, in which neither class of behaviors was targeted; (b) CRF for protests in light and DRO (of nonprotest behaviors) in darkness; (c) CRF for protests/cry in darkness and DRO in light; and (d) reversal or elimination of

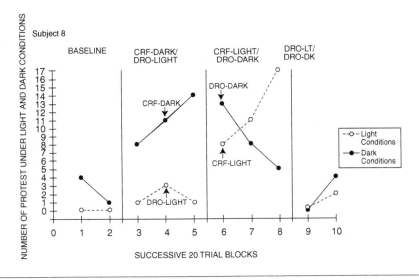

Figure 10.7 Maternal Responding to Infant Protests (CRF vs. DRO)

protest both in darkness and light contexts with DRO. The order of contexts and treatments was counterbalanced for the five other infants. Potentially elicited facial expressions of the infants confronting darkness were also recorded by infrared camera, and their vocal behavior (other than protests) was scored.

When protest frequencies were compared in subjects, every one of the 10 infants showed increasing and dramatically greater protest frequencies in the CRF than in the DRO treatment, separately in the light and in the dark conditions (see Figures 10.7 and 10.8). In addition, no difference in facial expressions for any one of the 10 infants was found between the light and the dark condition. Thus, it was demonstrated that what some take to be fear-denoting protests are as readily conditioned in light as in darkness by contingent maternal attention.

Fear of Strangers

Empirical studies have shown that not all children show a fear-of-strangers response, nor do all researchers conceive that fear of strangers is related to age or developmental level. The presumed ubiquitous fear of strangers was also explored in our lab, by Henry Lumlock, from a conditioning perspective (Gewirtz & Peláez-Nogueras, 2000). Six 8- to 10-month-old infants participated in a four-phase, single-subject design: (A1) baseline, (B1) parent attention contingent on infant approaches to female strangers, (A2) parent attention contingent on the infant avoidance of/withdrawal from the strangers, and (B2) a

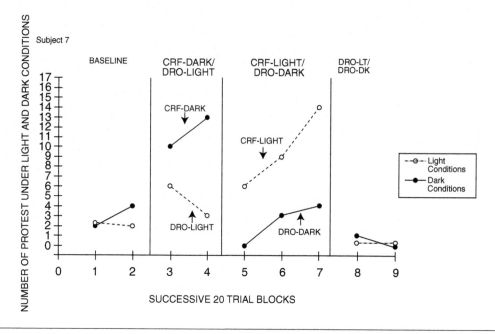

Figure 10.8   Maternal Responding to Infant Protests (CRF vs. DRO)

second phase in which parent attention is contingent on infant approaches to strangers. The baseline assessed the infant's initial approach rate to the female stranger in the absence of maternal-provided cues or contingencies. Under the two conditioning phases (B1, B2), infant locomotor approach responses to the stranger were shaped and maintained by the mother's contingent-attentive responding (on a CRF schedule). For the A2 reversal phase, attention was provided contingent on the infant's avoidance of the stranger. That is, differential attention reinforcement was provided for behaviors that were incompatible with approach (DRI). An incompatible response with "approaching" is "withdrawing."

In this study, each trial began with the infant on the right side of a playpen, beyond a red line that divided the playpen in two. The mother sat 2 feet away adjacent to the side where she could (under experimenter instructional control) provide cues and contingent (reinforcing) stimuli for her infant's approach and avoidance behavior to the approaches of a series of female "strangers." From a distance of 3 meters, a stranger female approached the infant on repeated trials, on each occasion initiating contact by smiling and talking. When the infant moved in the stranger's direction across the red dividing line, an approach was scored. When the infant moved away from the stranger, across the red dividing

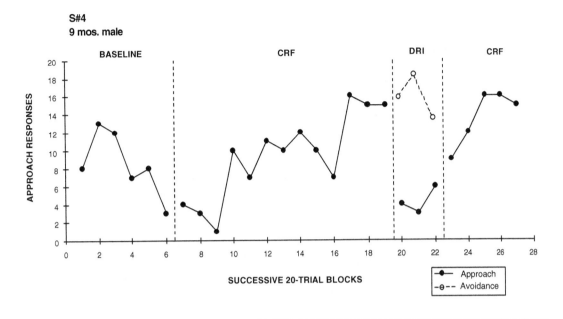

Figure 10.9   Fear of Strangers

line, or remained beyond the red line away from the stranger, an avoidance response was scored. In every session, three to six different strangers participated with each infant, rotating after five trials.

Figure 10.9 shows the approaches of each of the four infants. Their responses rise from base level in the first contingency phase, decline in the reversal phase, and again increase in the final contingency phase. This research illustrated how each infant learned to approach or avoid the female stranger depending on the discriminative and reinforcing stimuli provided by the mother. As with the work on infant fear of the dark, the results of this experiment suggest that behaviors denoting the fear of strangers in life settings may be strongly influenced by operant learning processes unwittingly provided by maternal behavior.

SOCIAL REFERENCING ●

One factor that seems to affect the child's response to strangers during this period is the behavior of familiar others, particularly the mother, but this has also been demonstrated with familiar same-age companions. As the stranger approaches, the child observes the facial expressions and physical and motor behavior of the familiar person. This looking at another's facial, vocal, or bodily expressions as a discriminative stimulus for one's own behavior is labeled **social referencing.** Traditionally, it has been suggested that the child references the person's emotional characteristics and must have the cognitive ability to interpret these with respect to his or her own behavior.

Behaviorally, we view social referencing as an example of social knowledge. With experience, the child learns that if the mother is smiling when the stranger approaches, reinforcement is likely. However, if the mother is cringing, crying may prevent the stranger from hurting her. Thus, the facial expression of the mother becomes a setting event that establishes the function of the stranger as being discriminative for positive or negative reinforcement. That is, if the mother is smiling, the stranger may evoke attention from the child; if the mother is showing concern, the stranger may evoke crying from the child.

Campos and Barrett (1984) have postulated that the responses and perceptions making up social referencing are "prewired" (i.e., unconditioned) and that social referencing mostly involves emotional components. We favor an alternative to that nativistic theory, which emphasizes that social referencing (whether instrumental or affective) can result from the infant's contingency-based learning. In our view, in ambiguous or uncertain contexts, maternal expressive facial cues come reliably to predict positive or aversive consequences for the infant's instrumental (reaching) responses (Peláez-Nogueras, 1992a).

The Conditioning of Meaningless Arbitrary Cues

Gewirtz and Peláez-Nogueras (1992c) conducted two studies to see if infants could learn to respond to maternal "expressive" cues in ambiguous situations.

In the first laboratory experiment, the mother's cues were chosen arbitrarily for being neutral for the expression of emotions. That is, the cues were originally meaningless. These cues were either palms-to-both-cheeks (in which the mother held her palms against the sides of her face) or fist-to-nose (in which the mother held her clenched right fist to her nose). Both cues were selected because they have no preexisting status as emotional cues. This enabled them to be acquired as social referencing cues through learning.

Twenty infants ranging in age from 9 to 12 months were seen daily with their mothers over a period of 8 to 13 weeks. On each trial, a covered, ambiguous object was placed before the child. The mother gave one of two initially neutral cues (originally meaningless) when the child turned and looked at her. When the child turned back, the object had been uncovered and moved within reach of the child. If the child reached for the object, one of two consequences was delivered, based on the cue (positive S^d, or negative S^Δ) given by the mother. For

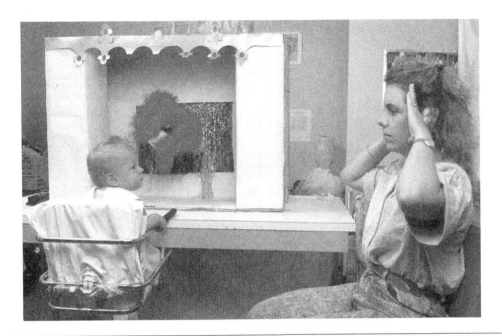

Figure 10.10   Positive Signaling

half the children, the mother's palms-to-both-cheeks behavior (S^d) was predictive of a pleasant consequence, and reaching was followed by a brief musical baby melody and slow movements of the object. For the other five subjects, the fist-to-nose (S^Δ) was predictive of an unpleasant consequence; a harsh door buzzer, concrete drill, or food blender sounds accompanied by rapid movements of the object.

The specific order of cue-response-consequence ($S^d \rightarrow R \rightarrow S^{r+}$) relationship was reversed between the two groups of five children. The results of the first experiment showed that young children learn to use the mother's cue as a discriminative stimulus for reaching, depending on the consequences that accompanied the given cue. Infants showed greater reaching than baseline rates when the palms-to-both-cheeks cue was associated with the pleasant consequence and less reaching when it was associated with the aversive consequence.

The Conditioning of Joyful and Fearful Originally Meaningful Maternal Cues

A follow-up experiment by Peláez-Nogueras (1992a) was needed to determine whether maternal facial-emotional expressions, such as *joyful* and *fearful*

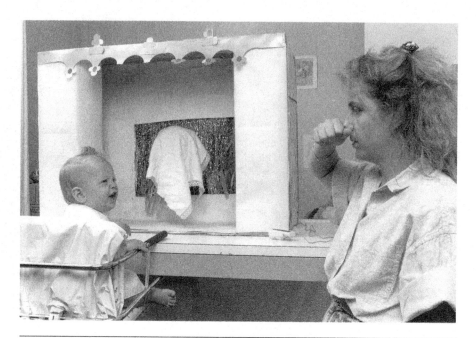

Figure 10.11   Negative Signaling

expressions, could also function as conditioned cues for infant referencing. Facial expressions are the most important cues in natural settings. Thus, a conditioning-reversal ($A_1B_1A_2B_2$) design was used with eighteen 4- to 5-month-old infants to demonstrate that maternal emotional facial expressions can become conditioned cues for infant referencing. (These infant subjects were much less advanced than the 1-year-olds with whom the social-referencing phenomenon has routinely been explored in the literature.)

Initially, during pretreatment assessment (A_1), the researchers found no difference in the incidence of infant reaching for ambiguous objects following either maternal joyful and fearful facial expressions. In the next phase, the conditioning treatment (B_1), the infants learned to reach for ambiguous objects when reaching was cued by a *joyful* maternal facial expression and followed by extrinsic positive (i.e., reinforcing) consequences, and to avoid those ambiguous objects when reaching was cued by a *fearful* maternal expression and followed by extrinsic aversive consequence contingent on their reaching. In the third phase of the experiment (withdrawal of treatment A_2) this differential reaching pattern in the presence of the two facial-emotional expressions was lost (i.e., extinguished). Finally, in the last reconditioning treatment phase (B_2), the cues recovered their predictive power. The results supported the

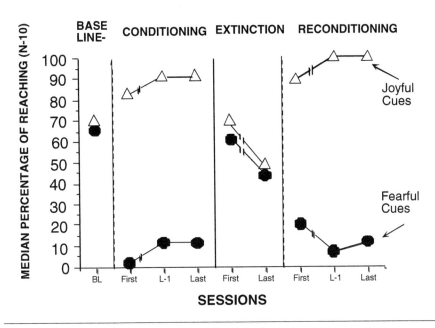

Figure 10.12   Results of the Learning of Social Referencing

hypothesis that maternal facial–emotional expressions became cues (S^ds) for infant social referencing and their approaching or avoiding responses in ambiguous contexts.

Thus, taken together, the two experiments show that any arbitrary stimulus could come to function as a discriminative stimulus whose function is much like that of the mother's facial expression in social referencing. Gewirtz and Peláez-Nogueras's (1992d) conclusions were that this is a laboratory metaphor for the way social referencing develops in the child's interactions with the parents in naturalistic settings. That is, the child learns through operant conditioning that the caregiver's facial expression of joy or fear becomes reliably associated with specific consequences (see Figure 10.12).

SIBLING RIVALRY AND JEALOUSY   ●

An example of how peers are entangled in a system involving themselves and their parents can be found in sibling jealousy or sibling rivalry. A common experience of parents (just ask them) with more than one child is the setting event of a telephone call or a neighbor coming to the front door. Suddenly, two children begin to act up, argue with each other, and make enough noise that the parent can't continue with the phone call or conversation. Conventional wisdom is that this is worse with twins, for whom the sibling rivalry is greatest. Because "sibling jealousy" or "sibling rivalry" are descriptive terms, they do not constitute true explanations of behavior. That is, to say that twins are acting up because they are jealous is tantamount to saying, "They're acting up because they're acting up"—a **circular explanation**.

Instead, to explain this behavior, it may be better to ask, "Under what conditions does the acting up occur?" In a laboratory analog of real-life jealousy, Roth and Gewirtz (1995) did exactly that. They reasoned that jealous behavior occurs in triadic (i.e., three-person) social contexts or setting events in which the mother's attention elsewhere becomes a discriminative stimulus for emitting jealous behaviors. Depending on the child's interactional history, the class of jealous behavior may take the form of crying, fussing, whining, screaming, whimpering, calling for the mother, hitting, punching, proximity seeking, reaching out to be picked up, staring, frowning, pouting, stiffening the body, placing the body between the mother and the other child, or even imitating the behavior of the rival. As an operant, the development of jealous behavior is under the control of its consequences. Regardless of topography, the functional class of jealous responses is aversive to the mother, and she is negatively reinforced for attending to them because when she does, the aversive jealous behavior stops. At the same time, mother's attention positively reinforces that child's jealous behaviors. A further problem with jealous behavior is that the rival observes the reinforcing consequences received by the other child, which makes the second child more likely to imitate jealous behavior as well.

The researchers used repeated-measures (reversal) procedures similar to those described above, but in this study, they worked with three sets of twins and their own mothers and looked at the interactions between the two dyads. One of each set of twins was put in a playpen, with each playpen placed 1.4 meters apart. Their mothers sat on a chair about a meter in front and equal distance between the playpens with their twins on either side. Each mother wore an earphone so that she could hear instructions from the experimenter.

Two conditions, CRF (continuous reinforcement of jealous behavior) and DRO (differential reinforcement of other than jealous behavior) were alternated between each twin over a total of three phases. In the first phase, after a brief period facing forward, the mother was asked to turn toward and speak to Twin 1 and thus reinforce this twin's nonjealous behaviors (DRO). When Twin 2 emitted a jealous behavior, the mother was instructed to turn to that infant and interact with that infant. In essence, that reinforced Twin 2's jealous behavior

(CRF). When Twin 1 showed nonjealous behavior, the DRO procedure was used, and that behavior was reinforced. The initial length of time with no protests required for Twin 1 to receive reinforcement was started at 2 seconds and was lengthened to 10 seconds. Thus, the DRO procedure also included shaping of a longer period of nonjealous behavior. In Phase 2, the contingencies were reversed, and in Phase 3 the contingencies were reversed again so that they were the same as Phase 1.

The contingencies of reinforcement determined the amount of jealous behavior shown by the twins. Under CRF conditions for jealous behavior, jealous protest behavior was high. When behavior other than jealous protests was reinforced, jealous behavior decreased. The study suggests that we may look at social behaviors, such as jealousy, as a class of operants reinforced by dynamical interactions in the family system rather than as individual traits.

SOCIAL COGNITION AND ENVIRONMENT ●

In her review in the *Handbook of Child Psychology,* Shantz (1983) referred to **social cognition** as "the development of social knowledge and reasoning." She went on to suggest that it focuses on "understanding the relationship between social behavior and cognitive development between thinking and behaving, between social and nonsocial knowing" (p. 495). From a behavioral systems view, we may analyze social cognition in the same way that we analyze other cognitive behavior (see Chapter 7). Therefore, we focus on three aspects of social cognition (Novak, 1987):

1. *Social knowledge.* Knowing about things in social situations. For example, saying "please" when asking for something or wearing the appropriate clothes for a rock concert versus a funeral.

2. *Social abilities.* Knowing how to do things of a social nature. For example, being able to initiate conversations or being able to play house.

3. *Social problem solving.* This involves manipulating public or private events (i.e., thoughts) to produce solutions to social problems. For example, both Mary and Marisa want to swing, but there is only one swing; Mary offers to let Marisa go first and to push her so that she can swing next.

Thus, in this view, social cognition is treated in the same way as other cognitive behavior. What is special about social cognition is that in these four-term

Figure 10.13 Carrying an Infant Facing Inward

contingencies, cognitive behavior is influenced by the behavior of other individuals. This means that cognitive behavior is a function of setting events, discriminative stimuli, and reinforcing stimuli, all or some of which may be social in nature.

Carrying Position Affects Infant Behavior

Field, Malphurs, Carraway, and Peláez-Nogueras (1996) conducted a study in which 3-month-old infants were carried by their mothers in a soft infant

Figure 10.14   Carrying an Infant Facing Outward

carrier. The carrier was designed for infants to be faced *either inward or outward* (see Figures 10.13 and 10.14).

A comparison of these two positions showed that when the infants were carried facing in, they spent significantly more time sleeping and were rarely actively awake and looking at the environment. In contrast, the infants in the facing-out position were more active, including more time moving their arms, head turning, kicking, and looking at their environment. Fathers typically hold and carry their infants facing out.

PROSOCIAL BEHAVIORS •
IN EARLY CHILDHOOD

Prosocial behaviors, such as cooperation, emphatic responses, and sharing, as well as more advanced moral standards, such as honesty, justice, loyalty, conscience, and public or private virtue such as **altruism**, are fostered very early in development. In appropriate environmental family contexts during the preschool years, the child is exposed repeatedly to behaviors of role models that can be characterized as "honest," "altruistic," and "just" and to caregivers who provide reinforcing consequences contingent on the child's *matching* responses.

In the same way, behavior denoting standards such as dishonesty, greed, corruption, or selfishness can be fostered by exposing the child repeatedly to the model's (parent or teacher) behavior patterns characterized as "dishonest," "greedy," "corrupt" and providing reinforcing contingencies on the child's *matching* responses (e.g., as in the case of "gang" or "terrorist" leaders functioning as models for the members of the group).

All these imitative behaviors then would become part of the individual's repertoire of moral and immoral behaviors. Later in development, during adolescence, the overt imitative behaviors of the young adult can occur in the absence of the original model(s) and maintained by consequences mediated by the behaviors of diverse others (e.g., peers) conforming to group norms and societal standards.

Empathy

"Ethologists see empathy as a primitive experience of affective sharing that has its early origins in the playful exchanges shared by mother and offspring" (Peláez, 2001b, pp. 12–13). Cognitivists see empathy as they do social referencing, being able to feel and interpret another person's expressions. Feelings of empathy originate very early in development, usually after social referencing has been acquired. The development of empathy is seen as multifaceted and relates to referencing and interpreting the emotional signals of others. It develops through very early learning experiences and emotional cues. Empathic behavior is important because it contains various motivational functions for human moral behavior.

● THE DEVELOPMENT OF MORALITY

In this section, we will contrast two main approaches to moral behavior: the behavior–analytic (Peláez, 2001b; Peláez-Nogueras & Gewirtz, 1992, 1995) and the cognitive–developmental (Kohlberg, 1969, 1976).

The Behavior–Analytic Approach to Morality

From a learning perspective, prosocial behavior and moral actions and judgments are viewed as under the influence of beneficial or detrimental consequences experienced or predicted by the individual (Peláez-Nogueras & Gewirtz, 1995). In our view, judgments and actions termed moral are not taken to involve romantic expressions of moral goodness or principled thinking but rather to involve an increasingly sophisticated sense of how to further one's long-term interests based on the predicted consequences of one's action. The child's moral development is based on an extensive repertoire of acquired moral rules. Thus, from a behavior–analytic approach, morality is conceived to be a system of rule-governed behavior, with the developmental question being how rules come to acquire discriminative control over the individuals' moral behavioral patterns.

Contextualism and Morality

The behavior–analytic approach to moral development is not mechanistic in the conventional sense but, rather, is *contextualistic* (see Chapter 2). One problem with mechanistic models is that they view the individual as passive and inherently at rest (Peláez, 1994; Peláez-Nogueras, 1992b). The external forces applied to the organism are seen as the only causes for behavior. Behavior analysis of development, however, does *not* see the child as a passive organism who does *not* contribute to his or her own development, or as molded by the environment without assuming any particular direction to development.

Instead, a behavioral systems view of development focuses on *sequential* and *reciprocal* influence in interaction between the individual's behavior and environmental stimuli (Morris, 1992, 1993b). Thus, *both* the organism and the environment are *active* and make up an inseparable interdependent unit (Bijou, 1979; Gewirtz & Peláez-Nogueras, 1991b, 1992a; Morris, 1988; Novak, 1998).

The historical context, or history of interactions, is crucial in analyzing moral development. This means that an individual's social-contingency history would be the major determinant or predictor of his or her subsequent moral behavior. The unique history of contingencies for each person results in individual differences in moral (and immoral) behavior patterns and in the development of the rules governing moral behavior. However, cultural and social rules and contingencies contribute to commonalities in moral behavior and reasoning. For example, the Judeo-Christian commandment "Thou shall not kill" states a common rule with a common implicit contingency (i.e., or you will go to hell).

The Cognitive–Developmental Approach to Morality

From a cognitive-developmental approach, Kohlberg (1969) proposed that the child's rule-governed behavior, and the pattern, quality, and extensiveness of his or her moral repertoire, depends on the child's being more or less "mature" or being at a higher or lower "stage" of moral development

Kohlberg (1969) conducted a longitudinal study with males ages 10 to 36 over a 20-year period to formulate his theory of moral stages. His theory, however, has been challenged by Carol Gilligan (1977, 1982), who has argued that Kohlberg's results were biased because his longitudinal sample included only males. Gilligan's view is that females develop a different orientation and special sensitivity with respect to moral dilemmas. Even so, Kohlberg's levels and stages for moral reasoning are very popular in mainstream psychology. His research consisted of interviewing children and adults using hypothetical moral dilemmas. The moral dilemmas consisted of "stories in which a character must make a crucial decision in a situation in which there is no clear right or wrong" (Haviland & Scarborough, 1981, p. 245). The participants' answers to the dilemmas were scored according to the level of complexity of moral reasoning they displayed—Level I: preconventional morality; Level II: conventional morality; and Level III: postconventional morality.

Level I: Preconventional Morality

In the first two stages of Kohlberg's theory, the child's moral reasoning and judgments are based exclusively on the tangible punitive consequences (Stage 1) or rewarding pleasurable consequences (the hedonistic Stage 2) of an act for the actor rather than on the relationship of that act to society's or culture's rules. Therefore, the child obeys orders and rules to avoid punishment or get rewards, and the greater harm done is what is considered "bad" without taking into account the intentions of the actor.

Level II: Conventional Morality

The third and fourth stages of moral reasoning and judgments are based on the child's desire to gain approval (the "good boy/girl orientation" Stage 3) or to support and follow laws and social rules that maintain the social order (e.g., the rules of legal authority). The reason for following the rules at this stage, according to Kohlberg, is not fear of punishment but the belief that conventional rules and laws help maintain a social order (Stage 4) that is worth keeping to benefit society and its members. The individual at Stage 4 typically thinks that he or she has to follow the rules regardless of feelings or special circumstances. This individual is very focused on those conventional rules and rarely breaks them or makes exceptions.

Level III: Postconventional Morality

The fifth and sixth stages of moral reasoning are based on *social contracts* and the idea of *democracy* (Stage 5). In the last and more advanced or "highest" moral stage, judgments are based on *universal principles* of ethics, such as justice and fairness (Stage 6). These abstract moral principles of universal justice and respect for the civil rights of all human beings must transcend any law or social order or contract that may conflict with these principles. It is the rare individual who achieves this stage and functions consistently in it.

As you can see, Kohlberg (1969) uses the concept of rules and rule-governed behavior at conventional stages for the most part. In the next section, we will contrast the meaning of rules between the behavioral and cognitive perspectives.

Similarities and Differences Between the Two Approaches

The cognitive–developmental and behavior–analytic approaches to moral development diverge on their orientations, being either *absolutistic* or *relativistic* (Kurtines & Gewirtz, 1984; Wainryb, 1993). Theories of moral development, like that of Kohlberg (1969), are absolutist, in that they stress universality of moral principles (e.g., justice) and thinking based on those principles. Morality is thought to be universal, and moral judgments are thought to be generalizable and prescriptive across social contexts and different situations. In contrast, the behavior–analytic approach can be seen as relativistic, in that it stresses the contexts and consequences of moral and immoral actions. We believe that, at *all* ages, individuals tend to change (contextualize, relativize) their moral judgments when they apply those judgments to groups and cultures with different informational beliefs and contexts (Wainryb, 1993).

From a behavior approach, prosocial behavior, moral actions, and moral judgments are viewed as behaviors under the influence of beneficial or detrimental consequences experienced or predicted by the individual. Many judgments and actions called "moral" are not romantic expressions of moral "goodness" or principled thinking, but, rather, they involve an increasingly sophisticated sense of how to further one's long-term interests based on the predicted consequences of one's actions (see also Liebert, 1984).

The cognitive–developmental and behavior–analytic perspectives also differ in how they approach and explain the "causes" (or processes) underlying action and whether or not a universal invariant progression of "stages" orders hierarchically moral development. The cognitive–developmental theories have been imprecise in accounting for the acquisition of, and changes in, the child's moral behavior patterns. They have linked implicit changes in cognitive schemes (see Chapter 7) to the child's moral behavior without really explaining how these "schemas" change behavior. On the other hand, behavioral approaches assume that the determinants of moral behavior can be isolated by an analysis of the contexts and observable contingencies that function to modify behavior. Such contexts and consequences and their interrelations provide the basis for understanding and predicting moral behavior without recourse to unobservable causes, inner activities, or complex theoretical constructs such as schemas.

Let us expand further on this important problem that the cognitivists have experienced for years. Cognitive theories rely on mentalistic constructs to explain **moral behavior** (Gewirtz & Peláez-Nogueras, 1993a). For instance, they have used mentalistic abstractions such as "expectancy" "schemas," "moral self," "stages" (Kohlberg, 1969; Kohlberg & Diessner, 1991) and "decentration" (Flavell, 1985) to explain behavior such as verbal reasoning and action. In contrast, behavioral approaches have concentrated on process variables that can be reliably observed and measured and that function as explanations. That is, we emphasize a functional relation between behaviors called "moral" and the social environment that produced the controlling contingencies.

Schlinger (1995) points out that a traditional view of morality is an essentialistic one in which some essence called morality is said to exist in each of us. Therefore, our behavior is only a reflection of this moral sense.

> The behavior analytic view, by contrast, views morality as a term that is evoked in people by a wide range of behaviors in social contexts. The behaviors reflect not some underlying or internal sense of morality but, rather, the cumulative effects of social contingencies of reinforcement and punishment. (p. 217)

For a behavior analyst, the most important question about moral behavior is not what happens or when it happens but, rather, how it happens. This means identifying the variables that determine the behavior (Schlinger, 1995). Behavior analysis attempts to clarify the meanings of some of these concepts and constructs encountered in developmental psychology, such as *cognition, learning,* and *scheme.* We attempt to clarify these terms to avoid the problem of reification discussed in Chapter 2 and to pursue a more coherent theory and practice (Schlinger, 2002).

Moral and Legal Contingencies

Immoral behavior and *illegal* behavior do not really differ fundamentally, but both usually harm society. In many cases, moral or ethical control is crucial. "Society needs to arrange for individuals to observe their own behavior and apply punishment and avoidant contingencies" (Malott, 2001, p. 1). If society cannot observe the behavior or its outcomes directly, it has no choice but to use moral control because moral development leads to control by indirect and long-delayed contingencies. Malott (2001) states that moral control is hard to maintain and often fails because of the weakness of the contingencies. The reason that legal control is more effective is because society fears the legal outcomes.

Contingency-Shaped Versus Rule-Governed Behavior

Direct **contingency-shaped behavior** is shaped directly by its consequences and may be under the control of nonverbal discriminative stimuli. Contingency-shaped behavior units ("operants") are given meaning and are strengthened by those of their *direct* consequences that function as reinforcing stimuli. On the other hand, **rule-governed behavior,** as described by Skinner (1966, 1969), is discriminative responding shaped by reinforcement of rule following. Although the two types of behaviors are similar in form, their functional properties and controlling variables are different (see Cerutti, 1989).

Once the child has acquired language, another way that he or she may learn from others is through verbal instruction or rules (always backed up, at least intermittently, by reinforcement or punishment) (Vaughan, 1989). Consider the following example: A child sees a new video game at the arcade. How does he or she learn how to play it? How does the child learn what to do to win? One approach would be to come in contact with the contingencies directly. That is, by experiencing the consequences of the behavior. The child could put money in and play. Some of his or her behavior would be reinforced, some punished, and some have no consequences. Gradually, the child would learn how to play the game through directly experiencing these consequences.

Direct contingency-shaped behavior could be a slow and expensive way to learn the contingencies of reinforcement. Alternatively, our game player could learn the contingencies from the rules about how the game works. By either reading the rules or by listening to a skilled player tell him or her the rules, the child could learn what behaviors are consequated and in what manner. Then actually playing the game and experiencing the consequences would strengthen the rule-following behavior. The child's behavior would be what Skinner (1969) called rule-governed behavior.

Rule-Governed Behavior

In Skinner's (1957) view, rules specify the contingencies of reinforcement and punishment. Furthermore, rules can usually be learned in less time than needed to derive the contingencies by direct trial-and-error experience (Skinner, 1974). Rule-governed behavior can be modified by altering its antecedents, its consequences, or both. In contrast, contingency-shaped behavior is modified only by its consequences. As the child's behavioral repertoire becomes more complex and language is acquired, the child's actions come more under the control of *verbal rules* (both formulated by others and self-formulated). The child learns to discriminate and respond differentially to *proximal* or *immediate* consequences versus *remote, indirect,* or *delayed* consequences for following or not following rules. That is, the child learns to predict the consequences of a given action—*which* consequences prevail in a particular setting and *how, when,* and *by whom* these consequences would be applied (Peláez-Nogueras & Gewirtz, 1995).

As for many other learning processes discussed in this textbook, rules are acquired first through basic imitation processes and later through generalized imitation of role models. Once the child learns the various rules, **rule generalization** may occur. Rule generalization is a process for acquiring new rules, as is transference of rules across various setting, individuals, and circumstances.

Taxonomies of Rules

In this section, we discuss two different taxonomies and dimensions of rules and rule-governed behavior that have been identified in the behavioral literature.

Zettle and Hayes Classification: Tracking and Pliance. Zettle and Hayes (1982) identified two styles of responding based on the relationship between rules and contingencies. The first is called **tracking**. People who track are sensitive to the natural environmental contingencies in effect. Rule following puts them on the right track, and then they track the actual contingencies in effect. For example, a tracker may take the rule "Walk—you'll get there just as soon" and follow it until she finds that she is usually late. At that point, her sensitivity to the contingency (e.g., losing out on some fun) will enable her to try the other behavior and to track whether it is better at producing reinforcing consequences.

In contrast to this is **pliance** (from the word *compliance*). Plyers learn to comply with the behavior specified by the rules, even if the rules do not accurately specify the contingencies in effect or those that are truly controlling the behavior. For example, given the same rule ("Walk—you'll get there just as fast), a plyer will continue to follow the rule, insensitive to the actual contingencies. Thus, tracking and pliance may be two different response styles characteristic of individuals. They are likely to develop under different conditions. One of these is the style of parental discipline used by parents, discussed in Chapter 12.

Taxonomy of Rules. The taxonomy proposed by Peláez and Moreno (1998, 1999, 2002) takes into account dimensions of an entire contingency arrangement specified in the rule and how these dimensions relate to rule-following behavior and child development. This taxonomy is based on four dimensions:

1. Explicitness: explicit versus implicit rule

2. Accuracy: accurate versus false or remote (cannot be confirmed)

3. Complexity: low versus high level of complexity

4. Source of the rule: provided by others versus self-derived
   - *Explicit* rules verbally describe the entire three-term contingency arrangement. They state that in the presence of a specified discriminative stimulus, the occurrence of a particular behavior will be followed by a specific consequence.
   - *Implicit* rules are incomplete in that neither the discriminative stimuli, the context, nor the consequence for the moral behavior in question are explicitly specified in the rule; they are only implied.
   - *Accurate* rules describe contingencies that, when followed, match or correspond to certain event–consequence relationships in the environment.
   - *Inaccurate (false or incongruent)* rules describe contingencies that do not correspond to those encountered in the environment or describe remote contingencies that cannot be falsified or verified, such as burning in hell.
   - *High complexity* refers to a complex relational network that specifies more than one contingency.
   - *Low complexity* describes no contingency, no conditions under which there are exceptions.
   - *Rules provided by others* means the speaker (other than the listener) specifies, implicitly or explicitly, the criterion for the listener's behavior.
   - *Self-provided rules* mean that the speaker and the listener is the same individual. Self-provided rules can be taught by others, self-generated, or derived or abstracted by the subject from learning experiences.

The four dimensions yield 16 possible types of rules ($4 \times 4 = 16$). For example, the rule "I shouldn't take the candy before dinner because mom will be angry," is an example of an *explicit, accurate, low-complexity, self-provided* rule. The probability that the child (the listener) will behave according to a rule would depend on these dimensions. For example, a rule given to a child could be explicit, accurate, and simple. At another time the rule provided by the parent could be implicit, inaccurate (or false), and complex. The latter type of rule requires a more advanced language repertoire for following or not following such rule.

For example, a younger child would first learn to follow explicit rules and later in development he or she would learn implicit rules (the implicit rules are those that do not verbally specify in the instruction the three-term contingency elements). An implicit rule is, for example, when the mom says, "Don't do it" and the child knows what behavior she is referring to and refrains from engaging in such behavior. The source of the rule is also another important dimension. Younger children learn to follow rules provided by others before they begin to generate or derive rules by themselves, their own rules, which are known as self-provided rules.

The accuracy and the complexity of a rule are two other extremely important dimensions. That is, the contingencies specified verbally in the rule should be accurate and match those that occur in the environment for the child to obey the rules. For example, a false rule would be a mother saying to her child too many times: "Don't run or you will fall! Don't run or you'll fall . . ." but in actuality, the child seldom falls or hurts himself or herself. Just as in pliance, the behavior is controlled not by the instruction but by the person providing the rule. When there are no consequences for not following the rule, the child learns to omit or discard the rule. If the rule is too complex (specifies too many contingency arrangements), younger children would have more difficulty following it compared with older children who have more advanced language (verbal) repertoires.

Rule following depends on the context in which the rule is provided, the child's developmental level, and the child's learning history with that or other similar rules. An experiment was conducted with 80 children in Mexico to test this taxonomy and its dimensions (Herrera, Peláez, Reyes, Figueroa, & Salas, 2001). The study was to determine whether the levels of psychological development and language comprehension were relevant to accuracy in rule following. To evaluate this assumption, the researchers created the Instrument of Rule Following (IRF-4D), a battery that comprises 16 types of rules based on the four rule dimensions described above. The battery was administered to children 4, 6, 8, and 10 years of age who were assigned to one of two groups: low and average level of language comprehension. The findings were consistent with the theoretical formulations of Peláez and Moreno (1998) on the different types of rules. The authors found a developmental progression of rule-following behavior along the four dimensions of the proposed taxonomy.

The fanatical behavior that we have seen in the early 2000s during terrorists and war times involves the following of moral rules. Let's examine this rule and the dimensions that describe the rewards that the Shahid, or martyr, would earn according to Islamic Tradition:

From the moment his first drop of blood spills, he feels no pain. And he is absolved of all his sins; he sees his seat in heaven; he is spared the tortures of the grave; he is spared the horrors of the Day of Judgment; he is married to a "black-eyed" [woman]; he can vouch for 70 of his family members to enter Paradise; he earns the crown of glory whose precious stone is worth all of this world.

Al-Hotari, who committed a suicide bombing in Tel-Aviv, left a will that expresses faith in the divine reward that awaits him:

There is nothing greater than being martyred for the sake of Allah, on the land of Palestine. Cry in joy, my mother, hand out candy, my father and brothers, for your son awaits a wedding with the black-eyed in heaven.

These two examples illustrate a rule that is explicit (specifies the martyred behavior), false (in the sense that cannot be confirmed by the listener—in this case, Al-Hotari), complex (because it specifies more than one outcome or relation—candy, wedding, heaven), and is provided by others (the Islamic culture or religion) (Peláez, 2001a).

Rule Compliance and Self-Instruction

In another analysis of rule following presented by Riegler and Baer (1989), the development of rule-governed behavior relies on five steps. These five steps need not occur in order but may, to some degree, happen simultaneously:

1. Early in the child's life, parents provide stimuli for **compliance**. These take the forms of requests, commands, rules, and the like. At first, children follow specific requests, demands, or rules given by the parent. The parent is likely to reinforce compliance of these specific rules or instructions.

2. These requests, demands, and other rules function as instructions. Because instructions specify what response will produce a reinforcing (positive or negative) consequence, they become discriminative stimuli. The result is that a child may engage in **generalized compliance**. That is, the child will follow nearly all instructions because of his or her history of reinforcement with responding to other members of this instructional stimulus class. This is maintained as long as there is a correspondence between the rules, behavior, and consequences in most cases.

3. Compliance generalizes to other aspects of the child's environment. Now the rules of grandparents, teachers, and others are followed in the same

manner as the parents' rules. The child can learn to discriminate those whose rules lead to reinforcement and those whose rules do not. Thus, the child may learn to not follow the rules of a culture (e.g., "Thou shall not steal."—but crime pays) or for drug use where adults say, "Just say no," while peers say it is fun.

4. The child generates his or her own rules and instructions from imitating the rule-giving behavior of adults. Adults may prompt the development of this **self-instruction** by asking the child, "What are you going to do?" and by reinforcing the child's overt self-instructions. Eventually, children are prompted and reinforced for making their instructional self-talk private rather than public.

5. The use of self-instructions generalizes so that the instructions can be used in novel situations. For example, the child can say to himself, "No, I shouldn't cheat on this test," without ever hearing another person saying that. Generalized self-instruction becomes the basis for a highly compliant child.

Moral Behavior as the Subject of Research

We believe that it is difficult to argue about moral development in infants, because moral development does not occur until the child can speak and reason with other human beings about abstract moral concepts and principles. Behavior analysis is concerned with lawful relations among *observable* events— we study the behavior of individuals in interaction with environment. The analysis can be extended to social interactions and also to private events, such as problem solving and thinking, but *only* after overt behaviors—reflecting those private events—are analyzed and understood (Schlinger, 1992). The advantage of behavior analysis is that, by emphasizing *external* variables and *observable* moral actions, the analysis moves away from those "inner" events that are inaccessible to the investigator (Gewirtz & Peláez-Nogueras, 1992a). Emphasis on these unobservables only complicates analyses of the actual processes and the contextual factors responsible for the child's moral behavior.

● SUMMARY

Social transactions can be conceptualized in terms of a four-term contingency. In this context, the behaviors of individuals serve as discriminative or reinforcing stimuli (or both) for each other, in a reciprocal manner. Such dynamical interactions affect the development of both parties in a social transaction. Understanding this process is necessary to understanding the development of *prosocial transactions*.

The newborn possesses a limited repertoire of behaviors that enable him or her to transact with others. Some of the child's physical characteristics and reflexive behaviors evoke caretaking behavior in others. These likely develop by means of natural selection because of their adaptive value. Although universal social reflexes (phylogenic in nature) are important in terms of survival of the species, social behavior tends to be more variable and relevant to the development of behavior over the life span (ontogenic in nature). Reflexive behaviors may develop into operant behaviors through reinforcement.

Social behaviors produce *social reinforcers,* which constitute a class of *secondary reinforcers.* Affection is likely to be a response that follows the performance of desirable behaviors and is an effective way to shape such behaviors. It follows that caretakers and their attentive behavior can become positive reinforcers. Attention-producing and jealous behaviors, however, can become problematic, particularly if undesirable behaviors are inadvertently reinforced. Such behavior can be extinguished through deprivation, differential reinforcement of other behavior, punishment by hurt, or punishment by loss. Some of these procedures, however, have drawbacks.

We learn through others in a number of ways. *Observational learning* refers to the change in behavior brought about by observing the behavior of others. Albert Bandura suggests that both behavior and emotional responses can be conditioned vicariously. Although Bandura asserted that new principles are needed to account for **vicarious learning,** others have posited that existing principles of operant learning are sufficient (particularly *generalized imitation*). Another example is verbal instruction. The learning of rules that specify the contingencies of reinforcement and punishment in effect is more efficient than the shaping of behavior through contingencies. Behavior is also taught through intuitive parenting, meaning that in interactions with their children, many parents unknowingly incorporate conditions that promote the development of learning.

Attachment is characterized by dynamical patterns of behavior focused on an attachment object (e.g., a caretaker). Both phylogenic and ontogenic factors are thought to be involved in the development of attachment, a view consistent with a dynamical systems approach. *Separation protests* with regard to attachment figures may develop as learned behavior during parent–child interactions in which the object constitutes a reinforcer. It has been suggested that fear of strangers can be the product of either a child's attempts to avoid disruption of reinforcement (i.e., interaction with the attachment object) or the association of strangers with aversive stimuli. During *social referencing,* a caretaker's facial expression constitutes a setting event establishing a stranger's function as a discriminative stimulus for either positive or negative reinforcement. *Empathy* is another prosocial behavior developed with the assistance of others through learning experiences and emotional cues. Its development is important with respect to its implications for human motivation and behavior. Similarly, *moral behavior* reflects the cumulative effects of social contingencies.

Social cognition has been defined as "the development of social knowledge and reasoning" and may be analyzed in the same way as other cognitive behavior—in terms of a four-term contingency where some or all components may be of a social nature.

● **NOTE**

1. A study conducted by Warner-Rogers, Taylor, and Taylor (2000) found that children exhibiting inattentive behaviors demonstrated greater adjustment problems in their classrooms. They were children who demonstrated low self-esteem in school and a greater need to have instructions repeated. When compared with the control group, those children classified as part of the *inattentive* group exhibited lower intellectual functioning and reading attainment. In summary, although there are effective methods for dealing with inappropriate and disruptive mands for attention, it is much preferred to promote more desirable ways to signal attention.

CHAPTER **11**

DEVELOPMENT OF ANTISOCIAL BEHAVIORS

O ne of the most important problems facing society is antisocial behavior, or aggression. Crime is one of the top issues in public opinion polls. By the middle of 2002, over 2 million people were imprisoned in the United States, or about 1 inmate for every 142 people (Harrison & Karberg, 2003). Violence intrudes into more lives each year. We all experience the effects vicariously from virtually every local news broadcast or newspaper front page. Increasingly, antisocial behavior is becoming more violent. All told, there were more than 12,943 murders in the United States in 2000, of which 8,493 were the result of the use of firearms.

Violent crimes against and by children have become a national concern. The violence of the 1999 Columbine High School shootings, in which two high school students took out their grievances on fellow students and teachers by using automatic weapons, seemed to focus attention on the problems of gun violence. Although they garner the most media attention, shootings in schools make up only 1% of the gun incidents committed by children and youth. Firearm injuries are not among the most frequent reasons for hospital emergency room visits for youth, but the high fatality rate from these injuries means that firearms are among the leading causes of death among youth. Every year, more than 20,000 children and youths are wounded or killed by firearms (Fingerhut & Christoffel, 2002), making firearms, by far, the second leading cause of death (after automobile accidents) in the 10- to 19-year-old age group (MacKay, Fingerhut, & Duran, 2000).

Of course, guns are not the only weapons of violence used by children and youth. In a well-publicized case, two Florida brothers, ages 13 and 16, admitted to beating their father to death with a baseball bat. But guns are the most lethal weapon in violent crimes because they are much more likely to result in death. For example, in robberies, guns are 3 times more likely to kill than are knives and 30 times more likely to result in death than other weapons (Cook & Ludwig,

2000). Of those under the age of 20 who go to an emergency room to be treated for an injury, only 1 of 760 die. For those being treated for a gunshot injury, the number of deaths is 1 for every 4.4 treated (Fingerhut & Christoffel, 2002).

Another problem in the United States with guns is that besides being highly lethal weapons, they are available to children and youth. An estimated 34% of children in the United States live in homes in which there are firearms (Schuster, Franke, & Bastian, 2000). Of male high school sophomores and juniors in a national study, 50% reported that it would be "little" or "no problem" to get a gun (Sheley & Wright, 1998). Moreover, another survey conducted in 1999 estimated that 833,000 American youths between the ages of 12 and 17 had carried a gun at least once during the preceding year (Substance Abuse and Mental Health Services Administration, 2002). In 2000, more than 20,000 children and youth under 18 years of age were arrested on charges of weapons carrying or possession, even though this reflected a 26% decline from 10 years earlier (Pastore & Maguire, 2001). The United States has the highest per capita rate of deaths due to firearm use. In addition, as Figure 11.1 shows, firearm death rates from homicide and suicides have a developmental trajectory that peaks in adolescence and early adulthood.

Homicides and violent crimes are the most dramatic cases, but the development of antisocial behavior begins early and its effects extend well through adulthood. More children are referred for psychological treatment for behavior disorders than any other condition. People fail to hold jobs, cannot maintain marriages, and run into trouble with the law because of their antisocial behaviors. This chapter looks at antisocial interactions as a developmental process.

WHAT ARE ANTISOCIAL INTERACTIONS? ●

Most people equate antisocial behavior with aggression. However, the term aggression is a social, not a psychological, term. Two characteristics are normally present when society deems an act aggressive. First, the behavior must be at a high intensity or rate. Hitting, biting, kicking, and hair pulling are high-magnitude behaviors in children. Verbal aggression and "passive" aggression (refusing to comply) are also intense behaviors, although the dimensions of such intensity are difficult to quantify.

Second, society requires that for an act to be aggressive, it must be intentional. Accidents are not considered aggressive. We infer intentionality from the aggressor's behavior, including facial expression and verbalizations. Our jury system acknowledges the importance of intention in sentencing a person for killing another: Manslaughter is the verdict if the act was an accident; murder if

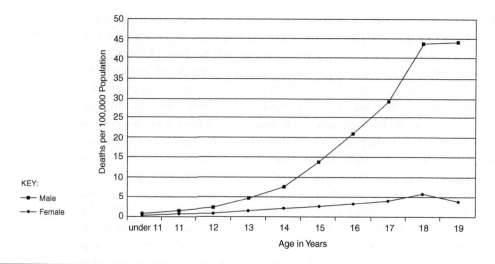

Figure 11.1   Firearm Death Rates by Age and Sex, 1997–1998

SOURCE: National Center for Health Statistics (2000).

the act was intentional (e.g., a first-degree conviction is found for premeditated acts of murder).

Psychologists have difficulty objectively studying intentionality because it must be inferred rather than directly observed. However, its presence seems crucial in a socially valid definition of aggression. According to the traditional mentalistic account, an intentional act is one preceded and caused by a specific mental act. For example, the thought about shooting an adversary causes the person with a gun to pull the trigger.

Although intention, per se, is not a behavior–analytic term, we speak of intentionality when we are concerned with behavior that is to be understood in terms of its consequences. Specifications of intentions include identifying what is intended; that, of course, is the assumed consequence of the behavior (Hineline, in press). Consider a situation in which Johnny bites his younger brother Bill and Bill then gives up his candy to Johnny. However, this is not a complete behavioral account. Johnny is also likely to have been punished in the past for biting his brother. For example, his parents might have grounded him for a night, resulting in his aggressive behavior decreasing dramatically for some time. In short, aggressive behaviors have participated in conflicting contingencies of reinforcement and punishment. How, then, does the behaviorist explain why at one moment Johnny intentionally aggresses and at another moment intentionally behaves nonaggressively?

Many explanations are possible. Johnny, although effectively punished in the past, may again aggress against his brother when the punishing agents (his parents) are out of the room. Or he may aggress when his parents are in the room because the reinforcing consequences (his brother has Johnny's favorite candy) outweigh the punishing consequences (being grounded for the night).

Let us consider how transactional development affects intentional acts of aggression. Active genotype–environment interactions may mean that Johnny may seek environments that reinforce aggressive behaviors. That is, Johnny may select situations in which his active behavior is reinforced by "weenie" children who cry, whimper, give him their candy, and then rat on him to his teacher. Although this may be facilitated by the genetic contributions to his large bodily build, as his genotype reciprocally interacts with his selected environment, these characteristics shift from being genotype–environment to person–environment interactions (see Chapter 9).

These characteristics have in fact been shown to be important in the development of childhood physical aggression involving peers. Recent research highlights the genotype–environment effect in that children identified as bullies are most often bigger than their classmates and receive social rewards (higher social status) for being a bully (Hawkins et al., 1998). In addition, investigators have found that victims of bullying also have common genotypic characteristics. Victims are usually weaker and younger than their aggressors (Hoover & Hazler, 1991). Recently, victims have been identified as playing an important role in peer aggression by evoking aggressive displays from their peers. It has been suggested that the reinforcement obtained in this process involves social recognition (Olweus, 1993; Slee, 1993). For some children, it appears that being a part of the group, if only to be victimized, holds more reinforcement value than being ignored by the peer group.

Box 11.1   What About the Mean Bully?

Bullying is an increasingly significant problem for children, their parents, and their teachers. Bullying is a pattern of antisocial behavior generally focused on younger, smaller, weaker, and isolated children. The bully's pattern of behavior is frequently stable over time. It functions in much the same way throughout the school years as Patterson, Littman, and Bricker (1967) describe in their classic study of the origins of bullying behavior in preschool. Here are some things that parents, teachers, and victims should know about bullying and how to deal with it.

What Is a Bully?

Someone who pushes others around
Someone who spreads
rumors about others

Someone who breaks the rules
Someone who starts fights
Someone who teases others

Where Does Bullying Happen?

In the classroom
In the cafeteria
At the park

On the playground
Walking home from school
On the bus

What Can You Do If You See Someone Being Bullied?

Let a teacher know
Let the principal know

Let a counselor know
Let an adult know

What Can You Do If You Are Being Bullied?

Yell for help
Stay in a group
Let your counselor know
Tell your parents
Find a new way home

Walk away **(DON'T FIGHT!)**
Let your teacher know
Tell your friends
Tell your older brother or sister

What Happens to Bullies?

They get in trouble
with the teacher
They get in trouble at home

They don't have many friends
They do poorly in school
They feel bad about themselves

How Does It Feel to Be Bullied?

You feel helpless
You feel disliked
You feel hurt
You feel angry
You feel nervous

Your self-esteem is lowered
You feel picked on
You feel sad
You feel weak
You feel scared

THE ORIGINS OF AGGRESSION ●

The Ethological Perspective

Ethologists view aggression as behaviors that evolved in species because of natural selection. In this view, aggression has adaptive significance for maintaining the species. Moyer (1967) identified seven types of aggression observed in the animal kingdom. He suggested that humans exhibit many of these behaviors as well. As you read about these types of aggression, see if you can apply them to human behavior too.

1. *Predatory:* Animals attack others that they will eat.

2. *Intermale, spontaneous:* Two male animals will fight to establish dominance. There is often a threat display preceding the aggression.

3. *Terror induced:* Animals that are cornered and under intense arousal will respond with violence.

4. *Irritable:* Animals respond with aggressive acts to eliminate an irritating stimulus.

5. *Territorial defense:* Some animals mark their turf and respond with aggression when their turf is invaded.

6. *Defense of the young:* (Mostly female) animals respond violently when their offspring are threatened.

7. *Instrumental:* Animals aggress to get something from their environment.

You can readily identify equivalent situations that elicit emotional arousal and evoke aggressive behavior in humans. These situations include teenage gangs marking their turf with graffiti and defending it with aggression, mothers defending their children at all costs, and armed robbers stealing money. Although Moyer's (1967) view is that these behaviors are unlearned instincts, it is likely that human behavior develops under the complex processes described in this book and that each class of behaviors is functionally distinct from the others because of the different classes of positive and negative reinforcers involved. For example, eating prey is distinct from keeping intruders off one's turf.

The Control of Aggression

An eminent ethologist, Konrad Lorenz (1966), argued that in addition to aggressive instincts, animals have also evolved unlearned mechanisms to inhibit aggression within their own species. Lorenz maintained that intermale, spontaneous aggression would have evolved through natural selection for survival of the fittest and, therefore, improvement of the species. However, taken to the extreme, uncontrolled intraspecies' aggression would result in elimination of much of the population, thus threatening the species. Natural inhibitors of aggression would have, then, adaptive significance for a species.

Lorenz suggested that there exist in species innate releasing mechanisms (or unconditioned stimuli) that elicit aggression inhibition. For example, timber wolves are very aggressive defenders of their turf against other timber wolves. Their fights are vicious and bloody, but not always lethal. There comes a point in the fight when the clear victor is atop his victim. Just as he is about to use his fangs to slash open the throat of his beaten foe, a strange thing happens. The victim, rather than protecting his vulnerable jugular, instead bears it to the top dog. A second strange thing then happens: Rather than slashing this exposed throat, the victor lets his victim go, perhaps to heal. Why should such strange behavior occur?

Lorenz argues that the unique white patch on the throat of the wolf serves as the innate elicitor of an aggression inhibition response. Do other animals, including humans, respond to unlearned aggression response stimuli? Has the technology of modern warfare removed us from the proximity of human cues—such as cries, screams, and facial grimaces—necessary to inhibit aggression?

● A BEHAVIORAL SYSTEMS APPROACH

Now consider a behavioral systems approach to aggression and other forms of antisocial behavior. In this approach, aggressive transactions develop because of reciprocal interactions between the person and the environment. Thus, developmental outcomes of aggressive behavior are a function of organismic and environmental transactions. First among the organismic factors, we consider the phylogenic ones: genetic makeup.

The Role of Genetic Makeup

Some biological theories of aggression suggest direct genetic causation. One such theory focused on men who had an extra Y chromosome, making them XYY. Some highly publicized murders were reportedly committed by men with the XYY genotype, and some studies reported that XYY men were more likely than XY men to engage in aggressive behavior and were overrepresented in the prison population (Jarvik, Klodin, & Matsuyama, 1973). These "supermen" were also described as being physically large and active. Subsequent research has brought into question the strength of the relationship between XYY chromosomes and aggression. Because of the small number of XYY men available for study (according to Jarvik et al., 1973, it is present in fewer than 1 or 2 people per 1,000), the studies are inconclusive (Goetz, Johnstone, & Ratcliffe, 1999). However, most individuals who are incarcerated for aggressive crimes have no known genetic or chromosomal cause, and although there may be a disproportionately larger number of XYY men in the prison population (Jarvik et al., 1973; Shah & Borgaonkar, 1974), the crimes they commit are more often against property and do not reflect an increase in aggressive crimes or aggressive behavior (Witkin et al., 1976). Furthermore, recent research suggests that the reported overrepresentation of XYY men in institutions is the result of sampling bias and other nongenetic factors, including legal and environmental ones (Ike, 2000).

Yet genetic makeup could contribute to the development of aggressive behavior, perhaps indirectly. Other factors, including mental retardation (Goetz et al., 1999) and larger physical size have been thought to be factors in the larger institutionalization rate of XYY men (Witkin et al., 1976). As Shah and Borgaonkar (1974) suggested, "An either/or approach, which appears to address the question in terms of nature *versus* nurture, does gross injustice to the complex and continuous interactions which take place between the genotype and its environment in determining the phenotype"(p. 357).

Again we return to the idea of **genotype–environment interactions**. Some children may inherit characteristics, including physical ones (e.g., size, muscles), that make them react to a physically stimulating environment. Eysenck (1964a) reported that individuals we now call sociopaths inherit a characteristic (i.e., psychoticism—see Chapter 9) that produces unresponsiveness to pain. This is based on research that suggests that compared with normal individuals, sociopaths do not learn paired associates when shock is used as a negative reinforcer. A genetic lack of responsiveness to pain is a passive genotype–environment interaction because individuals with this genotype do not react to aversive stimuli in their environments.

Inherited physical and behavioral characteristics also serve *evocative roles*. A big, robust, strong infant evokes (and reinforces) rough-and-tumble play behavior from the parents. These same characteristics likely reinforce more aggressive behavior. Children with certain genotypes actively seek environments that evoke and reinforce aggressive behavior. Thus, active genotype–environment interactions may also play a role in the development of aggressive behavior.

However, the role of genotype in aggression, as with other human behaviors, is not simple. Lore and Schultz (1993) have argued that although aggression occurs in most species, so too does control of aggression. Furthermore, they make a point for cultural determination for the control (or lack of control) of aggression. They point out, for example, that the risk of being murdered in the United States is 7 to 10 times greater than it is in most European countries. Among the crucial determining processes of the culture is the way parents control early aggressive behavior, which builds up a history of interactions between the child and the social environment.

The Role of Interactional History

Recall that in Horowitz's (1987) model (see Chapter 2), once the child has learned something as a function of environmental interactions, that which is learned becomes part of the organismic dimension. That is, our history of interactions becomes part of us. Early interactional histories then form the basis for later transactions. Thus, development involves ever-changing, dynamical interactions of the person and the environment. This is certainly true of the development of aggression.

Patterson et al. (1967) described the development of aggression in the preschool environment. They found that the typical preschool provides many opportunities for the development of aggression. Children who interacted with their peers at a high frequency and magnitude were most likely to be reinforced for aggressive behavior. Children's aggressive behavior toward other children was likely to be reinforced by victims who cried, gave up their toys, or were passive. If a child aggressed against another and the victim successfully counter-aggressed (i.e., retaliated or told the teacher), the aggressor changed victims. Rather than reinforcing the aggressor's behavior, this punished the behavior, so the aggressor switched victims. The aggressors tried another victim because they had learned that in the past, other victims had reinforced the aggression.

Not only are those who initially aggress against others more likely to aggress again because of reinforcement, but the victims who successfully engage in counter-aggression are also more likely to aggress in the future. The pattern that Patterson et al. found was (a) unassertive children were frequently the focus of aggression; (b) when a child successfully counteraggressed and terminated the aggressive behavior, the counteraggressive behavior was strengthened through negative reinforcement (i.e., it terminated the behavior of the aggressor); (c) the result of this dynamic transaction was that the formerly unassertive victim not only counteraggressed when attacked but also learned to initiate attacks on others.

The Role of Current Physiological Conditions

Physiological arousal is a powerful contributor to aggression. Emotional arousal is elicited by unconditioned stimuli, such as pain. Emotional arousal may also be elicited by conditioned stimuli. For example, someone may call the child a negative name (e.g., "You're a real jerk"), which serves as a conditioned stimulus for arousal. "Road rage" is another example. The arousal response includes increased heart rate, muscle tension, pupil dilation, a flushed feeling in the face, and internal changes, such as a release of adrenaline. This complex system of unconditioned or conditioned responses is called the **activation syndrome**. Some have termed this the **fight-or-flight reaction** because the bodily reactions facilitate vigorous action. Which operant behaviors are established by the emotional arousal depends on the situation. For example, the terror-induced aggression of a cornered animal (human or nonhuman) produces fight when the flight option is impossible.

A history in which aggression has been reinforced, as well as current environmental conditions, helps determine which behaviors are fueled by the "hot-blooded" arousal. Azrin, Hutchinson, and Hake (1966) found that aggression (in the form of severe biting) was the common response to an unconditioned electric shock. We shall see that physiological arousal plays a key role in escalating coercive family interactions and in changing physical punishment into physical abuse.

Current Environmental Condition Effects

Current environmental conditions may serve as *discriminative stimuli*, *consequences*, or *setting events* for antisocial behavior. A person's behavior or possessions may function as a cue for aggressive responses in hostile and instrumental aggression. Likewise, there is ample evidence that aggression, just as with other behavior, is susceptible to reinforcement. In the case of hostile aggression, it may be reinforced by inflicting injury or pain on the target of hostility. Victims who cry easily are good targets for such reinforcement. Children who give up their possessions positively reinforce antisocial behavior. Adults and others who attend to antisocial behaviors also positively reinforce the behaviors.

Much antisocial behavior is negatively reinforced; that is, it terminates or removes aversive stimuli. For example, hitting is likely to occur if hitting another child may get that child to stop calling the hitter names. Threats are likely to be frequent if they get the other child to back off. Because aversive stimuli also produce emotional arousal, we are likely to see an interaction between respondents and operants. For instance, name-calling may elicit the respondent emotional arousal we call anger; the operant aggressive act may be reinforced by terminating the same aversive stimulus.

Finally, consider the role of setting events or establishing operations as current environmental stimuli in aggression. Mood may make some operant contingencies more or less likely to occur. That is, a child who is in a good mood may respond to the name-calling by laughing. In a foul mood, the same child may lash out.

A basic research study suggests that aggressive behavior may be elicited when reinforcement is withheld. Flory (1969) showed that a pigeon whose key-peck responses were reinforced on a fixed-interval schedule will, during the time when the reinforcer is not available, attack another pigeon if one is present. That is, aggression is likely to occur in situations in which reinforcement is temporarily unavailable. This has some implications for physical child abuse (discussed later in this chapter) where parental job loss has been associated with greater risk of abuse.

There are some common setting events for antisocial behaviors in children. Consider a visit to the supermarket as a setting event for a preschooler's tantrums. One frequent setting event for child misbehavior is the presence of an adult. Besevegis and Lore (1983) observed pairs of children playing together under two different setting events: adult present and adult absent. The frequency of fighting and disagreements was higher with the adult present than when not. The presence of the adult increases the likelihood of reinforcement with attention for aggression. In many families, one of the surest setting events for child misbehavior is the presence of the mother talking on the phone. It seems that most children become sensitive to these environmental conditions.

Next, we examine the details of the behavioral contingencies affecting child–parent interactions before taking a look at the long-term development of antisocial behavior.

● COERCIVE FAMILY PROCESS: BASIC TRAINING OF ANTISOCIAL BEHAVIOR IN THE HOME

Gerald Patterson has spent a career researching the causes and treatment of antisocial behavior. Together with his colleagues, he has amassed a body of observational data from the laboratory and homes of antisocial children and their families. Their research has shown that if antisocial behavior in childhood persists through adolescence and into adulthood, it may ultimately be identified in individuals as Antisocial Personality Disorder. The research shows that the longer patterns of coercive interactions go on, the more difficult these patterns are to break. Thus, Patterson's work suggests that the most effective place to intervene in the development of antisocial behavior is at the beginning—in the home where it starts. It starts in the home through mother–child interactions that Patterson (1980, 1982) has deemed the "coercive family process." Figure 11.2 gives the outlines of these interactions. The small section on the left of the

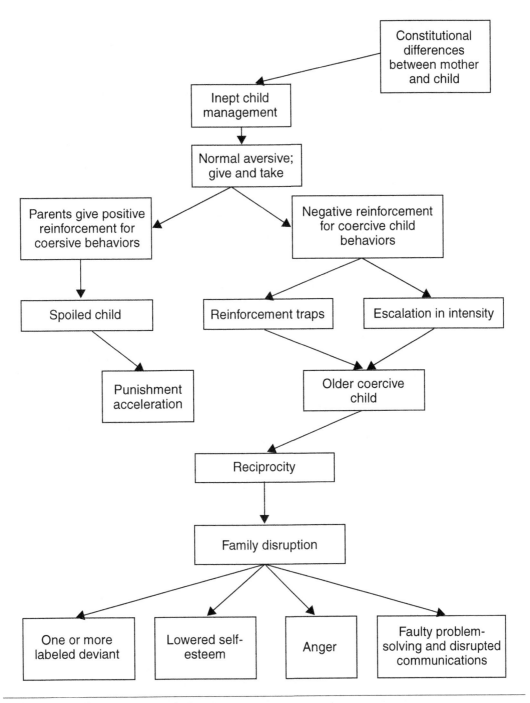

Figure 11.2 The Coercive Family Process

SOURCE: From Patterson, G.R. (1980), "Mothers: The unacknowledged victims," in *Monographs of the Society of Research in Child Development, 45*(5). Reprinted with permission of the Society of Research in Child Development.

figure diagrams the development of a "spoiled child." We focus on Patterson's path for the development of the antisocial or coercive child.

Constitutional Differences Between Children and Parents

The development of the coercive family process begins at the upper right of Figure 11.2. Genetic makeup and interactional history produce differences in temperaments and personality characteristics between children and their parents. Some mismatches may occur between the characteristics of the child and the personality of the mother. For example, a very active child may be a mismatch to a mother who is hypersensitive and finds a high activity level to be aversive. On the other hand, with a less sensitive mother, the same child's high activity level may not be problematic.

Inept Child Management

Parents of aggressive children have poor child management skills. They tend to be inconsistent, use many commands, threaten, and may use physical punishment, which is ineffective because it is delayed ("Wait till your father gets home!"). Mothers of aggressive children may even be less likely than mothers of normal children to identify obnoxious behavior as being obnoxious (Patterson, 1980). However, mothers of antisocial children are less likely to ignore minor annoyances and instead make an issue of these.

Normal Aversive Give-and-Take

Patterson (1980) has shown that even in homes where there are no antisocial children, there is a high level of aversive interactions. Minor aversives include whining, noncompliance, and verbal negatives. On average, there is a minor coercive exchange about once every 3 minutes. Major aversive exchanges may occur up to three times an hour. In families with aggressive children, the numbers increase to one minor event every three quarters of a minute. There are increases in major events as well.

In normal homes, parents mostly ignore minor aversive child behaviors. When they do act, parents in these "normal" homes are most likely to issue a "stop" command and to threaten punishment (Patterson et al., 1992). About 30% of the time, parents in these homes are likely to **natter.** This is Patterson, Reid, and Dishion's (1992) term for nagging or irritable scolding.

Parents of antisocial children are less likely to ignore minor child aversive behaviors. Instead, they are more likely to natter than are more successful parents. Although they may feel that their behavior is punishing the child, the effect of the nattering appears to reinforce it. In addition, the parents' nattering and irritability may actually serve to elicit and evoke more aversive child behaviors (Patterson et al., 1992). Antisocial children may react to the nagging and scolding with their own obnoxious behaviors.

At this point, we would like to point out that the term *punishment* has two different connotations. As we have used it throughout this textbook, punishment has the technical meaning of an operation that is defined functionally as a weakening of behavior. This is the way the term was introduced in Chapter 6 when we talked about positive punishment and negative punishment. The second meaning is a nontechnical one that is used in everyday language, where it implies retribution for a wrongdoing, irrespective of its effect on subsequent behavior. People often mistakenly believe that they are punishing a child even though what they do may actually increase or have no effect on the child's behavior. In behavior analysis, one punishes the behavior, not the child.

Negative Reinforcement for Coercive Child Behavior

Child coercive behaviors such as whining, yelling, and hitting are aversive stimuli for the parent. Parents are likely to drop their demands and terminate their own coercive behavior directed at the child. This increases the child's coercive behavior through negative reinforcement and may lead to a reinforcement trap.

Reinforcement Traps

The naturally occurring negative reinforcement of both child and parent coercive behavior constitutes a **reinforcement trap**. The participants trapped by negative reinforcement will likely engage and escalate in these behaviors toward each other in the future.

Escalation of Response Intensity

Listen to the following coercive transaction between a mother and her 6-year-old son, Attila:

Mom: "Atty, pick up your socks."

Attila: [Whining] "I'm busy."

Mom: "Atty, this is the last time I'm going to tell you: Pick them up!"

Attila: [Yelling] "NO, YOU DO IT!"

Mom: "I SAID THAT'S THE LAST TIME I'M GONNA TELL YOU—PICK THEM UP!!!"

Attila: [Screaming] "NO! PICK THEM UP YOURSELF!! "I'M NOT GOING TO!!!"

Mom: "THAT DOES IT. WAIT TILL YOUR FATHER GETS HOME."

(At this point, Mom picks up the socks.)

Notice the escalation of the coercion both in terms of threats and intensity of the voices. Patterson (1980) has observed that the child escalates his or her aversive behaviors faster and to a higher level than the mother. This increases the probability that it is the mother who will give in before the child does.

Older Coercive Child

The outcome of the preceding steps is an interactional history of coercion. When we proceed to Patterson and his colleagues' developmental model (Figure 11.3 in the section titled "The Development of Aggression"), we see the role this plays in later development.

Reciprocity

Patterson points out that the parents and children reciprocate, coercing against each other.

Family Disruption

This reciprocity of aversive attacks lead to family disruption in four ways.

1. *One or more family members are labeled as "deviant."* The child may be labeled as "aggressive," a "behavior problem," or "hyperactive." Siblings, parents, or both may be labeled as well.

2. *Lowered self-esteem.* Members of the family develop negative self-statements about themselves. Children acquire self-labels ("You're a real brat") from parents; parents may acquire labels ("You're a lousy parent,"

"You're mean") from children. Patterson (1980) reported that raising normal children produces **dysphoria** (negative mood states) in mothers. The amount of dysphoria increases in rearing aggressive children.

3. *Anger.* Anger in the above exchange should be apparent.

4. *Faulty problem solving and disrupted family communications.* Not only does anger fuel the coercive transactions, but it may have long-lasting effects that disrupt the family relationships. Family members become aversive stimuli that are to be avoided.

Modeling of Aggressive Behaviors

Aggressive models may be present in the form of an aggressive or abusive parent. Aggressive models may also be present from television, movies, and videos. Preschoolers may have aggressive playmates who serve as models as well.

Remember, it is not only the presence of models but the observed consequences of their behaviors that are important. Seeing an aggressive model leads to aggressive behavior if the child has a history of reinforced imitation of the model or observes the model's aggressive behavior being reinforced.

THE DEVELOPMENT OF AGGRESSION ●

Patterson, DeBaryshe, and Ramsey (1989) describe a sequence of steps leading to delinquency in adolescence (see Figure 11.3). Using data from a series of observational studies, Patterson and his colleagues have constructed a number of **structural equation models** that show the relationship between variables and the direction of influence over time (Patterson et al., 1992). They found that aggression, like charity, begins at home.

Phase 1. Aggression in Early Childhood: Basic Training in the Home

Patterson et al. (1989) found that aggression starts in early childhood. The sources of child conduct problems in early childhood are inept parental discipline methods and failure of parents to monitor their children. Patterson (1980, 1982) described the transactions that develop between the mother and aggressive children as a **coercive family process**. This process, which we looked at in detail above, begins with a breakdown of parental effectiveness in disciplinary conflicts.

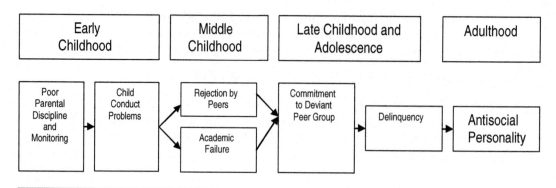

Figure 11.3   A Developmental Progression for Antisocial Behavior

SOURCE: From Patterson, G.R., DeBaryshe, B.D. & Ramsey, E. (1989), "A developmental perspective on antisocial behavior" in *American Psychologist, 44*, pp. 329-335. Copyright 1989 by the American Psychological Association. Reprinted with permission.

This breakdown allows for the development of coercive behaviors such as whining, lying, and threatening by children to get what they want from other family members (Patterson et al., 1992). These children become so aversive to the rest of the family that parental monitoring ends. The children are allowed, or even encouraged, to be out on the street unsupervised, where they will not bother the parents. They are likely to become part of a deviant peer group. Although the transactions that contribute to the development of coercive behavior happen many times each day, the family members are usually unaware of this coercive family process and accept it as the way families interact.

Phase 2. Middle Childhood: Rejection and School Failure

Returning to Figure 11.3, poor parental discipline and monitoring leads to child conduct problems (i.e., aggression, coercion, noncompliance) in early childhood. This takes us to the period of middle childhood.

Antisocial children do poorly in school (Hawkins & Lishner, 1987; Wilson & Herrnstein, 1985). Why is this? Patterson (1982) cites studies that suggest that the child's behavior problems, particularly noncompliance and undercontrolled behavior, directly interfere with learning. Furthermore, the aversive behavior of the child leads to rejection by the teacher.

Concurrent with school failure is rejection by the normal peer group. Normal peers dislike and avoid coercive children. Their behaviors are aversive to normal peers, who do not invite them to participate in their social activities.

Phase 3. Late Childhood and Adolescence: Deviant Peer Group Membership

School failure and rejection by normal peers mean that the opportunities to succeed academically and socially in school are minimal. These children become involved in a group of similarly failing and rejected peers. Membership in this deviant peer group is a nonfacilitative environment that has ominous effects on later development. Patterson et al. (1989) suggest that this deviant group serves as a source of modeling and reinforcement for the development of delinquent behaviors. Specifically, the deviant group shapes attitudes, motivation, and rationalizations for antisocial behavior. The group also provides opportunities to engage in specific antisocial behaviors. Buehler, Patterson, and Furniss (1966) showed that such peer groups positively reinforce deviant behaviors and punish conforming ones.

Dishion, Spracklen, Andrews, and Patterson (1996) videotaped the interactions of 186 13- to 14-year-old boys. The boys were placed into dyads based on whether both had been arrested (deviant), neither had been arrested (normal), or mixed deviant and normal. The topics they talked about were categorized as either rule breaking or normative and the listener's reactions as either a laugh or a pause. They found that the behavior of the youths followed the matching law (see Chapter 9), with the deviant boys matching the rate of rule-breaking talk to the amount of contingent positive feedback their behavior received. In the mixed and normal dyads, the normative talk matched the amount of laughing. The reinforcement of this talk in the dyads was observed to have an effect even 2 years later in the boys' self-reports of delinquency. Dishion and his colleagues concluded that this naturally occurring reinforced rule-breaking talk trains the delinquent in rule-breaking talk and plays a significant role in developing a common ground for committing to a deviant peer group.

Phase 4. The Adult Antisocial Personality

The outcomes of this deviant developmental path is a legacy of school dropout, substance abuse, employment problems, marital problems, multiple offenses, incarceration, and institutionalization (Caspi, Elder, & Bem, 1987; Huesmann, Eron, Lefkowitz, & Walder, 1984; Patterson et al., 1989; Robins & Ratcliff, 1979).

There is a great deal of evidence that the behaviors first learned in early childhood in the home continue through adulthood (see Huesmann et al., 1984). The coercive characteristics that have developed through adolescence mean that it is highly likely that the antisocial adolescent will continue to select and evoke environmental interactions that maintain antisocial behavior as an adult.

Patterson and his colleagues (Patterson et al., 1992) paint a picture of these antisocial adults as being society's "losers" maintaining a marginal existence. They have trouble holding jobs and are *downwardly* mobile. Not surprisingly, antisocial adults have unhappy marriages and higher divorce rates (Caspi et al., 1987). They are also more likely to have drinking and drug problems. Finally, they are more likely to run afoul of the law (Robins & Ratcliff, 1979).

The antisocial transactions between parents and children are the basis for lifelong dynamic transactions involving antisocial behavior in nonfacilitative environments. Patterson et al. (1992) summarize the legacy of the antisocial child: "Antisocial people tend to be lonely and loved by few" (p. 14).

● CHANGING THE BEHAVIORAL SYSTEMS: PARENT TRAINING

The evidence is reasonably clear that trying to reduce the antisocial behavior of adolescents is unsuccessful. With a long interactional history of antisocial transactions, it is difficult to make long-term changes in adolescent aggression (Kazdin, 1987). Consequently, most of the developmental work on preventing and reversing the development of antisocial behavior has focused on training parents of preadolescent and younger children. You will recall that inept parent management is one of the early factors in the coercive family process (Figure 11.2). Parental management skills affect many aspects of the child–parent systems. Good parenting skills can even reduce the effects of the mismatches between child and parent personality characteristics. With good parenting skills, the negative reinforcement, escalation, and reinforcement traps that characterize the coercive family process are less likely to occur. Thus, training parents how to interact with their children effectively has been the focus of most treatment approaches.

● THREE KEYS TO EFFECTIVE PARENTING

What characterizes effective parenting skills? Patterson et al. (1992) emphasize three key elements: Be positive, be contingent, and be consistent.

Be Positive!

As you have seen in the ineffective and inept parenting style depicted in the coercive family process, the entire family system is aversive. The result is that most behaviors are reinforced through negative reinforcement—that is, the behaviors that are strengthened are ones that terminate, remove, or avoid the other family members' aversive behaviors. Attempts at punishment, including physical punishment, occur frequently and are retaliated against with equally aversive behavior. Escalation, reciprocity, and disruption are the results of this inept style of parenting. Instead, Patterson's first key for effective parenting is to use positive reinforcement for desirable behavior and avoid aversives. This is captured in the phrase "Catch them being good!" If punishment is necessary, he recommends one that is only mildly aversive but effective: time-out. First we look at positive reinforcement.

Positive Reinforcement

The first key is to teach the parent to positively reinforce prosocial skills. By catching the child being good, prosocial skills should develop that are incompatible with antisocial ones. Patterson and his colleagues (1992) suggest that, unlike the use of contempt, guilt, and anxiety that some parents use to teach social skills, the use of positive reinforcers produces higher self-esteem. Probably the most highly effective positive reinforcers that parents have are their own proximity, positive attention, and affection. Praise is effective, particularly when the parent is associated with pleasant events rather than aversive events.

More specifically, Patterson and others have focused on specific parenting skills. Most of these deal effectively with eliminating or preventing the development of coercive family transactions. The procedures include training in the contingent use of positive reinforcement and punishment (time-out).

Punishment (Time-Out)

Even while the emphasis is on positive reinforcement of desired, prosocial behaviors, some antisocial behaviors still are likely to occur. This is particularly true of children who have already been part of long-term coercive transactions. The use of aversive stimuli, either of a physical (e.g., spanking) or verbal (e.g., threats, yelling, ridicule) nature, often does not have the expected effect of reducing the behavior but may increase it. If they do, they may also produce undesirable side effects, such as anger and fear. Therefore, both differential reinforcement of other behavior (DRO) and punishment by loss, in the form of time-out, are usually taught to parents as effective means to reduce undesirable child behavior.

Be Contingent

Being contingent means using the four-term contingency. It means reinforcing appropriate or desirable behavior and using DRO or time-out for undesirable behavior. Ineffective parents noncontingently reinforce behavior, strengthening undesirable behaviors as much as desirable ones. Contingent parents provide clear cues (S^ds) as to what is expected of children and follow the behavior with immediate consequences. Telling children that they will get a toy if they are good all week is far less effective than providing an immediate but small reinforcer such as praise. Similarly, dealing with undesirable behavior by threatening children with threats such as "Wait till your father gets home" is not an effective method of changing the behavior that warranted the threat.

To be contingent, it is important to monitor children and their behavior. Parents cannot see and impose consequences on their child's behavior if they don't know where the child is. Because antisocial children have behaviors that are aversive to parents, parents are negatively reinforced by letting the child be out of sight. Unfortunately, this is not a situation that promotes prosocial behavior. As you recall, poor parental discipline and monitoring are major factors in early childhood for setting children on a path for the development of antisocial behavior.

Be Consistent

The final key to effective parenting is consistency. This means that the contingencies are stable and do not change at the parents' whim. Consistency gives the child clear knowledge about what the contingencies are. Effective parents give their children clear cues and rules and provide consequences for desirable or undesirable behavior in a contingent and reliable manner. They ignore minor misbehaviors. Inept parents give their children mixed messages and then often fail to follow through with consequences. The child's behavior becomes unpredictable because the parents' behavior is also unpredictable.

● A BEHAVIORAL SYSTEMS VIEW OF PHYSICAL CHILD ABUSE

Child abuse is a form of antisocial behavior directed at children. It takes many forms, including physical abuse, psychological abuse, sexual abuse, and neglect. Many investigators have focused on a history of being abused as a child as a significant determinant of later abusiveness as an adult. However, most abused children grow to adulthood without becoming abusive to their children. The development of abusiveness is a complex developmental process. Ross Vasta (1982) offered a model for physical child abuse that incorporates many of the processes relevant to a behavioral systems approach to development.

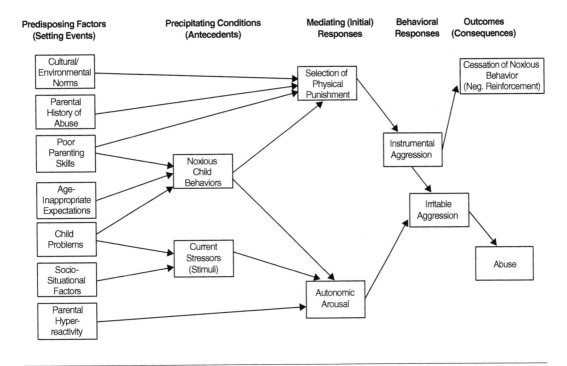

Figure 11.4 A Dual-Component Model of Physical Child Abuse

SOURCE: Adapted from Vasta (1982). Reprinted from *Developmental Review*, (2), Physical Child Abuse, 1982, p. 142, with permission from Elsevier.

Although, in fact, his model has multiple components, Vasta calls his a "dual-component" model of child abuse in the sense that it emphasizes the significance of (a) *operant* and (b) *respondent* behaviors. He also incorporates many of the known genetic, historical, and environmental contributors to abuse. Figure 11.4 shows Vasta's model. It is arranged into (a) **predisposing factors**, (b) **precipitating conditions**, (c) mediating (initial) responses, (d) behavioral responses, and (e) behavioral consequences. As shown in Figure 11.4, these factors are consistent with the four-term contingency.

Predisposing Factors

These are characteristics of the parent or characteristics of the child that may function as setting events. Various combinations of genetic makeup and histories of transactions produce these factors that make abuse more likely to occur.

1. *Cultural/environmental norms.* For example, there are wide cultural differences in the use of physical punishment in disciplining children. Some cultures emphasize physical punishment (e.g., "spare the rod, spoil the child"), and others, such as the Tasaday people of Mindinao in the Philippines, do not. Thus, what is considered too much or abusive punishment may vary from one culture to another.

2. *Parental history of abuse.* One of the most replicated findings in the literature on child abuse (e.g., Curtis, 1963; Spinetta & Rigler, 1972) is that abusive parents frequently have a history of being abused as children.

3. *Poor parenting skills.* Unskilled and insensitive parents are likely to have difficulty in controlling undesirable behavior in their children.

4. *Age-Inappropriate Expectations by Parent.* Some abusive parents have been found to lack knowledge of the sequence and timing of the development of their children (Blumberg, 1974). When this happens, they may expect a young child to behave in ways that the child is as yet incapable of doing. An example would be expecting a 5-month-old to be potty trained.

5. *Child behavior problems.* Children who have a history of being difficult to control, are aggressive, or otherwise present problems, are more likely to be the focus of abuse.

6. *Socio-situational factors.* This includes factors such as unemployment, socioeconomic status, and physical medical problems in the family. For example, in a study looking at 13,000 cases of abuse, Gil (1971) found that half the fathers were out of work in the year immediately preceding the child abuse incident.

7. *Parental hyperreactivity.* Because of their own transactional histories, some individuals are more sensitive to irritating stimuli than others. In addition, their reactions may be more intense than others. When child noxious behaviors occur, these parents overreact and are more likely to abuse than parents who are less sensitive to irritating stimuli.

Precipitating Conditions

These include both setting events (e.g., some current stressors) and discriminative stimuli. These are acute events that, when they occur, make it more likely that abuse will happen.

1. *Noxious child behaviors.* These are the whining, nagging, noncompliant, and oppositional behaviors identified by Patterson (1980). For example, under various setting events, a child's crying or whining may be a stimulus for abuse.

2. *Current stressors.* Among stressors, the loss of a job, marital problems, and death of a family member are a few of the major stressors.

Mediating (Initial) Responses

These are the initial behaviors of the abuser that are part of the chain leading to the abuse. These may be overt behaviors in the form of physical punishment or private events such as autonomic arousal.

1. *Selection of physical punishment as a response.* Note the arrows in Figure 11.4 that lead from specific setting events to noxious child behavior. Note, too, that cultural norms (i.e., whether the culture or subculture encourages corporal punishment or not), history of abuse of the parent, and poor parenting skills (see Patterson, 1980) increase the likelihood that the parent will select physical punishment as the response to the child's noxious behavior.

2. *Autonomic arousal.* Vasta (1982) noted that the consequences of physical acts against others that characterize abuse are far beyond that of simple negative reinforcement. If only negative reinforcement were involved, then abusers should terminate their attacks when the victim gives up. Vasta suggests that the fuel for the violence of abuse comes from **autonomic arousal** (including increased heart rate and breathing, perspiration, the feeling of heat from blood rushing into the face, and other physiological responses). The child's noxious behavior elicits the arousal. Some of these noxious behaviors may be unconditioned stimuli for arousal. Others, such as the child's voice, may acquire the role of conditioned aversive stimuli.

Behavioral Responses

Two components make this a **dual-component model**. One is an operant component (**instrumental aggression**) and the other, a respondent component (**irritable aggression**).

1. *Instrumental aggression.* This aggressive behavior is operant because it is reinforced by terminating the child's noxious behavior (negative reinforcement). For example, the parent slaps the child and the child stops crying.

2. *Irritable aggression.* This is respondent behavior. It is elicited by the child's noxious behavior. Both increased noxious child behaviors (crying, screaming, name calling) and the abuser's own aggressive responses can elicit even more irritable aggression. The result may be described as rage.

Behavioral Outcomes (Consequences)

Each component (operant and respondent) has certain outcomes that Vasta refers to as "consequences." However, in the technical sense, they are really only consequences for the operant component (see Chapter 6).

1. *Cessation of the child's noxious behavior (negative reinforcement).* This negative reinforcement is a consequence that strengthens the abuser's abusive behavior. Notice that the child's noxious behaviors serve as both antecedent and consequence (negative reinforcer).

2. *Physical abuse.* The result of the respondent component is that the operant behaviors are delivered with an increased intensity beyond what would occur without it. We deem these behaviors and their effects "abuse."

Vasta's (1982) model shows the complexity of the child abuse process. It involves the reciprocal interactions between the child and the parent. Both engage in reciprocal interactions based on their own unique genetic, historical, and current factors. When their paths of development collide, the developmental outcomes are poor.

Box 11.2   A DMZ in the Food Wars

One situation that often serves as a setting event for the coercive family process is mealtime. Move the setting to a public arena, such as Thanksgiving at Grandma's house or to a restaurant, and the conditions for even more disruptive behavior are substantially increased. Indeed, many families have given up altogether the very idea of eating out with the kids until it's time for their wedding rehearsal dinner. In an attempt to arm parents with effective strategies for taking children out to dinner, Bauman, Reiss, Rogers, and Bailey (1983) developed an advice package for parents.

This package includes 10 steps that parents should employ. What is of interest is that these steps cover all aspects of the four-term contingency, especially setting events and antecedents. The use of these procedures is designed to preempt child misbehavior by anticipating conditions likely to lead to misbehavior and to avoid these conditions from occurring in the first place. The steps are as follows:

1. Decide on what is appropriate behavior for the children in the restaurant and let them know what is expected of them. This specifies appropriate behavior to the children and to the parents and prevents on-the-spot debates and arbitrariness.

2. Find a table away from other people. This ensures a setting in which the children will get little attention from others.

3. Seat the children on the inside, next to the wall. This will limit their ability to interact with outsiders and get attention. The children will have to crawl over the parents to get into things.

4. If there is more than one child, separate them. This makes it more difficult for children to get each other going by hitting, pinching, and so on.

5. Bring along some crackers or other item as a premeal snack for the children. Even adults can get antsy waiting for their food to come. Don't expect children to be any better.

6. Order food that the children like. Parents are expecting their waiting behavior to be reinforced. They should make sure the children are reinforced by the food, too.

7. Provide small, interesting toys for the children to play with while waiting for the food. Parents may enjoy conversing with each other to pass the time. Don't expect children to be saints and just sit there.

8. While waiting for the food to come, remove the eating utensils from the children's reach. These are not toys—well, they're not supposed to be toys—so remove them before they become toys.

9. Remove the toys and return the utensils when the food comes. This makes it clear that food is the reinforcer and that eating, not playing, is the desired response.

10. Periodically praise the children for their good behavior. Don't expect the restaurant ritual to be as reinforcing to the children as it is to you—catch them being good.

Bauman et al. (1983) found this package to successfully reduce children's disruptive behavior in restaurants. Furthermore, they found that these procedures could be easily learned by parents, even by those reading them in a pamphlet provided on the table. Parents were observed as providing more praise and less disapproval of child behavior following their use of the advice package. Most of the families that were observed reported that the package was easy to use, it made the restaurant experience more pleasant, and they would probably use the steps in the future.

Many parents find that fast-food restaurants are the only refuges for eating out with their children. Interestingly, most fast-food places provide some of the conditions outlined above. For example, they often have special kids' meals that include toys and food that appeals to the little ones' palates. Because the food is served almost instantaneously, there is little waiting time to cause problems. As a last resort, parents can avoid all the problems associated with eating in public with their children by using the drive-through window. The package outlined above has been shown to provide parents with skills that can broaden their culinary pleasures and their family ones as well.

● SUMMARY

Antisocial behavior is commonly associated with aggression. Such behavior is typically characterized by (a) high intensity or rate and (b) intent. As with any other behavior, one's transactional history determines the development of aggressive behavior. What are initially genotype–environment interactions shift to person–environment interactions. Characteristics of the child evoke a response from the environment that is reinforced by and that reinforces a specific type of behavior. Subsequently, an individual actively seeks environments that evoke and reinforce that type of behavior. Physiological arousal is a potent determinant of aggressive behavior. Which operant behaviors are primed by emotional arousal depends on current environmental conditions.

Gerald Patterson (1980, 1982) attributes the development of antisocial behavior to a family dynamic termed the *coercive family process*. This process may be established as a result of constitutional differences in children and parents and may be maintained and exacerbated through (a) inept child management, (b) normal aversive give-and-take, (c) negative reinforcement for coercive child behavior, (d) *reinforcement traps,* (e) escalation of response intensity, (f) older coercive children, (g) reciprocity, (h) family disruption, and (i) modeling of aggressive behavior.

Patterson et al. (1989) developed a model of the development of delinquency in adolescence that begins in the home with the establishment of the coercive family process, progresses with rejection and failure at school, continues with membership in a deviant peer group, and culminates in the development of the adult antisocial personality.

Research has demonstrated that interventions aimed at antisocial behavior during adolescence are ineffective; therefore, the focus of such interventions has shifted to the training of parents and preadolescent children. With good parenting skills, patterns of interaction that characterize the coercive family process are less likely to develop. Effective parenting skills are characterized by the use of positive reinforcement (and, when necessary, use of mildly aversive punishment), the use of contingent consequences, and consistency.

Ross Vasta (1982) has posited a model of physical child abuse that highlights the importance of operant and respondent behaviors and gives consideration to known genetic, historical, and environmental contributors to abuse. Characteristics of the parent or child that may function as setting events include (a) cultural/environmental norms, (b) parental history of abuse, (d) poor parenting skills, (d) age-inappropriate expectations of the child by parents, (e) child behavior problems, (f) socio-situational factors, and (g) parental hyperreactivity. Precipitating events include current stressors and noxious child behaviors. Responses that mediate the behavior of the abuser are the selection of physical punishment as a response and autonomic arousal.

CHAPTER **12**

THE FAMILY SYSTEM

FAMILIES AS THE MEDIATORS ● OF SOCIETY AND CULTURE

In the human species, the family is the primary context in which a child develops. With some variation across cultures, the child will be raised in this family context for approximately 20 years. Yet the family influence is not likely to end when the child leaves home; rather, it changes. The adult is likely to create his or her own family context in which the original roles continue to be influential to some degree.

This continuous cycle of interaction illustrates the dominance of the family system for understanding human development. How shall we view the family? Modern developmental psychology treats the family as one system among many in which the child is embedded (Bronfenbrenner, 1979).

Bronfenbrenner has identified four levels of systems: microsystems, mesosystems, exosystems, and macrosystems. *Microsystems* are the smallest units functioning as complete systems. In Bronfenbrenner's view, the family, the school, and the child's peer group are three examples of microsystems. The child is in direct contact with and influences the microsystems that he or she is part of.

Mesosystems are intermediate system levels. The *combined* contexts of the family, school, and peer groups, as well as any other microsystems in which a child is embedded, are, collectively, a mesosystem. *Exosystems* are systems such as the government or the school system that the child does not experience directly but that affect the other systems. All these contexts make up the child's culture and society. Bronfenbrenner calls the level of system that involves the culture in which the other systems are imbedded the *macrosystem*.

The child is just one of the individuals who collectively make up the family microsystem. Family systems have their own dynamics that emerge from the dynamic reciprocal transactions of the individuals who constitute it. Recall the discussion in Chapter 1 about Seurat's *A Sunday on La Grande Jatte;* just as with a painting that we can analyze from different perspectives, we can look at development as occurring simultaneously at any of four levels of systems. At

Figure 12.1   The Family Dynamic

System Level 4 (society and culture), we are concerned with a system of systems. When analyzing at the level of the family (System Level 4), we see characteristics that are not present at the level of the individual (System Level 2) or even at the level of transactions between individuals (System Level 3).

● THE UNIVERSAL FUNCTIONS OF PARENTING

LeVine (1974) has noted that all families, regardless of the culture from which they come, have the same three basic goals and perform the same three basic functions of child development: (a) *survival*, (b) *economic goals*, and (c) *self-actualization*. Furthermore, these are arranged in a hierarchy, in which the more fundamental functions must be taken care of before higher level ones can be accomplished. We can conceptualize these universal functions of families as a pyramid in which the survival functions form the base on which economic functions and, finally, self-actualization functions may be built.[1] Until the more foundational functions are fulfilled, it may be impossible for the family to focus on higher-level goals. That is, unless the survival goals are met, higher-level functions are hardly relevant.

Consider a family in a war-ravaged nation. Neither self-actualization functions, such as promoting the study of music and literature, nor economic goals, such as basic education, may occur within the family. Instead, it is likely that all family functions will be concerned with survival goals, such as food, shelter, and safety.

THE SOCIAL AND CULTURAL ●
CONTEXT OF FAMILIES

One of the most important functions of the family (as is true with the schools, media, and peers) is to serve as a context for the transmission of societal and cultural influences. Some of the societal and cultural influences can be characterized as values. Values are the explicit and implicit contingencies specified by the culture. Explicit values may be moral or religious tenets such as "Honor thy father and thy mother," and "Do unto others as you would have them do unto you." Other values, such as a work ethic or having a large (or small) family may be promoted by modeling (e.g., a hardworking parent) or prompting (e.g., "So when are you going to have another child?") the desired behavior and then reinforcing the valued behavior when it occurs (e.g., "That makes us very happy; you're such a good son/daughter"). Family configuration (i.e., two-parent, nuclear family; single-parent family, etc.) is, in large part, a function of society and culture.

Family Structure

In modern American families, the traditional family, the *nuclear family*, consisting of a mother, father, and one or more children, is the dominant family structure. Yet in recent years, there has been an increase in other types of families in the United States. One of the largest recent increases is in the number of *single-parent-headed families*. In a single-parent family, the custodial parent provides the roles, or functions, that both parents provide in a nuclear family.

In *extended families*, grandparents or other adults are present and provide caretaking functions for children. Extended families may exist for a variety of societal and cultural reasons, many of which are economic. These are very common in farm-based cultures where it is an economic advantage to have different people available to work. If the mother is needed to do farm chores, the grandparents may take over child care functions. Wilson (1989) has noted the historical, marital, interpersonal, and socioeconomic factors that have made extended families a prominent part of African American culture. In this culture, uncles, aunts, cousins, grandfathers, and, particularly, grandmothers frequently provide support needed in low-income or single-parent families.

Yet another family structure is the so-called *nontraditional family* consisting of gay or lesbian partners and children. Finally, we may have a *reconstituted or blended* family consisting of children and parents from two previous family systems who spent time as single-parent families. Now they are combined into a new family with stepparents and stepbrothers and -sisters. Although all family systems are complex, the series of transitions in which members of reconstituted families have experienced different roles makes this one of the most complex and interesting developmental contexts.

What Is the Current Status of the American Family?

Households are defined as separate living groups, including families, single individuals, and unrelated individuals living together in the same housing unit. Figure 12.2 shows the changes in the relative numbers of the various family structure types in the United States from 1970 to 2000. Nuclear families, once more than 40% of all families, began a decline in the 1970s and in 2000 made up only 24% of all households. In 2000, there were 25.1 million married couples with children. In the same year, there were 11.4 million single-parent families, most of whom (9.9 million) were headed by mothers. Family size dropped from 3.14 in 1970 to 2.67 people per household in 2000. The 2000 census showed a slight increase in large families (over 5 people per household) although families with more than 4 children make up only about 6% of the U.S. households. Thus, the United States has seen a decrease in families with children, a decrease in the number of traditional nuclear families, and an increase in the number of mother-headed, single-parent families. The result of these structural changes has been a dynamical shift in the functions assigned to each member of the family system.

● THE FAMILY AS A SYSTEM OF SYSTEMS

It is common among psychologists to view the family as a system, whether functional or dysfunctional. Perhaps it would be better to view the family as a system of systems. That is, what emerges as a family is the interrelationship between

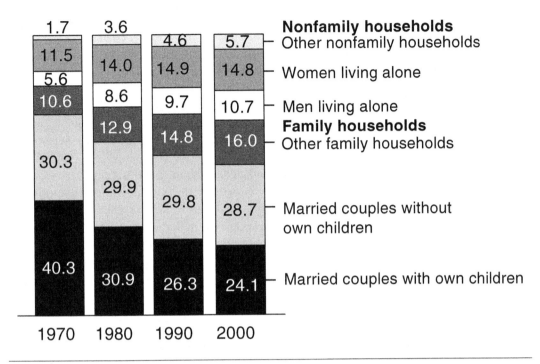

Figure 12.2   Households by Type: Selected Years, 1970 to 2000 (Percent Distribution)
SOURCE: Fields and Casper (2001).

more basic wife–husband, mother–child, father–child, and child–child relationships. Thus, at System Level 4, we are analyzing development at the level of systems of systems, which includes not only the family members but also the society and culture in which they are embedded.

Therefore, the family is a complex relationship built on other relationships. An example of this is the tremendous effect the arrival of a child has on the husband–wife relationship. The changes in interactions necessitated by redirecting attention to the needs of the baby pervade nearly every aspect of the spousal relationship, from eating meals to sleeping through the night. Years later, when left with an "empty nest," the spousal relationship may have to go through another period of readjustment to a new family system.

Indeed, the development of the family system is dynamical and may best be characterized by what Hetherington (1989) called "transitions." As family circumstances change, gradual adjustments or transitions occur in the family system. Some of these changing circumstances may be dramatic, such as divorce, death of a parent, or loss of family income. Other changed circumstances may have less impact, such as moving to a new town. Nevertheless, changes in conditions bring about changes within the family system that may initially be dramatic, but, eventually, the family system adapts to the changes.

From a behavioral systems view, the idea of transitions is an especially attractive notion. The family, from this perspective, is itself a dynamical system composed of the smaller systems of transactions between pairs of family members. The family patterns of transaction emerge as the results of reinforcement contingencies affect the members of the family. That is, the family system coalesces as the results of individual and two-way transactions are assembled by the contingencies.

Clarke-Stewart (1978) provided a good example of this. In her research, she found that a baby's cry might not directly be the antecedent for the mother to react to the baby. Instead, the baby's cry is more likely to bother the father who in turn requests the mother to respond to the baby, which she does. Thus, in family systems, transactions are not simply two-way transactions but involve multiway transactions between members of the family system. Changes in one part of the family may have subtle effects on all others, just as throwing a stone into a still pond produces ripples throughout.

Because the effect of the contingencies may require time to shape new behavior, the initial period following a dramatic change in conditions may be a period in which many previously reinforced behaviors are met with extinction and resulting variability and emotionality. This is a period of disruption in the interaction between individuals. Individual roles and functions may be unclear. Hetherington (1989) calls this a period of crisis. However, in our behavior systems approach, this is an example of a phase shift. Initially, changes in the system perturb the existing dynamic attractors (i.e., patterns of interaction). Eventually, the contingencies will gradually shape the individual interactions to a point at which the family system coalesces into a new one. At that point, the individuals in the family system will again be functioning to produce mutually reinforcing consequences.

Functional and Dysfunctional Families

Family systems theorists, such as Minuchin (Minuchin et al., 1975), draw a distinction between functional and dysfunctional families. Dysfunctional families are ones in which individuals support the maladaptive behavior of one family member. For example, Minuchin and his colleagues (Liebman, Minuchin, & Baker, 1974; Minuchin, Rosman, & Baker, 1978) see such dysfunctional systems as maintaining the eating disorder anorexia nervosa in teenage daughters. Because the severe loss of weight and other aspects of anorexia are maladaptive, families whose interactions result in reinforcement for reinforcing anorexic behavior are deemed dysfunctional.

Note, however, that as individuals, the members of a dysfunctional family system are functioning exactly as they should given the contingencies in effect. In the last chapter, Attila and his mother were clearly dysfunctional. That is, from the view of an outside observer, their behavior was maladaptive: they treated each other badly and were angry at each other. Yet as a system, this maladaptive behavior has come together, organized by natural contingencies of positive, but especially of negative, reinforcement. These contingencies shaped the "dysfunctional" system. Therefore, although in the value judgment of an outside observer this is a dysfunctional family system, as a system per se it is perfectly functional, with its component behavior patterns matched to their consequences.

In family systems therapy, it is common to view the maladaptive behavior of the family member as dependent. That is, much like in the case of addiction, the person with the problem is seen as dependent on other family members to maintain the maladaptive behavior. In turn, those whose behaviors are reinforced by maintaining the maladaptive behavior of the one seen as having the original problem are themselves viewed as having maladaptive behavior and are called codependent. It is most likely that a therapist would view Attila's behavior as maladaptive and dependent. His mother's behavior would then be seen as codependent.

From a behavioral systems view, the interactions between family members produce behaviors that are dynamic attractors. That is, characteristic patterns of interaction are loosely assembled by the contingencies. The family is functioning as it should given the conditions in effect. Remember, these conditions include the genetic makeup of the individuals, a long history of interactions between family members, and current physiological and environmental conditions. The results are many behavioral traps in which maladaptive, as well as adaptive, behaviors are reinforced by naturally occurring, but unintentional, consequences of reinforcement.

THE FUNCTIONS OF FAMILY MEMBERS ●

Mothers, fathers, children, and siblings have different functions in family life. Society and culture largely determine what these functions should be either through *verbal rules* or the *shaping process* called **socialization**. When we attach the functions to a specific person, we call the functions roles. When these roles are clearly defined and widely accepted by society, we have role stereotypes. Although roles are continually changing, in traditional nuclear families, mothers, fathers, and siblings have distinct roles. Roles define what the family member in that role prompts, models, and reinforces.

Let's test your views of traditional family roles. Next to each role, write down the words that describe the roles or functions provided by that family member.

Mother: _____

Father: _____

Older brother: _____

Older sister: _____

● LEVELS OF SYSTEMS: HOW SOCIETY INFLUENCES CHILD DEVELOPMENT

At this point, it is necessary to summarize the big picture of how society and culture exert their influences on the child. At System Level 4, society promotes values through mass media, local institutions (such as church and school), and family history. These values are modeled, and the behavior of family members that is consistent with societal values is reinforced. Thus, looking from the perspective of System Level 3, mothers, fathers, and siblings have been shaped to behave in accord with societal values by members of their society and culture. Among the behaviors they have developed are the teaching of socially appropriate behaviors to the child. Thus, mothers, fathers, and siblings model, prompt, and reinforce socially appropriate behaviors in the process called **socialization**.

At System Level 2, we view the child as developing appropriate (prosocial) or inappropriate (antisocial) behaviors. Finally, at System Level 1, we focus on the functions of basic process, especially operant learning, in the development of individual responses, some of which are social in nature. Just as the dots of paint construct the big picture, so, too, do basic learning processes bring societal and cultural values to fruition.

● WHAT HAPPENS WHEN THE ROLE IS ABSENT OR CHANGED?

In traditional (i.e., nuclear) families, individual members may have distinctive roles. What happens in families in which traditional roles change? What happens if one or more of the family members are absent, as in a single-parent-headed family? Changes in family systems, such as changing the "breadwinner" role, are increasingly more common in American families. Such changes may include those occurring through economic necessity or through personal decisions. An important change is frequently the absence of one of the family members because of divorce, death, or abandonment. What are the effects on the family system and the child when roles change or are missing?

Maternal Employment

A common, but dated, stereotype of the American family is the father as breadwinner. Reruns of TV shows from the 1950s and 1960s, starting with *Ozzie and Harriet,* through *The Honeymooners, Father Knows Best, Leave It to Beaver,* and ending with *The Partridge Family* and *All in the Family* provide evidence for the "father-as-breadwinner" role in years past. Perhaps this role is best summed up in Ricky's famous greeting to Lucy: "Honey, I'm home!" Our father-as-breadwinner depictions seem to have come full circle as aging swing bandleader Ozzie Nelson has been superseded some 50 years later by aging heavy-metal bandleader Ozzy Osbourne.

The role of the father as sole provider for the family has become an exception rather than the rule. By 1989 (Hoffman, 1989), most mothers, too, were wage earners. In 1990, 71% of two-parent American families had mothers employed outside the home, compared with only 43% in 1960. In 1996, 77% of mothers whose children had reached school age and 64% of mothers with preschool children were in the workforce. These figures are both more than 20% higher than they were 20 years earlier (Hayghe, 1997).

The change in the parental roles that has resulted from the increased likelihood of mothers working has been examined by Lois Wladis Hoffman (1989). Hoffman has looked at the effects on several components of the family system: the mother, the father, the marital relationship, and the child. As a part of a dynamical family system, the effects on individuals are ultimately determined by the combination of many factors. Simple effects that are true in all family situations should not be expected. Rather, the effects of maternal employment depend on complex interactions between many variables, including the cultural, economic, and social contexts in which the family is embedded. We first look at the effects of maternal employment on the mother.

Effects of Maternal Employment on the Mother

Hoffman (1989) found two major effects of maternal employment on the mother. First, for some mothers, outside employment serves as a "morale booster." Patterson (1980) found that the child-rearing role for some mothers brought on increased feelings of dysphoria. Mothers of difficult children seemed to be particularly helped by the "relief" of outside employment (Dienstag, 1986). Hoffman (1989) concluded that women who were able to gain employment because of lessened homemaking responsibilities or increased educational levels expressed higher levels of self-satisfaction than did nonemployed mothers. Increased satisfaction was expressed by both professional (Birnbaum, 1975) and blue-collar women workers (Feree, 1976).

Not all mothers receive a morale boost from outside employment, however. Although mothers who wanted to work outside the home did not show higher depression and stress scores (Hock & DeMeis, 1990), for some mothers, outside employment is just one more stressor in life. For these mothers, the demanding role of employee is added to the already demanding roles of mother, homemaker, and wife. For these mothers, work outside the home is one more role to assume.

Effects of Maternal Employment on the Father

Although influenced by the extent to which parents share household and caretaking responsibilities (Hoffman, 1989), the effects of the mother's employment on the father's life seem to be influenced by social–cultural factors. For some fathers, the increased economic and social benefits of maternal employment have positive effects. However, for fathers holding traditional role values, maternal employment tends to have more negative reactions. Specifically, fathers' self-esteem in blue-collar families is negatively affected because these fathers are more likely to feel they have failed in the breadwinner role that they value most highly (Staines, Pottick, & Fudge, 1986).

Effects of Maternal Employment on the Marital Relationship

These effects, too, are complex and dependent on the many specific factors in action in a particular family. Hoffman (1986) found positive effects on the relationships in dual-career families where both spouses value work. This was especially true in well-educated or middle-class families where the mother wants to work and the work is part-time. In these families, the mother's report of satisfaction with the relationship tends to be higher than the father's judgments of the marriage.

In contrast, maternal employment tends to influence negative judgments of the marriage in other family situations. The factors associated with negative marital satisfaction include families where the spouses have more traditional sex role values, in lower-class families, and in situations where either spouse resents the maternal employment.

Effects of Maternal Employment on the Child

In her review of available studies examining the long-term effects of maternal employment of child development, Hoffman (1989) concludes that mothers' employment has little lasting effect. The best-documented effect seems to be positive effects on daughters of working mothers. Daughters of working mothers seem to benefit from a working role model and are more likely to have higher self-esteem and reject traditional values of the limitations of women in the workforce. Furthermore, daughters seem to benefit from additional independence training that working mothers provide. Mothers who work have less time to dote on and make their children dependent.

Does the Mother's Work Role Change Her Role at Home?

Looking at maternal employment is a good place to see how a change in one part of the family system (i.e., the mother) changes interactions throughout the entire family system. Because in most American families mothers perform many, if not most, of the child-rearing and housekeeping functions, their removal from the home to work outside means that (a) someone else must assume these functions, (b) the functions must change, (c) the mother must perform both work and home functions, or (d) the functions will not be performed at all. The result of this change in function is a transition period in which the relationships between family members are disrupted. Relationships stabilize and become assembled again in some reorganized pattern in which roles are changed.

In general, studies show that there is a "modest" increase in father participation in household and child-rearing tasks when the mother goes to work (Hoffman, 1986). However, because this increase is the result of necessity rather than the father's seeking out increased participation because of a genuine interest in housework or child care, this situation may lower the father's satisfaction with the marriage (Hoffman, 1989).

One of the benefits of increased father participation in child care is that increased father involvement leads to higher academic and social development skills for both sons and daughters (Gottfried, Gottfried, & Bathurst, 1988). Apparently, father participation widens the range of skills and values taught to the children.

The children of working mothers spend more time in child care outside the home. Unfortunately, in most families, when the mother enters the workforce, the increase in paternal involvement or outside care does not entirely compensate for the mother's absence. In many cases, this means that the mother plays significant roles both at work and at home. Interestingly, the effects of the mother's outside work on the child are not linear. Part-time work for the mother seems to have more advantages for the family than having a nonworking mother. Negative effects on the children are generally not seen until the mother works more than a normal 40-hour workweek outside the home.

Paternal Job Loss

A downward trend in paternal employment has coincided with the increase in maternal employment seen in American society. This trend, which began in the 1980s (McLoyd, 1989), continued into the 1990s and may reflect a dramatic structural change in the U.S. economy.

Economic loss also includes reduction in wages as many fathers who are laid off from well-paying manufacturing jobs take jobs at reduced pay, when they can find work. Workforce reductions in manufacturing have disproportionately involved men. Furthermore, as a group, African American men have experienced proportionately more of the economic losses in jobs and wages (McLoyd, 1989).

McLoyd (1989) has proposed a model for the way in which paternal economic loss affects children. The model is consistent with a behavioral systems approach. It involves two sources of effects: (a) effects on the father and (b) effects on the child.

Effects on the Father

Unemployment is sometimes the result of individual choices. However, people sometimes lose jobs for reasons beyond their own control. Conditions in society leading to "downsizing" of the workforce may lead to termination of employment or underemployment. On the basis of research conducted during the Great Depression of the 1930s and also in the 1980 recessions, there is evidence that economic loss has clear effects on the head of the household. These effects may be positive or negative, depending on the circumstances surrounding the job loss and family configuration. Significantly, the appraisal of the cause of job loss affects the personality of the father.

Besides defining the father's role as breadwinner, the father's job helps structure his personality. To a large extent, the job environment determines who he is and how he acts. It is not surprising, therefore, that job loss may have a major impact on a father's identity. This effect is magnified in homes where there are dependent children because of the increased pressure that the financial stress applies (Scholzman & Verba, 1978).

Effects on the Child

McLoyd (1989) has focused on three areas of child development affected by the father's loss of employment: (a) socioemotional functioning, (b) the child's aspirations and expectations, and (c) physical health. These are mediated by the loss of family income and the effect that paternal job loss has on the interactions between father and child.

Socioemotional Effects. Paternal job loss and the resulting loss in economic status and embarrassment affect the personality and social interactions of the child. Children are likely to withdraw from existing social relationships because of embarrassment or because they no longer have the spending money to participate in social activities. McLoyd (1989) cites studies that associate paternal job loss with mental health problems (Werner & Smith, 1982), including loneliness and depression (Lempers, Clark-Lempers, & Simons, 1989). These effects seem to be enhanced by the reaction of the parents, which often is decreased monitoring and increased punishment (Lempers et. al, 1989).

Child Aspirations and Expectations. With the father's job loss, there is lower family income. This drop of income increases parental pessimism about the child's future. The parental responsibility to help with the child's career development and higher educational goals becomes an area of stress. The effect of such a change in a family's configuration results in lower aspirations for college and a career for the child. Girls' college and career expectations are particularly adversely affected by the father's pessimism (McLoyd, 1989).

Physical Health. Because job loss is often associated with loss of health insurance, reduced medical care, and poorer quality diets due to reduced income, children suffer physically. Margolis and Farran (1981) found a number of illnesses to increase when a parent loses a job.

Maternal Job Loss

In American society, the psychological effects are likely to have the most impact on the father who loses a job. These effects are due to the high reinforcement value placed on the breadwinner role of the father. However, as noted above, increasingly more mothers contribute to the economic well-being of the family through the workforce. Thus, there are increasingly more mother-headed families where the breadwinner role provides both critical economic and psychological reinforcers for the family. Maternal job loss, then, is likely to have similar significant effects on the child as does paternal job loss.

● THE EFFECTS OF DIVORCE

One of the most stressful events in a family system is the loss of one of its members. Children are particularly upset by the loss of a parent. Loss of a parent can occur suddenly, as with a death. Frequently, however, loss of a parent in a family system occurs through divorce, and the process may be a long one. One estimate is that a majority of children born in the late 1970s and 2000s will experience divorce. Because about 75% of divorced mothers and 80% of divorced fathers remarry (Hetherington, Stanley-Hagan, & Anderson, 1989), children of divorce experience a series of reorganizations of the family systems. In a sense, then, the members of the family go through a series of transitions. A family system disrupted by divorce experiences a period during which the new family functions coalesce into a new family system. In this new system, the child is likely living in a single-parent family, and further disruption may follow in remarriage because of a reconstituted family system.

It has long been assumed that divorce has a negative impact on all children. The work of Mavis Hetherington and her associates (Hetherington, 1989; Hetherington, Cox, & Cox, 1985; Hetherington & Kelly, 2002) has shown that some children are more vulnerable to the effects of family disruption than others. Some children may even have a better developmental outcome as a result of the divorce. Hetherington and her colleagues have identified which factors influence the effects of divorce on children. Three main areas stand out: (a) characteristics of the child, (b) characteristics of the family, and (c) factors outside the family (extra-familial), such as school and friends. Next, we look at how these factors exacerbate or moderate the effects of family disruption.

Child Characteristics

Each individual child's characteristics, the result of the coalescence of a history of interactions, may help determine the effects that divorce may have. Among those characteristics identified by Hetherington and her associates (Hetherington, 1989; Hetherington et al., 1989) are the following:

The Cumulative Amount of Stress the Child Has Been Under. Factors such as the amount of conflict in the home and stressful economic conditions are likely to influence the child's reaction to divorce. Emery (1982) has concluded that divorce may have beneficial effects when the predivorce environment was hostile and parents frequently engaged in fighting and other conflicts. Divorce, in these cases, actually reduced the amount of conflict the child was exposed to and had a beneficial effect. Likewise, divorced parents who cooperate on child-rearing issues and financial support are likely to reduce stress and have a positive impact on the child.

The Child's Temperament and Personality. Recall the characteristics of the difficult child. Hetherington (1990) has found that difficult children react more negatively to the stress of divorce than do easy-tempered children. Furthermore, the difficult child may elicit more negatives and place more stress on the custodial parent. Likewise, aggressive and noncompliant children with behavior problems may be a contributing factor to the divorce itself.

The Child's Developmental Status. The child's level of understanding of divorce may influence the reaction to it. Young children seem to react most negatively at first. They are more likely to blame themselves for being abandoned by a parent or for the divorce. However, with time, they seem to recover from the effects more fully. It is as if their limited level of understanding allows them to adapt better to the new circumstances. Older children may be better able to disengage from the turmoil of divorce, relying more heavily on peers and other support systems outside the home.

The Child's Gender. Boys and girls react differently to divorce. This gender effect is in part because 90% of divorced children live with the mother. Under these conditions, boys react more negatively than girls, showing higher incidence of behavior disorders and problems at home and in school. Effects continue longer for boys, with noncompliance being a problem even 3 years later (Hetherington, Cox, & Cox, 1982, 1985); but with most girls, little effect is seen after 2 years. The effects on girls are likely to take the form of personality disorders such as anxiety and depression (Emery & O'Leary, 1982).

As part of a family system, girls are in a very different position in relation to the mother. Hetherington (1990) reports that very often, girls adapt to the divorce by taking on the role of "friend" to the mother. The result is that the mother may treat the daughter as more of a peer as she relies on the daughter's help. Thus, daughters may have more difficulty with a remarriage than sons who are getting a new father. For girls, the men her mother dates may interfere with their new role as friend. Hetherington reports on daughters who stay up late waiting for their mothers to come home from a date, experiencing a kind of role reversal. When remarriages do occur, the daughter–stepfather relationship may be a particularly difficult one in our society. Neither daughter–stepfather nor stepfather–daughter behaviors are well defined. Hetherington's research (1990) suggests the consequence of this is that stepfathers are likely to withdraw from active interaction with their stepdaughters.

Family Characteristics

As mentioned, the amount of conflict present in the home prior to the divorce is a factor determining the effects on the child, and where there are high levels of conflict and fighting, divorce may actually benefit children. However, because divorce almost always results in a lower economic standard for the custodial parent, this too affects the child. In many cases, the custodial mother returns to the workforce for economic reasons, and the mother–child relationship changes dramatically. Hetherington (1989) finds that *lowered economic conditions* are also typically associated with the following: dependence on welfare and poorer quality of housing, neighborhoods, schools, and child care. In addition, the economic problems may lead to less stability, which results in the family's living with the consequence of loss of social support from accustomed friends, neighbors, and teachers.

When a custodial parent enters the workforce, the effects will, in part, depend on that parent's reactions to the new role. For example, high maternal satisfaction with work may influence the children positively. Remarriages significantly enhance the economic situation of the family. Although conflict over how to spend new resources may emerge, the effects of increased income have clear benefits for both parents and children (Hetherington, 1989).

Another area of concern in a divorcing family system is a period of *reduced child monitoring* by both parents (Hetherington, 1990). This may be the result of many factors, including parents' resentment toward one another, the parents requiring more time for their own adjustments, the belief by both parents that the other parent is paying attention to the child's behavior, or time spent filling other roles. In essence, the child is at risk of falling through the cracks. The effect of this lack of discipline on the child, as suggested by Patterson and his colleagues (Patterson, DeBaryshe, & Ramsey, 1989), is subsequent behavior problems.

Finally, the *presence or absence* of *grandparents* in extended families may exert a positive influence on the child. The engaged grandparent may take over some of the roles left absent by the missing parent (Hetherington, 1990). Grandparents can provide financial, emotional, and caretaking support. Crockenberg (1981) found that a responsive and sensitive grandmother can moderate the influences of an insensitive mother. Wilson (1989) found that the grandmother plays a particularly prominent role in African American single-mother-headed extended families.

Extra-Familial Factors

Finally, factors outside of the home can influence the effects a divorce will have on the child. Hetherington (1990) found two key factors: peers and the school.

Peers. Having a friend in whom the child can confide seems to moderate negative effects of divorce. The intimacy of the friendship seems to be even more important than the number of acquaintances the child has.

Schools. Hetherington found that structured schools had a moderating effect on the impact of divorce on children. Schools that provided consistency and pre-dictability in personnel and routines were better than unstructured schools.

The effective extra-familial factors seem to moderate divorce effects by pro-viding a consistency in the child's environment when the family system is in transition. This consistency and predictability enables the child to maintain a constancy in person–environment relationships no longer provided in the home. When contingencies are forming in the newly structured home, the already organized behavior patterns with friends and the school maintain some level of behavioral stability. The extent to which the transition period in the home affects the child is, of course, also dependent on the required change needed to stabilize the system. For example, a drastic change in parenting styles (discussed below) may have more of an effect than just a change of residence.

PATTERNS OF FAMILY DISCIPLINE ●

Diana Baumrind (1966) identified three distinct styles of parental discipline: **authoritarian, permissive,** and **authoritative**. Each of these differed along two identified dimensions of parental styles: warmth versus hostility and responsive-ness versus demandingness (Greenberger & Goldberg, 1989). These two dimen-sions form independent continuums along which parents may vary. Authoritarian, permissive, and authoritative styles fall on different quadrants of these dimensions.

Authoritarian parents are characterized by low warmth and high control. They strongly value virtue and favor punishment and negative reinforcement to control child behaviors not in accord with the authoritarian parent's strict views. Children are treated as submissive and to be kept in their place. Order and traditional values are reinforced; individualism and nonconventional behavior are punished. Children's views are not solicited and not considered. Right and wrong are viewed as absolute and originating from the laws of God. The authoritarian parent is high on demandingness and generally low on affection.

Permissive parents are accepting of children's behavior without attempting to modify it. They present themselves as resources for children to use, providing them with information and support, but they do not direct children's behavior. Unconditional positive reinforcement, where reinforcement is noncontingent on any desired behavior, is characteristic of permissive parents. They are low on demandingness and generally high on warmth.

Authoritative (not to be confused with authoritarian) parents are more reasoning. They consider the child's viewpoints and value them but remain in control. They view the child's behavior in relation to the context in which it happens, not in absolute terms. They are more directing than permissive parents. Authoritative parents use mostly positive reinforcement with some negative reinforcement, and only seldom do they punish. They tend more toward the responsive end of the continuum, but less so than do permissive parents. They may range along the entire warmth–hostility dimension, although hostility in authoritative parents is rare. Peláez, Pickens, Field, and Hart (2002) discussed a fourth type of parenting style—**disengaged** parents, who are aloof, withdrawn, and unresponsive to their children's cues and signals. They are insensitive to their children's needs, whereas permissive parents are overindulgent with their children.

What are the implications of differing parental styles? As mentioned above, the parental styles are likely to (a) be involved in different kinds of four-term contingency relationships with their children and as a result (b) differentially reinforce different kinds of behavior in daily interactions, which in turn influences the probability of these behaviors becoming organized behavioral systems.

Differing Contingencies in Parental Styles

Setting Events

The overall home environments established by parents with different child discipline styles are distinctive. These setting events provide different contexts that influence nearly all the discriminative stimulus–behavior and behavior–consequence relationships between parents and child. That is, an overall tone pervades nearly all interactions between the child and parent. Consider the differences in how the overall context affects the child in a home with two permissive parents versus a home in which both parents are strongly authoritarian. For example, take the phrase "My, don't you look handsome." In a permissive home, this compliment may be ineffectual because the child is satiated by parental approval. On the other hand, the same compliment coming from an authoritarian parent may be so unusual that its effect is very powerful. Unfortunately, in that context, it may be so unusual as to be taken as sarcasm that can result in the punishing rather than the strengthening of behavior. Thus, the overall different setting events prevalent in different styles of parenting may influence specific environment–behavior relationships.

Differences in Antecedents and Consequences

Authoritarian, permissive, and authoritative parents are likely to differ in the type of antecedents or discriminative stimuli they provide. Authoritarian parents, because they are more demanding are more likely to give commands. Permissive parents are least likely to give commands to children, but when they do, their commands are followed by fewer and less effective consequences. Instead, permissive parents are likely to tolerate more deviant behavior until a point at which they can no longer do so. Then, they are likely to handle the behavior ineffectively as is typical in Patterson's (1980) coercive family process (see Chapter 11).

Authoritative parents tolerate more freedom of child behavior than do authoritarian parents. In contrast to permissive parents, authoritative parents set limits that are clear to the child from both verbal statements and past actions. Thus, authoritative parents provide the conditions for the development of rule-governed behavior by specifying the contingencies and imposing consequences in a consistent manner. As in Patterson, Reid, and Dishion's (1992) examples of effective parenting practices, authoritative parents tend to ignore minor child irritations but are clear about what is acceptable and impose consequences immediately and effectively. Authoritative parents are more likely to use verbal rationales and nonphysical consequences, such as time-out or loss of privileges. Authoritarian parents are more likely to spank or paddle, and permissive parents are likely to try to reason with the child but not to use effective consequences.

Parents Differ in the Behaviors They Shape

Studies of Baumrind's (1966) three distinct parental discipline styles show that they have different effects on child behavior. The different effects occur immediately in the response of the child to the parent's behavior. These effects also follow a behavioral systems approach by building cumulatively over a long history of parent–child interactions. The results show clear long-term effects in the child's cognitive, as well as social and emotional, development.

Baumrind (1967) summarized the typical characteristics of children raised under different parenting styles. Authoritarian parents tended to have children who were fearful, apprehensive, moody, unhappy, easily annoyed, passively hostile, aimless, vulnerable to stress, sulky, and unfriendly. Permissive parents had children who were typically rebellious, low in self-reliance and control, **impulsive**, aggressive, domineering, aimless, and low in achievement. Finally, *authoritative* parents were likely to have children who turned out to be self-reliant, self-controlled, cheerful and friendly, able to cope with stress, cooperative, curious, showing purpose, and achievement oriented.

By middle childhood (age 8 to 9), the parenting style children received tended to affect their cognitive and social skills. As summarized by Baumrind (1977), the daughters of *authoritarian* parents had average social and cognitive abilities, and their sons had average social and low cognitive skills. *Permissive* parents were likely to have daughters who were low in cognitive and social skills and sons who were very low in cognitive and low in social abilities. Finally, the real winners were the daughters and sons of *authoritative* parents. Daughters of authoritative parents had *very high* cognitive and social abilities, and sons had high abilities in both domains.

These effects continue into adolescence. Dornbusch, Ritter, Leiderman, Roberts, and Fraleigh (1987) administered a questionnaire to high school students concerning their parents' discipline styles. The authors then correlated the three discipline styles to the students' high school grades. They found that an *authoritarian* parenting style was negatively correlated with grades, whereas the *authoritative* style was positively correlated. No relationship was found between a *permissive* style and high school grades.

Other investigators (Buri, Louiselle, Misukanis, & Mueller, 1988) have looked at the self-esteem of adolescents and the perceived parental style of their parents. Children who reported their parents had an *authoritarian* style had the lowest self-esteem, whereas those reporting being raised by *authoritative* parents had high self-esteem. *Permissive* parenting was unrelated to the self-esteem measure.

Clearly, authoritative parenting produces the most desirable outcomes in children. Authoritative parents allow their children to choose and participate within clear guidelines; use effective, but not strongly aversive, consequences; and encourage the development of achievement and self-reliant behavior.

Do parents change their style as the child develops? Apparently not. McNally, Eisenberg, and Harris (1991) administered the Child-Rearing Practices Report to a group of parents starting when their children were 7 or 8 years old, and for the last time when the children were 15 to 16 years old. They found a great deal of consistency in parenting behaviors across the 8-year period. Among the changes found was an increase in maternal control when the children hit mid-adolescence and a decrease in positive and increase in negative affect from the mothers as the children got older. Also, there were changes in specific discipline techniques as the child got older, with the use of isolation decreasing and deprivation of privileges being used more. Finally, as the children got older, mothers placed more emphasis on the child's achievement. However, the study suggests that, overall, the result of constant mother–child interaction maintained the mothers' parenting style throughout childhood and even into adolescence.

CHILDREN IN THE CONTEXT OF POVERTY ●

The family system is embedded in many contexts. One of the most pervasive and increasingly common is poverty. The lack of money for the family means that survival goals become important. Along with the lack of money come many setting factors that play havoc with the prospects of the child's development within the family. Horowitz (1989) considers poverty, along with other general conditions, such as race, a "social address." By this she means that poverty is a general condition that influences a child somewhere on the developmental path. As such, we may view it as a setting event—a context. Where that child ends up is not the direct result of poverty but, rather, of the kind of transactions that result from "residing" in poverty. Below, we explore some of the specific causal factors associated with poverty and their resulting effects.

The Extent of the Problem

The latest census of the United States (2000) lists the poverty rate for children at 16.1%, or about 12 million children living in poverty (Proctor & Dalaker, 2002). The rate of poverty for children in the U.S. is greater than the rate in Chile, Colombia, Jamaica, Costa Rica, and Cuba (Pollitt, 1994). The U.S. rate is 2 to 3 times higher than most other major Western industrialized countries (Song & Lu, 2002). The National Center for Children in Poverty (NCCP) estimated that 4 million children under age 6 live in poverty (Song & Lu, 2002). However, many more children's families live near that line.

Poverty is not spread uniformly over ethnic groups. The child poverty rate for white children is 9%; for African American children, 30%; and for Latino children, 28% (Proctor & Dalaker, 2002). The number of individuals living in poverty varies with the overall economic situation in the country, and, in the last decade, the number of individuals living in poverty has declined (see Figure 12.3). However, the number of mother-headed, single-parent families living in poverty has increased by the greatest percentage (Proctor & Dalaker, 2002). See Figure 12.4.

Huston (1994) identifies three reasons for these high numbers. First, structural changes in the U.S. economy have led to the loss of many well-paying industrial jobs for lower-skilled workers. These workers and their families have suffered serious income loss. Second, the percentage of children living with

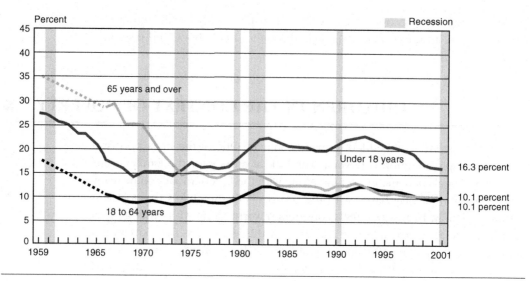

Figure 12.3 Poverty Rates by Age: 1959 to 2001

NOTE: The data points represent the midpoints of the respective years. The latest recession began in March 2001. Data for people 18 to 64 and 65 and older are not available from 1960 to 1965.

SOURCE: U.S. Census Bureau (2002).

single-parent mothers has increased dramatically. There is a high rate of poverty among these families. Third, government benefits declined during the 1970s and 1980s. This decline has continued at least through the 1990s and the 2000s as the percentage of families with poor children under 6 years of age receiving public assistance dropped from 53% to 36% (Bennett, Li, Song, & Yang, 1999).

In 1996, the U.S. Congress passed and President Clinton signed into law the Personal Responsibility and Work Opportunity Reconciliation Act (PRWORA). This act focused on employment for individuals receiving welfare and limited the number of years that welfare recipients could receive. Although some positive effects have been shown in getting parent into the workforce in a good economy, Duncan and Brooks-Gunn (2000) suggest that because deep or persistent poverty early in life has significant effects on children, these sanctions are likely to do harm if preventive actions are not taken. Recent data show that more than two thirds of poor children living in California are in families with at least one working parent (Song & Lu, 2002).

The Effects of Poverty on Children

Many disadvantageous conditions are associated with poverty. These include poor health care; inadequate housing (including, at its extreme, homelessness);

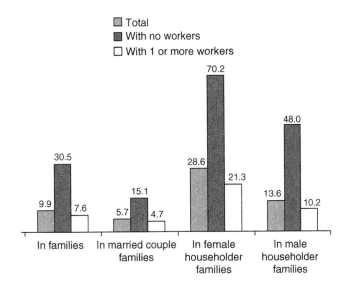

Figure 12.4 Poverty Rates of People in Families, by Family Type and Presence of Workers: 2001 (percentages)

SOURCE: Proctor and Dalaker (2002).

environmental toxins, such as lead poisoning; and neighborhoods that are violent or that provide little support (Huston, McLoyd, & Garcia Coll, 1994). Furthermore, there may be the effects of parental job loss described above. Because the conditions of poverty may affect organismic conditions (through lack of prenatal care and poor health care), they render the child impaired and vulnerable. And because the effects of these organismic conditions are likely to be exaggerated by a nonfacilitative environment, poverty puts the child in "double jeopardy" for poor developmental outcome (Parker, Greer, & Zuckerman, 1988).

Poverty and Nutrition

Nutrition is an example of how one variable may serve as a setting event influencing developmental contingencies. Studying a naturally occurring severe food shortage in Kenya that lasted several months, McDonald, Sigman, Espinosa, and Neumann (1994) found major effects on school-age children. Toddlers, whose food energy intake did not decline, did not exhibit the same effects. School-age children, however, showed less time spent in high-activity play, less positive peer interaction, less general activity, and poorer in-class attention. Their social and cognitive behaviors were affected during this famine. Thus, for the children whose food intake was reduced, lower energy levels reduced certain types of play and school interactions. In an interesting example of the complexity of family dynamics, toddlers were spared most of the effects of the famine by their families who made sure the toddlers were nourished. As a result, toddlers' behaviors were unaffected.

Poverty and Parental Discipline

Poverty also directly affects environmental conditions such as parental discipline. Sampson and Laub (1994) compared data collected on delinquent and nondelinquent adolescents during the Great Depression. They found that family processes were responsible for about two thirds of the effects of poverty on delinquency. Poverty seems to inhibit effective informal parental control (what Patterson, 1980, would consider "ept" parenting—monitoring and effective discipline) over adolescents. Indeed, delinquency increased directly in proportion to the amount of harsh and erratic discipline employed by parents. Furthermore, 83% of the adolescents in families showing low supervision or monitoring were delinquent. In contrast, only 10% of adolescents in families with good supervision were delinquent.

As suggested by Patterson's (1980) coercive family process (see Chapter 11), the influences are complex and multidirectional. That is, not only is the child's delinquency affected by the parents' poor monitoring and discipline, but the parents are affected by the child's coercive behavior as well. Sampson and Laub (1994) found that the child's difficult and antisocial behavior disrupts effective parenting. Having children who were difficult, showed misbehavior early in life, and had frequent violent tantrums led, as might be expected, to lower levels of maternal supervision when the children were adolescents. It is no surprise that these adolescents also had less attachment to their mothers (Sampson & Laub, 1994). Thus, this research supports a dynamical systems view in which both the child and parent reciprocal transactions determine development.

This view is also supported by Conger, Ge, Elder, Lorenz, and Simmons (1994). These authors studied families going through financial distress due to economic difficulties occurring in the Midwest. Conger et al. proposed a model for how poverty works. The model predicts that adverse economic conditions place economic pressure on the parents, which in turn leads to depressive moods resulting marital conflict. In this model, the economic pressure and marital conflict leads to parent–child coercion over economics and to parent hostility toward the adolescent. The result of this is a coercive family process with two outcomes: (a) Either the child withdraws, or (b) the child acts out problem behaviors. Thus, again, poverty may be seen as a setting event for poor developmental outcome. Poverty is an important variable that sets the conditions that make these types of behavioral transactions more likely.

Variability in Reactions to Poverty

As evidenced in the famine study described above (McDonald et al., 1994), not all children show negative effects of poverty conditions. Poverty may make certain conditions more likely, but its effects ultimately depend on the interaction of genetics, interactional history, current physiological conditions, and current environmental conditions, as described in Chapter 2. A study by Bradley et al. (1994) illustrates this. The authors found that of 243 premature, low birth weight children living in poverty, 26 were in the normal range for cognitive, social, health, and growth measures. This is not a high number. Yet it suggests that there may be some resiliency possible even under conditions of impairment and vulnerability. What facilitative environmental conditions produced these more favorable outcomes? The authors found that a responsive, accepting, stimulating, and organized environment "protected" these children. That is specific parent behaviors that encourage interaction between the child and the environment prevent many negative effects of poverty.

Preventing Poverty's Effects

What happens when home environments are nonprotective or nonfacilitative? Intervention programs, including early childhood education, may lead to better developmental outcome. Some preventive programs may focus on *early intervention*. For example, Grantham-McGregor, Powell, Walker, Chang, and Fletcher (1994) showed that even effects of early malnutrition can be overcome by teaching the mother to be more interactive and sensitive and to teach cognitive skills. Indeed, 14 years later, the malnourished children whose mothers received the training had children who were not significantly different from normal nutrition controls on IQ and school achievement. However, a group of malnourished infants whose mothers were not trained in interaction skills showed significant deficits in IQ and school achievement throughout school.

However, not all schools may be equally functional at overcoming the effects of poverty (see Chapter 13). Phillips, Voran, Kisker, Howes, and Whitebook (1994) found that school centers serving predominately low-income children were of lower overall quality than found in Head Start and public school-funded programs. Thus, children living in poverty may have less access to facilitative programs than they need.

**Box 12.1   Using Behavioral
Systems Approaches With Families**

Families living in poverty confront many problems. Solutions based on solving just one or two of these provide Band-Aid approaches to the family system. An alternative approach is a multifactor approach to the problems of low-income families. John Lutzker and his associates have taken such an approach in two well-documented programs, Project 12-Ways (Lutzker, 1984) and Project Ecosystems (Lutzker & Campbell, 1994). Both programs have developed systems of comprehensive services to families to prevent child abuse and neglect. These projects use what Lutzker calls an "ecobehavioral" approach (Lutzker & Campbell, 1994). The term *ecobehavioral* reflects the importance of changing behaviors in the real-world environments in which children and parents live.

Project 12-Ways was developed in 1979 at the University of Southern Illinois at Carbondale to provide services to rural families in 10 Southern Illinois counties. Adopting a systems approach, its primary focus is to teach children and their parents the skills necessary to get along together without abuse and neglect. It attempts to do this by reducing stressors and providing skills for family members. The comprehensiveness of this approach can be seen in the 12 ways in which these goals are approached:

1. Parent–child training

2. Assertiveness training

3. Basic skills training

4. Health maintenance and nutrition

5. Job finding

6. Family activities

7. Problem solving

8. Money management

9. Multiple-setting behavior management

10. Prevention of abuse (single parents)

11. Self-control

12. Stress reduction

In Los Angeles, Lutzker developed a new systems approach for the prevention of child abuse in the families of developmentally delayed children called Project Ecosystems. There are six components of Project Ecosystems:

1. *Parent–child relationship training:* There are two major components of the parent training. The first is *compliance training.* Compliance training emphasizes the use of antecedents, particularly instructions called *alpha commands.* Parents are taught to give these simple commands, which can be carried out by the child within a few seconds, rather than *beta commands.* For example, an alpha command such as "Johnny, please take the silverware out of the dishwasher and put it in the drawer" clearly specifies a task and how to do it. A beta command, such as "Johnny, please empty the dishwasher" or "Johnny, empty the dishwasher and then take the dog for a walk" is vague, open-ended, and much less likely to result in compliance.

A second important component of parent training is planned activities training (PAT), developed by Sanders and Dadds (1982, 1993). PAT teaches parents how to provide structured activities and good interaction skills to prevent misbehavior. By teaching parents to provide a reinforcing environment, much child misbehavior that serves as an antecedent for abuse can be avoided.

2. *Basic skills training.* Because many developmentally disabled children lack basic skills such as self-feeding, self-dressing, safety, and hygiene, counselors may train children directly. These counselors, who are college students, use basic behavioral methods to accomplish this; the control over the procedures is then gradually faded into the mothers' control.

3. *Behavioral pediatrics.* This program is designed to train parents in managing the often complicated medical procedures of developmentally disabled children. For example, a reinforcement system might be taught to the parent for increasing the child's taking of asthma medicine.

4. *Stress reduction.* As noted in Vasta's (1982) dual-component model, child problems, such as developmental disabilities, can be a setting event or an antecedent for abuse because they lead to a stressful household.

Stress reduction methods, including relaxation techniques, are taught to the parents to make the household less stressful.

5. *Problem solving.* Parents of developmentally disabled children in our society are confronted with frequent problems in child care and in obtaining the best services from agencies. Project Ecosystems has a training manual for the development of specific and general problem-solving skills to enhance the life of the parent and child.

6. *Assessment.* Like its predecessor, Project Ecosystems stresses ongoing assessment and evaluation of its own effectiveness. Individual, as well as projectwide programs, are evaluated for effectiveness, and improvements are made to ensure effectiveness.

Many published studies have demonstrated the effectiveness of these ecobehavioral approaches to preventing child abuse (e.g., Lutzker & Campbell, 1994; Lutzker, Campbell, Newman, & Harrold 1989). Despite the fact that the parents treated in Project 12-Ways were known abusers, during treatment there was an overall abuse rate of 2% versus a rate of 11% in a comparison group. A year after treatment, the Project 12-Ways rate was 10% compared with 21% for the comparison group. Among the first 75 families served by Project Ecosystems, only one case of abuse or neglect was reported (Lutzker et al., 1989).

Fortunately, many studies (e.g., Campbell & Ramey, 1994; Johnson & Layng, 1994; Lazar & Darlington, 1982; Weisberg, 1992, 1994) have demonstrated that effective early intervention and education can moderate the effects of organismic vulnerability and nonfacilitative environments. For example, Howard, Williams, and McLaughlin (1994) cite at least 18 studies that have successfully changed behavior problems of children prenatally exposed to drugs. These authors illustrate, in detail, how the four-term contingency may be effectively used with these children who have not only been prenatally exposed to cocaine and the impairment and vulnerability it may cause but have lived in a caregiver environment that is likely to be nonfacilitative due to the addiction of the mother. As Hart and Risley (1995) point out, the earlier the intervention begins, the more effective it is likely to be because of the cumulative amount of experience required to make up for lack of early facilitative experiences. "And the longer the effort is put off, the less possible the change becomes" (Hart & Risley, 1995, p. 203).

SUMMARY ●

The family is the primary context for child development. It is but one of many systems to which the child belongs; however, its primacy is evident in its influence on the child beyond leaving home. *Family systems* possess unique dynamics that emerge as the product of dynamical reciprocal interactions of the individuals that compose it. The dominant family structure of modern American families is the traditional nuclear family, consisting of a mother, father, and one or more children. However, in recent years, the number of families with non-traditional structures has been on the rise. The result has been a dynamical shift in the functions of family members. Such shifts typically instigate adjustments in the system necessary for adaptation. This conceptualization of the family system fits well with a behavioral systems approach. From this perspective, changes in the system upset existing dynamic attractors. Subsequently, new contingencies in effect shape interactions so that a new family system coalesces. A sort of equilibrium is achieved wherein family members resume functions that produce mutually reinforcing consequences. Family systems can be assigned value judgments such as "dysfunctional"; however, it is important to remember that even these families are functional in the sense that they work the way they should given the contingencies in effect.

Each member of the family has unique functions, many of which are determined by societal and cultural factors. When specific functions are attached to a specific person, these functions are called roles. When clearly defined and widely accepted, these roles become stereotypes. Roles determine what each family member prompts, models, and reinforces. When roles are absent or changed, the effects can be varied, depending on a number of factors, including cultural, economic, and societal contexts. The implications of one important disruption of the family system, *divorce*, depends on three main factors: (a) child characteristics (stress level, temperament, developmental status, gender), (b) family characteristics (conflict, economic status, amount of child monitoring, presence of extended family), and (c) extra-familial factors (e.g. school, friends).

Another important aspect of the family with diffuse effects on its functioning is the predominant method of discipline. Three styles have been posited by Diana Baumrind (1966): *authoritarian, permissive,* and *authoritative,* each of which is characterized by different parental behaviors and different outcomes for the child. A fourth style, *disengaged,* has been suggested as well. The authoritative style (characterized by acceptance, guidance, and use of positive reinforcement) is associated with the most desirable outcomes in children. It is suggested that this is the result of differences in the kinds of four-term contingency relationships parents have with their children that lead to differential reinforcement of different types of behavior. Finally, poverty is an important variable setting the conditions that make maladaptive types of behavioral transactions more likely, affecting developmental outcomes. Hope lies in the fact that the devastating effects of *poverty* can be moderated through effective early intervention and education.

● NOTE

1. Students of other fields of psychology may take note that LeVine's hierarchy is similar to Abraham Maslow's (1970) hierarchy of individual needs. In Maslow's theory, five levels of needs form a pyramid, starting with physiological needs at the base and ending with self-actualization needs at the apex. As in LeVine's approach, more basic needs must be met before we attempt to meet higher-level ones.

CHAPTER 13

SCHOOLS

● THE SCHOOLS AS AGENTS OF SOCIETY AND CULTURE

In the last chapter, we saw how societal and cultural values are transmitted through the actions of individuals in the family system. As mentioned, schools are an important source of societal transmission. Although the family continues to be a major source of influence, entry into the educational system exposes the child to extra-familial values. The school is part of one of the microsystems in which children develop. Schools tend to promote the values of the mainstream culture and the society in which a child lives. The culture as a macrosystem works through political systems to enact laws that sometimes dictate what other exosystems, such as school boards, pass on down the line to the microsystems that directly interact with the child. Even though an individual child does not come into contact with these larger systems, they substantially determine what is taught and how it is taught.

● THE FUNCTIONS OF EDUCATION

Schools developed out of society's need to extend the economic and self-actualizing goals of families beyond the home. In some societies, schooling continues in the home throughout childhood. Even in societies where there is public education, the child's first teachers are still the parents. Nevertheless, there are two main reasons for the development of extra-familial schooling. One is the extended knowledge and abilities of specialized teachers and educators that provide the child with more educational expertise than would be available from the parents alone. The second reason for the development of schools is largely economic: Sending the child to school enables both parents to work. A system with one teacher and 35 children is economically more efficient than one with one teacher (a parent) and one or two (or a few more) children.

However for many reasons, children may still be home taught. One increasingly popular reason is that some parents believe that they can do a better job meeting their children's individual economic and self-actualization goals than can the public schools.

The demand for early childhood education outside the home has increased in the recent years because of the increase in two-income families. In former decades, American society encouraged mothers to stay home until the children were of school age. This is no longer the case. In 2000, 64.6% of mothers who had children under the age of 6 were in the workforce (58.82% of single mothers and 53.3% of married mothers with children under the age of 1) (U.S. Bureau of

Labor Statistics, 2001). This is more than 3 times as many as were in the labor force 30 years earlier (Committee for Economic Development, 1993). Finding child care that is reasonably priced and environmentally enriching for a child is a taxing problem. Thus, a push for improved and affordable public child care (through early education) has come under recent political discussion.

If the purpose of schools is to provide for the economic and self-actualization goals for children, a primary function of education must be to increase the cognitive development of children. As you recall from Chapter 7, cognitive skills are knowledge (i.e., knowing about things), abilities (i.e., knowing how to do things), and problem solving. Fostering these is a function of education. A second, and often implicit, function is to promote the social development of children. Social development includes social knowledge, social abilities, and social problem solving. These social skills are generally considered the socialization function of education.

TYPE S AND TYPE F SYSTEMS ●

Schools are one of many organizations in society. Some, such as business organizations, are concerned with private matters and may have the interests of individuals not directly within the system, such as shareholders, as their major priorities. Others, such as the military, Congress, police departments, and schools, are public institutions. These are organizations concerned with "the common good" and exist for the purpose of furthering society's values. These organizations are medium- to large-scale systems that have been organized for some original function. Sometimes the organization formed because of a specific act of society, such as the formation of a three-branch government by a constitutional convention. Mostly, organizational systems have emerged because of the coalescence of factors driven by a goal or need to perform a function, such as the coming together of a Continental Congress to proclaim independence. As in our own nation's history, often more formal principles of organization follow the emergence of a system that has been assembled by the task at hand.

Schools are organizations that exist to further the society's values for the education of its citizens, especially children. Schools exist to further the family's (and society's) economic and self-actualization goals. Private and public schools emerged from these societal needs. Once schools emerged, structure was imposed on them with the purpose of enhancing their ability to meet their goals. Individual schools became part of school systems, with administrators assigned to enhance the function of the schools. The central question remains, however: "How well are schools doing in achieving their economic and self-actualization goals?"

434 ● CHILD AND ADOLESCENT DEVELOPMENT

In recent years, there has been great public debate on this question. Most of the conclusions drawn from the data show the educational system failing to meet society's goals. As part of the complex system of development, many factors determine the effectiveness of schools, including the teachers, the curriculum, societal values, the home system, and the child.

One interesting view of the role of the schools-as-systems was presented by Pennypacker (1994). Organizations, such as school systems, corporations, and governments, emerge due to the natural contingencies that exist in society. They coalesce around a task (e.g., education, profit, public services). Contingencies shape the formation and evolution of systems into their emergent characteristics. In Pennypacker's (1994) view, organizations can be classified into two types: Type S (or static) and Type F (or functional).

Type S (Static) Organizations

The original contingencies for either system may have been to solve a societal need. However, **Type S organizations** are under contingencies that shape and maintain the organization's survival, without regard for the organization's effect on the societal needs on which it may have been founded. For example, a government organization, such as Congress, would be considered a Type S organization if the contingencies determining the behavior of its members were to maintain their position (i.e., get reelected) rather than to serve the public. In Pennypacker's analysis, the self-survival contingencies in effect for Type S organizations select for certain characteristics that maintain the organization's status quo.

There are several characteristics of Type S organizations: First, the behavior of the organization is primarily controlled by avoidance contingencies (negative reinforcement). This means that the organization reacts to crises and meets deadlines to avoid aversive consequences. For example, a person in Congress may vote to pass a bill on terrorism to avoid appearing weak and being voted out of office. (Recall from Chapter 7 how the voting pattern in Congress shows the pattern of a fixed-interval schedule, with most of the activity coming just before the end of a session.) Likewise, a school system may bring in a new curriculum to show that it is doing something about increasingly lower test scores.

A second result of the self-survival consequences affecting Type S organizations is that they will do nothing that makes changes that might lead to their elimination, even if that would solve the problems they were organized to solve. For example, let us say that giving classroom teachers total judgment over curriculum leads to better test score results. A Type S school system would not allow this because it threatens the existence of the organization (its hierarchy of administrators), even though it furthers the purposes for which the organization was founded. The failure to enact campaign reform in Congress and the failure to control violence in media are examples of survival contingencies selecting the status quo.

A third characteristic of Type S organizations is that the selection by survival and avoidance contingencies produces reliance on the knowledge of "experts." This is what Pennypacker (1994) calls "invented wisdom". To maintain themselves, organizations depend on experts to state whether what the organization is doing is correct and effective. Such experts may rely on other experts (e.g., theorists, philosophers) and generate statistics or anecdotes to "prove" their point about what is being done or what further needs to be done. For example, the government may receive a report from a task force on crime, or a school system may adopt a curriculum for mathematics instruction based on a particular theory of cognitive development. By behaving in accordance with this invented wisdom of the experts, the organization can justify its existence. In this regard, Type S organizations are more rule governed than they are contingency shaped.

A fourth Type S characteristic is the development of a bureaucratic structure (indeed, Type S could stand for "structure" as well as "static"). A bureaucracy usually has a top-heavy layer of administration to generate the rules. A bureaucracy can create a web of rules and regulations (based on invented wisdom) that requires more bureaucracy for maintenance. This is the ultimate formula for self-survival and leads to the fifth and defining characteristic of Type S organizations: lack of variability and change.

Change threatens Type S organizations because it might lead to their demise. Solving a problem might lead to the elimination of personnel or other resources. This is a threat to survival that the Type S organization will try to avoid. The result is the status quo with little effective change in the practices of the organization. It is unlikely that Type S organizations will bring about effective changes to real problems.

Type F (Functional) Organizations

In contrast to Type S organizations, **Type F organizations** are controlled by the effects their actions have on the environment rather than by social control. Type F organizations are functional in the sense that they are controlled by contingencies associated with the problems that produced their emergence. Thus, a Type F government actually reduces crime, a Type F business actually makes a profit, and a Type F school system actually educates its students. In each case, the Type F organization does whatever is necessary to reach its goals. This may mean going against the collective invented wisdom in order to do something that works. What are the other characteristics of Type F organizations? According to Pennypacker (1994) there are five.

First, Type F organizations place a high value on the discovery of new knowledge that can be empirically verified. That is, Type F organizations constantly seek new technologies and methods, but they base these new developments on discovered knowledge that must be shown to be effective. In contrast, a Type S organization will implement methods based on the invented wisdom of experts and will rely on the testimony of experts about effectiveness.

Second, the contingencies maintaining the Type F organization are based on the cost versus the benefits of actions. Such cost–benefits contingencies involve both positive (producing benefits) and negative (avoiding societal costs) contingencies. Sensitivity to both cost and benefit contingencies means that Type F organizations place emphasis on positive reinforcing consequences where change and variability are likely to occur.

Because they are sensitive to contingencies that produce societal benefits rather than self-maintaining ones, if Type F organizations are successful, they will flourish. If they are very successful and solve the problems that led to their emergence, they may no longer be necessary and thus go out of existence. So for example, if the curriculum experts in a school system were to develop and implement a highly successful curriculum that maximized student learning, they would no longer be needed.

Finally, Type F organizations reinforce variability, not the status quo. Variability means that organizations will try out many things to find which ones work. Effective governmental, corporate, or educational practices will be selected by cost–benefit contingencies.

Clearly, the characteristics of Type F organizations are more beneficial to society. Unfortunately, all too often, self-maintaining Type S organizations gain a foothold and, by their nature, flourish to the detriment of the people they are supposed to serve. Much of today's cynicism toward our political and educational institutions may be traced to the public's frustrations with Type S organizations.

Project Follow Through

Cathy Watkins (1988) presents an example of the reluctance of educational organizations to change, even in the face of discovered knowledge. Her example is concerned with Project Follow Through, an educational experiment intended to study various curricula designed to maintain gains achieved by minority children in the preschool Head Start program. Project Follow Through became the most expensive experiment in education ever funded by the federal government, with costs totaling nearly $1 billion (Watkins, 1988).

Researchers had shown that within 3 years, gains in IQ and pre-academic skills acquired in Head Start were lost, leaving these minority children again below average. By following through with additional years of compensatory educational programs, educators hoped that these gains could be permanently maintained. The federal government paid to have more than a dozen curriculum models implemented in sites across the nation and to have the effectiveness of these models evaluated by independent agencies. These agencies (Stanford Research Institute collected the data and ABT Associates analyzed them) evaluated the programs in three areas:

- *Basic skills:* word knowledge, spelling, language, and math computation
- *Cognitive/conceptual skills:* reading comprehension, math concepts, and math problem solving
- *Affective measures:* self-concept

When the results were in, one curriculum model stood out: direct instruction, developed at the University of Oregon. It produced significant positive effects in all three areas. Two others, the behavior analysis developed by the University of Kansas and the Florida parent education model, produced smaller, but still positive, effects. Other than one positive significant effect, the remaining projects produced either no effect or actually produced effects that were even worse than the control condition of doing nothing special.

Did this lead to the adaptation of the direct instruction model for the implementation of Project Follow Through? It did not. The Office of Education ignored the data and, instead, averaged the results across all programs, which led to the conclusion that none of the programs worked. But because of the testimony of educational "experts" whose worldviews were consistent with the goals of the failed programs and out of line with the principles of the successful behaviorally based ones, instead of funding the programs that produced the best results, the government funded the programs that produced the worst results. Why would they do this? Watkins (1988) concluded that the programs demonstrated to be the most effective were also the ones that clashed with the views and opinions of the educational establishment . . . the experts. This is a case of invented wisdom, not discovered knowledge, guiding educational practice. Unfortunately, this is another case where taxpayers invested their educational dollars in the least effective schooling when demonstrably more effective alternatives were available. As Watkins concluded, "The educational establishment's vested interests have effectively prevented the largest experiment in history on instructional methods (costing almost one billion dollars) from having the impact on daily classroom practice that its results clearly warranted" (p. 10).

Many educators reject behavioral approaches to education because they see them as promoting academic achievement at the expense of social-emotional development. For example, DeVries and her associates (DeVries, Haney, & Zan, 1991; DeVries, Reese-Learned, & Morgan, 1991) compared observations of child–teacher and child–child interactions in kindergarten classrooms representing three types of instruction: direct instruction, constructivist, and eclectic. Their observations led to the conclusions that the direct-instruction teacher was more authoritarian and academically oriented.

The constructivist teacher (whose program was based on Piagetian principles and more likely to let the children determine what they did) was least authoritarian, least academically oriented, and most likely to encourage cooperation and reasoning. DeVries, Reese-Learned et al. (1991) also found that in interacting with their peers, kindergartners in the direct-instruction class used lower-level negotiating strategies, whereas those in the constructivist classroom more often used higher-level strategies. Two questions arise concerning these observed differences. First, are the differences real? Hatano (1991) and Gersten (1991) believe that these observations on interpersonal understanding are too narrowly focused. This type of focus resulted in a bias against the direct-instruction classroom, which had different goals than the constructivist classroom. As Hatano (1991) notes, it would be possible to provide a program for the enhancement of interpersonal skills in a direct-instruction program, if that were a goal that was deemed important.

Enhanced educational achievement is one goal shared by most educators. Gersten (1991) points out that the data presented on academic skills by DeVries and her colleague finds clear superiority for the direct-instruction classroom. The eclectic class was listed next for academic success and closely followed the direct-instruction class in style (DeVries, Haney, et al., 1991). The constructivist classroom showed the least improvement on academic skills. Thus, we should view the effects of educational programs on several dimensions but always taking the stated goals of the curriculum into account.

Indeed, the evaluation of Project Follow Through is evidence for goal-stated assessment. On the basis of its stated goals, each curriculum model was placed into one of three model categories. Both the direct instruction and behavior analysis models were placed into the basic skill model category. Other model categories were called cognitive–conceptual or affective–cognitive. An example of the latter was the Bank Street model developed by the Bank Street College of Education. Its primary emphasis was the development of positive self-image, creativity, and using language to express ideas. Contrary to the invented wisdom of the experts, all three of the basic skills models and one of the cognitive-conceptual models produced increases on the affective outcome measures. All the other models, including all the affective–cognitive programs, had significant negative effects on self-image. Apparently, providing children with *useful basic academic skills* has a much more positive effect on self-image and other affective measures than does a program focusing on building self-esteem without teaching basic academic skills.

Other researchers have supported the findings of positive outcomes in direct instruction and other behavioral programs. Weisberg (1988, 1994) has presented positive data on a preschool for poverty-level children that used direct instruction for reading.

If direct instruction and other behavioral methods have superior academic, cognitive, and affective outcome, why are they not more widely adopted by an educational system in search of more effective methods? One important reason for the rejection of behavior analysis in mainstream education is a difference in worldviews regarding the nature of children and the role of teachers. Watkins (1988) suggests that the educational establishment has a vested interest in the status quo, much as Pennypacker's Type S institutions do.

Box 13.1   Is Early Childhood Education Too Much Too Soon or Too Little Too Late?

As the discussion over Head Start curriculum suggests, a long-standing controversy exists over how to stimulate young children. As the Hart and Risley (1995) study on language influences (see Chapter 8) and other studies suggest, most children who have parents with middle-class incomes and educations are provided with facilitative early experiences that their cohorts from economically or educationally impoverished families do not have. Head Start was developed for, and continues to provide, services to children at risk for socioeconomic or physically based disabilities—so-called high-risk children. So although children who already have significant cognitive and social skills may benefit from a wide range of educational experience, it has been suggested that high-risk children may need a specialized environment to build in the apparent and hidden skills they lack that their colleagues may possess.

Recently, the debate over what is the most appropriate educational experience for children has enjoyed new life. Grover J. Whitehurst, a clinical developmental psychologist at the State University of New York at Stony Brook, was appointed Assistant Secretary of Education in the George W. Bush administration. He entered into a dialog with David Elkind, a professor at the University of Rochester, author and well-known proponent of waiting for the child to be "ready" before any formal education begins (see Elkind,

2001; Whitehurst, 2001).[1] Elkind's (2001) position was that preschool children who were taught pre-academic and academic skills, such as reading and writing their names, were put under too much pressure. The result of this, in Elkind's view, was that these children would later resent school and show only rote learning, not real skills. He based this on the work of cognitive-developmental theorists.

Whitehurst (2001) countered with research that suggested that children can acquire literacy skills without being forced to do so. He reasoned that Elkind's argument was based on expert wisdom rather than on the knowledge discovered from research. In the end, Whitehurst based his proposals for enhancing the learning environments of high-risk children on the data we already have and called for additional research to lead us to conclusions about any positive or negative effects of providing children with literacy-developing experiences.

● LEARNING AND TEACHING

As you recall from Chapter 6, learning is the relatively permanent change in behavior due to experience. By this definition, learning is a change in the behavior of a person, the student; but learning is a function of experience. Experience is the action of the environment on the student that produces the change. Experience is the action of the teacher on the student.

Structural Approach

In a structural analysis of teaching, teaching is anything that the teacher does to the student. Thus, giving a lecture, assigning homework, giving praise, even showing a film are defined as teaching. Teaching simply is what the teacher does.

Functional Approach

A functional analysis of teaching looks at the function of what the teacher does, and the effect it has on the student—learning. In this view, the teacher has taught when the student has learned. Therefore, teaching can be defined as creating conditions (i.e., experiences) that bring about the relatively permanent changes in behavior that we call learning. Thus, in a functional approach, lecturing, showing a film, assigning homework, and so on are considered teaching if, and only if, they have the function of changing the child's behavior (Skinner, 1992).

TEACHING AS APPLIED ● DEVELOPMENTAL PSYCHOLOGY

If we define teaching as the act of providing conditions that produce relatively permanent changes in behavior, we see the importance of understanding learning principles in education. From a developmental psychology viewpoint, teaching involves providing conditions that promote progressive changes in the interactions between the child and the environment. In both cases, teaching is producing changes, not just providing a stimulating environment.

From this viewpoint, teachers are actually applied developmental psychologists. Aided by the knowledge of both developmental and learning processes, they arrange conditions to bring about development in their students.

As applied developmental psychologists, teachers must be concerned with the two main questions of development: "What?" and "How?"

The Developmental Questions: "What?" and "How?"

Recall the two key questions in developmental psychology: (a) What?—or What develops? and (b) How?—or How does development occur? You may also recall that a better way of asking the "How?" question is, "Under what conditions does development occur?"

In viewing teaching as applied developmental psychology, the two same questions are relevant. The "What?" question is, "What should be taught?" This is curriculum. The "How?" question is, "How should it be taught?" This is the question about the appropriate educational practices or methods. Both are important questions in teaching. We turn first to the question of "What?" We address the question "How?" when we describe effective teaching methods below.

Worldviews and the Curriculum

How do we determine what should be taught to our students? Mostly, what is taught reflects the values of a society. What is taught reflects the current worldview of what society believes will best provide the child with the knowledge and abilities necessary for economic independence and personal development.

The specifics of curriculum reflect the society's worldview of what is necessary to fulfill these goals. For example, in contemporary technologically advanced and developing countries, computer literacy has become as important a part of the curriculum as reading. In agrarian cultures, computer knowledge and skills may be of little value and absent from the curriculum.

Who Determines Curriculum?

An official curriculum is developed by institutions specifically to address societal needs. This is called **explicit** (or formal) **curriculum** (Eisner, 1994) and is usually adopted by states or school districts after a long process involving parents, teachers, school administrators, and experts in subject matter areas. An example of formal curriculum is when a school system goes through a structured process and officially adopts the content of a sex education program. Formal curriculum may be developed by either Type S or Type F institutions. When developed by Type S institutions, formal curriculum is likely to reflect a structural approach to what is taught and ignore what students actually learn. The explicit curriculum is the subject matter that teachers are expected to teach and students are expected to learn. But this is not necessarily what happens.

Type F institutions are likely to develop functional approaches to curriculum. What is actually taught is influenced by the coming together of many social, political, and practical factors. For example, parents may want sex education changed to reflect a society's worldviews on what children should know about sex (e.g., teaching condom use to prevent HIV infection or emphasizing abstinence). Society's views, as reflected in the words and actions of parents, politicians (including school board members), and the media, are put into action by the individual teachers and local school administrators who interact with the children. Worldviews held by teachers, such as the use of the scientific method in problem solving (Proper, Wideen, & Ivany, 1988) or personal religious beliefs, may contribute strongly to what is actually taught. When what is taught is determined informally by changing community views or values, we call this **implicit** (Eisner, 1994) or taught (Cuban, 1995) **curriculum.** New lesson plans are implemented or discontinued as a society's implicit worldviews are reflected in teacher behavior. The explicit and implicit curricular are seldom identical.

Cuban (1995) identifies two other functional curricula. The **learned curriculum** is what the students actually learn. The **tested curriculum** is what is measured by the school or teachers. Again, there is usually some discrepancy among all these curricula so that what students learn is seldom what school officials or teachers intend. There may be additional disconnects in the curricula. For example, when California adopted a statewide assessment of the effectiveness of its schools, it used a general achievement test, the SAT-9 (Stanford Achievement Test), which was not aligned with the explicit curriculum. In subsequent years, the state developed its own tests that were more closely aligned measures of what was supposed to be taught, bringing the explicit, taught, learned, and tested curricula closer in agreement. Cuban (1995) suggests that closer relationships between these various curricula can be achieved when teachers who will be providing the taught curriculum are closely involved in the development of tests to measure what is learned.

WHAT MAKES FOR EFFECTIVE TEACHING ●

As suggested by the principle of equifinality (see Chapter 2), effective teaching practice will vary from situation to situation based on interactions between the child and teacher. However, some general statements can be made regarding effective teachers. Walberg (1990) generalized findings from more than 7,000 studies of educational practices from the United States and elsewhere. Walberg's findings show that practices that share many principles in common with dynamical systems and behavior analysis approaches are effective in educational settings. In fact, many findings are consistent with the four-term contingency (see Good & Weinstein, 1986).

Walberg (1990) titled the significant aspects of the teaching process as "cues, engagement, and reinforcement" (p. 471); he went on to state that the importance of these three terms is "enormous." You may recognize these as antecedent (cue), behavior (engagement of the reader into action), and consequences (reinforcement). Although he did not note setting events, Walberg does list some factors that function as the fourth term. Let us see what the educational research summarized by Walberg says about the importance of learning contingencies.

Effective Teaching and the Four-Term Contingency

Walberg found that the crux of the four-term contingency, the antecedent, response, and consequence relationship, were central to effective teaching. Greer (1994) has gone on to identify this contingency, which he calls a **learn unit**, as the most important measure of teacher performance. Using data collected from six different schools over a 7-year period, Greer (1992) found that the achievement of objectives was directly predicted by the number of three-term contingency learn units that the teachers provided and, subsequently, that the students performed. Greer and McDonough (1999) suggest that learn units are required more often in the early stages of teaching and become less necessary as the component operant skills are acquired. As students become more fluent, fewer learn units are required, but if the complexity of tasks increases before the necessary subskills are mastered, the student will flounder (Lindhart-Kelly & Greer, 1999). Thus, learn units are effective ways for teachers to create the requisite skills that can coalesce when all necessary conditions are present.

Antecedents or "Cues"

The function of cues or antecedents in teaching is to show the child what is to be learned. For example, the letter "d" is a cue for the sound "ddd" (which sounds similar to "duh"). Other cues include instructions, directions, and prompts. According to Walberg (1990), research shows that the effectiveness of cues is determined by their clarity and salience. Examples of effective cues given by Walberg include the following:

- *Advance organizers:* Give brief overviews that review old learning and relate it to what is to come.
- *Adjunct questions:* Provide the students with key questions that are most central to what is studied. These are particularly effective when they relate to similar, although not necessarily identical, questions on the posttest.
- *Goal setting:* These are specific objectives, methods, and standards that are made explicit. Like adjunct questions, these explicit objectives tell the students what they are supposed to know and what the standards are.
- *Learning hierarchies:* Presentations are structured along a hierarchical sequence based on logical or functional task analysis.
- *Pretests:* Not only do pretests allow the teacher to adjust instruction to the level of the student, but, according to Walberg, research shows that pretest information serves as cues to the child about what he or she knows and needs to know.

Active Responding or "Engagement"

The key term of effective teaching does not differ from the key term of the four-term contingency. It is, as Skinner (1984) stated, all behavior. Behavior analysts (e.g., Greenwood, Delquadri, & Hall, 1984; Greenwood, Hart, Walker, & Risley, 1994) have emphasized the importance of the teacher providing students with many opportunities to respond. Walberg (1990) labeled this behavior "engagement" of the student and found it to be central to effective teaching. As he summarized, "A high degree of engagement is indicated by an absence of irrelevant behavior and by concentration on tasks, enthusiastic contributions to group discussion, and lengthy study" (p. 471). Heward (1994) found three benefits of active student responding:

1. Active student responding generates more learning than a passive lesson of equal length.

2. Active student responding provides important feedback to the teacher.

3. Active student responding is related to more on-task and less off-task behavior. This means students are more attentive, less disruptive, and more pleasing to teachers.

Among the methods found to successfully enhance student learning though active engagement are the following (Walberg, 1990):

- *Frequent testing:* Tests stimulate greater effort and require studying responses by students. The effectiveness of smaller, more frequent quizzes is greater than that for final exams.
- *Questioning:* Teacher questions encourage student thinking and verbal responding. Furthermore, giving students time to think, rather than requiring immediate responding, may be most effective.

One problem with questioning in medium to large classes is that other students may be unengaged with only one student answering a question. We probably have all sighed with relief and stopped listening when the person next to us was called on to answer a tough question. At least two procedures have been devised to increase the active responding to questions of students in large classes. The first is choral responding (Heward, 1994). There are six key elements in choral responding:

1. The teacher provides clear directions and models one or two practice trials.

2. The teacher provides a pause for student thinking. Generally, the length of the pause is based on the complexity of the task and the students' level of skill.

3. The teacher uses a clear, consistent cue to signal students to respond. This might be a word such as "Class!" or "Now!" and may be helped with a visual prompt such as a hand signal or touching the chalkboard.

4. The teacher provides feedback for the majority's response. Offering praise when nearly all students are correct and repeating the answer provide reinforcement for correct responses. When a significant number of students give the wrong answer, a correction procedure such as giving the correct answer and then repeating the learning trial is used.

5. The teacher should occasionally call on a random individual student. This variable-ratio schedule is employed to prevent individuals from hiding behind the responding of others, such as the student who has the right answer but is 2 milliseconds slow.

6. The teacher should maintain a lively pace by preparing the materials ahead of time. This keeps the session moving and interesting. Choral responding can be fun but only if the teacher keeps it moving. Choral responding is a key element in direct instruction (e.g., Carnine, 1976; Engelmann & Bruner, 1988) and other behavioral teaching methods.

A second solution to encouraging responding in large classes is the use of response cards (Heward, 1994). Response cards are items such as cards, signs, or objects that students hold up on cue to indicate their understanding of a question. They are used like an instantaneous multiple-choice or true–false test. For example, students may be given a green card with the word "true" on it and a red one with "false" written on it. Students are taught the procedure that involves holding up one of the cards when given the appropriate cue. Then during lecture, a teacher may get feedback on the students' understanding of a concept by posing a question and looking at the number of correct cards held up by students. As with other forms of active responding this (a) enhances the likelihood that students will actively respond to the material, (b) provides feedback to the teacher about whether to go on or repeat material, and (c) keeps students on task. Similarly, multiple-choice answers and even pictures or words (e.g., "Hold up the word *elephant*") can be used as response cards. Again, this requires advance teacher preparation, but according to research summarized by Heward (1994) the procedure can be very successfully used for all grades.

The two active responding methods described above work well with groups but are best limited to material that has short answers (although response cards could have complex answers on them). Heward suggested a third active responding method: guided notes (Heward, 1994) or framed outlines (Bergerud, Lovitt, & Horton, 1988; Horton & Lovitt, 1989). Heward (1994) cites research showing that accurate note taking and studying of these notes leads to better test scores than those who just read a textbook and passively listen to a lecture (Baker & Lombardi, 1985; Carrier, 1983). Unfortunately, not all students are effective note takers. However, with guided notes, students are provided with handouts from the lecture in which key elements are left blank. There is space for students to complete the notes.

Greenwood and his associates (Greenwood et al., 1994) have identified seven components of active student responding. These components consist of writing, academic game play, reading aloud, silent reading, academic talk, answering questions, and asking questions. Taken together, these measures are associated with increased achievement test scores (Greenwood et al., 1981). This study compared the time spent in active engagement of inner-city fourth-grade children who were lower in IQ and standardized achievement with a group of suburban children. Greenwood and his associates (Greenwood et al., 1984) found the inner-city children actively engaging in academic tasks 12 fewer minutes per day than the suburban children. Although this may sound inconsequential, the 12 minutes per day comes to the equivalent of 1.6 additional school months when figured for the entire school year. Given the correlation of opportunity to respond, is it any wonder that the inner-city sample was behind intellectually and academically?

Consequences: Reinforcement and Corrective Feedback

Consequences are crucial because they strengthen some responses and weaken others. Without a strong and immediate consequence, behavior is not changed, and learning does not occur. Teaching therefore involves the planned application of consequences. In many cases, teachers may be able to arrange for the delivery of natural or logical consequences. For example, a wide variety of textures may naturally reinforce exploratory behavior of objects, or the plot of a story may reinforce reading. However, natural consequences may not always be possible or practical. In these cases, it is the teacher's role to provide consequences so that correct responses are strengthened and incorrect ones are weakened. Walberg (1990) identified two types of consequences that produced effective instruction: **corrective feedback** and praise.

Corrective Feedback. According to Walberg (1990), corrective feedback has moderate effects because it remedies errors by reteaching. Behaviorally, corrective feedback seems to serve two functions. First, it punishes the incorrect response. Second, it models the correct response. Engelmann and Carnine (1982) have developed several correction procedures that maximize the effectiveness of corrective feedback.

How to Praise. Praise is a common form of positive reinforcement. As with all reinforcement, praise is positive reinforcement only if it contingently strengthens behavior. Walberg (1990) finds praise to have a small positive effect on teaching effectiveness, possibly because it is used inappropriately. That is, praise may be used excessively and produce satiation. Furthermore, the praise from some teachers may be aversive or nonreinforcing because they have never established their praise as a secondary reinforcer. Finally, and surprisingly often, praise is used too infrequently by many teachers, thus not consequating many behaviors.

Good and Brophy (1984) have provided the following guidelines for the use of effective praise:

- Praise should be simple and direct.
- Use straightforward, declarative sentences, not "gushy" statements such as "Wow!" (Although even Good and Brophy might find "Cool!" cool.)
- Specify the particular accomplishment being praised and any effort, care, or perseverance the child shows (e.g., "That's really good. I like how you finished the whole thing").
- Vary your statements and the way you deliver praise.
- Have your nonverbal communication back up your vocal praise.
- Avoid ambiguous statements (e.g., "You were really great today"). Statements such as these do not reinforce specific behaviors.
- In sum, be sincere, be enthusiastic, and be contingent. Finally, remember, praise is a reinforcer only if it strengthens behavior.

Bill Hopkins (1994) related many of his experiences and, ultimately, his frustrations in making changes in the schools in Lawrence, Kansas (where he is a professor at the University of Kansas). He began as a consultant and found that getting teachers to provide frequent immediate positive reinforcement such as, "Good work, Mary," or "Great job, Johnny" had significant effects on the children's schoolwork. Teachers increased their praise and children increased their knowledge. Hopkins, as would most of us, thought that once teachers discovered the effectiveness of providing a little more frequent and a little more direct praise, they would be reinforced by the children's responses and increase their reinforcing behavior. This was not the case; once the consultants returned after a monthlong absence, the level of praise had declined, and so had student achievement.

Hopkins felt the solution would be to train the school principal in the procedure. He worked with the principal, who in turn supervised his teachers in the effective use of positive reinforcement. Results showed an increase in the teachers' level of praise as well as an increase in academic performance. However, weeks later, when Hopkins returned, neither the principal nor the teachers had maintained their behaviors. Finally, Hopkins ran for, and was elected to, the school board to be able to apply some contingencies to the larger system.

Hopkins' experience points out that even simple procedures that work may not work in the long run if they are not reinforcing to the person who must use them. Teaching, particularly with more than 30 children in a classroom, is hard work. Under the conditions in which most teachers work, praise may not come naturally, and finding the time and the opportunity to praise every child frequently may not occur. Hopkins admitted that he was somewhat naively expecting the use of praise to be a positive reinforcement trap in which the teacher would use praise because its use was strengthened by its natural consequences of increasing student performance. In fact, although praise did increase the children's performance, those effects were not sufficient to maintain the teachers' use of contingent praise.

Under what conditions are teachers and principals likely to adopt effective teaching strategies? One is to teach them how to evaluate the effectiveness of their work with children and to encourage them to monitor their students' progress. Bushell and Baer (1994) believe that close, continual contact with relevant outcome data or 3C/ROD (pronounced "three-cee-rod") would work. 3C/ROD means that teachers and administrators would determine objectives for each child and continually measure progress toward these goals. The kinds of measures that they suggest are not very difficult to collect.

As an example, they had a teacher identify, at the beginning of the year, how many pages of reading and what level of accuracy (at say, 80% accuracy) should be reached over a specified amount of time. Suppose 360 pages of reading in a 40-week school year was the goal. Each 10 pages would be a step. They had the teacher record the number of students who were reading at each step, and they graphed this. The graph provided a clear picture of class progress. As they summarized,

> The teachers always knew where they were in relation to the objectives, and in relation to where they had been last week and last month. Their teaching had been brought into close, continual contact with its most relevant consequences. If you asked those teachers if it had been a good week, and how it compared to the previous week, they could answer exactly. (Bushell & Baer, 1994, p. 6)

It is likely that there are extremely rare classroom teachers who actually do this on their own. It is seldom a part of the training teachers receive in their credentialing programs. However, the consequences for teachers are positive. The charts took about 20 minutes a week to prepare, which evoked a great deal of positive comment from the principal and other teachers. This led to the teachers' preparing charts for individual students. These progress charts were sent home so parents could see the progress of their children.

Bushell and Baer (1994) suggest that older children (their study was done with first graders) could be taught to graph their own progress. What function did the charts have apart from the positive reinforcement for teacher charting behavior? Coming into close, continual contact with relevant data means that a teacher knows what is and is not working and can make changes in the methods.

He or she knows which children are succeeding and which need further attention. This is truly a functional approach to teaching.

Training teachers to measure their effectiveness may be one way to provide them with positive reinforcement for effective teaching. Stokes, Fowler, and Baer (1978) found an unusual and less obvious way. They taught preschoolers social skills that got adults to praise them. In an even simpler demonstration of the bidirectional power of praise, when children complete a school unit, Don Bushell gives students a card to wear around their necks. The card has something written on it, such as "I can count to 20 by 2s!" This generally has one or two effects on adults. Either they praise the child's behavior, or else they ask the child to engage in the behavior and then praise it. Either way, Bushell (Bushell & Baer, 1994) reports that this has led to increased academic performance (and happy children and adults).

Natural (Intrinsic) Versus Contrived (Extrinsic) Contingencies. The role of natural (or intrinsic) versus contrived consequences is at the heart of the debate for those who take the "Do no harm!" approach to education. In the view of these educators, pushing the child too soon will destroy the child's intrinsic motivation and his or her love of learning.

The issue of natural versus contrived consequences was discussed in some detail in Chapter 7. As you may recall, it was suggested that contrived consequences be used only when intrinsic ones are absent. Unfortunately, in learning some things, **intrinsic reinforcers** are absent or very delayed. What is to be done in this case? Some suggest doing nothing—when the child is "ready" to learn he or she will. Others suggest that not using contrived reinforcers and other effective educational practices is a form of educational malpractice.

One group (the Association for Behavior Analysis, Task Force on the Right to Effective Education) believes it is the right of every child to receive effective education (Barrett et al., 1990). Their points are summarized in Box 13.3.

Over the past 30 years, more than 100 studies have been conducted to attempt to determine if extrinsic (contrived) reinforcement or rewards have an effect on the child's own "intrinsic motivation." Reviewing many of these studies, Dickinson (1989) concluded that when there are detrimental effects, these effects are short-lived and the result of using rewards, not reinforcers. Rewards are often given out inappropriately, without respect to children's performance, not as reinforcers contingent on the children's behaviors. Often, they are things, such as a "good citizenship" award that is more meaningful to the adult than to the child. On the basis of her review, she concludes that **extrinsic reinforcement** is clearly effective as long as it follows these guidelines: The reinforc ment is (a) noncompetitive, (b) actually shown to be reinforcing, and (c) contingent on realistic performance standards and not just the child's participation in the task.

Recently, a number of meta-analyses have been conducted to try to statistically summarize the results of the many studies looking at the effects of extrinsic rewards. A meta-analysis attempts to compare the results obtained from completed studies even though they have used different methods and different measures. This is done by first accepting a study based on some agreed-upon set of criteria and then using a statistically derived measure from the study called the standard effect size that can be compared against other standard effect sizes.

The first of these meta-analyses was conducted by Cameron and Pierce in 1994. These authors found no overall negative effects of extrinsic rewards on intrinsic motivation. They did find that there were some negative effects on free-time participation in an activity if the rewards were tangible, expected, and not contingent on meeting a level of performance but just generally distributed. An example of this might be if a child was playing with a video game and received stickers while playing, once the stickers were stopped, the child would be less likely to play with the video game.

Deci, Koestner, and Ryan (1999) questioned Cameron and Pierce's (1994) findings and conducted their own meta-analysis, including some other published and unpublished studies. They also estimated some uncalculable standard effect sizes. Furthermore, they focused on the effects on high-interest tasks, such as playing highly interesting video games. Using a broader set of criteria than Cameron and Pierce, Deci and his colleagues (1999) found a significant negative effect of rewards on whether the children continued with the high-interest task after the extrinsic reward was dropped. Other measures were also interpreted as showing pervasive negative effects of extrinsic reward on intrinsic motivation. Educators with a worldview that extrinsic rewards had a negative effect were quick to take the Deci et al. study as the last word.

But it was not the last word. Cameron, Banko, and Pierce (2001) later reanalyzed the studies included in the earlier two meta-analyses using stricter logical and statistical criteria to resolve the differences between the two earlier analyses. What Cameron et al. found is summarized as follows:

> Our results suggest that in general, rewards are not harmful to motivation to perform on a task. Rewards given for low-interest tasks enhance free-choice intrinsic motivation. On high-interest tasks, verbal rewards produce positive effects on free-choice motivation and self-reported task interest. Negative effects are found on high-interest tasks when the rewards are tangible, expected (offered beforehand), and loosely tied to level of performance. When rewards are linked to level of performance, measures of intrinsic motivation increase or do not differ from a nonrewarded control group. Overall, the pattern of results indicates that reward contingencies do not have pervasive negative effects on intrinsic motivation. (p. 1)

In conclusion, negative effects of extrinsic reinforcement seem to occur only when they are inappropriately applied. They should be used to help teach acquisition of behavior and maintain it where there are no existing natural or "intrinsic" reinforcers. They should not be used when existing natural reinforcers are effective. Still, despite the evidence, blanket prohibitions by educators about the evils of extrinsic rewards still exist. As Cameron et al. (2001) put it, "What is clear at this time is that rewards do not inevitably have pervasive negative effects on intrinsic motivation. Nonetheless, the myth continues" (p. 27).

From a developmental view, it is desirable to encourage the establishment of positive reinforcers and generalized positive reinforcers appropriate for the child's developmental history. For some, this may be accomplished by allowing the child to experience the "joy" of learning. In many cases, it involves the pairing of learning with praise and other effective positive reinforcers. In other cases, it may require the development of an effective teaching system in which both intrinsic and contrived reinforcers are effectively used. In addition, it is important to avoid making schooling aversive. Setting up conditions that lead to constant failure and the use of ridicule or other coercive behaviors is likely to punish learning rather than reinforce it.

In summary, praise and corrective feedback can change behavior. As Bushell and Baer (1994) state, "Criticism does not improve the outcome data nearly as well as praise reserved for good performance" (p. 8).

Box 13.2   A Model for Schooling

One comprehensive approach to education using dynamical systems and behavior analysis principles is seen in the Morningside Academy in Seattle, Washington (Johnson & Layng, 1994). The Morningside Academy started out as a broad series of programs for learners of all ages. Today, it is primarily a year-round school program for children with learning and attention problems who are below grade levels in academic achievement. One of the most unusual aspects about the Morningside Academy is its two academic money-back guarantees. For children who are 2 or more years behind in school and who would generally be classified as "learning disabled," the guarantee is that they will gain at least two grade levels per year or receive a tuition refund proportionate to the shortfall. The second guarantee is for children with problems such as distractibility, hyperactivity, and poor study skills who might generally be classified as Attention Deficit/Hyperactivity Disorder (ADHD) children. For these children, the guarantee is that they will increase their ability to stay on task (generally from their typical starting 1–3 minute attention span to 20 minutes or more) and increase their learning level to the 65th percentile nationally. In its history of offering guarantees (now more than 10 years), Morningside has never had to pay off on these guarantees! How has this remarkable feat been accomplished when most of the educational system is in crisis? The answer is in the use of behavioral and dynamical systems principles in its curriculum and methods.

Curriculum (What Is Taught)

The Morningside Academy approach to education follows a skills learning approach (see Chapter 7) to the development of intellectual behavior. What to teach is identified by task analysis. Conceptual behavior, defined as the behavior of identifying instances of events and things, forms the basic skills of the curriculum. Conceptual behavior is taught primarily through discrimination training in which a series of positive and negative examples of the concept is introduced and active responding is prompted. Correct responses are reinforced, incorrect responses are corrected, and discrimination-training trials are prompted again. Once basic concepts are learned, exercises are designed to produce generalization through relating and combining simple concepts into complex ones. Consistent with the hierarchy-of-skills learning approaches (see Chapter 7), the development of questioning and writing skills are further methods for producing complex conceptual behavior. The development of generalized and complex conceptual skills is planned rather than left to chance.

There is extensive use of the four-term contingency. Aside from providing motivation and facilitation through appropriate setting events, the Morningside Academy emphasizes three-term learn units. Responses are prompted by materials and teachers, and responses are consequated. Extensive use of natural contingencies and automatic reinforcement as well as teacher-provided reinforcement occurs.

Two key elements of the Morningside Academy approach are its emphasis on learning rate and fluency. Arguing that if slow learners continue at the same rate of academic development they will continue to fall farther and farther behind (the so-called cumulative deficit), Johnson and Layng (1994) focused on accelerating learning. By continually collecting data on each student, teachers could set goals and monitor the progress of individual students, effectively using the 3C/ROD principle. Thus, Morningside is able to correct instruction that is not working for its students.

Fluency is defined as behaviors that satisfy five criteria: retention, endurance, application, performance, and stability (REAPS). The REAPS criteria were discovered by teachers using a method called precision teaching that has been shown to produce long-lasting and powerful learning. It means that learning new concepts must occur until the REAPS criteria are obtained, rather than just simple acquisition. For example, a child who has only to spell "c-a-t" in response to a single picture of a cat has not met the REAPS criteria. Research shows that that child is less likely to be able to spell the word for other pictures, prompts, or over the long term. Meeting the REAPS criteria requires extended practice at a high level and in many situations. However, once the REAPS criteria have been met, fluency in a skill has been obtained.

For example consider your own language skills. You are likely fluent in at least one (let us say English). In addition, you may have studied another. At some point while you were studying that language, you were probably able to demonstrate some accurate skills but not to the extent to meet the definition of fluency specified by REAPS. Perhaps you were able to pronounce vocabulary or even carry out a formal greeting. Most students of a language have had the experience that they are able to use their acquired skills well enough to function within the confines of their classroom but fall completely apart the first time they have to talk to a native speaker in a real-life context. This difference in the ability of one fluent in a skill with one who is not is why the Morningside Academy emphasizes fluency.

Early on, it was discovered that by teaching to fluency, nonlinear phase shifts in skills often occurred. These "curriculum leaps" began to occur when fluent learners were challenged. This sudden combination of component skills has been called "contingency **adduction**" (Andronis 1983; Johnson & Layng, 1994) because the qualitatively different skill is assembled or adduced by the contingencies of reinforcement. As suggested by Skinner's (1974) writings on creativity, new behaviors may emerge under conditions in which the person is reinforced for unique combinations of existing knowledge and skills repertoires. You may recognize this as the same as the principle of coalescent organization introduced in Chapter 2.[2]

Because of the discovery that teaching skill fluency leads to emergent behaviors and acceleration of learning, the Morningside Academy curriculum emphasizes the fluency building of relatively few skills compared with the superficial learning of many concepts. Thus, although traditional schools may spend 70% in establishing skills and only 20% in practicing these, it is the reverse at Morningside. Here, 70% of student time is in practicing the skills to fluency and only 20% of the time is devoted to new skills. Because of the power of skills developed to the REAPS criteria, many new skills emerge without the need (and time!) to teach them directly.

Methods (How It Is Taught)

As already mentioned, most of the establishment of conceptual behavior is accomplished through discrimination training. Once a skill is acquired, practice sessions are used to establish fluency of the skills. Thus, unlike in other programs, much more time is spent on fluency building than on establishing skills. To accomplish fluency, a number of principles are followed. These steps are listed below:

1. Identify the component elements of instructional objectives. This is accomplished through task analysis and analysis of sequences of skills. For example, reading has prerequisite pointing, decoding, and scanning skills.

2. Measure the frequency of behaviors until true mastery (as identified by REAPS) of these behaviors is achieved. This is accomplished by initial pretesting and continual pretesting. Records of progress toward skill mastery are posted in public.

3. Establish a component behavior through highly interactive, contingent exchanges between learner and teacher. This is accomplished by small-group (12 or fewer students) instruction. Direct instruction, programmed instruction (including computer programs), and a personalized system of instruction are used. Instruction class size can be kept small by instructing only those deficient in the skills (based on pretesting) with those already possessing the skill engaged in practice rather than instruction. Once the skills are established, coaches interact with students to increase the student's speed on the skill in a method called "sprinting."

4. Build the component skills to fluency so as to ensure remembering. Once the skill is firmly established and strengthened, activities such as worksheets are used to bring the skill to fluency by practice on the basic skills and their combinations.

5. Build the endurance of component skills that are repeated in succession en masse in the real world. Once basic skills are fluent, composites are practiced to the REAPS criteria by extended worksheets and activities.

6. Include application activities that allow multiple-component skills to combine in ways that define the higher-level complex activities of an expert in a field. This is accomplished through activities, simulations, and games designed to strengthen composite skills and generalize them to new environments. Joe Layng has applied the Morningside model to college students at Malcom X College in Chicago who are lacking in necessary academic skills. For their final project in an art class, students must build a portfolio that will be accepted by and displayed by the curator of an art museum (Layng, 1995)!

7. Alter the procedures according to the data collected. A basic assumption of the Morningside model is that teaching is applied science and has a self-correcting mechanism built in. As with 3C/ROD, constant contact with the relevant outcome data will lead to the abandonment of ineffective practices and their replacement by effective ones.

The Fourth Term: Setting Events or Establishing Operations

Although many writers have specified the importance of the first three terms of the operant contingency, many educators have also focused on setting events or establishing operations. Recall, these are events that affect the contingency either by influencing the discriminative stimulus–response or the response–consequence relationship. General conditions such as the physical setting (e.g., whether a school room is bright and open or dark and in need of repair), the time of day (e.g., contingencies for difficult subjects may be more favorable early in the day than just before going home), and school breakfast programs (e.g., hungry children may have increased difficulty doing school work) affect learning. These are just a small set of the many conditions that influence the child's interactions with teachers, peers, and academic tasks. Together, the four-term contingency is a powerful determinant for learning. Effective teachers make maximum use of it.

**Box 13.3   The Association for Behavior
Analysis Statement on the Right to Effective Education[3]**

The current crisis in education and its destructive economic, social and cultural consequences are receiving international publicity. At the same time, research findings repeatedly demonstrating the superiority of specific instructional approaches and methods based on scientifically valid principles continue to be ignored. As a result, students are denied access to the most effective educational practices.

The Association for Behavior Analysis therefore issues the following position statement setting forth conditions and practices shown to maximize student gains throughout the course of their education.

Based on the principles that have been demonstrated to improve student learning and performance, the following are recommended educational entitlements for all students.

1. The student's overall educational context should include:
   a. Social and physical school environments that encourage and maintain academic achievement and progress and discourage behavior inconsistent with those goals;
   b. Schools that treat students with care and individual attention, comparable to that offered by a caring family;
   c. School programs that provide support and training for parents in parenting and teaching skills; and
   d. Consequences and attention at home that encourage and maintain success at school.

2. Curriculum and instructional objectives should:
   a. Be based on empirically validated hierarchies or sequences of instructional objectives and measurable performance criteria that are demonstrated to promote cumulative mastery and that are of long-term value in the culture;
   b. Specify mastery criteria that include both the accuracy and the speed dimensions of fluent performance;
   c. Include objectives that specify both long-term and short-term personal and vocational success, and that, once mastered, will be maintained by natural consequences in everyday living; and
   d. Include long-term retention and maintenance of skills and knowledge as explicitly measured instructional objectives.

3. Assessment and student placement should involve:
   a. Assessment and reporting methods that are sufficiently criterion-referenced to promote useful decision-making based on actual levels of skills and knowledge rather than on categorical labels such as "emotionally disturbed" or "learning disabled", and
   b. Placement based on correspondence between measured entering skills and skills required as prerequisites for a given level in a hierarchically sequenced curriculum.

4. Instructional methods should:
   a. Allow students to master instructional objectives at their own pace and to respond as rapidly and as frequently as they are able during at least some self-paced instructional session each day;
   b. Provide sufficient practice opportunities to enable students to master skills and knowledge at each step in the curriculum;
   c. Provide consequences designed to correct errors and/or to increase frequency of responding and that are adjusted to individual performance until they enable students to achieve desired outcomes;
   d. Be sensitive to and adjust in response to measures of individual learning and performance, including use of individualized instruction when group instruction fails to produce desired outcomes;
   e. Regularly employ the most advanced equipment to promote skill mastery via programs incorporating validated features described in this document; and
   f. Be delivered by teachers who receive performance-based training, administrative and supervisory support, and evaluation in the use of measurably effective, scientifically validated instructional procedures, programs, and materials.

5. Measurement and summative evaluation should entail:
   a. Decision-making via objective curriculum-based measures of performance, and
   b. Reports of objectively measured individual achievement and progress rather than subjective ratings, norm-referenced comparisons, or letter grading.

6. Assumption of responsibility for success should be such that:
   a. Financial and operational consequences for school personnel depend on objective measures of student achievement;
   b. Teachers, administrators, and the general educational program assume responsibility for student success and change programs until students achieve their highest performance levels; and
   c. Students and parents should be allowed and encouraged to change schools or school programs until their educational needs are met.

WHAT AND HOW TO ●
TEACH: FINAL COMMENTS

We end this chapter on schools by turning to comments by B. F. Skinner (1984). In his advice, Skinner outlined several basic points that apply to teaching at all levels:

- Be clear about what is to be taught.
- Teach first things first.
- Stop making all students advance at essentially the same time.
- Program the subject matter.

How do these points relate to dynamical systems and behavior analysis?

- *Be clear about what is to be taught.* By specifying the problem, you are specifying the solution. If you are clear about what you want, you can be clear about how to do it and how to assess your success.

- *Teach first things first.* More complex behaviors are built on basic ones. As suggested by Fischer's (1980) skill theory of cognitive development, complex cognitive skills emerge from the transformation of basic skills. This principle also relates, in general, to the principle of shaping or reinforcing successive approximations. By starting with simple responses that can be reinforced, teachers can gradually increase the standard for reinforcement to shape complex behavior.

- *Stop making all students advance at essentially the same time.* As individuals with unique genetics, interactional histories, and environments, students may require unique conditions for learning. Traditional education employs a group approach that is moderately effective for most students. However, not all fourth graders are equal. Group teaching is poor for optimizing the development and learning of each individual. Under group teaching conditions, most children will learn something, a few will learn much, and some will learn very little or not at all. Accepting the normal curve as the standard for teaching seems an admission that our educational approach is weak. After all, why should we be satisfied that teaching should produce the same kind of curve that can be found in nature without any special treatment? Shouldn't effective teaching produce better performance than that? Finding ways to individualize instruction (a difficult task with limited economic resources) should be a goal of educators.

- *Program instruction.* Teaching can be made more effective if what is to be taught and how it is to be taught can be programmed. Programming instruction means that what is to be taught is arranged in the most effective sequence so that basic concepts are taught first and form the foundation for complex consequences. This technology may be high-tech, in the form of multimedia

In summary, teaching is about student learning, and learning is the primary
subject matter of developmental psychology. We should use what we know

● SUMMARY

Schools constitute a major source of societal transmission, exposing children to
opment of children. Schools came about in response to societal needs. The
basic system, once assembled by the task at hand, became increasingly under
the influence of more formal principles of organization. Unfortunately, it can be
argued that school systems have come to resemble what have been referred to
as *Type S* (static) *organizations,* characterized by contingencies concerned with
an organization's survival to the detriment of issues it was created to address,
rather than *Type F* (functional) *organizations,* characterized by control through
consequences. As such, school systems have tended to choose relatively inef-

Learning is defined as a relatively permanent change in behavior that is the
result of experience. In this context, teachers provide the experience that
results in a child's change in behavior. From a functional perspective, a teacher
has taught only when the student has learned. Paramount concerns in teaching
are the curriculum and methods of teaching. Curriculum is determined by a
number of social and political factors. Four curricula—explicit, taught, learned,

Although there is some debate over what constitutes effective teaching
methods, in general, effective teachers make extensive use of the four-term contingency. Unfortunately, its effectiveness in and of itself does not always serve
to reinforce its use. One means of addressing this is to train teachers how to

The use of intrinsic versus contrived consequences in teaching has been a
heated source of debate. Although it may be preferable to use intrinsic reinforcers, they may be absent or too delayed to have reinforcing value in some
instances. In light of research indicating that use of contrived reinforcers does
not, in general, have a deleterious effect, it can be argued that the establishment

of positive reinforcers and generalized positive reinforcers should be encouraged, with the caveat that extrinsic reinforcement must be applied appropriately to be effective and avoid negative outcomes. Importantly, to facilitate learning it is imperative to avoid making school aversive.

Finally, B. F. Skinner (1984) has outlined several basic principles for effective teaching: (a) be clear about what is to be taught, (b) teach first things first, (c) stop making all students advance at essentially the same time, and (d) program the subject matter.

NOTES ●

1. Each author responds to the other in the "Forum" section of *Education Matters* (2001, Vol.1, No. 2, pp. 20, 21).

2. Contingency adduction and coalescent organization both describe the sudden emergence of new behavior out of basic component skills.

3. This statement was abstracted from a report by the Association for Behavior Analysis Task Force on the Right to Effective Education [members: B.H. Barret (chair), R. Beck, C. Binder, D.A. Cook, S. Engelmann, R.D. Greer, S.J. Kyrklund, K.R. Johnson, M. Maloney, N. McCorkle, J.S. Vargas, C.L. Watkins]. Ogden R. Lindsley was the original Council Liaison; he was followed in this capacity by Julie S. Vargas and Kennon A. Lattal. The full report of the Task Force was accepted by the ABA Executive Council and was published in *The Behavior Analyst,* 1991, Volume 14(1). This abbreviated statement was subsequently approved by majority vote of the general membership. It now constitutes official ABA policy.

CHAPTER 14

ADOLESCENCE

WHAT IS ADOLESCENT ●
BEHAVIORAL DEVELOPMENT?

Adolescence is a period of continued behavioral development along a pathway established in childhood. The notion of adolescence as a period of difficulties has existed since the publication of Hall's (1904) treatise on the topic. In this chapter, we discuss a number of physiological and sociobehavioral influences and transitions that occur during this period. We illustrate the positive as well as the negative environmental influences, such as adolescent physiology, schools, parents, peers, and risky environmental factors that produce changes that can perturb existing patterns of behavior.

Adolescence refers to those behavioral changes that take place between childhood and maturity/adulthood. This period is viewed as a time where biological, psychological, and social transitions take place. It typically occurs during the second decade of life when behavioral changes are related to sexual maturation, the emergence of more advanced reasoning abilities, the development of **rule-governed behavior,** greater social and emotional independence from parents, and changes in educational settings. Moreover, some have argued that adolescents also change in their behavioral "expectations" as they prepare for adulthood (Steinberg, 1996).

In this chapter, you will learn that during adolescence certain behavior patterns become more frequent These behavior patterns include greater involvement in peer interactions, increases in **risk-taking behavior,** conflicts between the adolescent and their parents, and marked increases in behavior patterns denoting depression and anxiety (Spear, 2000; Steinberg & Morris, 2001). Although adolescence may appear to be a period filled with distress, many problems are relatively transitory, and most adolescents adaptively make it through this transition.

In the following section, we describe events that occur during adolescence and that dynamically affect adolescents' transactions with environment. In every section, we explain how these physiological/organismic and environmental factors transact and affect behavior. We highlight some of the most commonly faced problems during this period as well as some of the most effective behavioral interventions for dealing with adolescent problem behavior.

● PHYSICAL DEVELOPMENT AND BEHAVIOR

Two major changes in physical development involve the adolescent **growth spurt** and puberty. The growth spurt refers to a dramatic increase in height and weight that characterizes the beginning of adolescence. On average, girls begin the growth spurt at age 10.5, and boys start this process between 12 and 13 years of age. During puberty, adolescents reach sexual maturity and become capable of having a child (Fabes & Martin, 2000.) Studies show that pubertal maturation is related to changes in adolescents' social behaviors during interactions. That is, adolescents who have reached pubertal maturation exert more influence in family decision making as well as more autonomy.

Hormonal Changes

Puberty is one of the most important organismic changes that occur during adolescence. During puberty, there is an increase in gonadal hormone production, which is responsible for the increases in the production of testosterone in males and estrogen in females and is also responsible for the growth spurt witnessed during this time. It may also have some effect on cognitive behavior. For example, Davison and Susman (2001) conducted a study that linked hormone levels (testosterone) to cognitive spatial ability. Three times over a 6-month period they collected cognition and hormonal measures. Higher levels of testosterone were associated with greater spatial abilities for all three occasions in both measures of mental rotation and block design in adolescent boys. For girls, higher testosterone levels were associated with higher mental ability scores in performance of mental rotation at the last session of data collection. This study suggests that testosterone is an organismic variable that may be related to behavioral functioning during puberty, especially in boys.

Organismic physiological variables such as the effects of hormonal changes on adolescents' behavior are important in the study of dynamic interactions in development. Increases in physical aggression have been seen more frequently in adolescents who show hormone deficiency (Finkelstein et al., 1997). However, most of the studies in this area are correlational and tend to exhibit weak associations between gonadal hormones and behavior. These results account for only a small amount of the variance in adolescent behavior and potentially suggest more bidirectional, reciprocal, and dynamic interactions rather than a unidirectional causal relationship between the aggressive behavior patterns and the release of hormones (Spear, 2000).

In fact, correlational studies comparing hormone level and behaviors in normal adolescents undergoing puberty suggest that gonadal steroids typically account for only 4% of the variance in negative affect among adolescents, whereas social events account for 8% to 18% of the variance (Brooks-Gunn, Graber, & Paikoff, 1994). These studies reflect the major impact that environmental factors have over adolescents' behaviors.

Timing of Physical Development

Differences in the timing and onset of physical maturation have been related to differences in behaviors in some adolescents. Early-maturing adolescents may be more popular among their peers but are at greater risks for engaging in risky behaviors, perhaps due to their friendships with older peers and, in the case of females, greater vulnerability to psychological distress (Steinberg & Morris, 2001). Also, the effects of pubertal timing differ significantly between boys and girls. Boys who mature late often fail to obtain positive reinforcement from peers (Bandura & Walters, 1963.) Early-maturing boys tend to be more confident socially and better athletes than late-maturing boys. Girls who mature early, however, appear to develop lower self-esteem and poorer self-evaluation than on-time-maturing girls. Although early-maturing girls tend to be more popular, they are also more likely to engage in delinquent behavior, use drugs and alcohol, and experience early sexual intercourse (Flannery, Rowe, & Gulley, 1993).

Early maturation has been related to problem behaviors among girls who have had a history of difficulties prior to adolescence (Caspi & Moffitt, 1993). Early-maturing females spend more time with older adolescents, particularly older boys, and these interactions appear to negatively influence them (Silbereisen, Petersen, Albrecht, & Kracke, 1989). The physical changes that accompany puberty affect self-perceptions, with studies implying that adolescent girls may already start to develop lower body-esteem around the ages of 12 or 13 that can last until their early 20s (Mendelson, Mendelson, & White, 2001).

● ENVIRONMENTAL FACTORS AFFECTING PUBERTY

In this section, we discuss how environmental factors affect the onset of puberty. For example, the age at **menarche** has shown a downward trend from what it was 100 to 200 years ago. In 1860, the average rate of menarche in the United States and countries of Western Europe was nearly 17 years. The differences reported from historical periods are probably accounted for by a dynamic interaction between genetic and environmental factors (Sommer, 1978). The environment also seems to be a major contributor to the development of puberty. *General health* and *nutrition* are two major factors in the environment that determine whether puberty will occur earlier or later. Healthy adolescents who have received adequate nutrition in previous years tend to experience puberty earlier than those who have been severely ill (Fabes & Martin, 2000.)

Quality of Family Interactions and Nutrition

The quality of family relationships may also affect the timing and course of puberty. In fact, girls who experience high levels of behavioral conflicts in the family tend to reach puberty about 6 months earlier than those who live in nonstressful homes (Belsky, Steinberg, & Draper, 1991). In sum, a great number of environmental factors, such as nutrition, exercise, and quality of family interaction, interplay to determine adolescents' physiological development.

Cognitive Development in Adolescence

The emergence of adolescence is associated with the development of mental abilities (e.g., abstract thinking, problem solving, hypothetico-deductive reasoning). Adolescents begin to use abstract and speculative critical thinking skills. They can formulate, test, and evaluate hypothesis through the use of hypothetico-deductive reasoning (Craig, 1999). According to Piaget (1954), adolescents, whom he placed in the formal operational stage, tend to focus more on themselves, and he called this **adolescent egocentrism**. Egocentric adolescents in the formal operational stage believe that their thoughts and ideas are unique and not understood by others, especially parents and teachers (Fabes & Martin, 2000).

As we have discussed earlier, Fischer (1980) proposed a theory of cognitive development by integrating behavioral and cognitive concepts called *skill theory* (this theory is described in greater depth in Chapter 7). Skill theory emphasizes the reciprocal interactions of adolescents' behaviors and the environmental factors affecting private behavior such as reasoning and problem solving.

MORAL BEHAVIOR AND REASONING ●

As a child approaches adolescence, he or she begins to develop the ability to generalize and conceptualize moral rules, values, and principles. The adolescent also may shift from moral realism to moral relativism. According to Jersild (1963), a child who is a moral realist tends to make a literal interpretation of the moral situation, whereas the moral relativist takes into consideration the intentions underlying the behavior as well as the practical consequences that follow. The relativist individual is more of a contextualist (who does not differ much from the pragmatist).

Moral judgments made by adolescents begin to come close to ones made by adults. According to Piaget, adolescents hold on to a morality of cooperation. The adolescent realizes that rules are created and can be changed as long as others agree (Haviland & Scarborough, 1981), especially in the case of rules adopted by convention.

In Chapter 10, you may recall that Kohlberg (1969) developed levels and stages for moral development by interviewing individuals and presenting them with moral dilemmas. The moral dilemmas consisted of "stories in which a character must make a crucial decision in a situation in which there is no clear right or wrong" (Haviland & Scarborough, 1981, p. 245). On the basis of an individual's response to the moral dilemmas, the adolescent's reasoning could be classified as following within three levels: Level I: preconventional morality; Level II: conventional morality; and Level III: postconventional morality.

Adolescents' **moral behavior** patterns, for the most part, are learned from societal practices, so their typical reasoning falls within the conventional level of morality. However, reasoning about moral issues may differ among adolescents and from culture to culture because of parental and societal contingencies of reinforcement and punishment, as well as systems of rule-governed behavior (Peláez-Nogueras & Gewirtz, 1995). Studies suggest that positive social reinforcement may enhance positive moral development, whereas conflicting reinforcement from societal members will lead to inner conflict and the personal adjustment of an adolescent's morality (Walker, Gustafson, & Henning, 2001).

● PERSONALITY DEVELOPMENT DURING ADOLESCENCE

Identity Formation

Erik Erikson (1950) described a series of eight psychosocial stages that reflect a struggle between two conflicting personality characteristics that present a crisis at every stage. Erikson's most relevant contributions to developmental psychology were the detailed explanation of stages that combined the social with the psychological factors. He recognized cultural differences and contributed considerably to the study of adolescents' personal **identity** (Fabes & Martin, 2000). According to Erikson (1968), identity formation is the major struggle that adolescents face. Identity refers to the self-questioning of who one is, where one is going, and how one fits into society. Erikson defined the **identity crisis** as the discomfort that adolescents experience as they question who they are and their role in society.

James Marcia (1980) expanded Erikson's theory and described *four* different states or statuses of identity formation. These statuses classify adolescents according to their decision making and commitment to specific choices, such as planning for a future occupation or profession. Research shows that the relationship between adolescents and their parents can have an effect on their identity formation—that is, on how soon the adolescent solves the crisis of who he or she is.

In *identity achievement,* adolescents who have achieved their identity or who are actively exploring identity issues seem to have freedom and a close relationship with parents. In *identity diffusion,* adolescents who have not yet questioned their identity are more likely to be distant from their parents than those adolescents in other statuses. In *identity foreclosure,* adolescents have committed to an identity without searching and fear rejection from their somewhat controlling parents. In *identity moratorium,* adolescents are indecisive, knowing about different identity options but not committing to any one.

The influence that attending college has over identity formation is not definitive. College attendance seems to set career goals and shape an adolescent's occupational commitments (Waterman, 1982). However, college students also seem to be behind in terms of establishing solid political/religious beliefs and ethical identities when compared with working peers (Munro & Adams, 1977).

Gender identity can be another struggle for many adolescents. Oftentimes, adolescents find that the immediate reinforcers involved in interactions with a compatible partner of the same gender can be more reinforcing than the delayed long-term and remote contingencies involved in producing a biological offspring. These feelings may immediately be reinforced or punished by society, thus creating a crisis that needs to be solved by the adolescent.

Autonomy and Social Influences

Rebellion, a central theme in adolescence, is prompted by a history of successful control of one's own "destiny" or path in life. This has long been a key figure in trying to understand adolescence. **Autonomy,** or the struggle for independence, affects humans throughout their lives, but in adolescence the first major step is taken toward freedom and away from parental authoritarian patterns. The way that parents handle adolescents' strivings for autonomy and self-efficacy patterns appears to influence high-risk behavior of adolescents (McElhaney & Allen, 2001).

PARENTING STYLE ●

The best outcomes of good parenting practices have been shown in adolescents whose parents who use an **authoritative** style of parenting. These parents set up and maintain contingencies, provide modeling and guidance, monitor their children, and exercise moderate control and high consistency. They also provide rules and rationales for implementing them.

Adolescents raised by parents with authoritative behavioral skills seem to develop higher self-esteem, reach higher levels of academic achievement, are more socially skilled, and behave more confidently than adolescents raised by authoritarian, permissive, or disengaged parents (Baumrind, 1991). The adolescent–parents relationship is bidirectional (Fabes & Martin, 2000) and dynamic. In other words, parents influence their adolescents' behavior, and adolescents also influence their parents' behaviors in various ways and directions. According to Ambert (1997), parents adapt their parenting practices to their adolescents' personalities and behaviors. For instance, it might be much easier for a parent to respond with an authoritative behavior style (where rationales for the contingencies or for the rule are given) to a responsible adolescent than to one who often displays rudeness, defiance, or noncompliance aggressive behaviors. Parental behaviors are maintained by the adolescent's responses through avoidance or escape mechanisms, as well as positive reinforcers, as discussed earlier in this book.

Figure 14.1   Adolescent Identity

The Parenting Style of Depressed Adolescent Mothers

A study was conducted by Peláez, Pickens, Field, and Hart (in press) to assess the "parenting styles" of adolescent mothers who either were or were not symptomatic for depression during interactions with their 1-year-old infants. Parenting styles of both depressed and nondepressed adolescents were classified as *authoritative, authoritarian disengaged,* or *permissive,* based on behavioral coding of a "compliance" task in which mothers instructed their infants to pick up toys from the floor and place them into a box.

In this study, the infant behaviors analyzed included following instructions, activity on task, noncompliance aggressive behavior, playfulness, protest/crying, and positive vocalizations. Elevated maternal behaviors signaling depression were significantly related to parenting style, as well as with the infants' task behaviors and play. The depressed adolescent mothers exhibited more authoritarian and disengaged styles compared with the nondepressed mothers who acted more permissively. Infants of depressed mothers also showed less on task and less playful behaviors compared with infants of nondepressed mothers. The authors concluded that the parenting style construct may be useful for classifying maternal behavioral interaction styles with infants and in turn appears to be related to the social and task behaviors of infants with their adolescent mothers.

Box 14.1 Polydrug-Using Adolescent Mothers and Their Infants Receiving Early Intervention

From a behavioral systems perspective, children born to drug-abusing mothers share the dual problems of physiological vulnerability due to exposure *in utero* and an increased environmental hazard due to the child-rearing behaviors of a substance-abusing parent. An effective research program on drug/social/educational/vocational rehabilitation for polydrug-using (alcohol and cocaine or marijuana) adolescent mothers was conducted at the University of Miami (Field et al., 1998). Although this program (initially funded by the National Institute of Drug Abuse) was originally devised to serve cocaine-using adolescent mothers, the majority of the drug-using adolescent mothers were using alcohol and marijuana instead of cocaine. The mothers were recruited at the birth of their infants and attended an all-day program designed to change the women's lifestyles. The program was housed in a vocational-training high school in inner-city Miami where the infants were also provided full-time day care. The participants were single mothers with extremely low-income status; 70% were African American, and 30% Hispanic.

This program was developed to accommodate more job-training opportunities for more adolescent mothers and to conduct a longitudinal assessment of their depressive moods. The program was offered in collaboration with the vocational high school, the university medical school clinics, and employers in the community. It served a total of 192 women (64/year over a 3-year period). Treatment consisted of a series of daily instructional activities and other interventions that included exercise, job opportunities, monetary incentives for maintaining their abstinence of alcohol and drugs, and massage therapy.

Outcome data for the 192 intervention women compared with the 96 control group women showed that the treatment program led to reduction in repeat pregnancy, reduction in drug use, completion of high school, increased job placement, housing, better health, and higher socioemotional status of the mother. Six-month follow-up data suggested that none have had a repeat pregnancy, 5% were continuing to use drugs, and as many as 33% obtained their high school diploma. Furthermore, 44% were still in school, and 61% were placed in jobs. In addition, the mothers were less depressed and had better interactions with their infants. The infants were better developed and had fewer illnesses. After the intervention, the infants of these mothers showed growth, positive social and cognitive development, and better health. Because of its potential cost-effectiveness, this model is recommended as a high school program for intervening with drug-using adolescent mothers.

● FAMILY AND SOCIAL SUPPORT SYSTEMS

Family systems are dynamic because the relationship between any two family members can affect the interaction of all other family members (Craig, 1999; Minuchin, 1974). During adolescence, most teenagers begin their quest for autonomy and independence. As a result, conflicts with parents become more common, centering on issues such as adolescents' choice of friends, physical appearance, and career choice.

Family and social behavioral support systems are extremely important to the adolescent, especially in times of stress. For example, a study was conducted with 220 college students to assess posttraumatic stress, depression, and their relations to family and social support after Hurricane Andrew. The authors found that students who reported having experienced the most severe impact damage from the storm also reported having experienced the most stress, anxiety, and depressive symptoms. Nearly half the students who sustained high damage to their dwellings were classified as depressed and low in social and family support. Regression analyses showed that material–economic and emotional–family social supports were significant predictors of anxiety and depression scores after the storm (Pickens, Field, Prodomidis, Peláez-Nogueras, & Hossain, 1995). Those adolescents with less family support reported the highest levels of anxiety and depression.

Figure 14.2   Peer Relationships

In addition to parental support, the process of renegotiation between parent and adolescent often occurs. Parents and adolescents must renegotiate their relationship from total parental dominance to a more egalitarian treatment, without adopting a very permissive or disengaged parenting style. That is, those parents who gradually give up control but keep monitoring their adolescents' behavior and support them when in need are likely to bring up well-adjusted adolescents that learn to monitor and regulate their own behavior.

Peer Relationships

During early adolescence, peer activities resolve around cliques, small groups of peers, usually of the same sex that interact frequently. By mid-adolescence, these same-sex cliques become mostly heterosexual. Adolescents also belong to crowds and large peer groups that share related activities and values (Craig, 1999). Adolescents tend to choose friends on the basis of their own values acquired from their parents' behaviors and rules. The adolescent's peer group then reinforces behaviors that tend to be approved by the parents (Bandura & Walters, 1963).

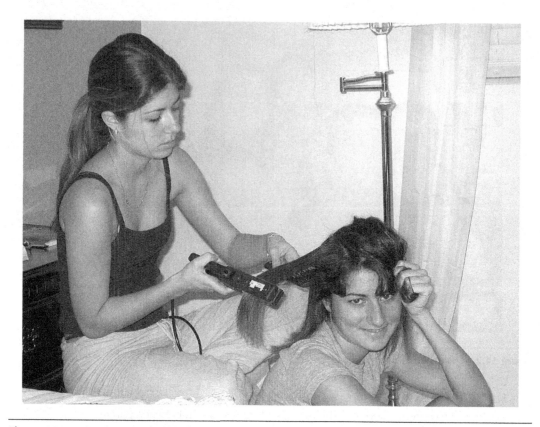

Figure 14.3   Peer Support and Influences

Let us give an illustration here. An adolescent girl is likely to have friends who value academic achievement because this value has been reinforced by her parents. These girls (Figure 14.3) would tend to behave in ways that maintain consistent environment and familiar cues for their behaviors. This helps explain why adolescents select friends who engage in behaviors that produce reinforcing consequences for themselves (e.g., hairdressing).

Adolescents spend much more time interacting with peers than with family members, which is why peers grow to have such a large influence on adolescent development (Spear, 2000). During a regular week, adolescents spend nearly one third of their time socializing with peers and roughly 8% with adults (Csikszentmihalyi, Larson, & Prescott, 1977). Peers provide a source of positive experiences for adolescents because they help develop adolescents' social skills through positive reinforcement. Peer groups can also serve as role models of maladaptive behaviors, such as delinquency, smoking, careless driving, and/or drug intake (Spear, 2000).

Researchers suggest that peer contact may predict problem behavior in those adolescents with a previous history of overt behavioral difficulties (see Steinberg & Morris, 2001). Jessor, Chase, and Donovan (1980) found that the strongest predictors of adolescent problem behaviors are friends' approval and access to potent idealized models (i.e., generalized reinforcers). For example, when high school students were asked how they would like to be remembered, only 31% of the boys and 28% of the girls wanted to be remembered as bright students (Coleman, 1961). Furthermore, more recent research shows that the adolescent is more preoccupied with showing those social skills (e.g., athletic, musical) that lead to being popular (Suitor & Reavis, 1995). However, a number of other factors, such as adolescents' age, socialization history, temperament traits, and personality, determine susceptibility to peer influence. Also, middle adolescents tend to be more influenced by peers than are early or late adolescents, perhaps because the latter group has already learned a system of rules.

BEHAVIOR DISORDERS DURING ADOLESCENCE ●

Antisocial Behavior

Antisocial behavior tends to be manifested as extreme physical aggressiveness, losing temper, arguing with adults, refusing to comply with adults' requests, deliberately doing things to annoy others, and being angry, spiteful, touchy, or vindictive (Davison & Neale, 1998). Antisocial behavior tends to be more common among adolescent males than females. Several studies have found a difference in the type of symptoms observed in each gender. Antisocial boys are more inclined to steal and display aggression, whereas girls tend to misbehave sexually (Robins, 1966).

The organismic and environmental factors known to place an adolescent at risk for antisocial behavior include parental psychopathology, dysfunctional aggressive and criminal behavior, alcoholism, and drug dependency (West, 1982). Antisocial youths tend to have parents who exercise harsh punishment as well as highly inconsistent discipline practices (Farrington, 1978).

Patterson's Coercion Model

We described Patterson's (1982) **coercive family process**, or *coercion model,* in some detail in Chapter 11. It serves as a framework to explain the interactive patterns between antisocial adolescents and their parents. As you recall, this theory is based on the view that aversive behaviors are inadvertently maintained by reinforcement contingencies, usually negative reinforcement.

Patterson, DeBaryshe, and Ramsey's (1989) developmental progression model for antisocial behavior speaks to the conditions in adolescence. (see Figure 11.3). According to these researchers, child conduct problems (i.e., coercion, aggression) manifest in early childhood as a result of poor parental discipline practices and monitoring of children. During middle childhood, children with antisocial behavior patterns tend to fail in school and experience rejection by their peers. In late childhood and adolescence, these children may become involved in a deviant peer group, which often provides a source of modeling and reinforcement for delinquent behaviors. Ultimately, these young adults exhibit an antisocial personality.

In sum, models that display aggressive behaviors can influence children to engage in similar behaviors. Abusive behaviors within family members (e.g., parents) can perpetuate aggressive behavior in children through modeling. A risk factor associated with antisocial behavior is academic deficiency. It is known that the relation between school problems and antisocial behavior is bidirectional and dynamic. Research shows that low scores on intelligence and academic achievement tests relate to the development of later delinquency (Farrington, 1978). This finding may be because antisocial behavior also relates to poor academic performance (Robins, 1966).

Conduct Disorder (CD)

Conduct Disorder (CD) is characterized as a group of behavioral and emotional problems in children and adolescents. Aggression, oppositional behavior, and other disruptive and rebellious behaviors are among the most common problems in CD (Wicks-Nelson & Israel, 2003). Adolescents with these behavior patterns have great difficulty following rules and behaving in a socially acceptable way. The typical behaviors exhibited are aggression to people and animals, destruction of property, deceitfulness, lying, stealing, and serious violation of rules, such as running away from home.

Behavioral Treatments for
Antisocial Behavior and Conduct Disorders

Containment. Containment is a frequently used time-out technique that ignores unacceptable behavior by coordinating all parties involved with the adolescent. This technique is difficult to implement with adolescents and may have some negative collateral undesired responses. However, time-out is implemented to ensure that the undesired behavior is not reinforced at all by the attention it usually commands.

Praise-and-Ignore Technique: Steps to Follow. The following is an illustration of how the "praise-and-ignore" technique can be implemented. First, ensure that everyone who deals with the antisocial adolescent comes together and objectively scrutinizes the adolescent's position in the conflict—for instance, examine under what conditions the adolescent's tendency to lie occurs. Second, create a contingency plan that everyone agrees to about the consequences for targeted behavior. A behavior modification plan can include negative and positive reinforcement consequences or punishment. Third, decide what target behaviors are going to be ignored (usually through a DRO, or differential reinforcement of other behavior, schedule as discussed in Chapter 6) and which behaviors will be reinforced, replacing the undesired target. Finally, try hard not to show any emotion when reacting to the inappropriate behaviors of the adolescent (Mash & Barkley, 1998).

Reinforcement and Punishment Combined. Multifaceted operant conditioning programs emphasize the use of reinforcement techniques combined with punishment contingencies to modify the behavior in question (e.g., Kazdin, 1985). The use of positive reinforcement together with mild punishment has shown to be more efficient in changing behavior than either of these techniques alone (Phillips, Phillips, Fixsen, & Wolf, 1971).

Achievement Place Home Program. One of the behavioral programs best studied with predelinquent youths is the Achievement Place Home Program. The program is managed by a trained couple, known as teaching parents, in a homelike setting (Kazdin, 1985). Adolescents are reinforced through a token economy in several areas, such as self-care, academic achievement, and social behavior. These youths earn points and obtain privileges, such as access to games and TV, for adaptive behavior. This program also implements punishment techniques (response cost) by taking away points for violation of rules, such as lying, or for failure to accomplish individual responsibilities, such as maintaining good grades. Compared with youths who participated in community-based programs (in the absence of behavioral techniques), adolescents in the Achievement Place program showed fewer criminal offenses (Kirigin, Braukmann, Atwater, & Wolf, 1982).

Functional Family Therapy. Functional family therapy (FFT) is another treatment program for delinquents and their families. FFT incorporates "behavioral–social learning, cognitive–behavioral, and family systems perspectives, and focuses on the interpersonal processes of the family system" (Wicks-Nelson & Israel, 2003,

p. 225). FFT's goals are to improve communication skills between the child and family, adjust expectations and attitudes, and establish new meanings of positive and constructive behavior.

Eating Disorders

Adolescent females seem particularly prone to developing eating disorders. We will discuss the reasons for these problems and emphasize two major types of eating disorders common during adolescence: Anorexia Nervosa and Bulimia Nervosa.

Anorexia Nervosa

Anorexia Nervosa (literally, nervous loss of appetite) is an eating disorder in which individuals starve themselves and have an intense fear of becoming overweight. Individuals with anorexia have a distorted body image and refuse to maintain normal weight. They try to lose weight by dieting, starving, exercising, and purging (Lask & Bryant-Waugh, 2000). Anorexic behavior takes two forms. The first is the *restricted type* where weight loss is achieved by restricting food. The second is the *binge-eating-purging type.* These individuals binge eat and then, when overstuffed, they purge the food by inducing vomiting (Israel & Wicks-Nelson, 2003). This eating disorder might affect 1 in every 200 adolescent girls, and it occurs more often in females than males (Fairbum, Welch, Norman, O'Connor, & Doll, 1996). Some behavioral changes in anorexics include depression, social withdrawal, irritability, and moodiness (American Academy of Child and Adolescent Psychiatry [AACAP], 2001).

Family dysfunction can perpetuate the maladaptive behavior of anorexics. Palazzoli (1974) has characterized families of anorexics as systems that are rigid. These parents also show inflexibility, overinvolvement, and conflict avoidance (Minuchin, Rosman, & Baker, 1978). Family members appear to provide the contingencies that enable anorexic behavior. At the same time, images in the culture and pressure to be thin are factors for the development of eating disorders. Many adolescent females are highly influenced by the typically thin models portrayed in the media. Interestingly, eating disorders are far more common in societies that value thinness than in those societies where thinness is not reinforced (Lask & Bryant-Waugh, 2000).

Behavioral Treatment for Anorexia Nervosa

The treatment for anorexics includes family therapy and the use of behavioral techniques to change these individuals' eating behaviors. Some of the behavioral techniques used in anorexic individuals include operant conditioning techniques, social skills training, and systematic desensitization.

Operant Conditioning Techniques. These procedures are employed by therapists to establish eating and facilitate weight gain for severe, hospitalized anorexic patients (Bachrach, Erwin, & Mohr, 1965). Operant conditioning techniques involve the use of positive and negative reinforcements, such as social praise and, later, hospital release, contingent on gradual increases in either food eaten or weight gain (Leitenberg, Agras, & Thompson, 1968). Operant procedures are most useful at the beginning of a comprehensive program and should not be used as a single treatment (Craighead, Kazdin, & Mahoney, 1981).

Social Skills Training. Social skills training is used to overcome deficits in social competence and problem-solving skills seen in anorexic and bulimic patients. Training in social skills may allow these adolescents to build up more self-control (Foreyt, Poston, Winebarger, & McGavin, 1998). They may also reduce anxiety in social situations.

Systematic Desensitization. This behavioral technique has been used to inhibit the anxiety associated with a morbid fear of weight and with irrational thoughts present in patients with eating disorders (Foreyt, Poston, Winebarger, & McGavin, 1998). As anxiety dissipates during the intervention period, there is an assumption that the expected behavioral change in the real-life setting would generalize and that the adolescents would gradually feel less anxious in different settings (Leitenberg et al., 1968).

Bulimia Nervosa

Bulimia Nervosa, also called binge-purge syndrome, is characterized by the reoccurrence of binge eating and purging activities such as self-induced vomiting and use of laxatives (AACAP, 2001). As with anorexics, bulimic individuals are overly concerned with their body image and getting fat (Fabes & Martin, 2000). A number of medical problems can occur with bulimia. Psychological and behavioral disturbances may include depression, low self-esteem, and intense mood swings (AACAP, 2001).

Behavioral Treatments for Bulimic Behavior

Bulimia is treated through behavior–analytic programs and behavioral techniques, such as antecedent control and self-monitoring techniques (Foreyt et al., 1998). These treatments are designed to reinforce intake and stop self-induced purging of the ingested food.

Antecedent Control. This behavioral technique consists of controlling factors previous to a binge. Particular feeling states, such as anxiety and food deprivation, may be some of the preceding factors setting factors or establishing operations. For example, food deprivation is the establishing operation, which leads to a smaller stomach that becomes full with less amounts of food. The discriminative stimulus is the adolescent feeling full, triggering the belief that he or she will get fat and ugly and be rejected by others. The response to this stimulus is the purging of the contents in the stomach, which leads to the reinforcing feeling that he or she is no longer full and will not get fat (the perceived consequence).

Self-Monitoring Techniques. Self-monitoring techniques are helpful for a majority of individuals with eating disorders, especially for bulimics. Through systematic self-monitoring, patients observe and record the specific environment involved in binge eating, including the tacting (labeling) of associated feelings of anxiety and previous thoughts (Foreyt et al., 1998). Tacting feelings of anxiety and previous thoughts are what we call private events in behavior analysis. Agras, Schneider, Arnow, Raeburn, and Telch (1989) conducted a study in which the effectiveness of self-monitoring techniques alone and cognitive behavior treatments that included self-monitoring techniques were compared. These researchers concluded that cognitive interventions, such as self-provided reinforcement, in conjunction with self-monitoring techniques were more effective in encouraging positive changes and reducing purging than self-monitoring techniques alone, although the latter were effective as well. Their study suggests that self-monitoring should be employed as part of the entire treatment of eating-behavior disorders.

Adolescent Depression

The most obvious aspect of **depression** in adolescence is a marked decrease in the frequency of certain behaviors and activities and an increase in the occurrence of **avoidance** and **escape** behaviors (Ferster, 1974). An example of avoidance and escape behaviors is staying in bed all day and not socializing or participating with others. In adolescents, the prevalence of clinical depression ranges from 4% to 12% (Kazdin & Marciano, 1998).

Behavioral Manifestations of Depression and Causes

The symptoms and behavioral manifestations of depression include social withdrawal, fatigue, difficulty in concentrating, expressed feeling of worthlessness, and dysphoria to name a few (AACAP, 2001). According to behavioral theory, most depressed people show a reduced frequency of emission of positively reinforced activities, such as lack of engagement in social situations, including talking to a friend (Friedman & Katz, 1974). Studies have showed that depression runs in families. Those adolescents with depressive parents (same environment) are more likely to suffer from depression (Kazdin & Marciano, 1998). Parents of depressed adolescents serve as models and tend to use more punishment, show less affection, and initiate more disagreement than parents of nondepressed individuals (Kaslow, Brown, & Mee, 1994). Thus, depressive behavior in adolescents could be directly related to negative family interactions where there are high levels of stress.

Explanations for the increase in the prevalence of depression and anxiety during adolescence take into account the various transitions the adolescent encounters during this time. Various critical changes occur during adolescence. Among the most important environmental and organismic factors are changes in physical appearance, school settings, the onset of dating, sexual pressure, greater peer influence, greater responsibilities, and preparation for employment and autonomy. If all these factors are faced gradually and experienced with family support, the adolescent may learn useful coping strategies, but if they're faced all at once, the adolescent may feel stressed and overwhelmed (Koenig & Gladstone, 1998).

For early-maturing females, these changes may appear too soon and in too synchronous a manner, taxing their coping resources beyond their abilities and resulting in depressive symptoms (Koenig & Gladstone, 1998). From a behavioral systems view, these changes disrupt the adolescent's patterns of interactions developed during childhood. The result of these disruptions is that existing behaviors produce less reinforcement until new patterns of interactions emerge.

Consequences Maintaining Depressive Behaviors

Neurochemical imbalances in serotonin, dopamine, cortisol, and epinephrine, as well an environmental difficulties such as social isolation, maltreatment, and anxiety, have been associated with depression. However, in this chapter we have emphasized the antecedents, the consequences, and the contextual determinants of behavior (e.g., organismic and physiological factors). All these factors for depressive behaviors in adolescents and their dynamic interactions need to be investigated to explain the depressive behavioral patterns. For instance, although a stressful environment may lead to certain depressive behaviors (e.g., crying, negative self-statements, sad affect, disrupted patterns of earlier behavior), familial reaction to such behaviors may also inadvertently reinforce such responses to stress, thus maintaining the depressive behavior. This is what we have identified as dynamic and reciprocal interactions.

Parents of depressed adolescents provide more sympathetic-type responses to depressive behaviors than do parents of nondepressed adolescents (Shecker, Hops, Andrews, Alpert, & Davis, 1998). For example, some studies have found that mothers were found to display increased problem-solving and facilitative behaviors (positively reinforcing behavior via attention, negatively reinforcing behavior via the elimination of the stressor). Fathers exhibited decreased aggressiveness (negative reinforcement functioning as avoidance for the adolescent), contingent on the adolescent's depressive behavior (Shecker et al., 1998). This process eventually serves to maintain maladaptive coping strategies in the young adult.

Cognitive–Behavioral Therapy for Depression

Adolescent perceptions of the family have been linked to the presence of both depressive and antisocial behaviors. High levels of negative perceptions of their families correspond strongly with depressive symptoms in the adolescent (Garnefski, 2000). This is why cognitive–behavioral therapy is often useful to treat the adolescent's perceptions (thoughts manifested in verbal behavior).

Because it is effective in treating self-generated verbalized misperceptions, **cognitive–behavioral therapy** is the most commonly used treatment for depression in adolescents. The main goal of cognitive therapy is to confront and alter maladaptive cognitive processes, such as misconstructions or erroneous perceptions of the self—for instance, when an individual is constantly thinking, "I'm a failure. I'm not good at anything." Behavioral therapy, on the other hand, focuses on increasing gratifying experiences and specific response repertoires—that is, on shaping replacement behaviors. Behavioral therapy provides response-contingent reinforcements for the social skills of depressed individuals. Although these two therapies have different goals, they are usually integrated to treat depression because "more adaptive cognitions are hypothesized to lead to more adaptive behavior patterns and vice versa" (Kazdin & Marciano, 1998, p. 226).

Acceptance and Commitment Therapy

Acceptance and commitment therapy (ACT) is a contemporary behavioral approach that takes a different approach to the treatment of depression and other psychological problems: The relationship between thoughts and feelings, on the one hand, and overt behavior, on the other, is itself to be understood *contextually*. Thus, rather than ignoring thoughts and feelings, avoiding them, or trying to change them, as traditionally done in cognitive–behavior therapy, an alternative is used. ACT recontextualizes the relationship between thoughts and feelings and overt behavior. In the ACT approach, the goal is to help depressed adolescents feel what they feel, think what they think, and do what needs to be done. Accomplishing these goals requires (a) challenging the verbal context in which the adolescent and the therapist construe the past and problems of the present and (b) finding potential solutions. The main goal is the adolescent's acceptance of private thoughts (or private events), the realization or clarification of his or her personal values, and an increased willingness to commit to behavior change that is recognized as needed.

ACT is theoretically based on **relational frame theory** (RFT) (see Chapters 7 and 8). The ACT approach has been used to treat multiproblem adolescent patients dealing with issues such as anxiety, substance abuse, and fears. It is a scientifically based approach to human behavior. The approach is receiving increasing attention from empirically oriented clinical psychologists, and there is supportive data for its use (e.g., Dougher, 2002; Wilson, Hayes, Gregg, & Zettle, 1991).

Other Behavioral Interventions

Behavioral treatment programs for the most part are based on a multicomponent approach (e.g., McLean, 1981). The treatment program for depression should improve the performance of depressed adolescents in the areas of social interaction, behavioral productivity, and reduction of high-risk behavior. Social interaction is a powerful source of social reinforcement because it allows the adolescent to obtain positive feedback from others, especially peers. At the same time, social interactions allow depressed people to engage in alternative activities, given that these tend to be incompatible with disturbing self-preoccupation.

Social skills should be shaped and encouraged in depressed adolescents. They should be reinforced especially because the adolescent tends to be self-absorbed and excluded from social interactions. To assist depressed adolescents, therapists help structure and plan positive social interactions as well as the types and number of them. Social skill training usually includes communication training between the patient and a significant other.

Behavioral productivity encourages depressed individuals to reinforce themselves, and it allows the individual to identify the problems associated with his or her ineffective performance. Behavior therapists usually follow these steps: (a) separate goals that need to be performed into small tasks, (b) make sure that the behavioral goals are significant to the client's needs, (c) ask clients to monitor daily behavior patterns and negotiate task assignments, and (d) give positive reinforcement contingent on successful performance. Because depressed individuals show cognitive distortions based on their descriptions of reality and negative thoughts such as "I am not worthy," cognitive control should be part of the treatment of depression. The behavior therapist will teach the patient to focus on solutions instead of the reason for the depression (McLean, 1981). (For further information on depression in adolescence, refer to Chapter 15.)

Adolescent Suicide

Along with increases in depression, suicide is a common problem faced during adolescence. Studies report that suicide claims the lives of nearly 2,000 teens each year and has become the third leading cause of death among teenagers. Gender differences show that females tend to attempt suicide with greater frequency than do males, but males are more successful in their attempts; homosexuals have higher suicide rates than the general population (Popenhagen & Qualley, 1998). Variables such as the presence of depressive and disruptive disorders, disadvantaged families, little support from parents and peers, low self-esteem, history of suicide in the family or friends—all increase the risk for attempted suicide in adolescents (Groholt, Ekebery, Wichstrom, & Haldorsen, 2000).

Intervention and Prevention of Adolescent Suicide

Interventions for crisis situations are also important given the incidence of suicide during adolescence. When intervening with suicidal adolescents, it is critical to create a no-suicide contract, instantly remove all potentially harmful objects from the home, refrain from using condescending statements, and, if necessary, employ hospitalization (Popenhagen & Qualley, 1998). Having strategies available for suicide prevention is recommended. The adolescent usually gives behavioral signals and cues that he or she may be considering suicide. These may include verbalizations of suicidal wishes, previous threats, and the giving away of previously important belongings. Parents and educators should be informed of the key symptoms related to adolescent suicide, become aware of the common myths associated with suicide, and never discard any verbal threats or wishes an adolescent might have of killing oneself (Popenhagen & Qualley, 1998). Imperative to suicide prevention is an awareness of the warning signs and the potential cries for help.

During an episode of depression, negative mood occurs alongside negative thinking and bodily sensations of fatigue and physical or mental weariness. Some of the best-known cognitive–behavioral research therapists (e.g., Segal, Williams, & Teasdale, 2002; Williams, 2002) claim that an association is learned between the various symptoms so that when small amounts of negative mood occur again (for any reason) they will tend to trigger all the other symptoms. There is now considerable evidence that these old habits of negative feeling and thinking are an important part of a "kindling" process that makes further full-blown episodes of depression conducive to suicidal behavior more easily triggered.

Mindfulness-based cognitive therapy (MBCT) (Segal et al., 2002) emphasizes the research finding that even when the adolescent may feel well, the link between negative moods and negative thoughts remains ready to be reactivated, and this is of enormous importance for effective treatment. It means that sustaining recovery from depression depends on learning how to keep mild states of depression and behavior associated with it from spiraling out of control (Teasdale et al., 2000).

High-Risk Adolescent Behavior

Adolescents tend to take more risks than any other age group. As a result, adolescents tend to have a higher incidence of mortality. In fact, accidents, suicides, and homicides account for more than 85% of all adolescents' deaths (Spear, 2000). Risk-taking behaviors can also escalate into deviant lifestyles, such as alcohol or drug dependency. However, most adolescents can survive the negative outcomes involved in risk-taking behavior. High-risk behavior has also been associated with some positive outcomes. For example, risk taking can sometimes be associated with gains in self-esteem, possibly because of reinforcement from peers engaged in similar behavior (Spear, 2000). Prevalence of high-risk behaviors may be due in part to the relative ineffectiveness of their natural contingencies' ability to prevent them. Malott (2001) argues that natural contingencies (which in this case include getting into an accident, drug overdose, contracting a sexually transmitted disease, etc.) are ineffective in controlling behavior if they involve outcomes that are (or are perceived to be) too improbable or remote. Adolescents might feel that possible negative consequences to their high-risk behavior are unlikely to occur to them, which renders these natural contingencies ineffective.

Substance Abuse

Many adolescents also engage in substance abuse. It is documented that the use of illicit drugs, alcohol, and cigarettes is quite prevalent in the United States. According to the National Institute of Drug Abuse, 50% of high school seniors have used marijuana, 65% have smoked cigarettes, and 82% have consumed alcohol (Spear, 2000). Adolescents can become physically and behaviorally dependent on these substances if taken in considerable amounts. Those adolescents who consume alcohol can experience escalating use toward abuse and have difficulty quitting.

Mid-adolescents who smoke cigarettes can show addictive signs to nicotine. Adolescents using drugs tend to be polydrug users, which may aggravate the effect of drugs. In fact, many adolescents who enter rehabilitation programs for drug and alcohol treatment also smoke cigarettes and show depressive behaviors (Field et al., 1998).

One factor that helps to initiate the use of alcohol and other drugs is adolescents' pursuing and accessing new reinforcers. Another factor is adolescents' level of stress and depression (Field et al., 1998). Changes in body composition, brain development, and organ functioning common during adolescence have also been linked to differences in adolescent drug responsiveness relative to an adult. Also, adolescents may exhibit insensitivity to certain drugs, which can result in greater use per occasion when compared with an adult (Spear, 2000).

Behavioral Treatment for Substance Abuse

Behavioral principles and procedures have been used to reduce or eliminate an individual's high-risk behavior.

Shaping. Shaping (Chapter 6) means reinforcing successive approximations of the target behavior. It is one of the most effective procedures used to create new repertoires or modify old behavior patterns (Mash & Barkley, 1998). Shaping involves reinforcing better and better patterns; for example, a therapist may reinforce an alcoholic adolescent for having four instead of five drinks, and subsequently, once this lower behavior intake is stable, the therapist will reinforce only for lower levels of the response—that is, three instead of four drinks a day. This process will continue until the adolescent stops drinking altogether. This is a technique known as differential reinforcement of low rate (DRL) of behavior (discussed in Chapter 6) and can also be implemented to reduce smoking behavior and any substance abuse.

Another technique used to change behavior involves establishing a behavioral repertoire, which involves teaching individuals skills to engage in alternate behaviors. This technique is known as differential reinforcement of alternative behaviors (DRA; discussed in Chapter 6) and is used to replace or modify the undesired target behavior. Eisler, Miller, Hersen, and Alford (1974) showed the effectiveness of teaching alcoholics assertive skills to refuse drinking (as cited in Sobell & Sobell, 1978).

Contingency Management Strategies. Contingency management is another behavioral principle widely used to modify maladaptive behavior. Contingency management involves arranging an individual's environment so that it provides positive consequences for desired outcomes and negative ones to undesired outcomes (Mash & Barkley, 1998). Hunt and Azrin (1973) provided evidence for the effectiveness of this technique by treating chronic alcoholics. They implemented a community reinforcement model in which social, familial, and economic rewards were delivered contingent on sobriety (not drinking alcohol).

They found that after 6 months, the community-reinforced group spent less time drinking, hospitalized, and unemployed than a matched control group.

Tangible reinforcers such as small amounts of money, tokens, show tickets, and vouchers for fast food have been successfully used to promote drug abstinence. Reinforcement can be contingent on clean urine tests, compliance with treatment plan recommendations, and attendance at treatment sessions. Success has been met by using schedules of reinforcement that can either be at a fixed ratio (same level of reinforcement for each negative drug test) or at a progressive rate (progressively increasing levels of reinforcement contingent on continuous negative drug tests) (Higgins et al., 1993).

High-Risk Sexual Behavior

Adolescents are more likely to have multiple and higher risk sex partners, engage in unprotected sex, and are among the age groups most at risk for acquiring a sexually transmitted disease. Social skills have been identified as possible factors that lead to healthy or unhealthy sexual behavior. Certain social skills have been identified as crucial to the engagement in healthy sexual behavior. These include the ability to appropriately initiate, maintain, or decline sexual activity; communicate important sexual information to a partner; carry through with safe sex practices; and make informed sexual decisions (Nangle, Carr, & Hansen, 1999).

Social Reinforcers in Sexual Behavior

Social reinforcers also play a role in the engagement of healthy versus unhealthy sexual behavior. Peer influence and acceptance of such behaviors have an effect on the occurrences of these behaviors. An example of this would be a case in which some teenage boys may engage in a competition to see who can sleep with the most girls. Elevated status or praise may function as reinforcers following the engagement in such high-risk behavior or while the behavior is occurring. In a similar way, the adolescent may also be more prone to engage in unhealthy sexual behavior based on the immediacy of the positive and pleasurable consequences (gratification and approval) relative to the delayed and remote negative or detrimental consequences.

Behavioral Intervention for High-Risk Sexual Behavior

Interventions incorporating the use of social skills training are very popular. Learning how to say "no" for abstinence or learning how to request and expect safe sex practices from a partner is crucial. The adolescent in these interventions is trained to accept the possible negative consequences that accompany healthy sexual decisions. It is true that such consequences may involve immediate rejection, embarrassment, and anxiety. But learning what to expect has shown promise in encouraging better decision making in the choice and number of sexual partners. Such interventions include the modeling of rule-governed behavior as crucial to engaging in safer-sex behavior. Examples of techniques also include (a) role-playing situations in which an adolescent proposes the use of a condom, discloses having a sexually transmitted disease, or rejects a sexual advance from a stranger and (b) a set of rules that outline the unhealthy consequences.

● LOVE AND ROMANTIC RELATIONS

In addition to the hormonal determinants of sexual initiation such as serum androgenic hormones, which motivate sexual behavior in adolescent boys (Udry, Billy, Morris, Groff, & Raj, 1985), it is important to understand the aspect of adolescence that involves romantic relations and love. The question of interest is, Why do we fall in love with a particular person? The answer lies in the contingencies of reinforcement, of course. We do not "fall in love" with just any person. Choosing a romantic partner among many other potential partners is a process of mate selection.

Researchers have found that we are most likely to fall in love with someone who is attractive to us, who has proximity to us, and who matches us in some characteristic, such as socioeconomic status, intellectual performance, educational history, ethnic practices, religious beliefs, or some combination of these. When we say that opposites attract, we may mean that even though some behavior patterns are not similar, they are still very reinforcing for each other. These characteristics are the sources of the most powerful reinforcers known to us. Cross-cultural studies on love attitudes and behavior patterns have shown the importance of partners in a culture matching all these behavioral characteristics.

Cross-Cultural and Gender Comparison of Love Attitudes in Late Adolescence

Despite the importance of romantic relations and experiences in adolescence, research on this topic has been surprisingly limited in psychology. This line of research (Rodríguez, Montgomery, Peláez, & Salas, in press) seeks to add to what is known about adolescents' romantic experiences by investigating "love attitudes and behaviors" in late adolescence. The authors conducted a preliminary study investigating dating experiences in a sample of 257 late adolescents whose mean age was 20 years across three Spanish-speaking cultures: adolescent students from Spain, Mexico, and the United States (Miami). The researchers (Rodríguez et al., in press) made comparisons using Spanish versions of the Love Attitudes Scale and the Dating Experience Scale, which indicate both gender differences and cultural differences on several subscales.

Findings of this study were interpreted in light of courtship-related socialization behavioral practices associated with intracultural traditions. The results revealed that both gender differences and cultural differences exist on several subscales. More important, the differences between adolescents' attitudes toward love and romantic relations related to gender-specific socialization practices in the different cultural traditions. For example, the extent of dating experience was greatest in students from Miami, Florida and least among students from Mexico.

ADOLESCENT ATTACHMENT AND SEPARATION ●

Just as with very young children, as we discussed on Chapter 10, adolescents often show attachment patterns and attachment disorders. Attachment patterns between romantic partners are learned. Separation protests are an index of attachment formation; this is a phenomenon that results from operant learning, and it is not exclusive to any particular age. The acquisition, shape, and rate of separation protests (behaviors such as crying, showing distress, or nagging upon departures) can be reduced or increased depending on the power of the reinforcing stimuli—that is, the contingencies provided by the romantic partner or attachment figure, just as in the case of mother–child separation protest documented in the developmental literature (Gewirtz & Peláez-Nogueras, 1991a, 1992b). Romantically involved partners may suffer from behaviors denoting anxiety, distress, and despair after separation, and they experience regaining joyfulness and proximity seeking after reunion with the loved one.

SUMMARY ●

The term *adolescence* pertains to behavioral changes occurring between childhood and maturity relating to sexual maturation, increasingly sophisticated reasoning abilities, development of *rule-governed behavior,* increased social and emotional independence, new educational settings, and changing behavioral expectations.

Increased gonadal hormone production produces *growth spurts* and has been associated with enhanced cognitive functioning. The onset of puberty takes place, during which the adolescent reaches sexual maturity. The consequences for timing of physical development vary with gender. Early-maturing boys generally experience more positive outcomes than their female counterparts. However, overall, early maturation is associated with an increased likelihood of engaging in risky behaviors. A number of environmental factors, including nutrition and quality of family interaction, may exert a significant influence on development during this time.

Adolescence is also marked by use of abstract and critical thinking skills. There is a shift from moral realism to moral relativism, and moral judgments approximate those made by adults. *Moral behavior* is learned behavior that can be shaped by social contingencies.

Another major theme during adolescence is the formation of *identity*. Identity refers to self-questioning regarding who one is, where one is going, and what one's place is in society. The term *identity crisis* refers to the sense of turmoil one experiences as a result of this questioning. The source of this crisis is thought to stem from the relative instability in factors influencing development during adolescence, including physiological changes, emerging physical characteristics, and a shift from family to peer influence. Struggles with gender identity may also contribute to the identity crisis. Although some suggest that the identity crisis characterizes the period of adolescence and results in the emergence of an entirely different person, others posit that development proceeds in a much more consistent manner, personality formation being more continuous. It is important to recognize that identity development is complex, highly variable, and characterized by both continuity and disturbances in the pathways of development.

Another important struggle during adolescence is the striving for *autonomy*. The style of parenting employed during this time can significantly affect behavior, particularly high-risk behaviors. The best outcomes have been associated with the use of an *authoritative* parenting style. During this time, the influence of peers also becomes salient. Although peers may help develop social skills, they may also model maladaptive behaviors. The influence of the parent is illustrated in the adolescent's choice of friends. As individuals tend to actively engage the environment so as to maintain consistency, adolescents will tend to choose friends on the basis of the values acquired from their parents.

Significant shifts in the complex interactions of factors affecting development can sometimes produce behavioral attractor states that are considered abnormal and that constitute behavior disorders. *Antisocial behavior* is thought to be the result of the *coercive family process* and may culminate with the development of an antisocial personality in adulthood. In adolescence, antisocial behavior may warrant a diagnosis of *Conduct Disorder,* characterized by aggression, oppositional behavior, and other disruptive and rebellious behaviors. Such disorders may be treated effectively with a range of behavioral techniques. The use of positive reinforcement combined with mild punishment has been shown to be more efficient in modifying behavior than the use of either technique alone. Behavioral programs and family therapy may also be used with success.

Adolescent females appear to be at greater risk than males of suffering from eating disorders such as *Anorexia Nervosa* and *Bulimia Nervosa.* Individuals with anorexia have a distorted body image, refuse to maintain a normal weight, and engage in either restricted type (e.g., starving) or binge-eating-purging behavior due to an excessive fear of becoming overweight. Families of such individuals are characterized by rigidity, overinvolvement, and conflict avoidance, and they often perpetuate maladaptive behavior through contingencies. External factors such as media and social pressure also contribute to the behavior of those with anorexia. Treatment for this disorder includes family therapy and the use of behavioral techniques, including operant conditioning, social skills training, and systematic desensitization. Bulimia Nervosa is characterized by cyclical binge eating and purging activities. The disorder also involves an obsession with body image and becoming fat. Medical, psychological, and behavioral disturbances are the result. Treatments for bulimia include behavior–analytic programs and behavioral techniques, such as antecedent control and self-monitoring techniques.

Adolescent *depression* is characterized by decreased frequency of certain behaviors and increased avoidance and escape behaviors. Depression has often been attributed to neurochemical imbalances. However, the consequences of depressive behavior can also explain depressive symptoms. From a behavioral systems perspective, the critical changes taking place during adolescence disturb patterns of interactions developed in childhood so that established behaviors result in less reinforcement. Families may inadvertently create contingencies that reinforce and maintain depressive behavior. *Cognitive–behavioral therapies* are often integrated in the treatment of depression because of their complementary effects on maladaptive cognitive processes and behaviors, respectively. Behavioral programs and cognitive–behavior therapies aimed at improving social interaction, behavioral productivity, and cognitive control or *acceptance* and *choice* may also be useful.

The presence of depressive and disruptive disorders, low self-esteem, and nonfacilitative environmental factors all increase the risk of attempted suicide for adolescents. Important aspects of suicide intervention include (a) the creation of a no-suicide contract, (b) removal of potentially harmful objects from the home, (c) refraining from the use of condescending statements, (d) consideration of inpatient hospitalization and (e) mindfulness therapy, among others. It is important for parents and educators to be aware of the warning signs and to treat verbal threats and wishes regarding self-harm seriously.

Adolescents tend to engage in more *high-risk behaviors* than any other age group. *Substance abuse* can turn into dependence and become highly problematic. Behavioral principles such as shaping, the establishment of behavioral repertoires that include alternate behaviors, and contingency management strategies may be useful in treating substance abuse. High-risk sexual behavior is also likely to produce negative outcomes for adolescents. Interventions that incorporate the use of social skills training include modeling of assertive behavior, and the use of role-playing can be effective in reducing such behavior in adolescents.

CHAPTER **15**

BEHAVIOR DISORDERS
OF CHILDHOOD

E arly in development, some children struggle to speak, listen, read, write, reason, or learn math. Others show difficulty in socializing with peers and adults or in regulating their emotions. Although variations in behaviors exist across children, for some children, their behaviors are sufficiently deviant and problematic to warrant attention. Numerous childhood behavior disorders and learning disabilities have been identified in the literature, and special educators have created the controversial category called "exceptional children" to label these individuals. Any textbook on exceptionalities lists dozen of definitions of diverse learning disabilities (e.g., Hallahan, Kauffman, & Lloyd, 2000). In contrast, we focus on those few behavior disorders and learning disabilities that posit serious lifelong threats to the child. These behaviors may serve as developmental cusps that when they occur have serious consequences for the behavioral of lifelong behavior problems. We discuss some early diagnoses and early behavioral interventions that are extremely important in precluding further developmental delays and that prevent the onset of other maladaptive behavior patterns. In our view, these behavior problems often arise from disparate organismic and environmental factors that dynamically interact.

As we emphasized in Chapter 2, a behavioral systems approach to development acknowledges both nature and nurture as determinants of behavior. Innate and acquired behavioral disabilities are a function of selection by consequences involving phylogenic and ontogenic contingencies. The ontogenic contingencies of learning have been stressed in this textbook, and we have argued that they contribute to the behavioral history of an individual, work their effects through the reinforcement of behavior, and bridge past and present via nongenetic biological factors.

In this chapter, we discuss the genesis of disorders arising in the interactions between genetic, physiological, and family–environmental components. We have selected the most prevalent childhood behavior disorders, including Oppositional Defiant Disorder, Conduct Disorder, Mental Retardation, Attention Deficit/Hyperactivity Disorder, autism, depression, and anxiety. Depression in adolescence was discussed in the previous chapter, but here we discuss the issues relevant to childhood depression. Other behavior disorders that also occur during childhood and adolescence such as anorexia, bulimia, suicidal tendencies, substance abuse, and sexually transmitted diseases were also addressed in the previous chapter.

● WHAT ARE BEHAVIOR DISORDERS?

The primary authority for the identification of behavior disorders is the *Diagnostic and Statistical Manual of Mental Disorders (DSM)* of the American

Psychiatric Association (APA). The current version, **DSM-IV-TR** (APA, 2000) is a text revision of the fourth edition and is the result of years of refinement by panels of psychiatrists, psychologists, and others in the clinical field. The next version, *DSM-V*, a further refinement, is due in 2010.

The *DSM-IV-TR* contains hundreds of identified disorders, most of which are oriented toward adults. Of most relevance here is the category called "Behavior Disorders Usually First Diagnosed in Infancy, Childhood, or Adolescence." The main categories in this area are as follows:

- Mental Retardation
- Learning disorders
  - Mathematics Disorder
  - Reading Disorder
  - Disorder of Written Expression
- Motor skills disorders
  - Developmental Coordination Disorder
- Communication disorders
  - Developmental Language Disorder
  - Expressive Language Disorder
  - Phonological Disorder
  - Mixed Receptive-Expressive Language Disorder
  - Stuttering
- Pervasive developmental disorders
  - Asperger's Disorder
  - Autistic Disorder
  - Childhood Disintegrative Disorder
  - Rett's Disorder
- Attention deficit and disruptive behavior disorders
  - Attention Deficit/ Hyperactivity Disorder
  - Conduct Disorder
  - Oppositional Defiant Disorder
- Feeding and eating disorders of infancy or early childhood
  - Pica
  - Rumination Disorder
- Tic disorders
  - Chronic Motor or Vocal Tic Disorder
  - Tourette's Disorder
- Elimination disorders
  - Encopresis
  - Eneuresis
- Other disorders of infancy, childhood, or adolescence
  - Selective Mutism
  - Separation Anxiety Disorder
  - Reactive Attachment Disorder of Infancy or Early Childhood
  - Stereotypic Movement Disorder

These disorders are most clearly developmental in nature, and, as mentioned earlier, the most prevalent of these will be the focus of this chapter.

Our definition of **behavior disorders** is that they are organized patterns of behavior, or **attractors,** that deviate from an arbitrary or socially determined standard or norm. According to this definition, these behaviors are not unique from nondisordered behaviors, but their frequency and the way they are organized make them of special interest. The individual behaviors we find in behavior disorders deviate from the accepted normal pattern in one of three ways: they may be excessive, deficient, or occur under the wrong circumstances.

Excessive Behaviors. These are patterns of behavior that occur at a rate or intensity that is considered above a normal range. For example, all children have some difficulty paying attention at times and move about and fidget. However, when this occurs excessively and causes difficulty with parents and teachers, the child may be identified with **Attention Deficit/Hyperactivity Disorder** (ADHD).

Deficient Behaviors. These are patterns of behavior that occur too infrequently, with too little intensity, or not at all. This category would include poor reading and math behaviors (i.e., learning disorders) and poor cognitive behaviors (i.e., Mental Retardation).

Behaviors Occurring Under the Wrong Conditions. Sometimes behaviors occur but to the wrong S^d or under the wrong setting event. **Selective mutism** is a condition in which a child may speak with a perfectly normal frequency at home or at play but does not speak at all in school. Similarly, even a single episode of public masturbation is problematic, although it would be a problem in private only if it were excessive.

● BEHAVIOR DISORDERS USUALLY FIRST DIAGNOSED IN INFANCY, CHILDHOOD, OR ADOLESCENCE

Individual behaviors become organized into patterns or attractor states much like we find in personality (see Chapter 9). Commonly occurring patterns of behavior have been identified and labeled. When a child's behavior fits into these attractor states, we often say that he or she "has" a behavior disorder. We must be cautious that we do not fall into the trap of *reifying* the behaviors and turning them into an entity. The behavior disorder labels are descriptions of these organized patterns of behavior. It is an error to take them as explanations. If we do so, we may erroneously treat behavior disorders as the cause of behaviors rather than what they are—descriptions of the organized patterns of behavior themselves. Thus, we want to avoid making statements such as, "He's banging his head because he has autism," or "She can't sit still because she has ADHD".

In Chapter 2, we introduced the problem of reification in developmental psychology. As you recall, reification is treating something abstract as if it is a real or physical thing. Reification is a common problem in the area of behavior disorders and is any easy error to make. It occurs when we diagnose a child's problem from the observed behaviors and then treat the diagnosis as a real entity. Thus, once we use the child's behaviors to give us the diagnosis of autism or ADHD, we start to say, "The child has autism" or "The child has ADHD" as if these were things inside the child, much like we say, "The child has the flu." Reification also occurs when we say, "The child is autistic." The problem is that we then use this "thing" in a circular manner to explain the behavior that was used to diagnose in the first place. So we easily fall into saying things such as, "Joey can't sit still because he has ADHD." Or we may say, "Mary won't interact with you because she's autistic." In fact, based on the diagnostic categories we have, what these children do "have" are certain organized patterns of behavior that coalesced under their own unique genetic, physiological, and environmentally established developmental histories.

A typical example of one of the *DSM* diagnostic categories is shown in Table 15.1. Two things are of particular note. First, the diagnosis or categorization of the disorder is based on observed behaviors of the child. That is, these are descriptions of behavior disorders. Second, there is variation in how the behaviors are organized. Not all autistic children have all the behaviors. Instead, each autistic child may have a unique organization of behaviors. That is the case with the other categories as well.

WHAT CAUSES BEHAVIOR DISORDERS? ●

It is our strong view that behavior disorders are the result of the same developmental process as other behaviors. They are the result of the constant interactions between the five factors we identified in Chapter 2: genetic–constitutional, historical, physiological, environmental, and behavior dynamical interactions. Although there are clear genetic–constitutional origins identified in some disorders, such as Down syndrome where there is an extra Number 21 chromosome, with many disorders there is, as yet, no known genetic or physiological cause. With others, such as Mental Retardation, there are hundreds of known genetic or chromosomal contributors, yet for most individuals diagnosed with Mental Retardation there is no known biological cause. Just as there is typically no single pattern with behavior disorders identified in *DSM-IV-TR*, there is unlikely to be a single cause. Behavior disorders are characterized by the same principles of multiple determinism and equifinality that apply to all development. Recall that multiple determinism means that many factors in interaction produce an outcome. Equifinality means that individuals with the same characteristics may have developed them through very different combinations of different factors.

Table 15.1   Diagnostic Criteria for 299.00 Autistic Disorder

A. A total of six (or more) items from (1), (2), and (3), with at least two from (1), and one each from (2) and (3):

1. Qualitative impairment in social interaction, as manifested by at least two of the following:
   a. marked impairment in the use of multiple nonverbal behaviors such as eye-to-eye gaze, facial expression, body postures, and gestures to regulate social interaction
   b. failure to develop peer relationships appropriate to developmental level
   c. a lack of spontaneous seeking to share enjoyment, interests, or achievements with other people (e.g., by a lack of showing, bringing, or pointing out objects of interest)
   d. lack of social or emotional reciprocity

2. Qualitative impairments in communication as manifested by at least one of the following:
   a. delay in, or total lack of, the development of spoken language (not accompanied by an attempt to compensate through alternative modes of communication such as gesture or mime)
   b. in individuals with adequate speech, marked impairment in the ability to initiate or sustain a conversation with others
   c. stereotyped and repetitive use of language or idiosyncratic language
   d. lack of varied, spontaneous make-believe play or social imitative play appropriate to developmental level

3. Restricted repetitive and stereotyped patterns of behavior, interests, and activities, as manifested by at least one of the following:
   a. encompassing preoccupation with one or more stereotyped and restricted patterns of interest that is abnormal either in intensity or focus
   b. apparently inflexible adherence to specific, nonfunctional routines or rituals
   c. stereotyped and repetitive motor mannerisms (e.g., hand or finger flapping or twisting, or complex whole-body movements)
   d. persistent preoccupation with parts of objects

B. Delays or abnormal functioning in at least one of the following areas, with onset prior to age 3 years: (1) social interaction, (2) language as used in social communication, or (3) symbolic or imaginative play.

C. The disturbance is not better accounted for by Rett's Disorder or Childhood Disintegrative Disorder.

SOURCE: Reprinted with permission from *The Diagnostic and Statistical Manual of Mental Disorders,* Fourth Edition, Text Revision. Copyright 2000 American Psychiatric Association.

Thus, several children identified as autistic may have developed their behavior disorders from various combinations of factors interacting over very different developmental histories. Because it is unlikely that there is any simple, single cause of a behavior disorder, it is unlikely that any simple, single treatment will remedy an entire category.

ASSESSMENT OF BEHAVIOR DISORDERS ●

Many behavior disorders are assessed using standardized tests or checklists. For example, Mental Retardation is usually assessed by administering an individualized intelligence test, such as the WISC (Wechsler Intelligence Scale for Children) and Stanford-Binet (see Wicks-Nelson & Israel, 2003). ADHD is commonly assessed by having parents and teachers fill out a behavior checklist on the child's behavior at home and in school, respectively (Barkley, 1998). Basically, these devices sample the behavior of the child either directly, as in an intelligence test, or indirectly through the reports of others, as in a checklist. The purpose of this type of assessment is to diagnose or place the child in a category.

Generally speaking, for a family to receive professional services for their child through insurance or, in some cases, to be put in special school programs, a child must be provided with a *DSM-IV-TR* diagnosis. Because the *DSM-IV-TR* categories generally require assessment of behavior patterns, this generally means that the child must be diagnosed by a professional trained in the *DSM-IV-TR*. The result is that to receive treatment, a structural assessment is made of the child's behavior disorder that describes the child's characteristics and places him or her in the diagnostic categories. Unfortunately, because the disorders may have developed due to very different conditions, this type of diagnosis does not generally help identify a unique effective treatment.

Behavior analysts take a different tack. They focus on specific behaviors and their functions. So if a child is diagnosed as autistic, behavior analysts focus on the child's unique behavioral excesses and deficits directly and on the conditions that cause them. For example, they may focus on one autistic child's excessive self-stimulation and the same child's lack of language. Similarly, they may focus on two children's excessive self-stimulatory finger waving, even though one was diagnosed as autistic and the other as mentally retarded. To determine what causes the behavior, the behavior analyst focuses on the function of the problematic behavior, rather than on just a description of it, by using what is called functional assessment.

Functional Assessment

Functional assessment is used to identify specific variables that predict and maintain problem behavior. It follows the model of the four-term-contingency. The variables it considers consist of the setting events (or establishing operations), antecedents (or discriminative stimuli), and consequences (or reinforcing stimuli) that shaped and maintain the behavior. Through the use of functional assessment, the behavior analyst is able to focus on improving the child's overall level of functioning and maintain adaptive behavior.

Functional Analysis

Functional analysis differs from functional assessment in that it uses arrangements that entail actual exposure to the identified variables to determine their influences on problem behavior. Functional analysis is done through systematic observation and manipulation of the independent variable (Horner & Carr, 1997). An example of this is an autistic girl banging her head on the wall when a toy is out of her reach. Her mother responds by giving her the toy. In this example, the consequence of head banging and the antecedent is the out-of-reach toy. After several recorded observations, the behavior analyst begins to detect a systematic causal relation between the antecedent, the targeted behavior, and the consequences. That is, when the girl sees the toy (S^d), she bangs her head (R), and mom hands her the toy (S^{r+}).

On the other hand, in functional assessment, manipulation of the independent variable or treatment is not always undertaken. Sometimes a functional assessment without manipulating suspected variables may suffice to determine if these variables are indeed operative. If a child has not had access to her toy for a while (deprivation/setting event) and these toys are currently out of reach (antecedent), then the analyst may predict that the problem behavior has a higher probability of occurrence. So if time without the toy increases and the head banging increases, a functional relationship between the toy and head banging is assumed. In other situations, it has proved important to manipulate the likely relevant factors to discern what is actually going on. In either case, the focus is on determining under what conditions the behavior problem occurs.

● TYPES OF BEHAVIOR DISORDERS

The *DSM-IV-TR* (APA, 2000) provides a major category composed of attention-deficit and disruptive behavior disorders. These patterns of behavior share a common feature: antisocial behavior. These behaviors have been described as **externalizing disorders** (e.g., Farmer, Compton, Burns, & Robertson, 2002) because they are directed primarily at others. In contrast, personality disorders, including anxiety disorders, are frequently referred to as **internalizing disorders** (e.g., Compton, Burns, Egger, & Robertson, 2002).

Disruptive Behavior Disorders

The two primary categories of disruptive behavior disorders are **Conduct Disorder** and **Oppositional Defiant Disorder**. Both disorders share similar behavior problems that arise from the type of antisocial interactions detailed in Chapter 11.

Developmental Progression for Antisocial Behavior

As you recall, Patterson, DeBaryshe, and Ramsey (1989) describe a series of steps concerning behaviors that emerge in early childhood and that may lead to delinquency during adolescence. Antisocial behavior can begin in early childhood if the child typically receives poor parental discipline and if parental monitoring is lacking. Coercive family interactions have also been associated with the development of children's antisocial behavior, which ultimately may contribute to the development of more serious conduct problems. Once the child enters middle childhood, he or she may experience rejection by peers and academic failure. These variables have been correlated with the child's becoming part of a deviant peer group that often exerts a powerful influence on delinquent-type behavior patterns and the onset of antisocial personality. This model was discussed in more detail in Chapter 11. Often, children who exhibit delinquent behavior and conduct disorders live in environments where the homes and family relationships are chaotic, unsupportive, and nonnurturing or are characterized by physical or sexual abuse (Campbell, 1995; Kazdin, 1998; Lavigueur, Tremblay, & Saucier, 1995). Studies suggest that peer aggression and victimization are also important problems faced by many school-aged children, and these patterns may also contribute to the development of antisocial behavior. Children who have been the victims of bullying exhibited higher rates of depressive behaviors, school refusal, and more generalized social anxiety (Branscum, 2000).

Conduct Disorder and Oppositional Defiant Behavior

Features of Conduct Disorder and Oppositional Defiant Behavior

The key feature of Conduct Disorder (CD) is a repetitive and persistent pattern of behavior in which the basic rights of others or major age-appropriate societal norms or rules are violated. The *DSM-IV-TR* lists four behavior categories in the diagnosis of CD: aggression, deceitfulness, serious rules violations, and destruction of property. All these behaviors can be shaped and maintained by the contingencies provided by family members, peers, and others. Studies have found that some other characteristics of CD include poor school performance, lack of interpersonal skills, and deficient cognitive problem-solving skills (Dodge, 1985; Ledingham & Schwartzman, 1984). There are notable differences in prevalence and age of onset for males and females diagnosed with CD. The American Psychiatric Association (1994) estimates that between 6% and 16% of males and 2% and 9% of females are diagnosed with CD. The age of onset for males is between ages 8 and 10, whereas for females it usually occurs later, between the ages of 13 and 15 (Toth, 1990).

In contrast to CD, which is marked by the child's violation of the rights of others and societal rights and norms, the essential features of Oppositional Defiant Disorder (ODD) are characterized by defiance and hostile behavior toward authority figures. Approximately 25% of children who exhibit oppositional defiant behaviors are at a greater risk for developing CD. ODD is one of the most serious and common behavior problems of children and youth. It is estimated to prevail in 4% to 10% of the child population (Kauffman, 2001). These children are also at risk for delinquency, criminality, and Antisocial Personality Disorder. Researchers have linked difficulty in parenting or inappropriate parenting practices to children displaying oppositional defiant behaviors or to children diagnosed with CD. The coercive parent–child interaction cycle occurs because of ineffective parental management practices and the negative reinforcement contingencies within these interactions. The cycle typically continues and increases in intensity, and thus aggressive behaviors of all family members are reinforced (such reinforcement can be produced by avoidance).

There are other theories that attempt to explain the development of aggression. For instance, Bandura's (1977b) social learning perspective viewed modeling and vicarious reinforcement as important factors for learning, and Novaco's (1978) theory appeals to a cognitive paradigm. But in the development of ODD, defiance becomes an effective behavior for children to escape tasks that they find effortful, boring, or unpleasant (Barkley, 1997). The defiant behavior exhibited by the child allows him or her to better predict the consequences of his or her environment. Also, instructions and rules may have aversive properties for both members of the dyad, and parent compliance with such child instructions can maintain behavior chains of increasing aversiveness during dyadic interactions (Wahler & Dumas, 1986).

Interventions for Conduct Disorder and Oppositional Defiant Disorder

Parent Training, Family-Based Interventions. Parent training, which focuses on breaking the cycle of coercive interactions and behaviors between parent and child, has proven to be the most effective intervention for treating CD and ODD (Farmer et al., 2002; Patterson, Chamberlain, & Reid, 1982). Family-based interventions, which train the parents to implement these interventions at home, include procedures such as tracking, response cost, token economies, role-playing, cueing, and modeling. These are used to create clear behavioral goals that include increasing positive behaviors while decreasing negative behaviors through consistent consequences. For example, positive behaviors are increased through the use of reinforcement and include prosocial interactions with peers, social skills such as respectful comments to adults, and appropriate expression of anger and self-regulation of emotions in general. A family-based intervention that has been very effective is called "parent child interaction therapy" (PCIT). This intervention has been shown to improve the long-term outcomes of young children with severe conduct problems (Snyder, Schrepferman, & St. Peter, 1997). In family therapy, the entire family learns new ways to communicate with one another in a constructive and effective manner.

School-Based Interventions. Effective classroom management typically involves token economies and contingency management contracts. These school-based interventions consist of adding adaptive behaviors to a child's repertoire or expanding on existing behaviors with the goal of replacing or reducing the exhibition of maladaptive behaviors (Del Valle, Kelley, & Seoanes, 2001). Other effective elements of classroom management for children with ODD include establishing clear rules and directions, pacing a student's progress at his or her own rate, positive and corrective feedback, time-out, and the use of differential reinforcement of replacement or incompatible behaviors.

Attention Deficit/Hyperactivity Disorder

In this next section, we discuss ADHD and two other behavior disorders associated with impairment in school and developmental functioning—Autistic Disorder and Mental Retardation.

One of the most common behavior disorders diagnosed in childhood is ADHD. It is estimated that 3% to 7% of the population could be classified as ADHD (APA, 2000). ADHD is most often detected in the classroom environment and tends to impair school functioning. There are two subtypes of ADHD: inattentive, or hyperactive/impulsive. The *DSM IV-TR* diagnostic categories are shown in Table 15.2. A child needs to show 6 of 9 behavioral symptoms to be classified in either subtype (Root & Resnick, 2003).

Most of the research on the etiology of ADHD has focused on several brain-related factors. Many researchers believe a main causal factor of ADHD to be neurological dysfunction (neurotransmitter disturbances, reticular activating system problems, and biophysical development) (Nussbaum & Bigler, 1990). Another theory of etiology focuses on environmental agents as the primary cause for ADHD. Studies have shown that lead poisoning is a toxin commonly found in children with ADHD (Barkley, 1987). For a small percentage of children, certain foods seem to cause a hyperactive allergic reaction. A study conducted by Halperin et al. (1997) suggests that several family variables (familial alcoholism, antisocial behavior, and clinical problems) are associated with hyperactivity in children. According to Nussbaum and Bigler (1990), an estimated 20% to 30% of children with ADHD have a parent or sibling with the disorder. As tempting as it may be to reduce the cause of ADHD to a more basic biological one, as with most behavior disorders, there is no known single biological cause of ADHD. Indeed, ADHD, as it is currently presented, is a descriptive term, describing children with a range of behaviors of unknown developmental origins. Furthermore, no single pattern of behaviors emerges in all children diagnosed with this disorder. Instead, the flexibility of the diagnostic criteria means that children identified with ADHD may have their own unique organization of behaviors, including extremes of normal behaviors, that meet the broad diagnostic criteria for ADHD.

The main criterion for ADHD is based on hyperactive, impulsive, and inattentive behavior. Impulsivity is the choice between concurrently available response alternatives that produce smaller immediate reinforcers rather than larger, delayed reinforcers (Neef, Bicard, & Endo, 2001). **Hyperactivity** is the high frequency of repetitive movement, and inattention is defined behaviorally as high-rate switching between response alternatives (Neef et al., 2001).

Several studies have reported that ADHD children tend to be more agitated, active, and fidgety than normal children (Teicher, Ito, Glod, & Barber, 1996). ADHD can be detected as early as infancy where infants exhibit lack of gaze, fussiness, and withdrawal behavior. Hyperactive behaviors are frequently associated with other problem conditions, such as learning disabilities, oppositional-defiant behaviors, CD, academic underachievement, and socials skills deficits (Mash & Barkley, 1998).

Table 15.2   Diagnostic criteria for Attention Deficit/Hyperactivity Disorder

A. Either (1) or (2):

  1. six (or more) of the following symptoms of inattention have persisted for at least 6 months, to a degree that is maladaptive and inconsistent with developmental level:

    a. Inattention

      (1) often fails to give close attention to details or makes careless mistakes in schoolwork, work, or other activities

      (2) often has difficulty sustaining attention in tasks or play activities

      (3) often does not seem to listen when spoken to directly

      (4) often does not follow through on instructions and fails to finish school work, chores, or duties in the workplace (not due to oppositional behavior or failure to understand instructions)

      (5) often has difficulty organizing tasks and activities

      (6) often avoids, dislikes, or is reluctant to engage in tasks that require sustained mental effort (such as schoolwork or homework)

      (7) often loses things necessary for tasks or activities (e.g., toys, school assignments, pencils, books, or tools)

      (8) is often easily distracted by extraneous stimuli

      (9) is often forgetful in daily activities

  2. six (or more) of the following symptoms of **hyperactivity–impulsivity** have persisted for at least 6 months, to a degree that is maladaptive and inconsistent with developmental level:

    a. Hyperactivity

      (1) often fidgets with hands or feet or squirms in seat

      (2) often leaves seat in classroom or in other situations in which remaining seated is expected

      (3) often runs about or climbs excessively in situations in which it is inappropriate (in adolescents or adults, may be limited to subjective feelings of restlessness)

      (4) often has difficulty playing or engaging in leisure activities quietly

      (5) is often "on the go" or often acts as if "driven by a motor"

      (6) often talks excessively

    b. Impulsivity

      (1) often blurts out answers before questions have been completed

      (2) often has difficulty awaiting turn

      (3) often interrupts or intrudes on others (e.g., butts into conversations or games)

B. Some hyperactive–impulsive or inattentive symptoms that caused impairment were present before age 7 years.

(Continued)

Table 15.2 Continued

C. Some impairment from the symptoms is present in two or more settings (e.g., at school [or work] and at home).

D. There must be clear evidence of clinically significant impairment in social, academic, or occupational functioning.

E. The symptoms do not occur exclusively during the course of a Pervasive Developmental Disorder, Schizophrenia, or other psychotic Disorder and are not better accounted for by another mental disorder (e.g., Mood Disorder, Anxiety Disorder, Dissociative Disorder, or a Personality Disorder).

F. Code based on type:

314.01 Attention Deficit/Hyperactivity Disorder, Combined Type: if both Criteria A1 and A2 are met for the past 6 months
314.00 Attention Deficit/Hyperactivity Disorder, Predominantly Hyperactive-Impulsive Type: if Criterion A2 is met but Criterion A1 is not met for the past 6 months
314.01 Attention Deficit/Hyperactivity Disorder, Predominantly Hyperactive-Impulsive Type: if Criterion A2 is met but Criterion A1 is not met for the past 6 months

SOURCE: Reprinted with permission from *The Diagnostic and Statistical Manual of Mental Disorders,* Fourth Edition, Text Revision. Copyright 2000 American Psychiatric Association.

CODING NOTE: For individuals (especially adolescents and adults) who currently have symptoms that no longer meet full criteria, "In Partial Remission" should be specified.

Interventions for Attention Deficit/Hyperactivity Disorder

The treatments for ADHD can be categorized into three different interventions: *pharmacological therapy, behavior modification,* and *cognitive–behavioral therapy.*

Pharmacological. The most common medications used for the treatment of ADHD are stimulants, in particular **methylphenidate** (Ritalin). Stimulants have been shown to be effective by improving symptoms in about 70% of hyperactive children (Forness, Kavale, Sweeney, & Crenshaw, 1999). Brown and La Rosa (2002) concluded that there was "compelling evidence-based support for both the safety and efficacy of stimulant medication for children and adolescents with ADHD and associated symptom" (p. 594). However, as Pelham and Gnagy (1999) point out, stimulants have their limitations. First, although stimulants have been shown to improve classroom performance, they have not been shown to enhance long-term academic achievement. Second, stimulants do nothing to improve parent–child relations in real settings in what are often dysfunctional families. Third, medication does not produce change in some children, and, finally, if a child responds positively to the medication, parents and teachers are less likely to pursue interventions that will teach the child the skills and behavior needed for long-term success.

Furthermore, there are some drawbacks to using medication; one being the risk of overprescribing and another being an enhanced likelihood of future substance abuse (Loney, Kramer, & Milich, 1981). Many children experience side effects such as mood swings, headaches, loss of appetite, and growth inhibition (Nussbaum & Bigler, 1990). Furthermore, although trial doses of stimulants are used to identify children as ADHD, the logic of doing so is questionable. The practice of diagnosing ADHD with trial doses of stimulants is premised on faulty assumptions, including (a) that there is a single, uniform drug reaction to any medication, including stimulants; (b) that stimulants stimulate all behavior, and thus hyperactivity should be exacerbated, not reduced; and (c) therefore, reduction of ADHD by stimulants is a "paradoxical" effect, so any child whose ADHD is improved by stimulants must "have" ADHD because the paradoxical reaction is "abnormal." What we do know is that not all individuals, including children and adults, react to stimulants exactly alike and that stimulants improve the attention of many individuals, including many "normal" adults. Thus, there is not strong evidence for an actual paradoxical effect, but drugs such as stimulants do affect behavior and may improve the behavior of some children with ADHD behaviors.

Behavior Treatments: Behavior Modification and Cognitive Behavioral Therapy for ADHD. Cognitive–behavioral interventions can help hyperactive children increase attention and decrease impulsivity. This approach focuses on self-monitoring behavior, self-talk, and problem solving (Harris & Schmidt, 1997).

Several behavior–analytic interventions that can be used to treat children diagnosed with ADHD, including correspondence training, self-management, token economies, and response cost, to name a few (Mash & Barkley, 1998). Barkley (1981, 1987) developed an intervention for parents that included the enhancement of parent attending skills, paying positive attention to appropriate independent play and compliance, and the management of child's behavior in public places. These behaviors are reinforced by parents using a home token economy. Behavioral interventions such as positive reinforcement programs and programs that use behavior reduction procedures such as differential reinforcement of other behavior (DRO) have proven to be very effective in treating children with ADHD as well (Reid, 1999). Reid (1999) also recommends that caregivers and teachers provide a well-structured environment with a regular routine for children with ADHD.

Typical behavioral approaches to treating ADHD have involved either parent- or teacher-training programs or both. Pelham and Gnagy (1999) provide a sample sequence of topics to be covered with parents and teachers over an 8- to 12-week period. They conclude that this type of parent-training clinical behavior therapy has been prove to provide "reliable, substantial, and clinically important improvement on multiple measures" (p. 228) in both home and school settings for most children with ADHD behaviors.

Another type of behavior–analytic treatment for ADHD children is called contingency management. **Contingency management programs** have mostly been implemented in school settings rather than in the home. As the name suggests, contingency management involves arranging the contingencies to reinforce desired school-related behaviors and the use of mild forms of punishment, such as time-out or response cost, to reduce undesirable ADHD behaviors.

Token economies involve the use of token reinforcers, such as poker chips or pencil marks that can be redeemed for backup reinforcers such as food or activities. Pelham and Gnagy (1999) conclude that when contingency management programs are in effect, they improve ADHD behavior to the same extent as low to moderate dosages of stimulants. Pelham and his associates (Pelham et al., 2000; Pelham & Hoza, 1996) devised an intensive 8-week summer treatment program (STP) of behavior–analytic treatment for ADHD children. The program ran 5 days per week from 8:00 a.m. to 5:00 p.m. A typical day involved 3 hours of classes taught by special education teachers and various social and recreational activities. The behavioral treatment components of the program involved a token economy point system with positive reinforcement and response cost, sports skills training, social skills training, daily report cards on specific individual target behaviors, and weekly parent-training sessions.

The effectiveness of such an intensive summer treatment program by itself was evaluated against the STP combined with stimulant medication (Pelham et al., 2000). Combining medication with behavioral treatment methods has become widely accepted by the mental health community. The most common combination for treating ADHD is the use of medication along with some behavior management or cognitive–behavioral technique (Forness et al., 1999). Pelham and his associates (Pelham et al., 2000) point out that there is little knowledge about what levels of each type of treatment are effective. Although behavioral intervention is usually implemented at the beginning of treatment in the form of parent training, and not continuously applied, stimulant medication is present over the entire treatment period. To examine effects of continued intensive behavioral treatment compared with continued medication, they conducted a study.

Fifty-seven ADHD children who were already on medication and 60 others who were not medicated participated in the STP over an 8-week summer session at six different sites across the United States. All children received the same intensive behavioral treatment program. The difference was that the children who were on medication continued to receive an average dosage of 30.5 mg of stimulant medication per day during the 8-week STP (combined treatment), whereas the other children received no drugs (behavioral treatment only).

Multiple measures were taken in different settings. These measures included observation of direct behavior related to the point system, such as following or violating rules, noncompliance, and negative verbalizations. The measures also included classroom-related behaviors, including completion, accuracy, productivity, and daily report cards. Ratings were also obtained from counselors, teachers, peers, and the children themselves.

The results showed that adding stimulant medication to behavioral treatment showed relatively little effect above and beyond the intensive behavioral treatment. Both conditions tended to produce improvements on most measures and brought behaviors within the normal range. Pelham's group concluded that about 25% to 55% of ADHD children will do well on behavioral treatment without medication. Furthermore, 43% to 70% will not be normalized on some important behaviors even when behavioral treatment is combined with medication (Pelham et al., 2000). A comparison of the combined treatment with the behavioral treatment showed only that although there were small benefits to adding the medication, the percentage-of-activity rule following the 8 weeks of the program was not very different. Parents, counselors, and teachers rated the changes in the children at the end of the program, and these ratings show that in some cases the behavioral intervention by itself was better than the combined treatment and, in general, there was not a clear advantage to adding the medication to the behavioral intervention.

The findings by Pelham et al. (2000), that there is no important advantage in adding medication to behavioral intervention, are in contrast to some studies (e.g., MTA Cooperative Group, 1999) that have found the combined treatments superior. Pelham et al. (2000) argue that the differences are that in those cases, the behavioral treatment was gradually removed during the study, but the medication continued at a high level throughout. Thus, the differences were attributed to differences in the intensity of ongoing behavioral treatment. As Pelham et al. (2000) suggest, chronic disruptive behavior disorders are ongoing, long-term problems that may require years of treatment. This view of behavior change is consistent with the behavioral systems approach presented in this textbook.

Anxiety Behavior Disorders

Although **anxiety** is a common and frequently studied behavioral problem, there is no single precise definition of anxiety. This is because in the clinical arena, definitions often encompass only internal states and do not identify clearly the behaviors involved. No one knows all exact causes for anxiety disorders; again, multiple determinism is the rule. However, two known factors—genetic factors and environmental stressors—contribute to the behavioral manifestation of this disorder. Children whose parents were diagnosed with anxiety disorders are more likely to have anxiety disorders than children whose parents are not diagnosed with the disorder (Turner, Beidel, & Costello, 1987), but this could be due to environmental or genetic causes or both. Environmental stressors seem to influence the development of anxiety disorders. It is known that children with high anxiety tend to experience more negative and stressful life events than those children with low anxiety (Kashani et al., 1990). However, studies attempting to determine the hereditary influences on anxiety disorders have not yet provided conclusive data.

In behavior analysis, we use the principles of respondent conditioning, social learning, and operant learning to explain the development of anxiety disorders as manifested in behaviors that are oftentimes dysfunctional. As the Little Albert (Watson & Raynor, 1920) study suggested, respondent–conditioning procedures mean that fears and anxious behaviors develop as a result of direct or indirect environmental pairings. In addition, escape and avoidance behaviors are often shaped through negative and positive reinforcement. For example, if a child sees a dog for the first time, she might be a little frightened (seeing a fury creature with sharp teeth and barking loudly). If the child's fright responses (e.g., crying, covering her eyes, etc.) are reinforced by her mother (e.g., the child is hugged, consoled, "It's okay . . . don't worry . . . mommy is right here."), this fearful behavior may be shaped and established. The social learning of fears may occur when children observe others in situations and learn the fear vicariously (see Chapter 9). For example, if a child sees another individual get bitten by a dog, he or she would learn to fear dogs or getting bitten by a dog. Nevertheless, the notion of vicarious learning is complex (see Gewirtz, 1971a, 1971b), and it appears that the learning of fears (e.g., fear of dark and fear of strangers) results from direct operant conditioning (Gewirtz & Peláez-Nogueras, 2000). We think behavior analysis provides more consistent, parsimonious, and empirical explanations of the model for the development of behavior signaling pain and other emotions, such as fear that emerge as a result of behaviors having phylogenic and ontogenic histories (Novak & Peláez, 2002).

Separation Anxiety Disorder

According to Bernstein and Borchardt (1991), Separation Anxiety Disorder (SAD) is characterized by excessive anxiety about separation from parents or attachment figures. According to Anderson, Williams, McGee, and Silva (1987), 2.4% to 3.5% of the community is diagnosed with SAD. In an infant study conducted by Gewirtz and Peláez-Nogueras (1993b), it was shown that separation protests by infants were learned responses. How the child reacted depended on how the mother responded to the child's protest when she was leaving. For example, if the mother hurried back to the child after hearing the child cry, the child learned that crying and protesting would bring the mother back.

Interventions for Separation Anxiety Disorder. Common interventions for treating separation anxiety and other anxiety disorders, including phobias, are systematic desensitization and counterconditioning. These principles are used to decrease fears and anxiety. Systematic desensitization was developed by Joseph Wolpe (1958) and consists of three steps: (a) learning relaxation techniques—for example, learning how to take long deep breaths; (b) establishing a hierarchy of feared stimuli—for example, making a list of what an individual fears, with the most-feared objects at the top of the list; and (c) exposing individuals to the feared stimuli and pairing the stimuli with the relaxation state, beginning with the lowest on the hierarchy. For example, in working with a girl who is afraid of dogs, we would (a) begin by teaching the child how to relax by taking deep breaths. (b) We might ask her questions about various experiences with dogs and ask her to rate how scared they made her, with 0 being not scared at all (e.g., watching *Scooby-Doo* on TV) and 100 being terrified (e.g., being surrounded by a pack of snarling pit bulls). Once rated, these various stimuli, which could be imagined or real, will become a fear hierarchy. (c) We would use the relaxation technique, then start with one of the lowest-rated stimuli on the hierarchy. When she showed no evidence of arousal or escape, we would move to the next highest stimulus on the hierarchy. We would proceed until the highest-ranking stimuli produced no arousal or escape.

Counterconditioning involves introducing the feared stimulus (conditioned stimulus, or CS) in the presence of stimuli-eliciting positive responses so that the feared stimulus elicits positive emotional responses rather than negative ones—for example, giving the child some candy when a dog is present. Thus, through respondent conditioning, the dog becomes a conditioned stimulus (CS) that produces the same pleasant feelings (CR) as the candy (unconditioned stimulus → unconditioned response). Some other common behavioral techniques used to treat SAD are shaping and modeling (Mansdorf & Lukens, 1987). For example, a peer child may show how petting the dog is fun, and the target child's successive approximations to petting (e.g., approaching the dog, putting out a hand but not touching) are reinforced.

Autism

Autism is considered a pervasive developmental disorder. The behaviors of children with autism can be categorized as stereotypic, self-injurious behavior, and hypo- or hypersensitivity (Scott, Clark, & Brady, 2000). These children show little emotional attachment; if they have speech, it is abnormal; their IQ is usually in the retarded range; and they often show ritualistic behaviors and aggression. The prognosis is very poor, and medical therapies have not proven effective (Lovaas, 1987). See Table 15.1.

Treatment of Autism

Early Intensive Behavioral Intervention. The field of applied behavior analysis has given rise to effective and efficient interventions for individuals with autism. Through the power of positive reinforcement, systematic generalization programming, functional assessment, and the teaching of established home-based early intervention programs, the lives of many persons with autism have been improved (Scott et al., 2000). Ivar Lovaas pioneered the treatment of autism at UCLA in the 1960s. His systematic program involving intensive early intervention has produced impressive results (Lovaas, 1987; McEachin, Smith, & Lovaas, 1993).

Lovaas's program has been detailed in many places (Lovaas, 2003; Lovaas & Buch, 1997). The program, developed as the UCLA Young Autism project, runs for 40 hours per week for 2 to 3 years, beginning when children are 2 or 3 years of age. The program involves extensive use of discrete-trial learn units (see Chapter 13) following the four-term contingency concept. Trained behavioral paraprofessionals serve as teachers, providing hundreds of these learn units per day in the home. Parents are also trained to provide additional teaching. The program curriculum is designed to build in key behavioral cusps, such as following instructions and imitation, early in the program. Communication skills are developed along a developmental path, from simple echoic behavior to spontaneous language usage. Social skills are also developed through the use of peers. Attempts are made to get children in normal preschool placements with the help of an aid to shadow the child and provide scaffolding-type assistance where needed.

Autism has been considered a permanent disorder, and there have been few reports of successes outside behavioral interventions. Follow-up data from an intensive, long-term experimental treatment group of 19 children treated in the UCLA program showed that when studied at age 7, 47% achieved normal intellectual and educational functioning, with normal-range IQ scores and successful first-grade performance in public schools. Another 40% were mildly retarded and assigned to special classes for the language delayed, and only 10% were profoundly retarded and assigned to classes for the autistic/retarded. In striking contrast, only 2% of the control group of 40 children achieved normal educational and intellectual functioning; 45% were mildly retarded and placed in language-delayed classes, and 53% were severely retarded and placed in autistic/retarded classes (Lovaas, 1987). A second follow-up when the treatment children were 13 years old showed that they had maintained the gains over the controls. The 9 most successful children tested at 7 years of age were found to be indistinguishable from average children on intelligence and adaptive behavior tests when they were 13, suggesting that the behavioral intervention made significant and important long-term improvement for many of the children diagnosed with autism at ages 2 and 3.

Lovaas's program is one of many behavioral interventions for autism that have been shown to be effective. Most of these involve EIBI, or early intensive behavioral intervention. Several programs focus on communication as the key to overcoming the language and cognitive deficits autistic children have. Others focus primarily on developing social interactions.

Communications-Based Treatments of Autism. Sundberg and Michael (2001) have suggested ways that Skinner's analysis of verbal behavior could be used to teach language to autistic children by emphasizing mand training early on; as you recall, mands are automatically reinforced by what they specify. Andy Bondy and his associates have developed the picture exchange communication system (PECS) (Bondy & Frost, 1994, 2001) as an alternative to more traditional language programs. PECS relies on Skinner's analysis of verbal behavior and starts with mand training (see Chapter 7). Rather than using vocal language, which is often extremely difficult for children with autism or Mental Retardation to master, the PECS uses pictures to teach children with autism a quickly acquired, self-initiated functional communication system.

PECS follows a prescribed sequence of phases. Possible reinforcers are identified, and during the first phase the child learns to give *any* of the picture squares to a staff member and receive a reinforcer. In a sense, the child is learning that the function of verbal behavior is to produce reinforcement, much like an infant without words does. This response is made more durable in Phase 2 by requiring the child to be more persistent and self-initiating. Once the undiscriminated picture exchange response occurs frequently and is initiated by the child, the next phase starts, in which the child has to give a *specific* picture to receive a *specific* reinforcer. In Phase 4, the child must construct "phrases" by putting two picture symbols together on a communication strip. Thus, the child learns the symbol for "I want" and that it goes with an object to be manded (e.g., "I want apple"). The entire communication strip is exchanged for the reinforcer it mands. In the next phase, the child is taught to use the previously learned phrases to answer direct questions put to him or her. Thus, the prompt from the staff, "What do you want?" is answered by the child's putting the "I want" and object pictures together. The final step involves tact training. In this phase, new symbols, such as for the phrase "I see," are introduced to questions about "What do you see?" The child must construct an appropriate "I see ____" to receive a reinforcer that, in the case of this tact, is not the object that is seen, but an arbitrary reinforcer. PECS has been shown to be effective in teaching functional communication. In addition, in one study, most autistic children who used it developed independent speech (Bondy & Frost, 1994), using expressive speech alone or combining speech with picture exchanges to express themselves.

Although many behavioral programs for autism focus on academic and cognitive behaviors, they also target social behaviors as well. Naturalistic interventions such as **pivotal response training** (PRT) (see Pierce & Schreibman, 1995) help children with autism engage in increased level of social behavior (Pierce & Schreibman, 1997).

Many autistic children benefit from being included in typical schools because they are less likely to have their atypical behaviors reinforced in natural settings. However, there may be differences in the kinds of interactions that the children have in a typical environment. Lynn and Robert Koegel and their colleagues (Koegel, Koegel, Frea, & Freeden, 2001) compared the social behaviors of autistic and typically developing children in schools. They found that although both autistic and typical children interacted with adults, autistic children showed much less frequent interactions with peers. Likewise, although both played with toys, the autistic children played with them a much shorter time. Thus, specialized help may be necessary to enhance the experiences of autistic children in typical environments. Weiss and Harris (2001) suggest that many behavioral interventions for increasing social skills in autistic children may be effective. These include direct social skills training programs, self-management training, classwide interventions in inclusion programs, and scripts for which children are given social parts to act out.

Positive Behavioral Support. **Positive behavioral support** (PBS) is an intervention that has evolved as an extension of applied behavior analysis. The central purpose of PBS is to have interventions target problem behaviors that are most effective when they fulfill an educative purpose. Changing behavior through PBS can result in broad changes in a person's lifestyle (Horner et al., 1990). Language is the most targeted behavior in children with developmental disabilities. In behavior analysis, there are many effective techniques in teaching language to children with Mental Retardation and autism. Among them are Sundberg and Partington (1998), who established procedures to identify alternative approaches to language assessment. These include teaching beginning imitation, echoic receptive and matching to sample skills, and tact and receptive skills.

When a student lacks rich behavioral repertoires, the same behavior may be used for different purposes. Here, a functional analysis is necessary to help teachers understand the behavior and turn it around (see Carbone, 2001).

Behavioral approaches employ the four-term contingency. Behavioral procedures most acceptable to educators include restructuring of setting events that empower students; antecedent procedures involving change in cues, prompts, and delivery strategies; reinforcement procedures involving change in content and schedules, noncontingent reinforcement, and differential reinforcement; and consequence and correction procedures that combine reinforcer removal with delivery of instruction (Scott et al., 2000).

Box 15.1   Science, Pseudoscience, and Antiscience in Autism Treatment

One of the most devastating things the parents of a young child can hear are the words "Your child has autism." These words are usually preceded by months or years of trying to find out what is wrong with the child and are often treated as the final pronouncement on an incurable disorder that will start the family system on a desperate search for a cure or at least an effective treatment. Unfortunately, in the case of autism, as is true with many physical and behavioral disorders, there are many misleading claims and false treatments with little or no evidence of support. At best, this takes time away from effective treatment; at worst, it can do actual harm. Gina Green, a long-time researcher on autism treatment, has been at the forefront alerting parents and professionals to the problems of bogus claims of treatment effectiveness and has documented many of the claims that take on some of the trappings of science or that are directly antagonistic to science. Real science differentiates opinions, beliefs, and speculations from demonstrated facts; claims are not made without supporting data. The data are based on direct observations.

In contrast, pseudoscience tries to lend credibility to beliefs, speculations, and untested assumptions by making them *appear* scientific—for example, by using scientific jargon, endorsements from individuals with "scientific" credentials, perhaps even some numbers or graphs. But instead of objective measurements from well-controlled experiments, pseudoscientists offer testimonials, anecdotes, and unverified personal reports to back up their claims. Antiscience is the outright rejection of the time-tested methods of science as a means of producing valid and useful knowledge. The extreme antiscientific view is that there are no objective facts; all knowledge is made up of personal interpretations of phenomena. (Green & Perry, 1999, p. 6)

One pseudoscientific treatment for autism that was popular in the 1990s is called "facilitated communication." This treatment was developed by a nurse in Australia for working with physically handicapped individuals. It was based on the unproven assumption that autistic children were actually extremely bright but were frustrated by an inability to communicate. The goal was to allow the autistic person to communicate with the help of a trained "facilitator" who was supposed to take the autistic person's hand and amplify the responses as the facilitator held the hand over a keyboard. The claim was that the autistic child could use the facilitator to express himself or herself. Many remarkable claims were made, including the writing of letters and poems. Many testimonials, both personal and professional, were offered about the effectiveness of facilitated communication, and a virtual cottage industry sprang up offering workshops and training.

Unfortunately, the effectiveness claimed was not based on any scientific evidence. When facilitated communication was finally investigated using double-blind procedures (where the facilitator and the child were seeing different test items) keyboard responses reflected the facilitator's stimuli, not the child's. This and other tests quickly proved that despite the firm convictions to the contrary of those who believed in facilitated communication, it was merely an elaborate Ouija board method where thoughts of the facilitator, not the autistic person, were expressed.

Recently, secretin, a drug for treating digestion problems, has come to be used as a treatment for autism. Its use is based on three poorly documented case studies published in an obscure journal. Despite the lack of any real scientific evidence for effectiveness, parents have had their children injected with doses of secretin that greatly exceed the recommended dosage for treatment of adults with the digestive problems. Recently, several double-blind controlled studies have been conducted (e.g., Carey et al., 2002; Corbett et al., 2001; Unis et al., 2002). The results of the studies show that, compared with using a placebo, there is no positive benefit to using secretin with autistic children.

Finally, there have been widespread, media-supported claims that at least some autism is caused by MMR (measles, mumps, rubella) immunizations. Part of this claim comes from a supposed correlation between the increase in autism and increase in the use of immunization in the past 30 years, and part comes through claims of individuals that their children developed autism shortly after receiving the MMR immunization. These claims have led many parents to avoid immunizing their children, despite a lack of any scientific evidence for the link.

Although the scientific evidence does not demonstrate a link between MMR vaccinations and autism (National Institute of Child Health and Human Development [NICHD], 2001), there are real health threats, including possible deaths, if children do not get immunized. Measles, which has been virtually eliminated by vaccinations in the United States, remains a serious health problem where immunizations are not widely provided. In 1964–65, before the vaccine for rubella was available, 20,000 babies were born to mothers who had rubella. Of those 20,000 born, 11,600 were deaf, 3,580 were blind, and 1,800 were mentally retarded (NICHD, 2001). Mumps has serious health risks if contracted as an adult. All told, the concern is that there is good scientific evidence for the problems resulting from not getting vaccinated. In sum, it benefits the family and society if we demand scientific evidence for treatment. Of course, parents of autistic children do not have the luxury of waiting for the evidence to come in. At this time, the treatment that has received the most scientific support for its effectiveness in treating autism disorder is early intensive behavioral intervention (EIBI). EIBI can normalize the behaviors of many children diagnosed with autism to the extent that they are considered "normal," but it has been less effective with others. Because EIBI is intensive (it requires at least 40 hours per week of paraprofessional or parent training) and works slowly by building skills over a period of years, EIBI is difficult to provide and is expensive. Still, it is currently the treatment of choice.

Mental Retardation

Although Mental Retardation has at its core deficits in cognitive and social skills, mentally retarded children may share many of the behavioral deficits and excesses seen in autistic children. Therefore, based on the specific behaviors targeted, they may benefit from many of the programs and procedures appropriate for autistic individuals.

Progression for Developmental Retardation

A hypothetical intergenerational progression to Mental Retardation has been proposed based on research data. The progression (Figure 15.1) provides one path for developmental retardation in terms of low academic achievement and early school failure. It includes (a) limited parenting practices (low amounts of stimulation) that produce low rates of vocabulary growth in early childhood (Hart & Risley, 1995), (b) behavioral instructional practices in middle childhood and adolescence that produce low rates of academic engagement during school years (Greenwood, Delquadri, & Hall, 1989), (c) lower rates of academic achievement and early school failure, (d) early dropout, and (e) parenthood and continuance of the progression into the next generation.

Interventions for Mental Retardation

Individuals classified as mentally retarded show a variety of behaviors that can be classified as excessive or deficient. In focusing on excessive behaviors, such as self-injury or self-stimulation, techniques that have been effective for reducing undesired behaviors typically shown by mentally retarded children are differential reinforcement, extinction, response cost, time-out, overcorrection, and positive practice (Foxx, 1982; Mash & Barkley, 1998). Extinction is the most widely used procedure for decreasing unwanted excessive behavior of developmentally delayed individuals. This is a procedure in which the reinforcer that has been sustaining or increasing unwanted or unconstructive behavior is withheld.

Differential reinforcement of incompatible behavior (DRI) is helpful in reducing hand flapping, self-injurious behavior, and other negative behaviors by reinforcing behaviors different from the unwanted ones. An example of this is a child who repeatedly hits himself or herself in the head. A good incompatible behavior would be keeping hands away from the child's head. Having the child scribble on paper for a few minutes can do this. If the child can keep his or her hands on the paper without hitting himself or herself on the head, the child is reinforced over periods of time.

Mentally retarded children show deficits in cognitive, language, self-help (such as feeding, toileting, and dressing), and social skills. Several comprehensive early-intervention programs have been developed to provide a curriculum for addressing these deficits. Most behaviorally based programs focus on assessing the child's level of the various skills, directly teaching the skills, reinforcing successive approximations, and generalizing skills to make them functional in real-life situations.

Language training with children with Mental Retardation has been shown to be enhanced through the use of observational learning and matrix-training strategies (Goldstein & Mousetis, 1989). In teaching toilet training, Azrin, Sneed, and Foxx

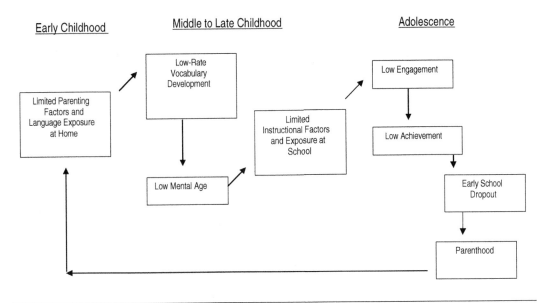

Figure 15.1   Progression for Developmental Retardation

(1973) found that positive reinforcement for correct toileting, positive practice for nighttime toileting, increased level of urination by prompting drinking, immediate detection of correct and incorrect toileting, and positive practice for accidents significantly reduced bed-wetting accidents.

Depression

Depression in Early Childhood

Behavior problems can begin at an early age. Infants show separation protest and anxiety as early as 6 months when they are separated from their caregivers and left at the nursery or day care center (Gewirtz & Peláez-Nogueras, 1993b). We know that children born of depressed mothers will behave in depressive ways by showing few smiles or even, at times, aggressive behavior. The use of behavior–analytic interventions has demonstrated that infants, when interacting with nondepressed trained caregivers, show less depressive and problem behaviors (Peláez-Nogueras, Field, Cigales, Gonzalez, & Clasky, 1994). Addicted mothers typically have children born with addictive behaviors. These are known as "colicky babies" who develop negative interactions styles that may ultimately lead to problematic behavior as well as to unconstructive and inhibited child–parent interactions. Coercive and synchronized mother–child interactions adversely affect the quality of child development and depressive-type behaviors.

Depression in Older Children

Depressed children may be very passive and show no interest in activities they used to enjoy doing. Some children, in addition, show cognitive symptoms (how they think of themselves), including negative beliefs and feelings of hopelessness, helplessness, and failure, and they do not respond in situations they can control. Depressed children may also show signs of academic dysfunction (inattention in class and lower school performance) (Cole, 1990).

The most easily observed symptoms of **depression** are the physical symptoms. For example, depressed children may show several somatic symptoms as well as fatigue and low energy levels. Research findings show that they tend to isolate themselves and avoid social interactions (Poznanski, Cook, & Carroll, 1979); changes in appetite are also common among depressed individuals.

Depression in Adolescence

You may recall from the discussion in Chapter 14 that the onset of depression in adolescents is at puberty. The occurrence of depressive behaviors is exhibited more frequently in girls than boys. According to Kazdin, the younger the child, the lower the incidence rate for depression (Kazdin, 1988). Furthermore, Rutter (1991) found that the incidence of depression increased considerably during adolescence.

Depressive Behaviors

Depressed adolescents show a wide range of symptoms, some of which we already discussed in Chapter 14. Emotional symptoms of depression include feelings of sadness, guilt, unimportance, boredom, and irritability, which we need to translate into behavioral terms. The relevant aspects of depression are manifested in behaviors such as crying, lack of participation in shared activities, low involvement, and withdrawal.

Some have argued that lack of positive reinforcement and depression are interrelated (Hoberman & Clarke, 1993; Hoberman & Lewisohn, 1985; Lewisohn & Gotlib, 1995). Depression appears to result from a person's social interactions not being reinforced. That is, children and adolescents who receive little positive reinforcement for their social interactions tend to be less responsive and less active. This results in a depressed mood. In turn, the depressed mood can cause low activity levels and other symptoms, such as low self-concept, negativity, and feelings of shame. These characteristics become a self-reinforced behavioral attractor state that others recognize as depression.

Situations leading to extinction and exposure to aversive settings have also been associated with the onset of depressive behaviors. For example, an event that causes extinction could be the death of a loved one or the breakup of a loving relationship. Such an absence means normal behaviors are neither prompted nor reinforced because the important source of these social stimuli is no longer there to provide them. An example of an aversive event producing depressive behaviors in children would be child abuse because it usually involves a long history of inescapable punishment (Dougher & Hackbert, 1994).

Treatment for Depression

The most common treatment for depression in children and adolescents is medication (tricyclic antidepressants). Several psychological and psychosocial treatments are also used to treat depressed individuals. These interventions include family therapy, cognitive–behavioral therapy, and social skills training (Peterson et al., 1993). Behaviorists Kohlenberg and Tsai (1994) have developed a different approach—**functional analytic psychotherapy** (FAP)—to treat depressive behaviors. FAP is a behavioral reconceptualization of cognitive therapy that uses the client–therapist relationship to bring about and change actual occurrences of the client's problematic behavior. This is a more intense and interpersonal therapy in which the therapist and the client affect each other in a meaningful way, and the therapy relationship is the primary vehicle for client change. FAP appears to more effectively address the diverse needs of clients because it is a behavioral approach to understanding, using the therapist–client relationship to help the therapist identify opportunities that typically are overlooked during traditional cognitive–behavior therapy.

Acceptance and Commitment Therapy. Another very useful contemporary approach in treating depressive behaviors is **acceptance and commitment therapy** (ACT). ACT is a behavior-analytic approach that targets the avoidance of events and increases the ability for changes in behavior (Hayes & Wilson, 1994). ACT promotes the acceptance of the behaviors of feeling depressed as part of normal living and encourages the individual to make choices and develop other behaviors, such as going out and enjoying oneself, that are incompatible with the depressive behaviors. The ACT model has considerable more breadth than is seen in conventional applications to psychological problems in childhood and adolescence.

According to a report from the U.S. Surgeon General's Office (U.S. Public Health Service, 2000), 1 in 10 children have a mental illness severe enough to cause impairment, and depression is one of the most prominent disorders. ACT has been used with children and their parents to treat depression (Murrell & Wicksell, 2003). This approach includes techniques and concepts such as looking at the relationship of suffering with verbal processes, emphasizing how these concepts specifically relate to children and adolescents; treatment components, such as valuing and cognitive diffusion; acceptance of "unacceptable" private events; establishing emotional approach instead of avoidance; experimenting with committed action; and involving parents in treatment across a wide variety of presenting problems. (Also see the discussion in Chapter 14 on adolescent suicide and other cognitive–behavioral interventions, such as mindfulness-based cognitive therapy for depression.)

School-Based Interventions. As discussed earlier, school-based interventions are also very useful in treating childhood depressive behaviors. As a part of treatment, children are taught and counseled in relaxation, social skills, problem solving, cognitive restructuring, and affective education (Hart, 1991).

● SUMMARY

For the purposes of the present chapter, *behavior disorders* are defined as organized patterns behavior that deviate from an arbitrary or socially determined standard. Strictly speaking, such behaviors may not differ from "normal" behaviors; rather, they may be differentiated in terms of the degree to which they are excessive, deficient, or have a tendency to occur under inappropriate circumstances. The labels given to behavior disorders are descriptions of organized patterns of behavior or *attractors*. As such, it is important to remember that they do not explain behavior. It is also important to recognize that the organization of behaviors varies and is subject to the principles of multiple determinism and equifinality.

Behavior disorders are often assessed with standardized tests or checklists. Unfortunately, the structural assessments that are often used to obtain a *DSM-IV-TR* diagnosis necessary for insurance coverage of treatment lack informative value in terms of selecting appropriate treatment. In contrast, behavior analysts favor *functional assessments* and *functional analyses*. The functional assessment identifies the factors that predict and maintain problematic behavior within the framework of the four-term contingency. The functional analysis is a procedure that involves actual manipulation of factors suspected to be maintaining behavior to determine the effects.

Conduct Disorder (CD) and *Oppositional Defiant Disorder* (ODD) constitute two primary categories of disruptive behavior disorders. The essential feature of CD is a repetitive and quite persistent behavioral tendency to violate the basic rights of others, to break major age-appropriate societal norms, and not follow societal rules. Aggression, deceitfulness, serious rules violations, and destruction of property are behavioral categories of interest in the diagnosis of the disorder. The essential features of ODD are defiance and hostile behavior toward authority figures. Children exhibiting oppositional defiant behaviors are at increased risk of developing CD. Interventions for these disorders include parent training and family-based interventions. *Parent training* focuses on interrupting the coercive family process, whereas family-based interventions teach parents to implement interventions at home and focus on developing more constructive means of family communication. *Effective school-based interventions* may involve token economies and contingency management contracts and may require the establishment of clear rules and directions, individual pacing, and the use of positive and corrective feedback, time-out, and differential reinforcement of incompatible behaviors.

Attention Deficit/Hyperactivity Disorder (ADHD) is one of the most commonly diagnosed behavior disorders in children. The two subtypes of this disorder are (a) inattentive and (b) hyperactive/impulsive. Assessment for ADHD focuses on hyperactive, impulsive, and inattentive behavior. Common treatments for ADHD include psychotropic medication (particularly stimulants), behavior modification, and cognitive–behavioral therapy. Although medications have been found to be effective, drawbacks include the potential for future substance abuse and side effects. Also, the rationale behind their use (the inference of a paradoxical effect) has been questioned by many. *Cognitive–behavioral interventions* focus on self-monitoring behavior, self-talk, and problem solving. *Behavioral interventions* include correspondence training, self-management, token economies, and response cost, among others. The use of positive reinforcement programs incorporating behavior reduction procedures have proven to be effective in treating children with ADHD. Parent and teacher training programs have also proven to be effective. Treatments that combine medication with behavioral treatment methods have become widely accepted in the mental health community. However, research suggests that the addition of medications to a behavioral program does not increase effectiveness of treatment significantly.

Anxiety usually refers to behavior denoting intense apprehension, uncertainty, and fearful behavior often resulting from the anticipation of a threatening event or situation and often to a degree that the normal physical, psychological, and behavioral functioning of the affected individual is disrupted. From a behavioral perspective, operant and respondent conditioning, in addition to social learning, provide an adequate account of the development of anxiety disorders. *Separation anxiety* can be seen as the child showing behaviors that denote excessive anxiety about departures and separations from parents or attachment figures. Typical interventions for a variety of anxiety disorders are systematic desensitization and counterconditioning. *Systematic desensitization* involves (a) the learning of relaxation techniques, (b) development of a fear hierarchy, and (c) exposure to feared stimuli until extinction occurs. *Counterconditioning* involves introduction of the feared stimulus in the presence of stimuli that elicit positive responses, the result being that the feared stimulus comes to elicit positive conditioned responses. Shaping and modeling may also be used in the treatment of anxiety disorders.

Autism is a pervasive developmental disorder characterized by stereotypic and self-injurious behavior, hypo- or hypersensitivity, lack of emotional attachment, abnormal speech, IQ in the retarded range, ritualistic behaviors, and aggression. Ivar Lovaas has developed an effective treatment program for children with autism that makes extensive use of discrete-trial learn units following the four-term contingency. Trained behavioral paraprofessionals administer hundreds of trials per day in the home, and parents are trained to provide additional teaching. Key behavioral cusps are built into the program, and communication skills are developed. Social skills are also developed through the use of peers. Other interventions, such as the Picture Exchange Communication System, pivotal response training, and positive behavioral support, have also proven to be effective. To be effective, *school-based interventions* should include restructuring of setting events, antecedent procedures, reinforcement procedures, and consequences and correction procedures that combine reinforcer removal with corrective instruction.

Children with *Mental Retardation* often exhibit cognitive, language, self-help, and social skills deficits. Many experience behavioral deficits and excesses similar to those of autistic children and may benefit from similar interventions. Additional techniques that have proven effective for addressing behavioral problems in children with Mental Retardation include differential reinforcement, extinction, response cost, time-out, overcorrection, and positive practice. Behaviorally based programs focus on assessing the child's level of skills in various domains, direct teaching of skills, shaping, and generalization to real-life situations.

The incidence of *depression* in children increases with age. Indicators of depression may include crying, lack of participation in shared activities, low level of involvement, withdrawal, cognitive symptoms (e.g., feelings of helplessness and hopelessness), academic dysfunction, somatic symptoms, fatigue, low energy, and changes in appetite. From a behavioral perspective, depression results from a lack of reinforcement from social interactions. In addition, situations leading to extinction or exposure to aversive events have also been associated with depression. Depression in children and adolescents is commonly treated with medication. Other interventions include family therapy, cognitive–behavioral therapy, social skills training, Functional Analytic Psychotherapy, Acceptance and Commitment Therapy, and school-based interventions that include the teaching of relaxation skills, social skills, problem solving, cognitive restructuring, and effective education.

GLOSSARY

ABAB reversal design An experimental research design with individual subjects in which a series of baseline (A) observations is followed by a series of observations in which the independent variable is introduced (B). This sequence is repeated until the control of the independent variable has been determined.

ability Knowing how to do things. An operant sequence in a certain order or an operant with a characteristic response topography cued by certain classes of discriminative stimuli. See *knowledge*.

acceptance and commitment therapy (ACT) A behavior–analytic approach that targets the reduction of avoidance of aversive events or thoughts and increases the ability for changes in behavior. ACT promotes the acceptance of the behaviors of feeling depressed as part of normal living and encourages behaviors that are incompatible with depressive behaviors. It is an alternative approach to traditional cognitive-behavioral therapy and consists of recontextualizing the relation between thoughts and feelings and overt behavior based on the person's discovered values and choice.

accommodation The modification of existing mental structures in accordance with newly assimilated information. One of Piaget's mental adaptation processes.

acquired reinforcers Stimuli that acquire the ability to reinforce behavior through being paired with primary reinforcers and other acquired reinforcers. Also called *secondary reinforcers* or *conditioned reinforcers*.

activation syndrome A complex system of conditioned or unconditioned responses that includes increased heart rate, muscle tension, pupil dilation, a flushed feeling in the face, and internal changes, such as a release of adrenaline.

activity reinforcers A behavior class of common acquired reinforcers that encompasses physical and mental actions.

adaptation In Piaget's theory, changes in mental structures occurring through the processes of assimilation and accommodation. Assimilation + accommodation = adaptation.

additivity Linear change characterized by accumulation of experiences.

adduction (contingency adduction) The production of novel behaviors in addition to the specifically reinforced behavior, as in coalescent organization.

adolescent egocentrism Piaget's term for a characteristic of adolescents, who tend to focus more on themselves and believe their thought and ideas are unique.

affordance The various features of an environment (such as objects to see or sounds to hear) that allow perception to develop.

allantois A structure that becomes the umbilical cord (the conduit for substances between child and placenta).

allele Any sequence of bases determining the form of the gene at a given site on a chromosome. For example, the sequence for blue eye color may be one allele and for green eye color another allele.

alternating treatments designs (also called multiple-treatment designs) An experimental research design with individual subjects in which a series of observations under one experimental condition are randomly interspersed with observations under another experimental condition.

altruism The principle or practice of unselfish concern for or devotion to the welfare of others.

amnion An inner membrane surrounding the embryo and containing amniotic fluid.

amodal Independent of the mode of perception (e.g., visual, auditory, etc.).

androgynous Possessing both masculine and feminine characteristics.

animism Giving human characteristics to inanimate objects.

Anorexia Nervosa An eating disorder in which the individual has a distorted body image and refuses to maintain a normal weight. Behaviors include starving oneself, binge-eating-purging behaviors, or both.

antecedent A stimulus that precedes some contingency; usually, a discriminative stimulus in a four-term contingency.

anxiety An aversive or unpleasant state involving subjective apprehension and physiological arousal of a diffuse nature.

applied behavior analysis The science in which the principles of behavior are used to make improvements in socially significant behaviors or learning.

applied research Research done to solve practical or clinical problems. See *basic research*.

assimilation A term used by Piaget to describe the process of distorting or ignoring discrepancies between an actual stimulus and the existing mental schemes so that the stimulus can be absorbed into the scheme. Modification of incoming information so that it will fit existing mental structures. Another component in Piaget's theory. See *accommodation* and *adaptation*.

attachment Organized social bonding (behavior patterns) that develops between infant and primary caregiver(s) or between two partners. Behaviors such as proximity seeking as well as protest and distress upon separation have been used as indexes of secure or insecure attachment.

Attention Deficit/Hyperactivity Disorder A disorder characterized by impulsiveness, overactivity, and difficulty paying attention.

attractor (dynamic attractor or attractor state) Organized patterns of behavior assembled by environmental contingencies. For example, an individual's pattern of walking, running, or talking.

authoritarian Parenting style characterized by efforts to control behavior and require obedience to an adult-determined standard.

authoritative Parenting style characterized by warmth and openness to children's inputs but also by the establishment of clear rules and boundaries and insistence on compliance with these.

Autism A pervasive developmental disorder characterized by self-injurious and ritualistic behaviors, hypo- or hypersensitivity, little emotional attachment, abnormal speech, low IQ scores, and little or no language.

autoclitic A unit of verbal behavior identified by Skinner based on or that depends on other verbal behavior by modifying the effects of that other verbal behavior on the listener.

automatic reinforcement A reinforcer related to a response in such a way that it is produced automatically by that response. For example, when sounds made by parents in their native language are presented with other reinforcers, the result is that those sounds acquire the ability to reinforce behavior that produces them. Thus, infant motor behavior that produces these sounds is automatically reinforced by the ability to hear the sounds. See *intrinsic reinforcement*.

autonomic arousal Increased physiological responses that may act as reinforcing stimuli. Such responses could include increased heart rate and breathing.

autonomy The capacity to behave and make decisions independently, serving as one's main source of reinforcement and management of life tasks without being overly dependent on other people. This is an important developmental skill for successful development in adolescence.

autosome Chromosome that is identical in length and carries the same gene location (22 pairs). Any chromosome other than a sex chromosome.

avoidance Refers to the process in which the responses of an individual are maintained by the prevention or reduction of the probability of aversive stimuli or circumstances.

backward chaining Chaining procedure that begins with teaching the last behavior in a behavioral chain and continues to teach each behavior in the reverse order that it occurs within the chain.

backward conditioning Type of conditioning that occurs when the unconditioned stimulus precedes the neutral stimulus (respondent, rather than operant, conditioning).

baseline The base rate of behavior before intervention against which an experimental manipulation is measured.

basic behavior analysis Typically conducted in the lab or under controlled conditions to eliminate or minimize possible confounding variables and to test basic principles of learning.

basic research Research designed to investigate fundamental principles. See *applied research.*

behavior An organism's interaction with the environment that produces a detectable change in the environment. The activity of a living thing in relation to the environment.

behavior analysis The study of the functions of behavior to achieve an understanding of behavior change. It is a natural science approach to understanding the environmental determinants of behavior and their functional relations. Prediction and control are the main goals in behavior analysis.

behavior–analytic psychology The scientific study of the interactions between the behavior of individuals and the events in their environment.

behavior chain A set of discrete behaviors sequenced in a particular order.

behavior disorders Organized patterns of behavior, or attractors, that deviate from an arbitrary or socially determined standard or norm. The behaviors are not unique but deviate from the accepted pattern in one of three ways: They may be excessive or deficient, or they may occur under the wrong circumstances.

behavioral contrast A change in a behavior pattern that is the result of an earlier change in the behavior. This change can be seen as a contextual variable or setting event.

behavioral cusp The emergence of a new behavior that is important for the development of many other behavioral paths.

behavioral genetics The field of study concerned with the effects genetics has on behavior.

behavioral gerontology Field of study concerned with contending developmental issues involving the aging process and the elderly.

behavioral pediatrics The application of psychological research findings to prevent and deal with developmental problems in medical settings.

behavioral schemes Child's first mental representation of stimulus–response reflexive reactions.

behavioral systems theory A natural science approach to development that combines dynamical systems approaches with behavior analysis and emphasizes constant, reciprocal, and nonlinear interactions between behavior and environment.

benefogen Physical environmental agents, such as the nutrient folic acid, that have a positive effect on development when present prenatally. See *teratogens.*

between-subjects designs Experimental research designs in which different subjects are used in different conditions.

blastocyst Hollow sphere of cells formed during the germinal period of prenatal development. It will differentiate into the embryoblast and trophoblast.

blastula   See *blastocyst.*

Bulimia Nervosa   An eating disorder characterized by cyclical binge eating and purging behaviors.

canalized (phenotype)   Originally applied to genetic determination: A deeply entrenched path of development from which it is difficult to deviate. The more highly canalized the phenotype, the more genetics has limited the environment's influence on the development of a given trait or characteristic. Recently, the effects of the environment of canalizing development have been acknowledged. See *experiential canalization.*

cephalo-caudal law of development   Principle of developmental direction stating that development occurs from head to tail (toe).

chaining   Process that involves the reinforcement of a set of discriminated operants sequenced in a particular order. Where one response may function as the discriminative stimulus for the next response.

changing-criterion design   An experimental research design with individual subjects in which a level of behavior is specified and used to shape a subject's behavior.

chaos   A branch of science dealing with nonlinear systems. Behavioral development can be considered a nonlinear system. Such systems are sensitive to multiple initial conditions, which means even small changes may have drastic effects.

child development   The study of the psychological, physiological, and social development of humans between conception and adulthood.

chorion   The protective membrane that surrounds the child and amnion.

chromosome   Strands of DNA; 23 pairs of threadlike bodies within the cell nucleus that carry the genes in a linear order.

circular explanation   Occurs when a description merely labels the behavior but offers no cause-and-effect relationship clarification. For example, the child cannot read because he has dyslexia: We know the child has dyslexia because he cannot read.

circular reactions   In Piaget's theory, the repeated patterns of behavior of the sensorimotor stage. See *primary, secondary,* and *tertiary circular reactions.*

classical conditioning   The pairing of an initially neutral stimulus with an unconditioned stimulus, which results in the neutral stimulus becoming a conditioned stimulus. Through learning trials, the conditioned stimulus comes to elicit the same response as the unconditioned stimulus in its absence (respondent conditioning).

clinical method   An approach to the study of psychology concerned with or based on actual observation and treatment of individuals rather than on experimentation.

coalescent organization   The dynamical process by which factors bring together coherent patterns of behavior. These factors include genetics, physical structure, previous experiences, hidden skills, and the environmental contingencies at hand.

codominance   Occurs when two alleles are of equal strength. Characteristics of both alleles are expressed in the phenotype.

coercive family process   A breakdown of parental effectiveness in disciplinary conflicts leading to the development of aggressive, coercive, and noncompliant behaviors.

cognition   The process of thinking or knowing. Cognition can be measured only indirectly or inferred from other public behavior.

cognitive behaviors   Traditionally, behaviors involved in thinking. In a behavioral systems approach, these include knowledge (knowing), ability (doing), and problem solving.

cognitive development   Progressive changes in one's knowing and thinking over the life span.

cognitive-behavioral therapy   The application of learning principles to change problematic public and private behaviors.

cohort   In research, comparison subjects of the same age or experience.

commitment   Behavior made more likely by our overall responding patterns. In self-control, early-choice behavior that allows for later choice of large delayed reinforcers.

comparative psychology The study of the evolution of behavior across species.

compliance Obeying requests, commands, rules, and so on that serve as stimuli when presented by a parent to a child.

concordance rate Commonly used measure of heritability. The concordance rate is the degree to which one individual's measure on a given test (e.g., IQ or personality test) correlates with another individual's measure on the same test. The more similar, the higher the concordance rate.

concrete operations stage (7–11 years) In Piaget's model, the stage of cognitive development characterized by the ability to engage in inductive reasoning, conservation, and seriation.

conditioned reinforcers Stimuli that become reinforcing due to the pairing with primary or secondary reinforcers. See *secondary or acquired reinforcers.*

conditioned response (CR) A learned response to a conditioned stimulus.

conditioned stimulus (CS) A previously neutral stimulus that is repeatedly presented with the unconditioned stimulus until it acquires the ability to elicit the same response.

Conduct Disorder (CD) A repetitive and persistent pattern of behavior in which the basic rights of others or age-appropriate societal norms or rules have been violated.

confluence of research methodologies Approach to the study of development that involves (a) naturalistic observation to identify the existence of the problem and potential causal variables in the real world, (b) bringing the phenomena under control in the laboratory environment to identify the processes involved, and (c) returning to the real world to verify that the processes found in the laboratory function in the outside world.

conjugate reinforcement Reinforcement that is proportional to the amount or intensity of behavior.

consequence A stimulus event produced by behavior. The effect of consequences will be to strengthen or weaken behavior. It is the environmental event or stimulus that follows the behavior in the four-term contingency.

conservation This is a characteristic that develops in Piaget's concrete operations stage of cognitive development. Specifically, this is the ability to recognize that the quantity, mass, or volume of an object does not change when the form of the object has been altered.

contextualistic approach to development A fundamental approach that views behavioral development as part of a greater whole. Contexts may be environmental or historical. Context gives behavior its meaning.

contiguity Nearness in time; next to one another. In respondent conditioning, the placing of the CS and UCS closely in time.

contingency An if–then relationship that involves a response and a consequence (if Response A occurs, then Consequence A will happen). The effect of the response, the consequence, the discriminative stimulus, and the setting event produces the contingency.

contingency management program Programs that involve arranging the contingencies to reinforce desired behaviors and the use of mild forms of punishment, such as time-out or response cost, to reduce undesirable behaviors. Commonly used in school settings with ADHD behavior.

contingency-shaped behavior Patterns of behavior that have been learned through the consequences resulting from that behavior, in opposition to rule-governed behavior.

contingent Consequence follows and depends on the occurrence of a response, as in the case of contingent reinforcement. Contrasts with "noncontingent."

continuous reinforcement (CRF) schedule A schedule of reinforcement in which every response within the operant class is reinforced. This leads to the most rapid acquisition of a response.

continuum of caretaking casualty The influence of the environmental dimensions mediated by the caretaker. This theoretical perspective suggests that interactions of environmental (caretaking), genetic, and historical bases are crucial to developmental outcomes.

control parameters The critical amount of a variable that determines the emergence of a behavior or characteristic. Small changes in control parameters (e.g., bone length, muscle strength, time of day) may produce phase shifts.

control procedures Methods used to eliminate irrelevant differences between control and experimental group treatments.

cooing The production of vowel-like sounds usually occurring under pleasant setting events, most often seen in infants around the second month of life.

corrective feedback A teaching method that punishes the incorrect response and models the correct one.

correlation The degree of relationship (or covariation) between two or more variables. Correlations range between +1.00 (positive) and −1.00 (negative). A correlation of .00 indicates no relationship.

counterconditioning Principle used to decrease fears and anxiety. It involves introducing the feared stimulus (CS) in the presence of stimuli eliciting positive responses so that the originally feared stimulus elicits positive emotional responses rather than negative ones.

counterimitation Occurs when an observer does not follow a modeled behavior. In fact, the opposite behavior of the modeled may be seen. The modeled behavior serves as a discriminative stimulus that signals a matching behavior could have unwanted consequences.

cross-sectional designs Developmental research methods in which age differences are assessed by using different subjects at different ages. See *longitudinal designs*.

crossing over Occurs during meiosis. It involves the actual exchange of parts of genetic material, as segments of one chromosome in a pair changes place with segments of its compliment. Crossing over increases genetic variability.

cultural tools A term used by Vygotsky for culturally shaped behaviors, such as language, that are used in developing cognitive behavior.

cusp See *behavioral cusp*.

deficient behaviors Patterns of behavior that occur too infrequently, with too little intensity, or not at all.

delayed conditioning The most effective type of conditioning. Respondent conditioning in which the conditioned stimulus is presented for some fixed, extended time period before the unconditioned stimulus is presented.

depression An affective or mood disorder characterized by behaviors that show at least one episode of feeling profoundly sad and hopeless and/or losing interest in almost all activities.

deprivation Reducing the quantity of a reinforcer. This condition may cause a positive reinforcer to become more effective (e.g., food).

derived relational responding A relation between stimuli that emerges from a learning history but that is not directly trained.

development A dynamical process of adaptation to the environment in which learning plays an important role by providing us with the flexibility to meet changing demands.

developmental momentum The principle of dynamical systems that states behavior moving in a particular direction at a particular rate will continue on its trajectory unless there is some disturbance.

developmental ontogenesis The study of the development or life history of an individual organism.

developmental phylogenesis The study of the development or evolutionary history of species.

developmental psychology The study of the progressive changes in the relationships between an organism and its environment over its life span.

developmental trajectories Long-run trends in behavior.

differential reinforcement of alternative behavior (DRA) Reinforcement that is delivered after a desirable behavior that is of a different form but that serves the same function as the target (undesirable) behavior.

differential reinforcement of high rate of behavior (DRH) A reinforcement schedule during which there must be a large number of responses during a given time period in order to deliver reinforcement.

differential reinforcement of incompatible behavior (DRI) A reinforcement schedule during which the targeted behavior is replaced by a behavior that cannot be performed at the same time as the target behavior.

differential reinforcement of low rate of behavior (DRL) Reinforcement that is delivered after a set time that is contingent on a behavior's frequency being equal to or less than a prescribed limit.

differential reinforcement of other behavior (DRO) Reinforcement that is delivered when a behavior other than the undesirable behavior occurs. DROs are often used to reduce undesirable attention-seeking behavior with reinforcement of another incompatible (desirable) behavior.

differentiation In reproduction, differentiation occurs when the cells of a zygote begin to divided into cells for specific functions.

difficult child Characteristic behaviors such as negative mood and short attention span that produce negative reactions by care provider. These reactions evoke environments (setting events) that are nonfacilitative. See *easy child.*

direct contingency-shaped behavior Refers to contingency-shaped behavior units (operants) that are given meaning and strengthened by those contingencies involved in their *direct* consequences.

discrimination Refers to differences in responding to different stimuli as the result of the contingency histories. Discrimination is a learning process in which an individual is said to discriminate among relevant stimuli.

discriminative stimulus An antecedent stimulus that cues or signals a response. The third term of the four-term contingency.

disengaged Refers to mothers who are detached, withdrawn, and unresponsive to infants' signals.

disequilibrium A principle of Piaget's cognitive development theory. Frequent mental state in which there is a discrepancy between what the child knows and the environment.

dizygotic twins Developed from two fertilized ova (also called fraternal twins).

DNA (deoxyribonucleic acid) A complex molecule configured as a double helix whose specific sequences determine the species' and the individual's genetic code.

dominant Term used to describe alleles that are stronger relative to other alleles and more likely to express themselves in the phenotype.

DSM-IV-TR *Diagnostic and Statistical Manual of Mental Disorders* (4th ed., text revision) of the American Psychiatric Association. It is the primary authority for the identification of behavior disorders.

dual-component model of child abuse Model offering an explanation of child abuse by identifying the transactions between the genetic, historical, and environmental factors of both the parents and the child. This model places emphasis on the significance of respondent and operant behaviors.

dynamical systems approach The analysis of development into bidirectional, inseparable, and interlocking systems. It emphasizes a nonlinear model of change in which initial interactions have been reorganized so that their effects on other components of the system are ever changing. More general than the behavioral systems approach that does include behavior–analytic learning principles.

dyslexia An impairment of the ability to read.

dysphoria A negative mood state (e.g., anxiety, mild depression).

easy child Child whose characteristics, such as moderate activity level, rhythmicity in biological functions, positive mood, and so on, make it easy to care for him or her. See *difficult child.*

echoic Response that matches the form of its verbal controlling stimulus.

echolalic babbling Babbling with the intonation of adult language.

ecological stimulus Intrinsic reinforcers of exploratory behavior involving the physical properties of various objects, social stimuli, or biological stimuli.

ectoderm Outer layer of the embryo from which the skin, hair, nails, and central nervous system develop.

ectomorph Body type of individuals who are thin, frail, and intellectual.

edible reinforcers Reinforcers that can be eaten.

EEG (electro encephalogram) A measure of the electrical activity of the brain.

egocentrism Seeing things from one's own point of view.

elicited Behavior provoked or caused by a specific stimulus. A characteristic of respondent behaviors, including reflexes. See *emitted.*

embryo Name for the human organism during the second (embryonic) period of development.

embryoblast The inner mass of cells that is the part of the blastula or blastocyst that will become the embryo itself.

embryonic period The second of three prenatal periods, beginning with implantation and ending when all of the basic bodily organs have developed.

emergent properties Characteristics of a phenomenon that appear at a higher level of analysis, but cannot be observed at a lower level of analysis.

emitted Refers to behaviors that simply occur as the activity of living things. Stimuli may signal them but do not provoke them. A characteristic of operant behavior. See *elicited.*

empiricism Viewpoint that states that we acquire perception through experience.

enactive representation A mental model of the world in the form of an action.

endoderm Innermost layer of the embryo from which the inner organs develop (e.g., digestive tract, respiratory system, pancreas, and liver).

endomorph Body type of individuals who are round, plump, and seek pleasure.

environmental contingencies Environmental events that provide reinforcing or punishing consequences.

environmental determinism Behavior is the result of environmental contingencies.

equifinality Situation in which similar developmental outcomes are the result of different interactions.

equilibrium Temporary mental state occurring when there is a match between what the child knows and the environment.

equivalence classes (stimulus or functional) A class of stimuli that serves the same discriminative or reinforcing function.

escape Refers to the process in which the responses of an individual are maintained by the termination of aversive stimuli or circumstances.

establishing operation (EO) Setting event that influences the degree to which a consequence is reinforcing or punishing.

evocative effect The effect produced by a discriminative stimulus; should not be confused with eliciting effect, which is triggered by an eliciting stimulus.

evoke To produce a response. This does not specify whether the response was elicited or emitted.

evolutionary psychology An approach to psychology that emphasizes the evolutionary source of current human behavior.

expansion The elaboration of a child's incomplete utterance by an adult into a (more) complete one (e.g., "Baby walk" into "Yes, the baby walks up the stairs").

experiential canalization A view that suggests that behavior can be organized by the action of environment (i.e., a learning history, not just genes).

experimental method The manipulation of a variable while controlling extraneous variables, and the measuring of changes in another variable to detect a cause-and-effect relationship between the variables.

experimental methodologies Scientific methods that involve the manipulation of independent variables under controlled conditions to see if these variables are the cause of development.

explanation To make clear a cause or reason. To specify the causal variables.

explicit curriculum Acknowledged curriculum that specifically addresses societal needs (formal curriculum).

exploratory behavior A sequence of operant interactions that is strengthened and maintained by contingent ecological stimuli under specifiable setting factors.

external locus of control Attributing the cause of one's behavior to someone or something that is relatively unstable and external to the individual.

externalizing disorders Antisocial behavior patterns, such as attention deficit and disruptive behaviors, that are directed primarily at others.

extinction See *operant extinction, respondent extinction.*

extinction burst An initial, temporary increase in responding, along with emotional behaviors, resulting from the withholding of reinforcement for a response.

extraversion A personality characteristic or trait characterized by being outgoing and seeking social interaction. Contrasted with introversion.

extrinsic reinforcers Environmental strengthening stimuli that must be presented by oneself or by another rather than occurring as an inherent consequence of a response.

fading A procedure of slowly removing one stimulus while introducing another to maintain stimulus control.

fetal period The third of three prenatal periods, beginning when all the bodily organs have developed and ending with birth. This period is characterized by growth and refinement of the fetus.

fetus Name for the human organism during the third (fetal) and longest period of development.

fight-or-flight reaction The activation syndrome in which physiological responses (e.g., heartbeat accelerations, adrenaline release, pupil dilation, etc.) to a threatening stimulus enhances the organism's ability to fight or escape from a threatening stimulus.

fixed-action patterns Elaborate patterns of unlearned behavior elicited by particular environmental stimuli.

fixed-interval schedule A schedule of intermittent reinforcement in which a reinforcer follows the first response after a specific time interval (e.g., 30 minutes, 24 hours) has elapsed.

fixed-ratio schedule A schedule of intermittent reinforcement in which a reinforcer follows a specific number of responses (e.g., every fourth response is reinforced).

formal operations stage (12 years and up) Piaget's stage of cognitive development characterized by the ability to engage in abstract reasoning.

forward chaining (or just chaining) Chaining procedure that begins with teaching the first behavior in the chain and continues teaching each behavior in the order that it occurs within the behavioral chain.

four-term contingency Contingent relationship involving four terms: (a) a response, (b) a consequence (reinforcement or punishment), (c) a discriminative stimulus, and (d) a setting event or establishing operation. The discriminative stimulus sets the occasion for the response, which in turn is reinforced or punished by its consequence. The setting event is the context in which the contingency occurs.

function What something does or how it is used.

functional analysis A procedure involving manipulation of factors or variables (the independent variable) suspected of maintaining, causing, or influencing the observed behavior (the dependent variable).

functional analytic psychotherapy (FAP) A behavioral reconceptualization of cognitive therapy that uses the client–therapist relationship to bring about and change actual occurrences of the client's problematic behavior. Frequently used to treat depression.

functional assessment Identifying the factors or variables that predict and maintain behavior within the framework of the four-term contingency.

functional environmental surround The part of the environment that affects the individual's behavior.

functional equivalence Behavior in which one response class can be substituted for another, producing the same functional contingencies.

functional knowledge Knowledge of how things work or change.

functional relationship Changes between an environment and behavior that usually occur at the same time and are dependent on each other.

functional response classes The grouping of responses based on their consequences. See *operant.*

functional stimulus classes The grouping of physically different stimuli according to the similar effects they have on behavior. See *operant.*

gametes The sex cells involved in biparental reproduction (the female's ovum and male's sperm).

generalization (operant) When a behavior occurs under different stimulus conditions, such as different settings. For example, when a behavior learned in school "generalizes" to the home environment.

generalization (respondent) Occurs when stimuli similar to the conditioned stimulus elicit the conditioned response.

generalized compliance Following instructions based on reinforcement history of previous responses to similar instructions.

generalized imitation Learning imitation as a response class. Occurs when the child's imitation of certain behaviors is reinforced and the child's imitation of other behaviors for which he or she was not reinforced for imitating increases as well.

generalized reinforcers Acquired reinforcers that have been associated with many other secondary and primary reinforcers so that they are reinforcing in many situations.

generative nature of language A view that language is not merely imitative or rote but characterized by an infinite number of grammatical utterances.

genes Locations along a chromosome that determine physical or behavioral characteristics.

genetic-constitutional makeup That which is inherited at conception, including gross physiological characteristics such as sex, physique, and race.

genome The complete genetic code of a species.

genotype One's actual genetic makeup.

genotype–environment interactions Types of relationships describing how two factors responsible for individual differences in development work together. There are three types: passive, evocative, and active.

germinal period The first of three prenatal periods, beginning with the establishment of the fertilized ovum (zygote) and ending with implantation of the blastula or blastocyst in the uterus.

gross–fine law of development Principle of developmental direction stating that general, unrefined characteristics develop into specific, refined characteristics.

growth spurt A dramatic increase in height and weight that characterizes the beginning of adolescence.

habituation Decrease in responding to a particular unconditioned stimulus as a result of repeated exposure to that stimulus. See *respondent extinction.*

heritability Statistical concept pertaining to the amount of the variability, across individuals, of a characteristic that can be attributed to genes.

heterozygous Two alleles from the same pair are of different values (e.g., one is dominant and the other recessive).

holophrase A single word utterance that stands for a complete idea.

holophrastic stage Stage of language development during which children use single words to stand for entire concepts.

homozygous Two alleles from the same pair are of the same value (e.g., bl, bl for eye color).

human genome The complete genetic code of the human race consisting of the sequences of genes on the chromosomes.

hyperactivity A high frequency of repetitive movement and inattention characterized by high-rate switching between response alternatives.

hypothesis A scientific statement in which the orderly relationship between complex sets of observations is summarized and opened to evaluation.

hypothetical constructs Fictitious factors created by theorists to explain difficult phenomena.

iconic representation Mental representation of the world in the form of an image.

identity (self) Refers to self-statements based on self-questioning regarding who one is, where one is going, and what one's place is in society.

identity (stimulus) In stimulus equivalence, a stimulus relation in which the stimulus is recognized as itself (e.g., A = A, B = B).

identity crisis Identity status characterizing individuals who have experienced identity issues and have not been able to resolve them.

implantation The embedding of the blastula or blastocyst into the uterus.

implicit curriculum Informal curriculum that emerges in an unplanned way and reflects societal worldviews (emergent curriculum).

impulsive Choosing between concurrently available response alternatives that produce smaller, immediate reinforcers rather than larger, delayed, or long-term reinforcers.

incompatible behavior A behavior that cannot occur during the presence of a different behavior (e.g., standing is incompatible with sitting).

incompatible response technique Reinforcement is provided contingent on responses that are incompatible with target behavior. The purpose is to reduce the frequency of the undesirable behavior by paying attention or reinforcing incompatible behaviors (e.g., talking to a child when he or she is sitting and ignoring when he or she is standing).

incomplete dominance Some of the characteristics of an allele showing incomplete dominance are expressed in the phenotype.

innate releasing mechanisms From ethological theory: Stimuli that elicit fixed action patterns.

instrumental aggression Operant aggressive behavior that is controlled by its consequences.

instrumental behaviors See *operant*.

interactional view The perspective that human development is the result of the interaction between the organism and the environment.

interaural time difference The difference in time it takes for sound to reach one ear versus the other. Used to identify the location of a sound. The interaural time difference is zero for objects located directly in front or directly in back.

intermittent reinforcement (partial reinforcement) schedule Schedule in which reinforcement does not follow every response. Also called partial reinforcement.

internal locus of control Attributing the cause of one's behavior to a relatively stable personal characteristic one possesses.

internalizing disorders Personality disorders that are not directed at others and are not easily observable internal events (e.g., anxiety disorders, depression).

intraverbal A verbal behavior whose controlling stimulus is the speaker's prior verbal behavior.

intrinsic reinforcement A strengthening consequence that occurs as a natural outcome of the response it strengthens. See *automatic reinforcement*.

intrinsic reinforcers Strengthening stimuli that are an inherent consequence of a response. See *automatic reinforcement*.

introversion A personality trait characterized by avoiding social interaction. See *extraversion.*

invariant Consistent; not changing.

irritable aggression Respondent aggressive behavior, usually displayed during intense autonomic arousal that is elicited by noxious child behaviors.

karyotyping Genetic analysis technique that identifies the chromosomal makeup of an individual.

knowledge Behaviors that demonstrate knowing about things. See *ability.*

language Formal or informal system of symbols forming the structure of verbal behavior.

language acquisition device (LAD) Hypothetical mental construct believed by psycholinguists to be responsible for the child's acquisition of language. Inferred to be part of innate human physiological makeup.

law of effect Thorndike's law, which states that reinforced behavior will likely occur again, whereas punished behavior is less likely to recur.

law of least effort Principle stating that one does the least effortful or difficult behavior that is reinforced.

laws of developmental direction Generalities about what physical features or motor behaviors develop before others.

leading parts Elements of a system, such as a mother in a nuclear family, that have the power to disproportionately affect the system.

learn unit A teaching episode consisting of one three- or four-term contingency.

learned curriculum What students actually learn from their school. See *explicit, formal, implicit,* and *tested curriculum.*

learning A relatively permanent change in behavior in relation to the environment that is due to experience.

linear model Developmental model that assumes that development proceeds in an incremental manner in which change is directly proportional to change in input. See *nonlinear model.*

linguistic competence The hypothetical rather than real ability of the child to form language constructions.

linguistic universals Aspects of language shared by all members of the human species due to the structure of human thought and neurophysiology.

literality Belief that concurrently occurring thoughts, behaviors, and feelings are the same as the behaviors and feelings themselves.

longitudinal designs Developmental research methods in which age differences are assessed by following the same individuals over time. See *cross- sectional designs.*

mand Operant behavior under the control of a setting event such as deprivation or aversive stimulation and reinforced by the stimulus that reduces this deprivation or aversive situation.

matching law Law stating that people closely match their behavior to the value of (e.g., amount or delay to) the consequences of each behavior.

maturation Physical and behavioral changes due to biological growth.

mechanistic Like a machine. Often applied to theories of behavior in which people are said to function like machines.

meiosis The type of cell divisions that take place in reproductive organs and reduce by half the chromosome number for the formation of gametes.

menarche A female's first menstrual period.

mesoderm Middle layer of the embryo from which the muscles, bones, and circulatory system develop.

mesomorph Body type of individuals who are muscular, strong, athletic, and energetic.

methylphenidate A stimulant commonly prescribed for the treatment of ADHD (e.g., Ritalin).

mindfulness-based cognitive therapy (MBCT) Involves moment-to-moment awareness invoked by tuning into one's breath and every other aspect of one's life. MBCT is developed by purposefully paying attention in a nonjudgmental way to what is going on in one's body and mind and in the surrounding world. Staying in touch in this way from one moment to the next—this shift in awareness—may lead to seeing things somewhat differently, perhaps to feeling less stuck, or to a sense of having more options, more strength, and more confidence in one's behavior. The main aim is to learn new ways to handle challenging physical sensations, feelings, behavioral moods, and social interactions. It has been used successfully for preventing relapse in depression.

mitosis Process involving the division of a cell into two new cells. Chromosomes are duplicated during this process so that each new cell has exactly the same genetic code as the original cell and all other cells.

modeling Demonstrating a behavior that serves as a prompt for an imitative response.

molar levels Levels of analysis that encompass large portions or units of behavior. Looking at behavior as a whole. The opposite of molecular analysis.

molecular levels Levels of analysis that focus on the specific individual units of behavior (e.g., stimulus–response analysis). The opposite of molar analysis.

monozygotic twins Identical twins. Develop from same ovum and sperm. See *dizygotic twins*.

moral behavior A behavior that can be shaped by sociocultural contingencies and that relates to the rightness or wrongness of an action.

morula The ball-like human organism when it reaches about 32 cells in number. After the Greek word for *mulberry,* which it resembles.

multifactorial Type of genetic influence on behavior involving many genes, each of which has a small effect by itself.

multiple determination The influence of many factors on the development of behavior. There are two categories of multiple determinants: organismic conditions and environmental conditions.

multiple-baseline designs A single-subject research design that establishes baseline levels of three or more independent behaviors and intervenes with each behavior sequentially. These measures may be of (a) different behaviors of the same individual, (b) the same behaviors of the same individual in different contexts, or (c) the same behavior of different subjects.

multiple-treatments designs See *alternating treatments designs.*

mutation The product of a "proofreading" error that resulted in the wrong sequence of DNA bases being formed during mitosis or meiosis.

naming Providing a formal label for an object or event.

nativism Proposes that perception is innate, that it is hardwired and present at birth.

natter Term for nagging, whining, or other aversive vocal behavior typically used by parents of antisocial children.

natural reinforcers Reinforcers that occur as natural consequences of behavior.

natural selection The process (based on overreproduction, genetic variability, and survival of the best-adapted organisms in a particular environment) that maintains or alters gene frequencies in populations and the survival of some species.

naturalistic approach Approach to the study of development focusing on the observation and description of development in its natural surroundings.

negative punishment (punishment by loss) A *response* is *weakened* because of the removal of a stimulus following the response.

negative reinforcement A *response* is *strengthened* when it removes, terminates, or avoids a stimulus event. Negative reinforcement is *not* punishment.

negative reinforcer A *stimulus* that strengthens a response that results in the removal, avoidance, or termination of the stimulus. The same stimulus may weaken a behavior that produces it.

neonatal imitation Newborns' ability to behaviorally match what they see someone else do.

neonate Newborn (term used until a child is about 2 weeks of age).

neutral stimulus In respondent conditioning, a stimulus that does not initially elicit a UCR or CR. With pairing with the UCS, it will become the CS.

nonarbitrary environment An environment in which objects and events must be labeled in a specific way.

nonlinear model A model of development that emphasizes bidirectional (reciprocal) interactions that result in reorganization of parts of the system. Development shows the sudden fits and starts of phase shifts.

nonlinearity Changes in behavior characterized by sudden changes that are often qualitative. See *phase shifts*.

nonshared environmental effects The unique effects the environment has on the individual.

nonuniversal behaviors Behaviors, unique to individuals, that are the result of learning opportunities determined by cultural values and variations in functional environments.

observational learning A type of learning based on Bandura's notion that children can learn by observation only, without the need of experiencing direct consequences for their actions via vicarious reinforcement. This idea has been challenged by behavior analysts.

one-trial conditioning Conditioning that occurs with a single pairing of a neutral stimulus with an unconditioned stimulus of a high magnitude or intensity.

ontogenic contingencies Factors effecting individual change. Learning.

operant See *operant behavior*.

operant behavior Behavior that operates on the environment and thereby affects and is affected by the environment.

operant conditioning The process of changing behavior through consequences.

operant extinction The weakening of behavior through the withholding of its reinforcement.

operant learning An enduring behavioral change produced as a function of the interaction between the individual's behavior and his or her environment. It refers to a class of behavior controlled (at least in part) by its consequences.

operational scheme Scheme or mentalistic term used in cognitive psychology to refer to a set of mental tasks that follow certain logical rules. A mental representation of how a procedure is performed.

Oppositional Defiant Disorder (ODD) One of the most serious and common behavior problems of children and youth; characterized by defiant and hostile behavior toward authority figures.

organismic Biological part of the individual that contributes to development (nature).

organismic characteristics The result of the organism's genetic makeup and repertoire of behavior.

osmosis The flowing of substances from a location of high concentration to one where there is low concentration.

overregularization Using the regular form of a verb (or noun) for an irregular verb (noun). For example, "The boy goed," or, "He has two left footses."

ovum The female germ cell or gamete. The egg.

parsimony A scientific criterion that states that a simpler explanation, based on a small number of established facts, is better than a complex one.

paternal twins Nonidentical or dizygotic twins.

Pavlovian conditioning See *classical conditioning*. Also called *respondent conditioning*.

perception Organized response to a stimulus. An integrated response to a sensation that results in a functional response.

permissive Parenting style characterized by an indulgent and accepting environment in which a child regulates his or her own behavior.

person–environment interactions Extension of genotype–environment interactions to behaviors that are clearly less genetically and more environmentally determined.

personality The organization of the unique behavioral equipment an individual has acquired under the special conditions of his or her development.

phagocytosis Process used by blastula to ingest nutrients, involving the absorption of nutrients through the cell membrane.

phase shifts A factor in dynamical systems approaches. These shifts are sudden changes in behavior that occur as a result of the organizing of behaviors into an emergent behavior that is topographically unrelated to the previous behaviors. Phase shifts result from coalescent organization.

phenotype The actual expression of a genetic trait that results from genotype and environment transactions.

phoneme A basic unit of sound in speech.

phylogenic contingencies Factors effecting species' change. Natural selection.

physical location as a response class The grouping of responses in accordance to *where* they occur, such as inside or outside the skin.

pivotal response training (PRT) A naturalistic intervention program that helps children with autism engage in an increased level of social behavior.

placental barrier A semipermeable membrane that serves as an interface between the blood supply of the mother and that of the child. It is the point of contact for the passage of nutrients into the child and the outflow of waste products from the child.

pliance Following instructions or a rule due to social contingencies rather than to the direct environmental events or contingencies.

polygenic inheritance patterns Occurs when a characteristic or behavior is the result of many genes rather than a single gene.

positive behavioral support (PBS) An applied behavior analysis intervention that targets problem behaviors that are most effective when they fulfill an educative purpose. Changing behavior through PBS can result in broad changes in a person's lifestyle (e.g., language).

positive punishment (punishment by hurt) A *response* is *weakened* because of the contingent addition of a stimulus following the response.

positive reinforcement A *response* is *strengthened* because of the addition of a stimulus following the response.

positive reinforcer A *stimulus* produced by a response that strengthens the response. Behavior can also be weakened if it results in loss of a positive reinforcer.

practice effects An effect created by testing and retesting.

pragmatics Study of the way language is used.

precipitating conditions of child abuse Acute setting events and discriminative stimuli that, when they occur, make it more likely that abuse may happen.

preconceptual period (ages 2–4 years) First part of Piaget's preoperational stage of cognitive development. The preconceptual stage is characterized by transductive reasoning, animism, egocentrism, and a poor understanding of cause-and-effect relationships.

precurrent behaviors In problem solving, the early part of a chain of behaviors produces the stimuli that produces the solution (behavior). For example, looking in a dictionary is a precurrent behavior that leads to finding the word that is the definition of a term. See *problem solving*.

predisposing factors to child abuse Characteristics of the parent or child that may function as setting events for abusive parental behavior.

prelinguistic sounds Sounds produced by infants prior to their production of words (e.g., crying, cooing, and babbling).

Premack principle Principle stating that any high-frequency behavior can be used to reinforce any low-frequency behavior.

prenatal period Time from conception to birth.

preoperational stage of development (ages 2–7 years) Piaget's preoperational stage consists of two substages: the preconceptual period and the intuitive period.

primary circular reactions Repetitive behaviors centered on the child's own body.

primary reinforcers Universal reinforcers that are functioning at birth due to genetic inheritance.

private events Behaviors that are observable only to the individual emitting the behaviors (e.g., thinking).

problem solving A behavioral chain that occurs when no reinforced response already exists. See *precurrent behaviors.*

prosocial transactions Involve acting in a sympathetic, cooperative, emphatic, helpful, comforting, and generous manner between two or more people. Learning these prosocial patterns is part of early moral development.

proximo-distal law of development Principle of developmental direction stating that things nearer to the center of the body (e.g., heart) develop before things that are more extreme (e.g., fingers).

psycholinguists Nativists who invoke biology as the primary mechanism for language acquisition, believing that a type of language acquisition device in the child's head is responsible for language development.

psychological androgyny Sex role flexibility characterized by an individual's possession of both masculine and feminine traits.

psychology The scientific study of behavior and the relationship of that behavior to the environment in which it occurs.

public events Observable behaviors.

punisher Stimulus that is presented (positive punisher) or removed (negative punisher) after a response and that decreases the frequency of the response.

punishment Any operation in which a response is weakened by its consequence.

random assortment The chance sorting of one of each pair of chromosomes, during meiosis. Random assortment ensures genetic variability.

recessive Term used to describe an allele that is masked by a dominant allele. Recessive alleles are expressed in the phenotype only when both alleles in a pair are present.

reciprocal Two-way interaction in which one person's behavior affects another person's behavior, and vice-versa.

reductionism The reducing of a phenomenon to a lower level of analysis. For example, giving a biological explanation for a psychological disorder.

reflexes Relationship involving the eliciting of an unconditioned response by an unconditioned stimulus.

reflexive Relationship involving the eliciting of an unconditioned response by an unconditioned stimulus.

reflexivity One aspect of stimulus equivalence characterized by being able to respond to a stimulus in terms of a derived (untaught) relationship with other stimuli.

reification Treating a hypothetical construct as real. A common problem that occurs when a child is diagnosed from observed behaviors and the diagnosis is treated as a real entity (e.g., "The child has ADHD").

reinforced behavior Behavior that has been strengthened by its consequence.

reinforcement Any operation that strengthens behavior.

reinforcement trap (involving negative reinforcement) Type of transaction whereby the mother's termination of behaviors that are aversive to the child is negatively reinforced by the child's cessation of behaviors that are aversive to the mother. (There are also positive reinforcement traps.)

reinforcer A stimulus that strengthens a behavior that it immediately follows.

relational frame theory (RFT) A modern behavioral approach to language and cognition built around the simple idea that derived stimulus relations define the core of human language and cognition. This contextualistic approach emphasizes that relating itself is learned and that what is new is the learned modification of learning processes (e.g., bidirectionality of the relationships).

relational frames A specific class of relational stimuli that (a) include contextually controlled qualities of mutual entailment, combinatorial entailment, and contextually controlled transformation of stimulus functions; (b) is due to a history of relational responding relevant to the contextual cues involved; and (c) is not solely based on direct nonrelational training with regard to the particular stimuli of interest or solely on nonarbitrary characteristics of either the stimuli or the relationship between them.

relational networks Combinations of relational frames, such as the following: A is more than B; B is the same as C; C is less than D.

relational repertoires All behavioral relationships shown by a particular person.

relational responding Responding to one stimulus relation in terms of another.

relativistic view of science View that one's conclusions, and even basic observations, are colored by his or her own worldview.

repertoire of behaviors (behavioral repertory) The sum total of response classes a person has emitted in the past.

replacement behaviors Behaviors selected by the experimenter to be reinforced in place of the targeted behavior to be reduced or eliminated.

reproductive risks Exposure to teratogens or other nonfacilitative conditions present prior to or during birth that are harmful to development.

resistance to extinction The ability for a behavior to continue once a consequence no longer occurs (an operant, rather than respondent, term).

resistance to temptation The ability to abstain from a behavior that results in a small, immediate consequence in order to obtain a larger, delayed consequence.

respondent A set of responses that are reliably *elicited* by certain stimuli.

respondent conditioning The pairing of an initially neutral stimulus with an unconditioned stimulus results in the neutral stimulus becoming a conditioned stimulus. The conditioned stimulus elicits the same response as the unconditioned stimulus in the absence of the unconditioned stimulus.

respondent extinction Occurs when the repeated presentation of the conditioned stimulus, in the absence of the unconditioned stimulus, results in the conditioned stimulus becoming a neutral stimulus that no longer elicits the conditioned response.

respondent learning See *classical conditioning*.

response Action that an individual takes or a change that an individual makes. The behavior of central interest when analyzing a four-term contingency.

response classes A group of responses that share a similarity. The similarity may be physical (i.e., the topography), functional (operates in same contingency), or geographic (i.e., public or private).

risk-taking behavior When adolescents engage in activities that involve danger or potential harm.

rubber band hypothesis Metaphor pertaining to the role of the environment with various genotypes. The rubber band represents different genotypes, varying according to their flexibility (range of reaction). The stretching of the rubber band is done by the environment. The more a characteristic can be influenced by the environment, the more stretchable the rubber band.

rule generalization Applying rules learned in one environment to other environments, other settings, or similar contexts.

rule-governed behavior Behavior that is under the influence of verbal instruction.

satiation Reduction of reinforcing effects by the constant or overused presentation of the reinforcer.

scaffolding Assistance or support, usually provided by a parent or teacher, in which cognitive, language, social, and behavioral development can occur.

schedules of reinforcement The pattern of reinforcement to responses. The basic schedules are fixed ratio, fixed interval, variable ratio, and variable interval.

scheme Mental representation or model of the world.

scientific method A system of making observations under well-specified conditions and using special techniques to summarize descriptions of those observations. The steps include (a) formulating a hypothesis; (b) conducting direct observations of the phenomena to test the hypothesis; (c) accepting, rejecting, or modifying the hypothesis; and (d) positing new questions from the data obtained. One of the basic principles of scientific method is that the outcome of a certain test or experiment cannot confirm a hypothesis unless it is possible that there could be another outcome or result that would have disconfirmed the theory.

secondary circular reactions Repetitive behaviors that produce consequences from the external environment.

secondary reinforcers Stimuli that acquire the ability to reinforce behavior by being paired with primary or other secondary reinforcers. Also called *acquired* or *conditioned reinforcers.*

selectionism An adaptation process in which new forms of behavior emerge and are selected by natural environmental contingencies. This process influences both phylogenic and ontogenic adaptations.

selective attrition Nonrandom withdrawal of participants in a study, resulting in a sample that is no longer representative.

selective imitation Behavior that matches some part of the model's utterance but is novel in another way.

selective mutism A condition in which a child may speak with perfectly normal frequency at home or play but does not speak at all in school.

self-as-knower The you that you know.

self-as-known Your personality as you think others see you.

self-awareness The part of a person concerned with knowledge about oneself.

self-concept The sum of all the self-statements an individual makes.

self-control The ability to alter one's behavior through commitment, despite the presence of immediate consequences.

self-editing Changing one's verbal behavior by using one's own feedback and consequences.

self-efficacy beliefs Self-statements about the ability to succeed in accomplishing specific behaviors.

self-esteem Evaluative self-statements about what one can do and how one appears to others.

self-instruction Teaching oneself to accomplish a task by imitation, guidance, talking through the steps out loud, and talking oneself through the task privately.

self-recognition Recognizing oneself in a photograph or mirror.

semantics The relationship of the situation or context to the meaning of an utterance.

sensation The stimulation of sensory receptors and their connections to neurons traveling to the sensory center in the central nervous system.

sensorimotor stage (birth to 2 years) First stage of Piaget's theory of cognitive development before the development of language.

separation protest Child behavior used as an index of mother–infant attachment.

sequential designs A research method that selects subjects of various ages and follows each one over time, thus discriminating age effects from developmental trends.

setting event The context in which the four-term contingency occurs. It influences an interactional sequence by altering the strength and characteristic of the particular stimulus–response functions involved in an interaction. Also called *establishing operation.*

sex chromosomes Chromosomes that determine the sex of the individual (XX for females and XY for males).

sex-linked characteristics Characteristics that occur more frequently in males than females. The Y chromosome of the male lacks sites for dominant genes that would mask the expression of recessive genes on the X chromosome.

shaping A procedure in which successive approximations of a terminal behavior are reinforced.

shared environmental effects   Facets of the environment that affect all persons in a home equally.

single-gene inheritance   Occurs when a characteristic is the result of one gene rather than many genes.

single-subject design   An experiment in which the subject serves as its own control.

slow-to-warm child   Child whose withdrawal, unpredictability in moods, and biological patterns evoke fewer detrimental reactions from the environment than the difficult child. See *difficult child, easy child.*

social behaviors   The responses of an individual that are strengthened or weakened by the reciprocal actions of other individuals or a group.

social cognition   The development of reasoning and social knowledge. Knowing what to do in social situations.

social referencing   Viewing a model's bodily expressions as a discriminative stimulus or cue for one's own behavior.

social reflex   Reflexes with the function of evoking parental caretaking.

social reinforcers   Characteristics of others that become acquired reinforcers that develop because they are associated with many primary reinforcers or previously established secondary reinforcers (e.g., physical contact, proximity, and verbal statements).

socialization   The process by which society teaches values and social skills to human beings.

somatotypes   The ectomorph, mesomorph, and endomorph body types, named after the embryological layer from which they are presumed to have originated.

sound localization   The ability to locate the source of a sound due to its intensity and interaural time difference.

species-typical environment   Environment that is normal for a given species.

spontaneous recovery   The reemergence of a conditioned response that occurs after a period of extinction.

stable–unstable traits   A learned attribute that views the source of control as being either internal (and therefore consistent) or external (and therefore varying).

stereotypes   A conventional, formulaic, and oversimplified conception, opinion, or image of someone's roles.

stimulus   An environmental change or event that has a functional relationship to a particular behavior.

stimulus equivalence class   A group of stimuli that are substitutable for each other in a given context. One is said to exist when identity, symmetry, and transitivity exist among the stimuli. See *identity, symmetry,* and *transitivity.*

strange attractors (also attractor)   The consistent organized patterns of behavior that are unique to individuals.

strong developmental question   Question that asks about the causal processes involved in the progressive changes in an individual over time.

structural equation models   Research-derived correlational models that show the degree of relationship between variables and their direction of influence over time.

structural knowledge   Knowledge about what aspects of development there are and how they relate to each other.

structure   The topography or morphology (form) of a response.

successive approximations   Small units of a complex behavior that are reinforced as they get closer to a final target behavior. See *shaping.*

supernormal stimulus   A stimulus that is more characteristic of its own stimulus class than are other members.

surface structure   The actual ordering of words as they are spoken or written.

symbolic gesturing   The act of using body movements to represent things. This generally appears around the beginning of the child's second year and corresponds with the same order and timing for the functions of requests as vocal words.

symbolic representation   Mental models of the world in the form of symbols or language.

symbolic schemes   Words or other mental stimuli that are arbitrarily related to the things they represent.

symmetry   One aspect of stimulus equivalence characterized by being able to respond to one stimulus in terms of another (e.g., the word *house* and a house).

synchronous reinforcement procedure   A method in which the onset of a response corresponds to the onset of the consequent stimuli.

syntax   The order of words in a sentence or phrase.

systematic desensitization   Common treatment used for phobias that involves the exposure to feared stimuli starting with the least feared and gradually progressing to the most feared. With each exposure, extinction of the fear elicited by the stimuli occurs.

tact   A class of verbal operants in which a response of a given form is evoked by a particular object or event or property of an event. Typically, a name or label.

tangible reinforcers   Objects that derive their reinforcing effects because they can be touched, viewed, smelled, or manipulated in a variety of ways.

task analysis   Procedure used to teach a behavioral chain. The discrete behaviors composing the chain and the sequence in which these behaviors occur are identified by the task analysis.

telegraphic stage   Stage of language development following the holophrastic stage, characterized by the use of as few words as possible to convey a message.

temperament   Style of behaving present at (or shortly after) birth.

teratogens   Substances present during the prenatal period, such as disease or drugs, that cause physical or psychological abnormalities.

tertiary circular reactions   In Piaget's theory, these mark the beginning of curiosity. The child accidentally produces a consequence and then varies the response to determine what behaviors produce the consequence.

tested curriculum   Student performance that is measured through classroom or schoolwide tests or other assessments.

textual   A verbal response whose discriminative stimulus is written or printed.

theory   A group of facts that allow for the prediction of additional facts. There are nine criteria for judging a developmental theory: accuracy, clarity, predictability, practicality, internal consistency, parsimony, testability, productivity, and self-satisfaction.

time-out   Procedure in which an undesirable behavior is weakened by removing the child from the opportunity for behaviors to be reinforced. The weakening of the undesirable behavior through this loss of reinforcement is a mild form of punishment.

token economy   A reinforcement schedule using tokens (such as markers, chips, etc.) as conditioned reinforcers that may be accumulated and exchanged for favored reinforcers.

topographic response class   The grouping of responses based on their form.

topography   The form of a response; its spatial configuration and sometimes its location.

trace conditioning   Occurs when the neutral stimulus is presented and terminated prior to the onset of the unconditioned stimulus.

tracking   Following instructions or a rule due to a history of the correlation between instructions and the direct environmental contingencies.

trajectory   The continuing pathway of development likely to follow one of three patterns: remaining stable, continuing to develop on the same linear or curvilinear path (up or down), or shifting suddenly (phase shifting).

transaction   Process involving reciprocal interactions in which the result of previous interactions determines current interactions.

transactional model   Model of development that views development as the product of reciprocal interactions involving mutual actions.

transductive reasoning   Thinking from specific to specific, unable to make generalizations. Said by Piaget to characterize the preoperational child's logic.

transformational rules   Simple rules for changing a sentence into another form (e.g., statement into question).

transitivity   One aspect of stimulus equivalence characterized by an emergent relation; that is, to be able to respond to an untrained stimulus in the same way as trained members of the class (e.g., A = B and B = C; therefore A = C).

trophoblast   Outer protective layer of the blastula or blastocyst that develops into the membranes surrounding the child (e.g., the amnion, chorion, placenta, umbilical cord, and allantois).

Type F organizations   Organizations controlled by the effect their actions have on the environment (functional organizations).

Type S organizations   Organizations under contingencies that shape and maintain the organization's survival without regard for its effect on societal needs (static organizations).

umbilical cord   The conduit for substances between the child and placenta.

unconditioned response   Response that is not the result of learning.

unconditioned stimulus   Stimulus that elicits an unlearned (reflexive) response.

universal behaviors   Behaviors that appear consistently across all members of the species.

variability   A characteristic of the action of all objects, including living beings. It is a necessary characteristic of behavior in order to make selection by consequences possible.

variable-interval schedule   A schedule of intermittent reinforcement in which the first behavior after a time interval has elapsed is reinforced. However, the length of the interval varies.

variable-ratio schedule   An intermittent reinforcement schedule in which the number of responses before reinforcement varies around an average.

verbal behavior   Behavior reinforced through the mediation of other persons.

vicarious consequences (vicarious reinforcement/punishment)   Principle of observational learning in which behavior changes without direct consequation of responses but, rather, by seeing another receive the consequence.

vicarious learning   Learning through the experiences of others. See *observational learning*.

visual cliff   A large, glass-covered table with a shallow and deep end used to study an infant's development of depth perception and fear.

visual preference method   A procedure used to assess visual capabilities in infants in which differences in the amount of time gazing indicate the ability to detect a difference between two stimuli.

vocables   Unique sounds of an infant that function as words.

within-subjects designs   An experiment in which a subject's behavior is observed repeatedly before and during experimental treatment. See *ABAB reversal design, alternating treatments designs, multiple-baseline design*.

worldview   An overarching general conception of the world.

yolk sac   The initial source of embryo blood cells.

zone of proximal development   The range of behavior between what a child can achieve independently and what can be achieved with the aid of a more competent member of the culture, such as an adult or another child.

zygote   Single-cell fertilized ovum.

REFERENCES

Acredolo, L. P., & Goodwyn, S. W. (1985). Symbolic gesturing in language development: A case study. *Human Development, 28,* 40–49.

Acredolo, L. P., & Goodwyn, S. W. (1988). Symbolic gesturing in normal infants. *Child Development, 59,* 450–466.

Acredolo, L. P., & Goodwyn, S. W. (1990). Sign language in babies: The significance of symbolic gesturing for understanding language development. In R. Vasta (Ed.), *Annals of child development* (Vol. 7, pp. 1–42). London: Jessica Kingsley.

Acredolo, L. P., Goodwyn, S. W., Horobin, K. D., & Emmons, Y. D. (1999). The signs and sounds of early language development. In L. Balter & C. S. Tamis-LeMonda (Eds.), *Child psychology: A handbook of contemporary issues* (pp. 116–139). Philadelphia: Psychology Press.

Agras, W. S., Schneider, J. A., Arnow, B., Raeburn, S. D., & Telch, C. F. (1989). Cognitive-behavioral and response-prevention treatments for bulimia nervosa. *Journal of Consulting and Clinical Psychology, 57*(2), 215–221.

Ainsworth, M., Bell, S., & Stayton, D. (1972). Individual differences in the strange situation behavior of 1-year-olds. In H. R. Schaffer (Ed.), *The origins of human social relations.* New York: Academic Press.

Ainsworth, M. D. S., Blehar, M. C., Waters, E., & Wall, S. (1978). *Patterns of attachment: A psychological study of the strange situation.* Hillsdale, NJ: Lawrence Erlbaum.

Ambert, A. M. (1997). *Parents, children, and adolescents: Interactive relationships and development in context.* New York: Haworth Press.

American Academy of Child and Adolescent Psychiatry. 2001. *Glossary of symptoms and mental illnesses affecting teenagers.* Retrieved August 14, 2003 from http://www.aacap.org/about/glossary

American Academy of Pediatrics. (1999). Policy statement: Folic acid for the prevention of neural tube defects (RE9834). *Pediatrics, 104*(2), 325–327.

American Psychiatric Association. (2000). *Diagnostic and Statistical Manual of Mental Disorders* (4th ed., text rev.) Washington, DC: Author.

American Psychiatric Association (1994). *Diagnostic and statistical manual of mental disorders* (4th Edition). New York: American Psychological Association.

Anastasi, A. (1958). Heredity, environment, and the question "How?" *Psychological Review, 65,* 197–208.

Anderson, J. C., Williams, S., McGee, R., & Silva, P. A. (1987). DSM III disorders in preadolescent children: Prevalence in a large sample from the general population. *Archives of General Psychiatry, 44,* 69–76.

Andronis, P. T. (1983). *Symbolic aggression by pigeons: Contingency coadduction.* Unpublished dissertation, University of Chicago.

Andronis, P. T., Layng, T. V. J., & Goldiamond, I. (1997). Contingency adduction of "symbolic aggression" by pigeons. *Analysis of Verbal Behavior, 14,* 5–17.

Anisfeld, M. (1991). Neonatal imitation. *Developmental Review, 11,* 60–97.

Anslin, R. N. (1987). Visual and auditory development in infancy. In J. D. Osofsky (Ed.), *Handbook of infant development* (2nd ed., pp. 5–97). New York: John Wiley.

Ashmead, D. H., DeFord, L. D., Whalen, T., & Odom, R. D. (1991). Sound localization and sensitivity to interaural time differences in human development. *Child Development, 62*(6), 1211–1226.

Azrin, N. H., Hutchinson, R. R., & Hake, D. F. (1966). Extinction-induced aggression.

Journal of the Experimental Analysis of Behavior, 9, 191–204.

Azrin, N. H., Sneed, T. J., & Foxx, R. M. (1973). Dry bed: A rapid method of eliminating bedwetting (enuresis) of the retarded. *Behaviour Research & Therapy, 11*(4), 427–434.

Bachrach, A. J., Erwin, W. J., & Mohr, P. J. (1965). The control of eating behavior in an anorexic by operant conditioning techniques. In L. Ullmann & L. Krasner (Eds.), *Case studies in behavior modification* (pp. 153–163). New York: Holt, Rinehart & Winston.

Baer, D. M. (1970). An age-irrelevant concept of development. *Merrill-Palmer Quarterly of Behavior and Development, 16,* 238–246.

Baer, D. M. (1976). The organism as host. *Human Development, 19,* 87–98.

Baer, D. M. (1993). On Morris's mechanisms. *The Behavior Analyst, 16,* 45–46.

Baer, D. M., & Rosales-Ruiz, J. (1998). In the analysis of behavior, what does "develop" mean? *Mexican Journal of Behavior Analysis, 24*(2), 127–136.

Baer, D. M., & Sherman, J. A. (1964). Reinforcement control of generalized imitation in young children. *Journal of Experimental Child Psychology, 1,* 37–49.

Bahrick, L. E. (1988). Intermodal learning in infancy: Learning on the basis of two kinds of invariant relations in audible and visible events. *Child Development, 59,* 197–209.

Bahrick, L. E. (1992). Infants' perceptual differentiation of amodal and modality-specific audiovisual relations. *Journal of Experimental Child Psychology, 53,* 180–199.

Bahrick, L. E. (1994). The development of infants' sensitivity to arbitrary intermodal relations. *Ecological Psychology, 6,* 111–123.

Bahrick, L. E. (2000). Increasing specificity in the development of intermodal perception. In D. Muir & A. Slater (Eds.), *Infant development: The essential readings* (pp. 119–136). Oxford, UK: Blackwell.

Bahrick, L. E. (2001). Increasing specificity in perceptual development: Infants' detection of nested levels of multimodal stimulation. *Journal of Experimental Child Psychology, 79,* 253–270.

Baker, L., & Lombardi, B. R. (1985). Students' lecture notes and their relation to test performance. *Teaching of Psychology, 12,* 28–32.

Baltes, M., & Reese, H. W. (1977). Operant research in violation of the operant paradigm? In B. C. Etzel, J. M. LeBlanc, & D. J. Baer (Eds.), *New developments in behavioral research: Theory, method and application* (pp. 11–30). Hillsdale, NJ: Lawrence Erlbaum.

Bandura, A. (1965). Influence of models' reinforcement contingencies on the acquisition of imitative responses. *Journal of Personality and Social Psychology, 1,* 589–595.

Bandura, A. (1977a). Self-efficacy: Toward a unifying theory of behavioral change. *Psychological Review, 84,* 191–215.

Bandura, A. (1977b). *Social learning theory.* Englewood Cliffs, NJ: Prentice Hall.

Bandura, A., Ross, D., & Ross, S. A. (1963). Imitation of film-mediated aggressive models. *Journal of Abnormal and Social Psychology, 67,* 527–534.

Bandura, A., & Walters, R. (1963). *Social learning and personality development.* New York: Holt, Rinehart & Winston.

Barkley, R. A. (1981). *Hyperactive children: A handbook of diagnosis and treatment.* New York: Guilford Press.

Barkley, R. A. (1987). *Defiant children: A clinician's manual for parent training.* New York: Guilford Press.

Barkley, R. A. (1997). *Understanding the defiant child: Program manual.* New York: Guilford Press.

Barkley, R. A. (1998). *Attention deficit hyperactivity disorder.* New York: Guilford Press.

Barnes, D. (1996). Naming as a technical term: Sacrificing behavior analysis at the altar of popularity? *Journal of the Experimental Analysis of Behavior, 65,* 264–267.

Barnes, D., McCullagh, P. D., & Keenan, M. (1990). Equivalence class formation in non-hearing impaired children and hearing impaired children. *Analysis of Verbal Behavior, 8,* 19–30.

Barnes-Holmes, D., & Barnes-Holmes, Y. (2002, Fall). Naming, story-telling, and problem-solving. *Behavioral Development Bulletin,* 34–38.

Barnes-Holmes, Y. (2001). *Analysing relational frames: Studying language and cognition in young children.* Unpublished doctoral dissertation, National University of Ireland, Maynooth.

Barnes-Holmes, Y., & Barnes-Holmes, D. (in press). Critical elements in the development of language and cognition. *Behavioral Development Bulletin.*

Barnes-Holmes, Y., Barnes-Holmes, D., Roche, B., & Smeets, P. M. (2001, Fall). The development of self and perspective-taking: A relational frame analysis. *Behavioral Development Bulletin,* pp. 42–45.

Baron-Cohen, S., Tager-Flusberg, H., & Cohen, D. (2000). *Understanding other minds: Perspectives from developmental cognitive neuroscience* (2nd ed.). Oxford, UK: Oxford University Press.

Barrett, B. H., Beck, R., Binder, C., Cook, D. A., Engelmann, S., Greer, R. D., et al. (1990, November). *The Association for Behavior Analysis position statement on students' rights to effective education.* Retrieved August 8, 2003, from http://www.abainternational. org/sub/membersvcs/journals-pubs/pssree/ index. asp

Barrett-Goldfarb, M. S., & Whitehurst, G. J. (1972). Infant vocalizations as a function of parental voice selection. *Developmental Psychology, 8,* 273–276.

Barton, S. (1994). Chaos, self-organization, and psychology. *American Psychologist, 49,* 5–14.

Bates, J. (1989). Concepts and measures of temperament. In G. Kohnstamm, J. Bates, & M. K. Rothbart (Eds.), *Temperament in childhood* (pp. 3–27). New York: John Wiley.

Baum, W. M. (1973). The correlation-based law of effect. *Journal of the Experimental Analysis of Behavior, 20,* 137–153.

Baum, W. M. (1994). *Understanding behaviorism.* New York: Harper-Collins.

Bauman, K. E., Reiss, M. L., Rogers, R. W., & Bailey, J. S. (1983). Dining out with children: Effectiveness of a parent advice package on pre-meal inappropriate behavior. *Journal of Applied Behavior Analysis, 16,* 55–68.

Baumrind, D. (1966). Effects of authoritative parental control on child behavior. *Child Development, 37,* 887–907.

Baumrind, D. (1967). Child care practices anteceding three patterns of preschool behavior. *Genetic Psychology Monographs, 75,* 43–88.

Baumrind, D. (1977, March). *Socialization determinants of personal agency.* Paper presented at the convention of the Society for Research in Child Development, New Orleans.

Baumrind, D. (1991). The influence of parenting style on adolescent competence and substance use. *Journal of Early Adolescence, 11*(1), 56–95.

Bayer, R. (1994). Ethical challenges posed by zidovudine treatment to reduce vertical transmission of HIV. *New England Journal of Medicine, 331,* 1223–1225.

Belin, H. (1989). Piagetian theory. In R. Vasta (Ed.), *Annals of Child Development* (Vol. 6). Greenwich, CT: JAI Press.

Bell, S. (1903). The significance of activity in child life. *Independent, 55,* 911–914.

Belsky, J., Steinberg, L., & Draper, P. (1991). Childhood experience, interpersonal development, and reproductive strategy: An evolutionary theory of socialization. *Child Development, 62,* 647–670.

Bem, S. L. (1974). The measurement of psychological androgyny. *Journal of Consulting and Clinical Psychology, 42,* 155–162.

Bem, S. L. (1975). Sex-role adaptability: One consequence of psychological androgyny. *Journal of Personality and Social Psychology, 31,* 634–643.

Bem, S. L. (1978). Beyond androgyny: Some presumptuous prescriptions for a liberated sexual identity. In J. A. Sherman & F. L. Denmark (Eds.), *The psychology of women: Future dimensions in research.* New York: Psychological Dimensions.

Bem, S. L. (1981). Gender schema theory: A cognitive account of sex typing. *Psychological Review, 88,* 354–364.

Bennett, N. G., Li, J., Song, Y., & Yang, K. (1999). *Young children in poverty: A statistical update.* New York: National Center for Children in Poverty.

Berger, S. M. (1962). Conditioning through vicarious instigation. *Psychological Review, 69,* 450–466.

Bergerud, D., Lovitt, T. C., & Horton, S. (1988). The effectiveness of textbook adaptations to life science for high school students with learning disabilities. *Journal of Learning Disabilities, 21,* 70–76.

Berko, J. (1958). The child's learning of English morphology. *Word, 14,* 150–177.

Bernstein, G. A., & Borchardt, C. M. (1991). Anxiety disorders of childhood and adolescence: A critical review. *Journal of American Academy of Child and Adolescent Psychiatry, 30,* 519–531.

Besevegis, E., & Lore, R. K. (1983). Effects of an adult's presence on the social behavior of preschool children. *Aggressive Behavior, 9,* 243–252.

Best, D. L., Williams, J. E., Cloud, J. M., Davis, W. S., Robertson, L. S., Edwards, S. R., et al. (1977). Development of sex-trait stereotypes among young children in the United States, England, and Ireland. *Child Development, 48,* 1373–1384.

Bijou, S. W. (1975). Development in the preschool years: A functional analysis. *American Psychologist, 30,* 829–837.

Bijou, S. W. (1979). Some clarifications on the meaning of a behavior analysis of child development. *Psychological-Record, 29*(1), 3–13.

Bijou, S. W. (1998). Exploratory behavior in infancy and early childhood. *Mexican Journal of Behavior Analysis, 24*(2), 215–224.

Bijou, S. W., & Baer, D. M. (1961). *Child development: Vol. 1. A systematic and empirical theory.* New York: Appleton-Century-Crofts.

Bijou, S. W., & Baer, D. M. (1965). *Child development: Vol. 2. Universal stage of infancy.* New York: Appleton-Century-Crofts.

Bijou, S. W., & Baer, D. M. (1978). *Behavior analysis of child development.* Englewood Cliffs, NJ: Prentice Hall.

Binder, L. M., Dixon, M. R., & Ghezzi, P. M. (2000). A procedure to teach self-control to children with attention deficit hyperactivity disorder. *Journal of Applied Behavior Analysis, 33,* 233–237.

Birnbaum, J. A. (1975). Life patterns and self-esteem in gifted family-oriented and career-committed women. In M. S. Mednick, S. S. Tangri, & L. W. Hoffman (Eds.), *Women and achievement* (pp. 396–410). Washington, DC: Hemisphere.

Bjorklund, D. F. (1987). A note on neonatal imitation. *Developmental Review, 7,* 86–92.

Bjorklund, D. F. (1989). *Children's thinking: Developmental function and individual differences.* Belmont, CA: Brooks/Cole.

Blumberg, M. (1974). Psychopathology of the abusing parent. *American Journal of Psychotherapy, 28,* 21–29.

Boller, K., Rovee-Collier, C., Borovsky, D., O'Connor, J., & Shyi, G. (1990). Developmental changes in the time dependent nature of memory retrieval. *Developmental Psychology, 26,* 770–779.

Bondy, A., & Frost, L. (1994). The Picture Exchange Communication System. *Focus on Autistic Behavior, 9,* 1–19.

Bondy, A., & Frost, L. (2001). The Picture Exchange Communication System. *Behavior Modification, 25*(5), 725–744.

Born, D. G., & Davis, M. L. (1974). Amount and distribution of study in a personalized instruction course and in a lecture course. *Journal of Applied Behavior Analysis, 7,* 365–375.

Bornstein, M. H. (1981). Psychological studies of color perception in human infants: Habituation, discrimination and categorization, recognition, and conceptualization. In L. P. Lipsitt & C. K. Rovee-Collier (Eds.), *Advances in infancy research* (Vol. 1, pp. 1–40). Norwood, NJ: Ablex.

Bower, T. G. R. (1977). *A primer of infant development.* San Francisco, CA: Freeman.

Bowlby, J. (1969). *Attachment and loss: Vol. 1. Attachment.* New York: Basic Books.

Bowlby, J. (1973). *Attachment and loss: Vol. 2. Loss.* New York: Basic Books.

Bowlby, J. (1980). *Attachment and loss: Vol. 3. Separation: Anxiety and anger.* New York: Basic Books.

Boyer, P. J., Dillon, M., Navaie, M., Deveikis, A., Keller, M., O'Rourke, S., et al. (1994). Factors predictive of maternal-fetal transmission of HIV-1: Preliminary analysis of zidovudine given during pregnancy and/or delivery. *Journal of the American Medical Association, 271,* 1925–1930.

Bradley, R. H., Whiteside, L., Mundfrom, D. J., Casey, P. H., Kelleher, K. J., & Pope, S. K. (1994). Early indications of resilience and their relation to experience in the home environments of low birthweight, premature children living in poverty. *Child Development, 65,* 346–360.

Brandenburg, G. C., & Brandenburg, J. (1919). Language development during the fourth year: The conversation. *Pedagogical Seminary, 26*(1), 27–40.

Branscum, E. (2000). *Early childhood social development. Multinformant examination of the bully–victim cycle.* Unpublished manuscript, Florida International University.

Branscum, E., & Novak, G. (1995, May). *The importance of compound stimulus presentation in language acquisition through dialogic reading sessions.* Paper presented at the 21st annual convention of the Association for Behavior Analysis, Washington, DC.

Brazelton Institute. (2000). *The neonatal behavioral assessment scale (revised).* Retrieved July 18, 2003 from http://www.brazelton-institute.com/train_r.html

Brazelton, T. B. (1984). *Neonatal behavioral assessment scale* (2nd ed.). Clinics in Developmental Medicine. No. 88. Philadelphia: Lippincott.

Bretherton, I. (1987). New perspectives on attachment relations: Security, communication, and internal working models. In J. D. Osofsky (Ed.), *Handbook of infant development* (2nd ed., pp. 1061–1100). New York: John Wiley.

Bridger, W. H. (1961). Sensory habituation and discrimination in the human neonate. *American Journal of Psychiatry, 117,* 991–996.

Bronfenbrenner, U. (1979). *The ecology of human development.* Cambridge, MA: Harvard University Press.

Bronfenbrenner, U., & Crouter, A. C. (1983). The evolution of environmental models in developmental research. In P. H. Mussen (Ed.), *Handbook of child psychology* (4th ed., Vol. 1, pp. 357–414). New York: John Wiley.

Bronshtein, A. I., & Petrova, E. P. (1967). The auditory analyzer in young infants. In Y. Brackbill & G. C. Thompson (Eds.), *Behavior in infancy and early childhood* (pp. 163–172). New York: Free Press.

Brooks-Gunn, J., Graber, J. A., & Paikoff, R. L. (1994). Studying links between hormones and negative affect: Models and measures. *Journal of Research on Adolescence, 4,* 469–486.

Brown, R. (1973). *A first language: The early stages.* Cambridge, MA: Harvard University Press.

Brown, R., Cazden, C., & Bellugi, U. (1969). The child's grammar from I to III. In J. P. Hill (Ed.), *Minnesota symposium on child psychology* (Vol. 2). Minneapolis: University of Minnesota Press.

Brown, R., & Hanlon, C. (1970). Derivational complexity and order of acquisition. In J. R. Hayes (Ed.), *Cognition and the development of language* (pp. 11–53). New York: John Wiley.

Brown, R. T., & La Rosa, A. (2002). Recent developments in the pharmacotherapy of attention deficit/hyperactivity disorder (ADHD). *Professional Psychology: Research and Practice, 33*(6), 591–595.

Bruner, J. S. (1964). The course of cognitive growth. *American Psychologist, 19,* 1–15.

Bryan, J. W., & Luria, Z. (1978). Sex role learning: A test of the selective attention hypothesis. *Child Development, 49,* 13–23.

Buri, J. R., Louiselle, P. A., Misukanis, T. M., & Mueller, R. A. (1988). Effects of parental authoritarianism and authoritativeness on self-esteem. *Personality and Social Psychology Bulletin, 14,* 271–282.

Burkholder, E. O., & Peláez, M. (2000). A behavioral interpretation of Vygotsky's theory of thought, language, and culture. *Behavior Development Bulletin, 9,* 7–9. Bushell, D., & Baer, D. M. (1994). Measurably superior instruction means close, continual contact with the relevant outcome data. Revolutionary! In R. Gardner et al. (Eds.), *Behavior analysis in education: Focus on measurably superior instruction* (pp. 3–10). Pacific Grove, CA: Brooks/Cole.

Bushell, D., & Baer, D. M. (1994). Measurably superior instruction means close, continual contact with the relevant outcome data. Revolutionary! In R. Gardner & D. M. Sainato & J. O. Cooper & T. E. Heron & W. L. Heward & J. Eshleman & T. A. Grossi (Eds.), *Behavior Analysis in Education: Focus on Measurably Superior Instruction* (pp. 3–10). Pacific Grove, CA: Brooks-Cole.

Caldwell, D. F., & Werboff, J. (1962). Classical conditioning in newborn rats. *Science, 136,* 1118–1119.

Cameron, J., Banko, K. M., & Pierce, W. D. (2001). Pervasive negative effects of rewards on intrinsic motivation: The myth continues. *The Behavior Analyst, 24*(1), 1–44.

Cameron, J., & Pierce, W. D. (1994). Reinforcement, reward, and intrinsic motivation. *Review of Educational Research, 64,* 363–423.

Campbell, F. A., & Ramey, C. T. (1994). Effects of early intervention on intellectual and academic achievement: A follow-up study of children from low-income families. *Child Development, 65,* 684–698.

Campbell, S. B. (1995). Behavior problems in preschool children: A review of recent research. *Journal of Child Psychology and Psychiatry, 28,* 835–845.

Campos, J. J. (1983). The importance of affective communication in social referencing: A commentary on Feinman. *Merrill-Palmer Quarterly, 29,* 83–87.

Campos, J. J., & Barrett, K. C. (1984). Toward a new understanding of emotions and their development. In C. E. Izard, J. Kagan, & R. B. Zajonc (Eds.), *Emotions, cognition, and behavior* (pp. 17–37). New York: Cambridge University Press.

Campos, J. J., Langer, A., & Krowitz, A. (1970). Cardiac responses on the visual cliff in prelocomotor human infants. *Science, 170,* 196–197.

Carbone, V. J. (2001). Teaching verbal behavior to children with autism and related disabilities. In M. L. Sundberg & J. W. Partington (Eds.), *Teaching language to children with autism or other learning disabilities.* Pleasant Hill, CA: Behavior Analysts.

Carey, T., Ratliff-Schaub, K., Funk, J., Weinle, C., Myers, M., & Jenks, J. (2002). Double-blind placebo-controlled trial of secretin: Effects on aberrant behavior in children with autism. *Journal of Autism and Developmental Disorders, 32*(3), 161–167.

Carnine, D. W. (1976). Effects of two teacher presentation rates on off-task behavior, answering correctly, and participation. *Journal of Applied Behavior Analysis, 9,* 199–206.

Carrier, C. A. (1983). Notetaking research: Implications for the classroom. *Journal of Instructional Development, 6*(3), 19–29.

Caspi, A., Elder, G. H., & Bem, D. J. (1987). Moving against the world: Life course patterns of explosive children. *Developmental Psychology, 23,* 308–313.

Caspi, A., & Moffitt, T. E. (1993). When do individual differences matter? A paradoxical theory of personality coherence. *Psychological Inquiry, 4*(4), 247–271.

Catania, A. C. (1984). Editorial: Conceivable book reviews. *Journal of the Experimental Analysis of Behavior, 42*(2), 165–169.

Catania, A. C. (1998). *Learning* (4th ed.). Englewood Cliffs, NJ: Prentice Hall.

Cattell, R. B. (1950). *Personality: A systematic theoretical and factual study.* New York: McGraw-Hill.

Cattell, R. B. (1965). *The scientific analysis of personality.* Oxford, UK: Penguin.

Caulfield, M. B., Fischel, J. E., DeBaryshe, B. D., & Whitehurst, G. J. (1989). Behavioral correlates of developmental expressive language disorder. *Journal of Abnormal Child Psychology, 17*(2), 187–201.

Cazden, C. B., & Brown, R. (1975). The early development of the mother tongue. In E. H. Lennenberg & E. Lennenberg (Eds.), *Foundations of language development: A multi-disciplinary approach* (Vol. 1). New York: Academic Press.

Centers for Disease Control and Prevention. (2003, February). Eliminating perinatal HIV transmission. *Program in Brief,* p. 1.

Cernoch, J. M., & Porter, R. H. (1985). Recognition of maternal axillary odors by infants. *Child Development, 56,* 1593–1598.

Cerutti, D. T. (1989). Discrimination theory of rule-governed behavior. *Journal of Experimental Analysis of Behavior. 51,* 259–276.

Chomsky, N. (1959). Review of B. F. Skinner's *Verbal Behavior. Language, 35,* 26–58.

Cigales, M., Field, T., Hossain, Z., & Peláez-Nogueras, M., & Gewirtz, J. (1996). Touch among children at nursery school. *Early Child Development and Care, 126,* 101–110.

Clarke-Stewart, K. A. (1978). And daddy makes three: The father's impact on mother and young child. *Child Development, 49,* 466–478.

Cohn, J. F., Campbell, S. B., Matias, R., & Hopkins, J. (1990). Face-to-face interactions of postpartum and nondepressed mother–infant pairs at two months. *Developmental Psychology, 26,* 185–193.

Cole, D. A. (1990). The relation of social and academic competence to depressive symptoms in childhood. *Journal of Abnormal Psychology, 99,* 422–429.

Coleman, J. (1961). *The adolescent society.* New York: Free Press.

Committee for Economic Development. (1993). *Why child care matters: Preparing young children for a more productive America.* A statement by the Research Committee of the Committee for Economic Development. New York: Author.

Commons, M. L. (1991). A comparison and synthesis of Kohlberg's cognitive-developmental and Gewirtz's learning-developmental attachment theories. In J. L. Gewirtz & W. M. Kurtines (Eds.), *Intersection with attachment.* Hillsdale, NJ: Lawrence Erlbaum.

Commons, M. L., & Miller, P. M. (1998). A quantitative behavior-analytic theory of development. *Mexican Journal of Behavior Analysis, 24*(2), 153–180.

Commons, M. L., & Rodriguez, J. A. (1993). The development of hierarchically complex equivalence classes. *Psychological Record, 43,* 667–695.

Compton, S. N., Burns, B. J., Egger, H. L., & Robertson, E. (2002). Review of the evidence base for treatment of childhood psychopathology: Internalizing disorders. *Journal of Consulting and Clinical Psychology, 70*(6), 1240–1266.

Conger, R. D., Ge, X., Elder, G. H., Lorenz, F. O., & Simmons, R. L. (1994). Economic stress, coercive family process, and developmental problems of adolescents. *Child Development, 65,* 541–561.

Cook, J., & Ludwig, P. J. (2000). *Gun Violence: The real costs.* New York: Oxford University Press.

Cooper, J. O., Heron, T. E., & Heward, W. L. (1987). *Applied behavior analysis.* Columbus, OH: Merrill.

Corbett, B., Khan, K., Czapansky Beilman, D., Brady, N., Dropik, P., Zelinsky Goldman, D., et al. (2001). A double-blind, placebo-controlled crossover study investigating the effect of porcine secretin in children with autism. *Clinical Pediatrics, 40*(6), 327–331.

Cowley, G. (1994, March 7). Locking HIV out of the womb. *Newsweek, 123,* 53.

Coyle, S., Arnold, H. M., Goldberg-Arnold, J. S., Rubin, D. C., & Hall, W. G. (2000). Olfactory conditioning facilitates diet transition in human infants. *Developmental Psychobiology, 37,* 144–152.

Craig, G. J. (1999). *Human development.* New Jersey: Prentice Hall.

Craighead, W. E., Kazdin, A. E., & Mahoney, M. J. (1981). *Behavior modification: Principles, issues, and applications* (2nd ed.). Boston: Houghton Mifflin.

Crampton, G., & Lucot, J. B. (1991). Habituation of motion sickness in the cat. *Aviation, Space, and Environmental Medicine, 62,* 212–215.

Critchfield, T. S., Haley, R., Meacropolis, G., Colbert, J., & Sabo, B. (in press). A half century of scalloping: Work habits of the United States Congress revisited. *Journal of Applied Behavior Analysis.*

Crockenberg, S. B. (1981). Infant irritability, mother responsiveness, and social support influences on the security of infant–mother attachment. *Child Development, 52,* 857–865.

Crockenberg, S. B. (1986). Are temperamental differences in babies associated with predictable differences in caregiving? In J. Lerner & R. Lerner (Eds.), *Temperament and interaction in infancy and childhood* (pp. 53–73). San Francisco: Jossey-Bass.

Csikszentmihalyi, M., Larson, R., & Prescott, S. (1977). The ecology of adolescent activity and experience. *Journal of Youth and Adolescence, 6,* 281–294.

Cuban, L. (1995). The hidden variable: How organizations influence teacher responses to secondary science curriculum reform. *Theory Into Practice, 34*(1), 4–11.

Curtis, G. (1963). Violence breeds violence. *American Journal of Psychiatry, 120,* 386–387.

Darwin, C. R. (1872/1965). *The expression of emotions in man and animals.* London: John Murray.

Davison, G. C., & Neale, J. M. (1998). *Abnormal psychology* (7th ed.). New York: John Wiley.

Davison, K. K., & Susman, E. J. (2001). Are hormone levels and cognitive ability related during early adolescence? *International Journal of Behavioral Development, 25,* 416–428.

de Villiers, J. G., & de Villiers, P. A. (1999). Language development. In M. H. Bornstein (Ed.), *Developmental psychology: An advanced textbook* (4th ed., pp. 313–373). Mahwah, NJ: Lawrence Erlbaum.

DeCasper, A. J., & Fifer, W. P. (1980). Of human bonding: Newborns prefer their mothers' voices. *Science, 208,* 1174–1176.

DeCasper, A. J., & Prescott, P. A. (1984). Human newborns' perception of male voices: Preference, discrimination, and reinforcing value. *Developmental Psychobiology, 17,* 481–491.

DeCasper, A. J., & Sigafoos, A. D. (1983). The intrauterine heartbeat: A potent reinforcer for newborns. *Infant Behavior & Development, 6,* 19–25.

DeCasper, A. J., & Spence, M. J. (1986). Prenatal maternal speech influences newborns' perception of speech sounds. *Infant Behavior & Development, 9,* 133–150.

Deci, E. L., Koestner, R., & Ryan, R. M. (1999). A meta-analytic review of experiments examining the effects of extrinsic rewards on intrinsic motivation. *Psychological Bulletin, 125,* 627–668.

Del Valle, P., Kelley, S. L., & Seoanes, J. E. (2001). The "oppositional defiant" and "conduct disorder" child: A brief review of etiology, assessment and treatment. *Behavioral Development Bulletin, 1,* 36–41.

Denney, J., & Neuringer, A. (1998). Behavioral variability is controlled by discriminative stimuli. *Animal Learning and Behavior, 26*(2), 154–162.

Devany, J. M., Hayes, S. C., & Nelson, R. O. (1986). Equivalence class formation in language-able and language-disabled children. *Journal of the Experimental Analysis of Behavior, 46*(3), 243–257.

DeVries, R., Haney, J. P., & Zan, B. (1991). Sociomoral atmosphere in direct-instruction, eclectic, and constructivist kindergartens: A study of teachers' enacted interpersonal understanding. *Early Childhood Research Quarterly, 6,* 449–471.

DeVries, R., Reese-Learned, H., & Morgan, P. (1991). Sociomoral development in direct-instruction, eclectic, and constructivist kindergartens: A study of children's enacted interpersonal understanding. *Early Childhood Research Quarterly, 6,* 473–517.

Dickinson, A. M. (1989). The detrimental effects of extrinsic reinforcement of "intrinsic motivation." *The Behavior Analyst, 12,* 1–16.

Dienstag, E. L. (1986, August). *The transition to parenthood in working and non-working pariparous mothers.* Paper presented at the annual meeting of the American Psychological Association, Washington, D.C.

Dietz, S. M. (1986). Understanding cognitive language: The mental idioms in children's talk. *Behavior Analyst, 9*(2), 161–166.

Dishion, T. J., Spracklen, K. M., Andrews, D. W., & Patterson, G. R. (1996). Deviancy training in male adolescent friendships. *Behavior Therapy, 27,* 373–390.

Dobson, V., & Teller, D. Y. (1978). Visual acuity in human infants: A review and comparison of behavioral and electrophysiological studies. *Vision Research, 18,* 1469–1483.

Dodge, K. A. (1985). Attributional bias in aggressive children. In P. C. Kendall (Ed.), *Advances in cognitive behavioral research and therapy* (Vol. 4, pp. 73–110). Orlando, FL: Academic Press.

Dolgin, K. G., & Azmitia, M. (1985). The development of the ability to interpret emotional signals—What is and is not known. In G. Zivin (Ed.), *The development of expressive behavior: Biology–environment interactions.* Orlando, FL: Academic.

Donahoe, J. W., Burgos, J. E., & Palmer, D. C. (1993). A selectionist approach to reinforcement. *Journal of the Experimental Analysis of Behavior, 60,* 17–40.

Donahoe, J. W., & Palmer, D. C. (1994). *Learning and complex behavior.* Needham Heights, MA: Allyn & Bacon.

Dornbusch, S. M., Ritter, P. L., Leiderman, P., Roberts, D. F., & Fraleigh, M. J. (1987). The relation of parenting style to adolescent school performance. *Child Development, 58,* 1244–1257.

Dougher, M. (2002). *Clinical behavior analysis.* Reno, NV: Context Press.

Dougher, M. J., & Hackbert, L. (1994). A behavior-analytic account of depression and a case report using acceptance-based procedures. *The Behavior Analyst, 17,* 321–334.

Duncan, G. J., & Brooks-Gunn, J. (2000). Family poverty, welfare reform, and child development. *Child Development, 71,* 188–196.

Dunn, J., & Plomin, R. (1990). *Separate lives: Why siblings are so different.* New York: Basic Books.

Dymond, S., & Barnes, D. (1994). A transfer of self-discrimination response functions through equivalence relations. *Journal of the Experimental Analysis of Behavior, 62,* 251–267.

Dymond, S., & Barnes, D. (1995). A transformation of self-discrimination response functions through the arbitrarily applicable relations of sameness, more-than, and less-than. *Journal of the Experimental Analysis of Behavior, 64,* 163–184.

Dymond, S., & Barnes, D. (1996). A transformation of self-discriminative functions in accordance with arbitrarily applicable relations of sameness and opposition. *Psychological Record, 46,* 271–300.

Eichorn, D. (1970). Physiological development. In P. H. Mussen (Ed.), *Carmichael's manual of child development* (pp. 157–283). New York: John Wiley.

Eimas, P. D., Siqueland, E. R., Jusczyk, P., & Vigorito, J. (1971). Speech perception in early infancy. *Science, 171,* 303–306.

Eisenberg, N., & Mussen, P. H. (1989). *The roots of prosocial behavior in children.* New York: Cambridge University Press.

Eisenberg-Berg, N., Boothby, R., & Matson, T. (1979). Correlates of preschool girls' feminine and masculine toy preferences. *Developmental Psychology, 15,* 354–355.

Eisler, R. M., Miller, P. M., Hersen, M., & Alford, H. A. (1974). Effects of assertive training on marital interaction. *Archives of General Psychiatry, 30,* 643–649.

Eisner, E. (1994). *The educational imagination: On the design and evaluation of school programs* (3rd ed.). New York: Macmillan.

Elkind, D. (2001). Much too early. *Education Matters, 1*(2), 9–15.

Emde, R. N., Gaensbauer, T. J., & Harmon, R. J. (1976). *Emotional expression in infancy: A biobehavioral study.* New York: International Universities Press.

Emery, R. E. (1982). Interpersonal conflict and the children of discord and divorce. *Psychological Bulletin, 92,* 310–330.

Emery, R. E., & O'Leary, K. (1982). Children's perception of marital discord and behavior problems of boys and girls. *Journal of Abnormal Child Psychology, 10,* 11–24.

Engelmann, S., & Bruner, E. C. (1988). *Reading mastery: Fast cycle (DISTAR).* Chicago: Science Research Associates.

Englemann, S., & Carnine, D. (1982). *Theory of instruction: Principles and applications.* New York: Irvington.

Engen, T., Lipsitt, L. P., & Kaye, H. (1963). Olfactory responses and adaptation in the human neonate. *Journal of Comparative and Physiological Psychology, 56,* 73–77.

Erikson, E. (1950). *Childhood and society.* New York: Norton.

Erikson, E. (1968). *Identity, youth, and crisis.* New York: Norton.

Etzel, B. C., & Gewirtz, J. L. (1967). Experimental modification of caretaker-maintained high-rate operant crying in a 6- and a 20-week-old infant (Infans tyrannotearus): Extinction of crying with reinforcement of eye contact and smiling. *Journal of Experimental Child Psychology, 5,* 303–317.

Eysenck, H. J. (1964a). *Crime and personality.* Boston: Houghton Mifflin.

Eysenck, H. J. (1964b). Principles and methods of personality description, classification and diagnosis. *British Journal of Psychology, 55*(3), 284–294.

Eysenck, H. J. (1967). *The biological basis of personality.* Springfield, IL: Charles C Thomas.

Eysenck, H. J. (1970). *The structure of human personality.* New York: Methuen.

Fabes, R., & Martin, C. L. (2000). *Exploring child development: Transactions and transformations.* Needham Heights, MA: Allyn & Bacon.

Fairbum, C., Welch, S., Norman, P., O'Connor, M., & Doll, H. (1996). Bias and bulimia nervosa: How typical are clinic cases? *American Journal of Psychiatry, 153,* 386–394.

Fantino, E., & Logan, C. A. (1979). *The experimental analysis of behavior: An experimental perspective.* San Francisco: W. H. Freeman.

Fantino, E., & Stolarz-Fantino, S. (2002). From patterns to prosperity: A review of Rachlin's *The Science of Self-Control. Journal of the Experimental Analysis of Behavior, 78,* 117–125.

Fantz, R. (1958). Pattern vision in young infants. *Psychological Record, 8,* 43–47.

Fantz, R. (1961, May). The origin of form perception. *Science, 204,* 66–72.

Farmer, E. M. Z., Compton, S. N., Burns, B. J., & Robertson, E. (2002). Review of the evidence base for treatment of childhood psychopathology: Externalizing disorders. *Journal of Consulting and Clinical Psychology, 70*(6), 1267–1302.

Farrington, D. P. (1978). The family backgrounds of aggressive youths. In L. A. Hersov, M. Berger, & D. Schaffer (Eds.), *Aggression and antisocial behaviour in childhood and adolescence* (pp. 73–93). Oxford, UK: Pergamon Press.

Feree, M. (1976). Working-class jobs: Housework and paid work as sources of satisfaction. *Social Problems, 23,* 431–441.

Ferster, C. B. (1974). Behavioral approaches to depression. In R. J. Friedman & M. M. Katz (Eds.), *The psychology of depression: Contemporary theory and research* (pp. 29–45). New York: John Wiley.

Ferster, C. B., & Culbertson, S. A. (1982). *Behavior principles* (3rd ed.). Englewood Cliffs, NJ: Prentice Hall.

Ferster, C. B., & Skinner, B. F. (1957). *Schedules of reinforcement.* Englewood Cliffs, NJ: Prentice Hall.

Field, T. (1984). Early interactions between infants and their postpartum depressed mothers. *Infant Behavior and Development, 7,* 527–532.

Field, T. (1986, Winter). Models for reactive and chronic depression in infancy. *New Directions for Child Development,* pp. 47–60.

Field, T. (1987). Affective and interactive disturbances in infants. In J. D. Osofsky (Ed.), *Handbook of infant development* (2nd ed., pp. 972–1005). Oxford, UK: Wiley.

Field, T. (1992). Infants of depressed mothers. *Developmental and Psychopathology, 4,* 49–66.

Field, T., Healey, B., Goldstein, S., Perry, S., Bendell, D., Schanberg, S., et al. (1988). Infants of depressed mothers show "depressed" behavior even with nondepressed adults. *Child Development, 59,* 1569–1579.

Field, T., Malphurs, J., Carraway, K., & Peláez-Nogueras, M. (1996). Carrying position influences infant behavior. *Early Childhood Development and Care, 121,* 49–54.

Field, T., Scafidi, F., Pickens, J., Prodomidis, M., Peláez-Nogueras, M., Torquati, J., et al. (1998). Polydrug using adolescent mothers and their infants receiving early intervention. *Adolescence, 33,* 117–143.

Fields, J., & Casper, L. M. (2001). *America's families living arrangements: March 2000* (Current Population Reports, Series P20–537). Washington, DC: U.S. Bureau of the Census.

Fields, L. (1993). Foreword: Special issue on stimulus equivalence. *Psychological Record, 43,* 543–546.

Fingerhut, L. A., & Christoffel, K. K. (2002). Firearm-related death and injury among children and adolescents. *The Future of Children, 12*(2), 25–37.

Finkelstein, J. W., Suman, E. J., Chinchilli, V. M., Kunselman, S. J., D'Arcangelo, M. R., Schwab, J., et al. (1997). Estrogen or testosterone increases self-reported aggressive behaviors in hypogonadal adolescents. *Journal of Clinical Endocrinology and Metabolism, 82,* 2423–2438.

Fischer, K. W. (1980). A theory of cognitive development: The control and construction of hierarchies of skills. *Psychological Review, 87,* 477–531.

Fischer, K. W., & Pipp, S. L. (1984). Processes of cognitive development: Optimal level and skill acquisition. In R. J. Sternberg (Ed.), *Mechanisms of cognitive development* (pp. 45–80). Prospect Heights, IL: Waveland Press.

Flannery, D. J., Rowe, D. C., & Gulley, B. L. (1993). Impact of pubertal status, timing, and age on adolescent sexual experience and delinquency. *Journal of Adolescent Research, 8*(1), 21–40.

Flavell, J. H. (1985). *Cognitive development* (2nd ed.). Englewood Cliffs, NJ: Prentice Hall.

Flory, R. (1969). Attack behavior as a function of minimum inter-food interval. *Journal of the Experimental Analysis of Behavior, 12,* 825–828.

Ford, D. H., & Lerner, R. M. (1992). *Developmental systems theory.* Newbury Park, CA: Sage.

Foreyt, J. P., Poston, W. S., II, Winebarger, A. A., & McGavin, J. K. (1998). Anorexia nervosa and bulimia nervosa. In E. J. Mash & R. A. Barkley (Eds.), *Treatment of childhood disorders* (pp. 647–691). New York: Guilford Press.

Forness, S. R., Kavale, K. A., Sweeney, D. P., & Crenshaw, T. M. (1999). The future of research and practice in behavioral disorders: Psychopharmacology and its school implications. *Behavioral Disorders, 24*(4), 305–318.

Foxx, R. M. (1982). *Decreasing behaviors of severely retarded and autistic persons.* Champaign, IL: Research Press.

Friedman, R. J., & Katz, M. M. (1974). *The psychology of depression: Contemporary theory and research.* New York: John Wiley.

Galbicka, G. (1992). The dynamics of behavior. *Journal of the Experimental Analysis of Behavior, 57,* 243–248.

Gallistel, C. R. (1980). From muscles to motivation. *American Scientist, 68,* 398–409.

Garnefski, N. (2000). Age differences in depressive symptoms, anti-social behavior, and negative perceptions of family, school, and peers among adolescents. *Journal of American Academy of Child and Adolescent Psychiatry, 39,* 1175–1180.

Gelman, S. A., Coley, J. D., Rosengren, K. S., Hartman, E., & Pappas, A. (1998). Beyond labeling: The role of maternal input in the acquisition of richly structured categories. *Monographs of the Society for Research in Child Development, 63*(1, Serial No. 253).

Gersten, R. (1991). The eye of the beholder: A response to "Sociomoral Atmosphere: A Study of Teachers' Enacted Interpersonal Understanding." *Early Childhood Research Quarterly, 6,* 529–537.

Gewirtz, J. L. (1969). Mechanisms of social learning: Some roles of stimulation and behavior in early human development. In D. A. Goslin (Ed.), *Handbook of socialization theory and research* (pp. 57–212). Chicago: Rand-McNally.

Gewirtz, J. L. (1971a). Conditional responding as a paradigm for observational, imitative learning and vicarious reinforcement. In H.W. Reese (Ed.), *Advances in child development and behavior* (Vol. 6, pp. 273–304). New York: Academic Press.

Gewirtz, J. L. (1971b). The roles of overt responding and extrinsic reinforcement in "self" and "vicarious-reinforcement" phenomena and in "observational learning" and imitation. In R. Glaser (Ed.), *The nature of reinforcement* (pp. 279–309). New York: Academic Press.

Gewirtz, J. L. (1972a). *Attachment and dependency.* Washington, DC: Winston.

Gewirtz, J. L. (1972b). Some contextual determinants of stimulus potency. In R. D. Parke (Ed.), *Recent trends in social-learning theory* (pp. 7–33). New York: Academic Press.

Gewirtz, J. L., & Boyd, E. F. (1977). Does maternal responding imply reduced infant crying? A critique of the 1972 Bell and Ainsworth report. *Child Development, 48,* 1200–1207.

Gewirtz, J. L., & Peláez-Nogueras, M. (1990). Social-conditioning theory applied to metaphors like "attachment": The conditioning of infant separation protests by mothers. *Mexican Journal of Behavior Analysis, 13,* 87–103.

Gewirtz, J. L., & Peláez-Nogueras, M. (1991a). The attachment metaphor and the conditioning of infant separation protests. In J. L. Gewirtz & W. M. Kurtines (Eds.), *Intersections with attachment* (pp. 123–144). Hillsdale, NJ: Lawrence Erlbaum.

Gewirtz, J. L., & Peláez-Nogueras, M. (1991b). Proximal mechanisms underlying the acquisition of moral behavior patterns. In W. M. Kurtines & J. L. Gewirtz (Eds.), *Handbook of moral behavior and development: Theory, research, and application* (3 Vols.; Vol. 1, pp. 153–182). Hillsdale, NJ: Lawrence Erlbaum.

Gewirtz, J. L., & Peláez-Nogueras, M. (1992a). B. F. Skinner's legacy to infant behavioral development. *American Psychologist, 47*(11), 1411–1422.

Gewirtz, J. L., & Peláez-Nogueras, M. (1992b). Infants' separation difficulties and distress due to misplaced maternal contingencies. In T. Field, P. McCabe, & N. Schneiderman (Eds.), *Stress and coping in infancy and childhood* (pp. 19–46). Hillsdale, NJ: Lawrence Erlbaum.

Gewirtz, J. L., & Peláez-Nogueras, M. (1992c). Infant social referencing as a learned process. In S. Feinman (Ed.), *Social referencing and the social construction of reality in infancy* (pp. 151–173). New York: Plenum.

Gewirtz, J. L., & Peláez-Nogueras, M. (1992d). Social referencing as a learned process. In S. Feinman (Ed.), *Social referencing and the social construction of reality in infancy* (pp. 151–170). New York: Plenum.

Gewirtz, J. L., & Peláez-Nogueras, M. (1993a). "Expectancy": Sleight-of-hand mentalism, not mechanism or process. *American Psychologist, 48,* 1156–1157.

Gewirtz, J. L., & Peláez-Nogueras, M. (1993b). Leaving without tears: Parents inadvertently train their children to protest separation. *Child and Adolescent Behavior Letter, 9,* 1–4. Reprinted in *Behavioral Development* (1993), *3,* 3–4.

Gewirtz, J. L., & Peláez-Nogueras, M. (1996). In the context of gross environmental and organismic changes, learning provides the main basis for behavioral development. In S. Bijou & E. Ribes (Eds.), *New directions in behavioral development* (pp. 15–34). Reno, NV: Context Press.

Gewirtz, J. L., & Peláez-Nogueras, M. (2000). Infant emotions under the positive-reinforcer control of caregiver attention and touch. In J. C. Leslie & D. Blackman, (Eds.), *Issues in Experimental and Applied Analyses of Human Behavior* (pp. 271–291). Reno, NV: Context Press.

Gewirtz, J. L., & Petrovich, S. B. (1982). Social and attachment learning in infancy in the frame of organic and cultural evolution. In T. M. Field, A. Huston, H. C. Quay, L. Troll, & G. E. Finley (Eds.), *Review of human development* (pp. 3–19). New York: Wiley.

Gewirtz, J. L., & Stingle, K. G. (1968). Learning of generalized imitation as the basis for identification. *Psychological Review, 75,* 374–397.

Gibson, J. J. (1979). *The ecological approach to visual perception.* Boston: Houghton Mifflin.

Gil, D. (1971). Violence against children. *Journal of Marriage and the Family, 33,* 639–648.

Gilligan, C. (1977). In a different voice: Women's conceptions of self and morality. *Harvard Educational Review, 47,* 481–517.

Gilligan, C. (1982). *In a different voice: Psychological theory and women's development.* Cambridge, MA: Harvard University Press.

Gleick, J. (1988). *Chaos: Making a new science.* New York: Viking.

Goetz, E. M., & Baer, D. M. (1973). Social control of form diversity and the emergence of new forms in children's blockbuilding. *Journal of Applied Behavior Analysis, 6,* 209–217.

Goetz, E. M., & Salmonson, M. M. (1972). The effect of general and descriptive reinforcement on "creativity" in easel painting. In G. B. Semb (Ed.), *Behavior analysis in education* (1972, pp. 53–61). Lawrence: University of Kansas Support and Development Center for Follow Through.

Goetz, M., Johnstone, E. C., & Ratcliffe, S. G. (1999). Criminality and antisocial behaviour in unselected men with sex chromosomes abnormalities. *Psychological Medicine, 29*(4), 953–962.

Goldberg, L. R. (1993). The structure of phenotypic personality traits. *American Psychologist, 48,* 26–34.

Goldiamond, I., & Dyrud, J. (1967). Behavioral analysis for psychotherapy. In J. Schlien (Ed.), *Research in psychotherapy* (Vol. 3, pp. 58–89). Washington, DC: American Psychological Association.

Goldsmith, H. H. (1996). Studying temperament via construction of the toddler behavior assessment questionnaire. *Child Development, 67,* 218–235.

Goldstein, H., & Mousetis, L. (1989). Generalized language learning by children with severe mental retardation: Effects of peers' expressive modeling. *Journal of Applied Behavior Analysis, 22,* 245–259.

Golombok, S., & Fivush, R. (1994). *Gender development*. Cambridge, UK: Cambridge University Press.

Good, T. L., & Brophy, J. E. (1984). *Looking in classrooms* (3rd ed.). New York: Harper & Row.

Good, T. L., & Weinstein, R. S. (1986). Schools make a difference: Evidence, criticisms, and new directions. *American Psychologist, 41,* 1090–1097.

Gottesman, I. I. (1963). Heritability of personality: A demonstration. *Psychological Monographs, 77*(9), 1–20.

Gottfried, A. E., Gottfried, A. W., & Bathurst, K. (1988). Maternal employment, family environment and children's development: Infancy through the school years. In A. E. Gottfried & A. W. Gottfried (Eds.), *Maternal employment and children's development: Longitudinal research* (pp. 11–58). New York: Plenum.

Gottlieb, G. (1991a). Epigenetic systems view of human development. *Developmental Psychology, 27,* 33–34.

Gottlieb, G. (1991b). Experiential canalization of behavioral development: Results. *Developmental Psychology, 27,* 4–13.

Gottlieb, G. (1997). *Synthesizing nature–nurture: prenatal roots of instinctive behavior.* Mahwah, NJ: Lawrence Erlbaum.

Grantham-McGregor, S., Powell, C., Walker, S., Chang, S., & Fletcher, P. (1994). The long-term follow-up of severely malnourished children who participated in an intervention program. *Child Development, 65,* 428–439.

Greco, C., Hayne, H., & Rovee-Collier, C. (1990). Roles of function, reminding, and variability in categorization by 3-month-old infants. *Journal of Experimental Psychology: Learning, Memory, and Cognition, 16,* 617–633.

Green, G., & Perry, L. (1999, Spring). Science, pseudoscience, and antiscience: What's this got to do with my kid? *Science in Autism Treatment,* pp. 5–7.

Green, L., Fry, A. F., & Myerson, J. (1994). Discounting of delayed rewards: A lifespan comparison. *Psychological Science, 5,* 33–36.

Green, L., & Snyderman, M. (1980). Choice between rewards differing in amount and delay: Toward a choice model of self-control. *Journal of the Experimental Analysis of Behavior, 34,* 135–147.

Greenberger, E., & Goldberg, W. (1989). Working, parenting, and socialization in children. *Developmental Psychology, 25,* 22–35.

Greenwood, C. R., Delquadri, J., & Hall, R. V. (1984). Opportunity to respond and student academic achievement. In W. L. Heward, T. E. Heron, D. S. Hill, & J. Trapp-Porter (Eds.), *Focus on behavior analysis in education* (pp. 58–88). Columbus, OH: Merrill.

Greenwood, C. R., Delquadri, J. C., & Hall, R. V. (1989). Longitudinal effects of classwide peer tutoring. *Journal of Educational Psychology, 81*(3), 371–383.

Greenwood, C. R., Delquadri, J. C., Stanley, S. O., Sasso, G., Whorton, D., & Schulte, D. (1981, Summer). Allocating opportunity to learn as a basis for academic remediation: A developing model of teaching. *Monograph in Behavior Disorders,* pp. 22–33.

Greenwood, C. R., Hart, B., Walker, D., & Risley, T. (1994). The opportunity to respond and academic performance revisited: A behavioral theory of developmental retardation and its prevention. In R. Gardner et al. (Eds.), *Behavior analysis in education: Focus on measurably superior instruction* (pp. 213–223). Pacific Grove, CA: Brooks/Cole.

Greer, R. D. (1992). L'enfant terrible meets the educational crisis. *Journal of Applied Behavior Analysis, 23,* 65–69.

Greer, R. D. (1994). The measure of a teacher. In R. Gardner et al. (Ed.), *Behavior analysis in education: Focus on measurably superior instruction* (pp. 161–171). Pacific Grove, CA: Brooks/Cole.

Greer, R. D., & McDonough, S. H. (1999). Is the learn unit a fundamental measure of pedagogy? *Behavior Analyst, 22*(1), 5–16.

Grimwade, J. C., Walker, D. W., Bartlett, M., Gordon, S., & Wood, C. (1971). Human fetal heart rate change and movement in response to sound and vibration. *American Journal of Obstetrics & Gynecology, 109,* 86–90.

Groholt, B., Ekebery, O., Wichstrom, L., & Haldorsen, T. (2000). Young suicide attempters: A comparison between a clinical and an epidemiological sample. *Journal of American Academy of Child and Adolescent Psychiatry, 39,* 868–875.

Grosch, J., & Neuringer, A. (1981). Self-control in pigeons under the Mischel paradigm. *Journal of the Experimental Analysis of Behavior, 35,* 3–21.

Guerin, B. (1990). Gibson, Skinner, and perceptual responses. *Behavior and Philosophy, 18*(1), 43–54.

Guthrie, R. D. (1976). *Body hot spots: The anatomy of human social organs and behavior.* New York: Van Nostrand Reinhold.

Hall, G. S. (1904). *Adolescence* (Vols. 1 & 2). Englewood Cliffs, NJ: Prentice Hall.

Hallahan, D. P., Kauffman, J. M., & Lloyd, J. W. (2000). *Introduction to learning disabilities* (4th ed.). Boston: Allyn & Bacon.

Halperin, J. M., Newcorn, J. H., Kopstein, I., McKay, K. E., Schwartz, S. T., Siever, L. J., et al. (1997). Serotonin, aggression, and parental psychopathology in children with attention deficit/hyperactivity disorder. *Journal of the American Academy of Child and Adolescent Psychiatry, 36,* 1391–1398.

Harlow, H. (1959). Love in infant monkeys. *Scientific American, 202,* 68–74.

Harmon, K., Strong, R., & Pasnak, R. (1982). Relational responses in tests of transposition with rhesus monkeys. *Learning & Motivation, 13,* 495–504.

Harris, J. R. (1998). *The nurture assumption: Why children turn out the way they do.* New York: Free Press.

Harris, K. R., & Schmidt, T. (1997). Learning self-regulation in the classroom. *ADHD Report, 5*(2), 1–6.

Harrison, P. M., & Karberg, J. C. (2003). *Prison and jail inmates at midyear 2002.* Washington, DC: U.S. Department of Justice, Bureau of Justice Statistics.

Hart, B., & Risley, T. (1968). Establishing use of descriptive adjectives in the spontaneous speech of disadvantaged preschool children. *Journal of Applied Behavior Analysis, 1,* 109–120.

Hart, B., & Risley, T. R. (1974). Using preschool materials to modify the language of disadvantaged children. *Journal of Applied Behavior Analysis, 7,* 234–256.

Hart, B., & Risley, T. R. (1975). Incidental teaching of language in the preschool. *Journal of Applied Behavior Analysis, 8,* 411–420.

Hart, B., & Risley, T. R. (1995). *Meaningful differences in the everyday experience of young American children.* Baltimore: Brookes.

Hart, B., & Risley, T. R. (1999). *The social world of children learning to talk.* Baltimore: Brookes.

Hart, S. (1991). Childhood depression: Implications and options for school counselors. *Elementary School Guidance & Counseling, 25*(4), 277–289.

Hart, S., Field, T., del Valle, C., & Peláez-Nogueras, M. (1998). Depressed mothers' interactions with their one-year-old infants. *Infant Behavior and Development, 21,* 519–525.

Hatano, G. (1991). Commentary. *Early Childhood Research Quarterly, 6,* 519–521.

Haupt, E. J., & Gewirtz, J. L. (1968). Analysis of interaction sequences between a focal person and other persons by contingency tables for any data coding scheme. *Behavioral Science, 13,* 83–85.

Haviland, J. M., & Scarborough, H. S. (1981). Moral development. In J. M. Haviland & H. S. Scarborough (Eds.), *Adolescent development in contemporary society* (pp. 240–255). New York: Van Nostrand.

Hawkins, J. D., Herrenkohl, T., Farrington, D. P., Brewer, D., Catalano, R. F., & Harachi, T. W. (1998). A review of predictors of youth violence. In R. Loeber & D. P. Farrington (Eds.), *Serious and violent juvenile offenders: Risk factors and successful interventions* (pp. 106–146). Thousand Oaks, CA: Sage.

Hawkins, J. D., & Lishner, D. M. (1987). Schooling and delinquency. In E. H. Johnson (Ed.), *Handbook on crime and delinquency prevention* (pp. 179–221). New York: Greenwood Press.

Hayes, S. C. (1986). The case of the silent dog—Verbal reports and the analysis of rules: A review of Ericsson and Simon's Protocol Analysis: Verbal reports as data. *Journal of the Experimental Analysis of Behavior, 45,* 351–363.

Hayes, S. C. (1987). A contextual approach to therapeutic change. In N. Jacobsen (Ed.), *Psychotherapists in clinical practice:*

Cognitive and behavioral perspectives (pp. 327–387). New York: Guilford Press.

Hayes, S. C. (1991). A relational control theory of stimulus equivalence. In L. J. Hayes & P. N. Chase (Eds.), *Dialogues on verbal behavior* (pp. 19–40). Reno, NV: Context Press.

Hayes, S. C. (1994). Relational frame theory: A functional approach to verbal events. In S. C. Hayes, L. J. Hayes, M. Sato, & O. Koichi (Eds.), *Behavior analysis of language and cognition* (pp. 9–30). Reno, NV: Context Press.

Hayes, S. C. (1996). Developing a theory of derived stimulus relations. *Journal of the Experimental Analysis of Behavior, 65,* 309–311.

Hayes, S. C., Barlow, D. H., & Nelson-Gray, R. O. (1998). *The scientist practitioner* (2nd ed.). New York: Allyn & Bacon.

Hayes, S. C., Barnes-Holmes, D., & Roche, B. (2001). *Relational frame theory: A post-Skinnerian account of human language and cognition.* New York: Academic Press.

Hayes, S. C., & Hayes, L. J. (1989). The verbal action of the listener as a basis for rule governance. In S. C. Hayes (Ed.), *Rule-governed behavior: Cognition, contingencies, and instructional control.* New York: Plenum.

Hayes, S. C., & Hayes, L. J. (1992). Verbal relations and the evolution of behavior analysis. *American Psychologist, 47,* 1383–1395.

Hayes, S. C., Hayes, L. J., & Reese, H. W. (1988). Finding the philosophical core. A review of Stephen C. Pepper's *World Hypotheses: A Study in Evidence. Journal of the Experimental Analysis of Behavior, 50,* 97–111.

Hayes, S. C., & Wilson, K. G. (1994). Acceptance and commitment therapy: Altering the verbal support for experiential avoidance. *The Behavior Analyst, 17,* 289–304.

Hayghe, H. V. (1997, September). Developments in women's labor force participation. *Monthly Labor Review,* pp. 41–46.

Hebb, D. O., Lambert, W. E., & Tucker, G. R. (1973, April). A DMZ in the language war. *Psychology Today,* 55–62.

Henderson, N. D. (1982). Human behavior genetics. *Annual Review of Psychology, 33,* 403–440.

Herrera, G., Peláez, M., Reyes, G., Figueroa, S., & Salas, M.W. (2001). Rule-following as a function of psychological development and language comprehension (Seguimiento de reglas en función del lenguaje). *Mexican Journal of Behavior Analysis, 27,* 403–429.

Hersen, M., & Barlow, D. H. (1976). *Single case experimental designs: Strategies for studying behavior change.* Oxford: Pergamon Press.

Hetherington, E. M. (1989). Coping with family transitions: Winners, losers, and survivors. *Child Development, 60,* 1–14.

Hetherington, E. M. (1990). Coping with family transitions: Winners, losers, and survivors. Presidential address at the meeting of the Society for Research in Child Development, *Annual progress in child psychiatry and child development* (pp. 221–241). New York: Bruner/Mazel.

Hetherington, E. M., Cox, M., & Cox, R. (1982). Effects of divorce on parents and children. In M. Lamb (Ed.), *Nontraditional families* (pp. 233–288). Hillsdale, NJ: Lawrence Erlbaum.

Hetherington, E. M., Cox, M., & Cox, R. (1985). Long-term effects of divorce and remarriage on the adjustment of children. *Journal of American Academy of Psychiatry, 24,* 518–830.

Hetherington, E. M., & Kelly, J. (2002). *For better or for worse: Divorce reconsidered.* New York: Norton.

Hetherington, E. M., Stanley-Hagan, M., & Anderson, E. R. (1989). Marital Transitions: A child's perspective. *American Psychologist, 44,* 303–312.

Heward, L. W. (1994). Three "low-tech" strategies for increasing the frequency of active student response during group instruction. In R. Gardner et al. (Eds.), *Behavior analysis in education: Focus on measurably superior instruction* (pp. 283–320). Pacific Grove, CA: Brooks/Cole.

Higbee, T. S., & Peláez-Nogueras, M. (1998). Reinforcer identification in infants. *Behavioral Development Bulletin, 7,* 10–14.

Higgins, S. T., Budney, A. J., Bickel, W. K., Hughes, J. R., Foerg, F., & Badger, G. (1993). Achieving cocaine abstinence with a behavioral approach. *American Journal of Psychiatry, 150,* 763–769.

Hineline, P. N. (in press). When we speak of intentions. In K. A. Lattal & P. N. Chase (Eds.), *Behavior theory and philosophy* (pp. 203–221). New York: Kluwer Academic/Plenum.

Hineline. P. N., & Wanchisen, B. A. (1989). Correlated hypothesizing, and the distinction between contingency-shaped and rule-governed behavior. In S. C. Hayes (Ed.), *Rule-governed behavior: Cognition, contingencies, and instructional control* (pp. 221–268). New York: Plenum.

Hoberman, H. M., & Clarke, G. N. (1993). Major depression in adults. In R. Ammerman & M. Hersen (Eds.), *Handbook of behavior therapy with children and adults: A developmental and longitudinal perspective* (pp. 73–90). Boston: Allyn & Bacon.

Hoberman, H. M., & Lewisohn, P. M. (1985). The behavioral treatment of depression. In E. E. Beckham & W. R. Lever (Eds.), *Handbook of depression: Treatment, assessment and research* (pp. 39–81). Homewood, IL: Dorsey Press.

Hock, E., & DeMeis, D. K. (1990). Depression in mothers of infants: The role of maternal employment. *Developmental Psychology, 26,* 285–291.

Hoffman, L. W. (1986). Work, family, and the child. In M. S. Pallak & R. O. Perloff (Eds.), *Psychology and work: Productivity, change, and employment* (pp. 173–220). Washington, DC: American Psychological Association.

Hoffman, L. W. (1989). Effects of maternal employment in the two-parent family. *American Psychologist, 44,* 283–294.

Holman, J., Goetz, E. M., & Baer, D. M. (1977). The training of creativity as an operant and an examination of its generalization characteristics. In B. C. Etzel, J. M. LeBlanc, & D. M. Baer (Eds.), *New developments in behavioral research theory, methods, and application: In honor of Sidney W. Bijou* (pp. 441–472). Hillsdale, NJ: Lawrence Erlbaum.

Hoover, J. H., & Hazler, R. J. (1991). Bullies and victims. *Elementary School Guidance and Counseling, 25,* 212–219.

Hopkins, B. L. (1994, October). *Behavior analysis and education.* Paper presented at the Second International Congress on Behaviorism and the Sciences of Behavior, Palermo, Italy.

Horne, P. J., & Lowe, C. F. (1996). On the origins of naming and other symbolic behavior. *Journal of the Experimental Analysis of Behavior, 65,* 185–241.

Horner, R. H., & Carr, E. G. (1997). Behavioral support for students with severe disabilities: Functional assessment and comprehensive intervention. *Journal of Special Education, 31,* 84–104.

Horner, R. H., Dunlap, G., Koegel, R. L., Carr, E. G., Sailor, W., Anderson, J., et al. (1990). Toward a technology of "nonaversive" behavioral support. *Journal of the Association for Persons With Severe Handicaps, 15,* 125–132.

Horowitz, F. D. (1987). *Exploring developmental theories: Toward a structural/behavioral model of development.* Hillsdale, NJ: Lawrence Erlbaum.

Horowitz, F. D. (1989). In the interest of the nation: A reflective essay on the state of our knowledge and the challenges before us. *American Psychologist, 44,* 441–445.

Horton, S. V., & Lovitt, T. C. (1989). Using study guides with three classifications of secondary students. *Journal of Special Education, 22,* 447–462.

Howard, V. F., Williams, B. F., & McLaughlin, T. F. (1994). Children prenatally exposed to alcohol and cocaine: Behavioral solutions. In R. Gardner et al. (Ed.), *Behavior analysis in education* (pp. 131–146). Pacific Grove, CA: Brooks/Cole.

Howlin, P., Baron-Cohen, S., & Hadwin, J. (1999). *Teaching children with autism to mind-read: A practical guide.* Chichester, UK: John Wiley.

Hoyert, M. S. (1992). Order and chaos in fixed-interval schedules of reinforcement. *Journal of the Experimental Analysis of Behavior, 57,* 339–363.

Huesmann, L. R., Eron, L. D., Lefkowitz, M. M., & Walder, L. O. (1984). Stability of aggression over time and generations. *Developmental Psychology, 20,* 1120–1134.

Hull, D. L., Langman, R. E., & Glenn, S. S. (2001). A general account of selection: Biology, immunology, and behavior. *Behavioral and Brain Sciences, 24*(3), 511–527.

Human Genome Program. (2001). *Genomics and its impact on medicine and society: A 2001 primer.* Washington, DC: U.S. Department of Energy, Office of Science.

Hunt, G. M., & Azrin, N. H. (1973). A community-reinforcement approach to alcoholism. *Behavior Research and Therapy, 11,* 91–104.

Huston, A. C. (1983). Sex typing. In E. M. Hetherington (Ed.), *Handbook of child psychology: Socialization, personality, and social development* (Vol. 4). New York: John Wiley.

Huston, A. C. (1994). Children in poverty: Designing research to affect policy. *Social Policy Report: Society for Research in Child Development, 8,* 1–12.

Huston, A. C., McLoyd, V. C., & Garcia Coll, C. (1994). Children and poverty: Issues in contemporary research. *Child Development, 65,* 275–282.

Ike, N. (2000). Current thinking on the XYY syndrome. *Psychiatric Annals, 30*(2), 91–95.

Izard, C. E. (1992). Basic emotions: Relations among emotions, and emotion-cognition relations. *Psychological Review, 99,* 561–565.

Izard, C. E., & Malatesta, C. Z. (1987). Perspectives on emotional development: I. Differential emotions theory of early emotional development. In J. D. Osofsky (Ed.), *Handbook of Infant Development* (2nd ed., pp. 555–578). New York: John Wiley.

Jacobson, S. W. (1979). Matching behavior in the young infant. *Child Development, 50,* 425–530.

Jacobson, S. W. (1998). Specificity of neurobehavioral outcomes associated with prenatal alcohol exposure. *Alcoholism: Clinical and Experimental Research, 22,* 313–320.

James, W. (1890). *The principles of psychology.* New York: Holt.

Jarvik, L. F., Klodin, V., & Matsuyama, S. S. (1973). Human aggression and the extra Y chromosome. *American Psychologist, 28*(8), 674–682.

Jeffrey, W. E., & Cohen, L. B. (1971). Habituation in the human infant. In H. W. Reese (Ed.), *Advances in child development and behavior* (Vol. 6). New York: Academic Press.

Jersild, A. T. (1963). Religion and morals. In A. T. Jersild (Ed.), *The psychology of adolescence* (pp. 373–392). New York: Macmillan.

Jessor, R., Chase, J., & Donovan, J. (1980). Psychosocial correlates of marihuana use and problem drinking in a national sample of adolescents. *American Journal of Public Health, 70,* 604–613.

Johanson, I. B., & Hall, W. G. (1979). Appetitive learning in 1-day-old rat pups. *Science, 205,* 419–421.

Johnson, K. R., & Layng, T. V. J. (1994). The Morningside model of generative instruction. In R. Gardner et al. (Eds.), *Behavior analysis in education: Focus on measurably superior instruction* (pp. 173–197). Belmont, CA: Brooks/Cole.

Johnston, J. M., & Pennypacker, H. S. (1980). *Strategies and tactics for human behavioral research.* Hillsdale, NJ: Lawrence Erlbaum.

Jones, M. C., & Watson, J. B. (1924). A laboratory study of fear: The case of Peter. *Pedagogical Seminary, 31,* 308–315.

Kagan, J. (1974). Discrepancy, temperament, and infant distress. In M. Lewis & L. A. Rosenblum (Eds.), *The origins of fear* (pp. 229–248). New York: John Wiley.

Kagan, J., Kearsley, R. B., & Zelazo, P. R. (1978). *Infancy: Its place in human development.* Cambridge, MA: Harvard University Press.

Kagel, J. H., Green, L., & Caraco, T. (1986). When foragers discount the future: Constraint or adaptation? *Animal Behaviour, 34,* 271–283.

Kantor, J. R. (1946). The aim and progress of psychology. *American Scientist, 34,* 251–263.

Kantor, J. R. (1959). *Interbehavioral psychology (rev. ed.).* Bloomington, IN: Principia Press.

Kashani, J. H., Vaidya, A. F., Soltys, S. M., Dandoy, A. C., Katz, L. J., & Reid, J. C. (1990). Correlates of anxiety in psychiatrically hospitalized children and their parents. *American Journal of Psychiatry, 147,* 319–323.

Kaslow, N. J., Brown, R. T., & Mee, L. L. (1994). Cognitive and behavioral correlates of childhood depression: A developmental perspective. In W. M. Reynolds & H. F. Johnston (Eds.), *Handbook of depression in children and adolescents* (pp. 97–121). New York: Plenum Press.

Kauffman, J. M. (2001). *Characteristics of emotional and behavioral disorders of youth and children* (7th ed.). Columbus, OH: Merrill Prentice Hall.

Kazdin, A. E. (1982). *Single-case research designs. Methods for clinical and applied settings.* New York: Oxford University Press.

Kazdin, A. E. (1985). *Treatment of antisocial behavior in children and adolescents.* Homewood, IL: Dorsey Press.

Kazdin, A. E. (1987). Treatment of antisocial behavior in children: Current status and future directions. *Psychological Bulletin, 102,* 187–203.

Kazdin, A. E. (1988). Childhood depression. In E. J. Mash & L. G. Terdal (Eds.), *Behavioral assessment in childhood disorders* (2nd ed., pp. 157–195). New York: Guilford Press.

Kazdin, A. E. (1998). Conduct disorder. In R. J. Morris & T. R. Kratochwill (Eds.), *The practice of child therapy* (3rd ed., pp. 199–230). Boston: Allyn & Bacon.

Kazdin, A. E., & Marciano, P. L. (1998). Childhood and adolescent depression. In E. J. Mash & R. A. Barkley (Eds.), *Treatment of childhood disorders* (pp. 211–248). New York: Guilford Press.

Kimble, G. (1961). *Hilgard and Marquis' conditioning and learning.* New York: Appleton-Century-Crofts.

Kirigin, K. A., Braukmann, C. J., Atwater, J. D., & Wolf, M. M. (1982). An evaluation of teaching-family (Achievement Place) group homes for juvenile offenders. *Journal of Applied Behavior Analysis, 15,* 1–16.

Klein, S. B. (1987). *Learning: Principles and applications.* New York: McGraw-Hill.

Koegel, L. K., Koegel, R. L., Frea, W. D., & Freeden, R. M. (2001). Identifying early intervention targets for children with autism in inclusive school settings. *Behavior Modification, 25*(5), 745–761.

Koenig, L. J., & Gladstone, T. R. G. (1998). Pubertal development and school transition: Joint influences on depressive symptoms in middle and late adolescents. *Behavior Modification, 22,* 335–357.

Kohlberg, L. (1969). Stage and sequence: The cognitive-developmental approach to socialization. In D. A. Goslin (Ed.), *Handbook of socialization theory and research* (pp. 347–480). Chicago: Rand McNally.

Kohlberg, L. (1976). Moral stages and moralization: The cognitive–developmental approach. In T. Lickona (Ed.), *Moral development and behavior: Theory, research and social issues* (pp. 31–53). New York: Holt, Rinehart & Winston.

Kohlberg, L., & Diessner, R. (1991). A cognitive developmental approach to moral attachment. In J. L. Gewirtz & W. M. Kurtines (Eds.), *Intersections with attachment* (pp. 229–246). Hillsdale, NJ: Lawrence Erlbaum.

Kohlenberg, R. J., & Tsai, M. (1994). Improving cognitive therapy for depression with functional analytic psychotherapy: Theory and case study. *The Behavior Analyst, 17,* 305–320.

Kohn, A. (1993). *Punished by rewards: The trouble with gold stars, incentive plans, A's, praise, and other bribes.* Boston: Houghton Mifflin.

Kolata, G. (1987). Early signs of school age IQ. *Science, 236,* 774–775.

Kolata, G. (1995, March 4). Vitamin can avert birth defect, but message goes unheeded. *New York Times,* p. 7.

Kurtines, W. M., & Gewirtz, J. L. (1984). Certainty and morality: Objectivistic versus relativistic approaches. In W. M. Kurtines & J. L. Gewirtz (Eds.), *Morality, moral behavior, and moral development* (pp. 3–23) New York: John Wiley.

Kymissis, E., & Poulson, C. L. (1990). The history of imitation in learning theory: The language acquisition process. *Journal of Experimental Analysis of Behavior, 54,* 113–127.

Lamb, R. E., & Bornstein, M. H. (1987). *Development in infancy: An introduction* (2nd ed.). New York: Random House.

Lask, B., & Bryant-Waugh, R. (2000). *Anorexia nervosa and related eating disorders in childhood and adolescence* (2nd ed.). East Sussex, UK: Psychology Press.

Lattal, K. A. (1975). Reinforcement contingencies as discriminative stimuli. *Journal of the Experimental Analysis of Behavior, 23,* 241–246.

Lavigueur, S., Tremblay, R. E., & Saucier, J. (1995). Interactional processes in families with disruptive boys: Patterns of direct and indirect influence. *Journal of Abnormal Child Psychology, 23,* 359–378.

Layng, T. V. J. (1995, February). *Crisis in education.* Remarks made at the Conference of the

Northern California Association for Behavior Analysis, Oakland.

Lazar, I., & Darlington, R. (1982). Lasting effects of early education. *Monographs of the Society for Research in Child Development, 47* (2–3, Serial no. 195).

Ledingham, J. E., & Schwartzman, A. E. (1984). A 3-year follow-up of aggressive and withdrawn behavior in childhood: Preliminary findings. *Journal of Abnormal Child Psychology, 12,* 157–168.

Leitenberg, H., Agras, W. S., & Thompson, L. E. (1968). A sequential analysis of the effect of selective positive reinforcement in modifying anorexia nervosa. *Behavior Research and Therapy, 6,* 211–218.

Lempers, J. D., Clark-Lempers, D., & Simons, R. L. (1989). Economic hardship, parenting, and distress in adolescence. *Child Development, 60,* 25–39.

Lerner, R. M. (1991). Changing organism-context relations as the basic process of development: A developmental contextual perspective. *Developmental Psychology, 27,* 27–32.

Levenstein, P., Levenstein, S., & Oliver, D. (2002). First grade school readiness of former child participants in a South Carolina replication of the Parent-Home Program. *Applied Developmental Psychology, 23,* 331–353.

Levin, G. R., & Kaye, H. (1964). Nonnutritive sucking by human neonates. *Child Development, 35,* 749–758.

LeVine, R. A. (1974). Parental goals: A cross-cultural view. *Teachers College Record, 76,* 226–239.

Lewis, M. (1987). Social development in infancy and early childhood. In J. D. Osofsky (Ed.), *Handbook of infant development* (2nd ed., pp. 419–493). New York: John Wiley.

Lewisohn, P. M., & Gotlib, I. H. (1995). Behavioral theory and treatment of depression. In E. Beckham & W. Leber (Eds.), *Handbook of depression* (2nd ed., pp. 352–375). New York: Guilford Press.

Lewkowicz, D. J. (1996). Perception of auditory-visual temporal synchrony in human infants. *Journal of Experimental Psychology: Human Perception & Performance, 22,* 1094–1106.

Lickliter, R., & Bahrick, L. E. (2000). The development of infant intersensory redundancy: Advantages of a comparative convergent-operations approach. *Psychological Bulletin, 126,* 260–280.

Liebert, R. (1984). What develops in moral development? In W. Kurtines & J. L. Gewirtz (Eds.), *Morality, moral behavior, and moral development* (pp. 177–192). New York: John Wiley.

Liebert, R. M., & Wicks-Nelson, R. (1981). *Developmental psychology* (3rd ed.). Englewood-Cliffs, NJ: Prentice Hall.

Liebman, R., Minuchin, S., & Baker, L. (1974). The use of structural family therapy in the treatment of intractable asthma. *American Journal of Psychiatry, 131,* 535–540.

Lindhart-Kelly, R., & Greer, R. D. (1999). *A functional relationship between mastery with a rate requirement and maintenance of learning.* Unpublished manuscript.

Lipkens, R., Hayes, S. C., & Hayes, L. J. (1993). Longitudinal study of the development of derived relations in an infant. *Journal of Experimental Child Psychology, 51,* 201–239.

Lipsitt, L. P. (1979). Infants at risk: Perinatal and neonatal factors. *International Journal of Behavioral Development, 2*(1), 23–42.

Lipsitt, L. P., & Kaye, H. (1964). Conditioned sucking in the human newborn. *Psychonomic Science, 1,* 29–30.

Loney, J. P., Kramer, J., & Milich, R. (1981). The hyperkinetic child grows up: Predictors of symptoms of delinquency and achievement at follow-up. In K. Gadow & J. Loney (Eds.), *Psychosocial aspect of drug treatment for hyperactivity* (pp. 232–252). Boulder, CO: Westview Press.

Lonigan, C. J., & Whitehurst, G. J. (1998). Relative efficacy of parent and teacher involvement in a shared-reading intervention for preschool children from low-income backgrounds. *Early Childhood Research Quarterly, 13*(2), 263–290.

Lore, R. K., & Schultz, L. A. (1993). Control of human aggression: A comparative perspective. *American Psychologist, 48,* 16–25.

Lorenz, K. E. (1966). *On aggression:* Harcourt, Brace & World.

Lorenz, K. Z. (1943). The innate forms of possible experience. *Zeitschrift fur Tier-psychologie, 5,* 233–409.

Lovaas, O. I. (1987). Behavioral treatment and normal educational and intellectual functioning in young autistic children. *Journal of Consulting and Clinical Psychology, 55*(1), 3–9.

Lovaas, O. I. (2003). *Teaching individuals with developmental delays: Basic intervention techniques.* Austin, TX: PRO-ED.

Lovaas, O. I., & Buch, G. (1997). Intensive behavioral intervention with young children with autism. In Singh, Nirbhay N. (Ed.) (1997). *Prevention and treatment of severe behavior problems: Models and methods in developmental disabilities* (pp. 61–86). Belmont, CA: Wadsworth.

Lundin, R. W. (1961). *Personality.* New York: Macmillan.

Lundy, B. L., Field, T., Carraway, K., Hart, S., Malphurs, J., Rosenstein, M., et al. (1999). Food texture preferences in infants and toddlers. *Early Child Development and Care, 146,* 69–85.

Lutzker, J. R. (1984). Project 12-Ways: Treating child abuse and neglect from an ecobehavioral perspective. In R. F. Dangel & R. L. Polster (Eds.), *Parent training: Foundations of research and practice* (pp. 260–291). New York: Guilford Press.

Lutzker, J. R., & Campbell, R. (1994). *Ecobehavioral family interventions in developmental disabilities.* Pacific Grove, CA: Brooks/Cole.

Lutzker, J. R., Campbell, R. V., Newman, M. R., & Harrold, M. (1989). Ecobehavioral interventions for abusive, neglectful, and high risk families. In G. H. S. Singer & L. K. Irvin (Eds.), *Support for caregiving families: Enabling positive adaptation to disability* (pp. 313–326). Baltimore: Paul H. Brookes.

Lyberger-Ficek, S., & Sternglanz, S. H. (1975, April). *Innate sex differences in neonatal crying: Myth or reality?* Paper presented at the meeting of the Society for Research in Child Development, Denver, CO.

MacCorquodale, K. (1969). B. F. Skinner's *Verbal Behavior:* A retrospective appreciation. *Journal of the Experimental Analysis of Behavior, 12,* 831–841.

MacCorquodale, K. (1970). On Chomsky's review of Skinner's *Verbal Behavior. Journal of the Experimental Analysis of Behavior, 13,* 83–99.

MacKay, A. P., Fingerhut, L. A., & Duran, C. R. (2000). *Adolescent health chartbook. Health, United States, 2000.* Hyattsville, MD: National Center for Health Statistics.

Madison, L. S., Madison, J. K., & Adubato, S. A. (1986). Infant behavior and development in relation to fetal movement and habituation. *Child Development, 57,* 1475–1482.

Major, B., Carnevale, P. J., & Deaux, K. (1981). A different perspective on androgyny: Evaluations of masculine and feminine personality characteristics. *Journal of Personality and Social Psychology, 41,* 988–1001.

Malott, R. W. (2001). Moral and legal control. *Behavioral Development Bulletin, 1,* 1–7.

Malphurs, J. E., Raag, T., Field, T., Pickens, J., & Peláez-Nogueras, M. (1996). Touch by intrusive and withdrawn mothers with depressive symptoms. *Early Development and Parenting Journal, 5,* 111–115.

Mansdorf, I. J., & Lukens, E. (1987). Cognitive-behavioral psychotherapy for separation anxious children exhibiting school phobia. *Journal of American Academy of Child and Adolescent Psychiatry, 26,* 19–36.

Marantz, S. A., & Mansfield, A. F. (1977). Maternal employment and the development of sex-role stereotyping in five- to eleven-year-old girls. *Child Development, 48,* 668–673.

Marcia, J. E. (1980). Identity in adolescence. In J. Adelson (Ed.), *Handbook of adolescence psychology,* New York: John Wiley.

Margolis, L., & Farran, D. (1981). Unemployment: The health consequences for children. *North Carolina Medical Journal, 42,* 849–850.

Marr, M. J. (1992). Behavior dynamics: One perspective. *Journal of the Experimental Analysis of Behavior, 57,* 249–266.

Marr, M. J. (1993a). Contextualistic mechanism or mechanistic contextualism? The straw machine as tar baby. *The Behavior Analyst, 16,* 59–65.

Marr, M. J. (1993b). A mote in the mind's eye. *The Behavior Analyst, 16,* 251–253.

Marr, J. (1996). A mingled yarn. *Journal of Applied Behavior Analysis, 19,* 19–33.

Mash, E. J., & Barkley, R. A. (1998). *Treatment of childhood disorders* (2nd ed.). New York: Guilford Press.

Maslow, A. H. (1970). *Motivation and personality* (2nd ed.). New York: Harper & Row.

Massad, C. M. (1981). Sex role identity and adjustment during adolescence. *Child Development, 52,* 1290–1298.

McDonald, M. A., Sigman, M., Espinosa, R. P., & Neumann, C. G. (1994). Impact of a temporary food shortage on children and their mothers. *Child Development, 65,* 404–415.

McEachin, J. J., Smith, T., & Lovaas, O. I. (1993). Long-term outcome for children with autism who received early intensive behavioral treatment. *American Journal on Mental Retardation, 97*(4), 359–372.

McElhaney, K., & Allen, J. (2001). Autonomy and adolescent social functioning: The moderating effect of risk. *Child Development, 72*(1), 220–235.

McGraw, M. (1935). *Growth: A study of Jimmy and Johnny.* New York: Appleton-Century-Crofts.

McGue, M., Bouchard, T. J., Iacono, W. G., & Lykken, D. T. (1993). Behavioral genetics of cognitive ability: A life-span perspective. In R. Plomin & G. E. McClearn (Eds.), *Nature, nurture, and psychology* (pp. 59–76). Washington, DC: American Psychological Association.

McGuffin, P., Riley, B., & Plomin, R. (2001). Toward behavioral genomics. *Science, 291*(5507), 1232–1249.

McHugh, L., Barnes-Holmes, Y., O'Hora, D., & Barnes-Holmes, D. (in press-a). Perspective-taking: A relational frame analysis. *Experimental Analysis of Human Behavior Bulletin.*

McHugh, L., Barnes-Holmes, Y., & Barnes-Holmes, D. (in press-b). Perspective-taking as relational responding: A developmental profile. *The Psychological Record.*

McLean, P. D. (1981). Behavioral treatment of depression. In W. E. Craighead, A. E. Kazdin & M. J. Mahoney (Eds.), *Behavior modification: Principles, issues, and applications* (pp. 223–242). Boston: Houghton Mifflin.

McLoyd, V. C. (1989). Socialization and development in a changing economy: The effects of paternal job and income loss on children. *American Psychologist, 44,* 293–302.

McNally, S., Eisenberg, N., & Harris, J. D. (1991). Consistency and change in maternal child-rearing practices and values: A longitudinal study. *Child Development, 62,* 190–198.

Meltzoff, A. N., & Moore, M. K. (1977). Imitation of facial and manual gestures by human neonates. *Science, 198,* 75–77.

Meltzoff, A. N., & Moore, M. K. (1983). Newborn infants imitate adult facial gestures. *Child Development, 54,* 702–709.

Meltzoff, A. N., & Moore, M. K. (1985). Cognitive foundations and social functions of imitation and intermodal representation in infancy. In J. Mehler & R. Fox (Eds.), *Neonate cognition: Beyond the blooming, buzzing confusion* (pp. 139–156). Hillsdale, NJ: Erlbaum.

Mendelson, B. K., Mendelson, M. J., & White, D. R. (2001). Body-esteem scale for adolescents and adults. *Journal of Personality Assessment, 76,* 90–106.

Michael, J. (1982). Distinguishing between the discriminative and motivational functions of stimuli. *Journal of the Experimental Analysis of Behavior, 37,* 149–155.

Michael, J. (1993). Establishing operations. *The Behavior Analyst, 16,* 191–206.

Midgley, B. D., & Morris, E. K. (1992). Nature = f(nurture): A review of Oyama's *The ontogeny of information: Developmental systems and evolution. Journal of the Experimental Analysis of Behavior, 58,* 229–240.

Midgley, B. D., & Morris, E. K. (1998). Nature and nurture in Skinner's behaviorism. *Mexican Journal of Behavior Analysis, 24*(2), 111–126.

Miller, P. M. (2001). Temperament, early experiences, and the behavior of mothers vs. strangers as influences on infant crying. *Behavioral Development Bulletin, 1,* 31–35.

Miller, S. A. (1987). *Developmental research methods.* Englewood Cliffs, NJ: Prentice Hall.

Minuchin, H. R. (1999). Understanding socialization: From unidirectional to bidirectional conceptions. In M. Bennett (Ed.), *Developmental psychology: Achievements and prospects* (pp. 272–288). Philadelphia: Psychology Press.

Minuchin, S. (1974). *Families & family therapy.* Oxford, UK: Harvard University Press.

Minuchin, S., Baker, L., Rosman, L., Liebman, R., Milman, L., & Todd, T. C. (1975). A conceptual model of psychosomatic illness in children. *Archives of General Psychiatry, 32,* 1031–1038.

Minuchin, S., Rosman, B. L., & Baker, L. (1978). *Psychosomatic families: Anorexia nervosa in context.* Cambridge, MA: Harvard University Press.

Mischel, W., Ebbesen, E. B., & Raskoff-Zeiss, A. (1972). Cognitive and attentional mechanisms in delay of gratification. *Journal of Personality and Social Psychology, 21*(2), 201–218.

Mischel, W., & Moore, B. S. (1973). Effects of attention to symbolically presented rewards on self control. *Journal of Personality and Social Psychology, 28*(2), 172–179.

Mischel, W., Shoda, Y., & Peake, P. K. (1988). The nature of adolescent competencies predicted by preschool delay of gratification. *Journal of Personality and Social Psychology, 54*(4), 687–696.

Moerk, E. L. (1983). *The mother of Eve—As a first language teacher.* Norwood, NJ: Ablex.

Moerk, E. L. (1986). Environmental factors in early language acquisition. In G. J. Whitehurst (Ed.), *Annals of child development* (Vol. 3, pp. 191–235). Greenwich, CT: JAI Press.

Moerk, E. L. (1989). The LAD was a lady and the tasks were ill-defined. *Developmental Review, 9,* 21–57.

Moerk, E. L. (1990). Three-term contingency patterns in mother–child verbal interactions during first-language acquisition. *Journal of the Experimental Analysis of Behavior, 54,* 293–305.

Moerk, E. L. (1992). *First language: Taught and learned.* Baltimore, MD: Brookes.

Morris, E. K. (1988). Contextualism: The world view of behavior analysis. *Journal of Experimental Child Psychology, 46,* 289–323.

Morris, E. K. (1992). The aim, progress, and evolution of behavior analysis. *The Behavior Analyst, 15,* 3–29.

Morris, E. K. (1993a). Behavior analysis and mechanism: One is not the other. *The Behavior Analyst, 16,* 25–43.

Morris, E. K. (1993b). Mechanism and contextualism in behavior analysis: Just some observations. *The Behavior Analyst, 16,* 255–268.

Morris, E. K. (1998). Mechanism, contextualism and the behavior analysis of development. *Mexican Journal of Behavior Analysis, 24*(2), 97–110.

Morris, E. K., & Midgley, B. D. (1990). Some historical and conceptual foundations of ecobehavioral analysis. In S. R. Schroeder (Ed.), *Ecobehavioral analysis and developmental disabilities: Toward the twenty-first century* (pp. 1–32). New York: Springer-Verlag.

Moyer, K. E. (1967). *Kinds of aggression and their physiological basis* (Report No. 67–12). Pittsburgh, PA: Carnegie-Mellon University, Department of Psychology.

MTA Cooperative Group. (1999). A 14-month randomized clinical trial of treatment strategies for attention deficit/hyperactivity disorder. *Archives of General Psychiatry, 56,* 1073–1086.

Munro, G., & Adams, G. R. (1977). Ego-identity formation in college students and working youth. *Developmental Psychology, 13,* 523–524.

Murrell, A. R. & Wicksell, R. (2003, August). The use of acceptance and commitment therapy with children, adolescents, and their parents. Paper presented at the First World Conference of ACT, RFT, and the New Behavioral Psychology, Linkoping, Sweden.

Nangle, D. W., Carr, R. E., & Hansen, D. J. (1999). Data-based clinical decision making in the treatment of an adolescent with severe conduct problems. *Education and Treatment of Children, 22,* 157–170.

National Center for Health Statistics. (2000). *Health, United States, 2000 With Adolescent Health Chartbook.* Hyattsville, MD: Author.

National Institute of Child Health and Human Development. (2001). Autism and the MMR Vaccine—Autism Research at the NICHD. *Health Publications.* Retrieved September 1, 2003 from http://www.nichd.nih.gov/publications/pubs/autism/mmr/ index.htm

Neale, J. M., & Liebert, R. M. (1980). *Science and behavior* (Vol. 2). Englewood Cliffs, NJ: Prentice Hall.

Neef, N., Bicard, D. F., & Endo, S. (2001). Assessment of impulsivity and the development of self-control in students with attention deficit/hyperactivity disorder. *Journal of Applied Behavior Analysis, 34*(4), 397–408.

Nelson, K. (1973). Structure and strategies for learning to talk. *Monographs of the Society for Research in Child Development, 38*(Serial No. 149).

Nelson, K. (1999). The developmental psychology of language and thought. In M. Bennett (Ed.), *Developmental psychology: Achievements and prospects* (pp. 185–204). Philadelphia: Psychology Press.

Neuringer, A. (1991). Operant variability and repetition as a function of interresponse time. *Journal of Experimental Psychology: Animal Behavior Processes, 17,* 3–12.

Neuringer, A. (1993). Reinforced variation and selection. *Animal Learning and Behavior, 21*(2), 83–91.

Neuringer, A. (1994). Behavioral variability and behavior analysis. Paper presented at the thirteenth annual conference of the Northern California Association for Behavior Analysis, Oakland, CA, February, 1994.

Neuringer, A., Deiss, C., & Olson, G. (2000). Reinforced variability and operant learning. *Journal of Experimental Psychology: Animal Behavior Processes, 26*(1), 98–111.

Nevin, J. A. (1992). An integrative model for the study of behavioral momentum. *Journal of the Experimental Analysis of Behavior, 57,* 301–316.

Novaco, R. (1978). Anger and coping with stress. In J. Forety & D. Rathjen (Eds.), *Cognitive Behavior Therapy: Research and Application.* New York: Plenum Press.

Novak, G. (1987, May). *Social cognition: A behavior analysis.* Paper presented at the Association for Behavior Analysis, Nashville, TN.

Novak, G. (1990, May). *The man behind the mask: J. B. Watson, Little Albert, and Santa Claus.* Paper presented at the 18th Annual Convention of the Association for Behavior Analysis, San Francisco.

Novak. (1993, May). *A behavior analysis of multilogic reading.* Paper presented at the 19th Annual Convention of the Association for Behavior Analysis, Chicago.

Novak, G. (1995, May). *Skill learning, dynamical systems, and the development of equivalencing.* Paper presented at the 21st Annual Convention of the Association for Behavior Analysis, Washington, DC.

Novak, G. (1996). *Developmental psychology: Dynamical systems and behavior analysis.* Reno, NV: Context Press.

Novak, G. D. (1998). Behavioral systems theory. *Mexican Journal of Behavior Analysis, 24,* 100–112.

Novak, G. (1999). Skills learning in behavioral epigenesis. *Behavioral Development Bulletin, 8*(1), 17–20.

Novak, G. (2001, November). *Fixed interval responding by students on a Web discussion.* Paper presented at the 1st International Association for Behavioral Analysis Conference, Venice, Italy.

Novak, G., Long, C., & White, H. (2000, May). *How babies become mentalists: Evidence from the first year.* Paper presented at the Twenty-Sixth Annual Convention of the Association for Applied Behavior Analysis, Washington D.C.

Novak, G., & Peláez, M. (2002). A behavior–analytic developmental model is better. *Behavior and Brain Sciences, 25,* 466–468.

Novak, G., & Scott, S. (1998, May). *Incidental teaching of stimulus equivalency to infants.* Paper presented at the Association for Behavior Analysis, Orlando, FL.

Novak, G., Staggs, D., & Jones, S. (1993, March). *Multilogic reading with Limited English Proficiency Children.* Paper presented at the biennial meeting of the Society for Research in Child Development, New Orleans, LA.

Nussbaum, N., & Bigler, E. (1990). *Identification and treatment of attention deficit disorder.* Austin, TX: Pro-Ed.

O'Hora, D., Peláez, M., Barnes-Holmes, D., & Amesty, L. (2003 accepted, in revision). *Derived relational responding and human language: Evidence from the WAIS-III.* Paper submitted to the Psychological Record.

Olweus, D. (1993). *Bullying at school: What we know and what we can do.* Cambridge, MA: Blackwell.

Oyama, S. (1985). *The ontogeny of information: Developmental systems and evolution.* Cambridge, UK: Cambridge University Press.

Palazzoli, M. S. (1974). *Self-starvation: From the intrapsychic to the transpersonal approach to anorexia nervosa* (A. Pomerans, Trans.). Oxford, UK: Chaucer.

Palmer, D. C. (1991). A behavioral interpretation of memory. In L. J. Hayes & P. N. Chase (Eds.), *Dialogues on verbal behavior: The First International Institute on Verbal Relations* (pp. 261–279). Reno, NV: Context Press.

Palmer, D. C. (1996). Achieving parity: The role of automatic reinforcement. *Journal of the Experimental Analysis of Behavior, 65,* 289–290.

Palmer, D. C. (2000). Chomsky's nativism revisited. *Analysis of Verbal Behavior, 17,* 51–56.

Pan, E., Gross, D., & Gross, A. (1996). Prenatal power: Education for life. *Public Health Reports, 111,* 541–545.

Papoušek, H., & Papoušek, M. (1987). Intuitive parenting: A dialectic counterpart to the infant's integrative competence. In J. D. Osofsky (Ed.), *Handbook of infant development* (2nd ed., pp. 669–720). New York: John Wiley.

Papoušek, H., & Papoušek, M. (1981). Fruhentwicklund des sozialverhaltens und der komunikation (cited in Papousek & Papousek, 1987). In H. Remschmidt & M. Schmidt (Eds.), *Neuropsychologie des Kindesalters.* Stuttgart: Enke Verlag.

Parker, S., Greer, S., & Zuckerman, B. (1988). Double jeopardy: The impact of poverty on early child development. *Pediatric Clinics of North America, 35,* 1127–1241.

Pastore, A. L., & Maguire, K. (2001). *Sourcebook of criminal justice statistics.* Retrieved August 21, 2003 from http://www.albany.edu/sourcebook

Patterson, G. R. (1980). Mothers: The unacknowledged victims. *Monographs of the Society for Research in Child Development 45*(5, Serial No. 186).

Patterson, G. R. (1982). *A social learning approach: Coercive family process* (Vol. 3). Eugene, OR: Castalia.

Patterson, G. R., Chamberlain, P., & Reid, J. B. (1982). A comparative evaluation of a parent training program. *Behavior Therapy, 13,* 638–650.

Patterson, G. R., DeBaryshe, B. D., & Ramsey, E. (1989). A developmental perspective on antisocial behavior. *American Psychologist, 44,* 329–335.

Patterson, G. R., Littman, R. A., & Bricker, W. (1967). Assertive behavior in children: A step toward a theory of aggression. *Monographs of the Society for Research in Child Development, 32*(Whole No. 113).

Patterson, G. R., Reid, J. B., & Dishion, T. J. (1992). *Antisocial boys.* Eugene, OR: Castalia.

Peckham, G. W., & Peckham, E. G. (1887). Some observations on the mental powers of spiders. *Journal of Morphology, 1,* 383–419.

Peláez, M. (1994). Contextualism in behavior analysis of development: Upon further reflection. *Behavioral Development, 4,* 8–12.

Peláez, M. (2001a, August). *Morality as a system of rule-governed behavior and empathy.* Paper presented at the Annual Convention of the American Psychological Association, San Francisco.

Peláez, M. (2001b). Morality as a system of rule-governed behavior and empathy. *Behavior Development Bulletin, 1,* 8–14.

Peláez, M., Gewirtz, J. L., Sanchez, A., & Mahabir, N. M. (2000). Exploring stimulus equivalence formation in infants. *Behavior Development Bulletin, 9,* 20–25.

Peláez, M., & Moreno, R. (1998). A taxonomy of rules and their correspondence in rule-governed behavior. *Mexican Journal of Behavior Analysis, 24*(2), 197–214.

Peláez, M., & Moreno, R. (1999). Four dimensions of rules and their correspondence to rule-governed behavior: A taxonomy. *Behavior Development Bulletin, 8,* 21–27.

Peláez, M., & Moreno, R. (2002). Una tassonomia delle regole e loro corrispondenze con il comportamento governato da regole [A taxonomy of rules and their correspondence to rule-governed behavior]. In P. Moderato, G. Presti, & P. N. Chase (Eds.), *Pensieri, Parole, e Comportamento: U'analisi funzionale delle relazioni linguistiche* [A functional analysis of linguistic relations] (pp. 171–184). Milan, Italy: McGraw-Hill.

Peláez, M., Pickens, J., Field, T., & Hart, S. (2002). *Parenting styles of depressed mothers with their 1-year-old infants.* Manuscript submitted for publication.

Peláez-Nogueras, M. (1992a). *Infant learning to reference maternal emotional cues.* Ph.D. dissertation, Florida International University Library, Miami, FL.

Peláez-Nogueras, M. (1992b). Recurrent issues in the study of behavior development: Meta-models. *Behavioral Development, 1,* 3–5.

Peláez-Nogueras, M. (1993). Alfie Kohn's attacks rewarded with money, praise, and recognition. *Behavioral Development, 3,* 5–6.

Peláez-Nogueras, M. (1996). Thought without naming: A commentary on Horne and Lowe's article "The origins of naming and other symbolic behavior." *Journal of Experimental Analysis of Behavior, 65,* 299–301.

Peláez-Nogueras, M., Field, T., Cigales, M., Gewirtz, J. Gonzalez, A., Clasky, S., et al. (1997). The effects of systematic stroking versus tickling and poking on infant attention and affect. *Journal of Applied Developmental Psychology, 18,* 169–177.

Peláez-Nogueras, M., Field, T., Cigales, M., Gonzalez, A., & Clasky, S. (1994). Infants of depressed mothers show less "depressed" behavior with their nursery teachers. *Infant Mental Health Journal, 15,* 358–367.

Peláez-Nogueras, M., Field, T., Hossain, Z., & Pickens, J. (1996). Depressed mothers' touch increases infant positive affect and attention in still-face interactions. *Child Development, 67,* 1780–1792.

Peláez-Nogueras, M., & Gewirtz, J. L. (1992). The behavior analysis of moral behavior. *Mexican Journal of Behavior Analysis, 18,* 57–81.

Peláez-Nogueras, M., & Gewirtz, J. L. (1995). The learning of moral behavior: A behavior–analytic approach. In W. M. Kurtines & J. L. Gewirtz (Eds.), *Moral behavior: An introduction* (pp. 173–199). Boston: Allyn & Bacon.

Peláez-Nogueras, M., & Gewirtz, J. L. (1997). The context of stimulus control in behavior analysis. In D. M. Baer & E. M. Pinkston (Eds.), *Environment and behavior* (pp. 30–42). Boulder, CO: Westview Press.

Peláez-Nogueras, M., Gewirtz, J. L., Field, T., Cigales, M., Malphurs, J., Clasky, S., & Sanchez, A. (1996). Infants' preference for touch stimulation in

face-to-face interactions. *Journal of Applied Developmental Psychology, 17,* 199–213.

Pelham, W. E., & Gnagy, E. M. (1999). Psychosocial and combined treatments for ADHD. *Mental Retardation and Developmental Disabilities Research Reviews, 5,* 225–236.

Pelham, W. E., Gnagy, E. M., Greiner, A. R., Hoza, B., Hinshaw, S. P., Swanson, J. M., et al. (2000). Behavioral versus behavioral and pharmacological treatment in ADHD children attending a summer treatment program. *Journal of Abnormal Child Psychology, 28*(6), 507–525.

Pelham, W. E., & Hoza, B. (1996). Intensive treatment: A summer treatment program for children with ADHD. In E. Hibbs & P. Jensen (Eds.), *Psychosocial treatments for child and adolescent disorders: empirically based strategies for clinical practice* (pp. 311–340). New York: American Psychological Association Press.

Pennypacker, H. S. (1994). A selectionist view of the future of behavior analysis in education. In R. Gardner (Ed.), *Behavior analysis in education: Focus on measurably superior instruction* (pp. 11–18). Pacific Grove, CA: Brooks/Cole.

Pepper, S. C. (1960). *World hypotheses: A study in evidence.* Berkeley: University of California Press. (Original work published 1942)

Petersen, G. A., & Sherrod, K. B. (1982). Relationship of maternal language to language development and language delay of children. *American Journal of Mental Deficiency, 86,* 391–398.

Peterson, A. C., Compas, B. E., Brooks-Gunn, J., Stemmler, M., Ey, S., & Grant, K. E. (1993). Depression in adolescence. *American Psychologist, 48*(2), 155–168.

Petrovich, S. B., & Gewirtz, J. L. (1985). The attachment learning process and its relation to cultural and biological evolution: Proximate and ultimate considerations. In M. Reite & T. Field (Eds.), *The psychobiology of attachment* (pp. 259–291). New York: Academic Press.

Phillips, D. A., Voran, M., Kisker, E., Howes, C., & Whitebook, M. (1994). Child care for children in poverty: Opportunity or inequity? *Child Development, 65,* 472–492.

Phillips, E. L., Phillips, E. A., Fixsen, D. L., & Wolf, M. M. (1971). Achievement place: Modification of the behaviors of pre-delinquent boys within a token economy. *Journal of Applied Behavior Analysis, 4,* 45–59.

Phillips, J. L. (1975). *The origins of intellect: Piaget's theory.* San Francisco: Freeman.

Piaget, J. (1952). *The origins of intelligence in children* (M. Cook, Trans.). New York: International Universities Press.

Piaget, J. (1954). *The construction of reality in the child.* New York: Basic Books.

Piaget, J., & Inhelder, B. (1971). *Mental imagery in the child* (P. A. Chilton, Trans.). New York: Basic Books.

Pickens, J., Field, T., Prodomidis, M., Peláez-Nogueras, M., & Hossain, Z. (1995). Posttraumatic stress, depression and social support among college students after Hurricane Andrew. *Journal of College Student Development, 36*(2), 152–161.

Pierce, K., & Schreibman, L. (1995). Increasing complex play in children with autism via peer-implemented pivotal response training. *Journal of Applied Behavior Analysis, 28,* 285–295.

Pierce, K., & Schreibman, L. (1997). Multiple peer use of pivotal response training to increase social behaviors of classmates with autism: Results from trained and untrained peers. *Journal of Applied Behavior Analysis, 30,* 157–160.

Platt, S. A., & Sanislow, C. A. (1988). Norm-of-reaction: Definition and misinterpretations of animal research. *Journal of Comparative Psychology, 102,* 254–261.

Pliskoff, S. S., & Goldiamond, I. (1966). Some discriminative properties of fixed ratio performance in the pigeon. *Journal of the Experimental Analysis of Behavior, 9,* 1–9.

Plomin, R. (1986). *Development, genetics, and psychology.* Hillsdale, NJ: Lawrence Erlbaum.

Plomin, R. (1988). The nature and nurture of cognitive abilities. In R. J. Sternberg (Ed.), *Advances in the psychology of human intelligence* (Vol. 4, pp. 1–33). Hillsdale, NJ: Lawrence Erlbaum.

Plomin, R. (1989). Environment and genes: Determinants of behavior. *American Psychologist, 44*(2), 105–111.

Plomin, R. (1999). Behavioral genetics. In M. Bennett (Ed.), *Developmental psychology: Achievement and prospects* (pp. 231–252). Philadelphia: Psychology Press.

Plomin, R., & Daniels, D. (1987). Why are children in the same family so different from each other? *Behavioral and Brain Sciences, 10*(1), 1–16.

Plomin, R., Reiss, D., Hetherington, E. M., & Howe, G. W. (1994). Nature and nurture: Genetic contributions to measures of the family environment. *Developmental Psychology, 30,* 32–43.

Pollitt, E. (1994). Poverty and child development: Relevance of research in developing countries to the United States. *Child Development, 65,* 283–295.

Popenhagen, M. P., & Qualley, R. M. (1998). Adolescent suicide: Detection, intervention, and prevention. *Professional School Counseling, 1,* 30–36.

Poulson, C. L. (1983). Differential reinforcement of other-than-vocalization as a control procedure in the conditioning of infant vocalization rate. *Journal of Experimental Child Psychology, 51,* 267–279.

Poulson, C. L., de Paula Nunes, L. R., & Warren, S. F. (1989). Imitation in infancy: A critical review. I *Advances in Child Development and Behavior, 22,* 271–298. New York: Academic Press.

Poulson, C. L., Kymissis, E., Reeve, K. F., Andreatos, M., & Richards, L. (1991). Generalized vocal imitation in infants. *Journal of Experimental Child Psychology, 88,* 1–21.

Powers, M. K., Schneck, M., & Teller, D. Y. (1981). Spectral sensitivity of human infants at absolute visual threshold. *Vision Research, 21,* 1005–1016.

Poznanski, E. O., Cook, S. C., & Carroll, B. J. (1979). A depression rating scale for children. *Pediatrics, 64,* 442–450.

Premack, D. (1959). Toward empirical behavior laws: 1. Positive reinforcement. *Psychological Review, 66,* 219–233.

Premack, D., & Woodruff, G. (1978). Does the chimpanzee have a theory of mind? *Behavioral and Brain Sciences, 1*(4), 515–526.

Proctor, B. D., & Dalaker, J. (2002). *Poverty in the United States: 2001* (Current Population Reports, Series P60–219). Washington, DC: Government Printing Office.

Proper, H., Wideen, M. F., & Ivany, G. (1988). World view projected by science teachers: A study of classroom dialogue. *Science Education, 72*(5), 547–560.

Prosser, C. J., & Hunter, W. S. (1936). The extinction of startle responses and spinal reflexes in the white rat. *American Journal of Physiology, 117,* 609–618.

Pryor, K. W., Haag, R., & O'Reilly, J. (1969). The creative porpoise: Training for novel behavior. *Journal of the Experimental Analysis of Behavior, 12,* 653–661.

Rachlin, H. (1976). *Introduction to modern behaviorism* (2nd ed.). San Francisco: W. H. Freeman.

Rachlin, H. (1995). Self-control: Beyond commitment. *Behavioral and Brain Sciences, 18,* 109–159.

Rachlin, H., & Green, L. (1972). Commitment, choice, and self-control. *Journal of the Experimental Analysis of Behavior, 17,* 15–22.

Rachlin, H., Raineri, A., & Cross, D. (1991). Subjective probability and delay. *Journal of the Experimental Analysis of Behavior, 55,* 233–244.

Ray, W. S. (1932). A preliminary report of a study of prenatal conditioning. *Child Development, 3,* 175–177.

Reese, H. W. (1994). Cognitive and behavioral approaches to problem solving. In S. C. Hayes, L. J. Hayes, M. Sato, & K. Ono (Eds.), *Behavior analysis of language and cognition* (pp. 197–258). Reno, NV: Context Press.

Reese, H. W. (1998). Utility of group methodology in behavior analysis and developmental psychology. *Mexican Journal of Behavior Analysis, 24*(2), 137–151.

Reese, H. W. (2002, September). *Behavior genetics: Much ado about (almost) nothing.* Paper presented at the Sixth Congress of Behaviorism and the Sciences of Behavior, Auburn, AL.

Reich, P. A. (1986). *Language development.* Englewood Cliffs, NJ: Prentice Hall.

Reid, R. (1999). Attention deficit/hyperactivity disorder: Effective methods for the classroom. *Focus on Exceptional Children, 32*(4), 1–20.

Revusky, S. H., & Garcia, J. (1970). Learned associations over long delays. In G. H. Bower (Ed.), *The psychology of learning and motivation* (Vol. 4, pp. 1–44). New York: Academic Press.

Reynolds, G. S. (1966). Discrimination and emission of temporal intervals by pigeons. *Journal of the Experimental Analysis of Behavior, 9,* 65–68.

Rheingold, H. L., Gewirtz, J. L., & Ross, H. W. (1959). Social conditioning of vocalizations in the infant. *Journal of Comparative and Physiological Psychology, 52,* 68–73.

Ridley, M. (1999). *Genome: The autobiography of a species.* New York: Harper Collins.

Riegler, H. C., & Baer, D. M. (1989). A developmental analysis of rule-following. In H. W. Reese (Ed.), *Advances in child development and behavior* (Vol. 21, pp. 191–219). New York: Academic Press.

Robins, L. N. (1966). *Deviant children grown up.* Baltimore: Williams & Wilkins.

Robins, L. N., & Ratcliff, K. S. (1979). Risk factors in the continuation of childhood antisocial behavior into adulthood. *International Journal of Mental Health, 7*(3–4), 96–116.

Rodríguez, I. A., Montgomery, M., & Peláez, M., & Salas, M.W. (in press). Love attitudes and dating experiences of adolescents in three different cultures. *Mexican Journal of Psychology, 20*(2).

Rogers-Warren, A., & Warren, S. (1980). Mands for verbalization: Facilitating the display of newly-taught language. *Behavior Modification, 4,* 361–382.

Rondal, J. A. (1979). Mama est au courant: Une etude des connaissances maternelles quant aux aspects formels du language de jeune enfant [Mommy is informed: A study of maternal knowledge about formal aspects of the language of the young child]. *Enfance, 2,* 95–105.

Root, R. W. I., & Resnick, R. J. (2003). An update on the diagnosis and treatment of attention deficit/hyperactivity disorder in children. *Professional Psychology: Research and Practice, 34*(1), 34–41.

Rosales, J., & Baer, D. M. (1994). A behavior-analytic view of development. In E. Ribes & S. W. Bijou (Eds.), *Recent approaches to behavioral development.* Guadalajara, Mexico: Editorial Universidad de Guadalajara.

Rosales-Ruiz, J., & Baer, D. M. (1997). Behavioral cusps: A developmental and pragmatic concept for behavior analysis. *Journal of Applied Behavior Analysis, 30*(3), 533–544.

Ross, A. O. (1976). *Psychological aspects of learning disabilities and reading disorders.* New York: McGraw-Hill.

Ross, A. O. (1980). *Psychological disorders of children: A behavioral approach to theory, research, and therapy* (2nd ed.). New York: McGraw-Hill.

Roth, W. E., Gewirtz, J. L. (1995). The role of contingent maternal attention in training jealous initiations in twin infants. Paper presented at the 21st Annual Convention of the Association for Behavior Analysis, Washington, D.C.

Rothbart, M. K., & Maccoby, E. E. (1966). Parents' differential reactions to sons and daughters. *Journal of Personality and Social Psychology, 9,* 353–362.

Rotter, J. (1966). Generalized expectancies for internal versus external control of reinforcement. *Psychological Monographs, 80*(Whole No. 609).

Rovee-Collier, C. (1987). Learning and memory in infancy. In J. Osofsky (Ed.), *Handbook of infant development* (2nd ed., pp. 98–148). New York: John Wiley.

Rovee-Collier, C. K., & Fagen, J. W. (1981). The retrieval of memory in early infancy. In L. P. Lipsitt & C. K. Rovee-Collier (Eds.), *Advances in infancy research* (Vol. 1, pp. 225–254). Norwood, NJ: Ablex.

Rovee-Collier, C. K., Griesler, P. C., & Earley, L. A. (1985). Contextual determinants of retrieval in three-month-old infants. *Learning & Motivation, 16,* 139–157.

Rowe, D. C., & Plomin, R. (1981). The importance of nonshared (E1) environmental influences in develop. *Developmental Psychology, 17,* 517–531.

Rubin, J., Provenzano, F. J., & Luria, Z. (1974). The eye of the beholder: Parents' views on the sex of newborns. *American Journal of Orthopsychiatry, 5,* 353–363.

Rutter, M. (1991). Age changes in depressive disorders: Some developmental considerations. In J. Garber & K. A. Dodge (Eds.), *The development of emotion regulation and dysregulation* (pp. 273–300). New York: Cambridge University Press.

Rutter, M. L. (1987). Continuities and discontinuities from infancy. In J. D. Osofsky (Ed.), *Handbook of infant development* (2nd ed., pp. 1256–1296). Oxford, UK: Wiley.

Sackett, G. P. (1987). Analysis of sequential social interaction data: Some issues, recent developments, and a causal inference model. In J. D. Osofsky (Ed.), *Handbook of infant development* (pp. 855–878). New York: Wiley.

Sagan, C. (1980). *Cosmos.* New York: Random House.

Sakabe, N., Arayama, T., & Suzuki, T. (1969). Human fetal evoked response to acoustic stimulation. *Acta Oto-Laryngologica, Supplementum, 252,* 29–36.

Sameroff, A. J., & Chandler, M. J. (1975). Reproductive risk and the continuum of caretaking casualty. In F. D. Horowitz, M. Hetherington, S. Scarr-Salapatek, & G. Siegel (Eds.), *Review of child development research* (Vol. 4). Chicago: University of Chicago Press.

Sampson, R. J., & Laub, J. H. (1994). Urban poverty and the family context of delinquency: A new look at structure and process in a classic study. *Child Development, 65,* 523–540.

Sanders, M. R., & Dadds, M. R. (1982). The effects of planned activities and child management training: An analysis of setting generality. *Behavior Therapy, 13,* 1–11.

Sanders, M. R., & Dadds, M. R. (1993). *Behavioral family interventions.* Needham Heights, MA: Allyn Bacon.

Sarbin, T. R. (1977). Contextualism: A worldview of modern psychology. In A. W. Landfield (Ed.), *Nebraska symposium on motivation* (Vol. 24, pp. 1–41). Lincoln: University of Nebraska Press.

Scarr, S., & McCartney, K. (1983). How people make their own environments: A theory of genotype–environment effects. *Child Development, 54,* 424–435.

Schlinger, H. D. (1992). Theory in behavior analysis: An application to child development. *American Psychologist, 47*(11), 1396–1410.

Schlinger, H. D. (1995). *A behavior analytic view of child development.* New York: Plenum Press.

Schlinger, H. D. (2002). Concepts in behavior development. *Behavior Development Bulletin, 1,* 1–8.

Scholzman, K. L., & Verba, S. (1978). The new employment: Does it hurt? *Public Policy, 26,* 333–358.

Schoneberger, T. (2000). A departure from cognitivism: Implications of Chomsky's second revolution in linguistics. *Analysis of Verbal Behavior, 17,* 57–73.

Schuster, M. A., Franke, T. M., & Bastian, A. M. (2000). Firearms storage patterns in U.S. homes with children. *American Journal of Public Health, 90*(4), 588–594.

Schusterman, R. J., & Kastak, D. (1994). A California sea lion (Zalophus californianus) is capable of forming equivalence relations. *Psychological Record, 43*(4), 823–939.

Schwartz, M. (1984). The role of sound for space and object perception in the congenitally blind infant. In L. P. Lipsitt & C. Rovee-Collier (Eds.), *Advances in infancy research* (Vol. 3, pp. 23–56). Norwood, NJ: Ablex.

Schweitzer, J. B., & Sulzer-Azaroff, B. (1988). Self-control: Teaching tolerance for delay in impulsive children. *Journal of the Experimental Analysis of Behavior, 50,* 173–186.

Scott, J., Clark, C., & Brady, M. (2000). *Students with autism: Characteristics and instruction programming.* San Diego, CA: Singular.

Segal, Z. V., Williams, J. M. G., & Teasdale, J. D. (2002). *Mindfulness-based cognitive therapy for depression: A new approach to preventing relapse.* New York: Guilford Press.

Shaffer, D. R. (1989). *Developmental psychology* (2nd ed.). Monterey, CA: Brooks/Cole.

Shaffer, D. R. (2002). *Childhood & adolescence: Developmental psychology* (6th ed.). Belmont, CA: Wadsworth/Thomson Learning.

Shaffer, H. R. (1999). Understanding socialization: From unidirectional to bidirectional conceptions. In M. Bennett (Ed.), *Developmental psychology: Achievements and prospects.* Philadelphia: Psychology Press.

Shah, S. A., & Borgaonkar, D. S. (1974). The XYY chromosomal abnormality: Some "facts" and some "fantasies"? *American Psychologist, 29,* 357–359.

Shahan, T. A. & Chase, P. N. (2002). Novelty, stimulus control, and operant variability. *The Behavior Analyst, 25,* 175–190.

Shantz, C. (1983). Social cognition. In J. H. Flavell, E. M. Markham, & P. H. Mussen (Eds.), *Handbook of child psychology: Vol. 3. Cognitive development.* (4th ed., pp. 495–555). New York: John Wiley.

Sharpless, S. K., & Jasper, H. (1956). Habituation of the arousal reaction. *Brain, 79,* 655–680.

Shecker, L., Hops, H., Andrews, J., Alpert, T., & Davis, B. (1998). Interactional processes in families with depressed and non-depressed adolescents: Reinforcement of depressive behavior. *Behaviour Research and Therapy, 36,* 417–427.

Sheldon, W. H., Dupertius, C. W. & McDermott, E. (1954). *Atlas of men; a guide for somatotyping the adult male at all ages.* New York: Harper.

Sheley, J. F., & Wright, J. D. (1998). *High school youth, weapons, and violence: A national survey.* Washington, DC: National Institute of Justice.

Sheppard, W. C., & Willoughby, R. H. (1975). *Child behavior: Learning and development.* Chicago: Rand McNally.

Shimp, C. P. (1982). On metaknowledge in the pigeon: An organism's knowledge about its own behavior. *Animal Learning and Behavior, 10,* 358–364.

Sidman, M. (1971). Reading and auditory-visual equivalences. *Journal of Speech and Hearing Research, 14*(1), 5–13.

Sidman, M. (1986). Functional analysis of emergent verbal classes. In T. Thompson & D. Zeiler (Eds.), *Analysis and integration of behavioral units* (pp. 231–245). Hillsdale, NJ: Lawrence Erlbaum.

Sidman, M. (1994). *Equivalence relations and behavior: A research story.* Boston: Authors Cooperative.

Siegler, R. S. (1994). Cognitive variability: A key to understanding cognitive development. *Current Directions in Psychological Science, 3,* 1–5.

Siegler, R. S. (1998). *Children's thinking* (3rd ed.). Saddle River, NJ: Prentice Hall.

Siegler, R. S. (2000). The rebirth of children's learning. *Child Development, 71*(1), 26–35.

Silbereisen, R. K., Petersen, A. C., Albrecht, H. T., & Kracke, B. (1989). Maturational timing and the development of problem behavior: Longitudinal studies in adolescence. *Journal of Early Adolescence, 9*(3), 247–268.

Siqueland, E. R. (1964). Operant conditioning of head-turning in four-month-old infants. *Psychonomic Science, 1,* 223–224.

Siqueland, E. R., & Lipsitt, L. P. (1966). Conditioned head-turning in human newborns. *Journal of Experimental Child Psychology, 3,* 356–376.

Skinner, B. F. (1931). The concept of the reflex in the description of behavior. *Journal of General Psychology, 5,* 427–458.

Skinner, B. F. (1935). The generic nature of the concepts of stimulus and response. *Journal of General Psychology, 12,* 40–65.

Skinner, B. F. (1938). *The behavior of organisms.* New York: Appleton-Century-Crofts.

Skinner, B. F. (1953). *Science and human behavior.* New York: Macmillan.

Skinner, B. F. (1957). *Verbal behavior.* New York: Appleton-Century-Crofts.

Skinner, B. F. (1966). The ontogeny and phylogeny of behavior. *Science, 153,* 1203–1213.

Skinner, B. F. (1968). *The technology of teaching.* New York: Appleton-Century-Crofts.

Skinner, B. F. (1969). An operant analysis of problem solving. In B. F. Skinner (Ed.), *Contingencies of reinforcement.* New York: Appleton-Century-Croft.

Skinner, B. F. (1974). *About behaviorism.* New York: Knopf.

Skinner, B. F. (1981). Selection by consequences. *Science, 213,* 501–504.

Skinner, B. F. (1982). Contrived reinforcement. *The Behavior Analyst, 5,* 3–8.

Skinner, B. F. (1984). The shame of American education. *American Psychologist, 39,* 947–954.

Skinner, B. F. (1989). *Recent issues in the analysis of behavior.* Columbus, OH: Merrill.

Skinner, B. F. (1992). The shame of American education. In R. P. West & L. A. Hemerlynck (Eds.), *Designs for excellence in education: The legacy of B. F. Skinner* (pp. 15–30). Longmont, CO: Sopris West.

Slater, A. (1999). Intermodal perception at birth: Intersensory redundancy guides newborn infants' learning of arbitrary auditory-visual pairings. *Developmental Science, 2,* 333–338.

Slee, P. T. (1993). Bullying: A preliminary investigation of its nature and the effects of social cognition. *Early Child Development & Care, 87,* 47–57.

Smith, R., Michael, J., & Sundberg, M. L. (1996). Automatic reinforcement and automatic punishment in infant vocal behavior. *Analysis of Verbal Behavior, 13,* 39–48.

Smith, W. I., & Moore, J. W. (1966). *Conditioning and instrumental learning: A program for self-instruction.* New York: McGraw-Hill.

Snow, C. E. (1972). Mothers' speech to children learning language. *Child Development, 43,* 549–565.

Snyder, J., Schrepferman, L., & St. Peter, C. (1997). Origins of antisocial behavior: Negative reinforcement and affect dysregulation of behavior as socialization mechanisms in family interaction. *Behavior Modification, 21*(2), 187–215.

Sobell, M. B., & Sobell, L. C. (1978). *Behavioral treatment of alcohol problems.* New York: Plenum Press.

Soken, N. H., & Pick, A. D. (1999). Infants' perception of dynamic affective expressions: Do infants distinguish specific expressions? *Child Development, 70*(6), 1275–1282.

Sommer, B. B. (1978). *Puberty and adolescence.* New York: Oxford University Press.

Song, Y., & Lu, H. H. (2002). *Early childhood poverty: A statistical profile.* New York: National Center for Children in Poverty.

Spear, L. P. (2000). The adolescent brain and age-related behavioral manifestations. *Neuroscience and Biobehavioral Reviews, 24,* 417–463.

Spelt, D. K. (1948). The conditioning of the human fetus in utero. *Journal of Experimental Psychology, 38,* 338–346.

Spence, J. T. (1982). Comments on Baumrind's "Are Androgynous Individuals More Effective Persons and Parents?" *Child Development, 53,* 76–80.

Spence, M. J., & DeCasper, A. J. (1987). Prenatal experience with low-frequency maternal-voice sounds influence neonatal perception of maternal voice samples. *Infant Behavior and Development, 10*(2), 133–142.

Spinetta, J., & Rigler, D. (1972). The child-abusing parent: A psychological review. *Psychological Bulletin, 77,* 296–304.

Sroufe, L. A. (1977). Wariness of strangers and the study of infant development. *Child Development, 48,* 731–746.

Staines, G. L., Pottick, K. J., & Fudge, D. A. (1986). Wives' employment and husbands' attitudes toward work and life. *Journal of Applied Psychology, 71*(1), 118–128.

Stein, J. (1973). *The Random House dictionary of the English language* (Unabridged ed.). New York: Random House.

Steinberg, L. (1996). Adolescent development in context. In J. Vaicunas, B. Kaufman, & J. R. Beiser (Eds.), Adolescence (pp. 1–20). New York: Mc Graw-Hill.

Steinberg, L., & Morris, A. S. (2001). Adolescent development. *Annual Review of Psychology, 52,* 83–110.

Stevenson, H. (1983). How children learn: The quest for a theory. In W. Kessen & P. H. Mussen (Eds.), *History, theory, and methods* (Vol. 1, pp. 213–236). New York: John Wiley.

Stokes, T. F., Fowler, S. A., & Baer, D. M. (1978). Training preschool children to recruit natural communities of reinforcement. *Journal of Applied Behavior Analysis, 11,* 285–303.

Substance Abuse and Mental Health Services Administration. (2002). *Results from the 2001 National Household Survey on Drug Abuse: Volume I. Summary of national findings* (NHSDA Series H-17, DHHS Publication No. SMA 02–3758). Rockville, MD: Substance Abuse and Mental Health Services Administration, Office of Applied Studies.

Suitor, J. J., & Reavis, R. (1995). Football, fast cars, and cheerleading: Adolescents gender norms, 1978–1989. *Adolescences, 20,* 256–272.

Sundberg, M. L., & Michael, J. (2001). The benefits of Skinner's analysis of verbal behavior for children with autism. *Behavior Modification, 25*(5), 698–724.

Sundberg, M. L., Michael, J., Partington, J. W., & Sundberg, C. A. (1996). The role of automatic reinforcement in early language acquisition. *Analysis of Verbal Behavior, 13,* 21–37.

Sundberg, M. L., & Partington, J. W. (1998). *Teaching language to children with autism or other learning disabilities.* Pleasant Hill, CA: Behavior Analysts.

Teasdale, J. D., Segal, Z. V., Williams, J. M. G., Ridgeway, V., Lau, M., & Soulsby, J. (2000). Reducing risk of recurrence of major depression using mindfulness-based cognitive therapy. *Journal of Consulting and Clinical Psychology, 68,* 615–623.

Teicher, M. H., Ito, Y., Glod, C. A., & Barber, N. I. (1996). Objective measurement of hyperactivity and attentional problems in ADHD. *Journal of the American Academy of Child and Adolescent Psychiatry, 35,* 334–342.

Thelen, E. (1991). Motor aspects of emergent speech: A dynamic approach. In D. M. Krasnegor, D. M. Rumbaugh, R. L. Schiefelbusch, & M. Studdert-Kennedy (Eds.), *Biological and behavioral determinants of language development.* Hillsdale, NJ: Lawrence Erlbaum.

Thelen, E. (1994). Three-month-old infants can learn task-specific patterns of interlimb coordination. *Psychological Science, 5,* 280–285.

Thelen, E., Kelso, J. A. S., & Fogel, A. (1987). Self-organizing systems and infant motor development. *Developmental Review, 7,* 39–65.

Thelen, E., & Smith, L. B. (1994). *A dynamic systems approach to the development of language and cognition.* Cambridge, MA: Bradford Books.

Thelen, E., & Ulrich, B. D. (1991). Hidden skills: A dynamic systems analysis of treadmill-elicited stepping during the first year. *Monographs of the Society for Research in Child Development, 56*(1, Serial No. 223).

Thomas, A., & Chess, S. (1977). *Temperament and development.* New York: Bruner/Mazel.

Thomas, A., Chess, S., & Birch, H. G. (1968). *Temperament and behavior disorders in children.* New York: New York University Press.

Thomas, A., Chess, S., & Birch, H. G. (1982). The reality of difficult temperament. *Merrill-Palmer Quarterly, 28,* 1–20.

Thomas, A., Chess, S., Birch, H. G., Hertzig, M. E., & Korn, S. (1963). *Behavioral individuality in early childhood.* New York: New York University Press.

Thomas, A., Chess, S., & Korn, S. (1982). The reality of difficult temperament. *Merrill-Palmer Quarterly, 28,* 1–20.

Thomas, R. M. (1985). *Comparing theories of child development* (2nd ed.). Belmont, CA: Wadsworth.

Thompson, R. A. (1999). The individual child: Temperament, emotion, self, and personality. In M. H. Bornstein & M. Lamb (Eds.), *Developmental psychology: An advanced textbook* (4th ed., pp. 375–409). Mahwah, NJ: Lawrence Erlbaum.

Thompson, S. K. C. (1975). Gender labels and early sex role development. *Child Development, 46,* 339–447.

Thorndike, E. L. (1911). *Animal intelligence: Experimental studies.* Oxford, UK: Macmillan.

Toth, M. K. (1990). *Understanding and treating conduct disorders.* Austin, TX: Pro-Ed.

Turkkan, J. S. (1989). Classical conditioning: The new hegemony. *Behavioral and Brain Sciences, 12,* 121–179.

Turner, S. M., Beidel, D. C., & Costello, A. (1987). Psychopathology in the offspring of anxiety disorders patients. *Journal of Consultation Clinical Psychology, 55,* 229–235.

Twitmyer, E. B. (1905). Knee-jerks without stimulation of the patellar tendon. *Psychological Bulletin, 2,* 43–44.

Udry, J., Billy, J., Morris, N., Groff, T., Raj, M. (1985). Serum androgenic hormones motivate sexual behavior in adolescent boys. *Fertility and Sterility, 43*(1), 90–94.

U.S. Bureau of Labor Statistics. (2001). *Employment characteristics of families in 2000.* Retrieved August 22, 2003 from ftp://ftp. bls.gov/pub/news.release/History/famee. 04192001.news

U.S. Census Bureau. (2002). *Poverty 2001 graphs.* Retrieved August 8, 2003 from http://www. census.gov/hhes/poverty/poverty01/graphs01. html

U.S. Department of Health and Human Services. (1998). Public Health Service Task Force recommendations for the use of antiretroviral drugs in pregnant women infected with HIV-1 for maternal health and for reducing perinatal HIV-1 transmission in the United States. *Morbidity and Mortality Weekly Report, 47*(No. RR-2).

U.S. Public Health Service (2000). *Report of the Surgeon General's Conference on Children's Mental Health: A national action agenda.* Washington, DC: Department of Health and Human Services.

Unis, A. S., Munson, J. A., Rogers, S. J., Goldson, E., Osterling, J., Gabriels, R., et al. (2002). A randomized, double-blind, placebo-controlled trial of porcine versus synthetic secretin for reducing symptoms of autism. *Journal of the American Academy of Child and Adolescent Psychiatry, 41,* 1315–1321.

Use of folic acid for the prevention of spina bifida and other neural tube defects: 1983–1991 (Morbidity and Mortality Weekly Reports). (1991). *Journal of the American Medical Association, 266,* 1190–1191.

Uzgiris, I. C. (1972). Patterns of cognitive development in infancy. *Merrill Palmer Quarterly, 19,* 181–204.

Valdez-Menchaca, M. C., & Whitehurst, G. J. (1992). Accelerating language development through picture book reading: A systematic extension to Mexican Day Care. *Developmental Psychology, 28,* 1106–1114.

Vargas, J. (2002). The baby tender. *A brief biography of B. F. Skinner.* Retrieved July 16, 2003 from http://www.bfskinner.org/bio.asp

Vasta, R. (1982). Physical child abuse: A dual-component analysis. *Developmental Review, 2,* 125–149.

Vaughan, M. (1989). Rule-governed behavior in behavior analysis: A theoretical and experimental history. In S. C. Hayes (Ed.), *Rule-governed behavior: Cognition, contingencies, and instructional control* (pp. 97–118). New York: Plenum Press.

Vaughn, M. E., & Michael, J. L. (1982). Automatic reinforcement: An important but ignored concept. *Behaviorism, 10,* 217–227.

von Eye, A. (1990). *Introduction to configural frequency analysis: The search for types and antitypes in cross-classifications.* New York: Cambridge University Press.

Vorhees, C. V., & Mollnow, E. (1987). Behavioral teratogenesis: Long-term influences on behavior from early exposure to environmental agents. In J. D. Osofsyk (Ed.), *Handbook of infant development* (2nd ed., pp. 913–971). New York: John Wiley.

Vygotsky, L. S. (1978). *Mind in society: The development of higher mental processes.* Cambridge, MA: Harvard University Press.

Vygotsky, L. S. (1987). *The collected works of L. S. Vygotsky: Vol. 1, Problems of general psychology.* New York: Plenum.

Wachs, T. D. (1999). The what, why, and how of temperament: A piece of the action. In L. Balter & C. S. Tamis-LeMonda (Eds.), *Child psychology: A handbook of contemporary issues* (pp. 23–44). Philadelphia: Psychology Press.

Waddington, C. H. (1957). *The strategy of the genes.* London: Allen & Unwin.

Wahler, R. G. (1969). Infant social development: Some experimental analyses of an infant–mother interaction during the first year of life. *Journal of Experimental Child Psychology, 7*(1), 101–113.

Wahler, R. G., & Dumas, J. E. (1986). Maintenance factors in coercive mother–child interactions: The compliance and predictability hypotheses. *Journal of Applied Behavior Analysis, 19*(1), 13–22.

Wainryb, C. (1993). The application of moral judgments to other cultures: Relativism and universality. *Child Development, 64,* 924–933.

Walberg, H. J. (1990). Productive teaching and instruction: Assessing the knowledge base. *Phi Delta Kappan,* 470–478.

Walk, R. D., & Gibson, E. J. (1961). A comparative and analytic study of visual depth perception. *Psychological Monographs, 75*(15, Whole No. 519).

Walker, L., Gustafson, P., & Henning, K. (2001). The consolidation/transition model in moral reasoning. *Developmental Psychology, 37*(2), 187–197.

Warner-Rogers, J., Taylor, A., & Taylor, E. (2000). Inattentive behavior in childhood: Epidemiology and implications for development. *Journal of Learning Disabilities, 33*(6), 520–536.

Waterman, A. S. (1982). Identity development from adolescence to adulthood: An extension of theory and a review of research. *Developmental Psychology, 18,* 341–358.

Watkins, C. L. (1988). Project Follow Through: A story of the identification and neglect of effective instruction. *Youth Policy, 10*(7), 7–11.

Watson, A. C., & Chase, P. N. (2002). Relational learning in preverbal infants: Evidence from developmental science. *Behavior Development Bulletin, 1,* 27–33.

Watson, J. B., & Rayner, R. (1920). Conditioned emotional reactions. *Journal of Experimental Psychology, 3,* 1–14.

Watson, J. S. (1969). Operant conditioning of visual fixations in infants under visual and auditory reinforcement. *Developmental Psychology, 1,* 508–516.

Watson, J. S. (1972). Smiling, cooing, and "the game." *Merrill-Palmer Quarterly, 18,* 323–339.

Watson, J. S., & Ramey, C. T. (1972). Reactions to response-contingent stimulation in early infancy. *Merrill-Palmer Quarterly, 18,* 219–227.

Webster, W. (1998). Teratogen update: Congenital rubella. *Teratology, 58,* 13–23.

Weinraub, M., Clemens, L. P., Sockloff, A., Ethridge, T., Gracely, E., & Myers, B. (1984). The development of sex-role stereotypes in the third year: Relationships to gender labeling, gender identity, sex-typed toy preferences, and family characteristics. *Child Development, 55,* 1493–1503.

Weisberg, P. (1963). Social and nonsocial conditioning of infant vocalizations. *Child Development, 34,* 377–388.

Weisberg, P. (1988). Direct instruction in the preschool. *Education and Treatment of Children, 11,* 349–364.

Weisberg, P. (1992). Education and enrichment approaches. In C. E. Walker & M. C. Roberts (Eds.), *Handbook of clinical child psychology* (2nd ed., pp. 919–932). Oxford, UK: John Wiley.

Weisberg, P. (1994). Helping preschoolers from low-income backgrounds make substantial progress in reading through direct instruction. In R. Gardner (Ed.), *Behavior analysis in education: Focus on measurably superior instruction* (pp. 115–129). Pacific Grove, CA: Brooks/Cole.

Weisberg, P., & Waldrop, P. B. (1972). Fixed-interval work habits of Congress. *Journal of Applied Behavior Analysis, 6,* 93–97.

Weiss, M. J., & Harris, S. L. (2001). Teaching social skills to people with autism. *Behavior Modification, 25*(5), 785–802.

Werner, E., & Smith, R. (1982). *Vulnerable but invincible: A study of resilient children.* New York: McGraw-Hill.

Wertsch, J. V. (1999). Cognitive development. In M. Bennett (Ed.), *Developmental psychology.* Philadelphia: Psychology Press.

West, D. J. (1982). *Delinquency: Its roots, careers, and prospects.* Cambridge, MA: Harvard University Press.

Whitehurst, G. J. (1989). Five Recommendations to SIG Members. *Behavior Analysis of Human Development SIG Newsletter, 2*(1), 1–4.

Whitehurst, G. J. (2001). Much too late. *Education Matters, 1*(2), 9, 16–19.

Whitehurst, G. J., Falco, F., Lonigan, C., Fischel, J., DeBaryshe, B., Valdez-Menchaca, M., et al. (1988). Accelerating language development through picture book reading. *Developmental Psychology, 24*(4), 552–559.

Whitehurst, G. J., & Novak, G. (1973). Modeling, imitation training, and the acquisition of sentence phrases. *Journal of Experimental Child Psychology, 16,* 332–345.

Whitehurst, G. J., & Valdez-Menchaca, M. (1988). What is the role of reinforcement in language acquisition? *Child Development, 59,* 430–440.

Wicks-Nelson, R., & Israel, A. C. (2003). *Behavior disorders of childhood* (5th ed.). Englewood Cliffs, NJ: Prentice Hall.

Willett, W. C. (1992). Folic acid and neural tube defect: Can't we come to closure? *American Journal of Public Health, 82,* 666–669.

Williams, M. (2002). *Suicide and attempted suicide: Understanding the cry of pain.* Harmondsworth, UK: Penguin.

Williams, R. D. (1994). FDA proposes folic acid fortification. *FDA Consumer, 28,* 11–114.

Wilson, J. G. (1973). *Environment and birth defects.* New York: Academic.

Wilson, J. Q., & Herrnstein, R. J. (1985). *Crime and human nature.* New York: Simon & Schuster.

Wilson, K. G., Hayes, S. C., Gregg, J., & Zettle, R. (1991). Psychopathology and psychotherapy. In S. C. Hayes, D. Barnes-Holmes, & B. Roche (Eds.), *Relational frame theory: A post-Skinnerian account of human language and cognition* (pp. 211–237). New York: Plenum Press.

Wilson, M. N. (1989). Child development in the context of the black extended family. *American Psychologist, 44,* 380–385.

Winokur, S. (1976). *A primer of verbal behavior: An operant view.* Englewood Cliffs, NJ: Prentice Hall.

Witkin, H. A., Mednick, S. A., Schulsinger, F., Bakkestrom, E., Christiansen, K. O., Goodenough, D. R., et al. (1976). Criminality in XYY and XXY men. *Science, 193,* 547–555.

Wolff, P. H. (1966). The causes, controls, and organizations of behavior in the newborn. *Psychological Issues, 5*(1, Whole No. 17), 1–105.

Wolff, P. H. (1969). The natural history of crying and other vocalizations in early infancy. In B. M. Foss (Ed.), *Determinants of infant behavior* (Vol. 4). London: Methuen.

Wolpe, J. (1958). *Psychotherapy by reciprocal inhibition.* Stanford, CA: Stanford University Press.

Zebrowitz, L. A., & Montepare, J. M. (1992). Impressions of babyfaced individuals across the life span. *Developmental Psychology, 28,* 1143–1152.

Zentall, T., Edwards, C. A., & Hogan, D. E. (1983). Pigeon's use of identity. In M. L. Commons, R. J. Herrnstein, & A. R. Wagner (Eds.), *Quantitative analyses of behavior: Vol. 4. Discrimination processes* (pp. 273–294). Cambridge, MA: Ballinger.

Zentall, T. R., & Urcuioli, P. J. (1993). Emergent relations in the formation of stimulus classes by pigeons. *Psychological Record, 43,* 795–810.

Zettle, R. D., & Hayes, S. C. (1982). Rule-governed behavior: A potential framework for cognitive-behavioral therapy. In P. C. Kendall (Ed.), *Advances in cognitive-behavioral research and therapy* (Vol. 1, pp. 73–119). New York: Academic Press.

Zevenbergen, A. A., & Whitehurst, G. J. (2003). Dialogic reading: A shared picture book reading intervention for preschoolers. In A. van Kleeck & S. A. Stahl (Eds.), *On reading books to children: Parents and teachers* (pp. 177–200). Mahwah, NJ: Lawrence Erlbaum.

Zigler, E., & Seitz, V. (1982). Social policy and intelligence. In R. J. Sternberg (Ed.), *Handbook of human intelligence* (pp. 568–641). Cambridge, UK: Cambridge University Press.

Zimmerman, B. J., & Whitehurst, G. J. (1979). Structure and function: A comparison of two views of the development of language and cognition. In G. J. Whitehurst & B. J. Zimmerman (Eds.), *The functions of language and cognition* (pp. 1–22). New York: Academic Press.

NAME INDEX

SUBJECT INDEX

Aggression development
  phase 1: aggression in early
      childhood, 387–388
  phase 2: middle childhood:
      rejection and school
      failure, 388
  phase 3: late childhood/
      adolescence, 389
  phase 4: adult antisocial
      personality, 389–390
  progression of, 388fig
  structural equation models
      of, 387
Alcohol
  abuse of drugs and, 485–487
  as teratogen, 120
Allantois, 111
Allels (dominant and recessive),
      88–89, 90
Alternating-treatments design
      (ABCBCB), 49
Altruism, 324, 357
Amnion, 111
Amodal features, 137
Androgyny, 306
Animism, 224
Anorexia Nervosa, 406, 478–479
Antecedents
  as discriminative stimuli,
      169–170, 179, 190–191
  effective teaching using, 444
  parenting discipline types and
      use of, 419
Antecendent control technique, 480
Anthropology, 9
Antireductionism, 13–14
Antisocial behaviors
  adolescent, 475–476
  antisocial interactions and,
      373–376b, 474
  behavioral systems approach to,
      378–382
  behavioral systems approach to
      physical child abuse,
      392–398b
  coercive family
      process/antisocial
      behavior in home,
      382–387
  development of aggression and,
      387–390, 474–475
  developmental progression for,
      501
  as externalizing disorders, 501
  firearm death rates
      (1997–1998), 374fig
  origins of aggression and,
      377–378
  parent training to reduce, 390

raising concerns with, 372–373
three keys to effective parenting
    to avoid, 390–392
See also Aggression
Antisocial Personality
    Disorder, 382
Anxiety behavior disorders,
    510–512
APA (American Psychological
    Association), 176, 494–495,
    502
Apgar test, 125–126t
Applied behavior analysis, 27
Applied developmental
    psychologists, 28
Art Institute of Chicago, 10, 11
Assessment
  of behavior disorders, 499–500
  functional, 500
  newborn, 125–127, 129
  perceptual capabilities, 129
Assimilation, 221–222
Association for Behavior Analysis
    Statement on Right to
    Effective Education, 450,
    456b–458b
Atlas of Men (Sheldon), 292
Attachment
  adolescent, 489
  development of, 337
  separation protests and,
      337–339, 340fig
Attention, 329–330
Attractors
  behavior disorders as organized
      patterns of, 495–496
  described, 67
  emergence of dynamic, 210
  skills as dynamic, 239b–240b
Authoritarian discipline pattern
  antecedents/consequences used
      in, 419
  behavior shaped by, 419
  described, 417, 418
Authoritative discipline pattern
  adolescent development
      and, 469
  antecedents/consequences used
      in, 419
  behavior shaped by, 420
  described, 417, 418
Autism
  described, 512
  science, pseudoscience, and
      antiscience in, 515b–517b
  treatments of, 512–515
Autistic disorder diagnostic
    criteria, 498t
Autoclitic verbal behaviors, 261

Automatic reinforcement
  language development and,
      267–268
  primary circular reactions
      producing, 223
Autonomic arousal, 395
Autonomy, 469
Avoidance behavior, 480
AZT (Zidovudine, ZDV), 116b

B. F. Skinner Foundation, 178
Babbling, 266, 267
Babinski reflex, 141
"Baby in a Box" (Skinner article),
    176b–178b
Back Street College of
    Education, 438
Backward chaining, 201
Backward conditioning, 161–162
Bank Street model, 438–439
Baseline phase, 49
Basic behavior analysis, 27
Behavior
  changes in interactions and, 4–5
  defining, 4
  developmental history of an
      individual and reinforced,
      18, 41
  evolution of species and, 14–15
  evolutionary significance of
      learning and, 22–23
  experiential canalization
      suggestions regarding,
      89–90
  exposure to species-typical
      environment, 24–25
  functional relationship of
      environment to, 149
  instrumental, 150
  learned, 147–148
  matching law on consequences
      and, 315
  moral, 362, 363–368
  multifactorial effect of genes
      on, 92
  nonuniversal, 99
  person-environment
      interactions and, 101–103
  repertoire of, 194
  resulting from multiple
      determination, 48, 55
  schemes and, 219–226
  stimulatory, 58–59
  universal, 63, 99, 137–138
  variability in, 66
  See also Operant behavior
Behavior analysis
  combining dynamical systems
      principles with, 3

Easy child, 298
Eating disorders
   anorexia nervosa, 406, 478–479
   bulimia nervosa, 479–480
Echoics, 260
Echolalic babbling, 266
Ecological stimulus, 232
Ectoderm, 111, 112
Ectomorphy, 292
Ectopic pregnancy, 117
Edible reinforcers, 196
Education
   curriculum and, 441–443
   debate over most appropriate,
      439*b*–440*b*
   functions of, 432–433
   learning, teaching and, 440–441
   Morningside Academy (Seattle)
      approach to, 452*b*–456*b*
   statement on right to effective,
      456*b*–458*b*–450
   See also Curriculum; Schools;
      Teaching
EEG (electroencelphalograms),
   127, 135
"Egocentric speech," 258–259
Egocentrism, 224
EIBI (early intensive behavioral
   intervention), 517*b*
Elicited stimulus, 151
Embryo
   illustration of, 111*fig*
   three layers of the, 111–112
Embryoblast, 109–110
Embryonic period, 110–112
Emergent properties, 59–60
Emitted operant behavior, 166–167
Emotional development. *See* Social/
   emotional development
Empathy, 358
Empiricism, 129
Enactive representation, 220
Endoderm, 111
Endomorph, 292
Environment
   aggression and current condition
      effects of, 381–382
   factors affecting puberty,
      466–467
   functional relationship to
      behavior by, 149
   interactions between genotypes
      and, 88–89, 100–101
   learning and exposure to
      species-typical, 24
   learning as relation between
      behavior and events of,
      148–149
   measurement error and
      influence of, 94–95

neonate's ability to respond to,
   127–135
nonshared factors of, 94
operant behavior emitted to,
   166–167
prenatal, 116–117
role in personality
   temperaments, 299–300*fig*
shared factors of, 94
social cognition and, 355–357*fig*
Environmental conditions, 98
Environmental contingencies, 236
Environmental determinism, 259
Environmental hazards, 121
EO (establishing operation),
   191, 192
Equifinality, 55–56*fig*
Equilibrium, 222–223
Equivalence classes, 236, 248
Equivalencing behavior, 247
Escape behavior, 480
Ethological perspective on
   aggression, 377
Events
   learning as relation between
      behavior and, 148–149
   responses to private, 183, 228
   responses to public, 183
   See also SE (setting event)
Evocative effect, 192
Evocative genotype-environment
   effects, 100
Evoked operant behavior, 167
Evolution
   history of the species and, 18
   parallelism between learning
      and, 23–25
   significance of learning in
      context of, 22–23
Evolutionary psychology, 15
Experiential canalization, 89–90
Experimental methodologies,
   26–27, 47–48
Explanation
   circular vs. true, 39–40
   description vs., 37–40
   prediction and, 37–38
   problem of reification and, 40
   reductionism used to
      produce, 13
Explicit curriculum, 442
Exploratory behavior, 232–233
External locus of control, 320
Externalizing disorders, 501
Extinction
   consequences and, 187–190
   of fear, 165
   reducing mands for attention
      by, 330
   resistance to, 209

Extinction burst, 190
Extraversion-Introversion, 293
Extrinsic reinforcement, 230
Extrinsic reinforcers, 450–452

Facial expressions, 325–326
Factor V, 293
Fading, 201–202
Families
   adolescent development and
      support of, 472–473
   codependency in, 407
   coercive family process in,
      382–390, 475–476
   current status of American, 404
   effects of divorce and
      characteristics of, 416
   functional and dysfunctional,
      406–407
   households by type
      (1970–2000), 405*fig*
   as mediators of society and
      culture, 401–402
   parent training to change
      behavioral system of, 390
   poverty rates (2001) by types
      of, 423*fig*
   social and cultural context of,
      403–404
   structure of, 403–404
   as system of systems, 404–407
   See also Mothers; Parents
Family discipline patterns
   differences in antecedents/
      consequences, 419
   poverty and, 424–425
   three styles of, 417–418
   types of behavior shaped by
      parents, 419–421
   See also Punishment
Family roles
   functions of, 407–408
   maternal employment and,
      409–412
   maternal job loss and, 413–414
   paternal job loss and, 412–413
Family system
   children in context of poverty
      and, 421–428
   dynamic of, 402*fig*
   effects of divorce on, 414–417
   functions of family members in,
      407–408
   impact of absent/changed role
      in, 408–414
   overview of, 404–406
   patterns of family discipline and,
      417–421
FAP (functional analytic
   psychotherapy), 521

FAS (fetal alcohol syndrome), 120
Fathers
    effects of job loss on, 412
    effects of maternal employment on, 410
    See also Mothers
Fears
    children's, 162–163
    counterconditioning, 163–165
    of the dark, 345–347
    extinction/systematic desensitization of, 165
    mother's "fearful" face, 163*fig*
    stranger anxiety, 344–345, 347–349*fig*
Fetal period, 112
Fetus
    getting ready for the world, 124–125
    habituation studies on, 151
    prenatal development of, 110–123
    teratogens affecting, 114, 117–123
    See also Newborns (neonates)
FFT (functional family therapy), 477–478
FI (fixed-interval) schedules, 205–206
Field of Dreams (film), 179
Firearm death rates (1997–1998), 374*fig*
First words, 270
Fisher's skill learning approach
    comparing Piaget's stages to, 237–238
    overview of, 234–241
Fixed action patterns, 23
Folic acid, 115*b*
Formal curriculum, 442
Formal operations stage (12 years and up), 225
Forward chaining, 200
Four-term contingency
    effective parenting using, 391–392
    effective teaching and the, 443–452
    food wars with children and, 396*b*–398*b*
    overview of, 180–181*fig*
    skill theory and behavior analysis using, 241
FR (fixed-ratio) schedules, 203–204
Free operant procedures, 178–179
FT (fixed-time) schedules, 206
Function vs. structure, 35–36
Functional analysis, 48, 500
Functional assessment, 500

The functional environmental surround, 98
Functional equivalence, 2424
Functional family therapy (FFT), 477–478
Functional knowledge, 35–36
Functional response class, 183

Gametes, 85
"Gaze aversion" signaling, 59
Gender consistency, 305
Gender differences
    CD onset and, 502
    described, 302–303
    effects of divorce and children's, 415–416
    firearm death rates (1997–1998) and, 374*fig*
    love and romantic relations and, 488–489
    personality and, 302–306
Gender identity, 305, 468–469
Gender sex chromosomes, 90–91
Gender stability, 305
Gender-related behaviors
    androgyny and combining roles of, 306
    development of gender-specific reinforcers of, 305
    development of, 303
    developmental changes in, 305–306
    parental expectations and reinforcement, 304
    reinforcement of appropriate, 304–305
    sex role stereotypes and societal/cultural expectations and, 303–304
General law of developmental direction, 113
Generalization, 157
Generalized compliance, 367–368
Generalized imitation, 282, 334
Generalized reinforcers, 196–197
Generative process of language, 256–257
Genes
    cell production signaled by, 92
    examining workings of, 78
    locations on chromosome, 83*fig*
    multifactorial effect on behavior by, 92
    overview of, 82–83
    proteins and, 81*fig*
Genetic code (DNA), 80
Genetic markup, 96
Genetic variability

alleles: dominant and recessive, 88–89
    codominance and, 91
    crossing over and, 85, 86
    development canalization and, 89–90
    genotype and, 88
    incomplete dominance and, 91
    mutations and, 85, 86–87*fig*
    overview of, 85
    random assortment and, 85, 86
    sex-linked characteristics and, 90–91*fig*
    single-genes/polygenic inheritance and, 92
Genetic-constitutional makeup, 96–97
Genetics
    aggression/antisocial behavior and, 378–380
    behavioral, 79–83
    biparental reproduction, 84–85
    chromosomes, 81–82*fig*
    development role of, 78–79
    field of behavior, 96*b*–97*b*
    genes, 81*fig*, 82–83
    language development and role of, 264
    meiosis, 85
    mitosis, 83–84*fig*
    reasons for study of, 79–80
    recessive hereditary diseases and, 89
    twin studies on, 93
    See also Heredity
Genital herpes, 118–119
Genome, 78
Genotype-environment interactions, 88–89, 100–101
Genotypes
    aggressive behavior and, 379–380
    described, 88
    influence on environmental transactions, 101103
    interactions between environment and, 88–89, 100–101
Germinal period, 109
Gross-fine law, 113
Growth spurt, 464
GSR (galvanic skin response), 335

Habituation
    defining characteristics of, 151–153
    described, 150–151
    infant studies on, 151
    nonhuman studies on, 151
    reasons for studying, 153

CPSIA information can be obtained
at www.ICGtesting.com
Printed in the USA
BVOW07s0923011217

501384BV00012B/44/P